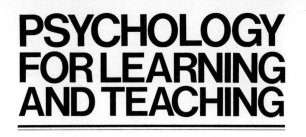

PSYCHOLOGY FOR LEARNING AND TEACHING

PSYCHOLOGY FOR LEARNING AND TEACHING

Charles Galloway
Professor of Education
University of Victoria, Canada

McGRAW-HILL BOOK COMPANY

New York   St. Louis   San Francisco   Auckland   Düsseldorf
Johannesburg   Kuala Lumpur   London   Mexico   Montreal
New Delhi   Panama   Paris   São Paulo   Singapore
Sydney   Tokyo   Toronto

PSYCHOLOGY FOR LEARNING AND TEACHING

Library of Congress Cataloging in Publication Data

Galloway, Charles.
    Psychology for learning and teaching.

    Bibliography: p.
    Includes index.
    1. Educational psychology. I. Title.
[DNLM: 1. Learning. 2. Psychology, Educational.
3. Teaching. LB1051 G174p]
LB1051.G218   370.15   75-25991
ISBN 0-07-022737-3

34567890 VHVH 7987

This book was set in Melior by Progressive Typographers.
The editors were Stephen D. Dragin and Phyllis T. Dulan;
the designer was Jo Jones;
the production supervisor was Judi Allen.
The drawings were done by Danmark & Michaels, Inc.
The cover illustration was done by Michelle Horowitz.
Von Hoffmann Press, Inc., was printer and binder.

to

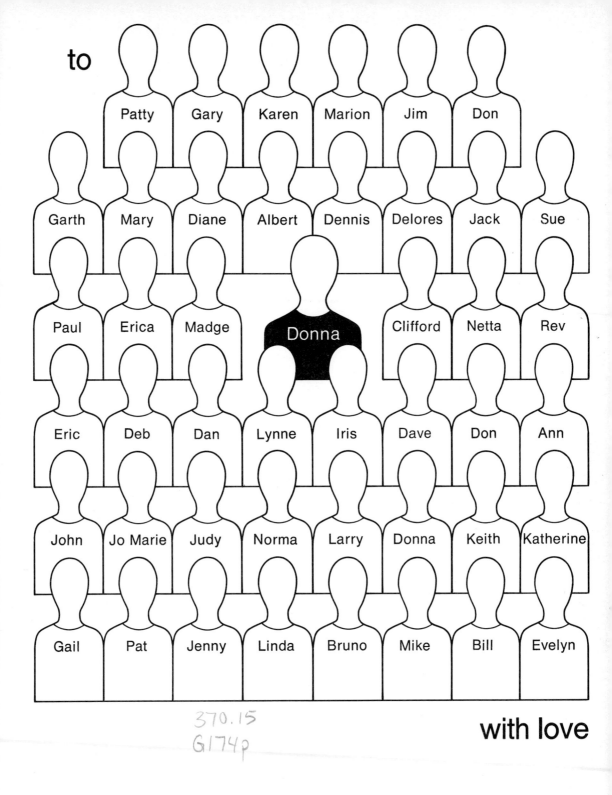

Patty	Gary	Karen	Marion	Jim	Don

Garth Mary Diane Albert Dennis Delores Jack Sue

Paul Erica Madge **Donna** Clifford Netta Rev

Eric Deb Dan Lynne Iris Dave Don Ann

John Jo Marie Judy Norma Larry Donna Keith Katherine

Gail Pat Jenny Linda Bruno Mike Bill Evelyn

with love

CONTENTS

PREFACE

Each year many children fail to learn or learn only poorly in our schools. But this condition does not surprise anyone, for failure in schools is historic; it is accepted and expected. In a way it is also respected, since the failure of at least a few children each year is seen by many teachers and administrators as an indication that sufficiently high standards of education are being maintained.

Yet, as teachers and parents, we feel disappointed when our children are not successful in school, and we spend great time and effort in search of the reasons for their failure. We "test" learners with a wide array of instruments designed to probe all manner of human dimensions: general health and physical condition, academic achievement, interests, general and specific learning abilities, personality, special aptitudes, and so forth. We have become quite effective at identifying good, average, and poor learners and at diagnosing and assessing learning difficulties. But identification, diagnosis, and assessment are only part of what is required to help children learn. We must also be effective at teaching, especially for those children whom we identify as poor learners, since the simple truth is that poor learning usually follows from ineffective instruction.

It is the thesis of this book that effective instruction is the major contributor to learning and that for a child who is not learning well, instruction is ineffective. The question for us, then, is how to become an effective teacher for each of our learners. This is what *Psychology for Learning and Teaching* is about.

Traditionally, teaching has been viewed as an art practiced by each teacher, often intuitively, according to his or her unique beliefs, values, abilities, and other personal characteristics. Only relatively recently has teaching come to be seen also as a science, that is, as a systematic application of the rules of a science of human behavior. Consequently, we are now beginning to remove from teaching some of the intuition, necessary perhaps for the practice of an art, but clearly insufficient for effective instruction.

In this text I have tried to present teaching as a humanistic activity experienced by persons knowledgeable in the rules of a science of human behavior and their application to classroom instruction. In this sense, the book is neither humanistic nor behavioristic; it is both. In a similar way, it does not focus primarily on theory or on practice; rather, it attempts to relate the two, with the practice of teaching *deriving* from theories of development and learning. This relationship between theory and practice in education is important for teachers to grasp. Once theory is understood, freedom for individuality in teaching becomes logically possible since there is an almost infinite variety of possible approaches, techniques, and methods of instruction that each of us can devise and make consistent with the rules of our theories about development, learning, and teaching.

A major hinderance to a logically based individuality in one's teaching approach has been the absence of a theory of instruction. One of the unique and potentially useful features of this book is the development of, and suggestions for, application of such a theory. Many examples from real classrooms are used throughout the text to illustrate logical, meaningful relationships between a theory of instruction and various approaches to instruction, ranging from free schools to open classrooms to mastery learning.

Another significant characteristic of this text that makes it different from other books in the area is that it *practices what it teaches.* The way its material is organized and presented gives one example of how the major ideas being learned about can be applied; that is, the book is designed to serve as an effective instructor. Goals and instructional objectives for all major levels of the cognitive and affective domains are stated, taught for, and evaluated; practice is distributed throughout the material with corrective feedback immediately available; many classroom examples are used to enhance meaningfulness; the arrangement of the book proceeds from general to specific and from simple to complex in hierarchical fashion, with each chapter building on and expanding the ideas presented in earlier chapters; and, as an effective teacher, the book emphasizes a synthesis of potentially useful ideas from various points of view rather than a selection of some and rejection of others.

In a single introductory text, it is impossible to attend to every topic in the psychology of learning and teaching to a depth satisfactory to every reader. Thus, this book, too, is selective, especially of those topics most directly related to the success of both the teacher and the learner in the school and classroom. For the topics selected, e.g., motivation and discipline, an effort has been made to operationalize their meaning in terms of teacher and learner behavior in order to avoid the vague and essentially useless definitions which traditionally define them.

Many people have contributed to the completion of this text and I thank them wholeheartedly for their wisdom and their willingness to share in its preparation. Their honest and helpful criticism added greatly to the quality and clarity of the ideas presented here. I extend a special note of appreciation to you, Beverly Timmons, for our almost-daily discussions about "the Book" and for the confidence you expressed in it. Also, my thanks go to several other of my colleagues, Fred Tyler, Geoffrey Mason, Vance Peavy, Don Knowles, Lloyd Ollila, James Vance, and Norma Mickelson for their helpful comments.

The entire manuscript was reviewed at various stages of its development by Professors Carolyn M. Callahan, Terry D. TenBrink, James H. Block, Ancel J. Tikasingh, Edward F. Ansello, Kaoru Yamamoto, and Glenn E. Snelbecker. Their criticism and suggestions for improvement were greatly appreciated.

At least a thousand students have a part of themselves reflected in the pages of this book. They have taught me that to become an effective teacher, I must also become an active learner with them, and that if I try to practice what I teach, each year my students will get a better teacher. I thank all of you for such an honest and obvious truth.

Elsie Coon, Linda Monteski, Beth Glassford, Patty Hughes, Aileen Harrison, Betty Christensen, Neela Cumming, and Valerie Kohler, thank you for your patience and skill in transforming my pencil scratches into neat, legible type. I realize the magnitude of the task and I appreciate the spirit with which you engaged in it.

Charles Galloway

PSYCHOLOGY FOR LEARNING AND TEACHING

PART I

CONTENT AND PROCESS OF LEARNING AND TEACHING

A MASTERY APPROACH TO LEARNING AND TEACHING

The truth is too great for any one actual mind, even though that mind be dubbed "the Absolute," to know the whole of it. The facts and worths of life need many cognizers to take them in. There is no point of view absolutely public or universal. Private and uncommunicable perceptions always remain over, and the worst of it is that those who look for them from the outside never know *where*.

William James
Talks to Teachers

CONTENTS

In the everyday sense, *education* is widely understood to mean a process of teaching and learning that results in changes in behavior. To educate means to change. *Teaching* refers to our attempts to effect certain desired changes in the behavior of our learners. When these changes are observed, we infer that *learning* has occurred, and we conclude that our instruction has been effective. We reckon that we are effective teachers.

BECOMING AN EFFECTIVE TEACHER

Becoming an effective teacher is a primary long-range goal of every person who embarks on a career of classroom teaching. Achieving the goal requires competencies of several related kinds, including knowledge and skills of (1) specific subject matter, (2) methods of instruction, and (3) the psychology of learning and teaching. Most programs of teacher education provide experiences in all three of these broad areas. Often, the experiences are closely integrated because, in actual practice, the competencies must blend together to compose the more general concept of effective teaching.

The Psychology of Learning and Teaching

In this text, we will be concerned primarily with the psychology of learning and teaching. Frequently, however, we will relate the psychology to specific methods of instruction in various subject areas because the psychology of learning and teaching is an applied psychology. It is the branch of psychology, often called educational psychology, that attempts to specify the conditions under which learning will occur most effectively in school settings. The conditions with which we will be most concerned are those that can be established from an application of the concepts and rules that derive from a science of human behavior.

Various Approaches to Effective Teaching

There are many ways to interpret the concepts and rules of a science of human behavior. Consequently, their application to the problems of school learning and teaching results in a wide variety of possible approaches or methods of instruction. One outcome has been that scores of studies have been done by educational researchers to determine whether certain methods are better than others. The results, however, have not supported the general superiority of any one method. With this in mind, you may want to begin thinking very soon about the types of approach you will possibly use with your learners. Throughout the text, we will use many examples to provide practice in applying the concepts and rules of a science of human behavior to at least four widely recognized approaches to learning and teaching: discovery, reception, auto-instruction, and mastery.

DISCOVERY APPROACH

The *discovery approach* is extremely popular among teachers as an effective way to help learners get the feel of how scientists go about their work. Jerome

Bruner, among others, has devoted much time and effort to the discovery approach to school learning. He believes that by engaging students in discussions in which questions, clues, and concrete materials are used in ways to provoke their curiosity and attention, they can be encouraged to discover ideas for themselves and to develop effective strategies of inquiry. Advocates of the discovery approach maintain that it causes learners to gain meaningful insight into the basic structure and processes of knowledge, the stuff of which "real and lasting learning" is made.

RECEPTION APPROACH

Quite different from the discovery approach is the *reception approach*, with David Ausubel as its outstanding spokesman. His view is that, although discovery learning is appropriate and desirable for achieving certain objectives, e.g., for ensuring meaningful associations for complex or abstract ideas, especially for young learners, it is unduly time-consuming and unnecessary for most learning of the school type.

In the reception approach, learners are presented with the content to be learned. They are not required to discover it on their own. The teacher's task here is to organize instruction so that the content will be received by the learner in a way and form that can be incorporated meaningfully and easily with previous learning. Usually this means proceeding from broad, generally inclusive ideas to more specific information that is subsumed by the general idea. In the reception approach, *advance organizers*, somewhat akin to topic sentences in paragraphs, provide broad introductory overviews for new material.

AUTO-INSTRUCTION

Another general approach, *auto-instruction*, usually consists of instructional materials, often prepared in steplike fashion, with answers that are immediately available and that are presented to learners by means of some electromechanical device. B. F. Skinner, one of the most visible advocates of auto-instruction, believes that it is one of the few approaches, outside of individual tutoring, that truly do individualize instruction for each learner. Programmed materials presented by teaching machines permit learners to proceed at their own rates with learning experiences that are appropriate for them at the time. Skinner maintains that a technological approach to making instruction optimal for each learner increases the effectiveness of teaching, since it releases the teacher from doing the kinds of activities that can be programmed. Thus, reasons Skinner, the teacher has more time to devote to other components of teaching, for example, to the humanistic or affective components that cannot presently be done by a machine.

MASTERY LEARNING

The fourth approach that you will learn about in this text is called *mastery learning*. It is an instructional approach developed by Benjamin Bloom from the theoretical ideas of John Carroll. Central to the mastery approach is the idea that most learners can learn well if given sufficient time to learn and if instruction is optimal for them. To meet these conditions, (1) the objectives of instruction must be clearly understood by the learner; (2) each learner must have acquired any prerequisites necessary for success in the present learning task; (3) the learner must be able to profit from the instruction; and (4) the learner must attend to the learning task long enough and well enough to learn the material. Operationally, in this approach a learner must demonstrate mastery of the objectives at one level of a learning task before being allowed to proceed to the next. Frequent testing with corrective feedback designed to help the learner master the objectives, rather than to attain a course mark, is an important and necessary part of this approach.

The Conditions of Learning

Although only the four general approaches to effective learning and teaching outlined here are discussed in *Psychology for Learning and Teaching,* it must be remembered that any number of general or specific approaches is possible. All approaches, however, regardless of how different they may be in terms of techniques, materials, or procedures, must meet certain requirements if they are to be effective in causing learning to occur. As you will learn later, these requirements are what Robert Gagné calls "the conditions of learning." They refer to such things as (1) clear objectives, (2) the meeting of prerequisites, (3) attention to the task, (4) the need for practice, and (5) knowledge of results. An important point to clarify is that *approaches* to instruction are simply methods of combining the required conditions of learning. Thus, any approach, if it is to be effective, must somehow account for all the conditions of learning necessary for a given learning task. This fact is perhaps the reason why educational researchers, such as John Stephens, have been unable to demonstrate the consistent and significant superiority of any one approach. Where differences in some studies have been noted, typically they have been associated with *teacher* variables, such as enthusiasm, knowledge, and skill with a particular approach rather than with the approach itself. This observation suggests that the variable of greatest importance relative to effective learning and teaching is the ability of teachers to incorporate the conditions of learning into their particular approach, and then how effective they can become at using it. Clearly, our search for effective approaches to teaching begins with the conditions of learning and ends with the teacher.

MY APPROACH

If I am to be an effective teacher for you, it follows that in writing this book, I should employ some approach within which I can incorporate the necessary conditions of learning and with the use of which I can become effective. Because a *mastery learning approach* lends itself well to learning about the psychology of learning and teaching, and because it is the approach with which I have had the most classroom experience, this textbook basically teaches from a mastery approach. Within this approach, however, we will find many occasions to apply Bruner's ideas about forming instructional strategies, Ausubel's suggestions for causing learning to be meaningful, and Skinner's rules of behavior for making instruction effective and efficient. My purpose is to help you synthesize major contributions to learning and teaching rather than to select some and discard others. Learning from a mastery approach will help you become effective with at least this one approach, should you decide to use it in your teaching.

USING A MASTERY APPROACH

Regardless of the general approach we elect to use in our instruction, we will always be trying to accomplish the broad purpose of education: to bring about changes in behavior. By changes in behavior I mean changes in a wide range of responses which include changes in *affect,* for example, feelings, attitudes, beliefs; *cognition,* that is, knowledge and capabilities in content areas such as reading, writing, and arithmetic; and *physical skills,* including singing, throwing, running, and jumping. The broad purpose I am trying to achieve with a mastery approach in this text is to change your affective and cognitive behavior relative to the psychology of learning and teaching.

Basic Assumptions and General Themes

My use of a mastery approach in this book implies the basic rule that *we learn what we attend to.* That is, as John Dewey frequently pointed out, we learn what we become involved in, what we do. More directly, we learn what we practice.

The term *attend* as we will use it carries the everyday meaning that is implied by the teacher's request: "Pay attention, please." Paying attention means more than just a physical orientation toward learning events. It also means responding to the stimuli relevant to a learning event and disregarding those stimuli that are irrelevant. More simply, attending means being appropriately and actively involved. If our learners do not attend, they will not learn what we want to teach.

Two extremely useful and general themes relevant to school learning can be derived from the basic rule: *"we learn what we practice."* They are used throughout the text as the central themes into which related topics can be integrated. The first of the two themes is that a teacher's primary task in bringing about changes in behavior is purely to cause learners to attend to appropriate learning events long enough and well enough to learn them. Since I am a teacher, my primary task in this text is to do the best I can, using a mastery approach to focus and hold your attention on the learning tasks I believe are important to help you learn about the psychology of learning and teaching.

The second major theme that continues throughout the text is related to the nature of practice. It is my belief that we need to practice doing the many things effective teachers do in addition to practicing reading, describing, and explaining about what they do. Therefore, an important part of my task is to try to cause you to practice *doing* these things in addition to causing you to practice *telling* about them. This means, of course, that I also need to practice doing these things as well as to tell you how you should do them. Therefore, I will continually (1) share with you my reasons for the things I do to help you learn, and (2) provide opportunities for you to practice many of the skills effective teachers find useful. If I am able to achieve my task, this text will "work" for you and your learners.

Organizing for a Mastery Approach

One of the requirements of a mastery approach is that for topics in which some material is prerequisite to later, more complex material, all the material must be arranged in a sequential and cumulative manner. The psychology of learning and teaching is a topic of this sort in the sense that knowing about the concepts and rules relative to learning and teaching is prerequisite to describing and explaining them. And, in turn, describing and explaining are prerequisite to analysis, to synthesis, and later, to evaluation of concepts and rules.

Consistent with this important requirement of a mastery approach, *Psychology for Learning and Teaching* is organized sequentially and cumulatively. This organization will be apparent to you both within the text as a whole and within each chapter.

PARTS AND CHAPTERS

The text is divided into four major parts. Part I, Content and Process of Learning and Teaching, helps you learn about aspects of learning and teaching that are mostly cognitive in emphasis. In Part II, Management of Classroom Behavior and Individual Differences, the emphasis is on affective components of effective learning and teaching. Part III, Development and Individual Differences, helps you pull together what you learn in Parts I and II into broad, useful theories of development and instruction. The experiences in Part III provide help in synthesizing your own approach to teaching. Part IV, Evaluation of Learning and Teaching, will help you learn how to check on the effectiveness of learning and teaching and how to go about improving your performance.

USING GOALS AND OBJECTIVES

Each chapter is designed to help you meet one general, long-range goal relative to the cognitive component and one relative to the affective component of becoming an effective teacher. The goals are suggested by the chapter titles. You will notice in the statement of these long-range goals the sequential and cumulative organization of the text material mentioned earlier.

The cognitive goals for the early chapters require you to describe, explain, formulate, interpret, and apply information relative to the psychology of learning and teaching. The goals for later chapters generally require the more inclusive and complex cognitive performances of analysis, synthesis, and evaluation.

In this sense, the learning process resembles a spiral. Concepts and rules introduced and learned about in early chapters reappear in later chapters as parts of increasingly inclusive concepts and higher-order rules. Early chapters are therefore prerequisite to later ones. As you can see, concepts and rules are never learned completely; we just keep learning more about them with each new experience. At the beginning of each chapter, the long-range goal is analyzed for its component parts. These parts are stated as the specific instructional objectives to be learned as a consequence of the learning experiences in the chapter.

The affective goals generally follow a similar type of progression from an emphasis on attending and responding in the early chapters to the more inclusive and complex affective performances in later chapters of valuing, organizing,

TABLE 1-1 Long-range goals for learning to be an effective teacher

To become an effective teacher, the learner should be able to:

COGNITIVE DOMAIN

Chapter 1	*Describe* a mastery approach to learning and teaching.
Chapter 2	*Explain* the importance of precision in learning and teaching.
Chapter 3	*Formulate* long-range goals and instructional objectives in cognitive, affective, and psychomotor domains.
Chapter 4	*Interpret* various laws and theories of learning.
Chapter 5	*Apply* the conditions of learning to teaching associations and discriminations.
Chapter 6	*Apply* the conditions of learning to teaching concepts and rules.
Chapter 7	*Apply* laws and theories of learning to teaching for transfer in cognitive, affective, and psychomotor domains.
Chapter 8	*Apply* the rules from a science of behavior to make instruction optimal for each learner.
Chapter 9	*Devise* instructional strategies, based on the rules of a science of behavior, to motivate learners.
Chapter 10	*Synthesize* instructional strategies from the rules of a science of behavior and the conditions of learning that help learners become self-managing.
Chapter 11	*Analyze* biologically based theories of developmental adaptation for their higher-order rules.
Chapter 12	*Synthesize* an approach to instruction that is personally satisfying and theoretically sound.
Chapter 13	*Evaluate* learner capabilities, classroom learning, and his own instruction.

AFFECTIVE DOMAIN

Chapter 1	*Recognize* the importance of becoming effective in whatever approach to learning and teaching that he chooses.
Chapter 2	*Accept* the challenge to be precise in teaching and learning.
Chapter 3	*Sustain attention* long enough and well enough to learn the skills of writing long-range goals and specific instructional objectives.
Chapter 4	*Participate* actively and thoughtfully in the activities related to the psychology of learning.
Chapter 5	*Practice* the rules relative to learning and teaching associations and discriminations.
Chapter 6	*Practice* the rules relative to learning and teaching concepts and rules.
Chapter 7	*Assume* responsibility for learning how to make instruction efficient for each learner.
Chapter 8	*Derive* satisfaction from learning about ways to make instruction optimal for each learner.
Chapter 9	*Commit* himself to the importance of capturing the attention of learners rather than demanding it.
Chapter 10	*Form* a personal and professional value system that emphasizes self-management of learners.
Chapter 11	*Develop* a broadly inclusive theoretical perspective of development from which can be derived higher-order rules with potential implications for making instruction optimal for individual learners.
Chapter 12	*Show a willingness to speculate* about the implications of higher-order rules of development for a theory of, and various approaches to, instruction.
Chapter 13	*Display confidence* in his ability to evaluate the effectiveness of his teaching, to judge the worth of his approaches to teaching, and to be willing to change when new information demonstrates the need to do so.

and integrating beliefs and actions relative to learning and teaching. The long-range goals for the cognitive and affective components of becoming an effective teacher are listed by chapter in Table 1-1.

SPECIFIC TECHNIQUES AND PRACTICES

Each chapter is organized around the two integrating themes *attention* and *practice,* and all chapters utilize techniques or apparatus that are consistent with a mastery approach. They are the techniques you will be learning about in this text to use in your own teaching. They are described here so that you will understand their use and purpose as we get started.

INTRODUCTORY QUOTE   The quotation introducing each chapter illustrates the theme of the chapter much as a teacher in a classroom might introduce a new topic with a pertinent picture, object, or reading.

ONGOING SUMMARY   The Ongoing Summary restates the major points encountered in previous chapters. They are always reviewed in relation to the integrating theme of helping teachers capture the attention of learners. This technique keeps in front of you a broad and meaningful overview of where we have been and helps you prepare for the next learning task.

ADVANCE ORGANIZER   Each Advance Organizer describes briefly and generally what the present chapter is about and how it relates to the main ideas presented earlier. Its purpose is to help ensure that the specific information of each chapter is learned meaningfully.

GOALS AND OBJECTIVES   The statement of the long-range goals and specific instructional objectives follows. Goals are the relatively broad, general outcomes of instruction that I hope you will gain by the time we finish the course. Specific instructional objectives, however, are the relatively immediate outcomes of learning for each chapter and are the specific things of various cognitive and affective levels you need to be able to do to achieve the long range-goals.

REVIEW GUIDES   In effective teaching, learning and evaluation always occur together. Review guides are concise test items distributed along the margins. The brief answers presented in the adjacent text will help you check on your acquisition and comprehension of the chapter content as you read it. Later, they will enable you to review the material quickly and to verify your retention of it.

CHECKPOINTS   Checkpoints represent a technique for combining evaluation and learning, especially learning that requires more than memory and comprehension of information. Most of the checkpoints contain questions and exercises that give you an opportunity to practice doing things teachers need to do to help children learn. Because corrective feedback is essential for effective learning, sample responses for all checkpoints are provided in the Appendix. They enable you to verify your own responses, and also serve as models to which you can refer as you learn to do relatively complex instructional skills.

IN PASSING   At the end of the content for each chapter is a brief section entitled "In Passing." In the same sense that the introductory quotation is intended to establish a mental set for the beginning of each chapter, In Passing is intended to sum up, in a nutshell, some important aspect of what the chapter was about, and to link it with the next one.

ACTIVITIES   The purpose of each chapter's Activities section is to provide practice with the ideas presented, especially in ways that you may need to handle the ideas as a classroom teacher. The last item in the Activities is always one called "Just for fun." Learning is a serious business, but it should also be fun. Sometimes you can combine both in the same encounter. This book tries to do so with this technique.

SUGGESTIONS FOR FURTHER READING   This text represents a biased point of view, and, since mastery learning is only one of many possible approaches, the Suggestions for Further Reading section draws to your attention annotated sources of points of view somewhat different from that presented in the text. References which either expand or show special application of certain main ideas also are presented.

A BRIEF STUDY GUIDE

It is suggested that you tackle each chapter in the following manner: First, get a broad overview of the major topic by noting the part and chapter headings. Read the introductory quote, then review the major ideas learned about so far by reading the Ongoing Summary. Get a feel for the main ideas to be learned next by reading the Advance Organizer. These ideas will become more meaningful for you if next you glance over Goals and Objectives, which summarizes the general long-range goals and the specific instructional objectives. Pretesting yourself with the objectives will help you know which sections of the chapter you need to study. You can keep at least a rough account of the results of your pretest by checking along the margins. Writing brief answers to the review questions in the margins will help ensure that you have absorbed basic factual information prerequisite to your learning later, often more complex information and skills. Completing the Checkpoints will help you achieve the objectives that require skills beyond memory and comprehension of information. If you need additional practice, especially of an applied nature, try any item in the Activities section that you believe will be helpful. When you feel you have mastered the material in the chapter, refresh your memory with the items in the review guide, then retest yourself with the objectives. If the experiences provided in the text are not adequate to help you achieve the objectives, or if you are interested in learning more about the topic, the Suggestions for Further Reading will guide you to additional information.

Space for practice is provided at places where only a brief response is required. For more extensive responses, you will need to use other paper.

PEOPLE

Many people over many years have been interested in the psychology of learning and teaching. And, although their contributions represent a wide range in point of view, one common goal has kept their efforts related. That goal has always been to improve learning. You will meet several of these people in this book.

Some of their names you will come to know quite well because of their work. But people are more than names and work, and learning and teaching are more than an exchange of ideas. This is an important point. Therefore, throughout the text I will try to keep the "peopleness" of learning and teaching visible. Since I am the first of the people you will meet, it seems appropriate to share some information about me.

About Me

I believe education is a human experience, the richness of which can be greatly enhanced through a willingness and an ability to engage in teacher-learner sharing. Education should be a pleasant experience among people. It should be honest, and it should be fun.

I was born on a small Missouri farm in 1933. After I had completed two years in a one-room school, my family moved to the state of Washington. We moved around a good deal in the next few years—by the time I graduated from grade twelve, I had attended thirteen different schools. I know firsthand what it feels like to be "the new kid."

After high school, I attended the community college at Yakima, Washington, and while there, worked at several outside jobs, including those of farm laborer, mail clerk in a bank, truck driver, nursery attendant, and salesclerk in a grocery store.

I then transferred to the University of Washington at Seattle, and also Donna and I married. Part-time jobs were in short supply, and for the first time in my life, I was unable to find one. Consequently, I dropped out of school—for the second time. I had dropped out once before when I was only five years old. I didn't like school when I first started, and since I kicked up such a fuss, it probably was easier to let me drop out than to try to keep me in!

During my three years away from the university, I had a variety of jobs and Donna delivered three of our four children. When I returned, it was in a program of teacher preparation at Central Washington State College. Soon I began teaching children. My first group was fifth grade, with sixty-six children on the class list by the end of the year. Yet, I never taught more than thirty-five at any one time. For the most part, they were children of migratory farm workers, people who cared about their children but who were not always able to provide well for them. These children and their parents taught me a lot about teaching, learning, children, and about myself.

After several years teaching children in grades four through twelve in the public schools of eastern Washington, we moved to Boston to study science education at Harvard. The following year found us back in Washington State and again teaching in the classroom. This time I was also acting as the counselor in a small secondary school.

The University of Southern California and the University of California at Berkeley were our next stops.

Ten years ago we moved to Victoria, British Columbia, Canada. I am on the Faculty of Education at the University of Victoria. Here I spend much of my time working with young people who want to become classroom teachers. Together, we learn about how to help children learn.

I have been fortunate in my lifetime. I have done many things, and I experience daily the privilege of knowing many persons well. My "teachers" have been good ones. In my beliefs about what I am, I have been influenced greatly by the teaching of Carl Rogers, B. F. Skinner, Saint Paul, my students, and migrant farm laborers. Among other things, they have taught me that to be most helpful, teachers must be as precise as possible, clear in their objectives, knowledgeable in their methods, and, at the same time, open, honest, and caring. It is my belief that all these things can, and must, occur in concert. Each is necessary and none is sufficient.

PRECISION IN LEARNING AND TEACHING

2

The teacher is a specialist in human behavior, whose assignment it is to bring about extraordinarily complex changes in extraordinarily complex material.

B. F. Skinner
The Technology of Teaching

CONTENTS

In Chapter 1 we learned that there are many approaches to effective teaching. We reviewed four general approaches that we will learn more about later. A mastery approach has been selected for the presentation of the material in this text. All approaches, however, have the same major goal: to change the behavior of learners. And all approaches must provide for the conditions of learning.

A basic assumption about learning and teaching is that we learn what we attend to and practice. Two continuing and integrating themes derive from this assumption: As teachers, (1) our primary task is to cause learners to attend to appropriate learning events long enough and well enough to learn them, and (2) we need to learn to do the many things effective teachers do.

We have learned about the basic components of a mastery approach and how they are applied in this text. The specific techniques and practices to be followed were outlined and a brief study guide was given. Together, the major goal of education, the basic assumption, the integrating themes, and the components of a mastery approach form a broad overview for our study of the psychology of learning and teaching. They are the Advance Organizer for the rest of the text.

ONGOING SUMMARY

Two main rules are presented in Chapter 2. First: *What we believe to be true is a function of our experiences and as our experiences change, our "truths" also change.* Our conception of "truth" is only our best abstraction and approximation of what "really is." We learn to adapt to a wide range of approximations.

ADVANCE ORGANIZER

At times, however, we act as if we believe our approximate truths were absolutes. As teachers with lasting influence on the lives of learners, we must understand the relative and approximate nature of those truths which we select for our learners' attention.

The second major rule is: *What we believe to be the cause of behavior is closely related to what we do to try to change behavior.* Central to this rule is the difference between *description* of behavior and *explanation* of behavior. Because the chief goal of teachers is to bring about changes in the behavior of children, teachers need to be as precise as possible about what constitutes only a description of behavior and what constitutes an explanation or cause of behavior. A teacher's primary task is to cause learners to attend to learning tasks long enough and well enough to learn them. Therefore, a precise explanation for attending and nonattending behavior is extremely helpful. Unless you can explain why a child fails to attend to learning tasks, you will not be able logically or systematically to improve that child's attention, and your efforts will at best be intuitive and random.

In later chapters we will learn much more about the importance of these two major rules for learning and teaching.

GOALS AND OBJECTIVES

Cognitive

To become an effective teacher, the learner should be able to explain the importance of precision in learning and teaching.

KNOWLEDGE LEVEL

Given the following terms, the learner is able to define them in writing: *behavior, relative, truth, description, explanation, cause and effect, relatively so and approximately true, circular reasoning.*

COMPREHENSION LEVEL

1. Given the situation of an automobile that will not start, the learner can explain why shouting at the automobile is not likely to cause the motor to start.
2. Given the following statements, the learner is able to explain how the statements are only relatively so and approximately true: "Larry Long is 5 feet 10 inches tall." "Our school is located one mile north of the police station."

APPLICATION LEVEL

Given the expression "Ben Sloe will not do his homework because he is too lazy," the learner is able to explain with an illustration how this is an example of circular reasoning.

ANALYSIS LEVEL

Given the situation that Tommy Shy does not answer an arithmetic question when called upon, the learner can identify the basic assumption(s) about cause and effect made by Tommy's teacher, who then proceeds to punish him for not answering.

SYNTHESIS LEVEL

Given the direction to provide at least two examples of his own making of circular reasoning involving the concept of cause and effect as it might occur in school settings, the learner is able to do so.

EVALUATION LEVEL

The learner is able to state, and support with reasons, whether he believes a mastery approach is an effective way to learn.

Affective

To become an effective teacher, the learner should be able to accept the challenge to be precise in learning and teaching.

RECEIVING (ATTENDING) LEVEL

The learner is aware of the potential confusion between *descriptions* and *explanations* of behavior.

RESPONDING LEVEL

The learner displays an interest in learning to be precise about human behavior.

VALUING LEVEL

The learner assumes responsibility for helping others learn rules of thumb relative to cause and effect in human behavior.

ORGANIZATIONAL LEVEL

The learner questions his prior usage of descriptive terms as explanations of human behavior.

CHARACTERIZATION LEVEL

In interacting with others, the learner attempts to be precise about the "truths" relative to cause and effect.

2

If one thing in education is abundantly clear, it is that there is little, if anything, that is abundantly clear. To suggest to you, therefore, that you should strive for precision within an area that is anything but precise seems almost a paradox. Yet, merely because we cannot be completely or absolutely precise, we should not keep ourselves from being as precise as possible.

THE RELATIVE AND APPROXIMATE NATURE OF TRUTH

A study of human behavior is really a study in approximation. In fact, it might be said that each of us lives—approximately. There is no such thing as the "right" or "good" or "best" life. In fact, in an absolute sense, there is no such thing as a "good" or "bad" teacher. We are good or bad, right or wrong, beautiful or ugly only in relation to something or someone else, and then only approximately so. As Albert Einstein pointed out years ago, everything is relative.

Perhaps in few areas of human activity is the relative and approximate nature of things more clearly seen than it is in the area of learning and teaching. Yet, even in relatively precise areas of study, such as physics and mathematics, there are no absolutes. There are only approximations. We come through our experiences to believe, however, that there are such measures as *exactly* 1 foot or 1 inch or a measure that equals 1 pound or one that is an absolute liter. During the intermediate grades in public school, we learn that there are such things as "equal" fractions and that there is such a thing as one-half and that one-half plus one-half equals one whole. The only place that these measures exist in an absolute sense is in our minds—in definition or in abstraction. Correspondence with reality is only an approximation. This is also the case with many of our other truths. The truth that everything has a beginning and an end is true relative to the extent of our experience. The world is only approximately round. The rule "Birds fly" is only approximately true; and so is all of what is said in this textbook.

The finer our measuring devices become, the closer and closer our approximations come to being precise. In science, measuring devices have become more precise than in other areas, such as in the study of human behavior. Consequently, the precision with which people are able to work within a discipline is relative to that discipline.

Throughout history, humans have searched for truth in an absolute sense because having general, lasting truths simplifies the whole business of living. Consequently, a good deal of human effort has been directed at abstracting absolutes or lasting truths from everyday experiences and at applying those "truths" to as many conditions of human activity as possible. However, as experience changes, so does truth. With experience, we see the earth as just another heavenly body, round, and then not so round. What goes "up" no longer has to come "down."

Persons who accept the responsibility for participating in the lives of children must question the nature of their own beliefs—especially those beliefs which have come to be regarded as absolutes. Education consists only of relative approximations and it demands that its teachers understand this clearly.

CAUSE AND EFFECT IN HUMAN BEHAVIOR

The civilized world has always been interested in observing human behavior, especially behavior that is atypical or that deviates from the expected. We have also been interested in describing and classifying behavior, making predictions about future behavior, and trying to explain and change it. As classroom teachers, you will be concerned with all these aspects of human behavior. When trying to understand why your learners behave as they do, try to keep in mind the rule that what you do to change their behavior is related to what you believe to be "true" about the causes of their behavior. Furthermore, remember that the effectiveness of your efforts to change behavior is limited by the precision and accuracy of your knowledge about the causes of behavior. Let us see how this rule has applied in historical perspective.

A Brief History

A brief review of humanity's interests in observing, describing, classifying, and modifying abnormal behavior will help to illustrate a teacher's need for accurate, detailed knowledge about the causes of the behavior. The following account is abstracted from Coleman's *Abnormal Psychology and Modern Life*.[1]

DEMONS AND SPIRITS

The earliest treatment for deviant behavior of which we have any knowledge was that practiced by Stone Age cavemen some half million years ago. For certain forms of mental illness, probably those where the patient complained of severe headaches and developed convulsive attacks, the early medicine man treated the disorder by means of an operation now called *trephining*. Crude stone instruments were used to chip away an area of the skull in the form of a circle until the skull was cut through. This opening presumably permitted the evil spirit which was believed to be *causing* all the trouble to escape. In some cases trephined skulls of primitive men show healing around the opening indicating that the individual survived the operation and lived for many years (Selling, 1943). This brain surgery left much to be desired in terms of technique, but it was even more inadequate in terms of the naïve, unscientific theory of demonology upon which it rested: "If an evil spirit is the cause of the abnormal behavior, then rid the body of the evil spirit in order to effect a cure."

References to mental disorders in the early writings of the Chinese, Egyptians, Hebrews, and Greeks make it clear that they too attributed severely atypical behavior to supernatural causes which had taken possession of the individual. For them, it seemed logical that good and evil spirits caused lightning, thunder, earthquakes, storms, fires, sickness, and many other events, including peculiar behavior, which primitive peoples did not understand.

Techniques used to rid the body of the unwanted evil spirit varied considerably among cultures and at different times. Typically, these techniques included

---

[1] James C. Coleman (1972). *Abnormal Psychology and Modern Life*, 4th ed. Glenview, Ill.: Scott, Foresman, Ch. 2. Reprinted with permission of the publisher.

prayer, incantation, noisemaking, and the use of purgatives. The purpose was either to lure the evil spirit out or to make the body such an unpleasant place that the evil spirit would no longer want to reside there. In extreme cases, flogging, starving, dunking, frightening, even burning an individual were used.

MENTAL ILLNESS

From the seventeenth to the nineteenth century demonology slowly gave way to the belief that people who behaved in abnormal ways were "sick" and should be called "patients." Monasteries and prisons gradually relinquished the care of mental patients to asylums, which were being established in increasing numbers. The care of patients in these asylums, however, left much to be desired. In 1547, the monastery of St. Mary of Bethlehem in London was officially designated as a mental hospital by Henry VIII. Its name was soon contracted to Bedlam and it became widely known for the deplorable conditions and practices that prevailed. The more violent patients were exhibited to the public for "one penny a look," and the more harmless inmates were forced to seek charity on the streets.

Treatment of mentally ill patients in North America was little better. Martin Deutsch gives a vivid description of the plight of the mentally ill during colonial times: [2]

> The mentally ill were hanged, imprisoned, tortured, and otherwise persecuted as agents of Satan. Regarded as sub-human beings, they were chained in specially devised kennels and cages like wild beasts and thrown into prisons, bridewells, and jails like criminals. . . . Even the well-to-do were not spared confinement in strong rooms and cellar dungeons, while legislation usually concerned itself more with their property than with their persons.

As modern experimental science gradually emerged, there was an increasingly more scientific and humane approach to the mentally ill. It must be remembered, however, that change does not always come easily. Even though great advances were being made in areas such as physics and medicine, demonology was still widespread. As late as 1768, the Protestant John Wesley made his famous declaration that giving up witchcraft is, in effect, giving up the Bible.

Following the humanitarian advances made by various European reformers, Benjamin Rush (1735–1814), called the Father of American Psychiatry, encouraged more humane treatment of the mentally ill at the Pennsylvania Hospital. But Rush did not escape entirely from the established beliefs of his time. His medical theory was tainted with astrology and his principle remedies were bloodletting and purgatives. In addition, he invented and used a torturelike device called the tranquillizer.

From the early 1860s, knowledge of anatomy, physiology, neurology, chemistry, and general medicine increased rapidly. These advances led to the gradual uncovering of organic pathology underlying many physical ailments, and it was only another step for these pioneer workers to jump to the conclusion that mental illness is a definite sickness based upon organic brain pathology. Impetus

[2] M. A. Deutsch (1946). *The Mentally Ill in America*. New York: Columbia University Press, p. 53. Copyright by the American Foundation for Mental Hygiene.

was given to intensive research in the physiological, medical, and allied fields in an attempt to isolate the brain pathology which was assumed to be the underlying cause of the various types of mental illness.

As early as the turn of the twentieth century, however, a new kind of psychiatric thought was challenging the belief in brain pathology as the sole cause of mental illness. This revolutionary view maintained that certain types of mental illness may be caused by psychological rather than organic factors; that the frustrations and conflicts common to everyday living may become so overwhelming that individuals will resort to the use of "unhealthy" responses in their efforts to adjust.

It was clear to many that there are mental disorders with psychological as well as organic causes, but one major question still remained to be answered: "How do psychologically caused mental illnesses come about?"

A DISEASE MODEL FOR BEHAVIOR

A common phenomenon of the growth and metamorphosis of an area of knowledge is the borrowing of information from related disciplines to help explain observations. This is seen especially in the development of knowledge of cause and effect in human behavior. The discovery within medicine of the etiology of certain diseases which follow a particular pattern, that of inner causes associated with outer observable symptoms, was generalized in an attempt to account for diseased behavior. Since it had been well established that a causal relationship exists between certain types of body abnormalities and certain deviant behaviors, it was only natural that a disease or "medical model," as it has recently come to be called, may also be used as a basis for trying to explain deviant behavior. This course of action shows up clearly in the work of Sigmund Freud (1856–1939).

Freud was a brilliant Viennese physician who first specialized in neurology, receiving an appointment as lecturer on nervous diseases at the University of Vienna. Perhaps his great contribution to the advancement of man's understanding of human behavior was his stress on the importance of early childhood experiences in later personality adjustment and maladjustment. Furthermore, he demonstrated that abnormal mental phenomena are simply exaggerations of normal phenomena, and that the patient's symptoms derive from attempts to meet personal problems as best as possible. With the realization that the same psychological principles are basic to both normal and abnormal behavior, much of the mystery surrounding mental illness was dispelled.

Freud believed that in order for an organism to respond, it must have an inner source of driving energy. He was unable to visualize that an individual's early experiences could relate *directly* to later experiences without operating through inner dynamic forces. Consequently, we see in Freud's work a reliance on the existence of hypothetical inner entities which are acted upon by early experience and which in turn give rise to, and direct, later behavior. Note how this line of thought parallels closely the one used to explain the cause of an infectious disease such as measles. This similarity is illustrated in Table 2-1.

You will recall our previous discussion about the relationship between what persons believe causes behavior and what they do to change it. In Freud's approach, the cause for maladaptive behavior is believed to lie somewhere in the early experiences of the individual. It is not these experiences themselves that

TABLE 2-1   Comparison of a medical model for disease and human behavior

ENVIRONMENT	BODY	SYMPTOMS
Disease		
Germs from the environment	→ enter the body and cause	→ the body to behave as it does, e.g., to experience fever, red spots, rapid heart beat, shallow breathing.
Behavior		
Early experiences in the environment	→ influence innate driving forces which cause	→ the person to behave as he does, e.g., share his lunch, steal coins, help the teacher, bite his fingernails.

are important in present behavior but their influence on innate and inner dynamic forces as they were striving for expression during the first years of life. These childhood experiences, in the Freudian view, lead to either a relatively normal or an abnormal balance among the driving forces which, thereafter, relate functionally to the ways in which an individual behaves. Consequently, any observed behavior, whether normal or abnormal, is considered to be only symptomatic of the balance or imbalance of inner forces. The observed behavior is not important in its own right, but rather, it is an indicator of some basic *inner* difficulty. Following this reasoning, we know by analogy that treating the symptoms does not make sense. Rather, we must treat the "real" cause of the disturbance which supposedly is within the body.

Cause and effect in human behavior means . . .   This line of thinking led to the development of a therapeutic technique, called *psychoanalysis,* for the psychological treatment of the mentally ill. This treatment is an intensive, long-range program of therapy which attempts to restructure the patient's personality in the direction of greater integration and more effective methods of coping with life's problems. The procedure for such a technique requires a person to talk freely about past experiences, especially early, traumatic ones. The procedure came to be called *free association,* and the term psychoanalysis was given to the principle involved in analyzing and interpreting what the patient does or does not say and do. Oversimplified here, the basic assumption is that if a person is able to gain logical insight into the nature of his difficulties, he will then achieve a proper balance of inner driving forces that will result in a more adequate adjustment to everyday problems. That is, the person's behavior will change.

A SCIENCE OF BEHAVIOR

It has been only in recent years that a Freudian type of medical model has shown some of its serious limitations as a useful tool for changing behavior. The most serious barrier has been the overextension of the analogy with medicine to the study of behavior.

**TABLE 2-2 Comparison of medical and psychological models
for human behavior**

ENVIRONMENT	BODY	SYMPTOMS
Medical model		
Early experiences in the environment	influence innate driving forces which *cause*	the person to behave as he does.
Psychological model		
Early experiences in the environment cause		the person to behave as he does.

Most, if not all, early interest in human behavior centered on maladaptive behavior. Only in the late nineteenth and the early twentieth centuries did a study of behavior apart from physical illness begin to be recognized as a legitimate and worthwhile enterprise in its own right. Following advances made in the investigation of the behavior of lower forms of animal life, human behavior came to be studied with increased scientific rigor.

From controlled psychological experimentation have come many simple and specific rules of behavior which do not rely on the assumption of inner entities as causes of behavior. Rather, the focus has begun to center on natural and observable events in the environment as probable causes. Furthermore, it has proved useful to consider that these events act *directly* on behavior rather than indirectly through inner agents. These differences in point of view are illustrated in Table 2-2.

The controversy created by this seemingly minor difference in point of "truth" has had far-reaching implications for school learning and instruction. We will examine these in detail in later chapters.

Description and Explanation in Human Behavior

Now we turn to another important problem relative to cause and effect in human behavior. Earlier, I mentioned that as classroom teachers, you will be interested in observing, describing, classifying, predicting, explaining, and changing the behavior of learners. To do this effectively, you need to be as precise as possible in your understanding and use of the terms which *describe* behavior and those which *explain* behavior.

THE MISUSE OF DESCRIPTION

One of the major difficulties we encounter regarding the concept of cause and effect is the misuse of "description" of behavior as "explanation" of behavior. The probable reason is that describing *how* a person behaves usually is much easier than explaining *why* a person behaves in a certain way.

Confusion of description with explanation is not always a problem, however.

If our purpose is to predict probable future behavior, describing precisely how a person has behaved in the past serves as a relatively good predictor for how that person is likely to behave later. Confusion between the two terms causes us problems only when our purpose is to *change* a person's behavior, because a description of behavior, even one which is carefully formulated and precise in detail, simply does not constitute explanation; it does not tell us *why* the behavior occurs.

Most of our firsthand experience in regard to human behavior has been descriptive in nature. What is immediately apparent about people and events is, of course, their behavior. And, as a consequence of the instant availability of observable data, we have established many detailed and complex classification systems to describe not only normal, but also abnormal, behavior. Much of the psychology which has derived from Freud's work is concerned with classification and labeling of human behaviors.

Confusion of description with explanation leads to . . . For the most part, however, we have had to rely on supposition and introspection for our explanations of why we behave as we do. Causes of behavior are not as immediately observable as are the behaviors themselves. One serious consequence is that we become careless in our use of descriptive terms. For example, we begin to believe that we have explained why Susie Brown shares her lunch with another person when we "explain" that she is kind and thoughtful. The weakness in this "explanation" is, however, that the words "kind" and "thoughtful" are descriptive words. The reasoning is circular. Another example of this type of circular reasoning is shown in Figure 2-1.

The point I want to make here is an extremely important one for teachers since what we do to change the behavior of our learners is a consequence of what we believe causes their behavior. Let me illustrate this point with examples.

SOME EXAMPLES OF THE MISUSE OF DESCRIPTION Suppose I place a clock in front of you and ask you what *causes* the clock to behave as it does, that is, why do the hands go around? Why does the alarm ring? We all know about clocks to one degree or another. We know about the relationship between what causes one to run and what we have to do to fix it or get it fixed when it stops.

Assume now that I place before you a toy car which has a springlike "engine" in it. You watch me wind the mechanism with a key. If I ask you what causes the car to behave as it does, that is, move across a table when it is released, most of you will probably mention the spring within the car that produces the forward-driving force on the rear wheels which propels the car across the table. Knowing the cause of the car's behavior enables us to be logical and systematic in changing its behavior.

Suppose we look at some behavior which is a bit more complex. This time, imagine another toy car placed on the table in front of you. It behaves differently. When I operate a small electrical switch on the side of the car, you observe that it moves in a straight line until it comes to the edge of the table. At that point, and just before it tumbles from the table, the car hesitates, reverses direction, and backs away. This kind of behavior occurs over and over, and it is easy to see. If we wanted to, we could describe and record the car's behavior with a high degree of precision. We could even give it a descriptive label which sums up its movements. The word cautious might be such a shorthand, descriptive label.

Now, if I ask you *why* the car does not fall off the table, no one will conclude that the car stays on the table *because* it is cautious. We know that the word "cautious" is just a shorthand way to describe the way the car moves. In other

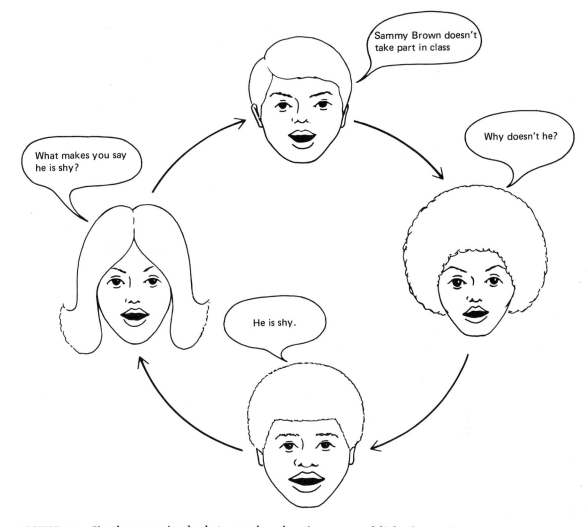

FIGURE 2-1 Circular reasoning leads to pseudoexplanations . . . and little chance of help for Sammy Brown.

words, to describe its behavior. "Cautious" is obviously not an explanation for its behavior. Most of us would be satisfied with such logical reasoning.

However, if I climb on the same table and behave in a manner similar to the car, that is, if I move cautiously to the edge of the table, and at the point just before tumbling off, I move quickly and carefully to the safety of the center of the table, some of you may conclude that I do not fall off *because* I am cautious. Does this reasoning make sense to you? It should not. It is circular.

Let us look at another bit of behavior. This time, imagine a small black box placed on the table in front of you. This box has a lid that hinges on one edge. Near the lid, there is a small receptacle which will receive coins. When a coin is placed in the receptacle, the box immediately begins to vibrate in place. Slowly the lid opens and a small plastic hand reaches up and out of the box. It grabs the coin, and as quick as a wink it disappears with it into the box just as the lid slams tightly closed.

We might *describe* the behavior of the box with a summary type of word, such as "sneaky," "clever," "cute," or "dishonest." As long as everyone understands that these words are being used solely to describe or classify the behavior of the hand, there is little argument with the usage. The problem occurs, however, when these types of descriptive words begin to be used in explanatory ways. When the cause of the particular behavior is not exactly clear, we begin to allow ourselves to think of descriptions of behavior as explanations. We say, for example, that people steal *because* they are dishonest. Few, however, would conclude that the little hand in the black box steals coins because it is either sneaky or dishonest.

So far in our discussion, we have been concerned with the relationship between our beliefs about the causes of behavior and what we do to modify behavior. Now, let us look at this idea again as it relates to the behavior of the hand in the black box. If I am interested in trying to change the behavior of the hand so that it no longer takes coins when they are placed in the receptacle, how may I go about modifying this behavior? Or, stated in more familiar terms, "How can I teach the hand not to steal?"

There are several things that I might try. If I were completely ignorant as to the workings of the box, I might have a little heart-to-heart talk with it and try to explain to the box that I simply will not accept its continuing to steal coins. I might even point out that in the long-run adjustment of the box in a society of essentially honest boxes, such behavior would not be tolerated. If this does not work, I might warn the box, scold it, or try shouting at it. If I cannot think of anything else to do, I will probably hit the box.

Most of you will admit that I would appear pretty stupid to try to change the behavior of the hand by such means. The question, however, is, why does my behavior appear stupid? It appears stupid because we all know, more or less, that the cause of the hand's behavior is the action of batteries, wires, levers, and so forth, and that there is no relationship between my talking to, shouting at, encouraging, or hitting the box and what causes it to steal coins. However, if the cause of the hand's behavior were not so obvious, I would not appear so foolish. In fact, I might not appear foolish at all if, for example, I was trying to change the behavior of children. Yet, at times what we do with children is just as foolish. You will remember some of the early "cures" for mental illness that appear foolish as we read about them today. Keep in mind, however, that they seem foolish solely because now we have the advantage of knowing more about cause and effect in human behavior than did the people before us. Also, what we do today to change the behavior of children will perhaps appear just as foolish to people tomorrow.

CHECKPOINT 2-1

Read the following set of comments made by classroom teachers, and try to identify those which reflect circular reasoning resulting from a confusion of description and explanation. "Sam won't do arithmetic because he doesn't like it"; "Karen can't learn to read because she has a low IQ"; "Joe doesn't pay attention because of his short attention span."

Laws of Behavior and Teaching

To change behavior, it is important to know its causes. And, in order to determine them, we need a way to determine lawful relationships between causes and effects in human behavior. Fortunately, this has been the objective of a branch of psychology that has addressed itself to the study of changes in human behavior.

The behavioral movement, as one recent approach to learning is called, has been directed toward isolating and specifying laws or rules of behavior. Early experimental efforts were concerned primarily with the behavior of lower animals for which strict and careful experimental controls could be effected. Out of such studies, which eventually included more and more aspects of complex human behavior, have come a few basic and simple laws of behavior, for example: "Responses that are rewarded are strengthened," and "Responses that are punished are suppressed." With laws such as these, we are beginning to arrive at more useful explanations of behavior and thus to be able to vary systematically the conditions which will effect desired change in behavior.

An important point, especially for teachers, is that laws of behavior which are reached experimentally are always open for further scientific inquiry. They constitute the means whereby we can get outside the circular arguments which make use of descriptive terms as pseudoexplanations for behavior. Thanks to a few comparatively simple laws of behavior, teachers are now in a position to search systematically and precisely for testable reasons why learners behave as they do. Laws of behavior permit us to intervene in the life of a learner in a logical and consistent way and to check on the effectiveness of what we are doing. We will begin to learn about these laws in Chapter 4.

Are laws of behavior descriptions or explanations?

QUESTIONS OF APPLICATION

Soon you will face the daily problems of a teacher concerned about the learning of students. You will have to make most of the important decisions of how best to go about the task of changing their behavior. How you choose to approach certain questions can make significant differences in whether you and the children are successful. For example, when a boy in your class does not attend appropriately to the learning task at hand, how will you go about causing him to attend? To what will you attribute the cause of his inattentiveness? What will you consider to be the problem? Is inattentiveness only symptomatic of some deeper inner disturbance within the child? Could inattentiveness be a behavior that has been strengthened because it has been rewarded? Once you have made a general decision about the cause of inattentiveness, what will you do about it? What techniques will you have available? Will you consider, as some teachers do, that inattentiveness is a phase through which all children go, and that if just left alone, they will soon grow out of it? Does your view of what causes the inattentiveness suggest that punishing the boy will help improve his behavior? That is, does it suggest that you might be able to beat or scare the bad, inattentive behavior out of the child? Does your reasoning suggest that gaining insight into the problem will help? Would a law of behavior?

CHECKPOINT 2-2

1. Following are comments made by classroom teachers about what they believe should be done to change the behavior of learners. State the beliefs about causes of behavior that are implied in the actions suggested. "The only way to keep Johnny Brown from stealing is to catch him at it and scare the hell out of him"; "If we can just make Sue understand that it isn't right to copy other children's work, I'm sure she will stop"; "If this doesn't stop Tom, I'm afraid we shall have to use corporal punishment."

2. What descriptive words have you previously used incorrectly as explanations of human behavior, but now question? (Related to Affective Objective, Organizational Level.)

PRECISION AND APPROACH

There are many approaches to, or methods of, changing the behavior of learners. All approaches, however, must be concerned in one way or another with laws of cause and effect as they relate to human behavior, even though specific methods may differ markedly. This means that laws or rules of behavior can be applied in many different ways.

Laws of behavior can be applied through . . .   As teachers, we are expected to play an important role in changing the behavior of children, that is, in affecting their learning. Furthermore, we are expected to be able to perform this role on purpose rather than by chance. We are expected to know what we are doing and why we are doing it. This is not to say that we must do all the same things, or indeed, that we should have the same goals for our learners. The important point is that we all understand as precisely as possible how the laws of human behavior can be employed effectively in whatever approach we elect to use.

A Note of Explanation

Now that you have read thus far in Chapter 2, reread the cognitive and affective goals and objectives. You will note that none of them asks you to learn specific names, places, dates, contributions, points of view, and so forth. The essential things to learn at this time are stated in the Goals and Objectives section. The specific content of the chapter is used only to help you learn about the relative and approximate nature of truth, about description and explanation in cause and effect, and about the relationship between beliefs and actions. The importance of the content is only illustrative. Whether you remember that Sigmund Freud was a brilliant Viennese physician is not vital (I do not know for sure that he actually was). The point is that once I decided what I believe is important to learn, Chapter 2 could have included a wide variety of specific information other than that which I chose to cover.

The difference in point of emphasis in *teaching the material* and *using the material to teach for certain objectives* may seem insignificant. The difference, however, can be tremendously important. For example, note the difference between using the story *A Christmas Carol* to help children learn some things about literature, and the alternative of teaching the story itself. Chapter 2 is not intended to be a lesson in history or a demonstration of mechanical toys. It uses toys and a few historical events that are only relatively so and approximately true to help us learn about becoming effective in changing the behavior of children. There may be times, however, when you want your students to learn actual material being presented. You will note that the material in Chapter 3 is used for this purpose. For the most part, what I hope you will learn *is* the material presented.

There is an important rule contained in knowing precisely what our objectives are. It is that when we do know, we are free to teach for those objectives in the best way we can. If, however, we do not know what we want our students to learn, we are not free to practice the art and science of teaching. We are tied to teaching the specific details of the material itself, whatever they may be. We have no reasonable or logical basis for doing otherwise.

I realize it may appear contradictory to suggest that freedom in teaching derives from structure. However, there is good reason to believe that it does. This will become increasingly evident as we proceed through Chapter 3.

Note the beliefs about cause and effect implied in the following account written by a teacher.[3] Notice also the implication that learners change *after* teachers change, and that what we practice is what we learn.

IN PASSING

Timothy was a talented youth, altho as his English teacher, I must confess that the mark I gave him at the end of each of the first two marking periods did not in any way reflect his inherent ability.

In the comments I penned on his report card, opinions were expressed concerning his indifference, his uncooperative attitude, and his lack of effort. When Tim's second report was returned to me, I noticed that Tim's father had written on the space reserved for parent's reaction the pithy comment, "I am dissatisfied too."

But the situation changed markedly in February. By chance I learned that Tim was interested in tennis. I asked him to stay after school, and in the conversation I mentioned some of the major tournaments I had seen.

Because of his interest, I invited him to my home on a Saturday afternoon to meet my eldest son, who had acquired some prominence as a local netster. When Tim left my home, after a demonstration of tennis strokes, he took with him a half-dozen books on court technics and strategy.

Frequently thereafter he stayed after school to talk to me about his reading. He developed an eagerness to give expository talks to his classmates on his hobby. He wrote several papers on tennis ethics and the lessons taught by the lives of great net stars. His paper on tennis ethics he must have rewritten at least a dozen times before it was accepted by the school literary magazine.

I believe no one in the class read or wrote more than he did during the next six weeks. His classmates obtained a liberal education in the romance of tennis.

When I totaled his grades for the next report card, I was surprised to see the great advances he had made in his knowledge of and skill in English. When I inscribed his mark on his card, I wrote:

---

[3] T. E. Robinson (1952). His teacher improved, too, *NEA Journal,* **41,** (1), p. 54.

"Timothy has made rapid advances recently as a student, and I congratulate him."

Back came the father's response. "You give my son too much credit, sir. It is you who should be congratulated for the rapid advances you have made recently as a teacher."

ACTIVITIES

1. Several broad, general ideas relevant to our understanding about changing human behavior were introduced in Chapter 2. These ideas can be stated as simple rules of thumb. As a way of summarizing the chapter, review the content and write rules of thumb for the main ideas presented.

2. In the personality survey *Thorndike Dimensions of Temperament*, several personality traits are assessed. Among them are traits labeled "planful," "impulsive," "placid," "irritable," and so forth. Traits such as these can be useful in explanation of why people behave as they do. Explain why you believe the preceding statement is true or false.

3. As an individual, small group, or entire class activity, provide examples of your own which involve circular reasoning that is based on the fallacy that description constitutes explanation. Have a colleague check your logic.

4. With the use of words, pictures, drawings, or real objects, help someone learn that statements such as the following are only relatively so and approximately true: "Swimming is fun"; "seeds grow." (You will know that your learner has learned when she can explain the idea to someone else.)

5. Just for fun:
The world is full of interesting information. Some of it is useful directly, for example in solving problems of daily living. Some, however, is useful just for the sheer pleasure of knowing. Both kinds of information serve the purpose of making school a good place to attend. Your learners will find it fun to know interesting things such as why manhole covers are round rather than square or some other shape. Do you know why they are round? A *relatively* good explanation can be found in Chapter 3—but it is only *approximately* true.

REFERENCES

Coleman, J. C. (1972). *Abnormal Psychology and Modern Life*, 4th ed. Glenview, Ill.: Scott, Foresman.
Deutsch, M. A. (1946). *The Mentally Ill in America*. New York: Columbia University Press.
Selling, L. S. (1943). *Men Against Madness*. New York: Garden City Books.
Skinner, B. F. (1968). *The Technology of Teaching*. New York: Appleton-Century-Crofts.

SUGGESTIONS FOR FURTHER READING

Staats, A. W., and C. R. Staats (1963). *Complex Human Behavior*. New York: Holt. Chapters 1 and 2 present an excellent discussion of the methods of science applied to a study of behavior. The treatment of the conditions necessary for explanation, and hence for control of behavior, is one of the best available. The chapter which considers personality as learned behavior further illustrates important differences between description and explanation of human behavior.
Ullmann, L. P., and L. Krasner (1965). *Case Studies in Behavior Modification*. New York: Holt, Rinehart and Winston. The first twenty-eight pages of the Introduction do an excellent job of contrasting the usefulness of medical and psychological models for effecting change in human behavior.
Skinner, B. F. (1971). *Beyond Freedom and Dignity*. New York: Knopf. In *Beyond Freedom and Dignity* Skinner shares with us some of the concerns he has about what he believes to be the tragic direction our world is taking as it (1) pursues a "truth" relative to individual freedom and dignity, and (2) evades the issue of dealing meaningfully with control of human behavior. Reading Skinner gives one a sense of what Sir Isaac Newton

must have felt as he "stood on the shoulders of giants," and thus was able to "see farther than most."

Gage, N. L. (1968). Can science contribute to the art of teaching? *Phi Delta Kappan,* **49,** 399–403. In his article, Gage expresses both pessimism and optimism about the contributions of science to the art of teaching. He presents reasons for both points of view and then tries to illustrate what might be done to alleviate some of the pessimism.

Skinner, B. F. (1974). *About Behaviorism.* New York: Knopf. Behaviorism has, for years, been widely misunderstood, often due to the behavior of the very persons who have tried to promote its acceptance, for example, that of John B. Watson. In *About Behaviorism,* Skinner answers some of the most common charges leveled, over the years, against behaviorism. Early in this course would be a good time to learn of these charges and how Skinner answers them.

STATING GOALS AND OBJECTIVES: COGNITIVE, AFFECTIVE, AND PSYCHOMOTOR

Regardless of how many failures a person has had in his past, regardless of his background, his culture, his color, or his economic level, *he will not succeed in general until he can in some way first experience success in one important part of his life.*

William Glasser
Schools Without Failure

CONTENTS

ONGOING SUMMARY

You will recall, from the somewhat general discussion in Chapters 1 and 2, that our major, long-range goal is that we will be effective in causing desired changes in learners' behavior. We have said that education means change, and that to cause it to take place in desired ways, we must be concerned with causing children to attend appropriately to learning tasks. Therefore, we must understand about cause and effect in human behavior, and we must be able to discriminate between *description* and *explanation.*

What children attend to must concern us, for, as we saw in Chapters 1 and 2, children learn what they attend to. We must remember that what we cause them to attend to is only relatively so and approximately true. At the same time, teaching and learning are concerned with specifics of human behavior, especially the specifics of what children should learn, that is, what they should attend to.

ADVANCE ORGANIZER

With Chapter 3, we begin our inquiry into the specifics of the first major question we must face as teachers: "What do I want learners to learn?"

Our attention will now be directed toward gaining mastery of the specific skills involved in completing task descriptions, that is, in breaking down broad areas of inquiry into specific, descriptive statements about what a learner is to learn. These statements are called goals and objectives. Because skills often require more practice than other types of learning, Chapter 3 includes more checkpoints for practice than other chapters.

All instructional objectives relative to school learning can be described in terms of a hierarchically ordered classification scheme known as a *taxonomy of educational objectives*. Within this taxonomy can be classified three major types of human behavior which include all the types relevant to school learning: (1) cognitive or "thinking" kinds of behavior; (2) affective behavior, i.e., attitudes, beliefs, values; and (3) psychomotor, or physical movements.

Although for convenience the three domains are usually considered separately, all behavior has components of more than just the domain within which it may conveniently be classified, and there is a great deal of overlap among domains. Only in point of emphasis can a behavior be classified in any one domain. For the cognitive and psychomotor domains, the emphasis is on the question: "*Can* the learner perform?" For the affective domain, it is: "*Will* the learner perform?"

Although these domains are only approximate guides, they can help us be relatively precise about what we want our learners to learn. But, until we know this clearly and precisely, the next question, "*How* can I help learners learn?" remains senseless.

Cognitive

GOALS AND OBJECTIVES

To become an effective teacher, the learner should be able to formulate long-range goals and instructional objectives in cognitive, affective, and psychomotor domains.

KNOWLEDGE LEVEL

Given the following terms, the learner is able to define them in writing: *taxonomy of educational objectives, cognitive domain, affective domain, psychomotor domain, goal, objectives, task description, task analysis, readiness, transfer.*

COMPREHENSION LEVEL

1. Given the major categories of the cognitive, affective, and psychomotor domains, the learner is able to describe typical behavior for each category.
2. When asked the question, "In what ways are specific instructional objectives useful for instructional purposes?" the learner is able to state their value prior to, during, and after instruction.

APPLICATION LEVEL

Given the terms "task description," and "task analysis," the learner is able to explain how to do these tasks with a specific example not mentioned in the text.

SYNTHESIS LEVEL

Given a topic of study, e.g., community helpers, fractions, business letters, or basketball, the learner is able to formulate one long-range goal and at least one related instructional objective for each major category of the cognitive, affective, and psychomotor domains.

EVALUATION LEVEL

Given the opportunity to teach either for specific objectives or for general goals, the learner is able to state reasons for choosing one rather than the other.

Affective

To become an effective teacher, the learner should be able to sustain attention long enough and well enough to learn the skills of writing long-range goals and specific instructional objectives.

RECEIVING (ATTENDING) LEVEL

The learner is willing to get involved with the "doing" parts of this chapter rather than just the "reading" parts.

RESPONDING LEVEL

The learner derives satisfaction from being precise in making a statement of instructional objectives.

VALUING LEVEL

The learner develops a keen interest in learning to be effective at the skills of task description.

ORGANIZATIONAL LEVEL

The learner accepts the challenge "not to be content to be mediocre in the skills of task description."

CHARACTERIZATION LEVEL

The learner takes on the responsibility of helping others learn to write objectives rather than trying to out-do them.

3

In Chapter 1 we said that education is a process of teaching and learning that results in changes in behavior. This is not an entirely adequate definition, however. For example, is education mostly learning factual information, knowledge? Is it a matter of learning how to learn? Does education mean acquiring certain kinds of attitudes and skills? Is it all these and more too?

In earlier times, school learning or formal education tended to be defined more specifically in terms of content than it is today. Within the past few years, there has been increased concern with the learning process itself, in some cases almost to the point that content is considered merely a means or mechanism to learn about learning.

Even more recently, there appears to be an increasing shift in emphasis to consider the importance of content along with the importance of process. A significant point has been the recognition that we must cause factual information to be meaningfully acquired by learners rather than acquired only in rote fashion. This means that factual information must be learned in a way relevant to other learning experiences, past and future. Acquiring factual information solely for the sake of having it has come under serious question.

As a teacher working within the definition of education as a combination of content and process, you may encounter the difficulty that the emphasis in your own education may have been on content. Working under changing expectations, you will need to make education for your own learners somewhat different from what it was for you.

FORMULATING LONG-RANGE GOALS AND SPECIFIC INSTRUCTIONAL OBJECTIVES

Although education for learners must be more than their memory of information, recall of information is not unimportant. It is just insufficient. Education that focuses on accumulation of knowledge becomes dull and routine. For the most part, tasks of the memory type lack intrinsic incentives, and learners find it difficult to attend to them. Over time, an education that emphasizes memory may actually foster and perpetuate loss of what Carroll (1963) and Trabasso (1968) maintain are key variables in learning: interest and attention. Furthermore, education that is only memory of fact is not a very useful education. It does not provide a good basis for further learning or for solving everyday problems. Such an education represents the minimal level of learning activity—acquire and repeat. To make education more than memory, however, requires broad and specific understanding of what society considers education to be, that is, understanding of its goals and objectives. It also requires that teachers be skilled in formulating goals and instructional objectives.

Two key variables in learning are . . .

A Need for Specific Objectives

During the past few years an increased effort has been directed toward establishing clear, usable definitions of what education should be. Researchers have explored our educational goals and objectives for learners; about what we want them to be able to do as a consequence of their experience in schools. Of course, there has always been concern about these goals and objectives, but in the past they were stated so vaguely and generally that they were relatively meaningless in terms of curriculum planning or even in planning day-by-day instruction. Consequently, the impact of these statements on curriculum or on what actually occurs in classrooms has usually been small. Outside observers, for example, may have difficulty in relating what they see taking place in a classroom to the school's philosophy or to its long-range goals for education.

Instructional objectives derive from . . .

Long-range goals are often stated in such general form that teachers can convince themselves, no matter what they do with their classes, that these are the goals that guide their teaching. Goals stated as imprecisely as "to have command of," "to understand," or "to appreciate" can be interpreted in a variety of ways. We must go beyond such vague statements. We must analyze general goals for descriptions of the behavior that pupils will be capable of carrying out when they "have command of," "understand," or "appreciate." When we know the expected results, long-range goals have exact meaning, and they become useful to us as we plan specific activities for our learners. Only then will we be able to answer with any precision the question, "What do I want learners to learn?"

ANOTHER POINT OF VIEW

Even though these points may form a convincing argument in favor of precision in goals and instructional objectives, one must not believe that everyone accepts them. There is, in fact, the point of view that applying the methods of science to human behavior can be dangerous—especially to human behavior as it relates to teaching and learning in school settings. Somehow, the feeling, expressed by Gilbert Highet (1957), is that if you specify too precisely what education should be, you may in fact run the risk of ruining it. He asks: "Must everything be defined, dissected and measured? Is there no room left in education for spontaneity, an *art* as practiced by an educated man?" Many believe that there is, and Highet presents the view that teaching is an *art*, not a science. He maintains that it is "very dangerous to apply the aims and principles of science to human beings as individuals."[1] He goes on to say:[2]

> It is necessary for any teacher to be orderly in planning his work and precise in his dealing with facts. But that does not make his teaching "scientific." Teaching involves emotions, which cannot be systematically appraised and employed, and human values, which are quite outside the grasp of science. A "scientifically" brought-up child would be a pitiable monster. . . . Teaching is not like inducing a chemical reaction: it is much more like painting a picture or making a piece of music . . . like planting a garden or writing a friendly letter. You must throw your heart into it, you must realize that it cannot all be done by formulas, or you will spoil all your work, and your pupils, and yourself.

Stephen's theory of spontaneous teaching states . . .

John Stephens (1965), an educational psychologist widely known for his views that combine science and common sense, has had a great deal to say about what he calls spontaneous forces in teaching. He believes that even though the teaching process is complex, "crude rudiments are taken care of by automatic tendencies found to some extent in all adults and conspicuously present in quite a few."[3] Furthermore, he says that we should take comfort in realizing that

[1] G. Highet (1957). *The Art of Teaching.* New York: Vintage Books, p. vii.
[2] Ibid., pp. vii–viii.
[3] John Stephens (1965). *The Psychology of Classroom Learning.* New York: Holt.

"in managing this complex and awesome process, you do not always have to manipulate, in deliberate and conscious fashion, each minute aspect of the learning process operating within the child. On the contrary, put yourself in a situation in which teaching is in order, let yourself go, and, by virtue of the spontaneous urges to be found within you, *some* teaching will probably take place."[4]

Criticism aimed at the specification of instructional objectives has also been raised with the contention that their precise specification leads to constriction of learners' interest, a rigidness in educational practices, and definite limitations on what is learned. This objection suggests that learners may stop learning when they feel they have met the specified objectives, whereas, when objectives are not precisely stated, learners may go beyond the objectives. In this view, specific instructional objectives may act as signals to stop learning.

Another criticism of specific objectives conjures up a mental image of a mechanical, factory type of process in which learners are stuffed with learning much as sausage cases are stuffed with meat.

EDUCATION IS MORE THAN EITHER/OR

It is tempting at this point to say that these statements pretty well sum up most of the differences of opinion about the relative place and importance of specific instructional objectives in education, and that as a beginning teacher, you will have to make up your own mind about what you will do. My preference, however, is in the direction of attempting to be clear and precise about what we consider important for learners to learn as a consequence of school experience. Edward L. Thorndike, early in the twentieth century, expressed a point of view that I urge you to consider. He was concerned that education was being looked upon by many people as either an art or a science. To him, this did not make a great deal of sense. Obviously, teaching was best considered *both*—not either/or. In his textbook *Principles of Teaching Based upon Psychology* (1906), he tried to give a scientific basis for the art of teaching and to show how it could be done. Yet, Thorndike was well aware of the importance of talking first about the *what* and *why* of education. This is the way Thorndike put it:[5]

Education is both an art and . . .

> If a teacher does not appreciate, at least crudely, the general aims of education, he will not fully appreciate the general aims of school education; if he does not appreciate the general aims of school education, he will not fully appreciate the aims of his special grade or of any one special subject; if he does not have fairly clear ideas of what the year's work as a whole or of what each subject as a whole ought to accomplish for the scholars, he will not know exactly what he is about in any particular day's work. . . . The teacher should often study how to utilize inborn tendencies, how to form habits, how to develop interests and the like with reference to what changes in intellect and character are to be made. The teacher should know about educational aims and values as well as about such principles of teaching as directly concern his own activities in the class-room.

Specifying precise instructional objectives for learners in no way reduces the freedom of teachers to be spontaneous, inventive, and enthusiastic about what they are doing. Indeed, knowing clearly what you want your learners to learn

---

[4] Ibid., p. 437.

[5] E. L. Thorndike (1906). *Principles of Teaching Based upon Psychology.* New York: Seiler, p. 2.

permits you a great deal of freedom and flexibility in terms of how you choose to get them to learn it. In fact, the teachers who are not free, that is, the teachers who are limited in their choice of materials, activities, and so forth with which to cause learners to learn are the very teachers who have not specified clearly what it is they want the learners to learn. If you do not know what you are trying to help your learners do, you must do as you see others do or as you are told to do by such directives as workbooks, textbooks, and curriculum guides. Spontaneity in teaching must derive out of design and purpose, rather than out of ignorance.

Specifying goals and objectives as best you can, realizing full well that you will need to modify them with experience, forms a reasonable basis from which to proceed. It provides clues as to the sorts of materials you should use; the kinds of questions you should ask; and the kinds of affective components you should keep in mind as you plan specific learning experiences. What we need to do at this point, then, is to begin learning the skills of writing goals and specific objectives.

A Way of Arriving at Goals and Objectives

To arrive at long-range goals and specific instructional objectives, we must start with questions about broad purposes of education and, from these, progress toward more specific goals and finally to specific instructional objectives. Goals and objectives at all levels of generality should reflect an internal consistency with broad definitions and broad statements of purposes. You will notice that this is essentially what Thorndike was saying back in 1906.

As an example of how this process works, let me describe my own procedure in building the goals and objectives for this text. I began by asking the broad question: "What is the purpose of education?"

Here I am talking to myself: I believe the broad purpose of education is to bring about changes in behavior. Of course, I don't know for sure whether this statement is adequate or sufficient. Yet, I must begin somewhere with what I know, believe, feel, or at least have a hunch about.

Now that I have a relative and approximate idea of what I believe to be the purpose of education, this idea brings me to the next question: "What must teachers be able to do to be effective in changing the behavior of learners?" For my answer, I can look to agencies which control teacher certification. Generally, teacher requirements fall into three major categories: (1) knowledge in subject matter areas, (2) knowledge and skill in methods of instruction, and (3) knowledge and skill in the psychology of learning and instruction.

I feel that I am beginning to zero in on what the goals and objectives should be for *Psychology for Learning and Teaching*. I can focus on them now by asking: "What is educational psychology?" "What can a psychology of learning and instruction provide a teacher in the task of bringing about changes in the behavior of children?" That is, "What do I believe teachers should be able to do as a consequence of their learning experience with this text?"

Answers to this last question should provide me with a statement of a broad, long-range goal. I can see that if next I ask: "What must the teacher be able to do to meet the long-range goal?" I will have a statement of long-range goals for the

TABLE 3-1   Specific instructional objectives derive from general, long-range goals

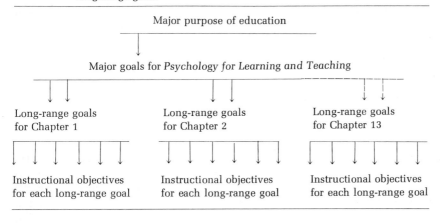

various topics that I believe combine to define what I mean by educational psychology. I can make these topics the major divisions in the text. Long-range goals can be written for each topic. If I put them all together, I will have my definition of what I believe to be important about the psychology of learning and instruction.

Now, if I ask one more question, I should arrive at a statement of specific instructional objectives: "What must the teacher be able to do to meet the long-range goals for each chapter?" When I answer this question, I will have the specific instructional objectives for each topic. These are the statements of the specific behaviors I believe you should be able to perform in order to (1) meet the long-range goals for each chapter, which then (2) help you meet the long-range goal of this text. This goal, in turn, helps define (3) what I believe you must be able to do to cause change in the behavior of learners, and (4) what I believe is the purpose of schools and of education.

At this point, I find myself recalling what Stephens (1965) said in favor of spontaneous schooling—just to "let it happen"—and I must admit it is tempting. But then I try to visualize what the everyday instruction of thirty children would be like without some sort of logically consistent way of approaching the question: "What do I want them to learn?" I also visualize what my efforts would look like through my learner's eyes. I decide to go ahead with building a logical and consistent structure, out of which I will try to derive spontaneity.

What I have said about arriving at long-range goals and objectives is shown in brief in Table 3-1. The diagram will give you both a general picture of what I mean and a way to verify your understanding of my verbal description.

AN EXAMPLE OF GOALS AND OBJECTIVES

The following example will help show the application of the questioning process just described. It consists of a set of long-range goals and specific instructional objectives for a unit of study for children in elementary school. The unit was developed by a student in a teacher preparation program and used in subsequent practice-teaching experience. Notice as you read through it how an example (concrete instance) adds meaning to the questioning sequence presented earlier.

SOCIAL STUDIES

THE COAST SALISH INDIANS[6]

What are Social Studies?

The *general* curriculum area to be studied in this unit is Social Studies. The Social Studies are those subjects which are concerned with the interactions of people in groups, and with their physical environment. Social Studies are a vitally important component of the entire school curriculum because their aims—to help children develop the necessary understandings, skills, and attitudes to become well-integrated, informed and responsible citizens—are virtually synonymous with the aims of the total school education—to make good citizens of our school, community, nation, and world. The school and Social Studies curriculum do, indeed, help children to reach self-actualization by allowing them to experience success and accomplishment and thus develop good citizens of tomorrow.

The topic of this particular unit is Indians—the Coast Salish Indians.

The Class

The class for which this Unit is intended is at the grade-four level and consists of about thirty-five pupils, all Caucasian, half girls and half boys. There are no children with noted emotional problems or physical handicaps. The subjective reading-ability levels range from upper grade-three to lower grade-five. I anticipate that it will take about three and one-half weeks to complete this unit.

The students have in earlier years studied their immediate environment (rural and urban), the physical environment (introduction of elementary geographical terms), and world folk (i.e., Holland, Switzerland). In grade-three they learned to study other people in relation to themselves (their climate, activities, etc.). Now that they are in grade-four, the students make their extended study of their community and nation with the historical background introduced. Thus, the topic of Indians, or more specifically, the Coast Salish Indians, because they are more typical of the native life of British Columbia than any other group.

Long-Range Goals

COGNITIVE

1. The student will gain knowledge and skills which will enable him to become a well-adjusted, well-informed and socially responsible citizen.

---

[6] By Susan Robbins, reprinted with permission of the author.

2. The student will develop skills in selecting important information from resource materials.

3. The student will develop skill in communicating with others through verbal and non-verbal means.

4. The student will become aware of how the environment influences the way people live.

5. The student will be able to transfer his knowledge of how Indians lived to how other groups of people live, (i.e., Dutch—how environment and technology affect past and current ways of life).

6. The student will become aware of how Indians lived in B.C. [British Columbia], food, clothing, shelter, tools and weapons, customs.

AFFECTIVE

1. The student will develop an appreciation, respect, and an elementary interest and understanding of our heritage, specifically of the contributions made by Native People.

2. The student will develop a sense of curiosity and a desire to learn.

3. The student will enjoy contributing and co-operating successfully with the rest of his classmates.

4. The student will value the idea that many people have contributed to our daily life as it occurs today.

5. The student will become committed to the belief that people are important.

Specific Instructional Objectives

COGNITIVE

KNOWLEDGE LEVEL

1. Given a map of [British Columbia] the student will be able to identify the approximate home of the Coast Salish Indians.

2. When asked to name and describe the dwellings in which the Coast Salish Indians lived, the student will be able to do so in a short paragraph.

3. The student will be able to identify four primary sources of food eaten by the Coast Salish Indians and explain how they are prepared.

COMPREHENSION LEVEL

The student will be able to write a definition in his own words of the following terms: *culture, long-house, totem pole, potlatch, tomtom, adze, harpoon, environment, technology, non-verbal communication.*

APPLICATION LEVEL

Given the knowledge of how the early Coast Salish Indians caught and used salmon, the student is able to write an article for the school newspaper entitled: "How to Survive on the [British Columbia] Coast."

ANALYSIS LEVEL

1. The student can compare and contrast in writing the means of transportation used by the Coast Salish Indians many years ago to the available means of transportation which we use today.

2. The student will be able to compare a day in the life of a Coast Salish Indian child to that of a day in his own life by writing an entry in a diary for both a Coast Salish child and himself.

SYNTHESIS LEVEL

1. Given the direction to construct a booklet on the Coast Salish Indians by using the materials and ideas presented in class, research materials, and pictures drawn or collected by the students, he will be able to do so.

2. The student will be able to provide four examples of his own making of what the Coast Salish Indians might have used for tools and how they may have used them.

EVALUATION LEVEL

When asked to give his opinion of the importance of the physical environment in which the Coast Salish Indians lived in terms of how it affected their way of life, the student is able to do so and give reasons to support his opinion.

AFFECTIVE

RECEIVING (ATTENDING) LEVEL

The student develops an awareness of the conditions under which the Coast Salish Indians lived (as compared to our present day conditions).

RESPONDING LEVEL

1. The student enjoys learning about Indian people.

2. The student enjoys participating in the activities which surround the study of the Coast Salish Indians, and he experiences feeling of worth and success as a result of his contributions.

VALUING LEVEL

1. The student enjoys working with others and thus develops consideration, respect and co-operation for and with his classmates.

2. The student develops a desire to learn more about the history of Indians of British Columbia and the rest of Canada, thereby becoming interested in other aspects of the history of our nation and the world.

ORGANIZATION LEVEL

The student develops tolerance for differences . . . physical, cultural and those which represent differences in point of view.

No doubt you noted that the instructional objectives in the example of the Coast Salish Indians have certain distinct characteristics. First, they are stated *from the learner's point of view*. Second, they refer to *specific learner behavior*. Third, they include any *qualifications* that specific behaviors must meet. Fourth, they represent a *variety of types of learner behaviors;* that is, some of the objectives require memory of information, whereas others require more than just memory. Long-range goals, on the other hand, are stated as broad, general outcomes of learning to which a study of the unit will contribute. These are important ideas relative to developing skill in writing long-range goals and specific instructional objectives. They will be elaborated upon in later sections. For now, let us check on your understanding of the differences between goals and objectives.

Which of the following represent goals, and which represent objectives?
1. At the end of the course, the learner will understand educational psychology. Goal____Objective____

2. Given the rule of behavior, "Responses that are followed by rewarding consequences are strengthened," the learner can give an example of how it may be applied. Goal____Objective____

3. Given appropriate learning conditions, the learner will appreciate poetry. Goal____Objective____

4. Given the statement, "Four groups of three items each," the learner is able to state the total number of items. Goal____Objective____

Writing Instructional Objectives

The idea of specific instructional objectives is far from new. Lists of objectives were developed in the early 1920s. What is new, as Burns points out, "is the increased realization that the quality of instruction, the quality of instructional materials, and the quality of achievement tests really demand that behavioral (instructional) objectives all be set forth prior to instruction."[7]

On first appearance, the task of writing specific instructional objectives may seem really not very difficult. However, Lindvall (1964) tells us, it requires careful thinking through for the precise meanings of vague statements such as "the student has command of some topic." We must ask more precisely what the student will be able to do to exhibit this command. "Does this merely mean that he will be able to repeat certain facts or generalizations? Or does it mean that he will be able to explain these ideas or be able to apply the principles so as to produce or explain certain results?"[8] Clearly, specifying the details involved in answering questions such as these requires a good deal of skill on the part of the teacher.

TASK DESCRIPTION AND TASK ANALYSIS

There are two major skills that teachers can master to help them prepare specific instructional objectives. These are the skills of (1) task description, and (2) task analysis. *Task description* is the process of breaking down long-range goals into specific instructional objectives. *Task analysis* is the process of specifying what the learner must be able to do to complete each of the objectives described. Much of this chapter is devoted to helping you acquire mastery of the skills of task description. Chapters 4, 5, and 6 will help you master the skills of task analysis.

Task description is defined as . . .

Task analysis is defined as . . .

---

[7] R. W. Burns (1972). *New Approaches to Behavioral Objectives.* Dubuque, Iowa: Wm. C. Brown Company Publishers, pp. 1–2.

[8] C. M. Lindvall, ed. (1964). *Defining Educational Objectives* (3). Pittsburgh: University of Pittsburgh Press, p. 2.

SPECIAL CHARACTERISTICS
OF INSTRUCTIONAL OBJECTIVES

In an earlier section, we discussed the procedure I used to arrive at goals and objectives for this text. This is essentially the process of doing a task description. To complete a task description, however, requires the skill of writing specific instructional objectives. We will need to master this skill before we can proceed, since it is prerequisite to later skills, e.g., to organizing for instruction.

We noted previously that the instructional objectives written for the unit on Coast Salish Indians reflect several distinct characteristics. They (1) are stated from the learner's point of view; (2) describe what the learner can do after instruction; (3) state qualifications; and (4) represent a variety of student behaviors. We will now examine each of these special characteristics in detail.

INSTRUCTIONAL OBJECTIVES ARE STATED FROM THE LEARNER'S POINT OF VIEW   In teaching and learning, the focus ought first to be on the learner's behavior. Instructional objectives, therefore, should be expressions of what the learners will be able to do if they have learned, rather than an expression of what the teacher is doing or is going to do. A quick look at the list of phrases below will show these differences. Each of these introductory phrases was written as an example of a specific objective rather than a goal. Many of them were written by experienced teachers, but many emphasize what the teacher is to do rather than what the learner is to do.

Inappropriate	Appropriate
To introduce . . .	The learner is able to name . . .
To give the . . .	The learner is able to identify . . .
To provide an . . .	The learner can apply . . .
To instruct . . .	The learner is able to analyze . . .
To acquaint the student . . .	The learner is able to sketch . . .
To demonstrate the . . .	The learner volunteers . . .
To develop within . . .	The learner is able to evaluate . . .
To promote a . . .	The learner is able to jump . . .

Let us check on your understanding of the first characteristic of instructional objectives.

CHECKPOINT 3-2

Which objectives are written from the learner's point of view?

1.   Given new spelling words, the learner will be instructed in their correct usage. Yes_____ No_____

2.   Given new spelling words, the learner will be able to use each one correctly in a sentence. Yes_____ No_____

3.   Given the chemical expression: $Na + Cl \rightarrow$, the learner will be given assistance in completing the statement. Yes_____ No_____

4.   Given the chemical expression: $Na + Cl \rightarrow$, the learner will be able to name the product formed. Yes_____ No_____

Notice in Checkpoint 3-2 that I wrote objectives 1 and 2, and 3 and 4 in parallel form. Notice also that each pair of objectives contains one written from the teacher's point of view and one from the viewpoint of the learner. This difference is often difficult for beginning teachers to discriminate. In order to help you see the difference, I have placed the objectives close together. This helps you discriminate them. Remember this when you try to help your learners tell the difference between stimuli that are potentially confusing, for example, between the letters b and d or between the words "affect" and "effect." We will learn more about this in Chapter 5.

INSTRUCTIONAL OBJECTIVES ARE SPECIFIC STATEMENTS OF LEARNER BEHAVIOR
Objectives are stated from the learner's point of view, and they are specific statements of student behavior. Being specific, however, is not always easy. Yet, the task of defining specific instructional objectives is basically one of facilitating communication, of using words and statements so that they have a clear and exact meaning (Lindvall, 1964).

There are many reasons for vagueness and generality in instructional objectives. For one thing, there are very few if any clear-cut and absolute answers to the question, what should learners learn? Is it important for children to be honest? If so, to what degree, and in what situations? Should children be conforming, different, dependent, independent, outgoing, or whatever? Teachers, however, are placed in the often unpleasant and vulnerable position of being responsible for the behavior of learners—cognitive, affective, and psychomotor. Being vague is usually the teacher's easiest way out of the difficulties these questions pose.

Another reason for vagueness in objectives is that we do not always know exactly what is necessary for a student to be able to do, even in such a task as using the dictionary, writing a friendly letter, or using proper grammar. There is simply lack of agreement in terms of content and even in the sequence with which the content ought to be learned. An additional difficulty is that, as teachers, we never have complete mastery of the material we teach. What we "know" is always only relatively so and approximately true.

It is not my intent to be pessimistic about teaching and learning but rather, to help you understand that working within the area of human behavior requires a willingness and an ability to work with changing approximations. Consequently, we must be able to modify our beliefs about what we consider important for learners to learn. The problem appears to be one of an apparent paradox: "How can one be specific and precise within the confines of vagueness, generality, and ever-changing approximations?"

There is nothing within a psychology of education that specifies the relative values of various kinds of learner objectives. These values must come from society in general and from the teacher's interpretation of society's values. Once a teacher has made these value judgments, however, a psychology of education offers a great deal in terms of being precise and specific about what children are to learn.

Burns (1972) points out that there are hundreds of terms that indicate exact behaviors, all of which can be learned in instructional settings. A few of the terms suggested in Burns's complete list are shown in Table 3-2.

Suppose that you are a classroom teacher and that you have stated the following objective: "The students will appreciate good music." The first requirement

TABLE 3-2 Terms that indicate exact behavior

Class 1 (Knowledges)			Class 5 (Attitudes)		
arranges	identifies	prints	accepts	enjoys	questions
bisects	indicates	recites	adopts	involves	rejects
checks	joins	shows		(oneself)	
chooses	lists	sorts	asks		seeks
counts	matches	states	attends	offers	suggests
defines	names	tells	chooses	participates	tolerates
gives	picks	touches	defends	praises	watches
groups	points to	writes			

Class 6 (Appreciations)
(See Attitudes)

Class 2 (Understandings)

contrasts	evaluates	interprets
designs	formulates	uses
discriminates		

Class 7 (Interests)
(See Attitudes)

Class 3 (Processes)

alters	draws	regroups
breaks down	formulates	rephrases
calculates	groups	restates
compares	makes	rewords
composes	matches	separates
concludes	orders	sequences
condenses	pairs	summarizes
constructs	pieces	weighs
contrasts	postulates	writes
diagrams	puts together	
divides	recalls	

Class 8 (Movements—without objects or tools)

bends	presses	swats
climbs	pulls	swings
crawls	pushes	taps
grips	runs	twists
hops	shakes	walks
leans	sits	wiggles
lifts	skips	
pitches	steps	

Class 4 (Strategies)
produces, step by step
proves, step by step

Class 9 (Movements—with objects or tools)

bats	hammers	saws
builds	holds	scrapes
catches	paints	stamps
constructs	pins	stirs
cuts	pours	tosses
draws	rolls	writes

for breaking down vague general statements into more precise ones is to ask: Exactly what is meant by the vague terms used in such statements? How can you determine when a student is in fact appreciating good music? Does it mean, for example, using some of the precise words suggested by Burns, that given various selections of music, children are able to distinguish between good music and bad music? Does it mean that students are able to describe various characteristics of good music—perhaps to contrast the qualities of good music with those of bad music? Does it mean that children are able to perform good music? Must they be able to read music? Does it mean that they are observed to spend spare time listening to good music? May it mean that, when given a choice of music to listen to, they select certain pieces?

When you can specify what you mean by terms such as "appreciate" and "good," you will be able effectively to plan specific learning activities, since part of the usefulness of stating objectives precisely in terms of learner behavior is that they provide clues for (1) the selection of teaching materials, (2) decisions about proper instructional activities, and (3) evaluating instruction.

CHECKPOINT 3-3

The following two examples of objectives are stated in vague, general terms. Try to visualize what each might refer to; how a learner who had met one or more of these objectives might behave. Decide which words in each objective need to be more precisely defined. Then, draw a circle around those words, and in the spaces at the right, list specific verbs that might be used to define more precisely the meaning of the general verbs. Check your verbs with a friend.

Example:

The learner understands what is meant by specific objectives.

can define
can explain
can state . . .

OBJECTIVES	SPECIFIC VERBS
1. The learner will become acquainted with the concept of transfer.	_____ _____ _____
2. The learner will be able to appreciate the importance of practice.	_____ _____ _____

SPECIFIC INSTRUCTIONAL
OBJECTIVES FOR LEARNER
BEHAVIOR MAY HAVE QUALIFICATIONS

Sometimes instructional objectives contain qualifications of the learner's behavior. There may be a time limit, an error limit, or restrictions about what may or may not be used as aids in the performance. For example, you may want your learners to be able to write, with 100 percent accuracy, multiplication facts for number combinations from $1 \times 2 = 2$ through $12 \times 12 = 144$, without figuring them out, and within a time limit of fifteen minutes. Or, you may want your learners to be able to speak extemporaneously on any topic, for one minute, without being coaxed or threatened.

As you can see, the inclusion of special qualifications causes you to think more precisely about what you want your learners to be able to do. It is obvious, also, that being precise about instructional goals provides specific clues for the teacher about the specific experiences that need to be provided in the learning situation, since, as we noted earlier, we learn what we practice.

CHECKPOINT 3-4

In the spaces provided, (a) indicate the qualifications for objectives 1 and 2, then (b) rewrite objectives 3 and 4 and include some qualifications.

Example:

Given appropriate typing materials and handwritten copy, the typist is able to type an average of fifty words	handwritten copy, average of fifty words per minute . . .

per minute with an average of no more than three errors   average error rate of three
per page.   per page. _____

OBJECTIVES   QUALIFICATIONS

1.   Given the directions to count aloud to 10, the learner is able to do so without   _____
assistance and within ten seconds.   _____
2.   Given a basketball, the learner is able to succeed in 90 percent of his throws   _____
by "shooting" with one hand from a distance of 20 feet.   _____
3.   Given the direction to name the products of South America, the learner is able to do so.

_____

4.   Given two literary works by different authors, the learner is able to compare them.

_____

SPECIFIC INSTRUCTIONAL OBJECTIVES
FOR LEARNERS CONTAIN QUALIFICATIONS
AND REPRESENT A VARIETY OF BEHAVIORS

As we saw earlier, all instructional objectives are either cognitive, affective, or psychomotor. However, they may vary considerably within each of these three major classifications. For example, instructional objectives of the cognitive type can be stated so that learners must do more with information than just remember it. They can be written so that learners must *translate, interpret, apply, analyze, synthesize,* and *evaluate* it.

In summary, educational goals are defined as . . .

Specific instructional objectives of the affective type can be defined for learners' behavior ranging from *receiving, attending, responding, valuing,* and *organizing* to behaving in *characteristic* ways. The objectives stated at the beginning of the chapters are examples of this variety of cognitive and affective functioning that instructional objectives can represent.

A variety of instructional objectives of the psychomotor type is also possible and desirable. Psychomotor objectives can range from simple *reflex* movements to *expressive* and *interpretive* movements.

In summary, instructional objectives are defined as . . .

Since various instructional objectives may occur within each of the three major types of educational experience, efforts have been made to classify these types. The result has been a taxonomy of educational objectives. However, before we move on to an examination of classification systems for educational objectives, I would like to draw your attention to a technique of learning that we have been using in the last few pages. Did you notice that each succeeding heading relative to special characteristics of instructional objectives incorporates the main idea of the previous one(s) and adds the next idea to be considered? This technique is sometimes called the progressive-part or *whole-part method of* learning. The chief idea is that of practice (repetition) in which a new part or unit of learning is added on as the learner reviews previously learned parts. All the parts tend to be learned together, rather than as separate and isolated bits and pieces. You might apply this technique to helping your learners learn new vocabulary words; postulates and theorems in geometry; a sequence of skills in physical education; poetry; words and melody for a new song. It is a widely useful technique that we will learn more about throughout the rest of the text, both by doing it and by reading about it.

A TAXONOMY OF EDUCATIONAL OBJECTIVES

Most of us are familiar with classification schemes in fields other than education. In biology, for example, the word "taxonomy" refers to a classification scheme that is hierarchical in its organization. The categories are defined so that succeeding categories are subsumed by those following. With such a system, those items that are classified within it range from specific to general. This sequence is seen in the biological taxonomies for plants and animals. The categories range from the narrowly inclusive ones of variety to the progressively more inclusive categories of species, genus, family, order, class, and phylum. Within education, a similar pattern may be used to derive specific instructional objectives. Thus, a taxonomy of educational objectives is a hierarchical classification scheme of the kinds of behavior that we want students to acquire in educational settings.

A taxonomy is . . .

As you recall, all school learning can be considered within the cognitive, affective, and psychomotor categories of experience. These domains therefore constitute the major divisions of the taxonomy of educational objectives. Within each domain are progressively more general and more inclusive categories of possible behaviors of learners. An overview of these categories is shown in Table 3-3.

The three domains of the taxonomy of educational objectives are . . .

Because the essence of what we want children to learn is embodied in the taxonomy of educational objectives, it is essential that we not only understand about the specifics of the taxonomy but also that we learn to use it. We will begin with the cognitive domain, although this does not suggest that educators

TABLE 3-3   The taxonomy of educational objectives

The six major categories of the cognitive domain are . . .

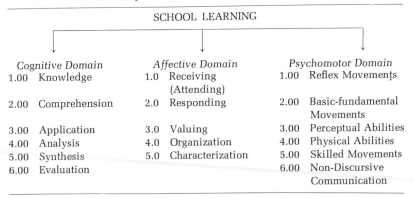

SCHOOL LEARNING

Cognitive Domain	Affective Domain	Psychomotor Domain
1.00 Knowledge	1.0 Receiving (Attending)	1.00 Reflex Movements
2.00 Comprehension	2.0 Responding	2.00 Basic-fundamental Movements
3.00 Application	3.0 Valuing	3.00 Perceptual Abilities
4.00 Analysis	4.0 Organization	4.00 Physical Abilities
5.00 Synthesis	5.0 Characterization	5.00 Skilled Movements
6.00 Evaluation		6.00 Non-Discursive Communication

believe it is more important than the affective or psychomotor domains. The cognitive domain simply is easier to work with. Experience with it should help you to understand about and use the others.

The Cognitive Domain

The *Taxonomy of Educational Objectives: Cognitive Domain* was published in 1956 by a committee of college and university examiners under the leadership of Benjamin S. Bloom. It can be divided into two major parts. The first part relates to the *acquisition* of knowledge. The second is concerned with the *use* of knowledge: comprehension, application, analysis, synthesis, and evaluation.

Now that you have a general picture of the major categories within the cognitive domain, let us add more specific detail which should enhance the meaningfulness for you of how the *Taxonomy* is organized. The six major divisions are subdivided, and each subdivision describes the kinds of behavior it classifies. Each category is assumed to require behavior which is more complex and abstract than that represented by the previous category. Consequently, an objective that is classified as *application* level requires both knowledge and comprehension of information before an application-level performance is possible. An objective properly classified as *evaluation* requires a learner to remember, comprehend, apply, analyze, and synthesize information.

Sample objectives written in the style originally developed by the authors of the *Taxonomy* are included in Table 3-4. Note that since 1956 we have become much more precise in stating objectives. As shown in Table 3-4, each subdivision provides examples of possible test items which may be used to evaluate learner's behavior for each category. We will return to this relationship between objectives and evaluation in Chapter 13.

Clearly, more can be done with information than to memorize it. It is also clear that writing objectives at more than a knowledge level requires that we know our subject matter, and knowing, as used here, is defined by the major categories of the *Taxonomy*. A rule of thumb is: *The more thoroughly a teacher knows his subject material, the greater the possibility that education for his learners can be more than memorization.*

Let us check your mastery of the ideas involved in classifying specific instructional objectives within the cognitive domain.

CHECKPOINT 3-5

The following instructional objectives are written in specific behavioral terms. Read each one and then classify it according to Bloom's six major categories. Refer to Table 3-4 if you need to. The objectives are based on the story "The Three Pigs."

OBJECTIVES   CLASSIFICATION

1.   Given a list of ten materials that include the ones used by the Three Pigs to build their houses, the child is able to select the ones used.   _____

2.   Given painting materials and a descriptive paragraph, the child is able to paint a picture of the Wolf.   _____

TABLE 3-4   The major and minor categories of the Taxonomy of Educational Objectives: Cognitive Domain*

1.00   KNOWLEDGE

Knowledge as defined here includes those behaviors and test situations which emphasize the remembering, either by recognition or recall, of ideas, material, or
phenomena.

Knowledge level means . . .

1.10   *Knowledge of Specifics*

The recall of specific and isolable bits of information.

1.11   *Knowledge of Terminology.* Knowledge of the referents for specific verbal and non-
verbal symbols.

Sample objective: To define technical terms by giving their attributes, properties, or
relations.

Sample test item: A spaniel is a type of:

(a) dog   (b) cat   (c) lace   (d) car   (e) coin

1.12   *Knowledge of Specific Facts.* Knowledge of dates, events, persons, places, sources
of information, etc.

Sample objective: Recall and recognition of what is characteristic of particular
periods.

Sample test item: (The term *operant conditioning* was coined by whom?)

1.20   *Knowledge of Ways and Means of Dealing with Specifics*

Knowledge of the ways of organizing, studying, judging, and criticizing ideas and
phenomena.

1.21   *Knowledge of Conventions.* Knowledge of characteristic ways of treating and presenting ideas and phenomena.

Sample objective: Knowledge of common rules of etiquette.

Sample test item: I believe he (1) done, (2) did, the best he could.

1.22   *Knowledge of Trends and Sequences.* Knowledge of the processes, directions, and
movements of phenomena with respect to time.

Sample objective: To develop a basic knowledge of the evolutionary development
of man.

Sample test item: The stages in the life history of the housefly are, in order,

1.   Larva-egg-pupa-adult   4.   Egg-larva-adult-pupa
2.   Pupa-larva-egg-adult   5.   Egg-larva-pupa-adult
3.   Pupa-egg-larva-adult

1.23   *Knowledge of Classifications and Categories.*

Knowledge of the classes, sets, divisions, and arrangements which are regarded as
fundamental or useful for a given subject field, purpose, argument, or problem.

Sample objective: To recognize the area encompassed by various kinds of problems
or materials.

Sample test item: Which of the following is a chemical change?

1.   Evaporation of alcohol   4.   Melting of wax
2.   Freezing of water   5.   Mixing of sand and sugar
3.   Burning of oil

1.24   *Knowledge of Criteria.* Knowledge of the criteria by which facts, principles, opinions,
and conduct are tested or judged.

Sample objective: Knowledge of the criteria for the evaluation of recreational
activities.

Sample test item: In the view of John Ruskin, the greatest picture is:

A.   That which imitates best
B.   That which teaches us most
C.   That which exhibits the greatest power
D.   That which conveys the greatest number of the greatest ideas

Table 3-4 (continued)

1.25   *Knowledge of Methodology.* Knowledge of the methods of inquiry, techniques, and procedures employed in a particular subject field as well as those employed in investigating particular problems and phenomena.

Sample objective: The student shall know the methods of attack relevant to the kinds of problems of concern to the social sciences.

Sample test item: A scientist discovers new facts by:
1.   Consulting the writings of Aristotle
2.   Thinking about the probabilities
3.   Making careful observations and conducting experiments
4.   Debating questions with his friends
5.   Referring to the works of Darwin

1.30   *Knowledge of the Universals and Abstractions in a Field*
Knowledge of the major ideas, schemes, and patterns by which phenomena and ideas are organized.

1.31   *Knowledge of Principles and Generalizations.*
Knowledge of particular abstractions which summarize observations of phenomena.
Sample objective: To know the major principles involved in learning.
Sample test item: If the volume of a given mass of gas is kept constant, the pressure may be diminished by:
1.   Reducing the temperature   4.   Decreasing the density
2.   Raising the temperature   5.   Increasing the density
3.   Adding heat

1.32   *Knowledge of Theories and Structures.* Knowledge of the body of principles and generalizations together with their interrelations which present a clear, rounded, and systematic view of a complex phenomenon, problem, or field.
Sample objective: To understand the basic structural organization of the local city government.
Sample test item: (True or false: If the human heart has two chambers at a very early developmental stage, this evidence is supportive of the theory of biological evolution.)

2.00   COMPREHENSION

Comprehension level means . . .

(Comprehension as defined here means an understanding of the literal message contained in a communication. In reaching such understanding, the student may change the communication in his mind or in his overt responses to some parallel form more meaningful to him, or change the communication so that it represents simple extensions beyond what is given in the communication itself.)

2.10   *Translation*
(Translation means that an individual can put a communication into other language, into other terms, or into another form of communication.)
Sample objective: Given geometric concepts in verbal terms, the ability to translate into visual or spatial terms.

Sample test item: A group of examiners is engaged in the production of a taxonomy of educational objectives. In ordinary English, what are these persons doing?
A.   Evaluating the progress of education
B.   Classifying teaching goals
C.   Preparing a curriculum
D.   Constructing learning exercises

2.20   *Interpretation*
(Interpretation means going beyond a part-for-part rendering of the communication. It means being able to identify and understand the major ideas which are included

Table 3-4 (continued)

as well as to understand their interrelationships. To do this, one must be able to abstract generalizations from a set of particulars.)

Sample objective: The ability to grasp the thought of a work as a whole at any desired level of generality.

Sample test item: (In a paragraph, explain how a teacher's major task might possibly be considered that of capturing the attention of learners.)

2.30 *Extrapolation*

(Extrapolation as it is used here means that the learner is able to translate as well as interpret a communication and, in addition, be able to extend the trends or tendencies beyond the given data and findings to determine implications, consequences, corollaries, effects, etc., which are in accordance with the conditions as literally described in the original communication.)

Sample objective: The ability to estimate or predict consequences of courses of action described in a communication.

Sample test item: Immigrants tend to settle in the slum areas closest to the central business districts of our large cities. Where are their descendants most likely to be found?

3.00 APPLICATION

(Application means that a learner is able to use an abstraction—a rule, a principle, or an idea—in particular and concrete situations.)

Application level means . . .

Sample objective: (Given the principle of operant conditioning, the learner can suggest how to make use of it to cause a child to attend to his spelling lesson.)

Sample test item: (The two legs of a right triangle are 3 inches and 4 inches in length. Find the length of the hypotenuse.)

4.00 ANALYSIS

Analysis emphasizes the breakdown of material into its constituent parts and detection of the interrelationships of the parts and of the way they are organized.

Analysis level means . . .

4.10 *Analysis of Elements.* (The learner is required to identify or classify the elements of the communication.)

Sample objective: The ability to recognize unstated assumptions.

Sample test item: There is one statement in the student's argument (presented in point form) for which reasons are offered, but which he does not offer as a reason for any other statement. That statement, his main conclusion, is

1. A   4. E
2. B   5. F
3. C

4.20 *Analysis of Relationships.* (The learner is required to make explicit the relationships among the elements, to determine their connections and interactions.)

Sample objective: Ability to distinguish cause-and-effect relationships from other sequential relationships.

Sample test item: Which of the following assumptions is necessary in order to determine the mass of a drop by the method described? (In a reading.)

1. The drop falls with uniform acceleration.
2. All the drops sprayed into the chamber are of the same size.
3. The drop is charged.
4. The drop is nearly spherical.
5. The electrical force is equal to the gravitational force.

4.30 *Analysis of Organizational Principles.* (The learner must recognize organizational principles, the arrangement and structure, which hold together the communication as a whole.)

Sample objective: Ability to recognize the point of view or bias of a writer in an historical account.

Table 3-4 (continued)

Sample test item: (Given a musical piece to listen to:) The theme is carried essentially by

1. The strings   3. The horns
2. The woodwinds   4. All in turn

5.00   SYNTHESIS

Synthesis level means . . .

Synthesis is here defined as the putting together of elements and parts so as to form a whole. This is the process of working with elements, parts, pieces, etc., and combining them in such a way as to constitute a pattern or structure not clearly there before.

5.10   *Production of a Unique Communication.* (The learner is required to communicate certain experiences and ideas. He may be interested in expression for its own sake. Usually, he tries to communicate to inform, to describe, to impress, or to entertain.)
Sample objective: Ability to tell a personal experience effectively.
Sample test item: (The learner is asked to tell about an experience which was important to him.)

5.20   *Production of a Plan, or Proposed Set of Operations.*
(The learner, given certain specifications or requirements, must produce a plan or set of operations which is new for him and which meets the requirements specified.)
Sample objective: Ability to plan a unit of instruction for a particular teaching situation.
Sample test item: (Given basic rules and concepts relative to the psychology of learning and teaching, the learner is asked to use them as a basis for planning a unit of study for children in a school setting.)

5.30   *Derivation of a Set of Abstract Relations.* The distinguishing feature of this subcategory is . . . the attempt to derive abstract relations from a detailed analysis. The relations themselves are not explicit from the start; they must be discovered or deduced.
Sample objective: Ability to formulate a theory of learning applicable to classroom teaching.
Sample test item: (Given certain laws of human behavior and conditions of classroom learning, show how these can be interrelated in the form of a theory of classroom teaching.)

6.00   EVALUATION

Evaluation level means . . .

(Evaluation is defined as the making of judgments about the value, for some purpose, of ideas, works, solutions, methods, material, etc. The judgments may be either quantitative or qualitative, and the criteria may be those either determined by the student or given to him.)

6.10   *Judgments in Terms of Internal Evidence.* Evaluation of a communication from such evidence as logical accuracy, consistency, and other internal criteria.
Sample objective: The ability to indicate logical fallacies in arguments.
Sample test item: (Given an argument, tell whether or not it is consistent, accurate, and carefully done. Give reasons for your judgment.)

6.20   *Judgments in Terms of External Criteria.* Evaluation of material with reference to selected or remembered criteria. . . . The criteria may be ends to be satisfied; the techniques, rules, or standards by which such works are generally judged; or the comparison of the works with the work of others in the field.
Sample objective: Skills in recognizing and weighing values involved in alternative courses of action.
Sample test item: (Given a television recording of a performance by a classroom teacher and her stated objectives, evaluate her performance in light of the major ideas presented in this textbook.)

* B. S. Bloom, ed. (1956). New York: McKay.
  The material enclosed in parentheses is an adaptation of that in Bloom's book. The rest of the material, including headings, is exactly as it appears in the *Taxonomy.*

3. When shown pictures from "The Three Pigs," the child can explain what is happening. _____
4. Given the task of choosing appropriate building materials for windy places, the child is able to do so. _____
5. When asked to say which pigs used adequate building materials, the child is able to do so. _____
6. Given the task of designing a house using the building materials mentioned in the story, the child can do so. _____
7. Given that the last page of the story was lost, the child is able to create a new ending. _____
8. Given the choice of which of the three houses she would prefer to live in, the child is able to state reasons for her selection. _____

ACQUIRING AND USING INFORMATION

As a beginning teacher, you may find it difficult to describe learning tasks so completely that you will be able to prepare instructional objectives for all the subcategories within the cognitive domain. Indeed, many experienced teachers cannot do it. Therefore, you will probably find it useful to begin by trying to write objectives that represent a reasonable balance among the six major categories. In fact, many educators argue that a significant improvement would be made over the predominantly memory nature of education if classroom teachers were to formulate objectives even in two major categories of the *Taxonomy: acquiring* information and *using* information. The example in Table 3-5, taken from a set of goals and objectives developed by practicing classroom teachers for a language arts program, shows objectives that cause children to acquire information and to use information. The objectives related to acquiring information are designated by a *K* (Knowledge), and those related to using information, by an *H* (Higher). The teachers state the long-range goals in abbreviated form under the heading "Program Description (Tasks)." Their instructional objectives define in precise, behavioral terms what they believe their learners must be able to do to meet the long-range goals.

WRITING COGNITIVE OBJECTIVES

If your knowledge of instructional objectives is to generalize, that is, to transfer to your classroom practice, it is not sufficient for you to function only at a knowledge level. You must be able to do more than explain what objectives are, state their importance, and classify them. Given a body of information, such as a study of South America, a study of the community, a unit on electricity, or a unit on music appreciation, you must be able to produce a set of specific instructional objectives which you believe are important outcomes for your learners. Consequently, if I want transfer to occur for you, I must help you learn to take a body of information and, through doing a task description, to produce specific instructional objectives representative of at least the major categories of the cognitive domain. Checkpoint 3-6 has been designed for this purpose.

TABLE 3-5   **An example of goals and objectives written by classroom teachers for a language arts program†**

PROGRAM DESCRIPTION (TASK)	SPECIFIC INSTRUCTIONAL OBJECTIVES
Word development Identifying Similarities and Differences	(a) Given a set of letters such as two h's, two c's and two m's on cards, the child can match the cards containing the same letters. (K)
	(b) Given three letters (two the same and one different), the child can show the one that is different. (H)
—match and differentiate	
—select a word	(c) Given a letter on a flash card, the child will be able to find this letter in a given word. (H)
—match capital and lowercase	(d) Given a set of capital and lowercase letter forms, the child will match each capital form with the correct lowercase form of the alphabet. (H)
Matching pictures and symbols Picture and word Picture and numeral Word and numeral Word and mathematical symbol	(a) When given a set of pictures and a scrambled set of word cards, the child can match the appropriate word with the correct picture. (K)
	(b) Given a picture of a set of objects and a series of numerals, the child is able to match the correct numeral with the set. (K)

† McKenzie Research Project, McKenzie Elementary School, Victoria, B.C., Canada. Reprinted with permission.

CHECKPOINT 3-6

Following is a simplified version of the popular children's story "The Three Bears." Read the story and then write one specific instructional objective for each of the six major categories in the *Taxonomy*. For your guidance, refer to the three questions below. (Since many possible objectives can qualify for each of the major categories, it is impossible to provide adequate feedback about the appropriateness of your objectives, but sample objectives in the Appendix will help you evaluate your own. Look at them after you have written yours.)

1. Is your objective written in specific behavioral terms and from the student's point of view, and does it state observable behaviors that you expect the learner to be able to perform after learning?

2. Do your objectives include qualifications?

3. Have you used words that suggest the type of cognitive performance you desire?

THE THREE BEARS

Once upon a time there were three bears. They lived in a little house in a wood.

Father Bear was a great big bear, Mother Bear was a middle-sized bear, Baby Bear was a little wee bear.

The three bears had three bowls. Father Bear's bowl was a great big bowl. Mother Bear's bowl was a middle-sized bowl. Baby Bear's bowl was a little wee bowl.

The three bears had three chairs. One was a great big chair. One was a middle-sized chair. One was a little wee chair.

The three bears had three beds. Father Bear's bed was a great big bed. Mother Bear's bed was a middle-sized bed. Baby Bear's bed was a little wee bed.

One morning the three bears went for a walk in the wood. They left their porridge on the table to cool.

Goldilocks was in the wood. She was picking flowers. She saw the home of the three bears. The door was not shut, so she pushed it wide open and walked in.

Goldilocks saw the bowls of porridge. She was hungry. She tasted the porridge in the great big bowl. It was too hot. She tasted the porridge in the middle-sized bowl. It was too cool. She tasted the porridge in the little wee bowl. It was just right. So she ate it all.

Goldilocks saw the three chairs. She was tired. She sat down in the great big chair. It was too hard. She sat down in the middle-sized chair. It was too soft. So she sat down in the little wee chair. It was just right. But the little wee chair broke. And down fell Goldilocks.

Goldilocks ran upstairs. She saw the three beds. She was sleepy. She lay down on the great big bed. It was too high. She lay down on the middle-sized bed. It was too low. She lay down on the little wee bed. It was just right. Goldilocks fell fast asleep.

The three bears came home. They were very hungry. They went to the table to eat their porridge.

Father Bear growled, "Someone has been tasting my porridge!"

Mother Bear called out, "Someone has been tasting my porridge!"

Baby Bear said, in his little wee voice, "Someone has been tasting my porridge and it is all gone!"

The three bears wanted to sit down.

Father bear growled, "Someone has been sitting in my chair!"

Mother Bear called out, "Someone has been sitting in my chair!"

Baby Bear said, in his little wee voice, "Someone has been sitting in my chair and has broken it!"

The three bears went upstairs.

Father Bear growled, "Someone has been lying on my bed!"

Mother Bear called out, "Someone has been lying on my bed!"

Baby Bear said, in his little wee voice, "Someone is lying on my bed now! And she is fast asleep."

Goldilocks woke up. She saw the three bears. She jumped up and ran downstairs. She ran out the door. She ran and ran and ran. She ran all the way home.

Traditional

Now that you are able to write your own specific instructional objectives, let us review what we have been doing. Did you notice that the instructional sequence leading up to this capability started back with Checkpoint 3-1, in which you demonstrated the ability to discriminate between goals and objectives? Next you learned how specific instructional objectives should be written. From there you practiced breaking down vague terms into precise, descriptive verbs. Then, you showed that you could qualify objectives if needed. Next, you used the major categories of Bloom's *Taxonomy* to classify objectives that were written for you. Now, you have just completed writing your own. Note your progressive sequence and how it reflects all the major categories of the *Taxonomy*. You have just done all the things we talked about.

Some people refer to this sort of sequence in terms of *readiness*. Learners are *ready*, for example, to write their own specific behavioral objectives when they have mastered the skills which come before, and are prerequisite to, the skills required to write one's own objectives. Note, further, that readiness in this sense is *learned*. You will need to help learners become ready for tasks such as doing division problems; working in the chemistry laboratory; managing their own behavior; playing a game; accepting constructive criticism. We will learn more about readiness as we go along.

DECIDING ON APPROPRIATE OBJECTIVES

Now that you are gaining mastery of the skills for doing task description, you may wonder whether the cognitive objectives you write are appropriate. You will probably have the same question when we consider objectives of the affective and psychomotor types. Appropriateness is hard to determine, since it may be interpreted many ways. Another difficulty in making the decision is our lack of certainty about what behaviors will either immediately or eventually prove useful for learners.

Appropriate objectives are those that . . . Burns (1972) suggests that appropriateness in a technical sense is related to the concept of validity. He says that validity is always relative to some predefined purpose; that an objective is good (valid) if it does well what it was intended to do. Burns continues by pointing out that objectives are developed (1) to communicate ideas, (2) to serve as a basis for selecting instructional activities, (3) to serve as a basis for evaluating learning, and (4) to define behaviors useful to learners.[9]

Objectives for all three domains should meet all these purposes. If we have effectively written our instructional objectives in specific, behavioral terms and from the student's point of view, and if we have included any special qualifications for the behavior desired, the first three requirements for appropriate objectives as stated by Burns are likely to have been met adequately. Whether an objective defines useful behaviors to be accomplished by learners is a more difficult question.

As we saw in Chapter 2, truth is relative, and in the present climate of rapid change, behaviors that may have been considered important in the past few years may in the next few years be useless or unnecessary. For example, some educators argue that there should be no formal study of arithmetic prior to grade

---

[9] R. W. Burns (1972). Op. cit., p. 67.

seven. Others contend that learning skills of penmanship is not useful since writing in longhand is likely to become unnecessary in the near future. Others argue against formal schooling of any kind.

Fortunately, each teacher need not be strictly self-reliant in making decisions about what should be learned. Most schools have a curriculum with some general guidelines about what the community believes is appropriate school responsibility at least within the subject matter areas. Many schools have adopted a philosophy of education and courses of study which teachers are encouraged to follow more or less. Consequently, a good deal of assistance is available as we try to answer the question: What shall I teach, cognitively, affectively, and psychomotorly?

The Affective Domain

When teachers are asked to name the most important goals for learners as a consequence of school experience, most cite things that have to do with affect. Yet, when asked to be more specific, many find it difficult to say precisely what they are trying to help learners do relative to affect. Furthermore, an emphasis on affective growth of learners is not always apparent from an observation of teachers' behavior in classrooms.

PROBLEMS WITH
AFFECTIVE GOALS AND OBJECTIVES

There must be some reason why teachers find it hard to be precise in describing affective objectives and why these objectives are not always apparent from what teachers do. Indeed, a large number of teachers direct a great amount of effort toward affective objectives, even though the objectives are rarely stated in precise, behavioral terms.

There are several probable reasons for a relative absence of specific behavioral objectives in affective areas. First, as we saw earlier: It is usually more difficult to feel confident about appropriate affective objectives than about appropriate cognitive objectives.

Second, attention, attitudes, values, opinions, interests, and feelings are usually more difficult to observe and measure than cognitive objectives, such as those dealing with acquiring and using subject matter. Even with the affective part of attending to learning tasks, it is not always easy to determine whether a particular learner is receiving the information being presented. For all practical purposes, the person may appear to be paying close attention, whereas, in reality, he may be attending to something entirely different.

Lack of emphasis on affective objectives is due to . . .

Third, many of the affective objectives that teachers develop for their learners are not immediately attainable. Often, they are the kinds of outcomes which appear to evolve over long periods of time, even over years. Consequently, a teacher may not be able to determine, other than on a subjective level, whether the objectives are being, or have been, met.

A fourth reason for the relative absence of affective objectives is the often-expressed reluctance of teachers to influence the value systems of other people, including those of their learners. The fact, however, is that, as teachers, we *do* influence the beliefs, attitudes, and values of our learners. Consequently, we need to teach specifically for changes in affective behavior. If we are to be effective at doing this, we must be specific about our affective objectives. Prerequisite to this is familiarity with the *Taxonomy of Educational Objectives: Affective Domain*.

BACKGROUND   It is probably fair to say that the *Taxonomy of Educational Objectives: Affective Domain* (Krathwohl, 1964) has not at this point has as widespread acceptance by classroom teachers as Bloom's *Taxonomy*, covering the cognitive domain. One likely reason is that it was completed some six years later. Also, education in North America, beginning in the late 1950s, experienced a rather dramatic swing toward greater emphasis on content and process of curriculum material, especially in the areas of science and mathematics. More recently, however, we are witnessing a reversal in the swing of the pendulum. Educators, as well as the lay public, are becoming increasingly concerned with each human as an affective being interrelated with the immediate environment. Questions of mounting concern center on a person's ability to relate affectively as well as cognitively toward social issues relevant to the individual's very existence, e.g., to war, pollution, population growth, food and energy, production and distribution.

Let us look at Table 3-6 and see how the major categories of the *Taxonomy of Educational Objectives: Affective Domain* are interrelated.

A NEED FOR PRECISION   At the classroom level, most instructors hope that their students will develop a continuing interest in learning. Consequently, they present material in as pleasant a manner as possible and use a variety of methods

TABLE 3-6   The major categories of the Taxonomy of Educational Objectives: Affective Domain‡

	MAJOR CATEGORIES	INTERRELATIONSHIPS
The five major categories of the affective domain are . . .	Receiving (Attending)	The affective continuum begins with the student's merely *receiving* stimuli and passively attending to it. It extends through his more actively attending to it,
	Responding	his *responding* to stimuli on request, willingly responding to these stimuli, and taking satisfaction in this responding, his *valuing* the phenomenon or activity
	Valuing	so that he voluntarily responds and seeks out ways to respond, his *conceptualization* of each value responded to, his *organization* of these values into systems,
	Organization of a value	and finally his organizing the value complex into a single whole, a *characterization* of the individual.
	Characterization by a value or value complex	

‡ D. R. Krathwohl, B. S. Bloom, and B. B. Masia (1964). New York: McKay.

TABLE 3-7   The major and minor categories of the Taxonomy of Educational Objectives: Affective Domain§

1.0   RECEIVING (ATTENDING)
(Receiving or attending, as the word is used here, refers to the learner's becoming sensitized to the existence of certain phenomena and stimuli; that is, that he be willing to receive or attend to them. Note that this is a narrower use of the term *attention* than that employed throughout our text.)   *Receiving means . . .*

1.1   *Awareness.* (Awareness means the learner will be conscious of something—that he take into account a situation, phenomenon, object, or state of affairs.)
Sample objective. (Awareness of the satisfactions that arise from mastery of skills, techniques, and so forth which relate to effective classroom teaching.)

1.2   *Willingness to Receive.* (This term describes the behavior of being willing to tolerate a given stimulus, not of avoiding it. At best, the learner is willing to take notice of the phenomenon and give it his attention.)

1.3   *Controlled or Selected Attention.* (In contrast to a willingness to receive, controlled or selected attention refers to the learner's controlling the attention so that the favored stimulus is selected and attended to despite competing and distracting stimuli.)
Sample objective: Listens carefully for, and remembers, names of persons to whom he is introduced.

2.0   RESPONDING
(Responding means a kind of "active attention." When a learner is responding, he is doing something with or about the phenomenon besides merely receiving it.)   *Responding means . . .*

2.1   *Acquiescence in Responding.* (Responding in this sense refers to compliance with directions, suggestions, rules, and so forth. It reflects a "going-along-with" type of response—even though the learner has not fully accepted the necessity for doing so.)
Sample objective: Obeys the playground regulations.

2.2   *Willingness to Respond.* (As used here, willingness to respond implies voluntary action. The learner responds "on his own" or voluntarily.)
Sample objective: (Assumes responsibility for helping to make the classroom a pleasant place to be.)

2.3   *Satisfaction in Response.* The additional element in the step beyond the *Willingness to Respond,* the consent, the assent to responding, or the voluntary response is that the behavior is accompanied by a feeling of satisfaction, an emotional response, generally of pleasure, zest, or enjoyment.
Sample objective: Takes pleasure in conversing with many different kinds of people.

3.0   VALUING
(Valuing, as used here, has the everyday meaning that a thing, phenomenon, or behavior has worth. An important element of behavior characterized by *valuing* is that it is motivated not by the desire to comply or obey, but by the individual's commitment to the underlying value guiding the behavior).   *Valuing means . . .*

3.1   *Acceptance of a Value.* (The term *belief,* which can be defined as an emotional acceptance of a proposition or doctrine, describes what may be thought of as the dominant type of behavior classified as acceptance of a value.)
Sample objective: Feels himself a member of groups which undertake to solve a common problem, whether local, national, or international.

3.2   *Preference for a Value.* Behavior at this level implies not just the acceptance of a value to the point of being willing to be identified with it, but the individual is sufficiently committed to the value to pursue it, to seek it out, to want it.
Sample objective: (Speaks to the teacher about learning conditions in the classroom if and when he feels strongly about them.)

3.3   *Commitment.* (Commitment refers to conviction and certainty. The person who displays behavior at this level is clearly perceived as holding the value. He tries to convince others and seeks converts to his cause.)

Table 3-7 (continued)

<table>
<tr><td rowspan="4">Organization
means . . .</td><td colspan="2">Sample objective: Loyalty to the social goals of a free society and a world community.</td></tr>
<tr><td>4.0</td><td>ORGANIZATION
Organization is intended as the proper classification for objectives which describe the beginnings of the building of a value system.</td></tr>
<tr><td>4.1</td><td>Conceptualization of a Value. (Conceptualization refers to the quality of abstraction. It permits the learner to see how the value relates to those he already holds or to new ones that he is coming to hold.)
Sample objective: Forms judgments as to the responsibility of the individual, various groups, and society for conserving human and material resources.</td></tr>
<tr><td>4.2</td><td>Organization of a Value System. Objectives properly classified here are those which require the learner to bring together a complex of values, possibly disparate values, and to bring these into some ordered relationship with one another.
Sample objective: Judges people of various races, cultures, national origins, and occupations in terms of their behaviors as individuals.</td></tr>
<tr><td rowspan="3">Characterization
means . . .</td><td>5.0</td><td>CHARACTERIZATION BY A VALUE OR VALUE COMPLEX
(The learner acts consistently in accordance with the values he has internalized: the attitudes and value system become a way of life.)</td></tr>
<tr><td>5.1</td><td>Generalized Set. (This term refers to a kind of unconscious tendency to act in fairly consistent and predictable patterns; a sort of basic orientation toward life.)
Sample objective: Views problems in objective, realistic, and tolerant terms.</td></tr>
<tr><td>5.2</td><td>Characterization. (Characterization reflects the peak of the internalization process. Here are found objectives which concern one's view of the universe, one's philosophy of life.)
Sample objective: Develops for regulation of one's personal and civic life a code of behavior based on ethical principles consistent with democratic ideals.</td></tr>
</table>

§ D. R. Krathwohl, B. S. Bloom, and B. B. Masia (1964). New York: McKay. All the material within the parentheses is an adaptation of the *Taxonomy: Affective Domain.* Everything else, including headings, is exactly as it appears in the *Taxonomy.*

in trying to capture their learners' attention. Much effort is spent trying to make the learning atmosphere both personal and attractive. Teachers hope that their learners will gain positive attitudes toward one another, toward themselves, and toward learning. Typically, however, such worthy but vague affective goals are left unspecified. Furthermore, as we saw in our discussion of cognitive goals, vagueness in hoped-for learner outcomes is likely to be associated with vagueness in the teacher's techniques and approaches.

Precision in stating affective objectives can encourage greater development of the affective components teachers say are so important in learning. There are guidelines which can help us plan more specifically for affective development. A look at the subsections of the *Taxonomy of Educational Objectives: Affective Domain* (Table 3-7) will give you some clues.

CLUES FOR PRACTICE   One of our basic assumptions is that practice increases the likelihood that learning and retention will occur. This is true not only for responses of the cognitive type but also for affective ones. Therefore, simply put, teachers organize learning situations that cause children to practice the kinds of responses they believe are important for children to acquire and to retain. And, if the importance of a child's affective development equals or exceeds the importance of his cognitive development, specific learning tasks must focus on the content to be learned and also on the affective conditions under which it is to be learned. Specific instructional objectives in the cognitive domain provide clues as to the kinds of learning conditions necessary to learn various cognitive behaviors. Affective objectives, if precisely stated, provide clues about how learning activities may be organized so that learners will want to participate, that is, so that they will be motivated to do so. Both must be specifically planned because both are too important to leave to chance. As Combs and Snygg point out, "How subject matter is taught may be even more important than what is taught."[10] Let us turn now to learning how to write specific affective objectives and how to get a feel for the approximate truth of what was just said.

Affective objectives provide . . .

WRITING AFFECTIVE OBJECTIVES

Writing affective objectives is similar in many respects to writing cognitive objectives. They should be precise statements that reflect a variety of learner behaviors, and they should have qualifications.

You have acquired the skill of analyzing vague statements for more specific descriptions of learner behavior. You have learned how to write instructional objectives that have qualifications such as degree of accuracy, time limit, or mode of performance. And you have learned to write cognitive objectives that reflect a variety of kinds of intellectual functioning. Because of the close parallel in the way the cognitive and affective domains have been organized into major and minor categories, your practice in writing cognitive objectives will generalize to writing objectives in the affective domain. This is an example of what we will come to refer to in Chapter 7 as *positive transfer*.

Let us check for the effects of positive transfer by writing affective objectives that reflect (1) specific behaviors, (2) the learner's point of view, (3) qualifications, and (4) variety of affective responses. Keep in mind that when children are learning, they are always doing so in the sense that cognitive and affective responses are occurring at the same time. Consequently, as you plan cognitive experiences for your learners, you should also plan affective ones. Therefore, as you practice writing affective objectives for each of the categories in the affective domain, you would be wise to think in terms of some cognitive task within the curriculum.

CHECKPOINT 3-7

For this checkpoint, suppose we think about a unit from the social studies, the Amazon Basin.

1. Write one specific instructional objective for each of the major and minor categories of the affective domain. Note that as you think about these objectives, they suggest ways of organizing instruction so that they may be met.

2. Were you willing to get involved in the activity of this Checkpoint? (Affective Objective, Attending Level)

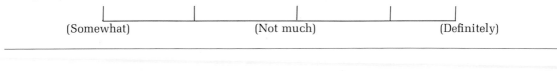

(Somewhat)   (Not much)   (Definitely)

[10] A. W. Combs and D. Snygg (1959). *Individual Behavior*, rev. ed. New York: Harper, p. 382.

The Psychomotor Domain

In addition to their interest in the cognitive and affective growth of learners, most classroom teachers are concerned with the physical development of children. Teachers at most grade levels consider that part of their work centers on helping learners to acquire and develop movement or motor skills. Physical development involves movements such as reflexes, walking, running, perceptual abilities, eye-hand coordination, balance, strength, endurance, the appropriate and proper use of a variety of instruments and tools, and expressive and creative actions. Many courses within the public school are established specifically for learning certain psychomotor skills; the courses focus, for example, on physical education, driver training, commercial skills, various manual arts, fine art, and music.

Psychomotor means . . .

LEVELS AND SUBCATEGORIES

Harrow (1972) organized the psychomotor domain into six major classification levels, with each major level further divided into subcategories and divisions. Her major levels and subcategories are shown in Table 3-8. A few objectives are included as examples of the types of objectives that can be written for behaviors in the psychomotor domain.

The six major categories of the psychomotor domain are . . .

Harrow describes the six major classification levels as the basic framework for her taxonomy of observable movement behaviors in the psychomotor domain. Ordinarily, classroom teachers will not need to formulate objectives for Harrow's first two levels—Reflex and Basic-Fundamental Movements—since most youngsters have developed adequate proficiency in these skills prior to entry into public schools. However, teachers of special education programs, e.g., for physically handicapped children, or of preschool programs such as nursery school, day care, or the increasingly popular Montessori classes, will need to become skilled at writing instructional objectives at the levels of Basic-Fundamental Movements.

Looking in broad overview at the psychomotor domain, we see that practice with corrective feedback is an important variable that distinguishes among the major levels. Through guided practice, learners progress from relatively gross bodily movements in level 2 to highly refined, complex, and creative-expressive movements in level 6.

Looking at the higher levels of all three domains—cognitive, affective, and psychomotor—one gets the feel for what we mentioned earlier: that the domains tend to blend together and overlap. For example, objectives at Harrow's level 6 of the psychomotor domain—Non-Discursive Communication—require an explicit cognitive component and, implicitly, an affective one. Cognitively, learners must be able to synthesize their own patterns or sequences of physical movement; then, psychomotorly, they must have previously acquired the skilled movements necessary to execute their patterns. Finally, affectively, the entire sequence of movements is to occur by choice in free response activities.

WRITING PSYCHOMOTOR OBJECTIVES

As you can see in Table 3-8, psychomotor objectives, like cognitive and affective objectives, are precise statements of learner behavior. They have qualifications

TABLE 3-8   Taxonomy for the psychomotor domain:
classification levels and subcategories¶

TAXONOMY CONTINUUM	LEVELS	DEFINITIONS	BEHAVIORAL ACTIVITY
1.10 Segmental 1.20 Inter-segmental 1.30 Supra-segmental	1.00 Reflex Movements	Actions elicited without conscious volition in response to some stimuli.	Flexion, extension, stretch, postural adjustments

Sample Objective: Objectives are not ordinarily written for this level of the Taxonomy.

2.10 Locomotor 2.20 Non-Locomotor	2.00 Basic-Fundamental Movements	Required: 1.00. Inherent movement patterns which are formed from a combining of reflex movements, and which are the basis for complex skilled movement.	2.10 Walking, running, jumping, sliding, hopping, rolling, climbing. 2.20 Pushing, pulling, swaying, swinging, stooping, stretching, bending, twisting. 2.30 Handling, manipulating, gripping, grasping finger movements.

Sample Objective: To improve, in the special-education children, the basic locomotor movements so that each child will be able to perform the following activities: sliding, walking, running, jumping with smooth movement patterns and gait so they do not deviate significantly from the mean performances of their peer group.

3.10 Kinesthetic Discrimination 3.20 Visual Discrimination	3.00 Perceptual Abilities	Required: 1.00–2.00 Interpretation of stimuli from various modalities providing data for the learner to make adjustments to his environment.	The *outcomes* of perceptual abilities are observable in *all purposeful* movement. Examples: Auditory: following verbal instructions.
3.30 Auditory Discrimination 3.40 Tactile Discrimination			Visual: dodging a moving ball. Kinesthetics: making bodily adjustments in a handstand to maintain balance. Tactile: determining texture through touch.
3.50 Coordinated Abilities			Coordinated: jump rope, punting, catching.

Table 3-8 (continued)

Sample Objective: To develop the eye-foot coordination of primary children so that one hundred percent of the children can successfully kick a stationary playground ball five times in succession and eighty percent can successfully kick a moving playground ball three out of five times.

4.10 Endurance	4.00 Physical Abilities	Functional characteristics of organic vigor which are essential to the development of highly skilled movement.	All activities which require strenuous effort for long periods of time. Examples: distance running, distance swimming.
4.20 Strength			All activities which require muscular exertion. Examples: weight lifting, wrestling.
4.30 Flexibility			All activities which require wide range of motion at hip joints. Examples: touching toes, back bend, ballet exercises.
4.40 Agility			All activities which require quick, precise movements. Examples: shuttle run, typing, dodgeball.

Sample Objective: To improve the agility of seventh-grade girls as determined by each girl's ability to increase by at least three the number of squat-thrusts performed during one minute and to decrease by two seconds the time to run the 40-yard shuttle run.

5.10 Simple Adaptive Skill	5.00 Skilled Movements	A degree of efficiency when performing complex movement tasks which are based upon inherent movement patterns.	All skilled activities which build upon the inherent locomotor and manipulative movement patterns of classification level two.
5.20 Compound Adaptive Skill			
5.30 Complex Adaptive Skill			These activities are obvious in sports, recreation, dance, and fine arts areas.

Table 3-8 (continued)

Sample Objective: To improve the typing skill of first-year typing students as measured by ninety percent of the class typing at least thirty words per minute during a five-minute typing test with no more than five errors.

6.10	Expressive Movement	6.00 Non-discursive	Communication through bodily movement ranging from facial expressions through sophisticated choreographies.	Body postures, gestures, facial expressions, all efficiently executed; skilled dance movements and choreographies.
6.20	Interpretative Movement			

Sample Objective: To develop in primary children the abilities to design their own series of movements in free response activities so that by the end of the year each child will be able to create a series of locomotor and non-locomotor movements and perform his choreography for one minute to music. The choreography must contain a minimum of three recognizable locomotor movements and at least four recognizable non-locomotor movements.

¶ A. J. Harrow (1972). *A Taxonomy of the Psychomotor Domain.* New York: McKay. The table is exactly as it appears in the *Taxonomy,* except that sample objectives from the text have been included.

and they reflect a variety of psychomotor behaviors. The same process of task description is used, that is, the process of asking: What do I really mean by the vague terms that are used in statements of general goals? Because of the similarities, what we have learned about writing cognitive and affective objectives should transfer to writing psychomotor objectives.

CHECKPOINT 3-8

1. Using the objectives in Table 3-8 as models, formulate at least one instructional objective that might be derived from the general goals given below. One way to check on those you write is to ask whether they are precise, are stated from the point of view of the learner, and include restrictions or conditions under which the behavior is to be performed.

   a. The learner will show improvement in physical condition.

   b. The learner will become well coordinated.

2. Have you tried to help anyone learn to write objectives? Yes_____ No_____ (Affective Objective, Organizational Level)

TEACHING FOR OBJECTIVES

Even though it is important to have a clear, precise idea of what you want your learners to learn, it is not always possible to say exactly what kind of objective you are teaching for. As we have just seen, the three domains presented in the three taxonomies of educational objectives are not entirely separate and discrete categories of behaviors. No objective will ever be entirely cognitive, affective, or psychomotor but will always contain elements of two or more domains. All objectives deal both with what the learner can *do* (cognitive, psychomotor), and with how he or she *feels* (affective) about being able to do it.

If an objective, for example, in the cognitive domain, is: "Given an appropriate literary passage, the learner is able to analyze it for evidence to support the behavior of the main character," there should also be affective objectives that relate to the learner's continuing attitude toward, and interest in, literature. Furthermore, in your teaching it is wise to include affective objectives that relate to how the child feels about himself as a consequence of being able to meet the cognitive objectives. As we have seen, some educators argue that the affective components of objectives are as important as, if not more important than, the cognitive objectives themselves. They maintain that what is being taught are *people*, and that information or psychomotor skills merely provide a useful matrix within which teachers can help learners become increasingly aware of themselves as living, responding, and valuing members of various and changing environments. Perhaps this is a rather thin hair to split; however, you surely will have difficulty in being an attending, responding, and valuing person if in fact you have not learned the information and skills important for success in your environment. As you begin writing objectives for your learners, it may be helpful to keep in mind that we do not teach, say, arithmetic; we teach learners about arithmetic.

Using Objectives before, during, and after Instruction

Objectives should be written prior to instruction because . . .

From our discussion so far, we should be able to draw a few generalizations about when instructional objectives should be written. The answer, of course, is that they should be written prior to instruction. There are several reasons for this and for sharing them with your learners before instruction actually begins. First, such preparation provides an answer to the question, What do I want them to learn? Next, it suggests the kinds of learning activities that may be helpful. It gives clues about the affective components which should be part of learning activity. It helps learners know what is expected of them and probably will provide an appropriate affective mental set for learning the new material. In this way, the material is likely to be learned meaningfully rather than rotely. Knowing the objectives will make it more likely that the interest and attention of learners will be captured by learning tasks rather than by the teacher's demand for them. Also, objectives provide a basis for pretesting learners in order to determine which learners need to learn what things, thus giving us information with which we can begin to individualize our instruction.

Specifically stated objectives are also helpful during and following instruction. A precise statement of learner outcomes permits both the teacher and the learners to know when they have completed the learning tasks. Instruction should end when the students have acquired the stated objectives rather than when time has run out or, as it is often the case, when most of the learners "seem to understand the main ideas covered." Also, it provides a definite basis from which to construct evaluation measures. That is, objectives help us know what to evaluate and how to go about evaluating; therefore, we need not have to rely on post hoc procedures of trying to guess at what we think learners may have gained from the instruction and what would be "fair" and "appropriate" questions to ask them.

AN EXAMPLE OF USING OBJECTIVES

Let me show you how you might use objectives before, during, and after instruction. Assume that you are teaching a group of learners about biology, and more precisely, helping them learn about plant cells, about the use of a microscope, and about themselves. Such teaching and learning might occur at any level—elementary school, secondary school, university, or even in a setting for adult education.

Among the objectives you have stated are the following:

Cognitive: Given a prepared slide of green-plant tissue, a microscope, and drawing materials, the learner is able to draw a typical green-plant cell and label the parts: cell wall, chloroplasts, nucleus, vacuole.

Affective: Given the opportunity to choose a laboratory partner, the learner chooses on the basis of ability to work cooperatively rather than on the basis of skin color, ethnic group, religion, or other dimensions irrelevant to the task at hand.

Psychomotor: Given a microscope and a prepared slide of green-plant tissue, the learner is able to operate the microscope so that he can see clearly the details of the plant cells.

If, prior to instruction, you share the objectives for each domain with your learners, all of you know the answer to the question: What do I want the learners to learn? Furthermore, thus sharing all your objectives helps everyone gain both a general and a specific overview of what is to be accomplished. As you discuss your objectives for the unit of work, you may find that some of them require modification. In this sense, the learners have a real part in the planning of their instruction.

Your statement of objectives suggests some clues about what the learning context may include. It tells you about the materials you will need and how the groups should be formed for the microscope activities. Obviously, the learners will be working in pairs (or larger groups) of their choice, with microscopes and with prepared slides of green-plant tissue. You will need to arrange the instruction so as to provide this situation.

Now that you know precisely how you should organize for instruction, the question arises as to whether all the learners are "ready" for this learning task. How can you find out? First, you must have some fairly clear idea of what the prerequisites are for the learning tasks as described by your objectives. What must a learner be able to do, for example, to operate the microscope so as to see clearly the cells within the green-plant tissue of the prepared slide? What must the learners be able to do to recognize a cell when it appears? What will they need to be able to do to choose partners on bases other than skin color or ethnic group?

If your teaching is to be more than a series of random efforts, and the learning more than rote, these questions must be answered. *Task analysis* is a technique that can be of great help. As we mentioned earlier in this chapter, doing a task analysis means essentially asking the question, over and over, What must the learners be able to do to do this thing, and then, what must they be able to do to do that thing?—and so forth. Answers for these questions not only help you specify your objectives, they form the basis for pretesting; they determine "readiness" for the next learning task. Finding out which learners have achieved the prerequisites for the present learning task allows you to modify your instructional materials and procedures to help each student acquire them.

Statements of your objectives in precise, behavioral terms help you and your learners know when instruction should terminate. It should end when the learners are able to demonstrate individually that they (1) have chosen laboratory partners, (2) can operate a microscope so as to see the details of plant cells, and (3) have drawn and labeled a typical green-plant cell. Instruction ends on purpose rather than on the basis of some more arbitrary variable such as the time running out, most of the learners learning it, interest seeming to lag, or the material being covered.

Having objectives stated in precise, behavioral terms removes the guesswork from the task of evaluating learning. At the end of the instruction you won't search for questions to ask the learners. This task has already been stated. Questions for evaluation derive directly from the objectives.

An approach to instruction such as that presented briefly in this example is straightforward, open, and honest. It virtually eliminates the situation in which teacher and learners are on opposing teams, trying to outguess and outflank one another in the classroom. It puts everyone on the same team, with everyone cooperating on the tasks to be learned.

At this time, you should return to the statement of goals and objectives for this chapter and see how well you have been able to meet them. If you need additional practice, try some of the items in the Activities section. Further information about objectives and criticisms of objectives can be found in the publications listed in Suggestions for Further Reading. We are now ready to learn more about learning itself and the skills of doing a task analysis. Chapter 4 will help us get started.

IN PASSING

MORNING IS YELLOW LIKE A DESK IS SQUARE

He always wanted to explain things.
But no one cared.
So he drew.
Sometimes he would draw and it wasn't anything.
He wanted to carve it in stone or write it in the sky.
He would lie out on the grass and look up in the sky.
And it would be only him and the sky and the things inside him that needed saying.
And it was after that he drew the picture.
He kept it under his pillow and would let no one see it.
And he would look at it every night and think about it.
And when it was dark, and his eyes were closed, he could still see it.
And it was all of him.

And he loved it.
When he started school he brought it with him.
Not to show anyone, but just to have it with him like a friend.
It was funny about school.
He sat in a square, brown desk
Like all the other square, brown desks
And he thought it should be red
And his room was a square brown room.
Like all the other rooms.
And it was tight and close.
And stiff.
With the teacher watching and watching.
She told him to wear a tie like all the other boys.
He said he didn't like them
And she said it didn't matter.
After that they drew.
And he drew all yellow and it was the way he felt about morning.
And it was beautiful.
The teacher came and smiled at him.
"What's this?" she said. "Why don't you draw something like Ken's drawing?
Isn't that beautiful?"
After that his mother bought him a tie.
And he always drew airplanes and rocket ships like everyone else.
And he threw the old picture away.
And when he lay alone looking at the sky,
It was big and blue and all of everything,
But he wasn't anymore.
He was square inside
and brown,
And his hands were stiff.
And he was like everyone else.
And the things inside him that needed saying didn't need it anymore.
It had stopped pushing.
It was crushed.
Stiff.
Like everything else.

   This poem was passed in to his teacher by a grade twelve student. Two weeks later, the poet took his own life. I wonder as I read the poem how teachers and learners can possibly get so far apart on their goals and objectives.

1. In order to summarize the general and specific ideas made in Chapter 3, complete the following two statements:

a. Generally, Chapter 3 is about: (State your answer, if you can, in the form of general rules of thumb).

b. More specifically, Chapter 3 makes the following points:

2. Explain to another person how a teacher's point of emphasis might differ if she were "teaching learners about physics" rather than "teaching physics." Refer to objectives in the cognitive and affective domains. Ask this person to write a brief statement that shows, to your satisfaction, that the person understood what you were teaching.

ACTIVITIES

3.   As an individual, small group, or entire class activity, try to complete a task description of the long-range goal commonly given by school districts as their primary goal of education: "The learner will become a worthwhile citizen."

4.   Prepare a set of specific instructional objectives that contains at least one objective representative of the cognitive, affective, and psychomotor domains. Classify the objectives. These objectives may be written for any kind of lesson at any grade level and they may be for one child or for a group of children.

Next, describe briefly an appropriate activity and the materials that can be used to help the learner(s) achieve the objectives stated. Explain how the activity would be organized and operated.

5.   Just for fun:

An approximately true answer to the question about manhole covers asked in Chapter 2 is this: Very simply, if they were not round, the cover could be dropped into the hole. As I understand it, manhole covers were square at one time, but not for long. The reason for their brief life can be explained in specific behavioral terms: Given a square-shaped manhole cover and one manhole, a mischievous person is able to lift the cover, turn it edgewise, and drop it through the square opening. Apparently this objective was relatively easy to meet!

Happily, education has a light side—if you can maintain a sense of positive affect. A mother sent the following note to the principal of the school attended by her children. Can you find the specific objective in the note? Or, can you describe the approximate behavior the principal should exhibit to show that he had met the objective?

Dear Sir:

In response to this note the principal should . . .

Michael is wearing a boot that is not ours. Someone took Robbie's yesterday by mistake so Robbie had to wear it home.

Today, Robbie took Michael's instead of the one that does not belong to us. Could you please ask Robbie's teacher for the one that is ours and give this one to her? And please exchange Michael's for Robbie's.

Thank you,
A Mother

REFERENCES

Bloom, B. S., ed. (1956). *Taxonomy of Educational Objectives. Handbook I: Cognitive Domain.* New York: McKay.

Burns, R. W. (1972). *New Approaches to Behavioral Objectives.* Dubuque, Iowa: Wm. C. Brown Company Publishers.

Carroll, J. A. (1963). A model of school learning, *Teachers College Record,* **64,** 723-733.

Combs, A. W., and D. Snygg (1959). *Individual Behavior,* rev. ed. New York: Harper.

Glasser, W. (1969). *Schools Without Failure.* New York: Harper & Row.

Harrow, A. J. (1972). *A Taxonomy of the Psychomotor Domain.* New York: McKay.

Highet, G. (1957). *The Art of Teaching.* New York: Vintage Books.

Krathwohl, D. R., B. S. Bloom, and B. B. Masia (1964). *Taxonomy of Educational Objectives. Handbook II: Affective Domain.* New York: McKay.

Lindvall, C. M., ed. (1964). *Defining Educational Objectives, (3).* Pittsburgh: The University of Pittsburgh Press.

Stephens, J. M. (1965). *The Psychology of Classroom Learning.* New York: Holt.

Thorndike, E. L. (1906). *Principles of Teaching Based upon Psychology.* New York: Seiler.

Trabasso, T. (1968). Pay attention, *Psychology Today,* **2,** 30–36.

Tyler, R. W. (1934). *Constructing Achievement Tests.* Columbus: Ohio State University Press.

——— (1964). Some persistent questions on the defining of objectives. In C. M. Lindvall (ed.), *Defining Educational Objectives,* (3). Pittsburgh: The University of Pittsburgh Press.

Eisner, E. W. (1967). Educational objectives help or hindrance? *The School Review,* **75,** 250–260. Eisner seriously questions the statement of objectives in specific terms, especially prior to instruction. He presents a convincing argument for following the interests of learners as they arise. He believes the statement of precise objectives narrows and constricts teaching and learning.

Mager, R. F. (1962). *Preparing Instructional Objectives.* Palo Alto, Calif.: Fearon Publishers, Inc. This small paperback (60 pages) is helpful for at least two reasons. First, it provides useful information and practice which can help you learn to prepare specific instructional objectives. Second, it presents the information in a programmed format. Thus, you both gain by the advantages of learning specific information through a programmed approach and you learn about programmed materials through experiencing them.

Stephens, J. M. (1965). *The Psychology of Classroom Learning.* New York: Holt. John Stephens has devoted much of his life to the questions of whether some approaches to instruction result in more effective learning than do others. He has concluded that effective learning is more a function of the teacher than of the approach. Furthermore, he concludes that much of a teacher's effectiveness is due to natural and spontaneous forces relative to teaching and residing in all of us. Consequently, Stephens presents a strong argument against detailed planning of each intricate step in a child's learning.

SUGGESTIONS FOR FURTHER READING

4

THE NATURE OF LEARNING

The will to learn is an intrinsic motive, one that finds both its source and its reward in its own exercise. The will to learn becomes a "problem" only under specialized circumstances like those of a school, where a curriculum is set, students confined, and a path fixed. The problem exists not so much in learning itself, but in the fact that what the school imposes often fails to enlist the natural energies that sustain spontaneous learning—curiosity, a desire for competence, aspiration to emulate a model, and a deep-sensed commitment to the web of social reciprocity. Our concern has been with how these energies may be cultivated in support of school learning. If we know little firmly, at least we are not without reasonable hypotheses about how to proceed. The practice of education does, at least, produce interesting hypotheses. After all, the Great Age of Discovery was made possible by men whose hypotheses were formed before they had developed a decent technique for measuring longitude.

Jerome S. Bruner
Toward a Theory of Instruction

CONTENTS

ONGOING SUMMARY

When there are observable changes in the performance (behavior) of an organism, we infer that learning has occurred. The major goal of teachers is to modify the performances of learners, that is, to effect learning. We have seen so far that to help learners learn effectively, we need to (1) capture their attention for an appropriate amount of time, in an appropriate manner, and to appropriate learning tasks; (2) be precise about cause and effect in human behavior, about description and explanation, and about the relative and approximate nature of the "truths" that capture the attention of learners; and (3) be precise about what we want our learners to attend to, the goals and objectives. Therefore, we must describe clearly and precisely what we believe are appropriate learning outcomes; and we must become skillful at doing so.

Helping learners learn effectively requires that we understand the concept *learning*. We must be able to interpret the concept of learning so that it will be useful at a level beyond simple recall, and we must be able to organize instructional frames of reference (approaches) that will result in optimal learning success for each child, not just the group in general.

ADVANCE ORGANIZER

There are several ways to interpret learning and unfortunately the differences among them have tended to be exaggerated. This tendency has caused observers to take sides rather than to utilize the best from each side, even though, obviously, no single interpretation adequately accounts for all the types of learning encountered in school settings.

Recently, however, there has been an important shift in the thinking about school learning, resulting in efforts to combine various interpretations of learning rather than to select certain ones. Your job as a teacher will be to arrive at interpretations that are *theoretically* sensible and that lead to approaches that are both practical and useful. As John Dewey pointed out, nothing is more practical than sound theory.

As we saw in Chapter 1, many approaches are possible. However, we will proceed by first looking broadly at the concept of learning, then at its history. After examining the various interpretations, we will see how they can be combined into a useful method of mastery learning.

When you finish this chapter, you will be ready to begin learning about the general and specific conditions necessary for your learners to succeed at the learning tasks you cause them to attend to.

Cognitive

GOALS AND OBJECTIVES

To become an effective teacher, the learner should be able to interpret various laws and theories of learning.

KNOWLEDGE LEVEL

Given the following terms or phrases, the learner is able to define them in writing: *learning, induction, deduction, connectionist interpretation of learning, cognitive interpretation of learning, classical conditioning, operant conditioning, insight, cognitive-field theory, Gagné's types of learning, task description, task analysis, Carroll's model of school learning, mastery learning.*

COMPREHENSION LEVEL

1. Given the following names of persons who have contributed to an interpretation of learning, the learner is able to describe each person's contribution:

Pavlov, Watson, Guthrie, Thorndike, Skinner, Wertheimer. Köhler, Bruner, Tolman, Gagné, Carroll, Bloom.

2. Given Figure 4-5, the learner is able to interpret it in terms of the basic assumptions involved in Carroll's model of school learning and in Bloom's model for mastery learning.

APPLICATION LEVEL

Given the principle (rule) of operant conditioning, the learner can provide an example of its application in a classroom.

ANALYSIS LEVEL

Given the terms task description and task analysis, the learner is able to compare and contrast them verbally so clearly that another person can explain how the terms are alike and how they are different.

SYNTHESIS LEVEL

Given the objective, "The learner is able to calculate $960 \div 32 = \square$," the learner is able to write a brief task analysis for the objective, using Gagné's types of learning as a guide.

EVALUATION LEVEL

Given the argument that mastery learning is a restrictive way to learn, learners are able to say why they agree or disagree.

Affective

To become an effective teacher, the learner should be able to participate actively and thoughtfully in the activities related to the psychology of learning.

RECEIVING (ATTENDING) LEVEL

1. The learner is willing to receive help and to help others learn about learning.
2. The learner is aware that he attends to those learning tasks that are accompanied by reinforcement (success).

RESPONDING LEVEL

The learner practices the checkpoint activities.

VALUING LEVEL

The learner is committed to the importance of being able to complete a task analysis.

ORGANIZATIONAL LEVEL

Learners become confident of their own ability to help themselves and others learn.

CHARACTERIZATION LEVEL

The learner is beginning to plan for his own future teaching in ways that are consistent with how he is learning.

WHAT IS LEARNING?

4

What do we mean by the term *learning*? Like so many other concepts, it appears easy to define until we try to do so. We saw this in Chapter 3 when we tried to define education. Even though these concepts are difficult to define precisely, we must attempt it. As you will recall from Chapter 3, Thorndike (1906) pointed out that if we do not understand clearly the general idea, we are not likely to know exactly what to do to help learners learn.

In your work as a teacher, it will be important for you to determine whether or not a child has learned something. How will you do this? The obvious answer is that you can consider learning has occurred when behavior shows some observable change. But note that in making such a statement, an inference has been made about something that has occurred within the individual. When the person performs differently, that is, does something now which he could not do earlier, we say that this person has learned. We cannot see learning directly. The only thing we have available for observation is the *performance* or the *behavior* of the individual.

Another important and general dimension of learning concerns the concepts *retention* and *transfer*. If I help Karen learn to spell a particular word today and find that tomorrow she is unable to spell it correctly, has learning occurred? Or, if I help Karen learn both to spell and to define the word correctly today, and find that tomorrow she is unable to use it correctly in a sentence, has learning occurred? Whether things learned are retained and transferred depends to a great extent on how the things were learned originally. We will discuss these important ideas in the next few chapters, but now let us try to learn more about learning itself.

Psychologists think of learning more broadly than we use the word in popular speech. Hill tells us that, in the way psychologists use the term:[1]

> What is learned need not be "correct" or adaptive (we learn bad habits as well as good), need not be conscious or deliberate (one of the advantages of coaching in a skill is that it makes us aware of mistakes we have unconsciously learned to make), and need not involve any overt act (attitudes and emotions can be learned as well as knowledge or skills). Reactions as diverse as driving a car, remembering a pleasant vacation, believing in democracy, and disliking one's boss, all represent the results of learning.

Learning is defined as . . .

A definition of learning, popular with psychologists and educators, considers learning to be a *relatively permanent change in a behavioral tendency that is a result of reinforced practice*. Although such a definition may be useful, we shall see that not everyone agrees with it. Some investigators have contended that learning is an all-or-nothing event and that practice serves the purpose of increasing the likelihood that what is learned will be retained. And not everyone agrees that reinforcement plays a part in learning.

Two Major Approaches to Learning: Deductive and Inductive

The deductive approach is . . .

Generally, the study of learning has taken two major approaches. One approach, the *deductive* method, has been to formulate general all-inclusive *theories* of

[1] W.F. Hill (1963). *Learning: A Survey of Psychological Interpretations.* San Francisco; Chandler, p. 1.

learning. This approach usually begins with certain postulates about learning which are derived from careful observation of behavior in naturalistic settings. From there postulates, more precise statements of theory, can be derived by a process of logical argument, and these statements of theory can be tested through experimentation to establish their adequacy or inadequacy.

The second major approach has been the *inductive* one. It begins with carefully controlled *experimental studies* from which observations are made. From the observations, laws of behavior are formulated. As experimentation continues, more useful laws are formulated. Laws of a specific nature, relative to specific experiments, often are grouped together to form more general laws. In time, general laws tend to be formulated into more general statements that may eventually constitute a theoretical position.

The inductive approach is . . .

From these two approaches to learning, the inductive and deductive methods, has risen the issue of whether it is more useful to consider learning from a *molar* or a *molecular* point of view. That is, from the standpoint of studying the total learning event intact, the cognitive approach; or of studying the specific and discrete components of the learning event, known as the connectionist (or behavioristic) approach.

The *cognitive approach* has tended to be deductive and to study learning on a *molar* basis, that is, through total behavioral acts, events, beliefs, patterns. Such an approach leads to an interest in *theories* of learning to account for what happens within an organism when learning occurs. At the same time, however, most proponents of the cognitive approach have been concerned in some way with controlled laboratory experimentation.

A cognitive approach tends to . . .

The *connectionist approach* has tended to be inductive and directed toward *molecular* study, that is, toward understanding the lawful relationships between specific, environmental stimuli and the responses of the organism when learning occurs. Consequently, the focus has been on laws of behavior relative to observable and measurable stimuli and responses. Yet, as we will see later in this chapter, people well known for their connectionist orientation have also developed theories of learning and have made rather extensive use of what have traditionally been known as concepts of a cognitive nature. Thus, those with an essentially connectionist point of view may be interested in behavior of a molar nature. Table 4-1 summarizes these ideas.

A connectionist approach tends to . . .

TABLE 4-1   The major approaches to learning overlap

DEDUCTIVE (Cognitive)	INDUCTIVE (Connectionist or behavioristic)
Natural observations (Molar)	Controlled experimentation (Molecular)
↓	↓
Postulates	Observations of experiments
↓	↓
Theories of learning	Laws of behavior
↓	↓
Experimentation (molecular)	General laws → theories (molar)

A HISTORY OF TRADITIONAL
INTERPRETATIONS OF LEARNING

Let us see how the concept of learning has come to be interpreted as it is today. Mostly, the history of learning falls into the two major approaches mentioned earlier, the cognitive (deductive) and the connectionist (inductive), and the following brief account is a selection and an approximation of what has really happened within each of these approaches. The difference in these approaches will be exaggerated somewhat to help illustrate some of the basic assumptions made from each point of view. Later in the chapter, we will see how the two approaches can combine effectively for school learning.

The history recounted here is biased by my own perceptions of what I believe to be important for future teachers to know about. The meaning I attach to each incident is biased by my past experiences, by the objectives set for you for this chapter, and by what, in my opinion, teaching and learning are about.

One of the difficulties in helping you to learn is that there is no way to be certain about what will be important for each of you to know in order to be an effective teacher. Yet as a teacher teaching about these materials, I must make these decisions as best I can.

First, I hope to help you gain a broad overview of what has happened to the concept of learning over time. Main ideas transfer better than specific detail; therefore, the focus will be on the main ideas that have been associated with this concept. Only as much specific detail will be included as I believe will help you gain the main ideas in a meaningful, as opposed to a rote, manner.

From the experimental and theoretical efforts of various investigators have come implications for what teachers might do in classrooms to help students learn more effectively. Our look at my history of learning will be concerned with these implications for classroom practice.

To begin our discussion, you will find it helpful to get an overall picture of the relationships, in terms of time, of the people we will be meeting. Presenting these men one by one in sequential order can be misleading, since it may give the impression that they followed each other in a time order. Actually, most of the men we will meet were contemporaries. This is shown in Figure 4-1 with a timeline.

PSYCHOLOGY IN THE
EARLY GERMAN TRADITION

The first psychological laboratory was established in Germany in 1879 by Wilhelm Wundt (1832–1920) and his colleagues. Their effort represented a merger of philosophy and physiology into what has come to be known as experimental psychology. Wundt and his followers were medical men who also had background in philosophy.

The kinds of data generated from early studies that attempted to probe the mental life of an individual were essentially subjective in nature. They relied heavily on the introspective comments of subjects, that is, the verbal descriptions about how one felt or what one thought about a particular experience. This approach to the study of psychology dominated in both Europe and North America until the early part of the twentieth century.

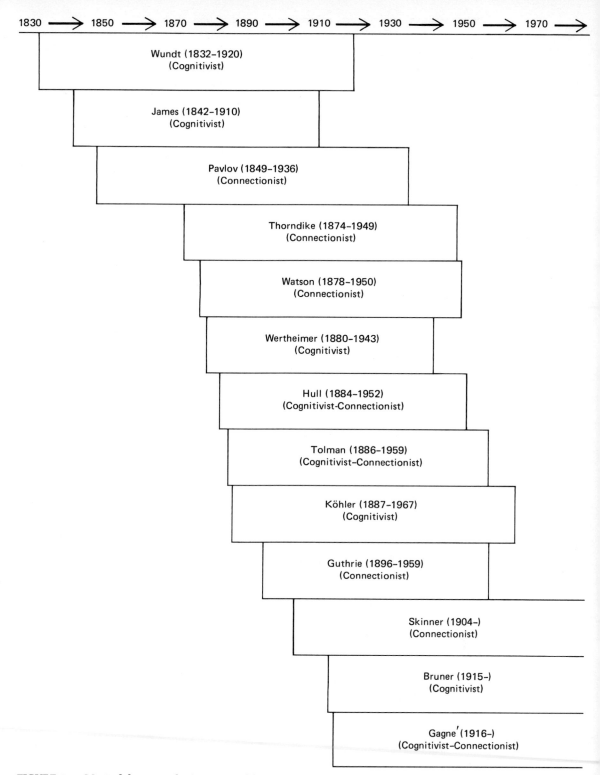

FIGURE 4-1 Most of the men who investigated learning were contemporaries.

In addition to being introspective in nature, psychology in the early German tradition was not necessarily directed toward practical uses. In fact, this very point became one of the critical issues that led to an eventual splitting away from the European tradition by various psychologists. William James (1842–1910) was one of the most influential in forcing the split. By the time he published his two volumes of the *Principles of Psychology* in 1890, interest was growing in what is now called applied psychology. James brought this rising trend toward practical applied psychology clearly into the open with the publication in 1907 of his book *Pragmatism: A New Name for Some Old Ways of Thinking.* He wanted the study of psychology to become an empirical science, and he wanted it to be useful.

Although William James was extremely interested in teaching and learning, the concept of learning itself was never studied in his psychology laboratory, the first of its kind to be established in North America. He did, however, give a great deal of attention to many of the variables related to learning and retention. Some of the chapter titles in his *Principles of Psychology,* volume I, will give you an idea of the kinds of topics James considered important for psychological study, and they are topics we still study today: chapter 4: "Habit"; chapter 9: "The Stream of Thought"; chapter 11: "Attention"; chapter 12: "Perception"; chapter 13: "Discrimination and Comparison"; chapter 14: "Association"; chapter 16: "Memory." If James were "alive today he would be delighted to discover how many of his hypotheses have stood the experimental test."[2] And he would be especially pleased to see the current merging trend of cognitive and connectionist points of view.

Learning in the Connectionist Tradition

A connectionist approach to the interpretation of learning considers learning to be a matter of bonds or connections between certain stimuli and certain responses.

In a strictly connectionist approach, certain stimuli are assumed to have a direct link or a direct connection with certain responses. Little if anything is assumed about unobservable occurrences that may take place within the individual and that may thus mediate between the stimulus on the one hand and the response on the other. You will recall from Chapter 2 that a medical model for cause and effect of human behavior is essentially a *cognitive* interpretation of learning, not a connectionist interpretation.

The variables considered important for investigation in the connectionist view are observable stimuli and observable responses. Attention is rarely given to inner elements such as thoughts, feelings, attitudes, and interests. A connectionist point of view does not deny the existence of such processes. Rather, it considers them subjective in nature. They must be inferred rather than observed directly, and they are difficult to measure and control. Consequently, they present almost insurmountable problems in terms of their usefulness for experimental investigation that might increase our understanding of the concept of learning.

The main difference between a connectionist and a cognitive interpretation of learning is shown in Figure 4-2.

[2] W. James (1958). *Talks to Teachers.* New York: Norton, p. 10.

A CONNECTIONIST INTERPRETATION

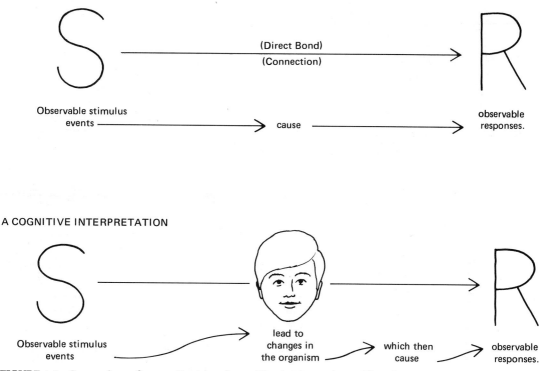

FIGURE 4-2   **Comparison of connectionist and cognitive interpretations of learning.**

Let us now meet some of the people who investigated learning from a connectionist point of view.

MEET IVAN PAVLOV . . .
CLASSICAL CONDITIONING OF ANIMALS

The theory of conditioning (of shaping or modifying behavior) was the result of the work of the famous Russian physiologist Ivan Pavlov (1849–1936). It is interesting to note that the first learning theorist was a physiologist. He was able to bring the precision and control of a laboratory approach to the study of learning.

Pavlov's contribution to our understanding of learning was essentially that responses (e.g., reflexes) which an organism is apparently able to make without having to learn to make them can be "conditioned" if certain procedures are followed. In Pavlov's well-known experiments, the concern was modification of the involuntary salivary response of a dog. Pavlov noted, actually by accident as he was conducting other experiments with dogs, that saliva would flow from a dog's mouth not only when the dog was fed but also at the mere sight of food. Previously, only food in the mouth, or chewing of food, had produced a flow of saliva. Somehow, something occurred that caused a dog to salivate not only at the taste of food but also at the sight of it. The question was: What occurred and under what kinds of conditions? Upon closer observation and experimentation,

Pavlov was able to specify the circumstances under which a reflex response might be conditioned.

Classical conditioning is . . .

A typical experiment that illustrates the principles of classical (or respondent) conditioning outlined by Pavlov is this one: A dog that has been deprived of food for a day or so is strapped into a harness. Then a buzzer or a bell is sounded. After a second or two, the dog is given a mouthful of meat powder. This process is repeated several times. Eventually, the sound of the bell alone becomes sufficient to cause the dog to salivate.

In variations of this basic experimental procedure, Pavlov discovered other important ideas about learning. He found that once a dog had been conditioned to salivate to the sound of a bell, similar sounds would also elicit the salivary response. The effects of one stimulus tended to *generalize* to similar stimuli. He also discovered that if he gave meat powder to the dog after the presentation of certain sounds and not others, he could soon cause the dog to salivate only in the presence of certain sounds. Pavlov was able to gain an additional measure of control over what was originally considered a reflex, or an involuntary, response. He had learned how to teach the dog to *discriminate*, or to tell the difference, between sounds.

Pavlov further discovered, with this simple design for conditioning a response, that as a result of following certain procedures, the conditioned stimulus (the sounding of the bell) appeared to lose its effectiveness. If the bell was sounded too many times without being followed by the unconditioned stimulus (food in the mouth, sometimes referred to as a reward or reinforcement), salivation would no longer occur.

This laboratory experiment is described here in detail because it illustrates many of the key ideas that formed the basis of the connectionist (behavioristic) approach to learning. Furthermore, as we will see, these key ideas can be of tremendous significance in your daily interaction with children in classrooms. They are important not only in a theoretical sense but also as logical extensions of theory to practice.

Pavlov's work is significant for another reason. Often, as teachers, we may think of a creative discovery as being generated "out of nothing." This assumption is a mistake. Pavlov's experiences had prepared him not only to attach significance to seemingly inconsequential detail but also how to deal with it, that is, how to ask the proper questions in the proper form in order to test the significance of a puzzling incident.

MEET JOHN WATSON . . .
CLASSICAL CONDITIONING OF CHILDREN

Sometimes in the history of change, the process is accelerated as much by the personality of the contributor as by his actual contribution. This was the case with John B. Watson (1878–1958), who, influenced by Pavlov's work, was an extremely vocal and vigorous opponent of the traditional psychology.

Watson was not really a learning theorist, although he did conduct several experiments based on Pavlovian conditioning. Perhaps his greatest contribution, in addition to his insistence on objectivity when studying behavior, was his generalization of Pavlovian conditioning to human subjects. He insisted that human behavior could be explained on the basis of conditioned reflexes. He argued that even complex types of responses were learned through the process of classical conditioning.

The best-known experiment conducted by Watson (Watson and Rayner, 1920) illustrated how the principles of classical conditioning could be used to modify certain natural responses of children. At the sound of an unexpected loud noise, most young children display a response characterized by withdrawal from the sound, whimpering, and crying. Watson chose this sort of natural (unlearned) response to illustrate classical conditioning with human subjects. A young boy, named Albert, was permitted to play with a white rat until he and the rat became quite "friendly." Later, in an experimental setting in which Albert was playing freely with the rat, an unexpected loud noise was sounded just as he reached his hand toward the rat. This occurrence was repeated several times. As you might expect, after several trials, the presentation of the rat even without the loud noise came to elicit a response of withdrawl, whimpering, and crying. The previously neutral, then positive stimulus (the rat) had somehow been modified or conditioned so that it now came to evoke a withdrawal and crying response, originally elicited only by the unconditioned stimulus (the loud noise).

In variations of the same experiment, Watson was able to demonstrate that generalization also occurs in human subjects. He showed that other stimuli, similar in various degrees to the rat, would also cause Albert to withdraw and cry. For example, a similar response occurred upon presentation of a rabbit, a dog, a sealskin coat, and a mass of absorbent cotton. Stimuli bearing no similarity to the rat, for example, wooden blocks, did not produce the response. After a month had elapsed, withdrawal and whimpering reactions to the rat, rabbit, dog, coat, and cotton were still evident, but they had decreased in intensity.

Watson, in all his enthusiasm to claim a sweeping victory for behaviorism, fell into the trap of overgeneralization and allowed his confidence to outdistance his information. He said, "Give me a dozen healthy infants, well formed, and my own special world to bring them up in, and I will guarantee to take any one at random and train him to become any type of specialist I might select—doctor, lawyer, artist, merchant-chief, yes, and even beggerman and thief, regardless of his talents, penchants, tendencies, abilities, vocations, and race of his ancestry."[3]

Before too long, however, it became apparent that, although Pavlovian conditioning was indeed a giant step forward in the interpretation of learning, there are aspects of learning for which classical conditioning could not account.

Even though Watson strived to remain strictly objective in his approach to learning, he was not able to convince himself completely that learning accounts for all behavior. In his system, which was never organized into a clear, consistent theory of learning, he recognized three patterns of emotional behavior that he attributed to inheritance. Those behaviors have come to be labeled fear, rage, and love. He held that a person's emotional learning involves a conditioning of these three patterns of inherited emotional response.

Watson's contribution to psychology was . . .

If, from the work of Watson and Pavlov, we abstract a rule or law of classical conditioning that we can apply to the learning of our students, it might be simplified and stated as a rule of thumb: "Stimuli that occur together come to elicit similar responses." This means, in a practical sense, that stimuli that occur together—that are contiguous or paired with learning tasks, for example, arithmetic, music, or social studies—come to affect the responses children make to

A rule of classical conditioning is . . .

[3] J. B. Watson (1925). *Behaviorism.* New York: Norton, p. 82.

these tasks. Children who experience success in learning tasks under these conditions are likely to express positive attitudes not only toward further learning tasks but also toward the school and learning itself. Unfortunately, the converse is also true.

Let us check your understanding of the rule of thumb relative to classical conditioning.

CHECKPOINT 4-1

1. In your own words, explain what the rule of classical conditioning is about. (Note that this item calls for an interpretation-level performance on your part, not just a knowledge-level one.)

2. Suppose you want your learners to learn to speak in front of the class. How might you apply the rule of classical conditioning to increase the possibility of their doing so?

MEET EDWIN GUTHRIE . . .
"WHAT WE DO IS WHAT WE LEARN"

Edwin Guthrie (1896–1959), like Watson, was interested in an interpretation of learning from an extension of Pavlov's work. He spent much of his life studying learning in a connectionist tradition. For more than forty years, Guthrie taught at the University of Washington, where he evolved and experimented with classroom implications of his theory of learning. Guthrie resembled Watson in that both were interested in the practical application of the principles of learning. Guthrie, however, was a good deal more rigorous than Watson in the formulation of a theoretical position about learning.

The basic and extremely simple postulate of Guthrie's theory relies on contiguity of stimuli and responses: *"A combination of stimuli which has accompanied a movement will on its reoccurrence tend to be followed by that movement."*[4] In other words, if a response is paired with a stimulus even once, it is likely to follow that stimulus if that stimulus occurs again; thus, learning will occur. Notice that this interpretation is far more simple and far more general than the interpretation of learning as classical conditioning. There is no mention of conditioned stimuli, unconditioned stimuli, reinforcement, generalization, or discrimination. It says nothing about the adequacy or appropriateness of responses or stimuli. All it says is, if stimuli and responses occur together, learning takes place.

Notice also that learning is considered to take place on one trial, a conclusion that seems contrary to our daily observations. We know that we perform better on certain learning tasks with practice. This fact suggests that learning is not a one-trial process, but rather, a continuous and cumulative process. Guthrie explains this phenomenon by saying that most behaviors we observe in everyday living are really examples of *molar* behaviors, consisting of a series of smaller, *molecular* learning events. For example, sharpening a pencil is comprised of a series of smaller, sequential actions (molecular events), each of which is learned

[4] E. R. Guthrie (1952). *The Psychology of Learning*, rev.ed. New York: Harper, p. 23.

on one trial. The function served by practice is that of linking or hooking each of the small stimulus-response bonds together in a chain of events so that a larger (molar) act is performed smoothly and without hesitation.

One of the major drawbacks of Guthrie's theory is the vagueness of his terminology. It is not always clear whether he is talking about specific stimulus-response pairings or about a series of such pairings. Consequently, it has been difficult to generate testable hypotheses based on his interpretations of learning.

Guthrie, in contrast to others, was more concerned with teaching than with doing research. His theoretical statements about learning have made their most important contributions in their implications for teaching. Stated as a rule of thumb in the informal language of the classroom, his theory is: "What a person does is what a person will learn." You will notice that this is essentially what the philosopher John Dewey said about learning.

Guthrie's simple rule of behavior is . . .

Guthrie's interpretation of learning can be useful to teachers, especially in terms of helping to establish habits, routines, or procedures. Suppose you wish your learners to follow a certain procedure on a routine basis. It might be moving as an orderly group from the classroom to the gym or playground, establishing a procedure for getting ready to work with microscopes, or working out a routine for getting chemicals from the store room. According to Guthrie's theory, if we want the procedure to be learned so that it flows smoothly, we should make sure the proper response occurs in the presence of certain stimuli, and we should practice the entire chain of events in proper order—from beginning to end. In this way, each piece of the chain serves as a stimulus for the next piece, and they all combine to make up the entire sequence. Guthrie warns that the chain should not be broken at any point. If it is, we should go back to the beginning and start over, rather than pick up in the middle and continue on.

To apply Guthrie's theory, you should . . .

Maintaining the chain of stimuli and responses can be another matter. Guthrie does not discuss the use of reinforcement of behavior, but as we shall learn, there are those who argue that only responses that are rewarded are maintained.

CHECKPOINT 4-2

1. Suppose a teacher wants her learners to learn to move in an orderly manner from the classroom, through the halls, and out to the playground. Describe how she might apply our rule of thumb relative to Guthrie's interpretation of learning to help her learners acquire this behavior.

2. As you did this activity, did you try to visualize how you might also use Guthrie's rule with your learners? (Affective Objective, Characterization Level)

MEET EDWARD THORNDIKE . . .
"REWARDED BEHAVIOR IS REPEATED"

Other theorists in the connectionist tradition have made provision for such concepts as reinforcement and punishment in their interpretation of learning. Perhaps the best known of these are Edward L. Thorndike (1874–1949), the Father of Educational Psychology, and B. F. Skinner (1904–). Thorndike was a student of William James, the Father of American Psychology. James's influence is reflected in Thorndike's practical interests, particularly in his application of psychology to education. The essence of Thorndike's approach can be gained from the following passage from his *Principles of Teaching Based Upon Psychology:*[5]

> Using psychological terms, the art of teaching may be defined as the art of giving and withholding stimuli with the result of producing or preventing certain responses. In this definition the term stimulus is used widely for any event which influences a person,—for a word spoken to him, a look, a sentence which he reads, the air he breathes. . . . The term response is used for any reaction made by him,—a new thought, a feeling of interest, a bodily act, any mental or bodily condition resulting from the stimulus. The aim of the teacher is to produce desirable and prevent undesirable changes in human beings by producing and preventing certain responses. The means at the disposal of the teacher are the stimuli which can be brought to bear upon the pupil,—the teacher's words, gestures and appearance, the condition and appliances of the school room, the books to be used and objects to be seen, and so on through a long list of the things and events which the teacher can control. The responses of the pupil are all the infinite variety of thoughts and feelings and bodily movements occurring in all their possible connections.

The key idea in Thorndike's law of effect is . . .

Like Watson and Guthrie, Thorndike was concerned that a study of learning be as objective as possible. The thing to be studied was what learners do, not what they feel. In this sense, Thorndike was every bit a behaviorist. Furthermore, his ideas followed closely in the connectionist tradition of focusing attention on the stimulus-response connection. Thorndike, however, differed from Guthrie in several important ways. First, he argued that practice in learning is important in that repeated trials lead to a strengthening of the bond between the stimulus and the response. Second, whereas Watson and Guthrie were not concerned with reinforcement, Thorndike interpreted reinforcement as one of the key ideas in learning. Thorndike set forward his law of effect as follows:[6]

> Of several responses made to the same situation, those which are accompanied or closely followed by satisfaction to the animal will, other things being equal, be more firmly connected with the situation, so that when it recurs, they will be more likely to recur; those which are accompanied or closely followed by discomfort to the animal will, other things being equal, have their connections with that situation weakened, so that when it recurs, they will be less likely to occur. The greater the satisfaction or discomfort, the greater the strengthening or weakening of the bond.

Two rules of Thorndike's theory are . . .

In brief, Thorndike's law of effect can be stated as two simple, very general rules: (1) *Responses that are rewarded are strengthened;* and (2) *Responses that are punished are weakened.*

Although his early law of effect tended to give equal emphasis to reward (reinforcement) and to punishment, in his later work Thorndike tended to emphasize reinforcement more and punishment less and less. Essentially, he came to see the role of punishment to be primarily that of producing *variable* behavior, thus giving a new response a chance to occur and to be reinforced. (We will want to remember this point of view when, in a later chapter, we consider the role of punishment in the problems of classroom management.)

Ivan Pavlov, one of Thorndike's contemporaries, captures the essence of Thorndike's experimental approach, typically with cats, in this passage from one

---

[5] E. L. Thorndike (1906). *Principles of Teaching Based upon Psychology.* New York: Seiler, pp. 5–6.
[6] E. L. Thorndike (1911). *Animal Intelligence.* New York: Macmillan, p. 244.

of his papers on conditioned reflexes. Pavlov writes:[7]

> In these investigations the animal was kept in a box, and food was placed out-
> side the box so that it was visible to the animal. In order to get the food the animal
> had to open a door, which was fastened by various suitable contrivances in the dif-
> ferent experiments. Tables and charts were made showing how quickly and in what
> manner the animal solved the problems set it. The whole process was understood as
> being the formation of an association between visual and tactile stimuli on the one
> hand and the locomotor apparatus on the other.

MEET B. F. SKINNER . . . OPERANT
CONDITIONING OF PIGEONS AND CHILDREN

Reinforcement means . . .

Although Thorndike's major contribution to an interpretation of learning was his emphasis on the principle of reinforcement, he never talked about the fate of responses which occur and *are not* followed by reinforcement or by punishment. Another investigator, B. F. Skinner (1904–) however, did address himself to this question and others relating to the place of reinforcement and punishment in learning. Furthermore, he questioned whether learning might be usefully considered as two types, rather than as the one type previously assumed by researchers in the connectionist approach.

Punishment means . . .

Whereas Thorndike may be thought of as a learning theorist even though he was not one particularly systematic in the use of a logically inductive or deductive method, Skinner states most emphatically that he is *not* a learning theorist. He believes that our understanding of learning can be pursued most fruitfully, at present, through a rigorous, systematic analysis of behavior based on the methods of science, rather than through attempts to construct widely general and inclusive theories of learning. He maintains that a scientific analysis of behavior can provide highly useful laws of learning. This has been his approach consistently for more than forty years, and in view of the tremendous amount of research both pure and applied that has generated from this premise, it is difficult indeed to argue with his position.

Two types of learning are . . .

Skinner points out some important differences between the two types of learning he proposes. The main difference is that each type represents a separate kind of behavior. One kind of behavior is *elicited* by stimuli, but the second is *emitted* by an organism. This second kind, *operant* behavior, is often molar, as opposed to molecular, in nature. It is the kind of everyday response that we emit in familiar contexts and situations. It seems to occur without being specifically associated with any given stimulus. Examples of operant behavior include such actions as sitting, standing, walking, talking, whistling, singing, eating, and looking. The word "operant" is used to describe this kind of behavior because, in an interpretation of learning that emphasizes the importance of reinforcement, the learning of a particular response depends upon how the environment *operates* on that response once it has been emitted. This idea is the core of operant (sometimes called instrumental) conditioning. In Skinner's view, most of our present behavior is the result of environmental conditioning that has occurred with the basic, generalized operants with which we are born, e.g., look-

Operant means . . .

[7] I. P. Pavlov (1926–1927). Conditioned reflexes: An investigation of the physiological activity of the cerebral cortex. In T. Shipley (ed.), *Classics in Psychology*. New York: Philosophical Library, 1961, pp. 762–763.

ing, reaching, stretching, grasping, flexing, vocalizing. In classical or Pavlovian conditioning, on the other hand, *pairing* of stimuli is the key idea.

Much of what Skinner has learned about the role of rewards and punishment in learning came from what is known as the Skinner box. As you might guess, following in the connectionist tradition of objectivity and precision of observation, Skinner's basic experimental design has been extremely simple. As you recall, Pavlov's experimental procedure involved a dog, a harness, and food. Thorndike's approach involved a cat, a box, and food. Skinner's technique calls for simplicity of the same order: a rat (or pigeon), a box, and food.

In a typical experiment conducted with a Skinner box, a white rat is placed in a closed box, one side of which is window glass. Within the box there is a small lever which is usually attached electromechanically to some outside recording device and a receptacle (food cup) for placing bits of food at appropriate times.

Prior to experimentation, the rat is allowed to become "hungry" (operationally defined as weighing 80 percent of its normal body weight). The experimenter decides under what special conditions a lever-pressing response will be followed by reinforcement (a bit of food delivered to the food cup). The recording device attached to the lever provides a continuous record of the rat's bar-pressing behavior. The basic process of operant conditioning is illustrated in Table 4-2.

By varying the conditions under which bar pressing is followed by reinforcement, Skinner has been able to derive a great number of principles of learning within the connectionist frame of reference. Many of these laws or principles have led to a better understanding of the acquisition and maintenance of particular responses and the conditions under which these responses decline or extinguish as a function of nonreinforcement.

Skinner has also been interested in the relationship of punishment to learning. In some of his experiments, the floor of the experimental box is electrified. Thus he is able to deliver aversive stimuli relative to the bar-pressing behavior of the rat. In this way he has been able to arrive at lawful statements about the relationship between punishment and behavior.

Skinner has been concerned not only with the establishment of principles of learning in the sense of a pure science, but also with the generalization of basic laws of learning to practical or applied settings, especially to learning in schools. We will see in Chapter 8 how the basic principles of operant conditioning, that is, the rules derived from a science of behavior, can be incorporated in teaching machines and in programmed instruction. In Chapters 9 and 10, we will learn about the application of these rules to strategies of motivation and discipline.

In recent years, the application of operant conditioning has been extended to a broad spectrum of human behavior, including many examples of social behaviors. The principles have been brought to bear on problems of changing human behaviors, ranging from learning to name the letters of the alphabet to learning to function appropriately as a member of society. Such diversity of application

TABLE 4-2   The processes of operant conditioning

AT PRESENT	IN THE FUTURE
Response emitted + reinforcement	→ Response strengthened
Response emitted + no reinforcement	→ Response weakened
Response emitted + punishment	→ Response suppressed

may appear to require quite a complicated statement of theory, yet the central ideas underlying the basic procedure developed for each specific instance of behavioral change are very simple and, in fact, not a great deal different from Thorndike's original law of effect: (1) Responses that are reinforced are learned, whereas responses that are not reinforced extinguish; and (2) responses that are punished are suppressed, and an organism avoids or escapes from punishment.

The rules of reinforcement and punishment are . . .

A SUMMARY OF THE HISTORY OF LEARNING IN THE CONNECTIONIST TRADITION

Throughout the remaining chapters, we will find numerous occasions to apply the extremely useful laws of behavior that derive from a connectionist interpretation of learning. Nearly everything we do as teachers and learners can be analyzed, at least in part, from the viewpoint of the rewards and punishments operating on our behavior. These laws cause us to direct our attention toward the specific environmental conditions within which children (and teachers) behave rather than toward some vague, inner conditions of learners. For example, if Tommy Brown does not attend well to his arithmetic, we are directed by the laws of reward and punishment to question the environmental elements which are present while this task is being presented in order to try to determine what the difficulty is. We are led to ask: "Why isn't attending to arithmetic *rewarding* for Tommy Brown?" "What can be *aversive* about it for him?" "How can I cause arithmetic to become *rewarding* for him?" We are not led to ask: "What is wrong with Tommy Brown?" The laws of reward and punishment imply that it is not children who are lazy or "wrong"—but that environments are.

Throughout our discussion to this point, from Pavlov to Skinner, we have focused on the stimulus conditions under which certain kinds of responses are likely to occur and on how the environment reacts to responses emitted, thus determining whether the response is learned, is changed, or declines. Nothing has been said about what happens within the individual. In the connectionist interpretation of learning, the organism is seen as if it were empty, void of any activity, or, as some have come to call such a supposed condition, as a black box.

In fairness to the connectionist point of view, it should not be inferred that those who investigate learning from a stimulus-response frame of reference actually believe that nothing happens inside the organism when behavior changes. Rather, what happens inside is open to subjective speculation, which is difficult if not impossible to test. Thus, these investigators "pretend" that, for the purposes of their investigation, there is nothing inside the organism. No doubt, as we become more sophisticated in our research methodology and as our knowledge grows in other branches of science, especially biology, biochemistry, and physiology, we can turn more to what goes on inside the body when learning occurs or fails to occur. In Chapter 11, we will have much more to say about this.

CHECKPOINT 4-3

Several rules of thumb can be generated from the laws of behavior in the connectionist interpretation. Two extremely useful ones are:
  a. "Don't leave well enough alone."
  b. "Catch kids being good." (Take "positive notice of" kids being good.)

1. Provide an interpretation of each of these rules in terms of your behavior as a teacher in the classroom.

2. Give a specific example of an incident or a classroom situation in which you might behave in accordance with each of these rules of thumb. (NOTE: This is a synthesis-level performance.)

Learning in the Cognitive Tradition

Now let us see what the history of learning has been like in the cognitive tradition. Many investigators have tried to account for what happens inside the learner when behavior changes, and this internal action has been a major focus of the cognitive approach to learning. It might be said that this approach attempts to go beyond specific stimuli and responses and to bring the *whole person* into an interpretation of learning. You will recall, however, that the connectionist and cognitive interpretations are not mutually exclusive. Persons categorized as connectionists have also tried to account for what they felt occurs inside the organism. Conversely, psychologists in the cognitive tradition have frequently made use of essentially connectionist ideas. We will meet some of these people later in the chapter.

A basic assumption of a cognitive approach is . . . An underlying assumption of a cognitive approach is that stimuli in the environment operate on the organism in the sense that they cause change to occur at the level of feelings, interests, attitudes, values, perceptions, and so forth. Changes in a person's thoughts, feelings, and attitudes are believed to bring about changes in the way a person behaves, and changed behavior is taken as an indication that learning has occurred, that is, that something has changed inside. In the cognitive interpretation of learning, it is argued that inner change results in change in observable behavior. We saw this idea compared with the connectionist view in Figure 4-1. The major difference in the two positions concerns the inclusion or the exclusion of what takes place within the organism when learning is believed to occur.

This difference may seem a relatively small point on which to spend a great deal of time. However, the implications for applications to problems of bringing about change in behavior are quite different with each approach. As you will recall from Chapter 2, what you believe about the *causes* of behavior is related to what you do to *change* behavior. Note the chief differences in the focus of attention within these approaches to changing behavior. From the cognitive approach, you must *first* work to change a person's perceptions, values, attitudes, and so forth. It is assumed that in so doing, the individual's observable behavior will also change.

A connectionist teacher focuses on . . . From the connectionist approach, to modify a person's behavior you would be instructed to arrange the environment so that if and when certain responses occur, they will be followed by appropriate consequences, either reinforcing, neutral, or punishing. No inferences are made about changes in how the person feels, what she believes, what her values are, and so forth.

Let us look more closely at an example of the implications for a teacher who wishes to be of assistance in changing some behavior of a child. Suppose that you consider it important for one of your learners to submit homework assignments on time and that a particular learner does not have a good record of having done so.

From the cognitive approach, your actions as a teacher will be directed to trying to change the attitude of the learner toward the importance of education, and to explaining how doing homework assignments regularly and consistently contributes to the overall significance of an education. The inference is that if the learner comes to display a more positive attitude toward the importance of school and toward the necessity of doing homework assignments, the frequency with which homework assignments are completed will increase.

A cognitive teacher focuses on . . .

Within a connectionist orientation, you, the teacher, would consider what the environmental consequences are when homework assignments are—or are not—completed, and particularly what the reinforcement contingencies are. Then, you would attempt to cause the response of submitting homework on time to be followed by reinforcing consequences, and to withhold reinforcement when homework assignments are late.

Note the difference in orientation of the two approaches. With the cognitive approach, the teacher's actions are primarily directed toward an examination of the inner workings (feelings, attitudes) of the learner. In the connectionist approach, the teacher's actions are primarily directed toward the environmental conditions under which a behavior either occurs or does not occur. We will learn more about both these points of view when we discuss management of classroom behavior in Chapters 9 and 10.

MEET MAX
WERTHEIMER . . . LEARNING BY WHOLES

From our history of the interpretation of learning in the connectionist tradition, you will recall that Watson was instrumental in stimulating interest in a more objective study of behavior. Watson was not the only person to question the direction which the early German school of psychology was taking toward an analysis of consciousness (thought) into all its basic parts (sensation, perception, images). One of the earliest of the rebels who spoke against the German school was Max Wertheimer (1880–1943). But his difference of opinion with the German psychology was not the same as Watson's. Remember, Watson insisted on objectivity, and he considered only behavior that consisted of observable stimuli and responses to be worthy of investigation. Wertheimer objected to analysis itself. His opinion was that to break a whole, or a molar, experience into pieces or molecular units destroyed its most important part: its wholeness. His position followed closely the idea in the statement: "The sum of the pieces does not equal the whole." Studying the pieces as isolated units of behavior is not equivalent to studying the total experience. Although Wertheimer did not use the following analogy, it conveys my impression of his position. In a study of elephants, if you break down the investigation into pieces, that is, if you investigate legs, body, head, trunk, tail, skin, bone, and cells, you will probably learn a great deal about legs, body, head, trunk, tail, skin, bone, and cells, but not much about what Wertheimer would consider the most important thing—elephants.

A cognitive-field theory approach focuses on . . .

The German word *Gestalt*, meaning pattern, form, or figure, describes what Wertheimer thought important for a meaningful study of learning. It was from his usage of the term that this approach to psychology got the name "gestalt psychology," and later, "cognitive-field theory," referring to the interaction of many forces on a person's behavior at any one time (Lewin, 1951).

MEET WOLFGANG KÖHLER . . .
INSIGHT IN PROBLEM SOLVING

Two of Wertheimer's colleagues, Wolfgang Köhler and Kurt Koffka, also became well known for their interest in learning from the cognitive point of view. They looked at learning as perceptions of problems as wholes, as gestalts. They believed that solution to problems occurred through acquiring meaningful insight, which was considered to occur gradually by trial and error, or suddenly, as in one flash.

Köhler (1887–1967) is probably best known for his study of problem solving in apes. In his famous experiments, it's interesting that, even though he approached learning in a cognitive rather than a connectionist way, his experimental apparatus was essentially the same as that of the connectionists: an animal, a box, and food. What he did, however, was considerably different. He was not really interested in looking at learning as connections between stimuli and responses, but rather, in terms of larger units of behavior, that is, acts or performances that might constitute what could be called problem solving.

The procedure Köhler used was essentially this: A hungry ape would be placed in a cage and faced with the problem of how to acquire food, usually a banana. Sometimes the banana would be placed at a certain distance outside the cage. When this was the case, a stick or sticks which could be joined together would be left within reach of the ape. The problem to be solved was that of how to use the sticks to reach the food. In other versions of the experiment, a banana would be suspended from the ceiling just out of reach of the ape. In the cage would be boxes that, when stacked, would serve as a platform from which the ape could reach the banana. Köhler would set up the experiment and then make careful notes about what the ape did as it went about solving the problem. Here Köhler describes one of his experiments:[8]

> In one of the experiments described previously . . . Sultan [an ape] came very near putting one box on top of another, when he found one insufficient [to reach a banana]; but instead of placing the second box, which he had already lifted, upon the first, he made uncertain movements with it in the air around and above the other; then other methods replaced these confused movements. The test is repeated . . . The objective [a banana] is placed very high up, the two boxes are not very far away from each other and about four metres away from the objective; all other means of reaching it have been taken away. Sultan drags the bigger of the two boxes towards the objective, puts it just underneath, gets up on it, and looking upwards, makes ready to jump, but does not jump; gets down, seizes the other box, and pulling it behind him, gallops around the room, making his usual noise, kicking against the walls and showing his uneasiness in every other possible way. He certainly did not seize the second box to put it on the first; it merely helps him to give vent to his temper. But all of a sudden his behavior changes completely; he stops making a noise, pulls his box from quite a distance right up to the other one, and stands it upright on it. He mounts the somewhat shaky construction, several times

---

[8] Wolfgang Köhler (1925). The making of implements. In T. Shipley (ed.), *Classics in Psychology.* New York: Philosophical Library, 1961, pp. 1090–1093.

gets ready to jump, but again does not jump; the objective is still too high for this bad jumper. But he has achieved the essential part of his task.

What Köhler was trying to show through such experiments was that learning involves the rearrangement of patterns of thought, that is, that problem solving requires a perception of new relationships, or insight. Furthermore, he was interested in illustrating that the solution to the problems faced by his apes did not occur as a consequence of conditioning or by trial and error, but rather, as a result of forming a rearrangement of previous experiences to new patterns of thought, that is, of gaining *insight* into a new relationship between boxes and the objective, the food.

Learning by insight means . . .

Learning theorists in the connectionist tradition would try to account for the solution to such problems in terms of reference to past experience with the various elements involved in the problem, for example, past experience with boxes, jumping, climbing, and bananas. Final solution to the problem would occur as a consequence of the chaining or linking together, perhaps by trial and error, of the smaller units of behavior. Yet, at this point, such an account hardly seems complete, especially in view that the solution to problems does often appear to come in a "flash of insight." Apparently something does happen within the learner when learning of this type occurs, which a purely connectionist interpretation finds difficult to handle adequately at this time.

Wertheimer's major contribution to school learning was perhaps his insistence that teachers put far too much emphasis on rote memorization and do little toward helping learners *understand* what they are learning. He would be pleased to witness today the increased emphasis being brought to bear to cause education to become more than memory of information through a taxonomy of educational objectives.

Both the cognitive and connectionist approaches to learning agree on the importance of stressing the use of cognitive processes beyond simple recall. However, note the differences in points of emphasis that a connectionist and a cognitive psychologist show in terms of a problem-solving task. Connectionists would ask: "What responses does the learner make, and how does the environment then operate on those responses?" Wertheimer, representing the cognitive point of view, would ask: "What does the learner understand about the problem?" The differences in point of view may seem slight; however, they do lead to different implications for what you, the teacher, do in trying to cause learners to become effective problem solvers.

Problem solving from a connectionist approach proceeds by . . .

Instructional procedures for problem solving from a connectionist standpoint would involve, first, an analysis of the problem to be solved in terms of the prerequisite information and skills necessary for solution. These would then be arranged in sequential order according to which information and what skills were considered to be prerequisite. In steplike fashion, the learner would be led, either by programmed materials, perhaps a teaching machine, or by teacher-prepared materials, through the sequence of learning tasks that were considered necessary to arrive at the solution. With the problem so analyzed, and perhaps programmed and presented to the learners by machine, they may then proceed more or less on their own, with help from the teacher as they need it.

Instructional procedures for problem solving within a cognitive approach rely heavily on what has come to be known as learning by discovery. Implicit in this term is the expectation that the learner will arrive at the solution to a problem

**Problem solving from
a cognitive approach
proceeds by . . .**

more or less as a consequence of personal initiative. The task for the teacher here is that of causing the learner to participate actively, with the teacher providing material and perhaps clues which, when manipulated in various ways, lead to discovery of possible solutions to the problem.

MEET JEROME BRUNER . . . STRUCTURE
AND STRATEGIES IN DISCOVERY LEARNING

Jerome Bruner (1915–) is one of the most widely recognized authorities on a cognitive-field theory approach, especially as it relates to school learning. He claims that discovery approaches that emphasize *structure* (interrelationships) of material rather than specific detail are likely to result in the learning of material meaningfully rather than rotely. Bruner believes that material so learned will have a high degree of usefulness (transfer value), that it will be more likely to be remembered, and that it will enable the learner to move easily, in spiral form, from an elementary consideration of a topic to a more advanced study of it later in the curriculum. Bruner sums up his view in this way:[9]

> A curriculum reflects not only the nature of knowledge itself but also the nature of the knower and of the knowledge-getting process. It is the enterprise par excellence where the line between subject matter and method grows necessarily indistinct. To instruct someone in [a] discipline is not a matter of getting him to commit results to mind. Rather, it is to teach him to participate in the process that makes possible the establishment of knowledge. We teach a subject not to produce little living libraries on that subject, but rather to get a student to think . . . for himself, to consider matters as an historian does, to take part in the process of knowledge-getting. Knowing is a process, not a product.

**Knowing as a process
means . . .**

As you might expect, not everyone agrees with this point of view. Few, however, disagree completely with the idea that a cognitive approach that relies heavily on a discovery procedure can be a useful way of approaching some of the kinds of learning tasks commonly encountered in school settings. The difference of opinion is more in degree than in kind. We will see how this is so later in the text when we combine Bruner's ideas with the rules from a connectionist science of behavior to form effective strategies for motivation, self-discipline, and a cognitive-connectionist theory of instruction.

MEET EDWARD TOLMAN AND CLARK
HULL . . . CONNECTIONS AND COGNITIONS

No history of the interpretation of learning, even a biased one like that presented here, could possibly be considered complete without the mention of two additional persons, Edward Chase Tolman (1886–1959) and Clark L. Hull (1884–1952). These two giants of learning theory are mentioned last because of their attempts to bridge the gap between a connectionist and a cognitive point of view. Each, in his interpretation of learning, approached the topic with a focus on objectivity and the observation of measurable responses. Each, however, also included, in his theoretical statement, essentially cognitive variables. Tolman, especially, expressed the view that our behavior is not merely responses to stimuli. It is also a function of our beliefs, attitudes, feelings, and goals or purposes.

In order to forge a link between a connectionist and a cognitive interpretation

---

[9] J. S. Bruner (1966). *Toward a Theory of Instruction.* New York: Norton, p. 72.

of learning, Tolman introduced the concept of an *intervening variable.* In Tolman's system, cognitive variables, i.e., thinking, feeling, valuing, and so forth, were admissible so long as they were considered an abstraction by the theorist and defined precisely. Intervening variables, for example, hunger, thirst, and desire, were defined in operational terms; e.g., a state of thirst is considered to exist within the organism when the organism has been deprived of water for a specified time. Thirst, thus defined, is thought to act as a drive or as a motivator for behavior that has as its purpose that of eliminating the condition of thirst. What we have in Tolman's theory is a combination of purposeful (cognitive) behavior and observable, measurable stimuli and responses (behaviorism). He called his approach a "purposive behaviorism."

Purposive behaviorism means . . .

Tolman's system emphasizes an increasing concern among theorists and practitioners alike with the inadequacy of any one approach to the interpretation of learning. Furthermore, it illustrates a continuing trend away from being labeled "connectionist" or "cognitivist." We will see later in this chapter how this is an important trend in terms of classroom practices of teachers.

Of all the theories of learning, Clark Hull's was probably the most ambitious. It is a complex, deductive system of basic postulates and their related correlaries from which theorms or laws of learning might be logically derived. His theory of learning reflects a personal background different from those of the other theorists we have reviewed. Its organization shows how a person's early experience influences later work. Most learning theorists had backgrounds in physiology or philosophy, but before Clark Hull became a psychologist, he was an engineer. His training is clearly reflected in his highly technical, elaborate, formal, and mathematically based interpretation of learning.

Hull did not intend that such a comprehensive theory would ever be complete. By its very deductive nature, it is always open to further investigation. However, he hoped that by establishing such an interpretation of learning, he would interest others in the same sort of theoretical approach.

Hull concerns us here for a reason beyond his particular interpretation of learning. Although his work did generate, during his lifetime, a great amount of interest in his approach to learning, with Hull we see the beginning of the decline in attempts to construct all-encompassing theories of learning. Perhaps such effort, as reflected in Hull's grand theory, was ahead of its time. The trend in recent years has been more toward the establishment of laws of learning and a better understanding of the special conditions under which certain desired kinds of learning occur. Perhaps, when we have exhausted the possibilities in this trend, we will once again return to the task of constructing a general and inclusive theory of learning. In one sense, the work of Tolman and of Hull has contributed a great deal toward bringing cognitive and connectionist interests into the same camp. This trend will come clearly into focus for you as we direct our attention more fully to learning in the classroom.

CHECKPOINT 4-4

Assume that you have this objective for your learners: "Given the direction to describe the wind, the learner is able to do so, using his own words and actions." From a cognitive interpretation of learning, outline what you would do to help your learners achieve the objective.

A Summary of the History of Learning

In summary, it might be well for us to remember that theories seldom give us solutions. Rather, they tell us where to look for solutions. Guthrie tells us to pay attention to the importance of making sure the pieces of a chain of responses in a habit or routine occur in the proper order, and that they are practiced sufficiently to link them firmly together. Skinner and Thorndike tell us to pay attention to the consequences of responses: Reward those we want to strengthen and ignore those we want to weaken. Bruner, Wertheimer, and Köhler advise us to attend to the arrangement of learning situations so that learners discover for themselves the real meaning of the experiences they live. Tolman and Hull warn us not to attend completely to either a cognitive or a connectionist interpretation of learning. They help us see the value of combining both views. The wisdom of this advice will become more apparent as we now look more closely at learning as it occurs in schools.

LEARNING IN SCHOOLS

The trend toward incorporation of ideas from both connectionist and cognitive interpretations of learning into a combined approach for classroom learning has gained recent recognition because of concern with the inadequacy of either approach to account exclusively for all varieties of learning phenomena. An important question, asked years ago by John Dewey (1938) and currently being asked again, is: "What are the alternatives to an either/or interpretation of learning?"

An Alternative to an Either/Or Interpretation of Learning

As classroom teachers, we must beware that we do not fall into the trap of either/or. To hold tenaciously to a particular point of view that we suspect is inadequate may appear to be scientifically pure. However, the advice given by P. W. Bridgeman (1950) about a purely scientific application of a scientific method is worth noting. This renowned physicist, referring to the method of science in one of his many papers, said that there is no one scientific method as such, but that the most vital feature of the scientist's procedure has been merely his obligation to do his utmost with his mind, *no holds barred*. Teaching, in large measure, has the same responsibility. When one approach proves to be inadequate for our purposes, we must look for ways to improve that approach—not necessarily to abandon it. Often it means modifying the approach by adding to it or by reorganizing it to include other points of view. This has been the method used by Robert Gagné (1916–) to interpret the types of learning that occur in schools.

MEET ROBERT GAGNÉ . . .
SIX TYPES OF LEARNING

Gagné's alternative to an either/or interpretation of learning attempts to identify different types or varieties of learning. Instead of only the two varieties—classical and operant conditioning—claimed by some connectionist theorists, Gagné (1965) proposed eight types. More recently, (1971), however, he has reduced the eight to only six varieties. The important point for us about Gagné's proposed approach to learning, especially school learning, is that his system allows us to use the best of both the connectionist and the cognitive interpretations of learning.

This is how Gagné (1965) described the problems in an either/or approach: "Somehow, they [the connectionist and cognitive points of view] came to be placed in opposition to each other; either all learning was insight or all learning was conditioned response. Such controversies have continued for years, and have been relatively unproductive in advancing our understanding of learning as an event.[10]

Let us turn to a closer examination of what Gagné has proposed and to a determination of what use we might make of it. His six types of learning range from simple to complex in a hierarchy; *chains, discriminations, concrete concepts, defined concepts, rules, and higher-order rules.* They refer primarily to cognitive learning, and only indirectly to affective or psychomotor learning. Generally, the types of learning that occupy the early positions in the hierarchy rely on a connectionist interpretation of learning, and those that occur later in the hierarchy tend to require both connectionist and cognitive interpretations.

Gagné's six types of learning are . . .

Each category or type of learning is assumed to be prerequisite for the next higher category. In this sense, the organization of Gagné's types of learning is similar to the organization in Bloom's *Taxonomy of Educational Objectives: Cognitive Domain.* See Figure 4-3.

FIGURE 4-3   Chains are the basic prerequisite for all six types of learning.

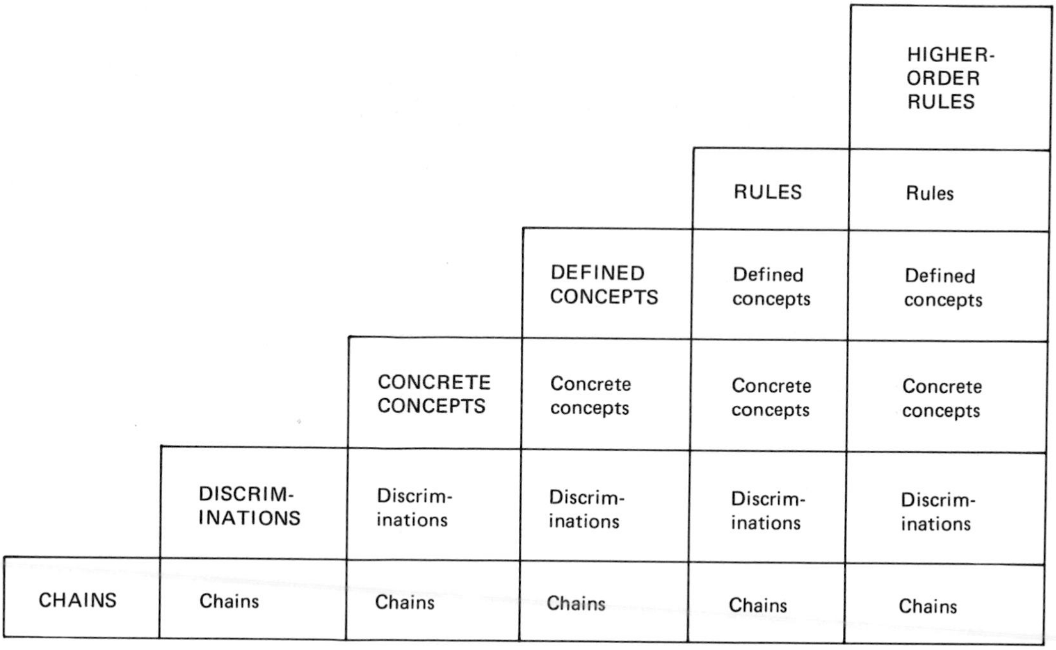

					HIGHER-ORDER RULES
				RULES	Rules
			DEFINED CONCEPTS	Defined concepts	Defined concepts
		CONCRETE CONCEPTS	Concrete concepts	Concrete concepts	Concrete concepts
	DISCRIM-INATIONS	Discrim-inations	Discrim-inations	Discrim-inations	Discrim-inations
CHAINS	Chains	Chains	Chains	Chains	Chains

[10] R. M. Gagné (1965). *The Conditions of Learning.* New York: Holt, p. 19.

Let us learn more about Gagné's six kinds of learning.[11] We will begin with the most simple and progress through the most complex.

CHAINS

A chain is . . .

A chain is *"a sequence of individual responses arranged in such a way that the entire set of responses reels itself off from start to finish."*

Chains may be of two varieties, *motor* and *verbal*. Chains of either type may be very short or exceedingly long. Examples of a motor chain include actions such as a linking together of all the individual responses necessary to hold a pencil, turn on a light, cut paper with scissors, kick a soccer ball, or ride a bicycle. Examples of verbal chains include the memorized sequences of words. These may be extremely simple, such as "Come here," "Help me," or "I don't want to," or they may be extremely complex, such as in the rote memorization of the letters of the alphabet, definitions for words, or perhaps all the words of a long poem. Note that this type of learning, the verbal chain, does not require the learner to make meaningful associations between the words and other aspects of reality. For example, the learner may be able to chain the words in a definition of an adjective, i.e., "An adjective is a word that modifies nouns and pronouns," and yet have no idea of the meaning of the definition or how to apply it.

DISCRIMINATIONS

To discriminate means . . .

To discriminate means *"to tell whether two things are the same or different."*

This means that the learner is able to distinguish between two or more stimulus objects—not that the learner can tell what the stimulus objects are or be able to name them. An example of discrimination as defined by Gagné may be seen when a child is able to point to, or pick out from, a collection of objects those which are alike or those which are different from one held up by the teacher. For instance, a child may be able to sort squares and triangles on the basis of their being the same or different without needing to know that squares are called "squares" and triangles are called "triangles."

CONCRETE CONCEPTS

A concrete concept is . . .

"A concrete concept is said to be learned when the individual can recognize or identify an object quality, like round or square, or an object, like chair, by its appearance."

Notice that in this use of the term *concrete concept*, it is necessary for a child to be able to discriminate or tell the difference between objects before being able to name them. The essential element in this type of learning is that in some way learners are able to let others know that they know what the object *quality* is.

DEFINED CONCEPTS

"A defined concept is learned when the individual can identify something for us by using a definition."

[11] The following definitions of Gagné's types of learning were presented in R. M. Gagné (1971). Defining Objectives for Six Varieties of Learning (a taped presentation). Washington: American Educational Research Association.

Gagné feels that most concepts learned in school fall into this category. These are the kinds of concepts that tend to be more or less abstract in nature, that is, they usually need to be defined through verbal description. Pointing or picking out is inadequate for these concepts. Examples of defined concepts include qualifications such as high, low, big, long, heavy, and angle. The occurrence of learning of this type is evident when learners are able to illustrate or to demonstrate, through words or actions, that they understand the concept in question, for instance, when they are able to compare two blocks and say which is the larger.

A defined concept is . . .

RULES (PRINCIPLES)

"A rule consists of a relationship between one or more concepts."

A rule is . . .

The point of importance in this type of learning is not the concepts themselves that make up the rule, but rather, the relationship between concepts. If we take a simple rule such as "Candy costs money," we see that, in this type of learning, the essential point is more than a child's being able merely to identify money, candy, or the concept of cost. It is the idea that if you want candy you must pay money. Obviously, this sort of learning is considerably different from, and more complex than, the mere identification of the concepts themselves.

HIGHER-ORDER RULES

What this usually means is that *"a higher-order rule is composed of two or more simpler rules. Often a learner puts together simpler rules into a higher-order rule in a problem-solving situation that is new to him. He discovers the higher-order rule."*

A higher-order rule is . . .

The type of learning involved in higher-order rules is illustrated in the following example. Suppose you set the problem from Chapter 2 for your learners: to explain why manhole covers are round. Further assume that your learners have never encountered this problem before (and it is likely they have not). To solve the problem, the learners will have to make use of simpler rules, which they may have already learned. Some of these rules may be: (1) "Heavy things fall"; (2) "the diameter of an object is the distance across it" (note that this is a definition and also a rule—many times, a defined concept qualifies for a simple rule); (3) "the diameter of a circle is a constant"; (4) "the diameter of a rectangle or some other irregular figure varies, depending upon where you measure it." To solve the problem, a higher-order rule must now be formed from the combined simpler rules. Such a rule will include a statement to the effect that a manhole cover of any shape other than a circle could be lifted and turned and dropped through the opening. Consequently, manhole covers are round. A similar progression could be outlined for learning other higher-order rules, for example, "plants grow," or "chemical compounds contain different elements."

In addition to combining a connectionist and a cognitive approach to learning, Gagné also provided another basis from which the teacher can derive answers to the question: "What do I want the learners to learn?" The six types of learning can be used very effectively as a basis for formulating specific learner outcomes for the intellectual skills that teachers want their children to acquire. Gagné's system provides an excellent guide for completing a task analysis, and from a task analysis a teacher derives a relatively precise statement of what the child must learn. The extremely useful part of Gagné's hierarchically arranged sequence of types of learning is that it helps us to recognize what things the child should learn *first*.

In addition to specifying six types of learning that take place in school settings, Gagné has devoted much effort to specifying the conditions which he considers necessary for each type to occur. These can prove very valuable to you as you set about the task of helping your children learn. We will examine these conditions in Chapters 5 and 6 when we direct our attention to specific instructional procedures. For now, let us learn more about completing task analyses.

Task Analysis Using Gagné's Six Types of Learning

Some authors believe Bloom's taxonomy of educational objectives: the cognitive domain to be so similar to Gagné's types of learning that they can be considered equivalent. This would mean that as a basis for arriving at specific learner outcomes in cognitive skills, a teacher might choose *either* of the systems. Some authors, on the other hand, while they consider the two systems as equivalent, consider Gagné's system more useful than Bloom's because Gagné's approach suggests definite clues to the conditions necessary for learning to occur. Fortunately, we do not have to choose, since both systems can be combined into a useful whole consisting of two processes: task description and task analysis. An example will help.

Suppose you have the job of preparing a unit of study dealing with South America. The first problem you must face is the question, "What do I want the learners to learn?" You must *describe,* in the form of instructional objectives, what you want the children to be able to do when they have finished the unit; you must describe in specific, behavioral terms what it means to "learn about South America." You will recall, from Chapter 3, that when you have completed this type of detailed description, you have completed a task description. With the use of Bloom's classification scheme, you can ensure that there is a reasonable balance in the types of intellectual skills required of your learners to meet the objectives.

Task analysis means . . .   By task analysis I mean *analyzing* each objective described to determine the types of learning required of the learner in order to meet each objective. In this sense, each objective is a learning task. Once the various types of learning required for a specific objective (task) have been determined, they can be placed in hierarchical order in keeping with Gagné's system. This means asking oneself, what specific chains, discriminations, concrete concepts, rules, and higher-order rules are required? Once this question has been answered, Gagné's system provides important direction as to the optimum learning conditions for the various subtasks the student must learn to perform. In everyday language, doing first a task description and then a task analysis can be said to involve asking these two questions: (1) "What are all the things that I want my learners to learn from a study of South America?" and (2) "What must the learner be able to do in order to meet each of the objectives I have described?"

It might be argued that either the system developed by Bloom and his colleagues or the system proposed by Gagné is sufficient for teachers' purposes.

Bloom's taxonomy, however, with its greater breadth and variety in the number and type of instructional objectives it offers and the terminology it uses, is probably an easier system to use in describing learner outcomes than Gagné's more restricted, yet more precise system. A major difference is that if only Bloom's *Taxonomy* is used, there are no guidelines as to the conditions necessary for the different types of intellectual skills to be learned. This is the advantage of using Gagné's system as the basis for performing a task analysis of each objective.

I am proposing, then, first, that the various categories within Bloom's *Taxonomy* be used as a basis for describing instructional objectives. Second, I suggest that Gagné's system be used as a basis for conducting a task analysis of the objectives formulated. This allows the teacher to answer the question: "Now that I have described the objectives and have included objectives representing appropriate categories of Bloom's *Taxonomy*, what must the learner be able to do to meet each of these objectives?"

Gagné's contributions are . . .

Let me give you an example of how this might work. Suppose, in completing a task description for a unit on measurement, you arrive at the following specific instructional objective at Bloom's *application* level: "Given a yardstick, the learner is able to find the area of his desk-top within an accuracy of 12 square inches."

Now, if we should apply Gagné's system of doing a task analysis of this instructional objective, we would begin by asking: "What must the learner be able to do in order to find the area in square inches of the desk top?" We would start at the upper level of the hierarchy of types of behavior by asking: "Are there any *higher-order rules* that are required in this task? If so, what are they?" Next, we would ask: "What are the *simple rules* or principles that must be learned in order to form the higher-order rules?" Next, we would ask: "What *concepts* (defined and concrete) must the learner know to form simple rules and, thus, higher-order rules?" Next, we would ask: "What *discriminations* and verbal and motor *chains* must be learned in order to form the concepts, rules, and higher-order rules required by the task at hand?"

Let us make sure we are still together. In Chapter 3, we saw the importance of formulating objectives and also having objectives stated in a precise behavioral form. In addition, we tried to formulate specific instructional objectives which would cause the learner to perform at several intellectual levels—from memory through evaluation.

In the present chapter, we have extended our discussion to learning about learning itself. We have seen that there have been differences of opinion with regard to interpretation of learning and that a single approach to learning, either connectionist or cognitive, is inadequate to account for all types of learning that commonly occur in school. This inadequacy has been recognized by a variety of investigators, the most recent being Robert Gagné. We have examined his system for classifying six different types of learning that include both connectionist and cognitive interpretations of learning.

Finally, I have illustrated a useful way of combining the best of Bloom's taxonomy and Gagné's system for classifying types of behavior into a way that can help a teacher describe instructional objectives and analyze what a learner must be able to do in order to meet them. At this point, then, we are still talking about the question: "What exactly do I want the learner to learn?" We have not yet addressed ourselves to the next major question: "How can I help learners learn?" The first question deals with instructional objectives. The second one concerns instructional procedures.

CHECKPOINT 4-5

1. Try to complete a task analysis, after Gagné, of the instructional objective stated earlier: "Given a yardstick, the learner is able to find the area of the desk-top within an accuracy of 12 square inches." List one higher-order rule you believe is required to complete the task, then list rules (principles), defined concepts, concrete concepts, discriminations, verbal and motor chains you feel are prerequisite to the higher-order rule. (You may find it helpful to refer to the task analysis in the Appendix.)

2. Did you allow anyone to help you, or did you offer to help anyone, to complete the checkpoints in this chapter? (Affecting Objective, Receiving Level)

A Model of School Learning

For specific instructional procedures to have an overall consistency and unification of purpose, we must first place them in a broad frame of reference, that is, a model for teaching and learning. One general model for school teaching is implied by the major questions we have to consider as teachers. These broad questions are shown in Figure 4-4.

However, one of the common weaknesses of general statements (or questions, as they are here) is the difficulty of identifying specific practices from broad statements. Within each area covered by the general questions in Figure 4-4, we need a way of organizing our instructional efforts so that they reflect consistently our point of view about learning.

Within the first major question, "What do I want learners to learn?" we have Bloom's taxonomy of educational objectives for the cognitive, affective and psychomotor domains, and we have Gagné's types of learning. We now need some way of organizing our instructional efforts as we consider the second major question: "How can I help learners learn?"

You will remember that, in Chapter 2, I emphasized that how you behave is related to what you believe to be true. This fact also applies to what we do when we organize for instruction. For example, if I believe that it is important to learn one thing before proceeding to the learning of another, this belief should be reflected in the way I organize instructional sequences which children then follow. If I believe that children should be, and are, capable of managing their own learning processes, my belief should also be reflected in my organization of instructional procedures. If I believe that the responsibility for learning rests primarily with the learner rather than the teacher, this conviction will influence

A model for school learning helps us . . .

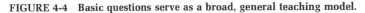

FIGURE 4-4   Basic questions serve as a broad, general teaching model.

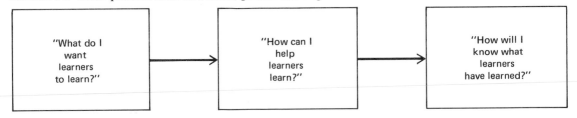

"What do I want learners to learn?" → "How can I help learners learn?" → "How will I know what learners have learned?"

how I organize for instruction and how I carry through with learning activities. If I believe that all my learners require the same amount and the same kind of instruction, I am likely to provide the same instructional procedures for everyone. If, however, I believe in individual differences among children in terms of the amount and the quality of instructional assistance required for learning, I will try to provide an organizational scheme that will ensure variety in time and quality of instruction.

The question is: "How will I do all these things?" If we turn to the work of John A. Carroll, *A Model of School Learning* (1963), and study it in conjunction with a more recent work of Benjamin S. Bloom, *Learning for Mastery* (1968), we will have an effective and consistent approach toward organizing instructional procedures that will begin to help us answer this question.

MEET JOHN CARROLL . . . ATTENTION
TO THE TASK AND QUALITY OF INSTRUCTION

Basically, Carroll's model of school learning states that if learners are allowed the time they need individually to learn to some level, and if they spend the required amount of time attending to the learning task, each one can be expected to attain the level of achievement set. On the other hand, if learners are not permitted sufficient time, the degree to which they can be expected to learn is a function of the ratio of the time actually spent attending to the learning task compared to the amount of time actually needed for the learning. Stated more simply, Carroll's model says that instruction is optional for each learner when you, as a teacher, direct the learner's attention long enough and well enough to the learning task for that individual to learn it. This means that your organization for instruction has caused the learner to practice as much as he needs to, and that the instruction has been organized well enough so that his practice results in efficient and effective learning.

Carroll's model of school learning says . . .

Carroll's model of school learning is shown as an equation in Table 4-3.

You will note that in Carroll's model tremendous importance is given to two variables: (1) the amount of time a learner devotes or attends to a learning task, that is, perseveres; and (2) the quality of instruction. Also, the time a learner needs to spend and in fact does spend attending to the learning task is related to the quality of the instruction provided. Aptitude for learning, in this sense, is defined as the amount of time needed to learn. Ability to understand instruction is related to general intelligence and prerequisites for the learning task.

TABLE 4-3   Carroll's model of school learning

$$\text{Degree of learning} = f\left(\frac{\text{time actually spent}}{\text{time needed}}\right)$$

or

$$\text{Degree of learning} = f\left(\begin{array}{l} \text{1. time allowed} \quad \text{2. perseverance} \\ \text{3. aptitude} \quad \text{4. quality of instruction} \\ \text{5. ability to understand instruction} \end{array}\right)$$

CHECKPOINT 4-6

Check your understanding of Carroll's model of school learning:

1.   Without looking back through the text, write the equation (formula) that expresses the relationship of the five variables included in the model.

2.   What is the major point made in Carroll's model?

3.   Although the model is not intended to relate directly to affective learning, indirectly it does. In what sense is this so?

4.   If Sally Sloe is not learning effectively, what does the model suggest a teacher ought to consider in trying to help her improve? (HINT: There are five variables to look at.)

5.   How may the rules of reinforcement and punishment relate to Carroll's concept *perseverance*—the willingness to attend to the learning tasks?

6.   What is the level of cognitive functioning required, according to Bloom's *Taxonomy*, of each of the five questions above?

7.   What type of learning tasks do you personally pay attention to and what type do you avoid or escape from? (Affective Objective, Receiving Level)

Learning for Mastery

Carroll's model of school learning raises practical questions of implementation for classroom teachers. They include: "How can I cause learners to *persevere* in regard to (attend to) the learning tasks?" "How can I organize my instructional procedures so as to provide the range of time for each task that is required by each individual?" "How can I help each child understand the instruction I provide?" We need some effective procedure for putting Carroll's conceptual model into operation so that a teacher can use it.

MEET BENJAMIN BLOOM
AGAIN . . . A MODEL FOR MASTERY LEARNING

A big step in this direction was taken by Benjamin Bloom (1968), who applied Carroll's model to the concept *mastery learning* that was first introduced by Carleton Washburne (1922) and Henry Morrison (1926). Mastery learning today does not differ greatly from that of fifty years ago; for example, the P.S.I. (Personalized System of Instruction) method developed by Fred Keller (1968) shows much the same approach as that of Morrison and Washburne:[12]

> The approach used short, teacher prepared study units through which students could proceed at their own pace. Each unit indicated the objectives the student was expected to master and suggested specific study procedures. At the end of each unit, students asked their proctor (a student who had already completed the course) for a short, ungraded essay test covering the unit's objectives. If the students exhibited mastery on each objective, the proctor commended his performance and allowed him to proceed to the next learning unit. If the student did not exhibit mastery of the

[12] J. H. Block, ed. (1971). *Mastery Learning: Theory and Practice.* New York: Holt, p. 120.

unit, the proctor briefly tutored him on the unmastered material and then asked him to review before returning for retesting. The use of proctors allowed repeated testing, immediate feedback of results, and tutoring and, in general, created a highly personal-social learning atmosphere. Lectures and demonstrations by the teacher were scheduled only after a sufficient number of students had mastered enough material to make them worthwhile. Final grades were determined by performance on a teacher prepared final examination, laboratory work, and the number of learning units completed.

Mastery learning is . . .

A mastery learning approach is designed to manipulate most of the variables in Carroll's model of school learning: (1) the expectation is set that the learner will be able to learn; (2) the amount of time needed for each learner to complete a task is allowed; (3) perseverence at the task is ensured through clear, specific, instructional objectives, through immediate feedback about performance, liberal use of reinforcement, personal interaction with each learner, and—success. Precise objectives, variety in instructional models, all serve to improve the quality of instruction and to increase the probability that learners will profit from instruction.

BASIC ASSUMPTIONS ABOUT LEARNERS IN MASTERY LEARNING

Now that you have a general understanding of what is meant by mastery learning, let us take a closer look at the basic assumptions underlying this approach and see how we might use it. One of the first assumptions is that most students can master what we have to teach them, and that it is our job as teachers to find the means that will enable our students to do so. As Bloom (1968) points out, this is not the typical assumption made by teachers as they begin a new term or course, since "Each teacher begins a new term (or course) with the expectation that about a third of his students will adequately learn what he has to teach. He expects about a third of his students to fail or to just 'get by'. Finally, he expects another third to learn a good deal of what he has to teach, but not enough to be regarded as 'good students.'"[13]

Basic assumptions of a mastery approach are . . .

The assumptions out of which this expected performance derives is that aptitude or ability to learn is a quality that is normally distributed[14] among learners. Bloom and Carroll both argue, however, that with respect to school learning, aptitude or ability to learn is best considered a function of the opportunity to learn (time spent attending to the task and the quality of the instruction). Their assumption is that if the quality of instruction is optimal for each learner and if each learner attends for the amount of time necessary for him or her to master the task, then achievement will not be normally distributed among the learners. It will be better. Most, if not all, learners will master it. In addition, there will be little or no relationship between aptitude, as commonly defined, and achievement. Aptitude in this view is simply the amount of time necessary for a learner

---

[13] B. S. Bloom (1968). Learning for mastery, *Evaluation Comment*, 1, (2). Los Angeles: University of California, Center for the Study of Evaluation of Instructional Programs, p. 1.

[14] *Normally distributed* means that, in things such as people's height or weight, or the width of oak leaves, most of the cases (observations, instances) will have "average" values, a small percentage will be below average, and a small percentage above average. It is the distribution one expects when the observations are infinite in number and are affected only by chance—hardly an acceptable distribution for success in school!

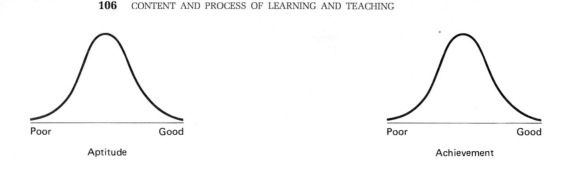

When *aptitude* for a task is normally distributed and *all* learners receive the *same instruction,* achievement will be normally distributed (above).

However,

When *aptitude* for a task is normally distributed and *each* learner receives *optimal instruction,* achievement will *not* be normally distributed; it will be better!

FIGURE 4-5   **Relationship between aptitude, instructions, and achievement.**

to learn when instruction is optimal. Figure 4-5 will help clarify what I am saying here.

PRECONDITIONS FOR MASTERY LEARNING

Preconditions for mastery learning are . . .

Bloom (1968) suggests that there are preconditions for mastery learning. He says that if we are to develop mastery learning in students, we must define what we mean by *mastery* and we must collect the necessary evidence to establish whether or not a student has achieved it.[15] In terms of what we have learned, Bloom's preconditions can be listed as (1) statement of specific, instructional objectives derived from a task description and available to teacher and learners; (2) task analysis of each objective; and (3) learner outcomes from the task analysis arranged in sequential or hierarchical order. Note that with these preconditions for mastery learning, the tests are not only prepared ahead of time, they are actually taught for.

[15] B. S. Bloom (1968). Op. cit., p. 8.

Another of Bloom's preconditions for mastery learning is that achievement criteria should not be primarily competitive. That is, achievement of a particular task or course should not be judged on the basis of a learner's relative position in a group. Rather, achievement criteria should be established in terms of standards of mastery and excellence apart from interstudent competition. This means a kind of "absolute" standard, e.g., the number of units completed at an acceptable level of mastery. Such a system leads to the possibility of all students receiving a mark of "A," or, alternately, perhaps of no students earning a mark of "A." What is important is that one student's mark is not directly influenced by the performance of other learners in the group.

It is not necessarily easy for teachers to arrive at absolute standards of learner performance, especially without a background of experience in teaching. Consequently, and perhaps fortunately, standards of learner performance should change as a function of experience with particular learning tasks or courses of instruction. One way that Bloom and his associates arrived at absolute standards was to inform their students that grades would be based on the standards—the levels of mastery—set by the previous group's performance. Thus, as Bloom pointed out, the students were not competing with one another for grades.

EVALUATING PERFORMANCE PRIOR TO, DURING, AND AFTER INSTRUCTION

Let us return to the question of evaluation within a mastery learning approach. In Chapter 3 we discussed the importance of preparing instructional objectives prior to instruction. Since the achievement we want to evaluate is contained within the objectives, it is easy to see how objectives written prior to beginning instruction are helpful in evaluation. Traditionally, however, instructional and evaluation procedures have followed a different pattern: First, teach the material for a unit or course, then test to determine which students have learned what things from the instruction. In such an approach, evaluation items are written after instruction and are kept secret from the learners. This procedure is considered not only appropriate but essential.

It is no wonder that only a small percentage of students learn well in this approach. In fact, "learning well" may be merely a reflection of the learner's ability to outguess the instructor.

In mastery learning, the purpose of evaluation is more than separating "good" learners from "poor" learners, and it occurs in three forms. First, there is pretesting. By pretesting I mean that the exam or a form parallel to it is given before instruction begins. The purpose of this is solely to determine which learners need what instruction. Without pretesting, teachers must make the assumption that all their students need all the instruction that they have prepared for them. This, in most instances, is not the case, and having information about each learner's knowledge of the objectives prior to instruction gives a basis for planning for individual differences of learners. In this way, a teacher is able to take a long step toward making instruction optimal for each learner.

Pretesting means . . .

The second form of evaluation in mastery learning is called *formative evaluation*. It is a kind of diagnostic-progress testing that can be used to determine whether individual learners have mastered a particular objective or sequence of objectives, and what, if anything, each one must still do to master it. Formative tests may be formal or informal, written or verbal, and results are usually not recorded as a part of a course mark. The purpose of such diagnostic-progress testing is to help each learner learn the material, not primarily to determine which students have or have not done so.

Formative evaluation also has a potential motivating effect on learners, causing them to attend to a learning task at the appropriate time and with sufficient effort to master it thoroughly, that is, to succeed. Here is Bloom describing the use of formative tests:[16]

> Each formative test is administered after the completion of the appropriate learning unit. While the frequency of these progress tests may vary throughout the course, it is likely that some portions of the course—especially the early sections of the course—may need more frequent formative tests than later portions. Where some of the learning units are basic and prerequisite for other units of the course, the tests should be frequent enough to insure thorough mastery of such learning material. . . .
>
> For students who lack mastery of a particular unit, the formative tests should reveal the particular point of difficulty—the specific questions they answer incorrectly and the particular ideas, skills and processes they still need to work on. It is most helpful when the diagnosis shows the elements in a learning hierarchy that the student still needs to learn. We have found that students respond best to the diagnostic results when they are referred to particular instructional materials or processes intended to help them correct their difficulties. The *diagnosis* should be accompanied by a very specific *prescription* if the students are to do anything about it. . . .
>
> These formative tests may also provide feedback for the teacher since they can be used to identify particular points in the instruction that are in need of modification.

Formative evaluation is . . .

Summative evaluation is the third type of evaluation in mastery learning. It provides information about how learners have changed by the end of instruction (Airasian, 1971). Its purpose within a mastery approach is to help arrive at final course marks. It is the type of testing with which most of us are familiar, e.g., unit, mid-term, or final exams.

Summative evaluation is . . .

We will have much more to say about formative and summative evaluation in Chapter 13. For now, let us look at a teacher-made example of mastery learning.

AN EXAMPLE OF MASTERY LEARNING

This example shows a teacher's efforts to improve learning for each student, and apparently it worked beautifully to capture the attention of learners.

The program was prepared by a teacher in his second year of classroom teaching. The topic is mathematics at the seventh grade level.

AN INDIVIDUALIZED PROGRAM
OF STUDY FOR GRADE SEVEN MATHEMATICS[17]

Overview to the Teacher

> This program is designed so that each of your students will have a better understanding of the concepts of grade-seven mathematics and a better understanding of his own abilities. It is designed on a Learning for Mastery approach and allows indi-

---

[16] Bloom (1968). Op. cit., pp. 9–10.
[17] Brian G. Usher, reprinted with the permission of the author.

vidual progress using the text, teacher, the community, and fellow students as resources.

Each program begins with a statement of the long-term goals that each student is trying to attain. Specific, short-term objectives are then given, with references to the specific areas of the text that will help him succeed with the objective.

Each student should mark his own work (*you* will not have time). When the student has completed all work in the unit he should use the scale beneath the objective to evaluate himself. This is important. It will cause a student to examine what he has done.

When a student has finished a program, his work should be checked by the teacher. This can be done easily by asking the student to explain 3 or 4 of the concepts stated while you examine his notebook.

There is a formative-type test for each program. The acceptable level of mastery is 80% success. The test *must* be marked *with the student present*. This is one of the best learning (tutorial) sessions available. If a student has less than 80%, I specify any work I feel will help him learn what *he* apparently has not learned so far. The student gets a rewrite on the questions he failed to master on the first test. (I use the original test and change parts of the questions.) When mastery has been demonstrated, the student moves on to the next unit.

Some of your students may have a problem deciding when they are ready to write the formative tests. You will have to set some time limits for them. For most students a progress chart on the wall is enough motivation. (No marks—just progress is shown.) They will want to keep up, or even get ahead.

I record the time each pupil spends on each program and his test results, *after* rewrites, if any. I keep each student's programs and tests in a separate envelope and give this to his grade-eight math teacher at the end of the year.

One word of warning: Be ready for a surprise! Your kids really will learn their arithmetic and *enjoy* doing so!

Contemporary Mathematics

Long-term Goals

1. I can successfully solve any problems involving decimals.
2. I am able to accept a challenge, organize my time, and do the job within the specified time.
3. I realize that with more thought, and more work on my part, I will be able to *plan my work* and *work my plan.*
4. I will not hesitate to ask for, or to give help when needed.
I will consider my long-term goals reached when I have completed the following short-term objectives:

Short-term Objectives

1. I realize that in order to do this work in the allotted time, my first short-term objective is to create a time schedule for my work:

:____:____:____:____:____:____:____:____:____:____:____:

(Very well met)   (Very poorly met)

2. I can name the value for any column in our decimal numeral system. i.e., $1.2 = 1 \times 1 + 2 \times \frac{1}{10}$ (pp. 176–177):

: : : : : : : : : : :
_____
(Very well met)   (Very poorly met)

3. I realize that decimal fractions are simply fractions with 10 or powers of 10 as the denominator (p. 178):

: : : : : : : : : : :
_____
(Very well met)   (Very poorly met)

4. I can write any decimal numeral as an improper fraction or as a mixed numeral (p. 177, #6; p. 179, #10):

: : : : : : : : : : :
_____
(Very well met)   (Very poorly met)

5. I can prove that $\frac{1}{10,000} = \frac{1}{10^4}$ (pp. 100–101, 178):

: : : : : : : : : : :
_____
(Very well met)   (Very poorly met)

6. I can write any decimal fraction as an expanded numeral, and I can do any question from #8 or #9 on page 178:

: : : : : : : : : : :
_____
(Very well met)   (Very poorly met)

7. I can change decimal numerals to fractions and can do #11, page 179:

: : : : : : : : : : :
_____
(Very well met)   (Very poorly met)

8. I can prove that:

: : : : : : : : : : : :

$$4.15 = \frac{400}{100} + \frac{10}{100} + \frac{5}{100} = 4 + \frac{10}{100} + \frac{5}{100} = 4\frac{15}{100} = 4\frac{3}{20}$$

: : : : : : : : : : :
_____
(Very well met)   (Very poorly met)

9. . . .nth

Now we are ready to begin learning more about the general and specific conditions necessary for learning to occur. This will help us answer the questions: "How should I go about instructing (teaching) so that my learners will learn the things I want them to learn?" "What should I do to help them learn the necessary motor and verbal chains, to make appropriate discriminations, to learn concrete and defined concepts, rules and higher-order rules?" In Chapters 5 and 6, we will direct our attention to the questions involved in arranging the appropriate conditions for learning. We will use Gagné's six types of learning as a guide.

As we learn about the general and specific conditions of different types of learning, we will try to understand how various instructional procedures can be meaningfully incorporated within a mastery learning approach, so that when we do capture the attention of our learners, they will learn efficiently—they will not fail.

You should now return to the goals and objectives for this chapter and see how well you have been able to meet them. Note especially the affective objective at the organizational level.

Those who fail in our society are lonely.

William Glasser
Schools Without Failure

1. List the main concepts and rules to be learned from this chapter.

2. Together with a friend, formulate two objectives each for the cognitive and affective domains that you believe relate to the long-range goals stated—*application* and *analysis*, and *responding* and *valuing*.

3. Explain in a paragraph or two how Gagné's types of learning rely on both cognitive and connectionist interpretations of learning. Ask a colleague to read your explanation, and revise it until he is able to show you that he understands your reasoning.

4. As an individual, a small group, or an entire class effort, use Gagné's six types of learning to complete a brief task analysis for the instructional objective: "Given $960 \div 32 = \square$, the learner is able to complete it accurately."

5. Explain in a paragraph or two how you might go about planning a unit of study based on a mastery learning approach. Do not actually plan the unit. Just explain how the planning would proceed.

6. Just for fun:

Share the following passage from *The Velveteen Rabbit*, by Margery Williams, with a friend. Then, just for fun, try to identify all the concrete concepts, defined concepts, rules and higher-order rules Margery Williams uses in this excerpt from a most powerful, insightful, and beautifully simple story.[18]

> The Skin Horse had lived longer in the nursery than any of the others. He was so old that his brown coat was bald in patches and showed the seams underneath, and most of the hairs in his tail had been pulled out to string bead necklaces. He was wise, for he had seen a long succession of mechanical toys arrive to boast and swagger, and by-and-by break their mainsprings and pass away, and he knew that they were only toys, and would never turn into anything else. For nursery magic is very strange and wonderful, and only those playthings that are old and wise and experienced like the Skin Horse understand all about it.
>
> "What is REAL?" asked the Rabbit one day, when they were lying side by side near the nursery fender, before Nana came to tidy the room. "Does it mean having things that buzz inside you and a stick-out handle?"
>
> "Real isn't how you are made," said the Skin Horse. "It's a thing that happens to you. When a child loves you for a long, long time, not just to play with, but REALLY loves you, then you become Real."
>
> "Does it hurt?" asked the Rabbit.
>
> "Sometimes," said the Skin Horse, for he was always truthful. "When you are Real you don't mind being hurt."
>
> "Does it happen all at once, like being wound up?" he asked, "Or bit by bit?"
>
> "It doesn't happen all at once," said the Skin Horse. "You become. It takes a long time. That's why it doesn't often happen to people who break easily, or have sharp edges, or who have to be carefully kept. Generally, by the time you are Real, most of your hair has been loved off, and your eyes drop out and you get loose joints and

[18] Margery Williams (1958). *The Velveteen Rabbit or How Toys Became Real.* New York: Doubleday, pp. 16–20.

very shabby. But these things don't matter at all, because once you are Real you can't be ugly, except to people who don't understand you."

"I suppose *you* are Real?" said the Rabbit. And then he wished he had not said it, for he thought the Skin Horse might be sensitive. But the Skin Horse only smiled. "The Boy's Uncle made me Real," he said. "That was a great many years ago; but once you are Real you can't become unreal again. It lasts for always."

REFERENCES

Airasian, P. W. (1971). The role of evaluation in mastery learning. In J. E. Block (ed.). *Mastery Learning: Theory and Practice.* New York: Holt.

Block, J. H., ed. (1971). *Mastery Learning: Theory and Practice.* New York: Holt.

Bloom, B. S., ed. (1956). *Taxonomy of Educational Objectives. Handbook I: Cognitive Domain.* New York: McKay.

——— (1968). Learning for mastery, *Evaluation Comment,* **1** (2). Los Angeles: University of California, Center for the Study of Evaluation of Instructional Programs.

Bridgeman, P. W. (1950). *Reflections of a Physicist.* New York: Philosophical Library.

Bruner, J. S. (1966). *Toward a Theory of Instruction.* New York: Norton.

Carroll, J. A. (1963). A model of school learning, *Teachers College Record,* **64,** 723–733.

Dewey, J. (1938). *Experience and Education.* New York: Macmillan.

Gagné, R. M. (1965). *The Conditions of Learning,* New York: Holt.

——— (1971). Defining Objectives for Six Varieties of Learning (a taped presentation). Washington: American Educational Research Association.

Guthrie, E. R. (1952). *The Psychology of Learning,* rev. ed. New York: Harper.

Hill. W. F. (1963). *Learning: A Survey of Psychological Interpretations.* San Francisco: Chandler.

James, W. (1911). *Pragmatism: A New Name for Some Old Ways of Thinking.* London: Longmans.

James, W. (1958). *Talks to Teachers.* New York: Norton.

Keller, F. S. (1968). Goodbye, teacher . . . , *Journal of Applied Behavioral Analysis,* **1,** 79–89.

Köhler, W. (1925). The making of implements. In T. Shipley (ed.), *Classics in Psychology.* New York: Philosophical Library, 1961.

Lewin, K. (1951). *Field Theory in Social Science.* New York: Harper & Row.

Morrison, H. C. (1926). *The Practice of Teaching in the Secondary School.* Chicago: The University of Chicago Press.

Pavlov, I. P. (1926–1927). Conditioned reflexes: An investigation of the physiological activity of the cerebral cortex. In T. Shipley (ed.) *Classics in Psychology.* New York: Philosophical Library, 1961.

Thorndike, E. L. (1906). *Principles of Teaching Based upon Psychology.* New York: Seiler.

——— (1911). *Animal Intelligence.* New York: Macmillan.

Washburne, C. W. (1922). Educational measurements as a key to individualizing instruction and promotions, *Journal of Educational Research,* **5,** 195–206.

Watson, J. B., and R. Raynor (1920). Conditioned emotional reactions, *Journal of Experimental Psychology,* **3,** 1–14.

——— (1925). *Behaviorism.* New York: Norton.

Williams, M. (1958). *The Velveteen Rabbit or How Toys Became Real.* New York: Doubleday.

SUGGESTIONS FOR FURTHER READING

Ausubel, D. P. (1969). *Readings in School Learning.* New York: Holt. In this volume Ausubel and his coworkers examine school learning relative to ideas such as meaningful versus rote learning; transfer of training; influence of experience; drill and practice; review; discovery learning; verbal learning; intention to learn; anxiety; cultural deprivation.

Block, H. J., ed. (1971). *Mastery Learning, Theory and Practice*. New York: Holt. Within the past few years a great number of mastery learning studies have been completed. Block's book presents an excellent annotated bibliography of some of these.

Bruner, J. S. (1966). *Toward a Theory of Instruction*. New York: Norton. The major idea developed by Bruner in this book is that specific instructional practices must derive from, and be consistent with, broad statements of basic assumptions about the development of learners, teaching, and learning. He has some pretty definite ideas about what he believes a theory of instruction should be. You will find they differ somewhat from the ideas relevant to instruction within the mastery learning approach.

Skinner, B. F. (1968). *The Technology of Teaching*. New York: Appleton-Century-Crofts. The theme of this volume relates to the methods and findings of science applied to school learning. Two chapters are particularly apt to the ideas developed in Chapter 4. They are chapter 2, "The Science of Learning and the Art of Teaching"; and chapter 5, "Why Teachers Fail."

Spence, K. W. (1959). The relation of learning theory to the technology of education, *Harvard Educational Review*, **29,** 84–95. Although this article is a bit old, it is still relevant to the current issue of the application of the methods and findings of science to the art of teaching.

5

LEARNING AND TEACHING ASSOCIATIONS AND DISCRIMINATIONS

March 21, 1961

Today Andy had a long, tough session with me. He finally solved the problem I had given him. But I can't help wondering what he learned. Not much; he certainly didn't gain any insight into the property of mulitplication in which I was interested. All that he had to show for his time was the memory of a long and painful experience, full of failure, frustration, anxiety, and tension. He did not even feel satisfaction when he had done the problem correctly, only relief at not having to think about it any more.

He is not stupid. In spite of his nervousness and anxiety, he is curious about some things, bright, enthusiastic, perceptive, and in his writing highly imaginative. But he is, literally, scared out of his wits. He cannot learn math because his mind moves so slowly from one thought to another that the connections between them are lost. His memory does not hold what he learns, above all else because he won't trust it. Every day he must figure out, all over again, that $9 + 7 = 16$, because how can he be sure that it has not changed, or that he has not made another in an endless series of mistakes? How can you trust any of your own thoughts when so many of them have proved to be wrong?

I can see no kind of life for him unless he can break out of the circle of failure, discouragement, and fear in which he is trapped. But I can't see how he is going to break out. Worst of all, I'm not sure that we, his elders, really want him to break out. It is no accident that this boy is afraid. We have made him afraid, consciously, deliberately, so that we might more easily control his behavior and get him to do whatever we wanted him to do.

John Holt
How Children Fail

CONTENTS

In Chapter 2 we set the stage with an overview of human behavior and the world's efforts to describe, explain, and change it. Chapter 3 helped us learn the skills of describing the behaviors we want to change. Then, with Chapter 4, we narrowed and directed our attention to a consideration of learning in school settings. So far, we have developed the point of view that certain prerequisites must be met before we actually begin instructing for change in a learner's behavior. They are (1) knowing clearly what you want learners to learn, and (2) having a general plan or approach for teaching and learning. Doing task descriptions and task analyses satisfies the first prerequisite to actual instruction. Applying a model of school learning to a process of learning for mastery is one way to meet the second prerequisite. When you have mastered these prerequisites, you are ready to learn about the conditions of learning and to begin organizing for instruction.

ONGOING SUMMARY

To organize for instruction you must know about the *conditions* for learning. Chapter 5 will help us begin to learn about these conditions. We will continue the task in Chapter 6.

ADVANCE ORGANIZER

Our first concern is *type* of learning. The conditions necessary for simple types of learning, such as motor chains, are somewhat different from those needed when learning the more inclusive and more complex higher-order rules.

Each of Gagné's six types of learning requires some conditions that are also required by all other types. In this text, we will refer to them as *general* conditions of learning. In addition to these general conditions, certain conditions are specific to each type. They will be referred to as *specific* conditions of learning.

The general conditions of learning can be stated briefly: The learners know what the objectives are; they attend to the learning task; they have learned and can recall any information or skills prerequisite to the learning task; they know whether or not their responses are adequate; and their correct responses gain reinforcement.

Specific conditions of learning usually relate to the proper order of stimuli in time and space. Appropriate contiguity of the important parts of a learning task ensures that practice will be effective.

In Chapter 5 you will learn about the conditions of learning motor and verbal chains and discriminations. Relative to these types of learning, we will examine the importance of meaningful learning as opposed to rote memorization.

Knowing about the general and specific conditions of learning will help you capture the attention of your learners. It will help ensure that the chains and discriminations they learn are meaningful for them. In addition, it will help make sure that they are able to use their learning effectively in further learning; that is, the learning should transfer.

Cognitive

To become an effective teacher, the learner should be able to apply the conditions of learning to teaching associations and discriminations.

KNOWLEDGE LEVEL

Given the following terms, the learner is able to define them in writing: *task description, task analysis, learning for mastery, conditions of learning, events of instruction, attention, prerequisite, feedback, reinforcement, contiguity, transfer, motor chain, verbal chain, discrimination, concrete concept, defined concept, rule, higher-order rule, meaningful learning, rote learning.*

COMPREHENSION LEVEL

1. Given the following clauses, the learner is able to complete each one so that a listener can repeat it to the satisfaction of both persons: "The general conditions of learning are: ____; the specific conditions of learning are: ____.
2. Given the general conditions of learning and the requirements for mastery learning, the learner can show how the requirements for mastery learning can be translated into general conditions of learning.

APPLICATION LEVEL

Given the general and specific conditions of learning chains, the learner can outline the events of instruction necessary to learn (1) the motor chains relevant to blowing up a balloon; (2) the verbal chain: "The circumference of a circle is equal to its diameter times π"; and (3) to discriminate between the appropriate use of "there" and "their".

ANALYSIS LEVEL

Given the general and specific conditions of learning chains and discriminations, the learner can compare and contrast the conditions required for the two types of learning.

SYNTHESIS LEVEL

Given a specific, instructional objective relative to learning chains and an objective from the affective domain, the learner can arrange the events of instruction so that the objectives from both domains are likely to be met.

EVALUATION LEVEL

Given an account of how a teacher plans to organize the events of instruction for meaningfully learning the motor chains relevant to "pouring hydrochloric acid," the learner is able to evaluate the probability of success.

Affective

To become an effective teacher, the learner should be able to practice the rules relative to learning and teaching associations and discriminations.

RECEIVING (ATTENDING) LEVEL

The learner "stays with" difficult learning tasks until he masters them, rather than only until he becomes familiar with them.

RESPONDING LEVEL

The learner is willing to participate in activities that require him to "perform as a teacher," e.g., to complete a task analysis.

VALUING LEVEL

The learner is confident that he can arrange the conditions of learning chains and discriminations.

ORGANIZATIONAL LEVEL

The learner organizes his beliefs about teaching and learning so that the importance of students is not lost among the chains and discriminations.

CHARACTERIZATION LEVEL

The learner treats others in ways consistent with his belief that how learners feel about what they know and can do is usually as important to them as what they know and what they can do.

Today is Tuesday. It is the one day each week that I set aside to teach learners in a public school setting. This year I have been teaching in a classroom in which there are twenty-one learners who have experienced only limited academic success. Most of these grade five and six learners have failed at least one year. They are described by their teachers as poor learners. They are known throughout the school as behavior problems. Seventeen of the learners are boys.

LEARNING FROM POOR LEARNERS

This is my tenth Tuesday with these learners and their teacher. Things appear to be running more smoothly today than they were the first Tuesday I was in class. I remember clearly that first Tuesday, especially the afternoon session. The teacher was trying to conduct a reading lesson with one group of learners. The rest of the class was supposed to be doing a seatwork assignment, but learners do not always attend to what teachers say they should.

Observing from the Back of the Room

Here is Karen slowly and deliberately walking along the top of a low, portable bookshelf-chalkboard that divides the room into two areas. With her hip, she is smudging Mr. Johnson's directions, written on the board, for the seatwork group. She has her head down so that Mr. Johnson will not be able to see her from where he is seated with the other group. Greg spies her first and demands loudly, "Get your ass off of there!" Without missing a step, Karen responds matter-of-factly, "Don't be a prick." Greg drags her down and they scuffle about until Mr. Johnson tells them to return to their seats. As he does so, he notices that Ricky has not yet started his seatwork. He sits carelessly in his desk and watches a crayon placed at the far edge of the desk roll quietly down the slight incline, over the assigned worksheet, and into his waiting hand. The crayon is placed for another roll, but Mr. Johnson intercepts it and questions Ricky about why he is not doing his work. With a quick, definite brush of his hand, Ricky sends the worksheet floating to the floor, and responds loudly, "I'm not doing that God-damned stuff!"

Mr. Johnson and Ricky look long and firmly at each other. Mr. Johnson moves back toward his reading group, which has begun to deteriorate in his brief absence. As he walks down the aisle, he stumbles over Melinda's shoes, which she has removed from her feet and placed beside her desk. Melinda and the rest of the class find it amusing to watch Mr. Johnson lose his balance. Mr. Johnson asks her to put them on the shelf near the coatrack. Part way to the rack Melinda thinks of a new game. It could be called "See if you can toss the shoes onto the shelf from halfway across the room." She initiates the game with gusto. By the time she has thrown two shoes, two new players have taken up the objective. Many shoes are removed from many feet, and almost instantly the air is filled with flying shoes, laughter, then arguments about whose shoes are whose and what are appropriate targets.

Ricky, however, isn't interested in the shoe game. Of course, neither is Mr. Johnson, who is doing his best to regain some sense of order in the room. Ricky sits sullenly sawing the edge of his desk with a knife dredged up from the depths of the debris that fills his desk to overflowing. As he moves past, Mr. Johnson confiscates the knife with the parting comment, "If you want to take the knife home tonight, O.K. If it's here tomorrow, you lose it."

Presently, shoes are sorted out and children are back in their desks. Ricky and Theresa are exceptions. Ricky is seated in another desk near the radiator. During the confusion, he has peeled the paper from three color crayons and has placed them on the radiator to melt into a thin wax. Theresa has taken the opportunity presented by the confusion of the shoe game to circulate among the class members to complete a list of the names of those children who owe her cigarettes. From the names on the list it would appear nearly everyone in the class is in her debt.

Observing Close Up

Eventually, most of the children seem to be making an effort to attend to the appropriate learning tasks. I leave my seat at the back of the room to try to help individual children.

As I try to help Buddy complete the part of the worksheet concerned with synonyms, he constantly glances at the clock and tries to catch the attention of his friend across the aisle. We are not getting much accomplished, so I ask Buddy why he keeps looking at the clock and at his friend. He looks deeply into my eyes for a brief instant—I think to determine whether he can trust me—then whispers to me that at two o'clock the children are allowed to leave the room for a drink of water or to go to the washroom. Only one child may be out of the room at a time, and Buddy likes to be the first one out. But, in order to do this, he must rely on his friend since, Buddy whispers, "I can't tell time."

There are many things the children in this room can't do. I find several filling in the blanks of the section dealing with synonyms, yet they apparently do not know what is meant by the word "synonym." The immediate objective seems to be merely filling the empty spaces. Many are not able to explain what the directions on the worksheet tell them to do. Some cannot read all the words. Others can pronounce the words but apparently connect little meaning to the sounds. Jim can read the word "pare" but hasn't a clue as to its meaning. Dereck seems to be doing a fair job filling the blank spaces with pencil marks, but neither he nor I can be sure of what his marks say. It seems impossible for him even to copy words accurately from a printed page. Punctuation, even that copied directly from the worksheet, appears on his paper in random fashion.

All these children have been in public school from five to eight years. Why have they apparently learned so little of what we consider important for them to learn? Is it impossible for them to learn? How does a teacher begin to organize the instruction for these children?

Today the lesson I'm helping with is arithmetic. Although progress in the language arts and in the general affect in the classroom is easily noticeable, we have not made much progress in arithmetic so far. I wonder why. Certainly a good deal of time and effort has been devoted to the subject.

TABLE 5-1 A worksheet for practice with fractions

ARITHMETIC

I Reduce to lowest terms

(1) $\dfrac{10}{12}$ = _____ (4) $\dfrac{32}{48}$ = _____ (7) $\dfrac{22}{48}$ = _____ (10) $\dfrac{125}{365}$ = _____

(2) $\dfrac{36}{72}$ = _____ (5) $\dfrac{39}{99}$ = _____ (8) $\dfrac{96}{120}$ = _____ (11) $\dfrac{72}{136}$ = _____

(3) $\dfrac{24}{48}$ = _____ (6) $\dfrac{44}{88}$ = _____ (9) $\dfrac{32}{98}$ = _____ (12) $\dfrac{40}{70}$ = _____

II Change to common denominators

(1) $\dfrac{2}{8} = \dfrac{N}{24}$ = _____ (6) $\dfrac{6}{12} = \dfrac{N}{48}$ = _____ (11) $\dfrac{24}{96} = \dfrac{N}{192}$ = _____

(2) $\dfrac{3}{7} = \dfrac{N}{14}$ = _____ (7) $\dfrac{7}{21} = \dfrac{N}{42}$ = _____ (12) $\dfrac{10}{35} = \dfrac{N}{140}$ = _____

(3) $\dfrac{7}{12} = \dfrac{N}{48}$ = _____ (8) $\dfrac{9}{18} = \dfrac{N}{54}$ = _____ (13) $\dfrac{5}{9} = \dfrac{N}{63}$ = _____

(4) $\dfrac{21}{36} = \dfrac{N}{72}$ = _____ (9) $\dfrac{4}{5} = \dfrac{N}{25}$ = _____ (14) $\dfrac{4}{12} = \dfrac{N}{36}$ = _____

(5) $\dfrac{24}{48} = \dfrac{N}{48}$ = _____ (10) $\dfrac{10}{18} = \dfrac{N}{72}$ = _____ (15) $\dfrac{3}{16} = \dfrac{N}{64}$ = _____

III Change to whole numbers or to mixed numbers

(1) $\dfrac{14}{12}$ = _____ (5) $\dfrac{29}{7}$ = _____ (9) $\dfrac{120}{35}$ = _____ (13) $\dfrac{29}{3}$ = _____ (17) $\dfrac{30}{20}$ = _____

(2) $\dfrac{35}{12}$ = _____ (6) $\dfrac{32}{6}$ = _____ (10) $\dfrac{63}{31}$ = _____ (14) $\dfrac{21}{5}$ = _____ (18) $\dfrac{66}{55}$ = _____

(3) $\dfrac{29}{2}$ = _____ (7) $\dfrac{75}{8}$ = _____ (11) $\dfrac{48}{7}$ = _____ (15) $\dfrac{32}{5}$ = _____ (19) $\dfrac{72}{24}$ = _____

(4) $\dfrac{36}{13}$ = _____ (8) $\dfrac{81}{9}$ = _____ (12) $\dfrac{44}{24}$ = · _____ (16) $\dfrac{36}{24}$ = _____ (20) $\dfrac{36}{8}$ = _____

IV Addition

(1) $\dfrac{2}{5} + \dfrac{7}{10}$ = _____ (3) $\dfrac{9}{45} + \dfrac{10}{15}$ = _____ (5) $\dfrac{4}{5} + \dfrac{6}{25}$ = _____

(2) $\dfrac{3}{16} + \dfrac{4}{32}$ = _____ (4) $\dfrac{32}{64} + \dfrac{3}{8}$ = _____

V Subtraction

(1) $\dfrac{10}{12} - \dfrac{3}{4}$ = _____ (3) $\dfrac{24}{36} - \dfrac{2}{9}$ = _____ (5) $\dfrac{20}{30} - \dfrac{2}{5}$ = _____

(2) $\dfrac{45}{55} - \dfrac{2}{11}$ = _____ (4) $\dfrac{10}{15} - \dfrac{2}{5}$ = _____

VI Solve this problem

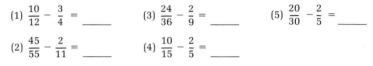

John works at the corner store after school each day. His job is to put peanuts
in bags. Each bag contains a fraction of one pound of nuts. One day Mrs.
Brononski bought two bags. One weighed ⅜ of one pound and the other ¼ of
one pound. How many pounds did Mrs. Brononski buy?

The activity for today is a worksheet for practice with the concepts and rules about fractions "learned" earlier (Table 5-1).

Mr. Johnson asks me to help those who are having difficulty. My general impression is that not many of the children are able to complete all parts of the worksheet. It is also obvious that not all are having the same difficulties. Some are not attempting the tasks at all. Others have started but have stopped after a few tries. Ricky has said that he is not going to do the work, but I notice that he has filled in the blanks for Part III. I also notice that Dan, seated in front of Ricky, has completed this part with answers the same as Ricky's.

John seems completely absorbed in the task. He has everything done correctly except for the problem of Part VI. He says he just cannot "figure it out."

Paul is at the blackboard drawing cartoons with colored chalk. I ask him why he is not doing his arithmetic. He says he can't be bothered, that he already knows it. It's too easy. "Cinchy," he says. Yet, when I ask him to tell me what a fraction is and to show me how he would solve an example from Part II, he is unable to do either. Furthermore, he is not much interested in trying, even though we are using red chalk and I'm trying to add meaning to the abstract ideas by talking about so many parts of apples and chocolate bars. Soon, he does not hear my words at all, even though I find I am speaking more and also more loudly than I was in the beginning. He is back to drawing cartoons. No longer will he attempt to think about fractions—adding, subtracting, or changing them—all that "cinchy" stuff.

I want to help these children learn about fractions, and I want them to gain pleasure from doing so, but they seem to have so many problems learning. How can I organize meaningful instruction for these children? Where shall I begin?

PREREQUISITES FOR INSTRUCTION

In Chapter 4 I presented the argument that completing task descriptions and task analyses was an important and necessary prerequisite to organizing for instruction. Consequently, this is where I must begin. Once the various behavioral requirements for a specific objective have been determined, they can be classified by type of learning and then arranged in hierarchical order following the system outlined by Gagné (1971). When I have completed these tasks, I will be ready to arrange the conditions necessary for each type of learning to occur; I will be ready to organize for instruction.

Meeting Prerequisites before We Proceed

It will be helpful for us first to check on our understanding and retention of the specific details relevant to the concepts *task description, task analysis,* and *mastery learning,* since knowledge, comprehension, and recall of these concepts are prerequisite to applying them.

CHECKPOINT 5-1

1. Following are several key words, phrases, and statements that relate to task description, task analysis, and/or mastery learning. Indicate the concept or concepts to which the statement is related.

TASK DESCRIPTION	TASK ANALYSIS	MASTERY LEARNING		KEY WORDS, PHRASES, STATEMENTS
————	————	————	(a)	Learning tends to be hierarchical.
————	————	————	(b)	Prerequisites must be met.
————	————	————	(c)	Receiving, responding, valuing, organization, characterization.
————	————	————	(d)	Knowledge, comprehension, application, analysis, synthesis, evaluation.
————	————	————	(e)	Chains, discriminations, concrete concepts, defined concepts, simple rules, higher-order rules.
————	————	————	(f)	Optimal instruction and attending to the learning task.
————	————	————	(g)	A basis for individualized instruction.

TYPE OF LEARNING		LEARNER BEHAVIOR
———— Chains, motor		The learner is able to:
———— Chains, verbal	(a)	Indicate when he hears a bell.
———— Discriminations	(b)	Hold a violin appropriately for playing.
———— Concrete concepts	(c)	Repeat the phrase, "catch children being good."
———— Defined concepts	(d)	Demonstrate that he can "catch children being good."
———— Simple rules	(e)	Define the term *affect*.
———— Higher-order rules	(f)	Explain what is meant by 2 + 2 = 4.
	(g)	Point to the heart of a dissected animal.

Writing Specific Instructional Objectives

Let us now look more closely at today's arithmetic lesson. First we will determine the objectives Mr. Johnson has for his learners, and then, what the learners must be able to do to meet them. Finally, we will want to organize instruction so that appropriate learning will occur.

If we should ask Mr. Johnson to describe his instructional objectives for his learners as reflected by the cognitive tasks assigned on the arithmetic worksheet, he would probably answer with a list of objectives somewhat like these:

COGNITIVE OBJECTIVES

Part I (Reduce to lowest terms): Given written examples of proper fractions, the learner is able to reduce each of them to its lowest terms.
Part II (Change to common denominators): Given written examples of proper fractions, the learner is able to convert them to other proper fractions of equivalent value.
Part III (Change to whole numbers or to mixed numbers): Given written ex-

amples of improper fractions, the learner is able to convert each of them to whole or mixed numbers.

Part IV (Add these fractions): Given written examples of two proper fractions, the learner is able to find their sum.

Part V (Subtract these fractions): Given written examples of two proper fractions, the learner is able to find their difference.

Part VI (Solve this problem): Given situations involving real-life problems, solution of which requires the learner to add or subtract proper fractions, he will be able to do so accurately.

AFFECTIVE OBJECTIVES

1. The learner *recognizes* that fractions are important parts of daily life.
2. The learner is *willing* to put forth the effort necessary to learn about fractions.
3. The learner is able to direct his *attention* so that other stimuli do not interfere with his study of fractions.
4. The learner *completes* his assignments.
5. The learner voluntarily *practices* those fractions for which he feels he needs practice.
6. The learner *enjoys* working with fractions.
7. The learner *wants* to become proficient with fractions.
8. The learner *volunteers to help others* learn about fractions.
9. The learner is *committed* to the value of arithmetic in personal and social life.
10. The learner *forms judgments* about the importance of arithmetic in his life.
11. The learner is *confident* of his ability to succeed.

Doing a Task Analysis

Having described instructional objectives, we are now ready to ask what the learner must be able to do to achieve each objective. In addition, we will want to ask: "What are the conditions necessary to learn these things?"

HOW TO PROCEED   Gagné (1970) has suggested that we should begin at the end; that is, by asking what the learner must be able to do to complete an objective as it is described. We should then continue by asking the question: "And what must he be able to do to do that—and, then that—?" Answers obtained from this kind of questioning define a *learning structure* or hierarchy for the topic being studied, in this case, fractions. A useful characteristic of a learning structure is that it gives us a way of determining the prerequisites for any given learning task. Knowing the prerequisites for a task allows us to establish a meaningful learning sequence for our learners. That is, it helps us determine what they need to learn first, then next, and so on. Typically, once the general idea has been grasped, the types of learning required in various learning structures progress from simple to complex, and from discrete bits of information to general, inclusive ideas or principles.

To do a task analysis, begin by . . .

Let us return to the worksheet assigned by Mr. Johnson. What must these children be able to do to meet the cognitive and affective objectives described? And what are the conditions necessary for learning to do all these "cinchy" things?

Look at a sample item from Part I. What must a learner be able to do to reduce a proper fraction, e.g.$\frac{10}{12}$, to lowest terms? Are there any higher-order rules involved? What simple rules are required? Does the learner need to know any concepts? Will it suffice merely for the learner to be able to identify concepts, for example, by pointing to various exemplars of proper fractions? What discriminations must the learner be able to make? Are there chains, verbal or motor, that are prerequisite to being able to do all the things required by the instructional objective? Clearly, there are many types of learning that are prerequisite to reducing a proper fraction to lowest terms.

GIVING IT A TRY   Although at this point we have had little experience doing task analyses, it is important that we begin to apply what we have learned even though it may be incomplete. As you will recognize, this is another way of applying the principle of part-whole practice. In Checkpoint 5-2, you are asked to attempt a task analysis. At the end of Chapter 6, you will be asked to do another one. Note that when you have completed the task analysis, you will have a useful guide to an effective learning sequence.

CHECKPOINT 5-2

1.   Using the following guide, complete at least a rough outline of a task analysis for the cognitive objective listed. It may be helpful to refer to the description of Gagné's six types of learning presented in Chapter 4.

Objective (task description): Given written examples of proper fractions, the learner is able to reduce them to lowest terms.

Specific task: Reduce $\frac{10}{12}$ to its lowest terms.

Learning Structure (task analysis): To reduce the proper fraction $\frac{10}{12}$ to lowest terms, the learner must be able to utilize:

    Higher-order rules: . . .
    Rules: . . .
    Defined concepts: . . .
    Concrete concepts: . . .
    Discriminations: . . .
    Chains: . . .
  a. Verbal: . . .
  b. Motor: . . .

2.   How well were you able to stay with this activity?

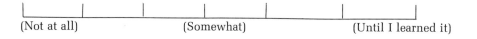

(Not at all)   (Somewhat)   (Until I learned it)

PREREQUISITES TO APPLICATION   Once we have described instructional objectives and have analyzed them in terms of a learning structure, we are ready to organize for instruction. How should we begin? For our purposes at present, let us continue with the learners in Mr. Johnson's class.

The children in this class vary widely in previous learning success, and consequently, in the types of learning they must now accomplish in order to successfully reduce a common fraction to lowest terms. Although the variation, both in cognitive and affective learning, is more apparent among these children than it might be in other groups, for our purposes of learning about teaching and learning, they are ideal. You do not learn much about teaching from "good" students. One of the first things poor learners such as these teach you is that, as a general rule of thumb, it is really wise to be wary of the quick assumption that learners have indeed learned and retained the cognitive, affective, and psychomotor skills and information that are prerequisite for any particular learning task.

Once you have pretested your learners and have a good idea of which ones need to learn which prerequisites, Gagné (1970) can help you arrange the important conditions necessary for different types of learning to occur.

CONDITIONS OF LEARNING

As we begin our discussion of the conditions necessary for each of Gagné's six types of learning (1971), we should recall the basic assumptions that are implied by Gagné's way of looking at learning: (1) No one interpretation of learning is adequate to account for all the types of learning that typically occur in school settings; (2) learning is hierarchical in nature, with some types more complex, general, and inclusive than others; (3) relatively simple and specific types of learning are prerequisite to more complex, general, and inclusive types of learning; and (4) for learning to be efficient and meaningful, the learner must have acquired, and be able to recall, specific prerequisite knowledge and skills.

Basic to Gagné's types of learning are the assumptions that . . .

Pretesting: Deciding Which Type of Learning is Needed

Here is Mike trying to reduce $\frac{32}{48}$ to lowest terms. He has completed three problems and is working on the fourth. This is what he has written on his paper so far:

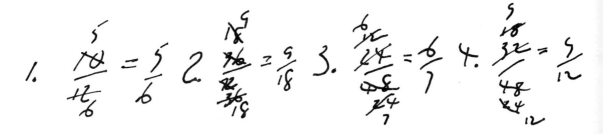

I ask him to show me what he is doing, even though he says he does not need help. He remarks that he is "doing fine." It is obvious that he is not doing fine, and I wonder how I can help him without causing him to lose his self-confidence.

His work is messy and his numerals are carelessly written. The general appearance of his work is disordered. It is unclear to me whether he actually has not acquired all the prerequisites necessary to reduce proper fractions, or whether he just gets lost in the confusion of his written work. To help Mike, I must help him isolate his problems and do something to improve them.

LEARNING FROM THE LEARNER   As I sit down with Mike, I recall what John Holt said about learning to be a teacher: "Everything I learn about teaching I learn from bad students."[1] By questioning Mike with the use of several examples, I conclude that he has an adequate grasp of the higher-order rule required to reduce proper fractions. He can explain the prerequisite rules and defined and concrete concepts. He can make the necessary discriminations between stimulus objects relevant to the task. I ask Mike to show me how he goes about solving these problems. He begins by writing the next problem on his paper: "$\frac{32}{78} =$ ___." He then looks at what he has written. (The problem is actually $\frac{32}{98}$.) He asks himself aloud: "What number will go into both 32 and 78? How many times does 2 go into 32?" On another piece of paper, he performs this sequence of division:

The purpose of pretesting is . . .

Next, Mike draws a line through the 32 and places the numeral 16 above it. He now has on his paper $\frac{16}{78} =$ ___. He repeats the division, this time dividing 16 again by 2. He writes "2)16," and says, "Now 2 goes into 16 how many times?" He guesses 8, and is pleased with himself when he multiplies 8 times 2 and remembers that it is indeed 16. He now crosses out the numeral 16 and places the numeral 8 above it. He seems confident as he proceeds. He knows what the problem requires and he feels he is able to do it. Without needing to go through the written process that he did to divide 32 and 16 by 2, Mike immediately crosses out the numeral 8 and writes 4 above it. Then he crosses out the 4 and writes 2 above it; then crosses out the 2 and writes 1. He knows what $8 \div 2$, $4 \div 2$, and $2 \div 2$ are equal to. He does not have to figure it out anew. His paper now looks like this:

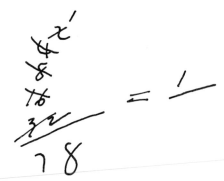

[1] J. Holt (1964). *How Children Fail.* New York: Pitman, p. 58.

We exchange smiles and he begins his attack on the denominator. "So 2 goes into 78 how many times?" I don't mention to Mike that the denominator actually is 98, and it does not occur to him to check the worksheet to make sure he has copied it correctly. He divides on his scratch paper:

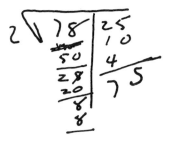

He concludes that 2 goes into 78 just 75 times, so he crosses out the 78 in the denominator and writes the numeral 75 below it. He looks at the numeral 75 and then back again at his last division sequence. He checks his work and decides there is nothing wrong, even though he mentions to me in passing that 75 seems to be "kind of big." He does not notice that he has placed the numeral 4 in the tens column. Satisfied that numbers do not lie, Mike continues. He writes "2)75" and then stops. He writes his answer to the problem: "$\frac{1}{75}$." I ask Mike why he did not divide 75 by 2. He replies with the simple rule: "Two won't go evenly into any number that ends with an odd number." I want to know if his answer seems reasonable to him, so I ask him how he feels about the size of it. He admits that it does look "kinda odd," but that it is "probably right."

Mike asks if he should begin the next problem. We have been on this one a little over three minutes. I suggest we do something else. I want to find out whether he "knows" his multiplication facts, and why he divides only by 2. Although it is a correct way to proceed, it is grossly inefficient, and has so many points at which error can creep in. Furthermore, if each problem takes Mike an average of three minutes to complete, the entire worksheet of fifty-eight problems will take him nearly three hours! Mike simply will not do it. He is defeated before he starts.

I begin by asking Mike number sentences, such as "7 times 6 equals what?" and "5 times 8 equals what?" He has little trouble with these. The combinations that he has forgotten are "remembered" with the help of his fingers as counting tools or by using his pencil and paper. However, when I ask Mike the reverse number sentences, for example, "42 divided by 7 equals what?" and "40 divided by 8 equals what?" he is lost. He does not know his "goes into's." I suppose that whoever organized the conditions of his instruction assumed that if Mike acquired the verbal chains in one way, he would automatically know them in other formats. Obviously, this did not occur with Mike. I wonder if it will with your learners.

KNOWING WHERE TO BEGIN   Mike's problems are clearly that the verbal and motor chains prerequisite to effective completion of the arithmetic task have been poorly or inadequately learned and retained. Consequently, as his teacher, I must arrange the conditions necessary for him to learn and recall them. The chains Mike needs to improve are those that will result in:

1. *Verbal chains:* a reeling off of the number sequences:
$2 \div 2 = 1, 4 \div 2 = 2, 6 \div 2 = 3, \ldots .144 \div 12 = 12$.
2. *Motor chains: (a)* neatly and legibly formed numerals and symbols, and *(b)* logical and useful written patterns or formats for use in work with fractions.

Let us now discuss the conditions of learning chains. Later, we will return to Mike and apply these conditions to help him learn these specific chains.

LEARNING MOTOR AND VERBAL CHAINS

Learning motor and verbal chains is essentially a matter of practicing the appropriate associations or connections between certain stimuli and certain responses. As such, learning to make chains of responses is a very simple and widespread type of learning. You will recall, from our discussion in Chapter 4, that learning a verbal chain of responses does not actually require learners to have meaningful associations among the links. That is, technically speaking, they do not need to understand or be able to explain the meaning of the individual links or of the complete chain. It requires only that the learner is able to make the responses in some appropriate pattern or sequence. For example, learning the verbal chain a, b, c, d, . . . z does not require an explanation of why b follows a, and so forth. The learning that is necessary is the ability to recite the series of letters in the proper sequence.

Similarly, as we saw in Chapter 4, for motor chains, learners need only *form* the letters in an appropriate manner. They are not required to say *why* the letters are shaped as they are. The conditions necessary for learning motor and verbal chains are essentially those required for stimulus-response learning in a connectionist tradition.

General and Specific Conditions

Gagné (1970) describes the conditions of learning in terms of those *internal* to the learner and those *external* to the learner or within the learning situation. In this text, I have chosen to talk about the conditions of learning Gagné's six types of learning in terms of conditions general to all types and those specific to certain types. Therefore, the general conditions for learning chains are those required of all six types of learning. The specific conditions are those most clearly related to learning motor and verbal chains.

The general conditions of learning are . . .

GENERAL CONDITIONS   The general conditions of learning can be expressed in point form as follows: (1) *clear objectives*—the learners know what their own performance should be like; (2) *prerequisites*—the learners have learned and can recall any information or skills necessary for the new learning task; (3) *attention to the task*—the learners become involved in the learning task; they respond, they try; (4) *knowledge of results*—the learners get feedback about their own performances; (5) *reinforcement*—correct responses are rewarded.

The specific conditions of learning chains are . . .

SPECIFIC CONDITIONS   The specific conditions of learning chains are: (1) *contiguity*—stimuli and their appropriate responses occur in close temporal relationship; (2) *repetition*—complete chains, with all links in proper order, are practiced.

Organizing for Instruction

If I want Mike to learn the motor and verbal chains listed earlier, I must organize his instruction so that both general and specific conditions of learning are met. This means that I must be sure that Mike knows what his final performances should be and that he has learned and can recall any information or skills prerequisite to learning these motor and verbal chains. I must organize Mike's instruction so that he will attend to the task long enough and well enough to learn it. I must make sure that he knows when his responses are correct and that correct responses are reinforced. The parts of the chains must be arranged so that they occur in appropriate association with each other. Also, I must organize his instruction so that he will practice the chains.

THE EVENTS OF INSTRUCTION   Obviously, the conditions of learning are closely related to the *process* of instruction. They specify what Gagné (1970) refers to as the *events of instruction*—the things teachers do to ensure that the conditions of learning are met. This is what is meant by *instruction*. Gagné (1970, 1974) describes these events in terms of *teacher actions* that (1) gain and control attention, (2) stimulate recall of relevant prerequisites, (3) inform the learner of the objectives, (4) present the relevant stimuli, (5) offer guidance for learning, (6) provide corrective feedback, (7) appraise performance, (8) provide for transfer, and (9) ensure retention through practice.

We should remember that conditions of learning refer primarily to learning in the cognitive domain. But, of course, this type of learning is not all that happens in instruction. As a teacher you must also teach for affective outcomes. I will have more to say about this when I try to illustrate how both these aspects of instruction can be applied in helping Mike learn motor and verbal chains that are prerequisite to the more complex types of learning required to reduce proper fractions to lowest terms. But first, let me alert you to a frequent abuse in teaching chains.

The events of instruction are . . .

A WIDESPREAD ABUSE OF LEARNING MOTOR AND VERBAL CHAINS   It is important that great care is exercised in organizing the conditions for learning chains of responses. Probably the greatest single abuse of educational practices as they commonly occur in classrooms centers on the learning of verbal chains. The *issue* is that although some learning tasks are legitimately of the simple association type, not all are. The *problem* is that many learning tasks which clearly involve learning potentially meaningful material frequently are organized so that learners learn the material rotely, as if it were a series of randomly associated links of a chain.

One does not need to look far for numerous and widespread examples of this abuse. Teaching learners to rise from their seats on cue when an adult enters the classroom is often accomplished as an essentially meaningless chain of motor responses. Diagraming sentences is another. Other examples that come readily to mind include instruction that causes pupils to learn to "read" words for which they have no meaningful associations; directing learners to "follow the rules" to get the "right" answer in doing long division or multiplication, balancing chemical equations, solving problems in physics, or reducing proper fractions. Instruction organized so that it causes students to memorize definitions such as "valence is the combining power of an element" is an example of the abuse of learning potentially meaningful verbal chains in a rote manner.

Motor and verbal chains are necessary parts of our learning experiences. However, they are most clearly appropriate either when acquiring material that is arbitrary in organization and content, or when the purpose is overlearning for retention and immediate recall. Arbitrariness, however, is a relative term. Whereas little school learning is completely arbitrary, that is, devoid of any logical association with other material learned, much is somewhat arbitrary in organization and content. The names of people, places, things, events, symbols, and so forth are relatively arbitrary. Usually such factual material is important in that it enables learners to complete other, more complex, and more meaningful learning tasks—solving problems, for example.

A learner often needs to reel off, from start to finish, verbal or motor chains of responses of varying degrees of meaningfulness, length, and complexity. These chains may contain material that is either relatively arbitrary or rich in potential meaning. The important point is that the learner is able to recall the necessary chains of responses when they are needed, and to perform them without hesitation. Tossing the ball toward the basket during a basketball game is one example of a motor chain that must be recalled and performed without hesitation as a part of a more complex and meaningful task. Being able to recall quickly that the letter d comes after c is necessary for the efficient use of dictionaries or encyclopedias. Saying "Twenty-five divided by five equals five" is an example of a verbal chain that must be recalled and performed from memory if problem solving is to be an efficient process.

As you can see, motor and verbal chains vary a great deal in the relative potential meaningfulness of their content. Although having potential meaningfulness, however, certain potentially meaningful content may not be meaningful to certain learners solely because they have not previously acquired the background skills or information necessary to make logical and relevant associations with the new material. One example occurs when a high school student learns the mechanics of balancing chemical equations without having a clear understanding of the reasoning from which these mechanics derive. Another is seen when learners learn rules or definitions that include words with which they have had no relevant experiences.

Because of the great differences in potential meaningfulness of various chains, an important distinction must be made with regard to how chains are learned initially. Motor and verbal chains with relatively arbitrary content, e.g., forming the shapes, names, and sounds of letters and numerals, saying the letters of the alphabet in order, and naming various symbols, can be appropriately and efficiently learned through repeated associations of stimuli and their responses. Motor and verbal chains with relatively meaningful content, e.g., higher-order rules, simple rules, and concepts, however, must not be learned in this manner. They must be learned so that their relevance to other parts of cognitive structure is emphasized. Only when the relevance has been grasped can the content appropriately be considered a motor or verbal chain which, for purposes of retention and recall, can be practiced through a process of repetition.

Briefly, then, the abuse in teaching motor and verbal chains occurs when the purpose for learning chains is confused. The conditions of learning chains are arranged for two purposes: (1) the initial acquisition of chains of essentially arbitrary content, and (2) retention and effective recall of potentially meaningful content, not for the initial learning of meaningful content.

We are now about ready to help Mike learn. You will recall from Chapter 3, however, that performing at a knowledge level is prerequisite to performing at

A widespread abuse of learning chains is . . .

Two purposes for learning chains are . . .

an applied level. Therefore, let us check on how well you have learned and can recall the general and specific conditions of learning chains. Moving ahead without mastery of the prerequisites can be a poor learning procedure for all of us.

1. General conditions are:

2. Specific conditions are: (Answers may be found in an earlier section.)

Instructing for Learning Chains

Mike is more fortunate than some pupils. He understands (knowledge, comprehension levels) the main ideas involved in reducing proper fractions to lowest terms, but he needs (1) to learn or relearn the appropriate motor chains (listed earlier) that will allow him to record the details of his thinking accurately and consistently in written form, and (2) to learn to practice the verbal chains $2 \div 2 = 1, 4 \div 2 = 2, \ldots 144 \div 12 = 12$.

As we help Mike learn, many rules of psychology will be at work. We have experienced some of them before, but some are new and we will learn more about them in later chapters. Because so much of what we learn is learned by observing the behavior of others, it is important to make sure we see beyond the immediately apparent, that we see the *why* of *what* is happening in instructional situations.

At the beginning of the next section you will see an application of Guthrie's rule about making sure all the links of a chain are appropriately connected and then practiced from beginning to end. If they are broken, that is, if the correct answer cannot be remembered, the rule is to give the learner the answer, then cause him to repeat the entire chain with the correct link properly placed and performed.

A little later on we will see once again *whole-part* or *progressive-part* practice. Four "new" elements, however, have been added. Observe first that practice occurs with those number sentences that are likely to be learned most quickly. Successful learning or relearning, as the case may be, has a good chance of happening early in the session, and success means reinforcement for attending behavior; the learner is likely to keep trying. Remember the "truth" according to the connectionists: "We avoid what we find aversive; we continue what is rewarding."

Whole-part practice means . . .

Second, practice occurs with four or five items at a time. Interference becomes too great a problem if a learner tries to learn many chains at once. The trouble is that each item in a set of, say, ten or more "new" number sentences is "interfered with" many times before it is repeated during a practice session. By the time an item comes around again, the correct response has been forgotten. As a rule of thumb for learning relatively arbitrary material, George Miller (1956) suggests that seven, plus or minus two, is a good number to remember as the upper limit of items to have learners try to learn in any one practice session.

Interference is a problem when . . .

Third, you will notice that I ask Mike to keep practice sessions relatively short and to distribute them over time rather than to mass them in one or two long sessions. Learning and retention of chains are usually more efficient when the practice is distributed than when it is massed. No one knows for sure why this is so. However, a good guess is that interference is less of a problem when practice of relatively rote learning tasks occur with a relatively small number of items, over a series of relatively short periods of time.

Distributed practice means . . .

Fourth, you will see that all the items to be practiced are occasionally shuffled so that the order is rearranged. The purpose is to make sure learners learn what we want them to learn and not other stimulus-response connections. If I do not rearrange the stimuli once in a while, Mike may begin to learn that the answer for one item is the stimulus for the answer to the next item. He might learn, for example, that for the item following the item whose answer is 8, the answer is 6. The response "6" then gets connected to the stimulus 8, rather than to the stimulus $24 \div 4 = 6$. Of course this is not what I want him to learn at all. Indeed, it is worse than useless to him; he believes that he is learning something useful when he is not.

Another rule relative to the defined concept *practice*, which you will see in operation in the next section, is that practice (drill or repetition) appropriately occurs only *after* the potential meaning of the material has been acquired. Practice does not take the place of meaning, not even for motor and verbal chains. A rule of thumb can be stated simply as: "Meaning first, then practice."

The rule "Meaning first, then practice" leads to . . .

Last, but far from least, you will see in the next section the operation of the rule that clues for the organization of instruction are to be found in our affective objectives. You will see the rule that guides teachers to practice being honest and caring with their learners so that learners will also learn to be honest and caring with one another and with themselves. As you will recall, the "truth" in the connectionist tradition is that what we practice is what we learn, about chains, and about people.

LEARNING VERBAL CHAINS

To apply these ideas to help Mike learn motor and verbal chains, I would begin by sharing with him what my objectives are for him. I would talk with him about why I believe these particular motor and verbal chains are important for him to acquire. If, in the past, I have been an honest, helpful person with Mike, he will know that I care about what he becomes and he will try to understand the meaning I offer him. If he does not understand fully, he will have learned to trust my judgment as a teacher; he will know that I will not hurt him.

At Mike's present state of readiness, it does not make sense to expect him to continue with learning tasks that require the prerequisite motor and verbal chains he has not yet learned. Consistent with a basic premise of mastery learning, I would not assign him further problems, such as those on the worksheet. Rather, I would organize instruction to help him learn the chains which are prerequisite for success in reducing proper fractions.

One way to meet the necessary conditions of contiguity of stimuli and responses (in this case, questions and answers) and of knowledge of results (in learning number sentences) would be to arrange the sentences on individual cards. On one side of each card would be incomplete number sentences, e.g.,

$36 \div 6 = \underline{?}.$ On the reverse side would be complete number sentences, e.g., $36 \div 6 = \underline{6}.$ I would ask Mike to practice the cards thus:

"First, read a sentence through the 'equal' sign. Then, if you are reasonably sure of the correct response, complete the sentence by saying or writing the answer. If you are unsure of the answer, do not guess. Turn the card over and check your answer. If correct, go on to the next card. If incorrect, reread the sentence including the correct answer. Do this three or four times before going on to the next card.

"As you proceed, place the cards in three stacks. One stack is for those number sentences you know really well. Another is for those you are not too sure of, and the third stack is for those sentences you need to learn. This last stack of cards is the one you must practice most. To begin with, however, practice four or five cards at a time from the second stack. As you become more sure of them, place them in the first stack. Occasionally review all the cards in the first stack so that, as you learn new number sentences, you do not forget those you already know. Each time you practice a stack of cards, reshuffle them into a new sequence. This will help you keep from learning the answers in order, rather than in response to the specific number combinations.

"As you go about learning all the chains, try to practice them so that your practice times are fairly brief (ten or fifteen minutes) and occur several times each day. Do not try to learn all the chains during one or two long practice sessions."

An immediate question arises. A fairly common characteristic of learners who learn poorly is that they do not always attend to the learning tasks as well as they should. Fortunately, there are many possible and positive ways to cause learners to practice verbal chains. You will remember, from earlier in this chapter and from Chapter 2, that affective objectives can help you decide how to organize instructions so that learners will want to attend to them. At this point, we should ask, "What guides can be gained from the affective objectives we assume Mr. Johnson has for these learners?" For purposes of example, look at objective no. 8: "The learner volunteers to help others learn about fractions." If I am to pay more than lip service to the importance of the affective development of learners, I must try to meet affective objectives as well as cognitive ones with Mike.

This affective objective implies that the learning situation should involve others if it is to result in Mike's wanting to help others learn. If there are other learners in Mr. Johnson's room who need to learn the number sentences that Mike does, I could group these children in twos or threes and have them help each other. This could be done over several short practice sessions each day. Indeed, this approach has been used effectively by teachers at all grade levels for hundreds of years.

It is not so easy, however, to arrange an instructional situation that is mutually helpful to each learner when the content was learned by most class members a year or so earlier. Furthermore, it can be humiliating for learners to have to practice verbal and motor chains that their peers recall and use with ease. They simply will not attend to the task and will not practice, and of course, practice is one of the important specific conditions of learning chains.

One effective way to get pupils to practice chains normally learned in earlier years is to arrange an instructional situation in which they help teach the chains

Affective objectives give us clues about . . .

to younger learners. Many learners find teaching younger children an extremely pleasant task, especially if it occurs during school time. Individual tutoring sessions can usually be arranged by asking teachers of young children who of their learners would profit from additional practice with specific motor or verbal chains. This is the approach I would try with Mike. I would ask him if he would be willing to spend a few minutes, three or four times each day, helping a child from a lower grade learn the verbal chains. I would not try to trick him into doing this, but rather, I would share with him that I feel the practice would help him learn the chains, and at the same time, he would perform a valuable service to a child who is having difficulty learning.

I would speak with the other teacher to ensure that the child with whom Mike is to work has a grasp of the *meaning* contained in the verbal chains to be learned. It will be Mike's task to provide guided practice for a learner who already understands the ideas inherent in the number sentences. It will not be his task to teach these ideas.

I would instruct Mike in how to proceed with his pupil. Because the instructions I give Mike are mostly verbal and motor chains themselves, he and I would practice them, with immediate feedback of his performance, until he had learned them well enough to perform smoothly and confidently in his role as a tutor.

I would give Mike a set of cards, as described earlier. To instruct his pupil, Mike would meet with him in a place relatively free of distracting stimuli. One at a time, in random order, Mike would show his pupil the stimulus side of each card. The pupil would be directed to read the sentence and supply the correct answer. Mike would tell his pupil not to guess if he was unsure of the correct response. If he cannot complete the sentence, he is asked to say so, and Mike will show him the complete number sentence on the reverse side. Mike would ask his pupil to read the sentence, including the correct answer. They would then go on to the next card.

In just the way I suggested to Mike earlier, they would proceed through the cards, first sorting them into three stacks and then practicing them. The practice will continue until the pupil is able to respond correctly and without hesitation to the stimuli on each card. As this process occurs, Mike will make a point of "catching his pupil being good." That is, he will reward correct responses, first by letting his pupil know that he is correct, and next, by showing his pleasure at his pupil's success. When his pupil is incorrect, Mike will try not to say things that may cause his pupil to feel stupid because of his ignorance of the correct answer. He knows from his own experiences of frustration and failure that how he *feels* about what he knows and can do is almost (if not always) more important to him than what he *knows* and what he can do.

When all cards are in the first stack, the pupil will have learned and be able to recall easily all the number sentences of the type $42 \div 7 = 6$, and of course, so will Mike. Of even greater importance, affective objective no. 8 will have been met. So will those numbered 1 through 7. Objectives 9, 10, and 11 will be closer to being met than they were before Mike "helped a friend."

LEARNING MOTOR CHAINS

You will recall that the general and specific conditions of learning motor chains are the same as those necessary for learning verbal chains: clear objectives, prerequisites learned and recalled, attention to the task, knowledge of results, reinforcement of correct responses, contiguity of stimuli and responses, and practice of properly ordered complete chains. Motor chains, like verbal chains, can be exceedingly short and simple, such as lifting one finger. They can also be long and complex, e.g., driving a car, operating a typewriter, completing a routine in gymnastics or dance. The general and specific *conditions* of learning each of these widely different motor chains, however, differ only in the degree to which the various conditions are necessary, and of course, nearly an infinite number of different approaches or methods of instruction may be used.

Any approach, however, will be most effective in helping us learn a motor chain, regardless of what the chain contains, when all the events of instruction have been provided: gaining and controlling attention, informing the learner of expected outcomes, stimulating recall of relevant prerequisite capabilities, presenting the stimuli inherent to the learning task, offering guidance for learning, providing feedback, appraising performance, making provision for transfer, and ensuring retention through practice (Gagné, 1970, 1974).

If I want to help Mike learn the motor chains described earlier, I must include all these events in the organization for his instruction. However, before I begin his actual instruction, I should ask myself whether Mike may possibly have already learned the motor chains that would permit him to form his numerals clearly and legibly on paper. Perhaps he has also learned appropriate formats to follow when trying to solve various problems in arithmetic. I need to pretest for these capabilities.

The conditions of learning motor chains are . . .

As a teacher, you never know exactly what pupils have learned merely by observing their performance. Mike may know how to perform the motor chains, yet does not do so. If this is the case, my task is not to help him *learn* the chains but rather to help him *reinstate* them. I can test Mike by asking him to form his numerals more carefully, perhaps in a way he may have learned to do them in the past, and to use a certain format when completing his arithmetic exercises. I will then follow up this direction by watching Mike's performance. If I learn that he can perform the chains, I will spend my efforts "catching Mike being good"—writing clearly and legibly, and following some acceptable format. I will try to withhold my attention from his performances which are not "good" ones. Over several trials, I will expect to notice a gradual improvement of Mike's written work in arithmetic as the previously learned motor chains are reinstated.

Let us assume that Mike has not learned to form his numerals neatly and legibly, that he is not just careless. Let us assume also that he has not learned useful patterns or formats to follow in his written work with fractions. My task is to help Mike learn these motor chains.

How should I begin? First, I will arrange a meeting with Mike to make sure that he is clearly aware of my concerns about his illegible and poorly organized written work. I want him to understand that I believe it is important for him to learn to perform as well as he can. In addition, I want him to be able to trust that I will teach in accordance with my present beliefs, even if it means extra effort for both of us. I will try to convey to him why I believe he is capable of improvement. However, I must try to be accurate in my assessment of his capabilities. He will know that I will not allow him to do less than he can. He will also know that I can be wrong in my belief about the importance of legibility and order in written work, and that he need not be afraid to intervene.

What I hope to accomplish through this and the countless other daily contacts with my learners is the avoidance of two of the saddest events that teachers can inflict on learners at all levels: (1) making demands that learners are unprepared or unwilling to meet; and (2) being unwilling to demand from learners the best of their performance.

Having established that we are both on the same team with the same objectives and similar motives, Mike and I will begin the task of his learning the motor chains. He will start with the motor chains involved with the forming of legible numerals. Mike and I will decide on what can be an appropriate style or form of numeral for him to learn. This will serve as his objective. In addition, a sample of numerals written in that particular style will provide comparative feedback about his success in trying to write in a similar style.

Gagné points out that "of utmost importance to the acquiring of (motor) chains is the requirement that each individual stimulus-response connection ($Ss{\rightarrow}R$) be *previously learned.* One cannot expect a (motor) chain like opening a door with a key to be learned in an optimal way unless the learner is already able to carry out the $Ss{\rightarrow}R'S$ that constitute the links."[2] What are the individual $Ss{\rightarrow}R$ links that Mike must have previously learned in order to form his numerals legibly? He must have learned to (1) hold a pencil and to position it in paper placed appropriately on his desk; (2) apply a pencil to paper in such a way that he is able to reproduce the basic writing strokes—curves, lines, loops—smoothly and automatically; and (3) perform these strokes in varying sizes and in varying relationships with each other. If Mike has learned to do all these things well, the task of learning to form numerals that are legible and of a particular shape should be relatively easy.

Practice per se is not sufficient. For each type of learning, it must be carefully arranged; it must have a particular purpose; and it must take a form that is consistent with that purpose. Later in this chapter, I will have more to say about these essential requirements in relation to more complex types of learning. For now, let us think through how the requirements of *purpose* and *form* of practice apply to helping Mike learn motor chains.

Practice in learning chains needs to be . . .   If Mike has not learned to reproduce the basic writing strokes of lines, curves and loops or to write them in desired sizes or interrelationships with one another, how can I help him learn to do so? Responses transfer best when they are learned and practiced in a way as similar as possible to the way in which they will be used. Therefore, Mike's basic strokes should not be practiced in isolation from one another, since this is not the way I want Mike to use them. I want him to chain all the appropriate strokes together so that he can write the entire numerals, not just the separate strokes which combine to form numerals. Consequently, I will arrange practice for Mike that will cause him to practice the basic strokes while he practices combining them into complete numerals.

Comparative models help by . . .   Especially valuable in learning motor and verbal chains are comparative models. Models do several things. (1) They provide information about what the desired performance should be like. Therefore, they should be immediately available to the learner. (2) They serve as comparative basis for assessing performance as the learning task proceeds. (3) They provide clues about how the next response should be modified to closer approximate the desired final performance. Delay in gaining knowledge of the adequacy of each performance causes inefficiency of learning and recall.

[2] R. M. Gagné (1970). *The Conditions of Learning.* New York: Holt, p. 128.

One way I can arrange instruction for Mike so that I will capture his attention, provide him a model, ensure immediate feedback, guide his practice, and provide for transfer is to present a model (numerals to be produced) on a sheet of paper with an attached overlay of clear plastic. I will give Mike a wax crayon or an erasable felt pen of some color that contrasts with the black color of the numerals in the model. I will tell Mike to trace over the numerals by writing on the plastic overlay. For repeated practice, the used plastic can be wiped clean or replaced with a new sheet.

If holding the pen and positioning the paper are prerequisite motor chains that have been poorly learned, I will first give Mike verbal directions and my own model to imitate. If necessary, I will guide his hand by placing my hand over his. In a very real sense, the kinesthetic stimuli, or the "feels" that accompany performance of the various links, are important parts of the total feedback necessary for learning motor chains. As Mike seems to get the feel of the appropriate motions of his hand and arm with the pen on the overlay, I will reduce the strength of my guidance. Eventually I will take my hand away completely. The same process can be used to help a learner acquire a certain stroke in tennis or swimming, or a certain movement with a wrench in auto mechanics.

Each time Mike practices tracing over a numeral, he can tell immediately how "good" his performance is. In addition, he can tell at what points it is "good" and at what points it is not.

As Mike's performance of the motor chains improves, I will gradually reduce the immediate availability of the comparative model. Rather than give him complete numerals as models to trace, I will begin giving him numerals that are to be copied rather than traced. I will ask him to look at the model numerals and then copy them in a blank space immediately below. He can then slip the overlay toward the top of the page so that the numeral he has written will cover the model. In this way he will gain corrective feedback. He will repeat this as many times as he needs to for the writing of his numerals to become smooth, neat, and automatic. Eventually, Mike will stop using the plastic overlay and write his numerals on regular lined paper.

By a process of gradually removing the cues supplied by the comparative model, and by gradually causing Mike to take the responsibility for making more of the total responses on his own, I will help him make closer and closer approximations of the desired final performance. You will recognize once again that this is yet another example of the part-whole process of practice.

Of course, I am not primarily interested in having Mike write numerals clearly and legibly on plastic overlays. I want this behavior to transfer to other parts of his work, especially to his written work in arithmetic. One way I can do this is by causing Mike's behavior to be reinforcing for him to form his numerals clearly and legibly in all areas of his written work. I will "catch Mike being good," and I will "not let well enough alone."

In addition to "catching Mike being good," I will withhold reinforcement for written performances I consider less than his "best" at that time. That is, I matter-of-factly will just not accept them. When they are improved, and indeed they will be if I really have been able to become a part of Mike's team, I will ignore the fact that they were not done "right" the first time. He and I will be pleased that now they are fine, and we will continue from there.

Did you notice, in the discussion of helping Mike reinstate previously learned, appropriate motor chains, that a very simple and powerful rule of human behavior was beginning to operate? That when I wanted Mike's written

To change the
behavior of learners,
first we must . . .

behavior to change, *first* I changed my own behavior toward his performance? I stopped ignoring his written behavior and began to see that the better parts of his written behavior gained reinforcement. My own behavior illustrated this rule of thumb: "If you want your learner's behavior to change, change your own behavior first." We will learn more about this rule as we go along. We will find it to be especially relevant to the topic of classroom management.

LEARNING MORE THAN
ONE CHAIN AT THE SAME TIME

One of the remarkable "truths" about learners is that they are capable of learning more than one thing at the same time. This, of course, can work to the advantage as well as the disadvantage of teachers and pupils since what is learned is not always appropriate. For example, as was illustrated earlier in this chapter and in Chapter 3, we learn to respond affectively to cognitive stimuli at the same time that we are learning cognitive responses. We tend to acquire positive affective responses for those cognitive and psychomotor stimuli for which we learn responses that are reinforced. The converse of this also occurs, with the result that learners attempt to avoid cognitive and psychomotor stimuli that have in the past resulted in punishment.

In addition to the possibility of cognitive, affective, and psychomotor learning occurring at once, it is possible that more than one learning outcome within one domain will occur simultaneously. It may also be true that more than one type of learning can occur at the same time. In other words, it is quite possible and often desirable to organize instruction so that more than one objective is being met at once.

Often several objectives that are being met simultaneously reflect learning that is representative mainly of only a single domain. For example, teachers of very young learners may wish to help the children learn the motor chains relative to skipping and to tracking moving objects with the eyes. Both these chains might be learned and practiced as a consequence of experience with one activity, skipping rope. Motor chains relative to timing would also be learned and practiced at the same time. The point is that separate and different organizations for instruction do not always need to be arranged for each objective. Learning motor chains relevant to appropriate eye-hand coordination in typing concurrently with learning motor chains relevant to proper stroking force and timing is another example of multiple objectives in a single domain being met simultaneously.

An example of meeting several objectives from different domains at once occurs when a teacher helps learners learn meaningful, cognitive associations relevant to such words as "around," "over," and "under" at the same time that they learn motor chains relative to body control by participating in an activity which pairs "saying the word" with appropriate body movements.

Precisely how many and what kinds of objectives can appropriately and effectively be "taught for" at the same time is an empirical question that will be answered for you through your own teaching experiences. In the meantime, let us think through how we might use the fact that more than one motor chain can be learned simultaneously. We could have applied this idea when we organized instruction for Mike to learn the motor chains that will result in his forming written numerals and symbols neatly and legibly. At the same time, we could have arranged his instruction so that he would have learned logical and useful written patterns to use in his work with fractions. This is the task for Checkpoint 5-4. It will help you learn to use the ideas involved in the conditions of learning chains. Think through how you might organize events of instruction so that Mike will achieve the objectives you have set for him. This will require you to expand or possibly revise the events of instruction that I described earlier for helping Mike. The events you will need to pay particular attention to are the ones whose functions are to (1) let Mike know what his final performance should be like, and (2) offer guidance for learning through verbal and nonverbal hints or prompts.

The final performance I have in mind for you in Checkpoint 5-4 is a written account of your arrangements for instruction that would help Mike learn both these kinds of motor chains at the same time. Although the specific details of your arrangements for Mike's instruction may be quite different from mine, they should be similar in the sense that each must somehow provide the necessary *general* and *specific* conditions of learning motor chains. You might use my response to this task as a comparative model.

CHECKPOINT 5-4

1. Construct a learning task for Mike so that he will learn the motor chains relevant to neatly and legibly formed numerals and symbols, and at the same time learn the motor chains relevant to an appropriate pattern or format to use in his written work with fractions.

2. As you think about doing this task, do you also think about potential affective objectives that you might help Mike meet? Yes_____ No_____

A Look at Our Own Learning

If I have done an adequate job of instructing to this point, you will have a clear idea of what our objectives are; you will have participated in the discussion; and you will have completed the checkpoints. You will have had sufficient feedback so that you know that you have learned and have not found it difficult to do so.

If these statements do not describe you, it is probably because my instruction was less than optimal for you. (Remember, from Chapter 4, what Carroll had to say about instruction needing to be optimal for each learner?) If learning is difficult, it is a good bet that the arrangements for instruction are less than optimally effective. If the conditions of learning have been adequately provided, learning should occur without difficulty. I know of no evidence that suggests purposely arranging the events of instruction so that learning that is difficult for most learners results in effective learning or of learning that is retained well. There is a good deal of evidence, however, to the contrary. The classroom is a place for well-organized arrangements of the conditions of learning, of optimal instruction for each learner. It is not an arena for haphazard and random assignments of learning tasks for which the necessary conditions of learning have not been met.

When the conditions of learning have been provided, learning . . .

LEARNING DISCRIMINATIONS

You will recall that learning *discriminations* means that the learner is able to indicate whether two or more stimulus objects are the same or different. It does not require learners to state why they believe they are the same or different or to describe or explain anything about the objects or their relationships with other stimulus objects. The learner may learn the names of stimulus objects as verbal chains, but this learning is not a prerequisite to being able to indicate whether they are alike or different.

Discrimination means . . .

The main idea involved in learning discriminations is that certain stimuli have certain responses that are more appropriately associated with them than are others. For example, a stimulus consisting of a blue spot is more appropriately associated with the responses "*blue*" or *blue spot*" than, say, "*red*" or "*red square.*" The task for the learner is to be able to keep separate which responses most appropriately go with which stimuli; the student needs to learn to "tell the difference."

A Meaningful Basis for Learning Discriminations

A good illustration of learning discriminations, as defined by Gagné, can be found in Part III of Ellen Reese's film *Behavior Theory in Practice* (1966). In this film a pigeon is taught to "read." Reading, in this instance, is operationally defined as being able to make different responses to different visual stimulus objects, printed words. Through a shaping process using principles of operant conditioning, the pigeon learns to "tell the difference" between different printed words. When the stimulus word "turn" is presented, the pigeon is rewarded with a small bit of food for making a turning response. When "peck" is presented, the pigeon is rewarded for pecking behavior. The pigeon is not rewarded when it fails to discriminate accurately between the two stimulus words. Within a relatively few trials, the pigeon's "reading" behavior is well established. It has learned to tell the difference between the stimulus words and to respond accordingly.

"Pigeon reading" results from . . .

I doubt, however, that the pigeon's "reading" involves any more than simple discrimination as described by Gagné. The words are just visual stimulus objects, each of which controls the occurrence of a specific response and the nonoccurence of others. The discriminations are learned rotely. Perhaps with pigeons this is about all one can expect. (Some investigators, however, including Harlow [1949], have found that chimps can learn to respond to tasks that require the use of concepts. For an interesting review of the research in this one area, see J. Fleming's articles (1973) in *Psychology Today*.)

With human learners we must do better. Yet, the ways in which many of the learners in Mr. Johnson's class attempt their arithmetic and their reading remind me of pigeons responding to stimuli they have learned to discriminate but not really to understand. Beth responds this way when she attempts to add proper fractions, such as $\frac{2}{5} + \frac{7}{10}$. When presented with these stimuli, she has learned that if she makes certain responses, she will get the "right" answer. I ask her to describe for me what she does to solve these problems and why it works for her. Beth does not mind talking with me about how she solves the problem. She just does not have much to say other than, "I don't really know why I do that. It just works if I do it."

Much of Tony's reading is "pigeon reading." He can pronounce the words pretty well but he does not understand many of their meanings. I remember asking him to read to me one day. His word-attack skills are obviously well developed for his grade in school. He reads material smoothly and easily that is beyond his present grade placement. I noticed, however, that his reading voice was flat. I mentioned the noticeable absence of expression and feeling to him and suggested that he try to put more expression into the words. He agreed to give it a try, and, indeed, he did get expression, but it did not occur where it should. Presently, I asked Tony what the matter was. He looked at the floor and in the same instant I was sorry I asked. He had trusted me and I had let him down. You see, he was bluffing and I caught him at it. "It's hard to put expression at the right places when you don't know what the words say," he confessed.

As teachers, you will find it necessary to help your learners learn many types of discriminations. Also, you will want to help your learners form meaningful relationships among the things they learn. Consequently, how you arrange instruction for learning discriminations is very important.

The sort of abuse so often committed when children rotely learn potentially meaningful verbal and motor chains can also occur when learning discriminations. The best way to guard against this happening, of course, is to ensure that your learners have a grasp of any potential meaning of the stimuli you want them to learn to discriminate. Therefore, you should arrange learning experiences that will also help them "know about" the stimuli between which they are learning to tell the difference.

General Conditions

To learn discriminations, the general conditions necessary for all types of learning must be provided. Learners need to (1) know what their final performance should be like, (2) be able to recall the prerequisite motor and verbal chains which they now must learn to discriminate, (3) attend to the task, (4) have feedback about the correctness of their responses, and (5) have reinforcement for appropriate responses.

The general conditions of learning discriminations are . . .

Specific Conditions

The specific conditions of learning discriminations are concerned mainly with practice of sets of motor and verbal chains learned previously. In order to learn to make a particular response to a certain stimulus object and not to make other possible responses to it, the learner especially needs to practice with sets of similar or related verbal or motor chains. The reason is that when more than one chain is learned, confusion tends to occur about which response goes with which stimulus object. The more nearly alike stimulus objects are, the greater the probability that interference will occur in learning and retaining discriminations.

The specific conditions of learning discriminations are . . .

Another point should be mentioned. As a rule, the more meaningful various chains can be made for the learner, the easier they are to learn and the easier they are later to discriminate from other similar or related chains. The potential meaningfulness of chains becomes increasingly important as the number of chains to be discriminated and retained becomes greater. It is easier to discriminate among a large number of potentially meaningful chains than among an equally large number of chains whose content is essentially arbitrary.

TWO RULES OF THUMB

Two rules for learning discriminations are . . . Knowing some of the important characteristics of stimuli relevant to learning discriminations enables us to state the following rules of thumb that are at least relatively so and approximately true: (1) *Make stimuli as distinctive as you can,* and (2) *Make stimuli as meaningful as you can.*

MAKE STIMULI AS DISTINCTIVE AS YOU CAN   This rule applies more to objects or events that are relatively arbitrary than to potentially meaningful material. Learning, discrimination, and retaining relatively arbitrary material is mostly a matter of repetition. Effectiveness can be increased by causing each stimulus to "stand out," to become distinctive or "different" from other stimuli. One good way to do this is to accent the important differences through auditory, visual, or physical means. This use of the senses helps the learner attend to the salient features of stimuli and to disregard less relevant features. In effect, there are fewer things to be learned, discriminated, and retained. Some "for instances" will help illustrate what I am saying.

Traffic control lights are comparatively easy to learn to discriminate because they usually rely on sharply contrasting colors. It is no accident that the colors are as distinctly different as red and green and that they consistently occur in the same relative positions.

Fire alarm bells are quite easy to discriminate from class dismissal bells if the two bells are extremely different in loudness, pitch, or pattern of ringing. Sirens are easily discriminated from other sounds because they are quite unlike other everyday sounds. Guidelines or grids superimposed on paper can be helpful in making discriminations between proper and improper placement and size of written, drawn, or painted responses. It is a useful technique is such tasks as pattern making in sewing, drafting in industrial education, drawing and painting in fine arts, to mention just a few.

When sounds, words, or phrases are used to help make stimuli distinctive, they become meaningful; and the first rule of thumb, *Make stimuli as distinctive as you can,* blends into the second rule of thumb, *Make stimuli as meaningful as you can.* As learners grow older and hence gain in verbal experience, they rely more on verbal prompts and cues in learning and retention. This is probably true for all types of learning including learning discriminations. It should be pointed out, however, that although verbal facility can greatly enhance the efficiency of learning and retention, it can be abused in the sense that one may easily fall into the practice of organizing for instruction as if *all* the conditions for *all* types of learning require *only* verbal experiences. This tendency becomes more and more likely with increased grade level of learners. You will recall that we spoke of this abuse earlier in terms of rotely learning potentially meaningful verbal chains. We will speak of it again.

"To" and "too" are two stimuli that learners often have difficulty discriminating. How would you apply the rule "Make stimuli as distinctive as you can" to these stimuli so that learners can discriminate them accurately and consistently?

MAKE STIMULI AS MEANINGFUL AS YOU CAN   We can think of many examples of how we frequently organize information with sounds, words, and phrases so that it is easily learned and discriminated from other information. Let us see how we add meaning to stimuli to make them easier to discriminate. Notice, in these examples I give, there is a progression of potential meaningfulness as the sounds and words change from those that have only "contrived" meaning to those that have logically or "naturally" meaningful associations with the information to be learned, discriminated, and retained.

"*Every Good Boy Does Fine*" is a mnemonic device that many of us use to discriminate the names of the lines on the treble clef in written music. We recall that E, G, B, D, and F are the names of the lines, not the spaces, because "Fine" rhymes with "line"—"Fine→(line)→Lines." In a similar manner, we discriminate the names of the spaces—F, A, C, and E—from "Face→(space)→Space." Of course, there is no logical association between the substance of the mnemonic devices and the names of lines and spaces. They are contrived verbal chains which have meaning only within themselves. The specific association depends simply on the similar sounds of the words "fine" and "line" and the words "face" and "space."

Rhythmetic jingles, such as "Thirty days has September, April, June, and November," are examples that involve more than contrived meaning. The arrangement of the words is contrived to produce a rhythmic pattern of sounds which tends to be relatively easy to recall. However, the substance of the words has meaningful associations with what is to be learned, discriminated, and recalled. Learners often form these associations on their own, and sometimes their efforts to "make sense" of what are, for them, largely verbal chains of "nonsense" are humorous; for example, youngsters may respond: "Our Father with Art in Heaven, Harold be thy name . . . "; "the Untied States of America . . . "; or "one nation, invisible, with liberty and just us for all."

"Make stimulus objects as meaningful as you can"; there is only one way I know of to accomplish this. It is by providing meaningful experiences for our learners, especially experience with concrete materials relevant to the stimulus objects we want them to learn, to discriminate, and to retain. Many of the children in Mr. Johnson's class have only vague, loosely formed associations with other parts of cognitive structure for the stimulus object "fraction." For some, the word is only a special pattern to be rotely followed when writing numerals called fractions. It is a pattern to be memorized and mechanically manipulated in a certain way when the "big" numeral is "above the line," and in a different way when the "big" numeral is "below the line." Only a few of the children really know the whys of what they do. Their responses when solving problems with fractions remind me of the responses pigeons make when "reading."

Most of these children, however, have meaningful associations for words related to the stimulus word "fraction." To "break into pieces," for example, is a stimulus expression common to their experiences. Therefore, helping them learn meaningfully may be simply a matter of associating "break" with "fracture," and then, with "fraction." It may best be done through the use of concrete materials, for example, by breaking (fracturing) an object such as an old plate or cup, or better yet, a huge bar of chocolate, and then distributing the "fractions" among the "hungry and attentive" learners. With such practice, learners will soon be able to discriminate meaningfully between what is a fraction and what is not.

CHECKPOINT 5-6

1. Following are two potentially meaningful rules of arithmetic that learners often have difficulty discriminating. How would you apply the rule of thumb *"Make stimuli as meaningful as you can"* so that learners would find it relatively easy to discriminate the rules accurately and consistently?

 a. To divide a number by a fraction, invert the fraction and multiply.

 b. To multiply a number by a fraction, do not invert the fraction. Just multiply.

2. At this point, your confidence in your ability to arrange conditions of learning chains and discriminations is (improving, staying the same, decreasing).

Meaning, the Basis of Concept Learning

The basis of concept learning is . . .   The experiences you provide relative to a particular stimulus object should be sufficiently varied so that a learner is able to determine whether other stimulus objects are logically associated with it. Such experience should also provide meaningful bases for determining whether a particular stimulus object is different in some significant way from other stimulus objects or whether it is representative of a class of certain kinds of stimulus objects. Once learners have acquired meaning for stimulus objects or events, they have taken a forward step in their learning. This acquisition of meaning is what is usually meant when it is said that a concept has been learned. A concept is learned (1) when the learner demonstrates that he can *identify* a stimulus object by its general characteristics, and (2) when he can *define* the important characteristics or properties of stimulus objects and the relationships among them. The former is similar to what Gagné (1970, 1974) calls "learning *concrete concepts.*" The latter is what he describes as "learning *defined concepts,*"

With concept learning we experience a type of learning that is difficult to explain in terms of a strictly connectionist interpretation of learning. Obviously, when concepts are learned, something happens within the learner that is more than a simple association between stimuli and responses. Learners now need to begin to "think about" what they are learning. That is, they need to apply, analyze, synthesize, and evaluate information rather than merely to acquire it.

Now that we have learned, and are able to recall, the conditions of learning chains and discriminations, we are ready to direct our attention to the conditions of learning concrete concepts, defined concepts, rules, and higher-order rules. These more cognitive types of learning form the substance of Chapter 6.

You should now return to the goals and objectives for this chapter and see how well you have met them.

MEANING BEFORE PRACTICE

IN PASSING

In the Midwest, a school system allows older students to work on regular building jobs. Recently, the music teacher designed a small building to house an auditorium and several practice rooms. She wrote a paper describing what special needs a music-teaching facility has to have and shared this with the students.

However, even before the foundation was poured, the students were required to interview sound engineers and read technical reports on acoustics. Permits for building, all necessary paper work for state, county, and city requirements had to be handled by the students. They had to read all the law necessary and meet with a local lawyer to be sure they understood the regulations.

For active students this was tiring and boring work, resisting it was natural, but the supervising contractor explained:

"They have to learn all about it, not just bang a hammer. I keep telling those boys that anyone can hammer nails: only a smart carpenter can build something useful. The boys like to tease me by saying 'You'd probably make us study chickens before we could build a chicken-coop!'"

Cynthia Parsons
"Series on Great Teachers"
Christian Science Monitor

1. Suppose you want to teach a friend about the contents of this chapter. (a) List the main ideas that you want this friend to understand; and (b) list the prerequisites for understanding these ideas.

ACTIVITIES

2. Look back through the checkpoints and state the level of performance, according to Bloom's *Taxonomy*, required of you for each item. See if some other student agrees with your decisions.

3. As an individual, small group, or entire class activity, do a task analysis of one of the specific objectives: (a) the learner can describe how to weigh an elephant. (b) the learner can tie her shoes. (c) Given an outline map that shows only the geographical features of an area (without names, cities, boundaries, and so forth), the learner is able to explain where major cities would likely be located.

4. As an individual, small group, or entire class activity, organize the events of instruction so that the conditions of learning one of the following are met: (a) The motor chains relevant to hopping on one foot or tying a shoe. (b) Meaningfully learning the verbal chain: "It is now ten minutes past three o'clock." (c) Learning to discriminate between "sarcasm" and "criticism."

5. Find a learner who has not yet learned to hop on one foot or to tie a shoe, or who does not understand the verbal chain in item 4. Use your organization for instruction in items 3 and 4 to help the learner acquire one of these chains.

6. Just for fun:

Here is a riddle familiar to many learners. See how many "correct" verbal chains (answers) you can make from it by discriminating various possible meanings for the key words. (The key words are in italics.) If you can think of six meanings for each key word, over a thousand "correct" chains will be possible: "What is *black* and *white* and *re(a)d all over?*"

	What is	*black* and	*white* and	*re(a)d*	*all over?*
Possible meanings for key words		*color*	*color*	*read*	*everywhere*
		danger	*fright*	*communism*	*completely*
		profit	*pure*	*embarrassment*	*finished*
		etc.	etc.	etc.	etc.

Possible chains (answers)   A newspaper; a completely frightened and dangerous Communist; a blushing nun; an embarrassed zebra; and so forth.

REFERENCES

Ausubel, D. P. (1963). *The Psychology of Meaningful Verbal Learning.* New York: Grune & Stratton.

Gagné, R. M. (1970). *The Conditions of Learning.* New York: Holt.

—— (1971). *Defining Objectives for Six Varieties of Learning* (a taped presentation). Washington: American Educational Research Association.

—— (1974). *Essentials of Learning for Instruction,* Hinsdale, Ill.: Dryden.

Fleming, J. D. (1973). Field report: state of the apes. *Psychology Today,* **7, 8** (31), 43–46.

—— (1973). The Lucy and Roger talk show, *Psychology Today,* **7, 8** (49), 50.

Harlow, H. F., and M. K. Harlow (1949). Learning to think, *Scientific American,* **181,** 36–39.

Holt, J. (1964). *How Children Fail.* New York: Pitman.

Miller, G. A. (1956). The magical number seven, plus-or-minus two: Some limits on our capacity for processing information, *Psychological Review,* **63** (2), 81–97.

Parsons, C. (1972). To build a chicken coop you should study chickens, *Christian Science Monitor,* Sept.

Reese, E. P. (1966). *Behavior Theory in Practice.* (Film.) New York: Appleton-Century-Crofts.

SUGGESTIONS FOR FURTHER READING

Ashton-Warner, S. (1963). *Teacher.* New York: Simon & Schuster. Sylvia Ashton-Warner, in a warm, human, and yet scholarly way, successfully addresses the concerns of meaningful learning, the use of models, and caring about learners as she describes a language-experience approach to teaching reading meaningfully.

Holt, J. (1964). *How Children Fail.* New York: Pitman. Teachers teach *children* about things and events. Often, however, we forget this and subject matter becomes an end in itself. Knowing about our learners and how they feel about themselves will help us prevent children not only from failing subject matter but also from failing themselves. Holt's little paperback gives many clues about how "to get inside the minds" of your pupils.

—— (1967). *How Children Learn.* New York: Pitman. In *How Children Fail,* Holt gives many glimpses into the minds of children who fail in schools. In *How Children Learn,* he suggests many ideas about how to help keep children from failing. Both books will give you clues about how to "see" children and to keep from losing them.

Stauffer, R. G. (1970). *The Language-Experience Approach to the Teaching of Reading.* New York: Harper & Row. The primary goal of this book is to help teachers ensure that learning to read is a meaningful experience for children. It is a "how to do it" book that transforms a simple idea into practical, everyday suggestions to help children avoid learning to "pigeon read."

LEARNING AND TEACHING CONCEPTS AND RULES

6

The most important day I remember in all my life is the one on which my teacher, Anne Mansfield Sullivan, came to me. . . .

The morning after my teacher came she led me into her room and gave me a doll. . . . When I had played with it a little while, Miss Sullivan slowly spelled into my hand the word "d-o-l-l." I was at once interested in this finger play and tried to imitate it. . . . I did not know that I was spelling a word or even that words existed; I was simply making my fingers go in monkey-like imitation. In the days that followed I learned to spell in this uncomprehending way a great many words. . . . But my teacher had been with me several weeks before I understood that everything has a name.

One day, while I was playing with my new doll, Miss Sullivan put my big rag doll into may lap also, spelled "d-o-l-l" and tried to make me understand that "d-o-l-l" applied to both. Earlier in the day we had had a tussle over the words "m-u-g" and "w-a-t-e-r." Miss Sullivan had tried to impress it upon me that "m-u-g" is *mug* and that "w-a-t-e-r" is *water*, but I persisted in confounding the two. In despair she had dropped the subject for the time, only to renew it at the first opportunity. She brought me my hat, and I knew I was going out into the warm sunshine. This thought, if a wordless sensation may be called a thought, made me hop and skip with pleasure.

We walked down the path to the well-house, attracted by the fragrance of the honeysuckle with which it was covered. Someone was drawing water and my teacher placed my hand under the spout. As the cool stream gushed over one hand she spelled into the other the word "water," first slowly, then rapidly. I stood still, my whole attention fixed upon the motions of her fingers. Suddenly I felt a misty consciousness as of something forgotten—a thrill of returning thought; and somehow the mystery of language was revealed to me. I knew then that "w-a-t-e-r" meant the wonderful cool something that was flowing over my hand. That living word awakened my soul, gave it light, hope, joy, set it free!

I left the well-house eager to learn. Everything had a name, and each name gave birth to a new thought. . . .

I had now the key to all language. . . .

Helen Keller
The Story of My Life

CONTENTS

ONGOING SUMMARY

With Chapter 5 we began the task of finding practical answers to the major question: "How can I help learners learn?" Prerequisite to attending to this question, we tried to answer the major question: "What do I want learners to learn?" And, prerequisite to this question, we examined questions relative to the overall purpose of education: to change human behavior.

We have tried to make sense of a great number of potentially meaningful terms and phrases. We have learned something about cause and effect, beliefs and actions, the relative and approximate nature of truth, taxonomies of goals and objectives, interpretations of learning, task description and task analysis, conditions of learning and the events of instruction, general and specific conditions of learning chains and discriminations, and meaningful and rote learning. With each new chapter, "old" terms have been recalled, expanded, and associated with "new" ones. We are now ready to continue this process.

ADVANCE ORGANIZER

In Chapter 6 we will see that the general conditions of learning are indeed constant for all Gagné's six types of learning. We will also see that the meaningful learning of concepts and rules depends on whether conditions of learning are adequately met.

Three important higher-order rules will become increasingly apparent in Chapter 6. First, although there are many possible approaches to organizing the events of instruction, each approach must ensure that the general and specific conditions of learning are met. To illustrate this, we will learn more about two major approaches to instruction: a discovery approach emphasized by Jerome Bruner and a meaningful reception approach described by David Ausubel. Each of these approaches relies on different instructional techniques and procedures, but both require the same conditions of learning. That is, stated as a higher-order rule, "Conditions of learning are independent of approaches to instruction."

A second higher-order rule that will become apparent as you combine the ideas in Chapter 6 with what you have learned earlier is that learning within a single topic is cumulative, as is learning in general. Consequently, if prerequisites are not meaningfully learned, new learning tasks are not likely to be learned meaningfully. Stated as a higher-order rule: "Learning is cumulative; so is not-learning."

A third higher-order rule we will learn about in Chapter 6 is: "Meaning enhances learning." Subsumed under this higher-order rule are simple rules relative to the general and specific conditions of learning.

In Chapter 6, we will continue to develop the theme that when learners are considered the most important condition of learning, they will attend to learning tasks long enough and well enough to learn them meaningfully.

GOALS AND OBJECTIVES

Cognitive

To become an effective teacher, the learner should be able to apply the conditions of learning to teaching concepts and rules.

KNOWLEDGE LEVEL

Given the following terms or phrases, the learner is able to define them in writing: *rote versus meaningful learning, reception versus discovery learning, problem solving, meaningless verbal chains, concrete concepts, defined concepts, simple and higher-order rules.*

COMPREHENSION LEVEL

1. Given the rule, "Conditions of learning are independent of approaches to learning," the learner is able to explain its meaning.
2. The learner is able to explain with examples how practice is different for learning chains and discriminations and for learning concepts and rules.
3. Given Figure 6-2, the learner is able to interpret it to a friend so that the friend, without looking at the figure, can reproduce it and explain its meaning.

APPLICATION LEVEL

Given a rule such as "heavy things fall" or "plants need nitrogen," the learner is able to complete a task analysis of the rule.

ANALYSIS LEVEL

Given the content of Chapters 5 and 6, the learner is able to analyze it for defined concepts.

SYNTHESIS LEVEL

Given the defined concepts in the analysis-level objective above, the learner is able to link them into higher-order rules of the conditions of learning.

EVALUATION LEVEL

Given the opportunity to review a colleague's lesson plans for a unit of study, the learner is able to judge whether the cognitive and affective objectives are likely to be meaningfully met.

Affective

To become an effective teacher, the learner should be able to practice the rules relative to learning and teaching concepts and rules.

RECEIVING (ATTENDING) LEVEL

The learner is aware that concepts and rules can be memorized rotely or learned meaningfully.

RESPONDING LEVEL

The learner is willing to share with others his ideas about arranging instruction to teach a learner a concept or rule.

VALUING LEVEL

The learner shares his belief about helping children learn meaningfully rather than rotely.

ORGANIZATIONAL LEVEL

The learner forms higher-order rules of thumb relative to his beliefs about the conditions of learning concepts and rules.

CHARACTERIZATION LEVEL

Given the opportunity to learn the material of Chapter 6 meaningfully or rotely, the learner chooses to learn meaningfully.

6 Within human learners there is a constant press toward economy of effort, toward maximizing the efficiency of learning and retention. Without the capability of maximizing such efficiency, learners would face an impossible task. If all things learned and retained had to be acquired and stored as discriminated and isolated motor and verbal chains, the quality and quantity of our learning would be seriously limited. Lyle Bourne, Jr., stated it this way: "If an individual were to utilize fully his capacity for distinguishing between things and were to respond to each event as unique, he would shortly be overcome by the complexity and unpredictability of his environment."[1]

Fortunately, it is not necessary for human learners to respond to each event, to each stimulus object in the environment as if it were unique. They are able to recognize and form logical and natural associations among the various events and objects that make up their experiences. Because of these associations, that is, because they possess potential meaning for each learner, the individual is able to respond to them on the basis of their *common properties* rather than because of their individual characteristics. When this occurs, the learner is said to have classified various events or objects according to some quality or characteristic common to each event or object but not to others. The distinctive quality is known as an *attribute*. It is the attribute or combination of attributes to which learners respond when they respond to a *class* of events or objects, when they respond in terms of *concepts* rather than individual stimuli.

LEARNING CONCEPTS

Learning concepts is essentially a task of learning attributes. It is directed toward the question: "What do all the various events or stimulus objects of a class of events or objects have in common?" As such, learning concepts requires the prerequisite learning of verbal chains and discriminations. In addition, learners must be able to indicate how certain groups of classes or events or stimulus objects are alike. They must show that they understand the bases for classifying various events or objects in some common category, which then usually has a verbal label attached to it. Such a verbal label can be considered a meaningful verbal label for the learner, since it stands for the associations common to various distinctive events or objects which permit them to be classified into a common category. Archer expresses this point of view when he comments that concepts "are meaningful words which label classes of otherwise dissimilar stimuli."[2]

Defining Concept Learning

Here is Paul drawing cartoons instead of "doing his fractions." Mr. Johnson tells me that Paul is able to do some of the manipulations with proper fractions so that he gets the right answer when he tries to reduce them to lowest terms.

---

[1] J. Bourne, Jr. (1966). *Human Conceptual Behavior*. Boston: Allyn and Bacon, p. 2
[2] E. J. Archer (1964). On verbalizations and concepts. In A. W. Melton (ed.), *Categories of Human Learning*. New York: Academic Press, p. 238.

A concept is defined as . . .

"But," Mr. Johnson continues, "I don't think Paul really understands the concept *fraction*. It's all pretty abstract for him."

I find myself wondering what it means to "really understand a concept," even concepts as simple and concrete as classes of familiar objects, such as chairs, tables, paper, chalk, books, boys, and girls. Where does "knowing a concept" begin and end? Does anyone ever learn all of what a concept can mean? That is, does anyone ever acquire all the possible associations between a concept and the stimuli that are potentially related to a class of stimulus objects or events? I think not. Kagan (1971) implies this when he comments that all a child's concepts "become more complex and more differentiated as he grows older."[3] Furthermore, much of the meaning of a concept is *relative* to the context within which it appears. Few if any, concepts have absolute, unchanging meanings. Kagan goes on:[4]

> The child himself is many things at once: he is a boy and the son of his father; he is the smallest child in the family but the largest child in the classroom; he is cleanest when he is in the street but dirtiest when he has just returned from play; he is the heaviest child in the classroom but the lightest person in the family. By working with familiar ideas that the child can grasp easily, the teacher can gradually persuade the child of the important principle that *the quality of an object is relative to its context.*

DeCecco adds: "In the final analysis, however, concepts. . . reside in individuals and are always idiosyncratic."[5]

What we usually mean when we say a concept has been learned is that only certain ones of all the associations possible have been acquired. For example, we say that a boy has learned the concept *chair* when he can look at a collection of objects that he has not seen before, one of which is a chair, and point to the chair. It is a mistake, however, to conclude that pointing to the chair, placed among other non-chair stimulus objects, constitutes all there is to learning the concept *chair*. The ability to identify a chair represents learning only at a knowledge level. The concept *chair*, however, can also be learned by relevant association to its use or function: its style or construction; comparison with near-chairs for some purpose, e.g., comfort, beauty, cost, availability; design for a new type of chair for a particular purpose; value or importance relative to any number of conditions, such as convenience, utility, economics, culture, tradition, and the future.

Concepts are never completely learned because . . .

It is useful to think of learning concepts first as learning attributes common among various stimuli and then learning an ever-expanding and probably infinite array of relationships among attributes not only of a particular concept but also of those which potentially are related to it. This is at the very heart of what I have been referring to as meaningful learning. It is a wise teacher who says to her learners: "Today we are going to learn something about things called chairs. Later, we will learn much more about them."

You will note, as we go from chapter to chapter, that your associations for various concepts—*learning, transfer, cognitive, affective,* and so forth—spiral

---

[3] J. Kagan (1971). *Understanding Children: Behavior, Motives and Thought.* New York: Harcourt Brace Jovanovich, p. 90.

[4] Ibid., p. 91.

[5] J. P. DeCecco (1968). *The Psychology of Learning and Instruction: Educational Psychology.* Englewood Cliffs, N. J.: Prentice-Hall, p. 400.

gradually up and out. They spiral up in the sense that you learn more in depth about these concepts, and out in that you learn more in breadth about these concepts each time they are repeated in a slightly different context. The extent of this spiral effect of "learning about" concepts is probably infinite, especially when you consider that the spiral of one concept can "touch" others and thus become associated in meaning with them. Our job as teachers is essentially to ensure that a learner's "spirals" do in fact "touch" one another, that what is learned is meaningfully associated. Overly simplified, the procedure resembles the spirals in Figure 6-1.

Learning Concrete Concepts

Gagné (1970, 1974) points out that there are several common meanings for the word "concept." He says, however, that its most fundamental meaning should be considered first. Therefore, we should consider first the observable qualities of classes of objects, such as their size, weight, color, shape, or the objects themselves. When we do this, we are referring to what Gagné calls "*concrete concepts, since they can be denoted by pointing to them; in other words, they are concepts by observation.*"[6]

GENERAL CONDITIONS

The conditions necessary for learning concrete concepts are those general conditions of all types of learning and those conditions specific to learning concrete concepts. If I want Paul to learn the concrete concept *fraction*, I must arrange his instruction so that all the general and specific conditions of learning concrete concepts are met. To satisfy the general conditions, I must be sure that Paul

The general conditions of learning concrete concepts are . . .

FIGURE 6-1 **Meaningful associations for concepts spiral up and out, and they touch.**

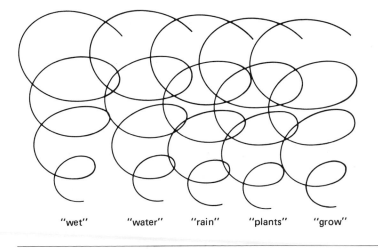

"wet"   "water"   "rain"   "plants"   "grow"

[6] R. M. Gagné (1970). *The Conditions of Learning.* New York: Holt, p. 172.

knows that his final performance will require him to show me that he knows what a fraction is. That is, given various examples of stimulus objects that he has not seen before, some of which are fractions and some of which are not, he will be able to pickout the fractions. If I have done a good job of clarifying the objectives for Paul, he will know that identifying fractions by pointing to them constitutes only the barest beginning of what he will eventually learn about the concept *fraction*.

Once the objective is clearly understood, I must be sure Paul is ready to learn the concept. This means that he has acquired the prerequisites to learning the concept *fraction*. They include verbal chains and discriminations. Paul must be able to say the verbal chain "This is a fraction," when it is appropriate. The verbal chain then needs to be associated with several concrete examples of stimulus objects that are fractions.

The next prerequisite is that Paul must be able to tell the difference between stimulus objects that are fractions and those that are not fractions. At this point, he need not be able to say in what way they are different, only that they are.

As I plan Paul's instruction, I must arrange other general conditions of learning. I must ensure that he attends to the task, that he responds, that he tries. I must make sure that he knows whether his responses are correct, and I must see to it that correct responses are rewarded. I will be pleased with his success and I will show it. Mostly, however, Paul will be reinforced by being successful.

SPECIFIC CONDITIONS

The specific
conditions of learning
concrete concepts
are . . .

The specific conditions of learning concrete concepts are primarily those of (1) reinforced practice with concrete stimulus objects that are representative of the actual range of the concept to be learned, and (2) directing the learner's attention toward the attributes common to the concept and away from those stimuli that are irrelevant to the class of stimulus objects as a whole. The latter is usually accomplished with verbal cues or prompts.

Gagné points out: "The great value of concepts as means for thinking and communicating is the fact that they have *concrete references*. The importance of this characteristic cannot be overemphasized."[7] The concept *fraction* refers to real things or events. This suggests to me that if I want to teach for transfer, that is, to help Paul "learn about" the concept *fraction* in a meaningful way, as opposed to his rotely acquiring essentially meaningless verbal chains, his instruction must include experiences with real fractions. Verbal reference to them will be helpful, but it will not be enough.

Before beginning to help Paul, I must decide what the range of the concept is, and what parts of that possible range will be helpful for Paul to acquire at this time. I must also determine whether the concepts needed to teach the new one are already familiar to Paul, e.g., *whole, break, piece, part*. Once I have done this, I am ready to begin the task of capturing his attention to the learning task.

The real fractions, near-fractions, and not-fractions I have selected will help me make these determinations. They can be seen, smelled, felt, manipulated, broken, torn, tasted, and eaten. That's the nice thing about real stimulus objects. We can experience them in so many "learningful" ways besides just seeing and

---

[7] Ibid., p. 186.

hearing about them, as is the case with the words we use to stand for them.

Let us now see how all these conditions of learning can be converted into what Gagné (1974) calls "delivering the events of instruction." I will demonstrate these events by helping Paul learn about fractions. However, the process used can also apply to teaching a variety of concepts at any grade level, e.g., teaching about elements in high school chemistry, certain tools in auto mechanics, or styles of clothing in home economics.

AN EXAMPLE OF CONCEPT LEARNING

Paul and I are seated at a table. Outside distraction has been reduced as well as I can manage it. A visual barrier has been placed between our table and the rest of the class. On the table are several stimulus objects. They are objects which I hope will be familiar to Paul and which will represent the "something" that I want him to learn today about the concept *fraction*. They also include objects that will provide the beginnings of associations Paul will make with a wider, more complex meaning of the concept as it spirals up and out for him with new experiences over time. I must remember to help Paul to know that today's "learning about" the concept will be only approximately true, and also relative only to those experiences he has had in the past and to those he is about to have now.

The stimulus objects I have gathered are string and scissors, a knife, a rose, a cracker, a fresh apple, a shriveled apple, and a picture of an apple tree laden with apples. I have other exemplars and nonexemplars of the concept *fraction* hidden in a box out of sight. Paul's prospects of being able to "learn by doing" and to "eat the lesson" capture his attention.

Concrete objects help learners by . . .

I know that Paul can already say the word "fraction," so he will not need to learn the verbal chain. He can discriminate between familiar objects that are "wholes" and those that are "less than" or "more than wholes." We need to begin by associating, in close contiguity, the word "fraction" with a variety of appropriate stimulus objects.

I ask Paul to "fracture" the cracker, to *break* it into pieces. He does so. Then, I point to one of the pieces and say, "This is a *fraction* of the whole cracker. It is a *part* of—the whole cracker." Next I point to another piece of the cracker and say, "This is also a *fraction* of the whole cracker. It is a *piece* of—a *part* of—the whole cracker. Next, I point to another piece of the cracker and say, "This is also a *fraction* of the whole cracker." I repeat the sequence by pointing to several other pieces. Then I point to another piece of cracker and ask Paul what it is. He responds by saying that it is a "fraction."

I ask Paul to take the knife and cut the fresh apple into four pieces. When he has done this, I point to a piece of the apple and say, "This is a *fraction* of the whole apple." Pointing to another piece, I ask him what this one is called. He says that it is also a "fraction." Then I fit all the pieces of the apple back together. I say to Paul, "This is the *whole* apple." Then, holding one piece, I say, "This is a fraction of the whole apple. Show me another *fraction* of the whole apple." He is able to do so. As we eat the fractions of the apple, we move on to other examples. It tastes good to learn.

Paul picks up the whole group of four cookies when I ask him to. He needs no coaxing or threatening to attend to this task. I say to him that he now has a *whole set* of four cookies in his hand. I ask him to show me a *fraction* of the whole set.

He breaks a piece from one of the cookies and holds it out. I start to "correct" him, then realize that his response is indeed correct, although it isn't the answer I had in mind. I expected him to hand me one whole cookie. I ask him what one whole cookie could be called in this case. He surprises me by saying that it is also called a "fraction." He decides to put the cookies in his pocket to save for lunch. We continue with another example.

This time, I hold up the rose. It has all its petals, 6 inches of stem and a couple of leaves. I say to Paul, "This is a fraction." He looks at the rose, and then at me and back at the rose. I think he is trying to determine whether this is one of those times when I try to "stretch a point" with him.

Presently, he nods in agreement. I ask him why he hesitated. He says he had to think what a "whole" rose was. He reasoned that the only way the rose I was holding could be a fraction was if I meant that the whole bush—roots, stems, thorns, leaves, and flower—was a whole rose. We never did come to a precise statement defining a whole rose. We did not feel too badly about it, however, when we noted that "lots of concepts are like that." Before we left the rose, we both enjoyed its fragrance, and we concluded that the smell must also be a fraction. I was pleased to move on, since I was afraid Paul might want to know whether the sight and feel of the rose might also be considered fractions. I felt this was beyond the "something about" fractions I was interested in having him learn today. Besides, I did not really know the answer to that question.

Next, I hold up the shriveled apple and ask if this is a "whole" or a "fraction." Before Paul can answer, I show him the picture of the apple tree heavy with apples. He comes through in great style. He answers through a wide smile, "It's a *whole* apple but it's also a *fraction* of an apple tree." It's easy to smile with him. I say, "Notice that this apple is shriveled. Some of the water has evaporated. It's dried up a bit. Is it less of an apple than the crisp one we ate earlier?" (At this point, I wish we had not eaten it. It would be nice to have it here now to make an actual comparison rather than a recalled and abstract one—but lessons do not always unfold the way they are planned.) Paul looks puzzled. He answers, "Yes, it's less, but it's still an apple. Only, some of it is missing." "Then is this a *whole* apple or a *fraction* of an apple?" I continue. Paul begins again. "Well, this apple is a whole apple, but it isn't as much of an apple as the crisp one, so—" (pause). He looks back at the picture of the tree with all its apples and then at me. He still looks puzzled. In his hand (and I think in his mind) the wrinkled apple is being turned over and over. Somehow he feels there must be an association between the concept *fraction*, wrinkled apples, and regular apples. Paul has not made the association yet, but I am sure he will.

I pick up the string and ask Paul to cut a small fraction from it with the scissors. We have set aside the unfinished business of apples and fractions, but not permanently. Paul knows there is "something more" to be discovered here, and he already has a feel for what it is. One day soon, when I ask him about it, he will respond, "cinchy," and of course it will be.

It is no problem for Paul to cut a fraction from the string. I ask him to cut another and this time to make it "equal" to the first one. He goes through a good deal of careful comparison with the first fraction he cut and then finally cuts another. When he holds them up together, they are not quite the same. He offers to "take a fraction off the longer one." I think he knows I am pleased with his verbal response. I am tempted to ask him if he believes it is always possible to remove a fraction from a fraction, but decide that the question might interfere with meeting the objective at hand. We will save it for another time. Paul cuts several fractions from the original string before finally concluding, "It can't quite be done—almost, sometimes, but not exactly."

From the box I have kept out of sight, I produce ten peanuts and place them on the table. He picks up one peanut and says, "This is a fraction."

"Show me another fraction that is the same as, or equal to, that one," I answer. He picks up another peanut and looks at me for confirmation of his response.

"Are you sure they are equal, Paul? This one seems larger than the other one."

Paul looks closely at both peanuts. He exchanges one of them for one of the eight left in the group, then trades again. Pretty soon, he says that many of them are *almost* equal but none are exactly the same. I suggest that maybe there really are no truly equal or identical fractions or wholes; that we just find it handy to pretend there are, since often the difference does not amount to much anyway. He says he will need to think about that for a while.

As the peanuts disappear into his pocket, I take other stimulus objects from the box, some exemplars and some nonexemplars of the concept *fraction*. The "new" objects are a toy car, the leg from an animal cookie, a marble, a piece of broken pencil, a worn eraser, a pin that is bent in two, and approximately one-half a pad of scratch paper. "Show me the fractions, Paul," I begin. He has no difficulty. He even includes the worn eraser as a fraction, saying that it is a fraction because some of it has been used and it's only part of what regular erasers are like. I find myself wondering if he will make the generalization from worn erasers to wrinkled apples.

Not much of this part of the lesson can be eaten, but at this point I do not worry about that. His attention has been captured and he has learned. Anyway, success is a far more reliable reinforcer for learning than apples and peanuts. I have learned this, but more important, I think Paul has too.

THE PROBLEM OF MEANINGFULNESS

It is not easy to know the precise point at which a learner has acquired the "something about" a concept that you want him to learn. For example, how many situations did we actually need for Paul to correctly identify the examples of "new" fractions I had hidden in the box? There probably is no adequate answer for this question. Much depends on the past experiences of the learner and whether what has been learned has been meaningfully acquired. No doubt the most important factor is the learner's ability to use language. The more highly this ability has been developed, the fewer actual situations needed to learn new concepts. For learning concepts, the worth of a cognitive structure made up of words that are rich in associational value cannot be overemphasized, since a meaningfully integrated cognitive structure releases the learner from relying directly on specific concrete stimulus objects. He will then be able to *think* about them in terms of general classes or groups, and in abstraction. That is, he can think and talk meaningfully about classes of objects or events—*concepts*—even in their absence simply through the use of their verbal referents.

Language facility aids concept learning because . . .

Another advantage to the overall economy of learning effort that accrues from concepts is that of *generalizability*. It is very different from the main characteristic of discrimination learning. In learning discriminations, it is important to attend to specific differences of stimulus objects or events that enable us to tell them apart. Important in concept learning is attending to the *general* similarities among stimulus objects or events in order to *group* them on the basis of *common* attributes. Once the common attributes have been learned for the specific exemplars used in learning a concept, they can be extended to new ones. For example, Mark Twain once said that "if just once a cat accidently sits on a hot stove, he will never sit on one again, and for that matter, he won't sit on a cold one again, either!"

As Mark Twain's observation suggests, generalization occurs without further specific practice. Once Paul has acquired the concept fraction through his experiences with crackers, cookies, string, apples, and so on, he can, without further learning, generalize this capability to new stimulus situations. He can point to and produce "fractions" in a wide variety of situations. Furthermore, because he has also acquired a verbal referent for what is meant by parts of wholes, he now can think, talk, and learn more about the concept *fraction* in the absence of concrete exemplars of the concept. Through learning concepts he is freed from control by stimuli that are specific and that must be physically present. Note, however, that discrimination learning is still of great importance, since the learner must be able to determine when a stimulus object is, or is not, an exemplar of a particular concept. The ability to generalize appropriately relies heavily on the ability to make accurate discriminations and on the extent of relevant past experience. This fact became especially meaningful for me while teaching preschool Indian children in an isolated fishing village on Vancouver Island one summer. I had asked a small girl to arrange four pictures of an apple so that they would show a progression of its being eaten. The pictures were (1) whole apple, (2) apple minus one bite, (3) apple half-eaten, and (4) the core. Her arrangement was correct and she could tell the story about what had happened to the apple. When I asked her what was left when the apple had been eaten, she answered, "The bones."

Verbal instruction is sufficient when . . .   The importance of verbal facility for learning concepts raises an important question for teaching: "Can concepts be learned meaningfully through instruction that is completely verbal?" Could Paul have gained the meaning of the concept *fraction* without experiencing the concrete objects I provided? The answer is, "Yes—if, *if* he had already learned a wide variety of such concepts as apple, cracker, cookie, and string, as well as all those concepts that are a part of the verbal instruction itself, e.g., break, fracture, part, piece, whole, and less than." A further "if" relates to whether, in his previous learning, he had experienced concrete referents of these concepts in meaningful associations as opposed to rotely learned verbal chains. *If* all these conditions are met, learning the concept *fraction* can be as simple a matter as being told: "A fraction is a quantity less than a whole; it can also mean an act of breaking or dividing."

It is obviously unwise to rely completely on verbal instruction for teaching concepts, since they can be learned as meaningless and useless verbal chains. The probability of this danger is more likely with very young learners than with highly verbal adults, although it can be a problem when any learner is trying to learn a new concept. We will learn more about this in Chapter 11 and in the next section about learning defined concepts.

Suppose you want learners to learn the concrete concept *triangle*:

1. What exemplars and nonexemplars can you use?

2. Which attributes will you help your learners attend to? Which ones are irrelevant?

3. How can you make the relevant attributes distinctive?

Did you try to (memorize, understand) the material about learning concepts?

Learning Defined Concepts

Concepts that cannot be pointed to or experienced directly are known as *defined concepts*. You will recall, from Chapter 4, that they are abstract in nature and that they usually require verbal definition. Evidence that a defined concept has been learned must include a demonstration or illustration of the meaning of the concept through the use of words or actions, or both. Pointing to or picking out certain stimulus objects is not sufficient.

Whereas the dimensions of concrete concepts are usually physical attributes of objects that learners can experience directly, defined concepts are usually not

Examples of defined concepts are . . .

FIGURE 6-2   **Some examples of concrete and defined concepts.**

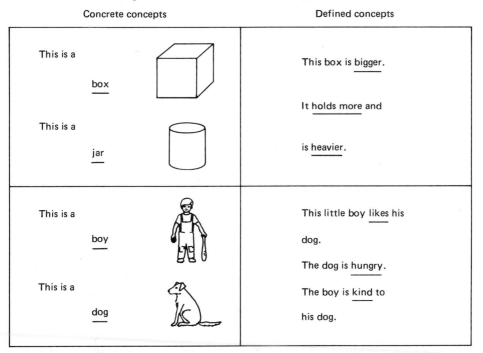

Concrete concepts	Defined concepts
This is a box This is a jar	This box is bigger. It holds more and is heavier.
This is a boy This is a dog	This little boy likes his dog. The dog is hungry. The boy is kind to his dog.

directly available to our senses. Typically, their dimensions refer to some relationship between concepts themselves, often concrete concepts. Consequently, defined concepts tend to be abstract because the meaning of a relationship is difficult to describe other than through verbal definition, illustration, or demonstration. Figure 6-2 shows some examples of typical concrete and defined concepts. Notice that the discrimination of the two types of concepts is enhanced by placing examples of them side by side.

COMBINING CONNECTIONIST AND
COGNITIVE INTERPRETATIONS OF LEARNING

Learning defined concepts is obviously more complex than learning concrete concepts, discriminations, or chains. Learning defined concepts involves more than forming connections between specific stimuli and responses. Some inner, purposeful activity also seems to occur that results in new arrangements of thought patterns. Specific information becomes rearranged into new relationships. Sometimes this rearrangement appears to be an outcome of deliberate thinking or reasoning. At other times the rearrangement occurs intuitively as a spontaneous insight, an "Ah-ha!"

You will recall from Chapter 4 that we talked about two major interpretations of learning—connectionist and cognitive. Each interpretation contributes to our understanding of human learning, but neither interpretation adequately accounts for all types of learning that take place in schools. This has been Gagné's belief, and it is a continuing theme of this book: "It is usually more useful for teachers to combine the best from several points of view than to choose among them."

A connectionist interpretation of learning provides an adequate account of learning individual links of motor and verbal chains and of hooking the links together into a total performance. Guided and reinforced practice with the specific stimuli and responses causes the chains to be learned and retained.

An explanation of discrimination learning is possible within a connectionist interpretation of learning when practice is differentially reinforced; that is, when a learner gains reinforcement for responding in a particular way to a stimulus but not for responding in other ways. You will recall that this is how Skinner shaped the operant behavior of experimental animals in his laboratory.

With concept learning, even the learning of concrete concepts, a strictly connectionist interpretation of learning becomes inadequate. When the exemplars of a particular concept differ markedly in their important physical characteristics, it becomes difficult to account for the extension of the concept to physically different exemplars solely on the basis of stimulus generalization.

Combining cognitive and connectionist interpretations of learning means . . . When we examine the conditions of learning defined concepts, we are even further removed from a strictly connectionist interpretation of learning. The learner obviously "thinks about" what she or he is learning. However, it is important to remember that, even though a connectionist interpretation of learning may be inadequate to account for all that happens when concepts are learned, it does provide a useful interpretation of how the prerequisites for concept learning— chains and discriminations—are learned. The point is that, beginning with the learning of concepts, a cognitive interpretation adds to our understanding of how more complex learning occurs. As the types of learning become

more complex, connectionist and cognitive interpretations of learning complement one another.

Learning a defined concept goes beyond simple discrimination, identity, and
labeling. Learners must increasingly look for the *meaning* of a concept more in
terms of its context and less in terms of absolutes. They must come to expect that
meaning itself varies, that it is conditional.

A couple of examples will help clarify what I am saying. Defined concepts,
such as *long, rough, heavy, honest,* and *above,* are meaningful only in a relative
or comparative sense. Their meaning derives from the relationship between stimulus objects or events. "Long" makes sense only when objects or events are compared. What is long in one situation is not long in another. Some objects are
"heavier" than others. No object is absolutely "heavy" or "above." No event is
absolutely "honest."

GENERAL CONDITIONS

The conditions for learning defined concepts must be arranged carefully to ensure that they become truly meaningful parts of cognitive structure. Because
learning defined concepts relies heavily on verbal instruction and since their
meaning derives from relationships between concepts, it is essential that
prerequisite concepts have been meaningfully learned. This is one of the most
important general conditions of learning defined concepts. And it is the one that
is the most likely to be neglected in classroom learning at all educational levels.
Frequently, learners are given verbal instruction that uses concepts for which
they have little or no meaningful referents. Jerome Kagan's opening paragraph to
the chapter on thought in his *Understanding Children* (1971) gives vivid but sad
testimony to the possible outcomes of verbal instruction that proceeds on the
faulty assumption that learners have meaningful associations for the words being
used:[8]

The general conditions of learning defined concepts are . . .

> A nine-year-old listens carefully as the teacher talks about the ancient Egyptian
> practice of placing dead pharaohs in large pyramids, but he is continually confused
> because every third sentence contains a word he does not understand. First it is
> "pyramid," then "mummy," then "Nile," then "desert." He eventually turns his
> attention to the scene outside the window, for he has lost the thread of the story. The
> teacher completes the presentation and asks the class to estimate how long it might
> take to build a pyramid. One child imagines thousands of Egyptian slaves dragging
> large pieces of stone to the site, intuitively judges that the task would take a long
> time, and offers the estimate of three years. A second child is completely at sea; no
> image comes to mind, and with no basis on which to make a guess, he sits quietly.
> When the teacher asks him directly he murmurs weakly, "I don't know," and upon
> prodding nervously whispers, "A month?"
>
> Although a child may be highly motivated to learn facts or to solve new
> problems, motivation is not sufficient. He must also have prior knowledge.

The defined concepts of *time* and *build* are meaningless for the second child
in this example. They are relative concepts that can have meaning only in terms
of meaningful relationships among the prerequisite concepts *pyramid, mummy,
Nile,* and so on. The child may rotely learn the verbal chain, "It took years to

---

[8] J. Kagan (1971). Op. cit., p. 81.

build the pyramids." However, that chain will remain in his cognitive structure only temporarily, and only as an isolated, sterile bit of information. It will not transfer.

There are other general conditions of learning defined concepts in addition to ensuring that prerequisite concepts, discriminations, and chains have been learned and can be recalled. The learner needs to know what the final performance should be like. She needs to know that she must be able to provide a verbal definition of the concept being learned, and to illustrate or demonstrate her understanding of it. Executing a simple motor or verbal chain, e.g., pointing to an object, or reeling off a rotely memorized verbal definition will not do.

As teachers, we must capture our learners attention to the task at hand. We must cause them to become actively involved, to think about the concept being learned. We must direct their attention to the relative and comparative qualities of the stimulus objects, events, and context in which they occur.

As our learners learn about a defined concept, they need to get feedback that lets them know how they are doing. Furthermore, correct responses need to be reinforced; learners need to be successful.

SPECIFIC CONDITIONS

Outstanding among the specific conditions of learning defined concepts is a variety of positive and negative instances of the concept being learned. Practice in learning defined concepts seems to have the function of helping the learner discriminate between relevant and irrelevant attributes of the concept. Practice does not seem to be important in the sense of strengthening connections between specific stimuli and specific responses, as it apparently does in learning chains and discriminations. As a consequence of varied practice, the learner is able to establish some basis for analyzing situations for the presence or absence of the concept. The basis for such analysis is probably verbal statements that the learner synthesizes as the concept is being learned, when the "pieces" begin to come together in a new and meaningful way: "Oh! I see; 'long' means. . . ." Or, "I get it! A 'chemical reaction' is . . . , whereas a 'physical reaction' is. . . ."

No one knows exactly what happens within a learner when concepts are being learned, but several people have made educated guesses. Some researchers believe that positive and negative examples of the concept may be used to (1) formulate and test hypotheses about the parameters of meaning of the concept, or (2) make appropriate discriminations and generalizations relative to the development of the range of meaning for the concept. Some psychologists disagree with these two views. They argue that formulating and testing hypotheses rest on the ability to make discriminations and generalizations. There is some consensus that the use of both positive and negative examples is a necessary condition of learning concepts, especially defined concepts.

The specific conditions of learning defined concepts are . . .

At this point, we should be able to state several specific conditions of learning defined concepts. You will note a close similarity between the specific conditions of learning defined concepts and learning concrete concepts. Read the next six items, then reread the account of our session with Paul. You will find that all six conditions are reflected in the events of his instruction.

1. Practice with positive and negative examples must be provided.
2. Positive and negative examples should be presented simultaneously. Re-

member, discrimination is easier when stimuli are presented in close contiguity, and less interference occurs when the learner need not rely on remembering specific characteristics of objects or events in order to discriminate among them.

3. Positive and negative examples should be varied enough so that they present the learner with the full range of the "things about" the concept you want the student to learn at this time. They should also be varied enough to form meaningful links with the "something more" that the student will learn about the concept at a later time. This is often called "teaching for positive transfer."

4. All examples of the concept should illustrate or demonstrate clearly its relevant attributes. Examples that contain a great deal of distracting or irrelevant information should not be used in the early stages of learning about the concept. If relevant examples are not immediately available, you should try to control for irrelevant information (Trabasso, 1968). You can do this through such devices as underlining; using bold or different print, different colors, arrows, and boxes; pointing to relevant information or blocking out irrelevant stimuli; putting emphasis in the voice or changing pace by adding pauses; physically assisting the movements of the learner; and giving verbal instruction that uses directives such as "Notice this," "Look here," "Disregard the. . . ," and "Pay attention to. . . ."

5. Positive and negative examples of the concept should already be meaningful to the learner. As a rule of thumb: *Begin with the familiar and concrete; proceed to the unfamiliar and abstract.*

6. Practice with positive and negative examples of the concept should closely pair verbal instruction with physical actions, illustrations, or demonstration that reflect the meaning of the concept. The learner should *do* the action in addition to hearing, watching, or reading about it.

RECEPTION AND DISCOVERY LEARNING

There are many ways of organizing the events of instruction so that the general and specific conditions of learning defined concepts are met. How best to organize the events of instruction, however, is an issue for which there is not complete agreement. Difference of opinion tends to polarize around two main approaches: (1) reception learning, and (2) discovery learning. Neither can be described precisely. Defined roughly, *reception learning* is an organization of the events of instruction that relies primarily on the teacher or on resource materials to instruct the learner—to direct his attention, form relationships for him, select information for him, and even tell him answers—at each step of the learning sequence. *Discovery learning* organizes the events of instruction with relatively less apparent teacher direction. This organization causes learners to form their own intuitive guesses or insights about objects, events, or problem situations; to discover ideas for themselves.

Reception learning means . . .

Discovery learning means . . .

Learning through lectures is usually receptive in nature. So also is programmed instruction. Tutorials, laboratory sessions, and discussion groups usually form the instructional modes for a discovery approach. There are many pros and cons about these two major approaches to organizing for complex types of learning. However, each approach, to be effective, must ensure that all the conditions of learning are met.

As an example of how a highly structured program of concept learning based on a meaningful reception approach can provide all the conditions of learning defined concepts, let us look at the Bereiter and Engelmann (1966) language program for deprived preschool children. Note, also, that I am using a meaningful reception approach to help you learn about defined concepts. In a later section we will see how a discovery approach works.

SOME EXAMPLES OF RECEPTION LEARNING   The Bereiter and Engelmann program, as you will note in the excerpts that follow, meets all the conditions of learning defined concepts. Bereiter and Engelmann refer to defined concepts as "second-order statements." Here they are talking about their program:[9]

> In the program . . . the children are learning new concepts—new ways of organizing experience or relating one experience to another. One cannot expose the child to a brief demonstration of the concept *long* and expect him to conclude, either consciously or unconsciously: "I get it. It means. . . ." For the typical deprived child, there is no way of completing the statement "It means. . . ." Demonstrations, therefore, play a much more vital role than they do in foreign-language learning. They must be chosen and used with great care, always being closely wedded to the language drill. The child is not merely learning how to express a concept in a new language or dialect. He is learning the concept through learning how to make the appropriate statements about illustrations and concrete objects.

Bereiter and Engelmann continue with an explanation of the progression in language abstraction from statements that *identify* to those that *describe*. In their program they provide specific directions for the teacher to use.

Prepositions can be considered defined concepts since they are *relational* words. That is, they convey a relationship between two or more concepts. In the same book, Bereiter and Engelmann describe in detail the organization for teaching prepositions in their program of language development. You will find all our conditions of learning defined concepts in the excerpt from their program presented in Table 6-1.

In your role as a teacher, you will need to teach many defined concepts. You will also need to help learners both combine concepts into simple rules or prin-

---

[9] C. Bereiter and S. Engelmann (1966). *Teaching Disadvantaged Children in the Preschool.* Englewood Cliffs, N. J.: Prentice-Hall, p. 139.

TABLE 6-1   Learning prepositions is learning defined concepts*

Through statements about position, the children learn to describe an object by locating it in relation to other things in its surroundings. The prepositional statement is similar in form to the other second-order prepositional statements. "This ____ is ____," with the first blank filled in with the name of a familiar object (This *chair* is ____) and the second filled in with a positional notation (This chair is *under the table*). . . .

  1. First, introduce the prepositions *on, over,* and *under* . . .
  2. Use three objects to demonstrate the idea of position—a chair, a book, and a table. Use only two of them (book and table) in the first part of the demonstration. After each object is identified and described in all of the detail that the children understand (This is a book; this book is red), place the book on the table and ask the positional question (which is new). "*Where* is the book? . . . The book is *on* the table." Ask the children to repeat the statement; then introduce the various *not* statements as answers to various positional questions. "Is this book *over* the table? . . . No, the book *is not* over the table.

Is the book *under* the table? . . . No, the book *is not* under the table. The book is *on* the table." The book is then moved to a position over the table. "Is the book *on* the table now? . . . No, the book is not on the table now. The book is *over* the table." Repeat the procedure with the book positioned under the table. Repeat the entire demonstration with the chair in place of the book (to make the point that positional references are not limited to books and tables).

3. After the initial demonstration, give the children practice in carrying out instructions, such as "Put your hand on the table." As soon as the children carry out the action, ask, "*Where* is your hand?" (or "Where is this hand?") Follow with questions that lead to *not* statements. All members of the study group can become involved in a variation of this task, the hand-piling task. Instruct one child to put his hand on the table. Ask the *where* question and answer it. "Tyrone's hand is on the table." Another child is required to put his hand on the first child's hand, and he is asked the *where* question. "Mary's hand is on Tyrone's hand." Continue until all the children have hands in the pile. To unpile, the teacher can introduce the idea of *off*. "Tommy, take your hand off."

4. Play positional games in which the emphasis is on statement production. Whisper instructions to a child. "Go sit *under* the table." With eyes closed, tell the other members of the class, "Now, I can't see where Harold is, so you'll have to tell me *where* he is. Don't point, because I can't see. Tell me about Harold. Harold is *where*?" A child can often be prompted by being presented with preposterous possibilities. "Tommy, you tell me where Harold is. Is he standing in the middle of the street? . . . Is he flying through the air? . . . Where is he?" Acknowledge correct answers, such as "He's over there," "He's here in the room," etc.

5. Introduce the other prepositions in a straightforward manner after *on, over,* and *under* have been mastered. The other positional concepts that should be taught are *in, in front of, in back of,* and *between.*

(*a*) A container should be introduced to demonstrate *in* and *not in.* After the initial demonstrations, tasks involving *in* can be created around doghouses, buildings, and pictures in books. "Is this man in the house? . . . Yes, he is in the house."

(*b*) Before *in front of* and *in back of* are presented, point out that buildings have a front and a back. A picture of a doghouse illustrates the point nicely. "See this door? This is the front of the doghouse." Questions about *in front of* and *in back of* can be asked about illustrations in books. If there is a picture of a house, present such questions as "Is the boy in front of the house? . . . No. Can you show me where he would be standing if he were in front of the house? . . . Good." Later, the idea of *in back of* and *in front of* can be extended to objects that do not have an identifiable front or back. . . .

6. Introduce plural prepositional statements as part of each of the tasks described above. After the children have mastered *on, over,* and *under,* freely introduce plurals, for example, by placing two hands instead of one hand on the table. "Where are the hands? . . . The hands are on the table."

7. After the children become facile in handling prepositions, ask them to make up *not* statements. Place an object on the table and ask the children to produce the appropriate statement. "The eraser is on the table." Next, ask them to "Tell me where the eraser is *not*. The eraser is not where?" "Creative" answers should be praised. "Come on, give me some silly ones, like 'The eraser is not in the closet.'" Through absurdly obvious examples of this kind, the fundamental assumptions about position are taught, and the children gain an appreciation of the various elements in a statement that can change.

8. Introduce multiple preposition statements. Point out that the eraser can be on the chair and in the room and in the school and in the city. Three or four objects can be positioned so that a variety of statements are possible. For instance, the book may be on the floor, under the table, and next to the eraser.

---

* C. Bereiter and S. Engelmann (1966). *Teaching Disadvantaged Children in the Preschool.* Englewood Cliffs, N.J.: Prentice-Hall, pp. 159–161.

ciples, and combine simple rules into higher-order rules as they solve problems of many kinds. You have just "learned about" the well-known Bereiter and Engelmann application of a *reception learning* approach to a complex learning task. Now I will try to illustrate how organization of the events of instruction can ensure that the conditions of learning rules are met through a discovery approach to learning. We will return to Mr. Johnson's class for the concrete examples necessary to make our learning meaningful.

CHECKPOINT 6-2

1. After reading the excerpts from the language program by Bereiter and Engelmann, outline specific instructions a teacher might follow, using a reception learning approach, to help a learner acquire the defined concepts *smooth* and *between*. Bereiter and Engelmann's specific directives for each of these concepts are given in the Appendix.

2. Did you talk with another person about how you would arrange instruction to help a learner acquire the concepts *smooth* and *between*? Yes_____ No_____

LEARNING RULES

As I move about Mr. Johnson's classroom during an arithmetic session, trying to help learners with their assignment, I am amazed by their inability to perform simple estimates with numbers. Mr. Johnson tells me that most of the children "just don't seem to be able to apply the rule for estimating even though they are able to explain generally that 'to estimate' means 'to guess'." He asks if I would teach a lesson on estimation to the class.

The instructional objectives we decide on are these: (1) The learners will be able to state a rule for estimation, and (2) the learners will be able to apply their rule for estimation accurately to the task of division of numbers.

I ask Mr. Johnson to group the children for me on the basis of those who know the rule and those who do not. He agrees to do so, and he will plan to go to the playground for a physical education activity on Tuesday with the children who already know about estimating with numbers while I work with those children who need further instruction.

A rule is learned when . . . As I prepare for the lesson, I try to remember that my objective is to help these learners gain what Gagné (1970, 1974) calls "rule-governed behavior," that is, to be able to respond to classes of stimuli with classes of responses. I want these learners to be able to respond to *any* situation that involves the defined concept *division* by being able to estimate *any* specific characteristic. Since they are currently learning about fractions, I should try to organize instruction so that what they learn about rules of estimation will transfer positively to problem-solving tasks such as reducing proper fractions to lowest terms, finding common denominators, and changing improper fractions. More important than learning about rules of estimation relative to arithmetic, however, I want these learners to learn about rules of estimation relative to people—to what we do with one another—rules that are based on mutual trust and caring rather than fear. I must not forget affective objectives.

Learning Simple Rules

A week has passed, and here we are ready to begin the lesson about estimation. I have decided to try a discovery approach. What I hope to achieve with each learner is something like this: He will make the insight, "Ahha! I see, when I estimate with numbers, the rule is to make a really close guess, without actually figuring it out, about the largest number of groups of some size that there are in a certain larger number." And the students will be able to demonstrate that they can apply the rule.

Throughout the next section, we will ask learners many questions. Evidence suggests that asking questions (1) before content is presented, (2) within the content, and (3) following the content facilitates learning (Bull, 1973). It is believed that questions direct and focus a learner's attention to the most relevant parts of learning tasks. Questions help keep learners "thinking about" what they are learning. Questions keep them involved.

DISCOVERING THE GENERAL
AND SPECIFIC CONDITIONS

I'm always a bit apprehensive when I become unafraid enough to share with others what I actually do in a classroom with learners. I believe the reason is that I am not always sure that what I am doing is consistent with what I say I am doing or, for that matter, with what I recommend you should do. Looking now at the learners waiting to begin our lesson, I realize that many of them are also a bit afraid, afraid that I might hurt them, especially if I become overly concerned about teaching arithmetic and forget about teaching children.

Even though I will use a discovery approach today, I must be sure my organization of the events of instruction provides all the necessary conditions, general and specific, of learning rules. If I have accomplished this, at the end of the lesson you should be able to describe what learners are able to do when they have learned a simple rule, and to state the conditions necessary for learning a simple rule. You should be able to do this without being told what to say. You should be able to infer, or to discover, what is meant by the term "learning rules" and what conditions are necessary for learning them. We can check on our performance at the end of the lesson.

AN EXAMPLE OF DISCOVERY LEARNING   I do not need to wait long for the learners' attention. They know from past experiences that I usually have something that is different, fun, tasty, or at times puzzling in the large paper bag I often bring along to class. There it is, sitting on the front table in full view of all fifteen pupils. I ask if anyone has a guess about what may be inside the bag today. Paul's hand is the first one up. So is his smile.

"Is it crackers?" he grins.

I think he is generalizing from our session about fractions. I smile too. It feels good to know that he remembers. "That's close," I reply. "Anyone else have a guess?" About a dozen hands are now up. Karen cannot quite make up her mind whether to get involved or not. When she notices me looking at her, I think I see a flicker of interest, and since it occurs so rarely for Karen, I dare not pass her by. "Do you have a guess, Karen?"

"Cookies," she answers, in such a matter-of-fact, positively certain way that I feel somewhat foolish for having asked. She must have been listening when Paul and I were working on fractions.

"That's right—cookies! Now that everyone knows there are at least cookies in the bag, can you estimate how many there may be?" I hurry to add the verbal cues: "You know about how big a cookie is, you can see how big the bag is, and you can see also that it's not completely full." I do not quite know how to respond to Karen, but somehow I feel that it is important for her to become involved. I think she is actually afraid of me, of being wrong, of being considered stupid—although her apprehension certainly does not show in her manner nor in her voice.

"Ten thousand," she replies flatly and firmly.

I search her face for a clue as to her intent, but I can find none. Several children begin to giggle. Greg says that the whole room wouldn't hold 10,000 cookies. Karen does not seem to hear. She just sits quietly and looks at me coldly.

"Do you really believe there could be 10,000 cookies in this bag, Karen?" I ask her.

"Yeah, I do! We don't know how big each cookie is just because you say we do. For all we know, they could be the size of thumbtacks." Several others nod in agreement.

"How would it be if I showed you what one cookie looks like? Would that help you make a better guess—a better *estimate*?" I ask the class. I notice that Karen nods in agreement, as do the other pupils.

"All right, this is what the cookies look like." I hold one up. "Now, Karen, how many do you *estimate* there are in the bag?"

"Fifty," she answers quickly. Something in the speed of her response and tone of voice tells me she has arrived at that number some time earlier. She smiles slightly. I manage to do the same even though it hurts a little. We both know she has made her point. She is right, of course, and she *is* involved.

Several other estimates are made. They range from as few as 15 to as many as 107. Mostly, the estimates cluster around 50. I think this makes Karen feel good about her estimate.

"What else do you guess may be in the bag?" I continue. The children ask me to shake it. It's easier to make a good guess if you have a clue. Shaking the bag results in sharp clicking sounds that give away the fact that I have brought along the familiar box of small plastic discs, (chips) that we have used before. I have one other item in the bag today. It does not rattle or occupy much space. Furthermore, it is something we have not worked with before—ten ropes of licorice. Each rope is approximately $\frac{1}{4}$ inch in diameter and 2 feet long. No one is able to guess this item. As I reveal the licorice, David wants to know, "What are we going to do with that?" I think I have found something that will hold his attention. The cookies, chips, and licorice are all placed on the table.

"Today, I want to help you learn two things. The first is something about the meaning of the words "to estimate." I want you to be able to explain what the words mean by telling me a rule I can follow if I want "to estimate." The second thing I want you to learn is to use your rule "to estimate" when you do division with numbers."

Earlier, I have written two objectives on the chalkboard and then unrolled a map to cover them. Now, I roll the map back and ask the children to look at the objectives. We read them together. It is important that they know what we are trying to accomplish.

The cookies, chips, and licorice are placed back in the bag. I begin with the verbal instruction, "Please look at the cookies I am again placing on the table." I have arranged the cookies (actually they are animal cookies) in five piles. In the first pile there are three cookies; in the second, fourteen; fifteen are in the third, sixteen in the fourth, and about fifty in the fifth pile.

"Look around the room. Try to get in your mind, without actually counting, about how many pupils are in here." Everyone looks around the room. Even Karen looks part way around.

"Now look at these five piles of cookies. On the piece of paper I have given you, write the number of the pile, 1, 2, 3, 4, or 5, that you *guess* has the correct number of cookies in it so that each pupil in here can have one cookie each, with no cookies left over."

The children glance back and forth from the piles of cookies to the pupils in the room. Ricky has already written his guess. I am surprised—so often I've heard him say, "I'm not doing this!" I see that now, while he waits for others to decide, he is busy trying to verify his guess. He has already counted the fifteen pupils in the room. When he notices me watching him trying to count the cookies in the third or fourth pile, he immediately looks away. In a few seconds he checks back with me. Children who believe they have been "caught" misbehaving always do this. When our eyes meet again, I try to send him a nonverbal message that says, "Don't feel badly. I'm glad you're involved." I think he understands.

The guesses are pretty evenly distributed among piles 2, 3, and 4. I ask Ricky if he can think of a way to check for the best estimate. I think he will reply; "Count the kids and count the cookies in each pile." He suggests, however, that he can take each pile of cookies and distribute them to the pupils present. The best estimate will be the pile that comes closest to providing exactly one cookie for each pupil. The class agrees that his way is better than mine. Dan adds that if any pile comes out "short," Ricky can make up the deficiency from the abundance of cookies in pile 5. It works out smoothly, and I am once again indebted to the basic wisdom of Robert Cullum (1967), who said in his book, *Push Back the Desks*, "Don't be afraid to be a beginner with your students."

As we eat our cookies and talk about the differences between "just guessing" and "estimating," I put away the leftover cookies and place the ten ropes of licorice on the table in even, parallel rows. I ask the pupils to write on their papers how many inches long they *estimate* the ropes to be. The estimates range from 15 to 36 inches. Most are approximately 24 inches. When I hold a yardstick so that everyone can see it and the ropes of licorice at the same time, the estimates cluster nearer and nearer to 24. Debra wants to know if it is "cheating" to change her estimate after seeing the yardstick and the licorice together. David volunteers, "The more you actually know about something, the easier it is to make a good estimate about it." He also volunteers the estimate that the ten ropes of licorice are enough so that everyone in the room can have "almost a whole one." I pretend not to hear his last comment and continue by asking the pupils to write on their papers the number of ropes of licorice they *estimate* it would take to reach completely around the outside edge of the table top. The table top has a perimeter of about 18 feet.

Debra wants to use the yardstick to measure the edge, but I remind the children that what we want to learn is just to estimate as closely as we can without actually measuring. When she asks if measuring isn't "really really" just an estimate itself, I get that feeling teachers have when a learner has made a great insight that was not intended for the present lesson. I tell her that she is certainly right and that her point is one we will want everyone to understand before we leave the topic of estimation. To remind us of the point, I ask Debra to make a brief note on the side board. We will return to her insight. For now, I explain that it is often helpful to make approximate estimates without the use of measuring tools, and that this is what we are trying to do now.

While Debra is at the board, I ask if she will tabulate each pupil's estimate. Greg offers to read his first. He estimates that it will take all ten ropes. I wonder if he really has tried to make an estimate or whether he figures that ten must be the correct answer since ten is the number of ropes I brought. So many of these children have learned the survival value of being able to outguess the teacher rather than attending to the important clues within the learning tasks themselves.

Debra asks for each pupil's estimate. Melinda is the tenth person to be asked. Each of the first nine estimates has been either eight, nine, or ten. When Melinda is asked her estimate, she whispers, "Eight." Her hand covers what she has written on her paper. Presently, as other estimates are given and recorded, Melinda quietly and privately erases her paper and writes "Eight." She checks to see if she has been observed. I look away, feeling that I have somehow taken advantage of her. Why must she feel so bad for being "wrong"? Why must she be so careful to keep others from finding out that she does not know?

When all estimates are recorded, I notice that no estimate is less than seven or greater than ten. As I move from the back of the room to where Debra has written the estimates, I go by Melinda's desk. I ask if she will help me verify the estimates. She hesitates for an instant, then, without lifting her hand from the paper where her estimate is hidden, she crumples the paper and follows me to the table. She gets rid of the evidence of her ignorance as she passes the wastebasket. I find myself wondering what her original estimate was. After school, when I am alone, I can remove her crumpled paper from the wastebasket and have a look. Perhaps she did not erase cleanly. I do not like that though very much, and besides, the number she wrote is not the point. The point is that she was afraid of being hurt for not knowing. I decide to let it be for now, but I will remember what I have just learned about her and will try to find a way to help.

Melinda and I measure the outer edge of the table top by laying the ropes of licorice end to end all the way around it. We report that nine ropes is the "best" estimate. Somehow I sense that Melinda is relieved to learn that her revised estimate was close, although not *exactly* correct.

As I place the licorice back in the bag, I ask Melinda if she and Tom will cut each pupil a piece of licorice when it is time to dismiss school for the day. I suggest that they try to give each person a piece about 12 inches long. To do so, they will need to estimate, not measure "exactly," except to check if they feel they need to.

A box of 100 red plastic discs, or chips, is the last concrete material I have in the bag. I place them all on the table, then take a handful (about twenty) and place them in a separate pile. Next I take one chip and place it alone about 12 inches from the pile. Then I ask the class to *estimate* how many groups of chips there are in the pile if each group has only one chip in it.

Debra says, "That's the same as asking how many chips are in the pile." I agree, and ask if she has an estimate. Other pupils volunteer their estimates. Melinda is one of the last to do so, but she does. We test the estimates by counting the chips. Alex will serve as our estimate tester.

Next, I replace the pile of chips and withdraw a larger handful, about thirty. I place two chips where the one has been before, then ask the pupils to estimate how many groups of two chips each that the larger pile can be divided into. Alex checks the estimates by dividing the pile of chips into groups of two chips each.

All the chips are returned to the box. I remove a pile of about twenty, then place two chips in a separate pile and five chips in another. I say to the children, "Estimate how many groups of two chips each the pile can be divided into. Then estimate how many groups of five chips each the pile can be divided into."

We repeat this procedure with groups of ten. I ask the class what they notice about the number of groups the pile can be divided into as the size of the groups increases. Several hands go up immediately. Debra looks as though she knows. Karen's hand is also up. Greg searches my face, as if that is the best place to look for the answer. I try to look blank. Melinda raises her hand, but her eyes look at the floor. I think she is afraid I may call her bluff. What a sad rule she has learned: "When you don't know, pretend that you do."

Dan is usually less than precise or to the point when a summary statement is needed, so I ask him for his. If he knows, it is at least a fair estimate that everyone knows. He responds in grand style, "As the groups get bigger, the number of groups that the pile can be divided into gets less."

We move from the chips to the chalkboard. We seem to be doing fine. I wonder if the children will be able to make the jump from the concrete to the abstract. We will give it a try. I draw a large circle on the board and write the numeral 11 inside. Outside this circle I draw, roughly to scale, a small circle and write the numeral 1 inside it. Next I draw a relatively larger circle and write the numeral 2 inside. Finally, I draw another even larger circle and place the numeral 5 inside of it. I then ask the pupils to write on their papers their estimates of how many groups of 1, 2, and 5 that the number 11 can be divided into. As they set about the task, I write Dan's rule on the chalkboard.

When they have finished their estimates, I ask if their results confirm Dan's rule. There is general agreement that they do.

On another part of the chalkboard, I draw another large circle. Inside it I write the numeral 24. Outside this circle I draw one small circle and four proportionately larger ones. Inside them I write the numerals 2, 4, 6, 8, and 12 respectively.

When I ask for estimates of the number of groups of each size that the number 24 can be divided into, I notice that some pupils quite suddenly are not paying much attention to the task. They do not seem to be working as independently as they were before. There is more wasted time, more sharpening of pencils, whispering, rummaging in desks, and so on. I find myself asking them to pay attention, to keep the noise down, to try harder. We have been at the lesson for about twenty minutes. I circulate among the pupils to check their estimates. Many have not completed all of them. Everyone has a good estimate for the groups of two, but for the other groups, there is a noticeable lack of accuracy and completeness. I explain what the "best" estimates are for each group. Everyone seems to listen carefully. I feel they are trying to understand what I am saying.

I decide to go back to the chips. "Here is a group of forty-eight chips." I place them in a pile in the center of the table. "Here are groups of two, three, four, six, eight, and twelve chips each.'' I place them in stacks around the large pile. "Into how many groups do you estimate that the large group of forty-eight chips can be divided by the number of chips in each of these smaller groups?''

The results are about the same as they were for the earlier example of twenty-four. Estimates are very good for groups of two but progressively worse for the other groups through twelve. When I ask Greg to tell me how he arrived at his estimate that the pile of forty-eight chips can be divided into forty groups of eight chips each, he says he did not know what else to do, so he just subtracted 8 from 48 and got an even 40. Apparently, having something on paper is somehow comforting for him, even if it does not make sense. Asking Greg to estimate the number of groups of eight chips each that a group of forty-eight can be divided into must be somehow like asking Kagan's (1971) small boy to estimate the length of time it took to build a pyramid. Both children simply have not acquired the information and skills necessary to estimate these *particular* things.

When I ask the class to try to state a rule that defines the term "to estimate,'' they are able to do so. Paul states it this way: "To estimate you try to guess something as closely as you can without really measuring it.'' For applying the rule to estimating about division, Ricky adds this: "To estimate about division, you try to guess, without measuring, as exactly as you can how many smaller groups there are in a large group.'' At this point, Debra refers to her note on the side board: "Measuring is really just estimating.'' I ask her if she will explain what she means by that. She does so simply and directly: "Rulers and scales aren't all exactly the same, and people can make mistakes when they use them. Even with a ruler, you can't measure the table top exactly. You just estimate it better than you can without a ruler.'' The rest of the pupils nod agreement with Debra's explanation. I do not know for sure whether they do so because they understand the meaning of Debra's insight or whether they know from past experience that Debra usually knows what she is talking about.

The rules for estimation these learners have arrived at, while perhaps grammatically weak, are nevertheless operationally useful rules. They reflect meaningful verbal chains. The children are able to illustrate or demonstrate the meaning of the rules. They are able to state them and to apply them to some situations. They are not, however, able to apply the rules successfully to all situations. Generalizing the rule for estimating about division seems to be limited by their lack of certain prerequisite capabilities relative to the operations of division. For example, many of these children have no idea of how many groups of 8 there are in 48—or how to go about finding out. Consequently, their illustration or demonstration of understanding of the rule is obviously limited by the degree to which they have acquired the relevant prerequisite capabilities. *A rule has meaning only relative to its prerequisites.* In more ordinary terms, rules, as concepts, are "learned about.'' Their meaning increases and generalizes as a function of experience. Therefore, they are never learned completely.

At this point, we decide to stop today's "learning about'' rules for estimating in division. The pupils have gone about as far as their prerequisite capabilities will permit. Before they can generalize their understanding of the rule for estimating about division to the solving of specific number problems, they will need to learn additional meaningful verbal chains, discriminations, and concepts relative to numbers and number values.

As the children prepare to go home, I notice that Melinda and Tom have taken up a position near the door. They have started the task of estimating and cutting the ropes of licorice into pieces approximately 12 inches long. I notice that they also have a ruler handy, just in case someone wishes to verify their estimates.

Let us check our performances. At this point, I hope you have *discovered* and are now able to complete the following:

1. A person who has learned a rule is able to. . . .

2. The general and specific conditions of learning rules are. . . .

Learning Higher-Order Rules

In this section we will attend to the conditions of learning higher-order rules, and by the end of the section, we should be able to infer the general and specific conditions of learning them. Our discussion will illustrate how discovery and meaningful reception approaches can be combined. Furthermore, as a consequence of having solved some of the problems relevant to learning about the general and specific conditions of learning chains, discriminations, concepts, and rules, we should be able to formulate some simple and some higher-order rules relevant to the conditions of learning and instruction.

If, as Gagné (1970, 1974) points out, rules are the stuff of our thinking, and if the ways they are used form our cognitive strategies, the major purpose of learning rules must be to form strategies for solving problems. Psychologists and educators use the phrase "problem solving" in a broad sense. Generally it means that a learner, when confronted with an unfamiliar problem situation, must *discover* some strategy that will solve the problem. The phrase is not confined to its more usual meaning of solving arithmetic problems that are assigned for practice of some rule, concept, discrimination or verbal chain. Problem solving, for the most part, involves analysis and a synthesis type of thinking that can occur in a variety of contexts. It can mean figuring out how to solve a particular problem in arithmetic, physics, chemistry, music, auto mechanics, and so on. It can mean trying to decide what to wear to a school dance or whom to invite to accompany you; planning how to spend a paycheck; what to cook for dinner; what to say to the boss; or when next to mow the grass—or how to avoid having to do so.

Rules form the basis of . . .

Although problem solving is most often referred to as a cognitive process, it is always more than that. Affect always accompanies problem situations. In fact, the affective component may be the most important one, for how we feel about solving problems is very much related to how effectively we solve them.

DISCOVERING RULES
THROUGH PROBLEM SOLVING

You will note in the following examples that active participation on the part of the learner is implied. Each example suggests the learner is purposefully doing something with information to arrive at a synthesis that can serve as a basis for action. Further, the examples suggest that the learners are confronted with problem situations for which they have not yet learned an appropriate behavior. Solution of the problems results in acquisition of new responses.

Problem-solving activity results in . . .

Newly learned responses have two important characteristics. First, they solve the immediate problem situation. Second, and of more general importance, newly learned responses that result from the solution of particular problems can be used repeatedly to solve other problems of the same general type. Furthermore, these newly learned responses can be linked with other responses to solve even more general and inclusive problems. Typically, the new learning that results from problem-solving activity has the characteristics of what Gagné calls a "higher-order rule:" a chain or synthesis of simple rules relevant to the problem situation. In the same way that concepts can be linked together to form simple rules, simple rules can be linked together, as a part of problem-solving activity, to form more complex and more generally inclusive rules.

It should be pointed out that problem solving refers to the thinking process that leads initially to a solution for a novel problem situation. Once this has occurred, technically speaking, problem solving has ended. The application of the resulting higher-order rule to the solution of other examples in the general class of problem situations does not constitute problem solving as it is defined here. This is more appropriately thought of as *generalization* or *positive transfer*.

Generally, a discovery approach proceeds by . . .

You will recall, from our earlier discussion about learning rules through a discovery approach, that the teacher's objective is to cause the learner to link relevant concepts together for himself. The teacher's role is to arrange verbal cues, prompts, leading questions, and concrete materials so that the learner "discovers" the important relationship among the relevant concepts. Essentially the same procedure is followed when teaching higher-order rules through problem-solving activity, that is, through a discovery approach. The teacher first ensures that prerequisite rules have been learned meaningfully and then provides the learner with any necessary guidance for solving a problem but without actually telling the learner what a correct solution is. It is the teacher's intent that the learner will independently discover the important relationship among the relevant rules and thus will solve the problem and at the same time learn a higher-order rule. An example will show more precisely what I am saying.

AN EXAMPLE OF LEARNING HIGHER-ORDER RULES BY DISCOVERY   Suppose that, in your high school physics class, you want your students to learn the higher-order rule that in a true vacuum all falling objects accelerate at the same rate. Suppose, further, that you believe it is important for the students to *discover* this higher-order rule. Therefore, you will arrange the events of instruction so that your students will find themselves in a problem-solving situation. The setting will likely be a laboratory if one is available, although this certainly is not a required condition. It is necessary, first, that your learners have meaningfully learned and can recall the simple rules and their prerequisite concepts that combine to form the higher-order rules to be learned, *since discovery is essentially an analysis and synthesis type of process*. Next, you must arrange some kind of problem situation, such as the following.

Let us assume that your instructional objective is this: The learner is able to state a higher-order rule that describes the relationship between the mass of objects and the rate at which they accelerate during free fall in a true vacuum.

Also, assume that your learners are given the following materials and experimental procedures to follow:

Materials
Vacuum tube
Vacuum pump
Coin
Feather
Block of wood
Rubber ball
Wad of paper
Ball of cotton

Procedures
1. Vacuum tube with air in it:
    (a) For each trial, place two objects in the tube, e.g., coin and feather, coin and wood, coin and rubber ball, or any other combination of objects. Quickly invert the tube and observe which object reaches the bottom of the tube first. Record your observations.
    (b) What conclusions can you draw about the composition of objects and the rate at which they fall in air?
2. Vacuum tube with air removed:
    (a) Repeat 1**(a)**.
    (b) What conclusions can you draw about the composition of objects and the rate at which they fall in a vacuum?
3. What are possible sources of error in your procedures for **1** and **2**? How do you account for the differences in your observations in part **1** and part **2**?
4. What inference can you make about the rate of acceleration of all objects in a true vacuum?
5. State your inference in **4** in the form of a general rule.
6. Suggest ways that you might verify the general rule stated in item **5**.
7. Suggest ways that your general rule might be applied in solving real problems that face mankind.

On completing the above activities, each learner can be expected to discover a meaningful relationship between less complex rules, such as "A vacuum is a space that has everything, including air, removed" (note that this is also a defined concept); "air exerts a buoyant force"; "the force of gravity operates on all objects"; "the weight of an object is its gravitational attraction." Discovery will result in meaningfully learning the higher-order rule: "In a true vacuum all falling objects accelerate at the same rate." And, because it is meaningfully learned, the rule can be expected to generalize, or transfer positively, to a broad class of problem situations involving the rule.

LEARNING RULES THROUGH
MEANINGFUL RECEPTION LEARNING

Higher-order rules, simple rules, and defined concepts need not be learned through a discovery approach, although it is true that they may be, and for certain purposes it is desirable that they are, thus learned. However, it is not necessary that *all* concepts, rules, and higher-order rules be discovered by the learner.

Let us consider how your instruction using a meaningful reception approach will be different from instruction using a discovery approach. You will recall that meaningful reception learning relies on instruction that informs, i.e., explains, relates, connects, and tells the learners of the meaning of the things they are to learn. A reception approach does not leave it to the learner to discover meaning.

AN EXAMPLE OF LEARNING HIGHER-ORDER RULES BY RECEPTION   Using the same instructional objective that we used in the example of discovery learning, let us think through how you might arrange the events of instruction using a meaningful reception approach.

The setting will probably be a classroom or laboratory. Your mode of instruction will likely be a lecture-demonstration. You *may* have concrete materials such as those listed unter "Materials" in the laboratory exercise for the discovery approach. There may be a chalkboard available. You may have prepared diagrams or pictures for use in the lesson. I emphasize the word "may" because the need for these concrete materials for learning the higher-order rule depends upon how well your learners have learned the concepts and rules prerequisite to learning the higher-order rule of the present lesson. Their use also depends upon your and your students' facility with language. If your cognitive structures and theirs are rich in associative meanings for the words relevant to learning about the present topic, the word pictures you are able to provide will suffice. I prefer to be conservative, however—to use at least some concrete materials—since, in addition to increasing the probability of meaningful learning, concrete materials serve to catch, direct, and focus the attention of learners. (It feels good, at least once in a while, to "kill two birds with one stone.")

Generally, a reception approach proceeds by . . .

Materials
1. Vacuum tube
2. Vacuum pump
3. Coin
4. Feather
5. Small block of wood
6. Rubber ball
7. Wad of paper
8. Ball of cotton
9. Chalkboard
10. Pictures or diagrams

Procedures
There are many ways of presenting an effective lecture-demonstration. However, the important points, regardless of approach, should include the following:

1. Presenting and explaining the objective for the lesson.
2. Recalling the relevant prerequisite rules, defined and concrete concepts.
3. Explaining or demonstrating the important relationships among the relevant concepts and rules; for example, (1) illustrating or demonstrating the defined concept *to accelerate* and the rule that air exerts a buoyant force on objects; (2) explaining that certain objects, because of their special physical characteristics, are more buoyed by air than are other objects.
4. Drawing inferences that are testable, e.g., "If there were no air in the tube, different objects released at the same time should fall at the same rate."

5. Devising and conducting a test of the inferences, e.g., placing two or more different objects in a vacuum tube, removing the air, quickly inverting the tube, and observing the results.
6. Pointing out or explaining possible sources of error in the test of inferences, such as failure to remove all the air from the vacuum tube.
7. Synthesizing the inferences to form a meaningful relationship, that is, a higher-order rule.
8. Suggesting possible ways that the higher-order rule might be applied (transferred) in solving real problems that face mankind.

By actively attending to all the instruction presented throughout such an approach of reception learning, your learners can be expected to learn the higher-order rule: "In a true vacuum all falling objects accelerate at the same rate." You can expect, also, that the rule will be a meaningful statement for them rather than only a meaningless verbal chain.

COMPARISON OF DISCOVERY AND RECEPTION LEARNING

There is nothing inherent in a reception approach nor, for that matter, in a discovery approach that guarantees meaningful learning. Meaningful or rote learning can result from either approach.

You will notice that there are four variables involved in the last two sentences: discovery, reception, rote, and meaningful. They represent two different and independent dimensions; consequently, they can interact with one another. That is, all six types of learning that we have considered in Chapters 5 and 6 can be characterized in any of the following four ways: (1) meaningful discovery; (2) meaningful reception; (3) rote discovery; and (4) rote reception. These possibilities are illustrated in Figure 6-3.

The fact that conditions and approaches interact implies . . .

Recently learning by discovery (Bruner, 1960, 1961, 1966, 1971) has received much emphasis. The interest has primarily been caused by widespread concern over lack of relevance or meaningfulness of educational experience. Learning by discovery has been seen by many as the logical answer to the assertion that the schools are doing too much "teaching" and the children too little "real

FIGURE 6-3   Two independent dimensions of all six types of learning.

	Discovery	Reception
Meaningful	Meaningful discovery	Meaningful reception
Rote	Rote discovery	Rote reception

learning." Those who support this position argue that teaching-by-telling results in rote memorization, whereas teaching-by-discovery produces meaningful learning. The relative truth, however, is that rote and meaningful learning can develop from either approach. The variable of primary importance is always you, the teacher, and how meaningfully you arrange the events of instruction within whichever approach you decide to use for whatever particular purpose.

Typically, in education and in psychology when one approach to learning is being exalted, others are being discredited. So it is at the present time regarding the relative merits of learning by discovery and learning by reception. In Chapter 3 we saw evidence of this phenomenon in relation to two apparently opposing interpretations of learning. Absolute positions of either/or are unfortunate, since questions of which *interpretation* of learning or which *approach* to instruction is "best" always call for answers that depend on the instructional objectives you are trying to meet. John Dewey (1938) reminds us that whenever we confront strongly argued positions of either/or, we should consider the possibility that each position is supported by a brilliant half-truth which is then overgeneralized. Just as no single interpretation of learning is adequate to account for all types of learning that occur in schools, no one approach to instruction is appropriate for meeting all the instructional objectives teachers have for learners. At all education levels, both approaches to instruction, discovery and reception, can be used. Effective teachers use both, as Schulman (1968) points out, commenting that a *guided discovery* approach "allows us to put the Bruner roller-coaster of discovery of the well-laid track of a Gagné hierarchy."[10]

GENERAL CONDITIONS

The general conditions of learning higher-order rules are . . .

At this point, we should be able to draw sufficient information from our examples of discovery and reception learning to infer the general conditions of learning higher-order rules. You will note that they are identical with those of learning any or all of the six types.

It is appropriate at this time to emphasize a point we have been developing over the last few sections. Stated in the form of a higher-order rule, it is: "Conditions of learning are independent of approaches to learning." *Different approaches do not require different conditions.* This suggests that a good way to begin planning the events of instruction for any learning outcome is by asking, first: "What are the conditions of learning that have to be met? Then we should ask: "What is an appropriate instructional approach for meeting this particular objective?" If these questions are answered effectively, learning will also be effective.

SPECIFIC CONDITIONS

The specific conditions of learning higher-order rules are . . .

Contiguity is an important specific condition of learning higher-order rules in the sense of linking prerequisite, simple rules. Usually the appropriate simple rules should be linked in relatively close temporal contiguity, especially in a meaningful reception approach. However, there is some reason to believe that in a discovery approach, some advantage is gained by "incubation" periods,

---

[10] L. Shulman (1968). Psychological controversies in the teaching of science and mathematics, *Science Teacher*, p. 90.

periods of time for relatively unstructured, unguided sorting and resorting of the component parts (simple rules, concepts) of the problem situation.

Practice is usually not considered an important condition of learning higher-order rules. If learning the rule is meaningfully accomplished, the learner does not appear to need to practice it. Furthermore, retention of meaningfully learned rules is extremely good.

Probably the most important functions of practice in learning higher-order rules, simple rules, and concepts are first for formulating and testing hypotheses about potential relationships among rules and concepts relevant to a problem situation. Few problems would be solved without practice of this sort.

Next, practice in learning higher-order rules helps a learner transfer a rule to other problem situations. Ideally, practice is unnecessary for a higher-order rule learned in one problem-solving situation to generalize to another. However, you will find this is true only when the past learning experiences have been ideal in their breadth, depth, and meaning relative to the problem situations involved. Past learning experiences for most learners, however, have been less than ideal. Many learners have learned the axiom: "Memorize just enough to get by, and don't worry about understanding the stuff." The children in Mr. Johnson's class have learned this adage well, and they have had sufficient breadth of practice with it so that it now generalizes to nearly all aspects of their lives. To believe that they do not need practice to generalize a higher-order rule learned in one situation to another, even another quite similar, is to miss the whole point about the necessity of meaningfully learned prerequisites for success in learning the task at hand.

The role of practice in learning higher-order rules is . . .

A Summary of Rules for Learning and Instruction

At this point, we should be able to generate simple and higher-order rules of learning and instruction. They will be helpful guides as we continue to learn more about learning and teaching.

First, simple rules regarding general and specific conditions of learning meaningfully:

1. Clear objectives are necessary.
2. Attention to the task is needed.
3. Prerequisites must be acquired.
4. Feedback of performance must occur.
5. Reinforcement of correct responses is required.
6. Practice, appropriately designed and sequenced, is necessary.

These simple rules can be synthesized into one higher-order rule of learning:

Meaningful conditions of learning result in meaningful learning.

Three higher-order rules of learning and instruction can be stated:

1. Many approaches to instruction are possible.
2. Approaches to and conditions of learning are independent.
3. General and specific conditions of learning are constant for all approaches to instruction.

There is one very important higher-order rule of optimism relative to school learning:

The learner is always the most important condition of all types of learning.

And there is one higher-order rule of caution relative to school learning that is more important than all the others:

Learning is cumulative—so is not-learning.

IN PASSING

One rainy afternoon late in the fall about twenty-five years ago, I was picking apples with a crew of migratory fruit workers. While we waited for a sudden shower to pass, we huddled together around the trunk of a tree that had already been picked. The boxes, each containing about a bushel of apples, were stacked nearby in a neat row four boxes tall and ten boxes long. As we waited, we talked, mostly about apple picking, how good we were at it, picking jobs we had done, and how this job compared with the others. Soon the rain ended and we went back to work. When my picking partner and I were alone, he said to me, "You know, while we were waiting out the rain back there, I discovered something, and I think it will work every time." He was really excited about his discovery, and continued, "Did you know that if you count the number of boxes *along* the stack and the number of boxes the stack is *high*, and then multiply them together, you will get the same number as when you count each box! I checked it on two other stacks and it came out right both times!"

I remember that at the time I thought the man was stupid. I found it difficult to keep from laughing at him. But I don't think about him in that way anymore. Rather, I find it sad that the part of his education related to the concept of multiplication must have been totally meaningless for him. "Four times ten equals forty"— a sterile and empty verbal chain as poorly associated with the rest of his mind as the child who rotely memorized it was now associated with the rest of the world.

We now turn our attention to a consideration in depth of the variables relevant to the question of whether learning does indeed become cumulative, meaningful, useful, and important to the learner. The topic of Chapter 7 is *transfer*.

ACTIVITIES

1. Implicit in the content of Chapters 5 and 6 are several higher-order rules relevant to the conditions of learning chains, discriminations, concepts, and rules. State these higher-order rules.

2. Throughout the first six chapters, several rules of thumb have been described and labeled. As an individual, small group, or class activity, list these rules of thumb. If the concept *rule of thumb* has been learned well enough, you will be able to generalize it to those rules of thumb that I have presented but have not identified as such. (Did you notice that this is an analysis-level task?)

3. In the early part of Chapter 5, you attempted a task analysis of an instructional objective. At that time you were ready to complete only a rough outline of a task analysis. Now you are ready to do more of what teachers do to organize instruction; that is, to describe instructional objectives, complete task analyses of the objectives, and arrange events of instruction so that the conditions of learning the required chains, discriminations, concepts, and rules are likely to be met. Therefore, as an individual or a small group activity: (1) select a topic of interest to you from the school curriculum; (2) describe appropriate cognitive, psychomotor, and affective instructional objectives; (3) select one or two of these objectives and complete a task analysis of each one; and (4) describe the events of instruction you would arrange so that the conditions of learning the necessary chains, discriminations, concepts, rules, and affective objectives are likely to be met.

4. Teach a learner the meanings of some of the following terms. (Note what you do as a teacher to help the person learn, that is, how you use general and specific conditions.) Balance of nature, watershed, watercycle, grassroots development, soil bank, speed of light, political machine, address, time, light, darkness, sun, love.

5. Just for fun:

Can you solve the following problem and at the same time generate a higher-order rule relative to solving problems?

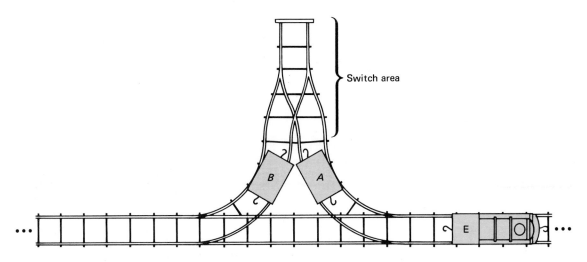

You are looking down on a railroad intersection where two boxcars, A and B, and an engine, E, have stopped. You are the engineer in the engine. Your task is to drive your engine along the tracks, pulling and pushing the boxcars, so that A trades places with B and the engine is back where it is now. There are a few rules that must be observed: (1) Only one boxcar can occupy the switch area at any one time; (2) the engine is not allowed in the switch area at any time; (3) the boxcars and engine each have connectors on both front and rear ends; (4) the boxcars and engine must make turns with the curvature of the tracks.

Do you know why this problem can be so difficult to solve, and why elementary school children often can solve it as easily as older and "more highly educated" people? A reasonably effective solution can be found in Chapter 7, where we will discuss some of the problems of mental set, facilitation, and inhibition as they relate to problem solving, learning, retention and transfer.

Archer, E. J. (1964). On verbalizations and concepts. In A. W. Melton (ed.), *Categories of Human Learning.* New York: Academic Press.

Bereiter, C., and S. Engelmann (1966). *Teaching Disadvantaged Children in the Preschool.* Englewood Cliffs, N.J.: Prentice-Hall.

Bourne, J., Jr. (1966). *Human Conceptual Behavior.* Boston: Allyn and Bacon.

Bruner, J. S. (1960). *The Process of Education.* New York: Vintage.

——— (1961). The act of discovery, *Harvard Educational Review,* **31,** 21–32.

——— (1966). *Toward a Theory of Instruction.* Cambridge, Mass.: The Belknap Press of Harvard University Press.

——— (1971). *The Relevance of Education.* New York: Norton.

Bull, S. G. (1973). The role of questions in maintaining attention to contextual material, *Review of Educational Research,* **43**(1), 83–87.

Cullum, R. (1967). *Push Back the Desks.* New York: Citation.

DeCecco, J. P. (1968). *The Psychology of Learning and Instruction: Educational Psychology.* Englewood Cliffs, N.J.: Prentice-Hall.

REFERENCES

Dewey, J. (1938). *Experience and Education*. New York: Macmillan.

Gagné, R. M. (1970). *The Conditions of Learning*. New York: Holt.

——— (1971). *Defining Objectives for Six Types of Learning* (a taped presentation). Washington: American Educational Research Association.

——— (1974). *Essentials of Learning for Instruction*. Hinsdale, Ill.: Dryden.

Holt, J. (1964). *How Children Fail*. New York: Pitman.

Kagan, J. (1971). *Understanding Children: Behavior, Motives and Thought*. New York: Harcourt Brace Jovanovich.

Keller, H. (1902). *The Story of My Life*. New York: Doubleday.

Shulman, L. (1968). Psychological controversies in the teaching of science and mathematics, *Science Teacher*, **35**, 34–38, 89–90.

Trabasso, T. (1968). Pay attention, *Psychology Today*, **2**, 30–36.

SUGGESTIONS FOR FURTHER READING

Kagan, J. (1971). *Understanding Children: Behavior, Motives and Thought*. New York: Harcourt Brace Jovanovich. Jerome Kagan provides an excellent example of the application of our theme: "Don't pick and choose, combine the best from many." His theoretical and practical contributions to our understanding of how children learn are at once connectionist and cognitive, humanistic and behavioral. "To educate a child one must arrange conditions. . . ; people, not objects, are the most persuasive agents whenever one is proselytizing a faith" (p. 10).

Bereiter, C., and S. Engelmann, (1966). *Teaching Disadvantaged Children in the Preschool*. Englewood Cliffs, N.J.: Prentice-Hall. This highly controversial book is a classic in several respects: (1) It begins with a broad, theoretical point of view—that cultural deprivation means language deprivation—and then translates theory into second-by-second teaching—learning activities for the classroom. (2) It is an example of a carefully completed task analysis, and (3) it is bold in presenting the position that caring about children is intensely active and completely involving, and at times it is even sternly demanding.

Hewett, F. M. (1968). *The Emotionally Disturbed Child in the Classroom*. Boston: Allyn and Bacon. It is one thing to teach chains, discriminations, concepts, rules, motor skills, and affect to children who are already "good" learners. It can be something else to teach these things to learners who either cannot seem to learn, do not want to learn, or both. One day you will face both kinds of learners. Hewett describes a developmental sequence of educational goals that places "attention to the task" on one end of the sequence and "achievement of the task" on the other. He also describes a learning triangle that places the task on one side, structure of the learning situation on another side, and reward for learning on the third side. The teacher and the child of course are located at the center of their triangles. You will find all of Gagné's conditions of learning in Hewett's many suggestions for classroom practices designed to help poor learners to learn.

TEACHING AND LEARNING FOR TRANSFER: COGNITIVE, AFFECTIVE, AND PSYCHOMOTOR

7

My older son Jay was almost four when we spent a summer in Mexico. He liked Mexico pretty well, except for the odd habit the Mexican kids had of speaking Spanish. We could see that he soon understood a lot of what they were saying and urged him, as parents will, to speak Spanish, but he always refused. Perhaps he thought it no good to encourage the Mexican kids in their stubborn ways.

A year later, in the normal course, he went to kindergarten back in the United States. He found it mildly disappointing. There were no toys, he said, and when they got to go outside to play, the teacher always went with them.

I was always asking him how things were going at school, and he was always answering, Fine. I pressed for details: What do you guys do there? One day he said, when we get there we line up, then we go in and sit down at our place, then we get up again, then we talk to the flag.

You talk to the flag?

Uh-huh.

I could see he thought the subject closed, but I said, Well, what do you say to the flag?

He turned on the TV. How do I know? he said. They're talking to it in Spanish.

The kindergarten, it seemed, had some odd habits too. Still, you could see he wasn't bothered by it. For the kindergarten didn't require him to talk to the flag himself, or to understand what they were saying to it. All it required of him was that he stand up and look as if he knew what was going on. That wasn't hard, and it didn't take long, and so he didn't mind doing it.

James Herndon
The Way It Spozed to Be

CONTENTS

ONGOING SUMMARY

When we finished Chapter 6, we concluded a task that could be called "Getting some basic tools relative to school learning." We have described these tools with labels, such as description and explanation of behavior, goals and objectives, interpretations of learning, types of learning, conditions of learning, models for learning, and approaches to learning. For the most part, we have learned about each of these tools in sequential order. Each was discussed, practiced, and related meaningfully to the others. Now, we must put them all together and try to use them as a teacher does, in concert.

ADVANCE ORGANIZER

All the tools relative to school learning that we have learned about through Chapter 6 can be meaningfully subsumed under the more generally inclusive topic "Transfer of Learning." Each tool, associated with others, helps to explain whether the learned material is retained and whether it enhances or interferes with further learning and retention in the same topic or in related topics. Our task in Chapter 7 will be to learn how this concert of tools can be synthesized and then translated into useful higher-order rules that can be applied to your classroom teaching so that learning is efficient and meaningful. Chapter 7 is a synthesis and a summary of the first six chapters. More importantly, it is also an advance organizer for Chapter 8, which discusses the application of these rules to optimizing instruction for each learner.

GOALS AND OBJECTIVES

Cognitive

To become an effective teacher, the learner should be able to apply laws and theories of learning to teaching for transfer in cognitive, affective, and psychomotor domains.

KNOWLEDGE LEVEL

Given the following terms or phrases, the learner is able to define them in writing; *transfer, dimension of transfer, theory of transfer, positive transfer, negative transfer, incidental transfer, vertical transfer, horizontal transfer, retention, cognitive structure.*

COMPREHENSION LEVEL

1. Given the expression "teaching and learning for transfer," the learner is able to explain verbally what it means.
2. Given Figures 7-1 and 7-2, the learner is able to interpret them so that a colleague, in a sentence or two, is able to summarize what each figure is about.

APPLICATION LEVEL

Given the higher-order rule, "Decide what you want to transfer," the learner can apply the rule to doing task descriptions and task analyses.

ANALYSIS LEVEL

Given examples of teaching situations such as those in Chapters 5 and 6, along with statements of the teacher's objectives, the learner is able to state whether transfer is likely to occur, and if so, what types of transfer will be evident.

SYNTHESIS LEVEL

Given the content material of the first seven chapters of this text, the learner is able to construct a line drawing or schematic that shows the sequential and cumulative nature of the major concepts and rules presented.

EVALUATION LEVEL

Given the first six chapters, the learner is able to state why he or she believes teaching for transfer has or has not been a primary objective of the author.

Affective

To become an effective teacher, the learner should be able to assume responsibility for learning how to make instruction efficient for each learner.

RECEIVING (ATTENDING) LEVEL

The learner is aware that as a teacher, he must organize instruction that transfers on purpose, not just by chance.

RESPONDING LEVEL

The learner finds it satisfying to know that he will be able to use what he is learning.

VALUING LEVEL

The learner defends the right of children to a "useful and relevant education" by insisting that "transfer must be taught for."

ORGANIZATIONAL LEVEL

The learner attempts to construct his own meaningful and useful higher-order rules that will help him teach for transfer.

CHARACTERIZATION LEVEL

Through active participation in learning activities, the learner demonstrates his belief in teaching and learning for transfer.

In Chapter 6 we mentioned a constant press within human learners toward an economy of effort, toward maximizing the efficiency of learning and retention. We related this idea chiefly to our efforts to maximize economy through learning concepts and rules. There is another way that our efforts at learning and retention can be maximized. It is through transfer.

WHAT IS TRANSFER?

Transfer refers to . . .

Transfer is not a new term for us at this point. We have been expanding this defined concept both "up" and "out" since Chapter 2. Generally, transfer refers to the facilitating and inhibiting effects that present learning can have on later learning and on our ability to retain what we learn now or what we learned earlier. We know that broadly inclusive and meaningfully learned concepts and rules transfer better than specific, isolated chains and discriminations. As Overman (1930) pointed out over forty years ago, we get our most dependable transfer from practical applications of general principles, from devices, and from rules of thumb. Knowing generally about transfer, however, probably will not be very useful to you in the classroom. You need to know specifically about this broad concept and to fashion useful rules and devices that are likely to transfer for you. Let us become more specific.

Dimensions of Transfer

The concept *transfer* is usually talked about relative to goals and objectives in the cognitive domain, for example, in connection with the effects on later learning and retention of subject matter now being learned. Transfer, however, is also related to learning and retention within the affective and psychomotor domains. The learning of certain attitudes, emotions, or feelings in one situation, for instance, affects later learning and retention. Also, learning of certain physical movements today influences next week's learning and retention of other physical movements.

The *kind* of transfer is another dimension of the concept. That is, present learning may facilitate, or it may hinder, later learning and retention. Consequently, transfer is often classified as *positive* or *negative*.

Four dimensions of transfer are . . .

Two other dimensions of transfer should be mentioned briefly here. Then, later in the chapter, we can look at all the dimensions together and discuss each more fully. These dimensions have to do with (1) whether transfer is *planned directly* or whether it just occurs more or less *incidentally,* and (2) whether transfer occurs *within* some certain topic in a *vertical* sense, or *among* related topics in a *horizontal* sense.

All the dimensions we have mentioned are interrelated. The way I see their interrelationships is shown in Figure 7-1. You will note that the classification scheme can help us plan the events of instruction so that positive transfer is likely to occur in all domains, not just the cognitive one. Furthermore, this scheme identifies various forms of transfer, and knowing these forms should enable us to be more systematic in our attempts to teach for transfer.

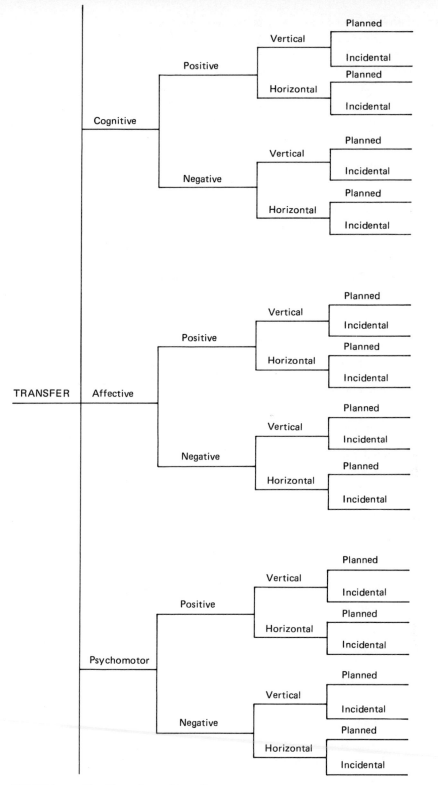

FIGURE 7-1 The dimensions of transfer.

SOME EXAMPLES OF
VARIOUS TYPES OF TRANSFER

As a general rule, our objectives are to cause positive transfer to occur and to prevent the occurrence of negative transfer. Some examples of both positive and negative transfer within each of the three domains will help us learn how their dimensions are interrelated. Moreover, seeing the contrasting examples close together will help you learn to discriminate among the various types of transfer possible. You will recall from Chapters 5 and 6 that this is one of the specific conditions of learning discriminations and concepts.

Although space will not permit examples of all twenty-four types of transfer identified in Figure 7-1, we will look at enough for you to get an idea of what the various types are about.

COGNITIVE, POSITIVE, VERTICAL, AND PLANNED   When a teacher says to her learners: "Today you are going to learn something about fractions, and later, you will learn more about fractions," she is planning for positive and vertical transfer in the cognitive domain. She does this in the sense that when she now helps a student learn meaningful associations for the concept *fraction,* she at the same time ensures that the learner will later be able to solve story-type problems that require an understanding of the concept.

> **Cognitive transfer means . . .**

A teacher of home economics teaches for this type of transfer when she helps her learners acquire meaningful rules relative to types of stitches and threads to use for specific purposes. This learning transfers to the later task of making an article of clothing.

COGNITIVE, NEGATIVE, VERTICAL, AND PLANNED   "Planned" in instances of negative transfer usually refers to a conscious attempt to cause transfer *not* to occur. A teacher uses this type of *cognitive, vertical, negative,* and *planned* transfer when helping children learn to discriminate between the spellings of homonyms such as "their" and "there" or "pair" and "pare." What the teacher does is try to prevent the occurrence of negative transfer, that is, to prevent the learning of the first word from interfering with the later learning of the correct but different spelling of the homonym.

> **Negative transfer means . . .**

Another instance of the same type of transfer occurs when a chemistry or physics teacher instructs his learners so that they do *not* apply a particular rule or principle learned earlier to a later problem situation that is similar but yet different. For example, the students learn not to apply Newton's laws of motion to problems involving atomic particles moving at high velocities.

COGNITIVE, POSITIVE, HORIZONTAL, AND INCIDENTAL   Examples of this type of transfer are readily available in most classrooms, for instance, when a teacher helps learners in arithmetic to construct tables or graphs with legends or keys for them. Later, and without actually being taught to do so, the children learn relatively easily to read legends and keys for maps in social studies. Another example is seen when a teacher helps learners to construct sentences that are grammatically correct, and in the learning-practice process, incidentally includes descriptive words that they then begin to use appropriately in other written work, such as reports of science projects.

> **Positive transfer means . . .**

AFFECTIVE, POSITIVE, VERTICAL, AND PLANNED   Several types of transfer are possible within the affective domain. Often, however, the transfer within this

> **Affective transfer means . . .**

domain is not planned for as carefully as it might be. This is unfortunate, since surely many of the important long-range goals we have for education are essentially affective in nature.

Let us look at transfer that is *affective, positive, vertical,* and *planned.* Mr. Johnson teaches for this type of transfer when, in an arithmetic lesson, he asks Melinda to help him verify the estimates made about the number of licorice sticks necessary to reach completely around the rim of a table. What he hopes to accomplish is that in later situations like this, Melinda will be willing to respond and will gain satisfaction from doing so.

AFFECTIVE, NEGATIVE, HORIZONTAL, AND PLANNED   This type of transfer occurs when teachers arrange the events of instruction so that learners do not use the same values or system of forming judgments for all situations. For example, the teacher may help learners become committed to the importance of being critical, probing, and constructively suspicious when learning about some scientific topic, but not when trying to become acquainted with a classmate. Or teaching may be planned so that, in creative writing, learners do not apply habits of caution and reservation, of detailed and critical analyses appropriate in science.

Horizontal transfer means . . .

AFFECTIVE, POSITIVE, HORIZONTAL, AND INCIDENTAL   Because "Incidental" implies lack of specific purpose, this type of transfer may be expected to occur without a teacher's actually planning for it. Because incidental transfer, both positive and negative, does occur, we must be aware of how it can happen. When a learner begins to be successful in one part of her school life, for example, she begins to behave in ways that suggest she believes arithmetic is important; she completes assignments, tries to understand what she is doing, participates in discussions about arithmetic, asks questions, and so forth. A teacher may conclude that *affective, positive, horizontal,* and *incidental* transfer is occurring if he notes that the learner also begins to complete assignments, ask questions, and participate in discussions in social studies, language arts, or some other part of her school life.

Incidental transfer means . . .

PSYCHOMOTOR, POSITIVE, VERTICAL, AND PLANNED   An instance of *psychomotor, positive, vertical,* and *planned* transfer occurs when a learner learns to form letters with a pencil. The teacher knows that learning to hold a pencil and form letters properly will make learning to write words and sentences easier than it would be if the learner did not know how to hold the pencil and form letters well.

Vertical transfer means . . .

Helping a student learn to make the physical manipulations necessary to focus a microscope is another example of how transfer can be *psychomotor, positive, vertical,* and *planned:* Learning to be able to focus one microscope is likely to enhance learning to focus similar viewing instruments, even more complex ones. Similarly, learning the psychomotor skills required to pat-bounce a ball can be expected to transfer positively to learning to dribble a basketball during a game.

PSYCHOMOTOR, NEGATIVE, HORIZONTAL, AND PLANNED   Some psychomotor skills interfere with learning others. Consequently, a teacher planning for psychomotor transfer of this type will attempt to prevent learners from applying movements learned in one skill to learning the appropriate movements for another skill. For example, a teacher may try to prevent children from applying psychomotor skills acquired in learning to letter or write numerals to the task of

Planned transfer means . . .

learning to draw or paint. Or, she may help students learn to ignore what one eye sees as the other observes through the lens of a microscope.

PSYCHOMOTOR, POSITIVE, VERTICAL, AND INCIDENTAL   In the psychomotor domain, instances of transfer that are positive, vertical, and not specifically planned can be seen when children learn to roller-skate and then, later, find it relatively easier to learn to ice-skate, or when they learn to "track and kick" a rolling ball and then, later, have little difficulty learning to kick the ball in soccer. Learning to operate one type of power saw in an industrial arts program is likely to transfer positively to learning to operate other types of power saws used in building a house. Learning to operate one type of sewing machine in a class of home economics can be expected to transfer positively to learning to use other types of sewing machines.

Psychomotor transfer means . . .

CHECKPOINT 7-1

The previous sections presented examples of various types of transfer within the cognitive, affective, and psychomotor domains. Following are three of the types that we did not discuss. Give an example of each type. (NOTE: The type of transfer I am hoping will occur here for you is *cognitive, positive, vertical,* and *planned.*) (1) Cognitive, positive, horizontal, and planned; (2) Affective, positive, vertical, and incidental; (3) Psychomotor, negative, vertical, and planned.

Viewpoints about How Transfer Occurs

You will note that, so far in our discussion of the defined concept *transfer,* we have described, rather generally, what transfer is, and then we described quite precisely a classification scheme for various types of transfer. However, you will remember from Chapter 2 that even detailed and precise description does not constitute explanation. This means, in our study of transfer, that if we are satisfied only to *describe* transfer, our task is pretty well completed at this point. If, on the other hand, we also want to *cause* transfer to occur with our learners, we must go beyond description and must *explain* how transfer occurs. Knowing that, we will be able to cause transfer to occur on purpose rather than leave it to chance.

There are several theoretical points of view about how transfer occurs. Some of them have gained widespread attention and are identified with labels such as "formal discipline," "common components," and "generalization." Let us examine these views to see what use we can make of them.

In Chapter 2 we saw that what we believe to be true is relative to, and changes with, our experiences. We also saw that what we do in our daily lives is closely related to what we believe to be true. We now meet these ideas again as we consider what we believe to be true relative to how transfer occurs and to what we might do in order to increase the probability of its positive occurrence.

FORMAL DISCIPLINE

At one time general areas of the brain were believed responsible for various mental activities, such as logical reasoning, imagination, attention, judgment, and aesthetic appreciation. It was the early belief that these brain areas, or faculties, as they were called, could be strengthened through practice, much as muscles can be strengthened through exercise. It follows, then, if this is "true," that vigorous study of difficult material should generally strengthen related faculties, that is, transfer should occur.

The theory of formal discipline states . . .

Such a belief led to an emphasis on the study of difficult subject matter for the development of general faculties rather than more directly on the potential usefulness of school subjects to meet specific problems encountered in living. The belief also generated a great deal of research effort, most of which suggests that little transfer occurs as a consequence of trying to strengthen the general faculties of the brain through exercising it with difficult and tedious subject matter or with extended drill of essentially rote material. What does occur, as you might expect from our rule of thumb that we learn what we practice, is that learners become proficient in those things they study and in the methods they use to study them. For example, if learners memorize lists of words, they become good at remembering those words but not necessarily at remembering. If learners practice difficult problems in mathematical logic, they become good at mathematical logic, but not necessarily good at logic involved in balancing a budget or planning a lesson.

A rule that is suggested by what we have learned over the years about transfer relative to a theory of formal discipline is this: We are not likely to be very successful if we try to teach for transfer in a general sense. We will probably be more successful in teaching for relatively specific types of transfer and in having learners practice specifically those things that we want them to learn, remember, and transfer. Later in the chapter we will return to this rule.

COMMON COMPONENTS

A theory of common components states that transfer of learning from one situation to others will occur to the extent that *components* or *elements* of one situation are perceived by the learner as similar to those of other situations. In this view, components can refer to skills, content, specific procedures or processes, objectives, and so forth. And transfer can occur as any of the twenty-four types shown in Figure 7-1. This can be illustrated with a couple of examples.

According to the theory of common components, knowledge of number values is a component common to the processes of both multiplication and division. A meaningful knowledge of number values enhances learning to multiply and divide meaningfully. Being able to spell correctly is a component common to spelling and writing. The task of writing sentences is made easier by facility with spelling.

Within the affective domain, according to a theory of common components, being committed to the value of attending well to learning tasks improves the probability that learners will respond appropriately and willingly to instruction. Attention is a component common to successful responding in all school tasks.

Within the psychomotor domain, the same theory suggests, for example, that tracking a moving object with the eyes is a component common to activities such as baseball, tennis, soccer, badminton, and tether ball.

Relative to school learning, the common-components theory has several implications for instruction. If it is at least approximately true that transfer occurs to the extent that various learning situations include common components, then

The theory of common components states . . .

teaching for transfer means first arranging the events of instruction so that the conditions of learning are met meaningfully. Central to this view is the requirement that specific prerequisite skills, content, procedures, processes, attitudes, habits of attending, responding, and so forth (the common components) have been mastered meaningfully and have been retained.

All these observations sound familiar to us because we already "know about" Gagné's cumulative-learning model (1970, 1974) that incorporates a theory of transfer based on the notion of common components. That is, the learning of new tasks is enhanced to the degree to which the components of previous learning tasks that are prerequisite to the new task have been learned.

We saw examples of positive and negative transfer occur with children in Mr. Johnson's class. *Affective, negative, vertical,* and *incidental* transfer occurred with Paul, the boy who spent most of his arithmetic time drawing cartoons. He had learned to avoid attending and responding to arithmetic. His affective behavior regarding arithmetic, of course, transferred to later work in arithmetic, with the result that "not-learning" accumulated for him. Learning about arithmetic became increasingly difficult for him since it became harder and harder for him to attend to it. Cognitively, this was also true, since not learning the content of arithmetic very effectively ensured that the prerequisites, or the common components, of later and more complex tasks in arithmetic were not learned and consequently were not available for transfer.

Later in Chapter 6 we illustrated positive transfer. Once Paul had experienced a learning situation in arithmetic that was meaningful and successful for him both cognitively and affectively, he began acquiring the common components necessary for transfer to another learning situation in arithmetic. The type of transfer that occurred for Paul made the later experience of learning rules of estimation easier and more pleasant. The types of transfer that occurred were (1) *affective, positive, vertical,* and *planned,* and (2) *cognitive, positive, vertical,* and *planned.*

Instances of psychomotor transfer that occurred with children in Mr. Johnson's class can also be interpreted in terms of the same theory. You will recall from Chapter 5 the difficulty Mike had writing numerals legibly and accurately. His poor motor performance transferred negatively, that is, it interfered with the task of solving written problems with fractions. We could teach for transfer in this case by following Gagné's advice. We would help Mike master the component motor chains prerequisite to writing the numerals needed for solving problems with fractions.

Although a theory of common components has been a useful explanation of transfer, it has created a few problems. The main one has been that many teachers have concluded that teaching for transfer, in this view, means isolating the components common to various learning tasks and teaching them as if they were isolated facts, skills, or attitudes. Consequently, much drill and practice with low meaning have occurred. Children have rotely memorized multiplication facts, procedures for calculations, rules for potentially meaningful relationships, and so forth. Teachers, believing that "commitment to learn" is a component common to all learning tasks, have tried to motivate children simply by "doing something exciting" only at the beginning of otherwise dull, meaningless lessons. Components of learning to read, for example, a left-to-right progression, have been identified and then taught in isolation in the belief that such skills would later transfer to the task of reading. Many "reading readiness" programs operate essentially from this point of view. You will recall that in Chapter 5 we talked about this kind of abuse in education as it relates to rotely learning potentially meaningful motor and verbal chains.

A rule that derives from what we have learned about a theory of common components is that such a theory can be useful to us as long as we remember that it is not the learning of the components themselves but the *meaningful relationships* between the components and the rest of the learning situations that provide the basis for transfer. Consistent with Gagné's tenet, prerequisites must be meaningfully learned.

GENERALIZATION

Learning about a theory of transfer by generalization should be relatively easy for you, since this theory is an extension of a theory of common components. This will be "true," however, only if your learning about a theory of common components has been meaningful rather than rote.

In a theory of common components, emphasis is placed on the fact that specific elements are common to more than one learning task. As we saw in the previous section, a component can consist of particular bits of information such as number combinations, particular responses like not attending to the arithmetic lesson, or certain motor skills such as writing numerals. In a theory of transfer by generalization, however, emphasis is given to the importance of generalizations, that is, to rules or higher-order rules that are common to more than one learning task. Belief in this point of view implies that when teachers teach for transfer, they should organize the events of instruction so that learners will acquire an understanding of relationships among defined concepts, rules, and higher-order rules rather than simply acquire meaning for, and among, individual chains, discriminations, and concrete concepts.

If you want to teach for transfer by generalization, you should try to help your learners understand the general principles of the topic rather than specific examples. We saw an instance of this type of teaching in Chapter 5, when students learned a higher-order rule for objects falling in a vacuum through approaches of discovery and meaningful reception learning. Having meaningfully learned this rule, students should find solving real-life problems relative to space travel less difficult than if they had not learned the rule.

Causing you to learn rules of thumb such as "Catch kids being good" is an attempt to teach for transfer by generalization. Helping children in Mr. Johnson's class learn rules of estimation is another example. You will recall from our discussion of that lesson, however, that the extent to which the children were able to generalize their rules of estimation was limited by their specific knowledge regarding the situations in which the rule might be transferred. The children knew what they should do to apply the rule, but they had not acquired the prerequisite information that would permit them actually to transfer a meaningfully learned rule to a new situation.

The theory of generalization states . . .

An important message for us, in this experience of Mr. Johnson's learners, concerns a point we have made before, namely, that it is usually more useful to combine the best from related points of view than to try to choose a single best one from among them. This means that if learning in all three domains can indeed be considered hierarchical in nature, then, as Gagné's cumulative learning model (1970, 1974) implies, transfer involving a higher-order rule requires more than just understanding that rule. It means understanding the simple rules, which requires understanding the concepts, which in turn requires a meaningful understanding of the discriminations and chains relative to all the situations in which transfer is expected to occur. Clearly, teaching for transfer involves aspects of all the views we have discussed. Let us see how this works.

From a theory of formal discipline we can first borrow the idea that practice is important for transfer, even if only in the restricted sense that practice is necessary for learning and retention of the specific common components that are prerequisite to rules and higher-order rules. Also, we can incorporate the rule that what is practiced is what is learned.

From the theories of common components and generalization, we derive the clues that tell us to look for those specific elements common to the learning tasks within which we hope transfer will occur. Therefore, when teaching for transfer, we should try to cause learners to practice those specific things that we believe are the important common components of other learning tasks, and we should try to cause the practice of these things to occur in ways similar to those in which the information skills or attitudes will be later used. This is another way of saying that practice will be meaningful.

We have just examined several theories about how transfer occurs. A theory of common components tends to derive from a connectionist interpretation of learning, whereas a theory of generalization tends to be a cognitive interpretation. Another theory of transfer, not yet discussed, derives chiefly from a cognitive viewpoint of learning. Checkpoint 7-2 asks you to speculate about it.

CHECKPOINT 7-2

Using your knowledge of a cognitive interpretation of learning, (1) suggest a name for this "other" theoretical viewpoint about how transfer occurs, and (2) describe some of its possible arguments.

LEARNING, RETENTION, AND TRANSFER

So far in this chapter we have described the concept of transfer, and we have examined four points of view that attempt to explain how transfer occurs. From these views, we have derived simple rules that borrow ideas from each. I have tried to help you learn these rules in a meaningful way by relating the concept *transfer* to what we learned earlier about Gagné's cumulative-learning model. If now I want to teach so that you will transfer what you have learned about transfer to your teaching, I should help you to derive higher-order rules about transfer and to practice applying them. I believe we can do this by noting the potentially meaningful relationships among Gagné's conditions of learning (1970, 1974), Bloom's taxonomy of cognitive objectives (1956), Krathwohl's taxonomy of affective objectives (1964), Harrow's taxonomy of psychomotor objectives (1972), and the major concepts associated with learning, retention, and transfer that we have learned about so far.

A Synthesis of Major Concepts

Bloom (1956), Gagné (1970), Krathwohl (1964), and Harrow (1972) provide a meaningful basis for illustrating the relationships among the major concepts we

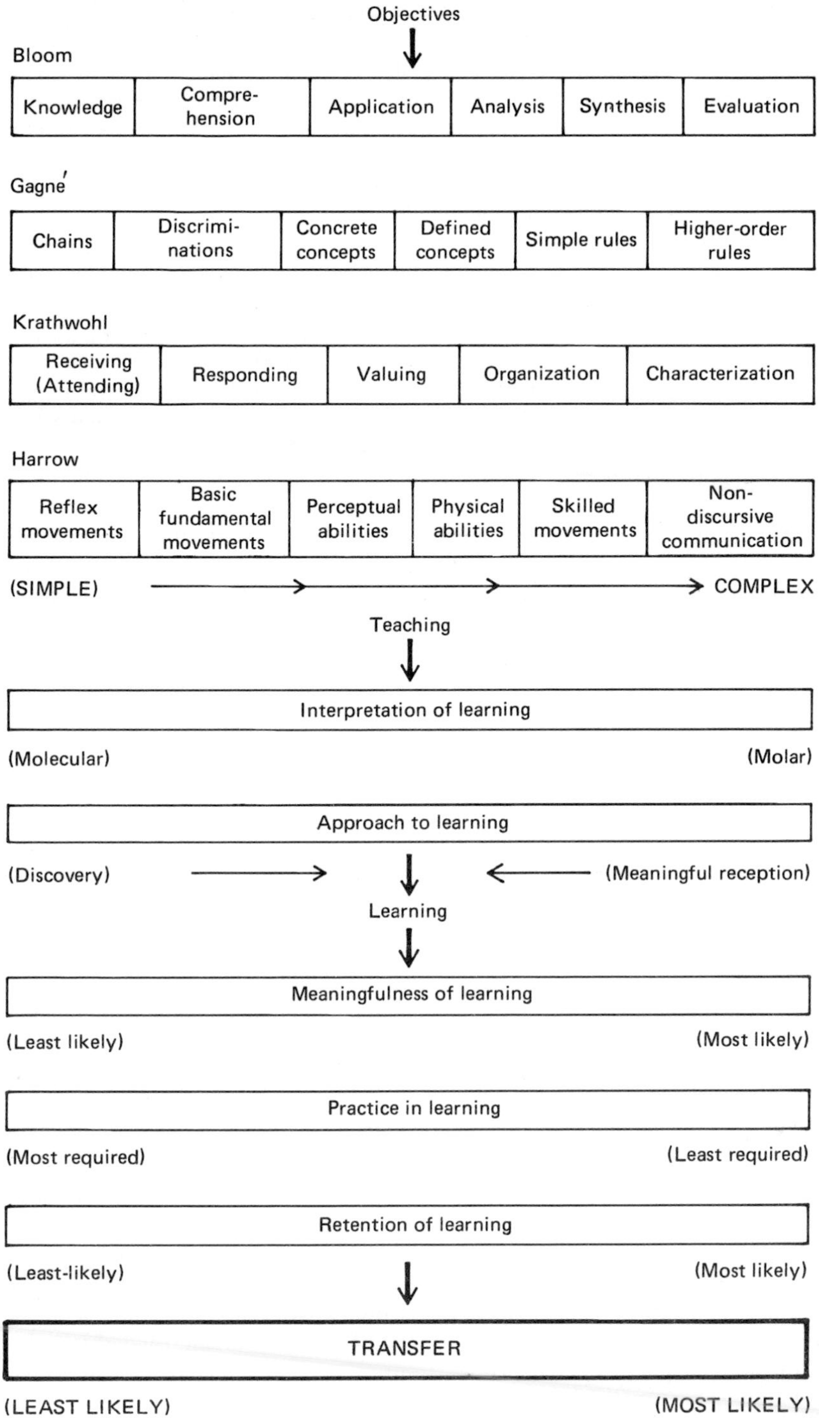

Objectives

Bloom

Knowledge	Compre-hension	Application	Analysis	Synthesis	Evaluation

Gagné

Chains	Discrimi-nations	Concrete concepts	Defined concepts	Simple rules	Higher-order rules

Krathwohl

Receiving (Attending)	Responding	Valuing	Organization	Characterization

Harrow

Reflex movements	Basic fundamental movements	Perceptual abilities	Physical abilities	Skilled movements	Non-discursive communication

(SIMPLE) ——————————————————————————→ COMPLEX

Teaching

Interpretation of learning

(Molecular)   (Molar)

Approach to learning

(Discovery) ——————→   ←———— (Meaningful reception)

Learning

Meaningfulness of learning

(Least likely)   (Most likely)

Practice in learning

(Most required)   (Least required)

Retention of learning

(Least-likely)   (Most likely)

TRANSFER

(LEAST LIKELY)   (MOST LIKELY)

FIGURE 7-2   A summary of Bloom, Gagné, Krathwohl, and Harrow relative to major concepts in teaching and learning for transfer.

have learned about relative to learning, retention, and transfer. These relationships are summarized in Figure 7-2.

You will notice that two progressions of a cumulative nature are evident in Figure 7-2. One is the progression of simple to complex relative to learning *outcomes*. This progression is seen by reading from left to right. The other is a cumulative progression in terms of learning *processes*. The sequence begins with objectives at the upper part of Figure 7-2, moves to teaching and learning in the center, and ends with transfer at the lower part of the figure.

There are several implications for teaching and learning suggested by Figure 7-2. Pictured this way, it is easy to see that teaching for transfer is a sequence that begins when the teacher formulates goals and objectives and ends when the learner applies what has been learned to new learning tasks. Another implication is that learning which concentrates at the levels of knowledge, receiving, and basic movements (1) is not likely to be meaningful, (2) will require a great deal of drill and practice, (3) will not be retained well, and (4) will have low transfer value. Furthermore, Figure 7-2 implies that for complex learning to be meaningful, both less complex and prerequisite learning must also be meaningful.

Let us examine more closely the implications that derive from each of the major concepts relative to teaching for transfer shown in Figure 7-2. First, we will examine those that are mostly teaching for transfer. Then we will look at the implications that derive from the major concepts more directly related to learning for transfer.

Briefly, Figure 7-2 shows that . . .

TEACHING FOR TRANSFER

Once goals and objectives have been stated, teaching for transfer requires that the teacher pay attention to interpretations of learning and to approaches to instruction.

INTERPRETATION OF LEARNING   Teaching for transfer involves both molar and molecular interpretations of learning. That is, teaching for transfer within each of the three domains, cognitive, affective, and psychomotor, requires cognitive and connectionist interpretations of learning in terms both of connections between the parts and of learning experiences as wholes. An interpretation that combines both points of view, such as that of Gagné for the cognitive domain, is likely to be optimally useful to teachers. Having learners strengthen the connections between specific stimuli and responses—for instance, having them name the bones of the body through drill and practice sessions while also understanding about the overall purpose, design, material, and so forth of the skeletal system—is an example of combining molecular and molar interpretations of learning in teaching for transfer. Learning that results from such teaching has a good probability of transferring *positively*, *vertically*, and *horizontally* to later learning tasks.

Teaching for transfer means . . .

A molecular interpretation of learning, as you will recall from Chapter 4, emphasizes practice of specific common components. A molar interpretation emphasizes the total pattern or entire context of the present and related learning situations. Combining the two views implies that to teach for transfer, you should emphasize practice of the common components in the total context of the learning situations rather than in isolation. For learning in the cognitive domain, for example, learners would learn to name some country's manufactured products not by drill with a list of its products, but rather, by practice in trying to put themselves in the place of the people in that country. By trying to "live" as they do, learners would learn about the general conditions of the country and its relationship with the rest of the world. The specific names of manufactured products would be learned as a meaningful part of the total experience with the people of that country (Bruner, 1960).

A combined interpretation of learning can also apply to teaching for transfer in the affective and psychomotor domains. Teachers constantly provide opportunities for learners to practice attending and responding to specific and appropriate learning tasks. Usually such practice is a part of some total learning experience. Occasionally, however, a teacher encounters learners who attend and respond poorly. In such instances, he might apply a molecular interpretation of learning, for example, a shaping process using principles of operant conditioning, to increase the frequency with which the learners remain in their seats, attend to the task, answer questions, and so forth. If maximum transfer is to occur, however, such specific affective behaviors must be learned in the context of the total school experience and not allowed to become connected only to arithmetic lessons, discussion sessions, or the teacher's presence. This means that teaching for transfer of affective learning requires practice while *living* in schools and not just *practicing* in schools for future living. School learning *is* living, not just practice for living. This "truth" is seen most clearly in teaching for transfer at the organization and characterization levels of affective objectives. We will learn more about combining molecular and molar interpretations of learning in the affective domain when we discuss classroom management in Chapters 9 and 10.

Examples of teaching for transfer that involve a combination of molecular and molar interpretations of learning are often more apparent in the psychomotor domain than in the other domains. This is probably because much that constitutes a total motor performance can actually be seen. For example, playing basketball, the parts—dribbling, passing, pivoting, shooting—are visible. A teacher who wants the learners to play well uses molecular and molar interpretations of learning when teaching for transfer. The coach causes the learners to drill and practice the many components of the game. Often drill and practice of the components is in isolation from other components and from the total performance of playing the game. There is drill in shooting baskets, passing, dribbling, and so on. The wise teacher, however, knows that transfer of these isolated motor skills to the later playing of the game will occur best if practice also occurs in the total context of the game. This is the reasoning behind the practice game.

A molecular interpretation of learning can be misused in learning motor skills much as it can in learning cognitive and affective skills. Isolated practice of the common components, even in large amounts, is not likely to result in effective transfer. Typists become expert at typing not just by doing readiness drills but by practicing the kinds of materials they eventually will need to type. Students in driver training learn to drive by driving, not just by practicing the isolated readiness skills of steering, braking, signaling, and so on. In like manner, children can be expected to become good at reading not just by practice of readiness skills but also by practicing reading.

APPROACHES TO TEACHING FOR TRANSFER   Teaching for transfer can be accomplished through many different approaches to instruction. Research does not support the superiority of any one approach to teaching for transfer. As we saw in Chapter 6, the approach you use should be determined by your objectives, by what you want to transfer. If the cognitive objectives you want your learners to acquire and transfer are concerned with practices, techniques, procedures, or processes of problem solving, probably you will choose a discovery or guided-discovery approach such as that described in Chapter 6. If, however, your objectives are primarily content, you will likely choose a meaningful reception approach, although it certainly is not necessary that you do. Learners can and do learn content through a discovery approach, and they can learn about processes, techniques, procedures, and processes of problem solving without actually discovering them.

As you know, a great deal of controversy has focused on the relative merits of discovery and meaningful reception learning. For example, it has been argued that discovery learning is "active," whereas reception learning is "passive." In this view, learners using a discovery approach are pictured as actively and meaningfully practicing what they are learning. Learners using a reception approach, on the other hand, are described as not practicing but rather passively and rotely absorbing what they learn. You would conclude from this argument that greater transfer might result from discovery learning than from reception learning. As you may guess, however, this point of view has not been accepted by everyone.

Teaching for transfer requires both . . .

David Ausubel (1963) takes us to the very center of this controversy. His point of view has been that meaningful discovery learning may result in greater learning, retention, and transfer than meaningful reception learning. However, it is neither necessary nor desirable to arrange the events of instruction so that learners discover everything they learn. It is simply too time-consuming to do so. Furthermore, reception learning can be meaningful. Ausubel (1969) points out that in meaningful reception learning, the learner actively associates the substance (meaning) of new chains, concepts, and so forth with relevant components of previous learning. Learning is meaningful provided that the learner has a "set" to connect the learning material to existing cognitive structure, and that the material is potentially meaningful, that is, logically relatable.

When you plan what you will do to help your children learn, retain, and transfer skills and knowledge in the cognitive domain, the two viewpoints mean that you will need to decide which of your objectives most appropriately can be met through the usually time-consuming discovery approach and which ones through the more efficient approach of meaningful reception learning. You no doubt will make frequent use of both approaches.

There is one major difference in the organization of instructions depending on the approach you use, however. A discovery approach usually proceeds from simple to complex or from specific to general. A meaningful reception approach, on the other hand, usually moves from general to specific. A couple of examples will show this difference.

Suppose you are teaching children in the primary grades. For social studies, you have described instructional objectives that require your learners to name six community helpers and to describe their duties. Teaching for transfer in this case means that, later, the learners will be able to apply the concrete concept *community helper* to solving the problem of deciding where to get certain kinds of assistance or service in similar communities where the learners may move or visit. Solving such problems will result in learning the rule: "Communities like ours have similar community helpers."

Teaching for transfer through a discovery approach involves arranging the events of instruction so that the conditions of learning concrete concepts are met. You share your objectives with the learners: "Today we will begin learning about certain people who help others in our community. When we finish this part of our learning, you will be able to name these people and to describe how they help others. Later, we will learn about the 'helping people' in other communities like ours."

Your instructional procedure will likely begin with concrete experiences with specific "helping" persons in the community. Pictures, stories, films, interviews, field trips, and other aids relative to each helping person will be used to give your learners a meaningful understanding of the concept *community helper*. You guide your learners with clues and questions toward a meaningful definition of the concept, e.g., "a community helper is a person who. . . ." To demonstrate that they have learned the concept meaningfully rather than rotely, you have them generalize the concept by determining whether another person, unfamiliar to them, can be classified as a community helper. You may do this by describing for them what service is performed by that person.

Teaching for transfer through an approach of meaningful reception learning also requires that you arrange the events of instruction so that all the general and specific conditions of learning concrete concepts are met. As with a discovery approach, you begin by sharing your objectives with your learners. You may even say the very same words you used in that approach.

From this point on, however, the instructional procedure for a meaningful reception approach is quite different from that for a discovery approach. Rather than begin by arranging concrete experience with specific examples of community helpers, you start with broad, general, concrete experiences indicating interdependent needs that exist within the community. You may, for instance, begin with the statement: "When many people live close together in a community like ours, they have to help one another." This remark can be made meaningful to your learners by relating the general idea of interdependence to the interdependence of children within the classroom. The services performed by room monitors, e.g., keeping clean chalk boards, attractive and useful bulletin boards, comfortable room temperature and ventilation, and available supplies of sharpened pencils, can be used as meaningful examples of how people who live together help one another.

From the broad, general statement, you then proceed toward increasingly specific details subsumed by the general statement. Eventually, you will provide concrete experiences with specific examples of community helpers.

Either approach can be expected to lead to transfer as long as the learning experiences have been meaningfully related to previous learning and can be associated meaningfully with specific components or generalizations of them in other learning situations.

My own preference in using approaches to learning is to emphasize a discovery approach during the early school years. This approach is more likely to result in the children's experiencing direct contact with concrete materials than is a reception approach. If we believe that learning tends to be cumulative, it follows that if later and more complex learning is to be meaningful, early learning experiences must also be meaningful. This requires that learning experiences include contacts with concrete materials, the "real" and physical world, not just abstractions of it. In Chapter 11, we will learn about Jean Piaget's explanation of why this is true.

LEARNING FOR TRANSFER

Learning for transfer means . . .

Once the teacher (1) has described goals and objectives, (2) can apply the important ideas from various interpretations of learning to the provision of the conditions of learning, and (3) has selected appropriate approaches to learning, the major focus of teaching for transfer shifts to what the learner does. Gaining meaning from the instructional process is the learner's central task. As Figure 7-2 shows, when learning is meaningful, (1) transfer is likely, (2) the necessity of practice is low, and (3) retention is high. Let us look more closely at each of these variables in connection with learning for transfer.

MEANINGFULNESS OF LEARNING By this time you have learned a great deal about the defined concept *meaningfulness,* and it should now transfer efficiently to learning the higher-order rule: *The single most important prerequisite for transfer is a rich and meaningfully organized cognitive structure.*

As a teacher, I want this rule to be meaningful for you. However, I know that if it is, the prerequisites for the rule must also be meaningful for you. The components or concepts that form the rule must represent word-pictures in your mind that are logically associated with other, relevant, and meaningful concepts. Remember, in Chapter 6, the line drawing of concepts spiraling up and out, touching as they become more complex and interrelated? The concepts in this rule must have these interconnecting links if the rule is to be meaningful for you.

As I examine the parts of the rule and review what we have done together, I must decide whether additional instruction will be helpful. You will need to do exactly the same thing many times with your learners. One way to decide what to do at points such as this is to evaluate how meaningful the concepts are for your learners. Setting a problem-solving task or asking questions is the usual way to go about testing for meaningfulness. We can use a checkpoint exercise for this purpose. The examples I give for each item should provide additional instruction that you may need relative to the concept of meaningfulness and teaching for transfer.

As you do Checkpoint 7-3, note that testing situations that give immediate feedback are really both testing and learning sessions. We will examine this fact more completely in Chapter 13.

CHECKPOINT 7-3

1. Define the term *prerequisite* and give an example to show that you can use it appropriately.

2. Construct simple line drawings that illustrate your understanding of the terms "meaningfully" and "rotely" learned material.

3. With words and line drawings, show your understanding of: "A rich and meaningfully organized cognitive structure."

4. Learning about transfer is:

(Boring)   (Nothing to me)   (Satisfying)

PRACTICE IN LEARNING   When teaching for transfer, it is useful to remember the rule "We learn what we practice," because it explains why we should have our learners practice what we want to transfer, and in the context in which it will later be used.

Two additional points about the role of practice in learning, retention, and transfer should be made. First, as Figure 7-2 shows, learning that is less meaningful—knowledge-level, chains, receiving (attending), and basic movements—usually requires more practice than does learning that is potentially more meaningful—synthesis or evaluation-level, rules or higher-order rules, organization of or characterization by values, and nondiscursive communication. Second, the less meaningful learning tends to be, the more the practice should be distributed in small amounts over time, rather than massed, say, at two or three hours at one time. This essentially means that there is likely to be an overall economy of learning and greater retention and transfer if practice occurs after or during the establishment of meaning. Learning to name the products of some country and then solving problems about the country's involvement in world trade, for example, is likely to require less practice and to result in greater transfer when learning about the country's products is meaningfully accomplished rather than when they are memorized from a list. Learning chemical equations, laws of physics, procedures for dismantling an engine, and so on also tends to require less total practice and to transfer better when practice occurs after or in conjunction with the acquisition of meaning than if learned as isolated facts.

RETENTION OF LEARNING   Figure 7-2 summarizes the idea that learning that is generally inclusive in nature is more likely to be retained than learning that is comparatively simple and less inclusive. The implication for teaching for transfer is that, whenever possible, we should try to instruct so that our learners acquire general, inclusive concepts, rules, attitudes, and motor skills. This brings us to an extremely important question for classroom instruction: "Since general ideas seem to transfer best, is it necessary that learners retain *any* specific information, chains, attentional responses, values, basic movements?" The answer is, *certainly*. Note that my ability to write the word "certainly" and to italicize it so that it speaks to you loudly and surely requires specific skills that I must be able to recall and reproduce quickly and accurately. Although our lives tend to be regulated by general concepts, rules, organizations of values, and motor skills, we live, in and out of school, in terms of specifics. Our specific learnings are the tools we have ready at hand that permit us to apply the general ideas to living. **Learning for transfer requires . . .** Consistent with the continuing theme of combining ideas expressed throughout this text, teaching for transfer is not a matter of teaching for the retention of either specific detail or general ideas. It is a matter of teaching for both.

Remember Mike from Chapter 5? He understood the meaning of the broad, general concepts and rules related to reducing fractions to lowest terms. He knew in general what division was about, yet he was unable to reduce specific fractions. The reason he could not was that he had not drilled and practiced sufficiently with the appropriate number combinations so that they were retained well enough to be recalled clearly and quickly when he needed them.

The problem you will have to face in teaching for transfer is trying to decide what specific information, values, and basic movements should be drilled and practiced so that they are retained and can be recalled precisely and quickly. Of course, there is no specific answer to this problem. The best I can do is show you where to find the answer. As you have probably guessed, the answer is in the instructional objectives you describe for your learners and in the analysis you make of the objectives described. When you have stated what you want learners to learn and what they must be able to do to learn it, you will have a reasonably good idea of what specific information, affect, or motor skills they will need to learn and practice so that it will be retained and recalled in order for transfer to occur.

CHECKPOINT 7-4

If my teaching is to be consistent with what I have been teaching about teaching, learning, and transfer, I should help you to formulate meaningful higher-order rules of thumb and to practice applying them. Therefore, for this checkpoint:

1. Review the information presented so far in this chapter, including Figures 7-1 and 7-2. Then state as many rules of thumb as you can that will provide general guidance for you and your learners as you teach and learn for transfer in a school setting.

2. For each rule, give an example of how you might apply it. The rules of thumb I have thought of, with examples of application, are in the following section. (NOTE: This is a synthesis-level task, and completing it provides a measure of your commitment to the importance of learning to teach for transfer.)

3. Suppose that, in your first year of teaching, one of your senior colleagues remarks, "teaching for transfer is all right in theory, but teachers really haven't time to worry about doing so in the real world of the classroom." What will be your response to this teacher's claim?

A Synthesis of Higher-Order Rules for Teaching and Learning for Transfer

Implied in the expression "teaching for transfer" is the idea that transfer does not happen automatically. Generally speaking, this is true. However, as we saw early in this chapter, transfer frequently occurs as an incidental part of learning experiences in all three domains. It is useful for us as teachers to be aware of the fact that incidental transfer, both positive and negative, often results from our instruction. It is more important, however, to have mastered the prerequisites for planned transfer. In other words, it is more valuable to meaningfully learn the general and inclusive higher-order rules relevant to teaching and learning for transfer, and also to learn to be able to recall the specific information and skills necessary to apply the rules when we need to, than it is to allow transfer to happen just by chance. As we learned earlier, we need to learn and retain *both* general rules and specific details if we are to teach for transfer and help learners to learn for transfer.

The higher-order rules of thumb for teaching and learning for transfer that I have synthesized from our discussion are presented in the next five sections and illustrated with examples. This "rule-example" technique of presentation is commonly used in a meaningful reception approach to learning. Here are the rules: (1) Teach for transfer in all three domains. (2) Decide what you want to transfer. (3) Make the learning meaningful. (4) Practice what is to be transferred. (5) Emphasize generalizations.

"Rule-example" is a technique for . . .

TEACH FOR TRANSFER
IN ALL THREE DOMAINS

Teaching for transfer is closely related to our statement of objectives, and, as you recall from Chapter 3, objectives in more than one domain are usually being met at the same time. This rule does not mean necessarily that you should plan to teach for transfer in all three domains at once, although this is entirely possible. Let me provide an example of how this might occur.

Suppose you are Mr. Johnson and you want Melinda to learn to (1) estimate lengths accurately, (2) measure with a ruler, and (3) gain satisfaction from responding in arithmetic class. Teaching for transfer in this instance involves at least three types of transfer. Can you describe the three types of transfer I am talking about here? If you can, two things have transferred for you. First, you have transferred the general idea of types of transfer to this specific instance. Second, you have meaningfully learned the specific prerequisites (parts of the general idea) and have practiced them enough so that they are retained with sufficient clarity and precision to be recalled separately from the more inclusive and general idea.

The three types of transfer I had specifically in mind are these: (1) *cognitive, positive, vertical,* and *planned*; (2) *psychomotor, positive, vertical,* and *planned*; and (3) *affective, positive, vertical,* and *planned*. Others are possible. Incidental transfer could have occurred in each domain. Transfer could have been horizontal in the sense that (1) skill in estimating could generalize to areas other than arithmetic; (2) skill in manipulating a ruler could easily transfer to measuring, for example, in sewing or art work; and (3) satisfaction in responding would be likely to transfer to areas other than arithmetic, especially to those in which responding is reinforced.

Five higher-order rules for teaching and learning for transfer are . . .

DECIDE WHAT YOU WANT TO TRANSFER

Reaching a decision on what you wish to transfer is an impossible task until you have (1) described your goals and objectives in all domains, and (2) completed a task analysis of them. "Teaching for transfer" is an essentially meaningless verbal chain until you know what the learner needs to learn *now* and how what he now learns will relate to what he will learn about later. Only one type of transfer is at all logically possible when you do not know clearly your goals and objectives, and when you do not know what the learner needs to learn to meet them. Any transfer that occurs will necessarily be incidental. An example will help us understand how teaching and learning for transfer relies on task description and task analysis.

Here we are, back again with Mr. Johnson's class. The children are trying to work the arithmetic problems on the practice worksheet we looked at in Chapter 5. Remember John? He is completely absorbed in the activity and has finished everything except the story problem in Part VI. A look of confusion clouds his face as he says to you, "I just can't figure it out." He continues, "Is this problem a 'change' problem or is it an 'add' problem? Something in his manner suggests that he believes asking for help is cheating. He watches your face for a clue and waits for your answer.

Obviously, John has not learned for transfer. When the problems are already set up for him, as they are in Parts I through V, he knows what to do. This suggests that his learning and practice of "change" and "add" problems have been restricted to set-up problems. Implicit in instruction for John has been the notion that skill in solving set-up problems will transfer automatically to solving story-type or application problems. Hence, practice relative to teaching for transfer has been out of context. That is, the common components have been identified and practiced in isolation from the situations in which they are to be used later.

A statement of goals and objectives and a task analysis of them could have resulted in teaching and learning for transfer. A task analysis of a specific instructional objective might have related to solving problems that require application of knowledge of how to reduce, change, and add fractions and mixed numbers. It would have shown a progressive and cumulative sequence of the prerequisites required to meet the objective. The sequence would also have provided clues about appropriate contexts in which teaching and learning for transfer would occur. The sample task analysis of the instructional objective presented in Checkpoint 5-2 illustrates these points.

MAKE THE LEARNING MEANINGFUL

As we have seen, there are many factors that determine whether learning is meaningful. Teaching and learning for transfer require that it is.

At this point, we should be able to express these factors as simple, applicable rules: (1) Share your goals and objectives with your learners. (2) Sequence learning tasks in a cumulative way. (3) Make sure prerequisites have been meaningfully learned. (4) Practice what is to be transferred.

SHARE YOUR GOALS AND OBJECTIVES WITH YOUR LEARNERS   Objectives give learners a basis from which to form a purpose or intent to learn meaningfully: "Today we are going to learn about. . . . When we finish, you will be able to. . . . Later you will learn more about. . . . "

SEQUENCE LEARNING TASKS IN A CUMULATIVE WAY   In brief, you should first make sure that learners are able to associate what is now to be learned with broad and meaningful concepts or rules they have learned about before. Then you should help them learn the less general concepts and specific chains that are logically subsumed under the relatively broad concepts and rules. At the point of learning new concepts and chains, you should make sure that your learners experience concrete examples of what is being learned about. The sequence progresses from general to specific like this:

> What we are going to learn about today is related to how people in the world learn to behave toward one another. (Teacher leads general discussion.) . . . One way of looking at why people do what they do is known as a connectionist interpretation of learning. (Teacher provides a broad view.) . . . Central to a connectionist interpretation of learning is the rule. . . . (Teacher explains overall rule.) B. F. Skinner has spent much of his lifetime learning about the specific characteristics of the parts of this rule. (Teacher defines details.) The term *positive reinforcement* means. . . . (Teacher explains.) To illustrate what I mean by *positive reinforcement*, let us. . . . (Teacher cites examples.)

MAKE SURE PREREQUISITES HAVE BEEN MEANINGFULLY LEARNED Your task analysis will tell you the prerequisites for any new learning task. If you follow Gagné's system for conducting a task analysis, they will be listed in the form of his six types of learning. Testing for meaningfulness of chains, discriminations, concepts, and rules can be accomplished by applying Gagné's criteria for determining whether learning of a particular type has occurred (refer to Chapter 4); e.g., "Mike, in order for you to divide by two numbers, you must be able to *estimate* with numbers. Explain to me what 'to estimate' means. . . . Estimate the number of groups of five cookies each that are contained in this larger group of cookies." Or, in the affective domain, as a prerequisite to gaining satisfaction in responding, Melinda must have meaningfully learned about the topic being discussed. That is, she must have learned something meaningful, with which she *can* respond.

PRACTICE WHAT IS TO BE TRANSFERRED Subsumed under this higher-order rule are several simple rules, some of which we have practiced before: (1) Practice in context. (2) Distribute practice. (3) Practice through application.

Practice in Context We saw an example of this rule in Chapter 5 when Mike practiced forming numerals legibly and accurately in the context of solving problems in arithmetic. Learning vocabulary words of a foreign language in the context of speaking the language is another example. Practicing a left-to-right progression while picture reading is another.

The rule "Practice in context" means . . .

Distribute Practice This rule is especially relevant for retention and transfer of material that cannot be acquired with a high degree of meaning, e.g., names of places and people, value for π, unusual spellings of some words, and geographical and historical facts. Such learning should be practiced (reviewed) frequently in context and usually in the form of whole-part learning and review. This technique results in what is called overlearning, that is, in practice of material beyond the point at which it is barely learned. Material that is overlearned is highly resistant to forgetting.

Practice Through Application This rule derives from a combination of the previous ones. That is, practice of what is to transfer should be distributed, and applied in a variety of contexts. Practice of the skills of adding or subtracting fractions should be distributed, in the form of whole-part review and applied to solving various kinds of story problems. Practice of the motor skills of bouncing and passing a basketball should be distributed and applied in progressively more complex, simulated, and actual game situations. In like manner, within the affec-

The rule "Practice through application" means . . .

tive domain, becoming committed to a value or a value system requires distributed and varied practice of what is to transfer. For example, your becoming committed to the value of specific instructional objectives for effective teaching and learning has the prerequisite that you understand what objectives are and how they can be used. It also requires that you distribute your practice of them and that you practice applying objectives to a variety of situations of teaching and learning.

EMPHASIZE GENERALIZATIONS

The previous discussions have shown that information, values, and motor activities of a general, inclusive nature have greater possibility of transfer than do specific facts, attitudes, or motor chains. Consequently, teaching and learning for transfer should have the long-range goal of causing learners to form meaningful generalizations relative to their school experiences in all three domains of learning. The important point here is that meaningful generalizations are *not* formed from nothing. They are the culmination of sequences of less inclusive learning experiences that are rich in meaning.

The one major generalization, that is, the higher-order rule, I hope you have gained from our work together in these first seven chapters, is that if transfer is to occur more than just by chance, we must teach for it. This rule will transfer to your classroom teaching *if* the less inclusive ideas subsumed by it have been meaningful for you and *if* you have had sufficient practice with them to master and retain them.

We now turn our attention to a practical part of teaching for transfer—ways and means in which a teacher can help each learner practice what and when he needs to so that his learning is indeed efficient and meaningful for him. Chapter 8 is about the application of the rules from a science of behavior to the provision of instruction that is optimal for each learner.

IN PASSING

Can you see any possibilities for transfer in the example of instructions on page 207 that have been programmed?

ACTIVITIES

1. So far in the course, we have proceeded from general to specific in keeping with an approach of meaningful reception learning. Illustrate this progression with a line drawing or schematic that shows how the general and specific ideas we have worked with in the first seven chapters connect with one another in sequential and cumulative fashion. Note that the connections represent the meaning, in summary form, that you have gained from our work through Chapter 7. Compare and contrast your line drawing with that of a colleague or with one provided by your instructor.

2. Explain to a colleague how this text attempts to teach for transfer. (NOTE that your explanation calls for an analysis-level performance.)

3. For review, as an individual, a small group, or the entire class, describe briefly the major contributions to teaching and learning made by the people we have met in the first seven chapters: William James, Sigmund Freud, Benjamin Bloom, David Krathwohl, Anita Harrow, Ivan Pavlov, John Watson, Edwin Guthrie, Edward Thorndike, B. F. Skinner, Max Wertheimer, Wolfgang Köhler, Jerome Bruner, Edward Tolman, Clark Hull, Robert Gagné, John Carroll, John Holt, David Ausubel.

4. Teach a learner for transfer. First, decide what you want him to learn now and later

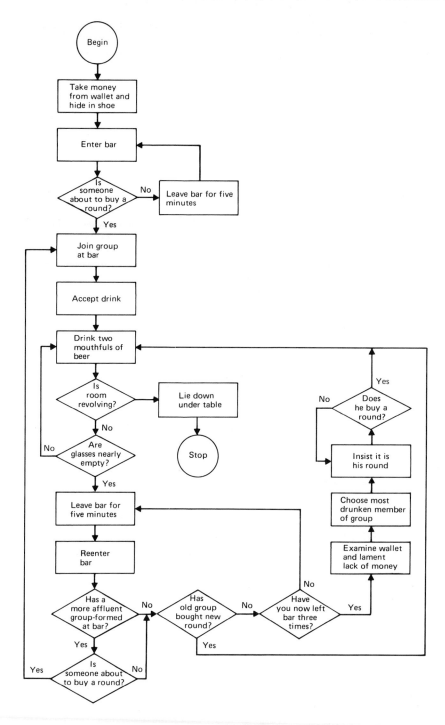

(objectives); second, do a brief task analysis of the objectives to decide what you want to transfer; and third, apply our higher-order rules of thumb relative to teaching and learning for transfer; that is, state how you will make the learning meaningful, how practice will be used, and what generalizations to emphasize.

5. Just for fun:

Here is one reasonably effective solution to the railroad problem in Chapter 6. Your learners will find others. "Drive engine to boxcar A. Push A into the switch area. Unhook. Drive engine back and across to boxcar B. Push B to A and hook them together. Pull both A and B back on main track. You have E-B-A on the main track. Push B and A to far right. Unhook A and leave it there. Pull B to left and push it past its original position and into switch area. Unhook and leave B there. Back E to main track and across to right side. Drive past where A was originally and hook on to B. Pull B to original A position and unhook. Back E to A. Hook on to A and drive across to left side. Push A to original position of B. Unhook. Drive E back to original position on main track."

One reason you may have had difficulty with this problem is negative transfer. To solve the problem, you had to overcome past learning relative to problems that appear similar to this one, problems that can be solved by moving *directly* to the solution. In the railroad problem, this approach does not solve the problem. Therefore, past experiences interfere with solution. Note how this may have occurred with you. You probably first tried to solve the problem directly by pushing A into the switch area, unhooking, pushing B to A, hooking them together, pulling A to the original position of B, and then unhooking it and leaving it there. This, of course, is the most obvious and direct thing to do in light of past experience. But it will not work in this instance. To solve the problem, you must overcome negative transfer. You must move A and B past the obvious solution.

Do you now have a clue as to why children in elementary school can often solve the problem as easily as older and "more experienced" people?

A higher-order rule that comes to my mind when solving "difficult" problems is simply: "If what I'm trying doesn't work, try another approach."

REFERENCES

Ausubel. D. P. (1963). *The Psychology of Meaningful Verbal Learning*. New York: Grune & Stratton.
——— (1969). *Readings in School Learning*. New York: Holt.
Bloom, B. S., ed. (1956) *Taxonomy of Educational Objectives: Handbook I: Cognitive Domain*. New York: McKay.
Bruner, J. S. (1960). *The Process of Education*. New York: Vintage.
Gagné, R. M. (1970). *The Conditions of Learning*. New York: Holt.
——— (1974). *Essentials of Learning for Instruction*. Hinsdale, Ill.: Dryden.
Harrow, A. J. (1972). *A Taxonomy of the Psychomotor Domain: A Guide for Developing Behavioral Objectives*. New York: McKay.
Herndon, J. (1968). *The Way It Spozed to Be*. New York: Simon & Schuster.
Krathwohl, D. R., B. S. Bloom, and B. B. Masia (1964). *Taxonomy of Educational Objectives, Handbook II: Affective Domain*. New York: McKay.
Overman, J. R. (1930). An experimental study of the effect of the method of instruction on transfer of training in arithmetic, *Elementary School Journal*, 31, 183–190.

SUGGESTIONS FOR FURTHER READING

Duncan, C. P. (1953). Transfer in motor learning as a function of degree of first-task learning and intertask similarity, *Journal of Experimental Psychology*, **45**, 1–11. Duncan, in a cleverly designed study of motor learning, demonstrates that transfer can be attributed to a combination of generalization of responses and learning how to learn.
Ellis, H. C. (1965). *The Transfer of Learning*. New York: Collier-Macmillan. This small volume (200 pages) provides an excellent review of research on transfer, with both prac-

tical implications and theoretical significance. See also Ellis on transfer and retention, in M. H. Marx, ed. (1969). *Learning Processes*. New York: Macmillan, chaps 17–20.

Hendrickson, G., and W. H. Schroeder (1941). Transfer of training in learning to hit a submerged target. *Journal of Educational Psychology*, **32**, 205–213. This study is a replication of an earlier classic study by C. H. Judd (1908). The relation of special training to general intelligence, *Education Review*, **36**, 28–42. It illustrates the transfer value of knowledge of general principles to solving specific problems.

Logan, T. H., and K. H. Wodtke (1968). Effects of rules of thumb on transfer of training, *Journal of Educational Psychology*, **59**, 3, 147–153. This study is important because it points out clearly that rules of thumb of only limited generality can result in negative transfer if learners are not taught to discriminate when the rule applies and when it does not.

Maier, N. R. (1930). Reasoning in humans. I. On direction, *Journal of Comparative Psychology*, **10**, 115–143. Many years ago, Maier demonstrated with his famous two-string problem that experience alone is not sufficient for positive transfer to occur; such a transfer is best when experience is directed, that is, when transfer is taught for.

8

TECHNOLOGY IN EDUCATION: A BASIS FOR INDIVIDUALIZED INSTRUCTION

August 3, 1876

Up to the age of thirty, or beyond it, poetry of many kinds . . . gave me great pleasure, and even as a school-boy I took intense delight in Shakespeare, especially in the historical plays. I have also said that formerly pictures gave me considerable, and music very great delight. But now for many years I cannot endure to read a line of poetry: I have tried lately to read Shakespeare, and found it so intolerably dull that it nauseated me. I have also almost lost my taste for pictures or music. . . .

My mind seems to have become a kind of machine for grinding general laws out of large collections of facts, but why this should have caused the atrophy of that part of the brain alone, on which the higher tastes depend, I cannot conceive. . . . [I]f I had to live my life again I would have made a rule to read some poetry and listen to some music at least once every week; for perhaps the parts of my brain now atrophied would thus have been kept active through use. The loss of these tastes is a loss of happiness, and may possibly be injurious to the intellect, and more probably to the moral character, by enfeebling the emotional part of our nature.

Charles Darwin
The Autobiography of Charles Darwin

CONTENTS

ONGOING SUMMARY

In the first seven chapters we talked at length about the content and process of learning and teaching. The issues which have concerned us can be summarized by chapter.

In Chapters 1 and 2 we argued for the general issue of precision in a science of behavior, pointing out that description does not constitute explanation of behavior, and that a mastery approach is one way to cause learning to be efficient and meaningful. The argument for precision continued in Chapter 3, where we stressed the importance of specific instructional objectives.

Chapter 4 emphasized combining points of view as opposed to choosing from among them. We maintained that a meaningful synthesis of ideas relative to school learning is usually more helpful than are isolated ideas that result from choosing and rejecting among several alternatives.

The value of combining viewpoints was illustrated in Chapters 5 and 6, and the issue relative to possible confusion of approaches with conditions of learning was presented. We argued that regardless of the approach used to capture the attention of learners, the conditions of learning must be met.

Chapter 7 continued the argument for combining rather than selecting points of view. Teaching for meaningful learning, retention, and transfer requires more than an analysis of points of view. It demands a synthesis of approaches with the conditions under which learning will occur.

ADVANCE ORGANIZER

Performing just the right synthesis to ensure that classroom instruction is optimal for each learner is a tremendously difficult task. Fortunately, a much-needed technology of education is currently evolving from the rules of a science of behavior. With its evolution comes the hope that eventually teachers will be able to individualize instruction.

The expression "technology of education" refers to the application of the rules of a science of behavior to problems encountered in teaching and learning. The potential contribution of such a technology is its ability to devise ways to improve a teacher's effectiveness through techniques, materials, and strategies that help a teacher perform the many and varied teaching functions.

The teaching aids that have been a part of the technology have been mostly programmed materials and electromechanical devices that enable a learner to self-instruct, that is, to learn without the teacher's being immediately present. More recently, the rules of a science of behavior have been extended to instructional strategies that a teacher may develop into ongoing teaching behaviors *without* the use of programmed materials or self-instructional devices.

We must keep in mind, however, that programs and machines are techniques and materials of instruction, and to be effective, they must ensure that conditions of learning are met.

Arguments have been raised whether the teacher can, or should, be replaced by programmed materials presented by self-instructional machines. It is the type of either/or argument we have encountered before. Here it takes the form of "*either* teachers *or* machines." We will continue to argue, however, for combining, for synthesizing teachers *and* machines. The issue of either/or is trivial compared with the issue of how real, live, and warm teachers can use cold, impersonal, and matter-of-fact machines to help make instruction optimal for each learner. Chapter 8 is directed toward the latter question. Chapters 9 and 10 will deal with the extension of the rules of a science of behavior to instructional strategies for self-management.

Cognitive

To become an effective teacher, the learner should be able to apply the rules from a science of behavior to make instruction optimal for each learner.

GOALS AND OBJECTIVES

KNOWLEDGE LEVEL

Given the following terms or phrases, the learner is able to define them in writing: *science of behavior, technology, technology of education, teaching, individualized instruction, reinforcement, differential reinforcement, schedule of reinforcement, shaping, auto-instruction, programmed instruction, linear and branching programs, teaching machines, instructional strategy.*

COMPREHENSION LEVEL

1.   The learner is able to explain how a science of behavior can be combined with the art of teaching so that instruction will be optimal for each learner.
2.   Given Figure 8-1, the learner is able to interpret its meaning so that another person understands it well enough to list additional examples of each type of reinforcer.

APPLICATION LEVEL

Given the rules of a science of behavior, the learner can suggest ways they may be applied to his own teaching behavior.

ANALYSIS LEVEL

Given examples of programmed instruction, the learner is able to explain how the rules of a science of behavior are being applied.

SYNTHESIS LEVEL

The learner is able to construct simple, programmed materials that strengthen and maintain behaviors learned previously.

EVALUATION LEVEL

The learner is able to state, with reasons, whether he believes classroom instruction can be individualized without the use of a technology of education.

Affective

To become an effective teacher, the learner should be able to derive satisfaction from learning about ways to make instruction optimal for each learner.

RECEIVING (ATTENDING) LEVEL

The learner is aware of the difficulties of providing individualized instruction.

RESPONDING LEVEL

The learner derives satisfaction from knowing that he can program some of his instruction.

VALUING LEVEL

The learner argues that each student is entitled to optimal instruction.

ORGANIZATION LEVEL

The learner tries to form an overall approach to teaching that has the long-range goal of individualizing instruction.

CHARACTERIZATION LEVEL

The learner consistently searches for ways to apply a science of behavior to the art of teaching.

Every teacher must try to provide instruction that is optimal for each learner. This idea, of course, is not entirely new to us. You will recall, from Chapter 4, that John Carroll's model of school learning (1963) requires that instruction be optimal for each learner. The "something new" about this idea that we are now ready to learn about is the question: "How can we ensure that instruction is optimal for each learner?"

Individualized instruction means . . .

The present answer to this question is that so far we do not know for sure. That is, we do not yet know enough about teaching to meet *all* the individual differences, cognitive, affective, and psychomotor, of *all* learners *all* the time. This is, however, the ideal long-range goal toward which we are constantly striving. And, even though we have not yet achieved it, many things have been done which have moved us a bit closer. For example, the clear and precise objectives that derive from task descriptions increase the probability that instruction will be optimal. Task analyses help ensure that learning events are sequenced so that learning occurs efficiently and meaningfully. Knowing about the conditions of learning helps maximize the probability that each learner will learn. Teachers for years have grouped learners so that they will profit from instruction. Individual assignments, tutoring, and so forth have always been part of the constant effort to make instruction optimal for each learner.

A higher-order rule of all learning and teaching is . . .

There is, however, an underlying and limiting higher-order rule relative to all situations of teaching and learning. It is this: "Optimal instruction and teaching effort are directly proportional." This means that meeting more individual differences of more learners more of the time requires more time and effort. For us, the question of importance that derives from this rule is: "What can be done to increase our teaching efficiency without reducing our effectiveness?"

One place to turn for help in solving problems of efficiency and effectiveness in teaching and learning is a science of behavior. From this source, we can identify rules that can be applied to the art of teaching, that is, to changing behavior relative to school learning. These rules form the bases for the development of a wide variety of techniques, activities, and strategies that teachers can use with learners.

Technology of education means . . .

What I am describing is known as a technology, the application of science to the solution of practical problems of living. Ultimately, most of science has the objective of applying its body of knowledge to the improvement of the human condition. Thus, a *technology of education* has the purpose of improving education through the application of a science of behavior to maximizing the probability that learning will be optimal for each learner.

SCIENCE OF BEHAVIOR AND ART OF TEACHING

A science of behavior supplies more than a basis for efficiency in teaching and learning. It provides reasons for teacher action, lawful explanations for *why* we do *what* we do to help learners. Note that once again we are faced with the issue of *explanation* and *description*, presented first in Chapter 2.

One of the most pervasive abuses that exists in teaching at all levels is the adoption and use of materials, methods, procedures, techniques, and activities for reasons other than those that logically derive from instructional objectives and from a science of behavior. "I saw this idea for art in a magazine." "The film was in the building." "I thought a visit to the museum would be good for them." "Do the problems in rows 6 through 8—that's about all the time you will have." And so forth. These are the "reasons" too often given as "explanations" for why we do what we do when we practice the art of teaching. Obviously, such "reasons" are inadequate.

Let us see how a science of behavior can move us a bit closer toward optimal instruction for each learner. From its rules we should be able to derive reasons for our teaching behavior, and also develop a technology for improving our efficiency and effectiveness.

A Science of Behavior

Learning activities should not occur randomly, by intuition, chance, or to "fill up time." They should be undertaken on purpose and by design. Instructional objectives tell us what kinds of learning activities are likely to be appropriate ones. The conditions of learning help us know what is required for different types of learning to occur, and a science of behavior gives us clues about the rules of learning that are a part of all learning activities. Knowing these rules and how they need to be arranged so that learning is efficient and effective for each learner helps us to develop ways of *applying* these rules, that is, to develop a technology of teaching and learning.

For the most part, a science of behavior from which a technology of teaching and learning has developed has been a connectionist interpretation of learning. You will recall, from Chapter 4, that a connectionist interpretation of learning, with the exception of the work of Clark Hull and possibly that of Edward Tolman, has been concerned more with the rules of learning than with theories of learning. These rules have been derived from natural observation and controlled experimentation in which events believed to be related to learning could be systematically varied and their effects on learning objectively recorded. The point of emphasis of this interpretation of learning has been the conditioning or modification of respondent and operant behaviors. Thus, the science of behavior in a connectionist tradition consists mainly of the rules of respondent and operant conditioning.

Science of behavior means . . .

Although many persons have contributed to the discovery and development of these rules, the contributions of B. F. Skinner are most widely known. For more than forty years, he has studied operant behavior for the purpose of discovering, interpreting, refining, and applying the rules by which human behavior is learned and regulated. It is largely from his efforts that a technology of education has been possible.

RULES OF OPERANT CONDITIONING

Because the rules of reinforcement and punishment are central to operant conditioning, the rules of the science of behavior relevant to a technology of education are essentially the contingencies of reinforcement and punishment, that is, the conditions under which reinforcement and punishment result in learning.

Generally speaking, the rules of reward and punishment are the higher-order

Two rules of reward and punishment are . . . rules we learned about in Chapter 4: (1) Responses that are reinforced are learned, whereas responses that are not reinforced extinguish; and (2) responses that are punished are suppressed, with the result that an organism avoids or escapes from punishment.

Stated generally, these rules are not immediately useful in developing a technology for their application. They are like long-range goals and do not provide specific guidance for our actions. Before we can make systematic use of them, we must learn *what* acts as reinforcers and punishers; *when* reinforcement or punishment should occur; *how much* reinforcement or punishment is needed; *how often* it should occur; *under what conditions* it will be effective; and *what undesirable effects* possibly are associated with the use of reinforcement and punishment.

Much experimentation has been done in the past forty years to try to determine these specific facts relative to operant behavior. The contingencies of reinforcement, however, have been studied more than the contingencies of punishment. Consequently, for the remainder of this chapter, we will devote our attention to learning about a technology of education that makes use of the rules of positive reinforcement. Actually, punishment has become a part of the developing technology only in the sense that withholding reinforcement can be thought of as punishment. Systematic application of the rules of punishment has largely been avoided. We will learn a great deal more about the effects of both positive reinforcement and punishment when we consider classroom management in Chapters 9 and 10.

Reinforcement is defined as . . . WHAT ACTS AS A REINFORCER?   In the past few years, the term "reinforcement" has been used regularly by many people, especially teachers. It is widely accepted to mean an act of strengthening or increasing the frequency of occurrence of responses. Any object or event (stimulus) that has this effect on a response is called a *reinforcer*. Thus, any stimulus can possibly act as a reinforcer, since reinforcers are defined only in terms of their effects on responses. That is, if a stimulus increases the strength or frequency of the response with which it is associated, by definition, that stimulus is a reinforcer for that response.

Because reinforcers are recognized only by their effects on responses, it is impossible to be certain, prior to an act of potential reinforcement, whether a stimulus will act as a reinforcer for a given response. Only by experimenting can we know whether it will do so. Fortunately, a great deal of experimentation has been done and several classes of stimuli have been identified that *usually* act as reinforcers, but not always.

The major classes of stimuli that act as potential reinforcers are usually identified on the basis of whether (1) they seem to be naturally reinforcing (unlearned) or have acquired reinforcing properties as a result of learning, usually of classical conditioning; (2) they are tangible or intangible in nature; and (3) they occur internally or externally to the organism. These three dimensions of potential reinforcers, along with a few examples, are shown in Figure 8-1. Although this representation is only approximately true, it provides a generally useful way of organizing stimuli that can act as reinforcers. (Some examples can be included in more than one category, e.g., learning, since initially learning may be inherently reinforcing.)

Figure 8-1 shows simply that there is a wide range of stimuli that can act as potential reinforcers for the responses we want our learners to acquire and re-

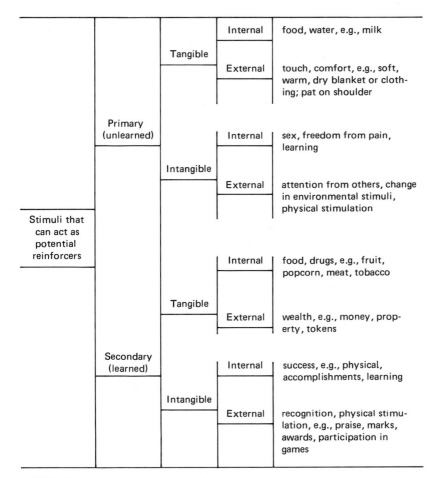

		Tangible	Internal	food, water, e.g., milk
	Primary (unlearned)		External	touch, comfort, e.g., soft, warm, dry blanket or clothing; pat on shoulder
		Intangible	Internal	sex, freedom from pain, learning
Stimuli that can act as potential reinforcers			External	attention from others, change in environmental stimuli, physical stimulation
		Tangible	Internal	food, drugs, e.g., fruit, popcorn, meat, tobacco
	Secondary (learned)		External	wealth, e.g., money, property, tokens
		Intangible	Internal	success, e.g., physical, accomplishments, learning
			External	recognition, physical stimulation, e.g., praise, marks, awards, participation in games

FIGURE 8-1   Dimensions of potential reinforcers.

tain. Clearly, potential reinforcers come in many forms. However, relative to school learning (and probably most other aspects of living), the single most promising potential reinforcer, classified here as *secondary, intangible,* and *internal,* is *success,* that is, in *knowing,* and in *knowing* that we know. We will have much more to say about this later in this chapter and in Chapter 11.

Lists of examples of stimuli that can act as potential reinforcers have been compiled by various persons. Here are a few from the list drawn up by Clifford and Charles Madsen (1972). Many of them are readily available to classroom teachers. (See Table 8-1.)

The most important reinforcer is . . .

Figures 8-1 and Table 8-1 do not tell us when, how much, how often, and under what conditions to reinforce and what possible undesirable effects may accompany reinforcement. We will have to look further.

WHEN SHOULD REINFORCEMENT OCCUR?   There is an old saying that a "poor" paymaster is one who pays before the job is done, or who never pays. By

TABLE 8-1   A variety of stimuli acts as potential reinforcers*

Words and sentences (verbal and written)

Yes	Exactly	I'm glad you're here.	You're doing fine.
Good	Great!	That shows thought.	This is the best yet.
Perfect	Of course!	Show us how.	Show this to your father.

Facial and bodily

Looking	Chuckling	Smiling	Rolling eyes enthusiastically
Winking	Clapping hands	Nodding	Signaling O.K.
Grinning	Thumbs up	Opening eyes	Hugging self

Nearness and touching

Standing alongside	Hugging	Eating next to the child	Touching hand
Ruffling hair	Shaking hands	Patting head	Squeezing hand
Patting shoulder	Walking alongside	Touching arm	Quick squeeze

Activities and privileges

Running errands	Displaying child's creative work or award
Choosing activities	Collecting materials (papers, workbooks, assignments, etc.)
Sharing a story	Helping other children
Reading a story	Making gifts

Things

Book markers	Play money	Books, appropriate level	Money (exchangeable, token)
Buttons	Wall decorations	Pencils with names	Stationary
Stars	Money	Chips	Collections (coins, rocks, glass, leaves, stamps, etc.)

Food

Popcorn	Sugar-coated cereals	Animal crackers	Candy bars
Peanuts	Fruit	Milk	Potato chips
Cookies	Crackers	Marshmallows	

Success

"Being able to do," and "knowing that you know."

---

* C.K. Madsen and C.H. Madsen, (1972). *Parents/Children/Discipline: A Positive Approach.* Boston: Allyn & Bacon. Reprinted with permission.

When should reinforcement occur?

implication, a "good" paymaster is one who pays as the job progresses, or who pays promptly upon its completion. As a rule of thumb, this pretty well answers the question of when reinforcement should occur. In most instances, it should occur immediately following the emission of appropriate responses.

Application of this rule to the effective use of reinforcers poses few problems for rats and pigeons learning relatively simple behaviors in Mr. Skinner's experimental boxes. However, a classroom teacher, when helping thirty or more students learn complex, cognitive, affective, and psychomotor behaviors in complicated school environments, will find it difficult, if not impossible, to apply the rule effectively without assistance. As we will see later in this chapter, a technology of education offers many suggestions that will increase the teacher's effectiveness at reinforcing each learner *when* reinforcement should occur.

HOW MUCH REINFORCEMENT IS NEEDED?   The answer to this question is always empirical, that is, we should use "just enough to get each job done." I know this is not a very definite answer, but the difficulty in being more precise is that stimuli which act as potential reinforcers vary in their reinforcing values. For one thing, reinforcers, like most currencies, are most valuable when in reasonably short supply and when they can be obtained for a reasonable amount of effort. Their value tends to decrease when available in such abundance that they become satiating. For example, reading poetry for a few minutes to your students, right after lunch when they return to class, causes them to come promptly and pleasantly to attention for the class session. However, unless you are an extremely gifted reader and constantly have interesting material, you can expect that reading to your students will lose some of its effectiveness if you begin stretching the reading sessions to fill the entire class period. In the same sense, other potentially reinforcing stimuli, for example, food, praise, attention, and games, may lose their effectiveness with overuse. Often, however, loss in effectiveness is only temporary. Usually a period of deprivation of the stimuli is enough to reinstate their reinforcing properties.

I should use as much reinforcement as . . .

We still have not really answered the question of just how much reinforcement is needed. Actually, the best I can say here is that your own judgment is your best guide. Give it a try, keeping in mind that moderation is a good target to aim for and that it is probably better to err initially on the side of not quite enough reinforcement than on the side of too much.

HOW OFTEN SHOULD REINFORCEMENT OCCUR?   There are several parts to the answer for this question. For the most part, however, frequency of reinforcement is related to whether a new response or series of responses is being learned or whether an old response is being maintained. As a rule of thumb, when new responses are being learned, as often as possible ensure that *each* appropriate response is immediately reinforced. This pattern of reinforcement is called a "schedule of continuous reinforcement."

As the new response or sequence of responses becomes established, however, the schedule for reinforcement should be altered so that only some of the appropriate responses are reinforced. This pattern is known as "intermittent reinforcement." It is a pattern that has the property of maintaining responses in strength over long periods of time. Classic examples of the operation of this schedule of reinforcement are seen in games of chance, such as cards, pinball, and slot machines, in which reinforcement occurs only "once in a while." Other examples, although not quite so obvious, can also be found; e.g., shooting baskets in basketball; fishing, with the occasional good catch; asking or coaxing, which frequently results in successful persuasion; working on the job, with the weekly or monthly paychecks; responding to school tasks; and, being "correct" at least occasionally.

How often should reinforcement occur?

A useful guide in using intermittent reinforcement is to remember that once your learners acquire new responses, it will not be necessary to reinforce each and every response. Reinforcement that occurs once in a while, even at some later time, will be sufficient.

UNDER WHAT CONDITIONS IS REINFORCEMENT EFFECTIVE?   The general answer is that potential reinforcers are effective when they follow a response immediately and when they occur in moderation. But, as we have seen, there are exceptions to this rule. For example, reinforcement that occurs on a continuous schedule tends to lose some of its effectiveness once the new response has been learned. Also, a potential reinforcer loses its value as the learner becomes satiated by that stimulus.

Differential reinforcement means . . . An important condition relative to the effectiveness of reinforcement is that only certain responses are reinforced. Thus, reinforcement is selective, not random. That is, responses are treated differentially. Only those appropriate to the task are reinforced. Responses irrelevant or detrimental to meeting the desired objective are not reinforced.

SHAPING BEHAVIOR THROUGH REINFORCEMENT

The principle of selective or *differential reinforcement* is a primary condition of shaping new behaviors. Since your job as a teacher is essentially that of changing or shaping behavior of learners, it will be extremely helpful to know how this principle operates. Briefly, it works thus:

Seven basic steps of shaping behavior are . . .
1. A learning task is described in precise, behavior terms (task description, after Bloom, Krathwohl, Harrow).
2. The learning task is analyzed (task analysis, after Gagné).
3. Conditions of learning are established.
4. Events of instruction are planned.
5. Responses consistent with the objective are reinforced. Others are not.
6. Gradually, only closer and closer approximations of the complete, final performance required by the objective are reinforced. Eventually, only the complete, final performance itself is reinforced. Approximations are not.
7. The new behavior is maintained in strength by intermittent reinforcement.

Let us see how an actual example of shaping new behaviors might work in your classroom.

1. *A learning task is described.*
Given the direction to compose her own examples of declarative, imperative, exclamatory, and interrogative sentences, the learner is able to do so in writing. (This is a synthesis-level performance.)
2. *The learning task is analyzed.*
"What must the learner be able to do to complete the objective as described? Several types of learning are involved, each of which requires certain conditions of learning. The following outline shows what the learner must be able to do.
(a) *Motor chains*
   (1) Manipulate tools and materials for writing.
   (2) Form letters, words, and symbols of punctuation, and space them appropriately in sentences.
(b) *Verbal chains*
   (1) Connect appropriate letters to form words; connect words to form sentences, and insert symbols of punctuation in places appropriate to the kind of sentence being written.
(c) *Discriminations*
   (1) Discriminate, e.g., by pointing, between letters, words, and symbols of punctuation.
   (2) Discriminate the intent or purpose of the four kinds of sentences.
   (3) Tell which type of punctuation is suitable for which kind of sentence.
(d) *Concrete concepts*

(1) Point to examples of symbols of punctuation, e.g., period, exclamation mark, question mark, comma.

(2) Point to examples of upper case and lowercase letters.

(3) Show knowledge of what a sentence is by picking complete sentences from a collection of sentences and not-sentences (e.g., phrases).

(4) Identify written examples of sentences as declarative, imperative, exclamatory, or interrogative.

(e) *Defined concepts*

(1) Show by demonstration, e.g., through actions, that she understands what is meant by the defined concepts *declaration, exclamation, question,* and *imperative, directive* or *command.*

(2) Illustrate, e.g., by definition, explanation, or action, the intent of sentences of each of the four kinds.

(f) *Rules*

(1) Illustrate that he knows the meaning of the rule: A sentence is a word or group of words that expresses a complete thought.

(2) Illustrate, by giving examples, that he knows the meaning of the rules:

A declarative sentence expresses a statement of information.

An imperative sentence expresses a directive or a command.

An exclamatory sentence expresses a statement of information and also some form of affect.

An interrogative sentence asks for information.

(3) Demonstrate his understanding of the rules:

A declarative sentence begins with an uppercase letter and ends with a period.

An imperative sentence begins with an uppercase letter and ends with a period.

An exclamatory sentence begins with an uppercase letter and ends with an exclamation mark.

An interrogative sentence begins with an uppercase letter and ends with a question mark.

(g) *Higher-order rules*

Demonstrate understanding, e.g., by explanation or examples, of the rules:

There are at least four kinds of sentences.

The kind of sentence used is determined by the intent or purpose of the communication.

3. *Conditions of learning are established.*

Chapters 5 and 6 described the conditions of learning chains, discriminations, concepts, and rules. The same conditions are applied to learning the specific chains, discriminations, concepts, and rules the learner must acquire to meet the instructional objective given in the task description.

4. *Events of instruction are planned.*

The events of instruction are organized so that the conditions of learning the specific chains, discriminations, concepts, and rules necessary to complete the objective are met. This means, as you will recall from Chapters 5 and 6, that the teacher needs to *(a)* gain and control the attention of the learner, *(b)* inform him of expected outcomes, *(c)* stimulate recall of relevant prerequisite capabilities, *(d)* present the stimuli inherent to the learning task, *(e)* offer guidance for learning, *(f)* provide feedback, *(g)* appraise performance, *(h)* make provision for transfer and ensure retention through practice.

5. *Responses consistent with eventually meeting the objective are reinforced; others are not.*

In our example, for each type of learning—chains, discriminations, concepts, and rules—only those responses that are approximations of the performance required are reinforced. All others are ignored. For example, consider that your learner has demonstrated that she does not know what a sentence is. You are at a point in the instruction of helping her learn this concrete concept. She will probably not learn it on one trial. Therefore, her learning will need to be *shaped* toward this end. You can help her learn by reinforcing only those responses that are approximations of the performance—that indicate to you that she knows what a sentence is. This may mean letting her know immediately following her response that the collection of words she has just selected from other collections of words is indeed a sentence or nearly a sentence (see Table 8-1 for possible ways to let her know she is correct). Responses that are not approximations of the final performance, such as looking out the window, walking around the room, pointing to single letters or parts of words, should not be reinforced.

6. *Gradually, only closer and closer approximations are reinforced; eventually, only the final performance is reinforced.*

In shaping the learning of your pupil, you must gradually and consistently raise the standard of performance for which reinforcement can be gained. For example, in the early attempts to write interrogative-type sentences, you may reinforce your learner for merely copying such sentences accurately, or even nearly so. Later, however, as her learning progresses, you will not reinforce her for copying, even if she does so accurately. She will need to compose and write an interrogative-type sentence of her own, although, at first, her attempts may only be approximately accurate. Later, approximations will not be reinforced. Only accurately composed interrogative sentences of her own will be followed by positive reinforcement. As much as possible, the sequence of shaping will progress on a schedule of continuous reinforcement.

7. *The new behavior is maintained by being reinforced intermittently.*

Once your learner has demonstrated that she can compose and write sentences of the four types described by the instructional objective, you can help her maintain this capability by providing practice that at least once in a while gains reinforcement. This can take a variety of forms: positive comments written from time to time on her daily work or special reports; requests that she write these types of sentences within the contexts of various subject-matter areas. (Teach for transfer)

One observation always strikes me when constructing or examining an instructional sequence designed to shape some new behavior. It is the tremendous amount of detail that consistently must be attended to by the teacher and the learner. For example, in meeting the objective described in our example, literally thousands of specific responses must be made by the teacher and the learner, first in preparing the events of the instructional sequence, then in teaching and learning all the behaviors required to meet the objective. Even in those rare instances in which the learning of only one essentially average pupil is being shaped, the teacher's task can become really complex in the sense of (1) causing the learner to attend to the task; (2) clarifying the objective; (3) helping her recall or learn prerequisite knowledge or skills for the task at hand; (4) presenting just the right stimuli at just the right time so that she can respond appropriately; (5) guiding or prompting her responses so that she will be successful; (6) providing information that tells her immediately whether her responses are correct; and (7)

The seven events of instruction are . . .

providing sufficient and varied practice so that this learner can verify for herself that she really has learned and can recall the new learning well enough to use it in further learning. And, if learning is to be efficient and effective, all these teacher responses must be done correctly and at the appropriate time.

But, most of us do not teach only one essentially average learner at a time. We find it necessary to teach many at once, and often we are not very effective or efficient at doing so. The important question is, of course, "How can we increase the probability that our instruction will be optimal for *each* learner whom we must teach?"

A technology of education provides many useful clues about the answer to this question. However, before we turn to the application of the rules of a science of behavior to teaching and learning, we would be wise to do two things. We should practice doing a shaping sequence, this time, perhaps, for an objective within the affective domain. And we should consider the undesirable effects that might possibly accompany use of reinforcement in a technology of education. Let us look first at a shaping sequence for affective behaviors.

The principle of differential reinforcement central to shaping behaviors in the cognitive domain is also central to shaping behaviors in the affective and psychomotor domains. It is most apparently a part of shaping complex psychomotor skills such as dancing, driving a car, shooting a basket, hitting a ball, writing, and painting. However, attending, responding, valuing, and so on are affective behaviors that are also shaped as a consequence of differential reinforcement.

When you check with my responses for Checkpoint 8-1, you will see that I had some difficulty with steps 2 (task analysis), 3 (conditions of learning), and 4 (events of instruction). My difficulty resulted from the fact that at present we simply do not have much information available about teaching and learning affective behaviors. The same is true for psychomotor behaviors. Of course, we have always been learning behaviors of the affective and psychomotor types; it is just that we do not know the precise conditions that are necessary for such learning to occur.

As teachers, a substantial part of our job involves helping children learn to attend, respond, value, and so on, as well as to learn a wide range of psychomotor skills. Somehow we have managed fairly well even in the absence of specific and detailed statements of the conditions of learning these types of behavior. Even though our attempts to teach affective and psychomotor behaviors at times have been inefficient, nevertheless, as Stephens (1965) points out, teaching and learning have occurred, probably as a consequence of the spontaneous tendencies toward teaching to be found within each of us. Stephens reminds us that[1]

> even the most ordinary mother directs speech at her child. Without realizing what she is doing, she motivates and stimulates him. She talks to him for many reasons—for fun, to get him to stay out of the mud, or to come to dinner. But whatever her intention, these comments do act on the child as verbal stimuli. Similarly, when he comes out with "dada" or some other approximation to a recognizable word, she shows her spontaneous delight, and thus, without thinking, reinforces this behavior and makes him more likely to use the expression again. Similarly, without thinking, she supplies the phrase for which he is groping, thus supplying guidance. Very often she may also spend some time showing him how much better it is to express himself in this way rather than that.

[1] J. M. Stephens (1965). *The Psychology of Classroom Learning.* New York: Holt, pp. 436–437.

Viewed in this sense, teaching must certainly be considered an art. However, in Stephens's description, we see reference to ideas that are familiar to us as part of a science of behavior and Gagné's conditions of learning cognitive-type behaviors. This suggests that since few if any behaviors are strictly cognitive, affective, or psychomotor, the conditions of learning the affective and psychomotor types of behavior are probably similar to those for learning cognitive-type behaviors. Therefore, transfer should occur for us in Checkpoint 8-1.

CHECKPOINT 8-1

1. Following is an instructional objective at the characterization level in the affective domain: "Through consistent and careful listening to the comments of others, the learner demonstrates his belief that each person has a right to express a point of view." Organize an instructional sequence that uses the rules of differential reinforcement to shape the behavior described in the objective. Use the outline that appears early in this section for shaping cognitive behavior in a school setting. It should transfer to the present task.

2. I feel that individualizing instruction for my learners will be:

(Easy)   (About the same as   (Difficult)
                          group instruction)

WHAT UNDESIRABLE EFFECTS CAN POSSIBLY ACCOMPANY THE USE OF REINFORCEMENT?   There is nothing inherent in the concept *reinforcement* nor in the rules for its use that ensures it will be handled effectively and positively. It can be misused as easily as, or perhaps even more easily than, it can can be used wisely, since using reinforcement effectively requires a good deal of knowledge and skill, whereas its misuse relies only on ignorance.

Probably the most likely undesirable effects that can accompany reinforcement are those that result from (1) its use toward ends that are generally at odds with society, e.g., use of drugs, reinforcement of dependent, conforming behavior; and (2) trying to substitute, in the classroom, "a bag of goodies" for good teaching. The latter result has a high probability of occurring when (1) we have done a poor job of arranging the events of instruction so that conditions of learning are not met; (2) we have done a poor job of arranging the contingencies of reinforcement for shaping or maintaining certain behaviors; or (3) we have done both of these jobs poorly.

Often our attempts to rely on contrived reinforcers rather than on effective instruction to change our learners' behavior result in something like this: The instructional program does not follow a progressive, developmental sequence that permits learners to be successful; learners stay with the learning tasks only as long as contrived reinforcers are forthcoming; contrived reinforcers—foods, games, privileges, money, and so forth—tend to lose their effectiveness, so that more and better ones must be used to keep learners on task; punishment—aversive consequences—tend to become an increasingly frequent consequence of not studying; and learners find ways to avoid or escape from study situations, thus reducing the already-remote probability of learning.

The overall undesirable effect of substituting "a bag of goodies" for good teaching is that when instruction is poorly organized, most learners do not experience the powerful and intrinsic reinforcement that results from being successful, that is, from learning. Success is not a contrived reinforcer; consequently, it maintains its effectiveness. Furthermore, reinforcement that results from success in learning tasks tends to eliminate the necessity of using contrived reinforcers and punishment.

Contrived reinforcers are defined as . . ., and they should be used only . . .

We should not conclude from this discussion, however, that contrived reinforcers should never be used. As a rule of thumb, the better we organize instruction so that it is optimal for each learner, the less we will need contrived reinforcers to keep our learners on task. Contrived reinforcers, nevertheless, can be extremely useful when used wisely. By used wisely, I mean (1) used initially on a continuous schedule, and (2) later used intermittently as a part of a total plan of shaping new responses and maintaining others. Let us look briefly at how this might work. In Chapters 9 and 10, we will examine specific examples in detail.

Suppose you have an analysis-level objective: "Your learners will be able to describe the relationship between the part of the world in which people live and the type of clothing they wear." To meet this instructional objective, you could provide your learners with reading material and possibly an opportunity to discuss the question in small groups. Suppose, however, that the past experiences of your learners with social studies have been painful. Consequently, they will avoid reading or try to escape the material. Contrived reinforcers can be used to get them started. Foods, games, privileges, and so forth can be made contingent on attending to the reading material, initially on a continuous schedule, e.g., so many minutes of reading earns so many minutes of a special privilege. On following days, contrived reinforcers are made contingent on studying behaviors only once in a while. Eventually, they occur only rarely and then most appropriately as *natural parts of the learning events themselves;* for example, sampling small bits of Dutch cheese during a study of Holland or, in the psychomotor domain, playing games that children in the hot wetlands often play.

The key to the wise use of contrived reinforcers is effective organization of instructional sequences so that learners are successful—they learn when they do attend. Effective teaching reduces the necessity of a "bag of goodies" (or punishment) to cause a learner to attend, to become involved, to learn.

APPLYING A SCIENCE OF BEHAVIOR TO TEACHING AND LEARNING

Clearly, if we are to provide optimal instruction for each learner, we must use whatever is available to arrange the specific details of the events of instruction peculiar to *each* learner for *each* learning task encountered. Furthermore, we must arrange the special contingencies of reinforcement under which each learner will (1) attend to the learning tasks, (2) respond to the stimuli presented, and (3) practice sufficiently and appropriately so that what is presented will be learned efficiently and meaningfully. Indeed, this is an awesome task for a teacher even for the instruction of one pupil. It seems an impossible assignment for an entire classroom of thirty students. Fortunately, a good deal of assistance is available.

Let us review briefly some of the assistance that is available in making instructional optimal for each learner. First, we have the ideas and skills for doing task descriptions and task analyses. We know about the conditions of learning cognitive-type behaviors and have made educated guesses about the conditions of learning affective and psychomotor-type beahviors. We have acquired knowledge and skills in arranging the events of learning sequences so that the prerequisites must be mastered before going on to the next part of the task.

In Chapter 2, and now in Chapter 8, we have learned about a science of behavior, especially one that has been developed in a connectionist interpretation of learning. Essentially, this science of behavior has specified the contingencies of reinforcement under which learners learn.

In more concise terms, we now know how to do a pretty good job of (1) describing our objectives precisely; (2) analyzing and sequencing the tasks described; (3) arranging the events of instruction so that the conditions necessary for learning are met; and now, with a science of behavior, (4) arranging the conditions of reinforcement that will cause learners to attend and respond to learning events in ways appropriate to efficient and effective learning. These are the operations that define teaching as described by B. F. Skinner: "Teaching is the arrangement of contingencies of reinforcement under which students learn."[2] For the rest of this chapter, we will see what use we can make of Skinner's definition. In Chapter 12, we will modify it somewhat with Bruner's more cognitive ideas about a theory of instruction.

Skinner's definition of teaching is . . .

With the addition of a science of behavior to what we know about task description, task analysis, mastery learning, conditions of learning, and the events of instruction, we have the basic prerequisites for the development of a technology of education—for the application of the knowledge of a science of behavior to the practical problems of teaching and learning.

There are two major ways a technology of education can be helpful in making instruction optimal for each learner. One way is the application of the principles of reinforcement through instructional media, that is, through audiovisual aids, auto-instructional devices, and programmed materials. The other is a more direct application of the principles of reinforcement through instructional strategies, through the teacher's ongoing daily behaviors. Ideally, both methods of application occur together; the teacher makes effective use of instructional media, and at the same time manages the classroom—the learning environment—in ways consistent with logical and systematic application of the rules of positive reinforcement. As you can see, a technology of education is not a matter of *either* instructional media *or* teachers. Optimal instruction for each learner in a classroom setting requires both.

Two ways technology of education can be useful are . . .

First we will look at the application of a science of behavior through instructional *media*. In this chapter, we will look only briefly at the rules for instructional *strategies* for effective arrangement of appropriate contingencies of positive reinforcement. We will examine strategies that arrange contingencies of reinforcement in Chapters 9 and 10.

Application through Instructional Media

Instructional media can be classified in two main groups: (1) those that just *present* instructional material, and (2) those that both present and *teach* instruc-

---

[2] B. F. Skinner (1968). *The Technology of Teaching*. New York: Appleton-Century-Crofts, p. 64.

tional material. The first type are the familiar audio-visual aids found today in most schools. They include phonographs, listening centers, tape recorders, television sets, film projectors, pictures, and charts. The chief function of these devices is that of presenting material to the student. Presenting material, however, should not be confused with teaching.

The act of presenting material to learners and then holding them responsible for learning it is really an act of selection, not teaching. It selects those who have learned to teach themselves from those who have not. Teaching is more than just presenting material and then handing over learning responsibilities to students. While it may be true that some students do learn under these conditions, they do so solely because they have acquired the capability of learning without being taught. The result, of course, is that with just presentation of material, a few **Auto-instruction** students learn well, most learn only marginally, and a few learn only poorly **means . . .** (Skinner, 1968; Bloom, 1968).

According to Skinner, teaching requires not only presenting material, but also arranging appropriate conditions of reinforcement.

A technology of education is concerned with improving learning. Consequently, efficient and effective ways of presenting material is only part of the technological task. The other part is devising ways of *teaching* the material. Programmed materials and teaching machines, classified as *auto-instruction*, are the most familiar forms in which a technology of education has been expressed.

PROGRAMMING LEARNING EXPERIENCES

B. F. Skinner (1963) describes the process of programming knowledge and skills as the construction of carefully arranged sequences of contingencies leading to the terminal performances which are the objectives of education. He explains that the teacher begins with whatever behavior the student brings to the instructional situation and, by differential reinforcement, he changes that behavior so that a given terminal performance is more and more closely approximated.[3]

Suppose that you are interested in programming learning experience for your students. Although actually constructing a program will likely be a new experience for most of us, we already know a great deal about how to proceed. We can make some good guesses about what must be included in programmed materials that teach and about the steps required in constructing them. Checkpoint 8-2 provides an opportunity for you to try to anticipate the experts on programming.

CHECKPOINT 8-2

1. Programmed materials that teach must include:

2. The steps required in constructing programmed materials that teach are:

3. I (believe, do not believe) that each learner is entitled to individualized instruction.

[3] B. F. Skinner (1963). Reflections on a decade of teaching machines, *Teacher's College Record*, **65**, p. 169.

TABLE 8-2 A set of frames designed to teach a third- or fourth-grade pupil to spell the word "manufacture"†

1. Manufacture means to make or build. *Chair factories manufacture chairs.* Copy the word here:

    □ □ □ □ □ □ □ □ □ □

2. Part of the word is like part of the word "factory." Both parts come from an old word meaning *make* or *build.*

    m a n u □ □ □ □ u r e

3. Part of the word is like part of the word "manual." Both parts come from an old word for hand. Many things used to be made by hand.

    □ □ □ □ f a c t u r e

4. The same letter goes in both spaces:

    m □ n u f □ c t u r e

5. The same letter goes in both spaces:

    m a n □ f a c t □ r e

6. Chair factories □ □ □ □ □ □ □ □ □ □ □ chairs.

---

† Adapted from B. F. Skinner (1968). *The Technology of Teaching.* Reprinted by permission of Appleton-Century-Crofts, Educational Division, Meredith Corporation.

TABLE 8-3 A few early frames from a program designed to teach parents methods of behavior modification‡

4. Food and money are not the only important rewards. Other kinds of reinforcers are far more effective. One of the most powerful reinforcers for a child is the love, interest, and attention of his mother and his father. Listening to the child, hugging him, smiling at him, or talking to him are all _____, the kind that are given thousands of times *every day* to most children.	reinforcers
5. When you are talking, your friends reinforce you by being good listeners. In this case, their _____ is a positive reinforcer.	listening
6. If they stopped listening to you, you would probably _____ talking or change the subject. If they did this to you very often, you would probably find new friends.	stop
7. It is the people who provide a great deal of positive reinforcement for us that we generally choose as _____.	friends

‡ G. R. Patterson and E. G. Gullion (1968). *Living with Children, New Methods for Parents and Teachers.* Champaign, Ill.: Research Press. Reprinted with permission.

SOME EXAMPLES OF PROGRAMMED MATERIALS   Two examples of programmed materials that teach are presented in Tables 8-2 and 8-3. An analysis of Tables 8-2 and 8-3 shows that the major characteristics of programmed materials agree quite well with what we anticipated: (1) There is a logical, step-by-step progression of the material; (2) the learner is required to respond frequently; (3) prompts and cues are built into the material to ensure correctness of responses; (4) answers are immediately available; (5) reinforcement for correct responses occurs with every step (frame); (6) the material progresses so gradually that few, if any, errors occur; and (7) with each succeeding step, there is a gradual shaping of the learner's responses toward the terminal behavior until it is performed without assistance.

Programmed materials are characterized by . . .

You will notice in the examples that the method of presentation differs in each case, although the basic format is essentially the same. Each step in the progression is small enough so that, with prompts and cues, the learner is not likely to make errors. This type of program is usually called a *linear* program—the learner moves slowly, constantly, and directly toward the terminal objective.

A linear program is constructed so that . . .

There is another type of program with a different format. It is called a *branching* program. An example of it is shown in Figure 8-2. It is part of Crowder and Martin's programmed textbook (1961) for an introductory course in trigonometry. At the beginning of their book they address this note to the reader:

NOTE TO THE READER

This is not an ordinary book. The pages are numbered in the usual way, but they are not read consecutively. You must follow the directions which you find at the bottom of each page.

You will find that reading this book is very much like having an individual tutor. The book will continually ask you questions and correct errors as well as give you information.

Your progress through this course will depend entirely on your ability to choose right answers instead of wrong ones—and by your endurance. The course is divided into chapters, and a number of short learning sessions produces better results than a few long ones.

Follow the instructions and you will find it's impossible to get to the final page without mastering the fundamentals of Trigonometry.

CHAPTER II (page 35)
The Importance of the Right Triangle

We are about to see how the ideas of ratio and proportion apply to the triangle.

You should know that an *angle* is a geometric figure formed by two line segments drawn from the same point, or vertex. Thus

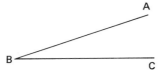

FIGURE 8-2.   **An instructional sequence from a branching program designed to teach a student of trigonometry that there are 90° in a right angle.** From N. A. Crowder and G. C. Martin (1961). *Trigonometry A Practical Course.* Garden City, N.Y.: Doubleday. Reprinted with permission.

An angle usually is designated by capital letters placed at the vertex and the sides of the angle, as shown above. In this case, we might speak of the diagram as showing angle ABC (with the vertex letter in the middle), or as ∠ ABC, or just as ∠ B.

Angles as you know, are measured in *degrees*. A circle contains 360 degrees (360°).

You should remember the answer to this question:

How many degrees are there in a right angle?

Answer:

  45° go to page 29

  90° go to page 38

100° go to page 42

Your answer: There are 45° in a right angle.   (Page 29)

No.

A right angle is sometimes called a square angle. The floor of a room makes a right angle with the wall, etc. When something stands "straight up", it makes a right angle with the level ground.

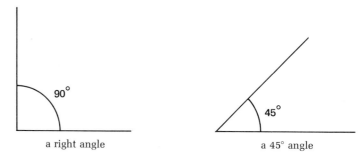

a right angle   a 45° angle

The unit of angle measurement, the degree (°), is so chosen that there are 90° in a right angle. (This unit of angle measure started with the ancient Babylonians.) Your answer, 45°, would be half of a right angle.

Now return to page 35 and choose the right answer.

Your answer: 90°   (Page 38)

You are correct. The unit of angle measurement is so chosen that a square or right angle contains 90°.

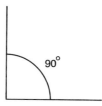

One side of a right angle is said to be *perpendicular* to the other side. A perpendicular line is at right angles (plural) to a base or foot, because adjacent angles would both be 90°.

FIGURE 8-2 **(Cont.)**

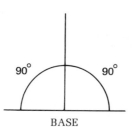

BASE

In this book, when we wish to call particular attention to the fact that a particular angle is a right angle, we will mark it with a small square as shown below.

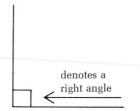

denotes a
right angle

Now we know what an angle is. A triangle (*tri* = three + *angle*) is a closed geometric figure constructed with just three lines and containing three angles. What do you suppose we mean by a right triangle?
Answer:
A triangle with a right angle in it. Go to page 41.
A triangle with all right angles in it. Go on to page 45.

Your Answer: A right angle is 100°.
No.   (Page 42)
A right angle is sometimes called a square angle. The floor of a room makes a right angle with the wall when something stands "straight up", it makes a right

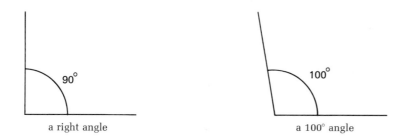

a right angle   a 100° angle

The unit of angle measure, the degree (°), is so chosen that there are 90° in a right angle. (This unit of angle measure started with the ancient Babylonians.) Your answer, 100°, would be a larger angle than a right angle.
Now return to the question on page 35 and try again.

FIGURE 8-2 (Cont.)

**A branching program
is constructed so
that . . .**

The writers of branching programs are not overly concerned about learners' making errors. When errors are made, the program merely directs the learner to a remedial "branch" of the program for additional instruction. When the learner has corrected his error, he is then returned to the main trunk of the program and he continues on.

One apparent advantage of branching programs is that each learner does only the part of the program that he needs to. If he is a "fast" learner, he tends to move in a linear fashion straight through the program. "Slower" learners do remedial branches as required. In linear programs, all learners do all the frames. Actually, this may not be so much of a handicap for rapid learners as it appears, since in most programs each student is allowed to progress at his own speed.

For the beginning teacher, writing linear programs is probably easier than writing branching ones, although writing effective programs of either type is not an easy task since, as you remember, any program designed to teach new behavior must include all the conditions and steps we discussed in Checkpoint 8-2. Programmed instruction is only an *approach* to learning. Consequently, it also must ensure that the conditions of learning are met.

Learning how to write programs that teach new behavior is beyond the scope of this textbook. There are several excellent sources available, however. Some of them are listed in Suggestions for Further Reading at the end of the chapter. Because of their availability and also because of the time and expertise required to write effective programs that teach new behavior, beginning teachers are probably wise to look first for commercially prepared programs before trying to write their own. A handy guide for the selection of published programs has been prepared in booklet form by P. Jacobs, M. Maier, and L. Stolurow (1966). Included in their booklet is the following checklist:[4]

A CHECKLIST FOR EVALUATING A SELF-INSTRUCTIONAL PROGRAM

	Yes	No
Is it really programmed instructional material?	___	___
How does the program fit into the curriculum?	___	___
A. Does it cover the appropriate topics?	___	___
B. Does it develop the appropriate skills and knowledge?	___	___
C. Is it at the appropriate difficulty level?		

	Yes	No
How well would the program teach in your situation?		
A. Are the conditions under which the available data were collected relevant to your situation?	___	___
B. How well does the program meet your objectives?	___	___
Can you afford it?		

[4] P. I. Jacobs, M. H. Maier, and L. M. Stolurow (1966). *A Guide to Evaluating Self-Instructional Programs.* New York: Holt, p. 28.

Although in this text we will not learn to write programs that teach new behavior, we can gain a feeling for doing so by writing a few frames of a linear program.

CHECKPOINT 8-3

1. Using Skinner's program for teaching a child to spell the word "manufacture," construct five or six frames to teach a learner to spell the word "bicycle." (This task requires an _____ level performance, and it relies on transfer of the _____ type.)

2. Knowing that I can program some of my instruction makes me feel _____.

TWO MAJOR PURPOSES OF SELF-INSTRUCTIONAL MATERIALS   Two major purposes can be realized through programmed instruction: (1) learning new behavior, and (2) maintaining behaviors that were learned previously. We have just examined three examples of programs designed to teach *new* behavior. Preparing self-instructional materials to *maintain* and *strengthen* previously learned behaviors is likely to be an easier task for the beginning teacher, since practice of the material learned is the essential purpose of such materials. The problems you will face in preparing practice materials are, first, those of *purpose* of the practice, and next the *conditions* under which practice should occur. As you can see, these are questions related to retention and transfer of learning.

The major requirements of self-instructional materials for maintaining and strengthening behaviors are (1) directions (written or taped) for use of the materials; (2) materials arranged so that they are practiced in the context and form in which they will later be recalled or used; and (3) feedback about correctness immediately available following each response. Once we know the major requirements for preparing these types of materials, it is relatively easy to devise practice for a variety of topics. This practice can take many forms. For example, it may consist of a stack of cards, each of which states an item of information to be practiced. Answers are written on the reverse side. See Figure 8-3.

Two major purposes of self-instructional materials are . . .

The information on the cards in any stack can represent factual (knowledge-level) information relative to arithmetic, proper grammatical construction or punctuation, geographical or historical knowledge, and so forth. Directions for study, individually or with others, instruct the students first to read the front side of a card and to respond verbally or in writing, then to turn the card over and verify their responses. If correct, they are instructed to go on to the next card. If incorrect, they are to repeat the *entire* item in proper sequence (reread the question *and* include the proper reponse). (Remember what Guthrie taught us about linking all the parts of a molar response in proper sequence.) Then, they go on to the next card. As each student practices the cards, he places those he can do in one stack. Those he can complete only with deliberation are placed in a second stack, and those he cannot remember at all go into a third stack. The cards in the latter two stacks are the ones he needs to practice at the present time.

Do you notice that this procedure sounds familiar? It is essentially the same procedure that Mike, In Mr. Johnson's class, used to help his pupil learn and retain verbal chains in arithmetic.

If learners practice in pairs or small groups, a useful way to motivate them to

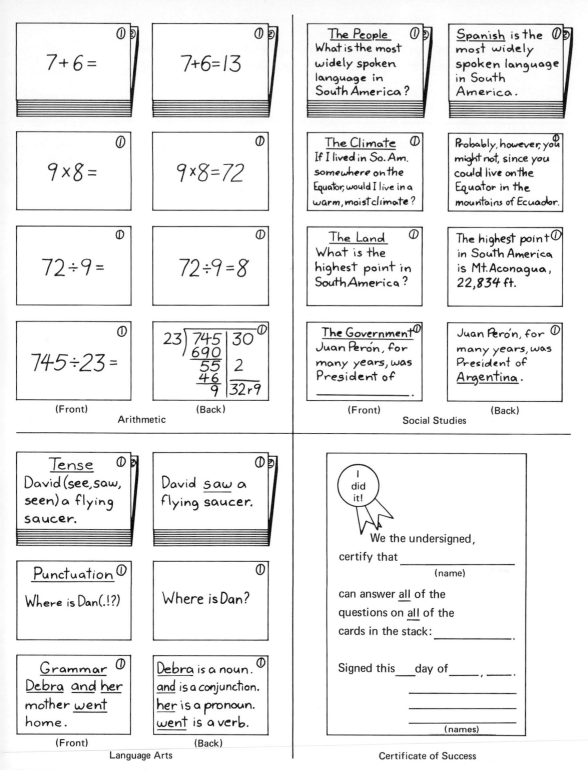

FIGURE 8-3 Practice cards programmed to maintain and strengthen behaviors learned previously.

practice is to allow the learners to be responsible for their own performance. "Certificates of Success" is one way to do this. (See Figure 8-3.) The certificate is issued when all members of the group are satisfied that the person knows and can recall the information on all the cards. "Knows and can recall" can be defined operationally as being able to respond correctly to each card three times consecutively. A grid for recording performance on each card can be printed on the reverse side of the Certificate of Success.

There are other forms of self-instructional materials that maintain and strengthen behaviors learned previously. One form that is increasingly popular with teachers is the recording of material to be practiced on audiotape. Children can then practice without direct teacher assistance. The format of the prerecorded verbal material usually begins with directions on how to respond. Responses can be oral, in writing, or by some other performance, e.g., moving certain objects. Next, the material to be practiced is presented, a bit at a time— say, words to be spelled correctly—"Number one." (Pause.) "Spell the word 'fracture'." (Longer pause.) Then, correct answers are given—"'Fracture' is spelled f-r-a-c-t-u-r-e." The word is repeated. (Pause.) The learner checks his response and corrects it, if he needs to, by rewriting the entire word. Then the tape continues: "Number two." And so on.

Another form of self-instructional material that maintains and strengthens behavior is illustrated in Figure 8-4. The main idea in this type of teacher-made material is to cause the learner to practice the *application* of some concept or rule already learned. Notice that this type of task requires the learner to do more with information than just remember it. In the example used in Figure 8-4, practice means applying the rule for forming compound words. The procedure is first to pair cards containing simple words in order to form compound words; then to check the answer sheet for verification. Or, to cite another example, subjects and predicates of sentences can be written on separate cards. The cards can be matched to form a sentence and then checked with an answer sheet. The same form can also be used to practice applying rules of physics to problems encountered in everyday life; i.e., rules can be written on some cards and descriptions of problem situations on others.

Let us look at another example of the many possible forms that can be used in self-instructional materials that maintain and strengthen behavior learned previously. It uses a simple, homemade electromechanical device and also illustrates the powerful motivational effects that are often associated with such instructional devices.

Ms. Garret is a teacher of children in grade four. They are described as a heterogeneous group of youngsters—a few "slow" learners, a few "fast" learners, and the rest "average." Many of these children have difficulty solving story problems because the number skills prerequisite to successful problem solving have been poorly learned and recalled. Typically, as a child tries to solve the problems, she has to learn or rediscover simple sums, differences, products and quotients, usually by counting on her fingers, using counting sticks, or marking on paper. By the time she arrives at the appropriate sums, differences, products or quotients, she has often forgotten why she was trying to remember them! Eventually, and usually only after a good deal of frustration, at least an approximate answer to the problem is obtained by most of the children.

Ms. Garret believes the process can be made more efficient. Lately, she has been trying to cause the children to recall, quickly and accurately, (1) all the num-

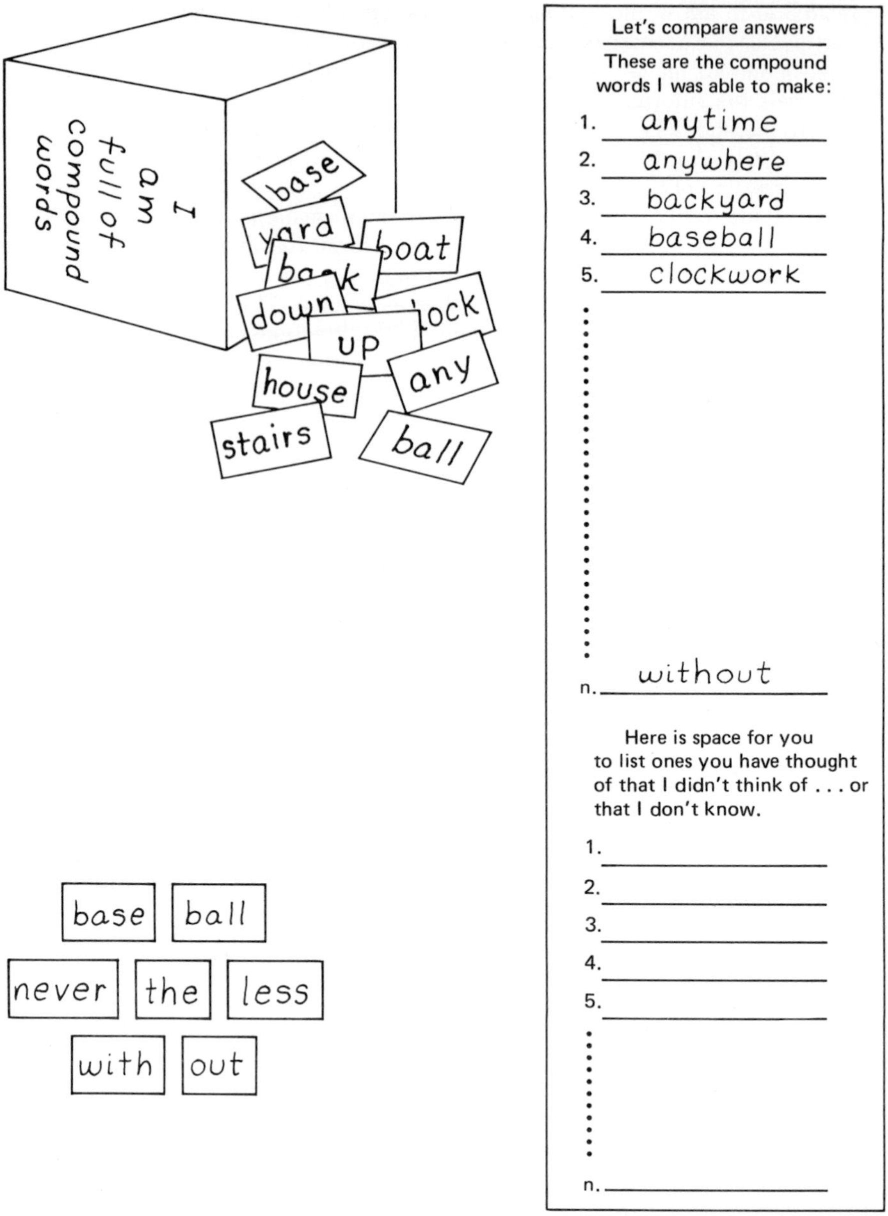
I am full of compound words
base
yard
boat
down
up
house
any
stairs
ball
base ball
never the less
with out
Let's compare answers
These are the compound words I was able to make:
1. anytime
2. anywhere
3. backyard
4. baseball
5. clockwork
n. without
Here is space for you to list ones you have thought of that I didn't think of . . . or that I don't know.
1.
2.
3.
4.
5.
n.

FIGURE 8-4 Practice can be programmed at the application level.

ber sums and differences up to and including $10 + 10 = ?$, and $20 - 1 = ?$; (2) all the products of the number combinations from $1 \times 1 = ?$ through $12 \times 12 = ?$; and (3) all the quotients of the number combinations from $1 \div 1 = ?$ to $144 \div 12 = ?$ She has asked the children to practice these combinations using paper and pencil. Ms. Garret knows that many of the children would study more effectively if she could give them individual attention, but she cannot possibly manage to do so. Consequently, a few group study periods have been given for practice, as have several individual detentions after school, since only a few of the better learners really do attend to the task appropriately during class time. These maneuvers tend to be somewhat painful for the children, and they are not exactly pleasant for Ms. Garret, either. As you might guess, everyone tries as hard as possible to avoid these sessions. The result is that practice for most is only sporadic, as are retention and recall of the material. Ms. Garret believes there must be some way to provide the individual attention each of her children needs. Her solution to the problem is shown in Figure 8-5.

With the use of the electromechanical device, that Ms. Garret constructed, and the program cards she wrote, each child in her class of over thirty children practiced sufficiently, without being coerced, so that, within a few weeks, problems of recall of sums, differences, products, and quotients were virtually eliminated. The reason it took as long as a few weeks was that Ms. Garret had made only one device. The children had to take turns using it. It is interesting to note, however, that when one child operated the device, others watched and practiced vicariously—and learned immediately if their responses were correct.

To practice the items that Ms. Garret wrote on the program cards, one of the boys, for example, would first choose the cards he needed to review. Then he would feed the card into the lower end of the slot in the device and push it upward until the information appeared in the window at the top. As you can see from the diagram, alternative responses, including the correct one, appear in the three lower windows. Pushing the button below the window in which the correct answer appears illuminates a red light bulb attached to the device above the windows. Pushing other buttons does not light up the bulb, since the electrical circuit is completed only when the button can make contact, through the card, with a terminal on the back of the device. This contact is made possible by punching a hole in the card at a place directly under the button for the correct answer. No holes are punched below incorrect responses. In this way, only correct responses are reinforced. Thus, incorrect ones begin to extinguish while correct ones strengthen. (Can you imagine the affective and psychomotor objectives that were being met by these children at the same time they were meeting the cognitive ones?)

You will have noticed from our discussion so far that the application of a science of behavior to teaching and learning through materials for self-instruction often involves some instructional device of a mechanical or electromechanical nature. Such devices can be extremely useful to you as you try to extend your capabilities as a teacher to meet more and more of the individual differences of your learners. We need to have a closer look at these devices as we continue to search for ways to make instruction optimal for each learner.

CHECKPOINT 8-4

1. Here are excerpts from materials assigned to students for study. Do they qualify as programmed materials that (1) teach new behavior, or (2) maintain and strengthen behavior learned previously? Give reasons for your answers.

A simple teaching machine

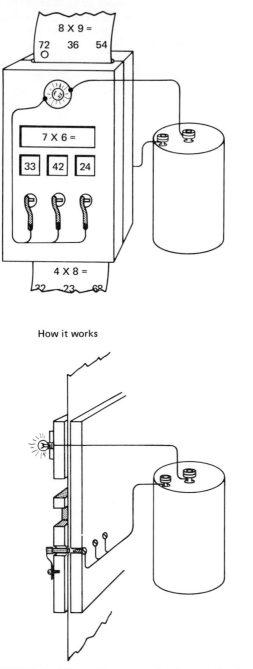

A sample program card

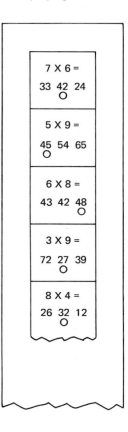

How it works

FIGURE 8-5   A form of programming for practice that captures the attention of learners.

MATERIALS A: CONSTRUCTING PROGRAMMED MATERIALS
1.   Begin with *objectives*.
2.   Next, *provide the information* necessary for the learner to meet the objectives.
3.   Next, decide on a logical *sequence* for the learning experiences to follow.
4.   Write items for the learner to *respond to* according to the sequence you choose.
5.   Provide *feedback* so learners will know if their responses are correct.
6.   Tell the learner *what to do next:*
(a) If *correct,* direct him to the next step in the program.
(b) If *incorrect,* give more information, and tell him what to do with it.
(c) Test him on the additional information; let him know if he is correct or incorrect. If *correct,* direct him to the next step in the program. If *incorrect,* direct him to consult with the teacher.

MATERIALS B: GETTING GOOD AT DIVISION
1. $6 \div 2 = \square$; $8 \div 4 = \square$; $32 \div 8 = \square$
2. $15 \div 6 = \square$; $34 \div 8 = \square$; $96 \div 6 = \square$
3. $120 \div 5 = \square$; $260 \div 7 = \square$; $876 \div 9 = \square$
4. $110 \div 10 = \square$; $356 \div 25 = \square$; $974 \div 94 = \square$
5. $3{,}240 \div 120 = \square$; $6{,}893 \div 345 = \square$; $9{,}876 \div 847 = \square$

2.   As I study this chapter, I think of how I might use the ideas presented to help individualize instruction for my learners. Yes_____ No_____

USING INSTRUCTIONAL DEVICES

When we think of instructional devices, we usually picture some form of mechanical or electromechanical device, usually of an audiovisual nature. Usually, these devices are called teaching machines. This is a somewhat unfortunate misnomer since, technically speaking, a machine does not teach. It just provides a convenient, time-saving way to bring materials that do teach into a one-to-one tutorial with learners that is often impossible for a teacher to achieve unassisted (Skinner, 1968). The special contribution of a teaching machine is that it permits the teacher to arrange certain contingencies of reinforcement for each learner. The teacher can thus present materials that have been programmed in an appropriate, developmental sequence. She can guide, prompt, and cue each learner's responses. She can ensure that the rate of progression is optimal for each learner, and she can make feedback immediately available following each response.

Moreover, the machine allows the teacher to tutor an indefinite number of students, and at the same time. The machine receives the learner's responses, gives feedback about the correctness of the responses, and delivers reinforcement, e.g., by informing the learner when the response is correct or, in addition, by delivering reinforcement in the form of tokens, edibles, words of praise. Skinner draws the comparison with a private tutor, pointing out that:[5]

> (1) There is a constant interchange between program and student. Unlike lectures, textbooks, and the usual audio-visual aids, the machine induces sustained activity. The student is always alert and busy. (2) Like a good tutor, the machine insists that a

---

[5] B. F. Skinner (1968). Op. cit., pp. 37–39.

A teaching machine is like a tutor in that it . . .

A teaching machine is unlike a tutor in that it . . .

given point be thoroughly understood, either frame by frame or set by set, before the student moves on. Lectures, textbooks, and their mechanized equivalents, on the other hand, proceed without making sure that the student understands and easily leave him behind. (3) Like a good tutor the machine presents just that material for which the student is ready. It asks him to take only that step which he is at the moment best equipped and most likely to take. (4) Like a skillful tutor the machine helps the student to come up with the right answer. It does this in part through the orderly construction of the program and in part with such techniques as hinting, prompting, and suggesting, derived from an analysis of verbal behavior. . . . Lastly, of course, the machine, like a private tutor, reinforces the student for every correct response, using this immediate feedback not only to shape his behavior most efficiently but to maintain it in strength in a manner which the layman would describe as "holding the student's interest."

SOME EXAMPLES OF INSTRUCTIONAL DEVICES   When we know the characteristics that teaching machines must have, we can imagine many and varied examples that could be constructed. They range from very simple devices like the one Ms. Garret constructed to elaborate systems of computer-assisted instruction, such as the Stanford CAI system described by Richard Atkinson (1968). O'Leary and O'Leary (1972) point out that teaching machines come in many shapes and sizes, ranging from the simple, and inexpensive Min-Max, consisting of a plastic box, a roller, and a display window, to the tremendously expensive (about $50,000) Talking Typewriters of O. K. Moore and the computer-assisted instruction complex of Suppes and Atkinson of Stanford, with its individual consoles in schools as far away as New York. O'Leary and O'Leary add this comment:[6]

> In addition to implementation in regular classrooms, Computer Assisted Instruction (CAI) has been used in schools for the deaf where the visual computer materials have a distinct advantage over the usual teaching techniques. In New York City some 24,000 students receive CAI Dial-A-Drill arithmetic lessons at home via telephone. CAI differs in one important aspect from previously discussed programs—it responds to the nature of the child's errors automatically by presenting remedial materials specific to the error before permitting the child to proceed through the main program.

Certainly many varieties of teaching machines are possible. And just as certainly, there are differences of opinion about their usefulness. Let us look more closely at some of the arguments on both sides of the issue.

Arguments for and against Programmed Instruction

Advocates of a technology of education argue that without the instrumental support provided by programmed materials and instructional devices, it is practically impossible to individualize instruction for more than a very few of our learners. Some of the potential advantages claimed by the proponents of individualized instruction are summarized by Daniel and Susan O'Leary:[7].

---

[6] K. D. O'Leary, and S. G. O'Leary, eds. (1972). *Classroom Management: The Successful Use of Behavior Modification.* New York: Pergamon, pp. 404–405.
[7] Ibid., pp. 401–402.

The major arguments for auto-instruction are . . .

(1) The child can learn the material at his own rate. The slow child is not lost as his teacher and classmates forge ahead. Similarly, the bright child can avoid the boredom of waiting while others catch up. (2) Learners may also learn better, e.g., they may learn faster and retain the material for a longer period of time. (3) The teacher can effectively teach more children. (4) Learners become more responsible, i.e., they become less dependent on the teacher's directions. (5) The teacher can deal with each child at his own level rather than teach to the average child and lose the rest of the class. (6) Programed instruction may be a partial solution to the problems of some disruptive children since behavior problems are often correlated with academic problems. Consequently, a learner who is experiencing a great deal of failure in his academic work may disrupt the class. Through programed instruction a learner may experience success in learning tasks since he works at a level that is appropriate for him.

It should be noted that most of the arguments in support of individualized auto-instruction, summarized by the O'Learys (1972), are, at this point, just claims. There is no clear evidence that programmed materials presented by a machine are better able to instruct a learner than is a real, live teacher. Of course, it is not really necessary that an instructional device be superior to a teacher in order to be useful to a teacher. We will return to this idea a little later.

Several objections to a technology of education have arisen. Here are some of the most frequent objections, and B. F. Skinner's replies (1968) to them:[8]

OBJECTION: Since most of the early work relative to a science of behavior was done on lower animals, e.g., pigeons and rats, aren't the procedures appropriate only to animals? To use them in education is to treat the student like an animal.

SKINNER'S REPLY: So far as I know, no one argues that because something is true of a pigeon, it is therefore true of a man. There are enormous differences in the topographies of the behaviors of man and pigeon and in the kinds of environmental events which are relevant to that behavior. . . . Experiments on pigeons may not throw much light on the "nature" of man, but they are extraordinarily helpful in enabling us to analyze man's environment more effectively. What is common to pigeon and man is a world in which certain contingencies of reinforcement prevail. The schedule of reinforcement which makes a pigeon a pathological gambler is to be found at racetrack and roulette table, where it has a comparable effect.

OBJECTION: The use of contrived contingencies of reinforcement seems somehow synthetic, spurious, or even fradulent.

SKINNER'S REPLY:[9] The objection to contrived reinforcers arises from a misunderstanding of the nature of teaching. The teacher expedites learning by arranging special contingencies of reinforcement, which may not resemble the contingencies under which the behavior is eventually useful. Parents teach a baby to talk by reinforcing its first efforts with approval and affection but these are not natural consequences of speech. . . . The contrived reinforcement shapes the topography of verbal behavior long before that behavior can produce its normal consequences in a verbal community. . . . The real issue is whether the teacher prepares the student for the natural reinforcers which are to replace the contrived reinforcers used in teaching. The behavior which is expedited in the teaching process would be useless if it were not to be effective in the world at large in the absence of instructional contingencies.

---

[8] B. F. Skinner (1968). Op. cit., p. 84.
[9] Ibid., pp. 85–86.

OBJECTION: Programmed instruction tends to narrow and focus a learner's attention. When following a program he is not likely to be learning how to study, how to work under puzzlement, and so on.

SKINNER'S REPLY:[10] It is true that a program designed simply to impart knowledge of a subject matter does not do any of this. It does not because it is not designed to do so. Programming undertakes to reach one goal at a time. Efficient ways of studying and thinking are separate goals. A crude parallel is offered by the current argument in favor of the cane or related aversive practices on the ground that they build character; they teach a boy to take punishment and to accept responsibility for his conduct. These are worthwhile goals, but they should not necessarily be taught at the same time as, say, Latin grammar or mathematics. . . .

It is important to teach careful observation, exploration, and inquiry, but they are not well taught by submitting a student to material which he must observe and explore effectively or suffer the consequences. Better methods are available. . . .

When a teacher simply tests students on assigned material, few ever learn to study well and many never learn at all. One may read for the momentary effect and forget what one has read almost immediately; one obviously reads in a very different way for retention. As we have seen, many of the practices of the good student resemble those of the programmer. The student can in a sense program material as he goes, rehearsing what he has learned and glancing at a text only as needed. These practices can be separately programmed as an important part of the student's education and can be much more effectively taught than by punishing the student for reading without remembering.

OBJECTION: Programmed instruction produces regimentation and limits creativity. It may even be detrimental to thinking.

The major arguments against auto-instruction are . . .

SKINNER'S REPLY:[11] We fear effective teaching, as we fear all effective means of changing human behavior. Power not only corrupts, it frightens; and absolute power frightens absolutely. We take another—and very long—look at educational policy when we conceive of teaching which really works. It has been said that teaching machines and programmed instruction will mean regimentation (it is sometimes added that regimentation is the goal of those who propose such methods), but in principle nothing could be more regimented than education as it now stands. School and state authorities draw up syllabuses specifying what students are to learn year by year. Universities insist upon "requirements" which are presumably to be met by all students applying for admission. Examinations are "standard." Certificates, diplomas, and honors testify to the completion of specified work. We do not worry about all this because we know that students never learn what they are required to learn, but some other safeguard must be found when education is effective.

It could well be that a technology of teaching will be unwisely used. It could destroy initiative and creativity; it could make men all alike (and not necessarily in being equally excellent); it could suppress the beneficial effect of accidents on the development of the individual and on the evolution of a culture. On the other hand, it could maximize the genetic endowment of each student; it could make him as skillful, competent, and informed as possible; it could build the greatest diversity of interests; it could lead him to make the greatest possible contribution to the survival and development of his culture. Which of these futures lies before us will not be determined by the mere availability of effective instruction. The use to which a technology of teaching is to be put will depend upon other matters. We cannot avoid

[10] Ibid., pp. 87–88.
[11] Ibid., pp. 90–91.

the decisions which now face us by putting a stop to the scientific study of human behavior or by refusing to make use of the technology which inevitably flows from such a science.

Most of the arguments for and against a technology of education seem to be based on the question of whether a machine can replace the teacher in the classroom. The issue appears to be one of either/or. This is unfortunate since it tends to encourage "choosing and rejecting" rather than "combining." A more useful question is how teachers can use a science of behavior to make instruction optimal for each learner. The task is to determine what teaching functions can be handled by machines in order to save time and effort for a teacher to do those things that machines cannot. As Skinner points out: "In assigning certain mechanizable functions to machines, the teacher emerges in his proper role as an indispensible human being."[12]

We have so far, in this chapter, seen some of the "certain mechanizable functions" of teaching that can be assigned to machines. In the next section, and especially in Chapters 9 and 10, we will see some ways a teacher can apply a science of behavior, without the use of machines, to the many teaching behaviors "that emerge in his role as an indispensible human being."

Application through Instructional Strategies

One of the nice things that occur when we have discovered the rules of a science is that understanding them permits us a degree of freedom beyond just description, classification, and prediction. Our discovery gives us the freedom to intervene, logically and systematically, in what happens to us. Understanding the rules opens the door to our ingenuity, cleverness, inventiveness—all the things that make up an art—to devise techniques, methods, and materials for applying these rules to the problems we encounter. This is possible because the basic rules of a science are independent of the specific approaches, methods, techniques, or materials devised for their application. You will recall an example of this higher-order rule in Chapter 6, when we learned that specific approaches to learning—e.g., discovery and reception—were independent of the general and specific conditions of learning. We now see another instance of this rule relative to the laws of a science of behavior and the means devised to apply them to the problems of individualizing instruction. Since the techniques, methods, and materials we can be clever enough to invent are independent of the rules of a science of behavior, we should be able to find many ways to apply the rules to problems of classroom learning other than through the use of programmed materials and self-instructional devices. We should also be able to apply the rules to our own behavior as we go about the functions of teaching and managing a class, that is, through our instructional strategies, remembering that although the rules are few, the methods, techniques, and materials for application are limited only by our ability to be inventive. Perhaps this is what William James was talking about when he implied that teaching is an art derived from a science of psychology.

The term "instructional strategies" means . . .

---

[12] Ibid., p. 55.

SOME RULES FOR
INSTRUCTIONAL STRATEGIES

In an earlier section of this chapter, we learned about a science of behavior when we discussed the rules of reinforcement. What remains to be done at this point is to translate the substance of that earlier discussion into useful rules of thumb. (Remember what we learned about the transfer value of general rules?) When we have formulated these rules, we will be ready to apply them through instructional strategies to the problems of classroom management. This will be our task for Chapters 9 and 10.

Two higher-order rules for instructional strategies that derive from a science of behavior are . . .

HIGHER-ORDER RULE: *Responses that are reinforced are learned, whereas responses that are not reinforced extinguish.*

SIMPLE RULES:

1. Since almost any stimulus can act as a reinforcer, the behavior of your learners will tell you if your reinforcers are working.

2. Usually, you should reinforce immediately following appropriate responses.

3. Use only enough reinforcement to get the job done. Keep your learners "hungry."

4. To begin with, reinforce each and every appropriate response. Gradually, reinforce only intermittently.

5. If necessary to cause initial responding, use reinforcers of the primary, tangible, and internal type. Move as quickly as possible to the secondary, intangible, and internal (success) type. However, do not move so rapidly that you "lose" your learner.

6. Reinforce only appropriate responses. Withhold reinforcement from inappropriate responses.

7. Do not try to change the behavior of your learners in one big step. Follow a shaping procedure; expect gradual changes.

8. Do not try to substitute a "bag of goodies" for good teaching. Regardless of your approach, you must arrange the events of instruction so that conditions of learning are met.

HIGHER-ORDER RULE: *Responses that are punished are suppressed, with the result that an organism avoids or escapes from punishment.*

Up to this point, we have not learned any simple rules about the use of aversive stimuli, that is, punishment, relative to classroom learning. The potential effects of punishment on learning and on learners, however, is a topic that you will want to understand well. Although punishment can have potentially positive effects on learning, its continuing widespread and frequent misuse is indeed a shocking testimony of our ignorance about the concept. Our discussion in Chapter 10 will provide us with the information necessary to formulate simple rules relating to the higher-order rule about punishment.

We are now ready to direct our attention to the topic of devising positive strategies to capture the attention of our learners. We will move now from our essentially cognitive concern in Part I with the *content* and *process* of teaching and learning to the more affective concern in Part II, *managing classroom behavior,* that is, to whether our learners attend and respond appropriately to instruction that has been planned well, and whether learning is valued.

THE BRIDGE BUILDER

An old man going along the highway came in the evening cold and grey to a chasm vast and deep and wide.

The old man though in the twilight dim the sullen stream had no fear for him but he turned when faced on the other side and built a bridge to span the tide.

"Old man," said a fellow pilgrim near, "you are wasting your strength with your building here. Your journey will end with the ending day." "You never will again pass this way. You have crossed this chasm deep and wide why build you this bridge at evening tide?"

"Good friend in the paths I have crossed" he said "there followeth after me today, a youth whose feet must pass this way."

"This chasm which has been but aught to me to that fair-haired youth may a pitfall be."

"He too must cross in the twilight dim, good friend, I am building this bridge for him."

Anonymous

1. To summarize the main ideas presented in this chapter, compare the requirements for programmed instruction, mastery learning, Gagné's events of instruction, and the conditions of learning.

2. Find a programmed text or programmed materials presented by some form of teaching device. Study them for an hour or so, then write your reactions to the experience as they relate to the arguments for and against programmed learning discussed in this chapter.

3. List the teaching functions you believe can best be handled (a) through programmed learning, and (b) by the teacher.

4. Construct programmed materials to maintain or strengthen some behavior learned previously, e.g., practice in the application of the rules for (a) finding words in a dictionary, (b) finding areas of two-dimensional geometric figures, or (c) balancing chemical equations.

5. Ask one or more learners to do the program you prepared for item 4. Modify your materials as necessary so that they teach your learner(s).

6. Just for fun:

In our home we have a black cat. Her name is Lizzy. Somehow, over the past few months she has acquired an annoying habit. When we forget to let her out of the house at night, she persistently scratches and meows at the bedroom door between four and four-thirty the next morning until I get up, go to the front door, and let her out.

Since I find the situation irritating, I have accepted the responsibility of trying to change it. I have decided to try to apply some of the principles of a science of behavior through an instructional strategy. My specific instructional objective is this: "Lizzie will stop scratching and meowing at my bedroom door at four o'clock in the morning."

Just for fun, assume that *my* problem is *your* problem. Describe how you would apply rules of a science of behavior in some strategy to meet the objective. At the end of Chapter 9, I will share with you how I finally managed the situation.

Atkinson, R. C. (1968). Computerized instruction and the learning process, *American Psychologist,* **23,** 225–239.

Bloom, B. S. (1968). Learning for mastery, *Evaluation Comment,* **1**(2). Los Angeles: University of California, Center for the Study of Evaluation of Instructional Programs.

Crowder, N. A., and G. C. Martin (1961). *Trigonometry: A Practical Course.* Garden City, N.Y.: Doubleday.

Darwin, C. (1958). *The Autobiography of Charles Darwin.* London: Collins.

Jacobs, P. I., M. H. Maier, and L. M. Stolurow (1966). *A Guide to Evaluating Self-Instructional Programs.* New York: Holt.

Madsen, C. K., and C. H. Madsen, Jr. (1972). *Parents/Children/Discipline: A Positive Approach.* Boston: Allyn and Bacon.

O'Leary, K. D., and S. G. O'Leary eds. (1972). *Classroom Management: The Successful Use of Behavior Modification.* New York: Pergamon.

Skinner, B. F. (1963). Reflections on a decade of teaching machines, *Teacher's College Record,* **65,** 168–177.

——— (1968). *The Technology of Teaching.* New York: Appleton-Century-Crofts.

Stephens, J. M. (1965). *The Psychology of Classroom Learning.* New York: Holt.

SUGGESTIONS FOR FURTHER READING

Anderson, R. C., R. W. Kulhavy, and T. Andre (1971). Feedback procedures in programmed instruction, *Journal of Educational Psychology,* **62**(2). Subjects who received knowledge of correct response (KCR) *after* they responded learned more than subjects who received no KCR or who could peek at KCR before they responded.

Davis, R. H., I. N. Marzocco, and M. R. Denny (1970). Interaction of individual differences with modes of presenting programmed instruction, *Journal of Educational Psychology,* **61**(3), 198–204. Modes of instruction do not seem to affect learning outcomes. Subjects who chose their own mode did not learn any better than those whose mode of instruction was prescribed.

Gagné, R. M. (1973). Educational technology and the learning process, *Educational Researcher,* **3**(1), 3–8. Gagné presents the conception of learning as a series of processes occurring in stages. Implications for instruction are considered relative to the characteristics of instructional media.

Pacztar, J. (1972). *The Theory and Practice of Programmed Instruction.* Paris: UNESCO. This book is significant because it describes not only techniques for preparing programmed materials but also the broader scientific basis from which the techniques derive.

Seltzer, R. A. (1971). Computer-assisted instruction—What it can and cannot do, *American Psychologist,* **26**(4), 373–377. Seltzer provides three criterion statements with which to judge the computer's place in instruction. He points out that simulation and gaming are very good uses for the computer in teaching.

The following books are good sources on how to write programmed materials:

Lysaught, J. P., and C. M. Williams (1963). *A Guide to Programmed Instruction.* New York: Wiley.

Markle, S. M. (1964). *Good Frames and Bad: A Grammar of Frame Writing.* New York: Wiley.

Pipe, P. (1966). *Practical Programming.* New York: Holt.

PART II

MANAGEMENT OF CLASSROOM BEHAVIOR AND INDIVIDUAL DIFFERENCES

A POSITIVE APPROACH TO MOTIVATION

9

As I become a person unafraid, I pray I do not become the source of another's fear

An interpretation of an insight made by an old
Indian man of genius, passed on to me by a friend.

ONGOING SUMMARY

So far we have discussed (1) the learning process, (2) goals and objectives, and (3) how to organize for effective instruction. We have learned how major points of view can be combined into powerful and useful approaches to the task of helping children learn. We have seen how a science of behavior can contribute to teaching through a technology of education. Chapter 8 illustrated the value of a technology by demonstrating how warm and caring teachers can use cold and matter-of-fact machines to make learning optimal, that is, individualized, for each learner.

The ideas presented in the first eight chapters are usually referred to as the process and content of school learning. Usually, they are treated as topics of cognitive importance, although, as we have seen, affect is always associated with them.

Process and content, however, do not account for all school learning. The affective management of learning is a very real part of effective instruction. Optimal learning occurs only when learners attend and respond to well-organized sequences of instruction. Causing them to attend and respond to instruction and to value learning requires more than appropriate organization of content. It is also a question of motivation, discipline, and individual differences.

ADVANCE ORGANIZER

Getting learners to want to learn and knowing what to do if they do not causes many teachers more concern than anything else related to school learning. Much of the confusion with the concepts *motivation* and *discipline*, however, is a misunderstanding of cause and effect in human behavior, especially in learning behavior. You will recall, from Chapter 2, the rule that expresses the relationship between what we do to try to change behavior and our beliefs about the causes of behavior. Confusion about this rule lies at the very heart of the dilemma about motivation and discipline of learners. In Chapters 9 and 10, we will see the practical value of being scientific about cause and effect.

There are several points of view about what causes (motivates) learners to attend and respond to instruction and to value learning. In Chapter 9, we will first consider more traditional ways of looking at the concept *motivation*, and then see how those views can be combined with our rules of positive reinforcement from Chapter 8 to form useful *strategies of instruction* that do indeed motivate learners. The theme we have been developing in the first eight chapters—the application of a science of behavior to the art of teaching—is the idea we will keep central to the development of these strategies. Consequently, the task for Chapter 9 will be to learn how our rules of positive reinforcement can be combined with rules from other points of view about motivation and the properties of various approaches to instruction, especially simulation and games approaches. We will learn how to synthesize instructional strategies that cause learners to attend to, respond to, and value learning without being coerced. In doing this, we will see the blending of the cognitive and affective components of school learning.

GOALS AND OBJECTIVES

Cognitive

To become an effective teacher, the learner should be able to devise instructional strategies to motivate learners that are based on rules of a science of behavior.

KNOWLEDGE LEVEL

Given the following terms or phrases, the learner is able to define them in writing: *instructional strategy, motivation, needs, hierarchy of needs, drives, simulation, game, simulation game, academic games, games model.*

COMPREHENSION LEVEL

Given Maslow's theory of motivation, the learner is able to explain how a hierarchy of needs is central to the theory.

APPLICATION LEVEL

The learner is able to apply the rules of positive reinforcement to specific instances of causing learners to attend and respond to learning tasks.

ANALYSIS LEVEL

Given an example of an instructional strategy for motivation, the learner is able to state whether it is based on rules of positive reinforcement.

SYNTHESIS LEVEL

The learner is able to devise an instructional strategy based on the rules of positive reinforcement and the properties of simulation games for causing students to attend to, respond to, and value learning.

EVALUATION LEVEL

Given the opportunity to choose among various points of view of motivation or a synthesis of view points, the learner is able to present arguments in support of his choice.

Affective

To become an effective teacher, the learner should be able to commit himself to the importance of capturing the attention of learners rather than demanding it.

RECEIVING (ATTENDING) LEVEL

As the learner reads about motivation, he tries to synthesize the various points of view presented.

RESPONDING LEVEL

The learner is willing to try to find positive, logical, and consistent strategies of motivation.

VALUING LEVEL

The learner wants to help others meet their basic needs.

ORGANIZATION LEVEL

The learner tries to plan specific instructional strategies that provide both the content to be learned and methods of motivation.

CHARACTERIZATION LEVEL

Through his interactions with others, the learner demonstrates his belief that capturing attention is preferable to demanding attention.

9

The bell has just signaled the end of the lunch hour and the students in my grade ten English class are beginning to find their desks for the Friday afternoon session. No one hurries. "Probably because it is Friday," I tell myself. "These children are repeaters. They do not like English. All of them failed it last year—not motivated enough to learn it."

This is my first teaching position and it has not been going well. We are six weeks into the term and the students have not yet settled down to work. My instruction has been reasonably well planned. I know what I want them to learn. I have provided a variety of study materials, have told them what to study, and how to study it.

I have gone to great lengths to provide practice with the material. Written homework assignments are given regularly. I consistently do my part of the homework, being careful to mark each paper completely and fairly. However, only a few of the students ever complete an assignment. Most do not listen well in class even though I tell them they must. I give well-organized and concise lectures but only a few students take notes, and then only if they believe the material will appear on the next test. Lately, even the prospect of failing a test seems to be losing its effect, and their test papers are getting worse rather than better. Time is being wasted in class and I am needing to "clamp down" on them more and more. But my rebukes do not help. I find myself wondering: "Does the new teacher always get the unmotivated learners? What will I finally have to do with these students to make them pay attention, practice, and learn? Will they never become motivated?"

I remember the details of this particular class that met on a Friday afternoon nearly twenty years ago, not because it was special, but rather because it was typical.

"All right now! Let's settle down! You heard the bell ring." Some do, but most pay little attention as they continue to talk, sit on their desks, loiter near the door and at the desks of friends.

"Quiet! Let's have it quiet in here! Clifford, Madge, Donna—please take your seats." "How would you like to come in after school and carry on that conversation, Dan?" I walk toward the place on the chalkboard where I usually write the names of those who misbehave and thus earn a detention. Dan stops talking. I turn to the rest of the class. "I'm waiting. I'm waiting. We will not begin until it is absolutely quiet in here, even if we have to wait all afternoon."

A long pause follows. Most of the students interrupt their various activities long enough to give me at least a vague feeling of being listened to.

"I have some notes for you today about—"

"Is this going to be on the test?" interrupts Linda.

"Of course it is. It's important."

"I don't have any paper," replies Linda.

"Then borrow some. Quickly, now, we're wasting valuable time."

"Don't begin until I get some," begs Linda. "Who has a hunk of paper I can borrow?"

"You mean steal!" quips Barry. Linda gives him a sour look as she leaves her desk to wander about the room in search of a paper donor. Several others take her cue and do likewise. Within seconds, many students are moving about trying to borrow paper and pencils. Several find the disturbance a convenient opportunity to take up the conversations I had interrupted earlier.

"O.K., now that everyone finally has paper and pencil, quiet down and let's get started. Head your paper in the usual way with today's date and the topic 'Grammatical Usage'."

"What's the date today, sir?" comes a loud voice from the back of the room.

Momentarily, I have forgotten the date, and I ask if anyone knows what day it is.

"Friday." says Kent, and everyone begins to laugh.

"No, I mean the *date*. We all know it's Friday."

Several dates are offered by several voices, and we finally settle for the fifteenth, since that is the number that has the loudest support.

"Quiet! I want it quiet in here! All right, that's better. Now, head your paper 'Grammatical Usage'."

"Grammatical? How do you spell 'grammatical'?" blurts out Peggy.

"You have a hand, Peggy. When you want to speak, please raise your hand," I reply, not really trying very hard to hide my annoyance. I find myself wondering what it is that motivates this girl. I write the word "Grammatical" on the board and wait for Peggy to copy it. I notice that several others are also copying from the board. Perhaps I should have written it there in the first place. I do not get much time to think about this because I know if I hesitate even for a few seconds, they will lose what little motivation they seem to have at this point. I hurry on.

"Now, the first thing to remember about grammatical usage is—"

"Wait, sir! I'm not quite ready," continues Peggy.

"Wait, sir! I'm not quite ready, sir!" mocks Dan. Several of the boys snicker. I wonder what inner need such sarcastic behavior must meet for Dan. Peggy is somewhat more explicit in her response to Dan's behavior.

"Shut your mouth, Dan, you smart ass!" she retorts.

"That's enough of that, Peggy, Dan. I again move toward the chalkboard, threatening to issue detentions. Things settle down somewhat and once again I try to begin, this time talking over the noise that lingers on.

"Mr. Galloway, could I move my desk?" asks Judy. "There's so much noise I can't hear you."

"I don't like the noise any better than you do, but we have a job to do and we're going to get it done whether it's noisy or not," I reply, trying to sound firm and calm.

"But, can I move, sir?" continues Judy.

"*May,* Judy. You mean, *may* I move."

"Yes, sir. Can I?"

"All right, Judy, if you *can* do it quietly and quickly, you *may*."

As Judy slides her desk closer to the front of the room, general confusion again spreads throughout the class. Several desks exchange places and the noise level gets out of hand.

"Quiet! Come on, people, won't you please keep it down? We've got to get on with these notes."

Why do we always have to take notes?" demands Peggy, again without bothering to raise her hand before raising her voice. I decide to say nothing about the hand, but respond to her query about notes.

"Because you need the notes for the term exam, which, as you know, is only four weeks away."

"Is everyone finally ready now? Do you realize that we have been seventeen minutes just trying to get started? I really don't know what's the matter with you people. Each day it seems to take you longer to get down to work. Now, as I was saying, the first thing to remember about grammatical usage is that it is a term widely defined to mean—what's that, Jerry? Does 'usage' have an *e* in it?''

Over the years, I often find myself reflecting on that beginning year of teaching, especially as I try to learn more about the concept *motivation* and to help others such as yourself learn about it.

The concept is indeed an elusive one. It has been used in several ways to explain why people behave as they do. Sometimes it is used to refer to something innate within the individual, a kind of energizer or driving force, a desire or an urge that causes the individual to perform. Often, these inner forces are described as drives, or attempts of the individual to meet basic needs, to establish and maintain states of equilibrium.

At other times, motivation refers to external stimuli, either positive or aversive, that can be applied to individuals to cause them to perform certain actions. For example, we talk of using motivation to get a learner to complete an assignment, to listen to directions, or to take part in a physical activity; and eventually, to perform the desired activity on his own.

Recently, the concept has become part of a science of behavior and thus has lost many of its occult qualities. Motivation is defined simply in terms of the observable conditions that can be shown to control attending and responding. Essentially, these are the conditions of reinforcement.

Motivation has not been a great concern relative to an interpretation of learning. Mainly, the concept has been of interest in a practical sense relating to the conditions under which learned behaviors are performed. In the everyday language of the teacher, the concern with motivation has been to discover how to cause learners to attend and respond appropriately to learning tasks so that learning itself becomes a source of motivation.

Motivation can be defined as . . .   As we begin to learn about the concept of motivation, you will notice that our efforts will relate mostly to objectives in the affective domain. You will also notice the operation of the higher-order rule discussed in Chapter 2: "What we believe about the cause of behavior is related to what we do to try to change behavior." We will want to keep this rule in mind as we consider various points of view about what causes learners to strive toward the objectives that we, as teachers, hope they will attain.

MOTIVATION: TRADITIONAL VIEWS

Traditional views of the concept *motivation* typically rely on internal states or entities of the organism. In these views, inner conditions are hypothesized to mediate between physiological and environmental events or conditions on the one hand and consequent behavior on the other. Physiological and environmental stimuli are believed to produce certain inner conditions which in turn "motivate" the organism to behave in certain ways. This view of motivation is similar to a medical model of infectious diseases (Table 2-1) and a cognitive interpretation of learning (Figure 4-2). The similarity is not surprising, since a traditional interpretation of cause and effect in human behavior is based on the mediating properties of hypothetical inner constructs which have been postulated as necessary elements in the many cognitive theories of human behavior, including those of motivation.

William James described the task of the teacher who views motivation in a traditional way, saying that "in teaching, you must simply work your pupil into such a state of interest in what you are going to teach him that every other object of attention is banished from his mind; then reveal it to him so impressively that he will remember the occasion to his dying day; and finally fill him with devouring curiosity to know what the next steps in connection with the subject are."[1]

In this view, motivating students calls for manipulating the conditions of their inner states. Typically, these inferred inner states are described as *inborn tendencies* and *needs*.

Inborn Tendencies

You will recall, from our discussion in Chapter 2, that a Freudian psychology requires an inborn and inner source of driving energy to respond. In this view, there is constantly available within the person a potential driving force of a psychosexual nature, ever ready to be released for various kinds of behaviors, mental and physical. In this sense, a person is constantly in an energized state, that is, "motivated" to behave. The motivational problem to be solved by each individual is not *establishing* a driving force. Rather, the task is to hold in check, guide, and channel a driving force that is innate to each of us. This is accomplished by hypothesized logical and moral censoring mechanisms, the ego and the superego.

Thus, in a Freudian view, an individual is always in a potential state of motivation. This state is much like a wound clock spring. It is potentially "ready" to make the hands move or the alarm ring, depending on the direction in which its energy is released by the regulating mechanisms within the clock.

From a Freudian view of motivation, the teacher's task is essentially that of helping learners to keep their energies in check or to channel them in directions that are logically and morally acceptable. Since the chief method for doing this is verbal, what a teacher actually does is carry on discussions, with learners, individually or in groups, that will help them to think through the advisability, both logical and moral, of various courses of action. Motivation in this sense is seen as helping learners decide how to behave by helping them choose among possible alternatives.

Freud was not the only person to believe in the inborn nature of motivation. Maria Montessori (1912) urged teachers to plan their instruction around the natural and spontaneous behavior of children; to let the child's natural tendencies toward learning lead the way.

Jean Piaget's theory of intellectual development (1952) insists on the biologically based intrinsic tendency of all living things to act and to know. Jerome Bruner (1966) also believes that nearly all children have an inborn "will to learn," usually shown as natural curiosity about their surroundings and a tendency to achieve competence in what they do and to work with others cooperatively.

Others, for example, Berlyne (1957), Fowler (1965), and Harlow (1950), have done extensive research on natural curiosity and exploratory behavior of animal and human subjects. The results of their studies suggest that subjects seek both

Proponents of inborn tendencies toward motivation maintain that . . .

---

[1] William James (1899). *Talks to Teachers*. New York: Norton, 1958, p. 25.

stimulation and change in stimulation from their environments. Novel, complex, surprising, unfamiliar, and changing stimuli seem to capture a subject's attention better than usual, simple, familiar, and static stimuli.

As teachers, we can take advantage of these findings to motivate our learners by making sure that our instructional materials and approaches are at least occasionally new, different, challenging, and enlivened with an element of surprise or mystery.

Needs and Drives

Needs are defined as . . .

It is common knowledge that living organisms have physiological requirements such as food, water, oxygen, elimination of wastes, and protection from environmental extremes. These requirements are frequently called *needs*. According to theories of motivation based on the idea of *need gratification*, when these needs are unsatisfied, stimuli, called *drives*, occur within the organism. Drives elicit responses that result in the needs being fulfilled. For example, an unsatisfied need for food produces drive stimuli that "motivate" the organism to behave in ways that eventually result in the taking of food into the body. Such behavior sat-

Drives are defined as . . .

isfies the physiological need and also reduces the drive stimuli. Such theories of motivation are often called drive-reduction or need-gratification theories.

One such theory is that of David McClelland (1961, 1965). He believes, like Bruner (1966), that human beings have a need for achievement. However, McClelland suggests that this general inner need is a learned motive. Believing achievement motivation can be increased, he has done research in which he applied rules of reinforcement to demonstrate increases in the achievement behavior of adults. McClelland's work, however, "gives limited attention to the situational contexts that affect achievement."[2] Therefore, the concept is somewhat difficult to work with in the sense of knowing what to do to cause a given learner to attend and respond more appropriately to a certain learning task.

Atkinson (1960, 1964) believes that an explanation for achievement behavior must include both the rules of reinforcement and the rules of punishment, that is, a need to avoid pain of failure. Both of these points of view are also found in Abraham Maslow's (1908–1970) theory of a hierarchy of needs. Maslow (1954, 1968) was one of the chief contributors to a theory of motivation based on gratification of needs. His work in the area of motivation led him to conclude that need gratification is "the most important single principle underlying all development. . . . The single, holistic principle that binds together the multiplicity of human motives is the tendency for a new and higher need to emerge as the lower need fulfills itself by being sufficiently gratified."[3]

Maslow was a student of Edward Thorndike, who, as you will recall from Chapter 4, played a significant part in the development of a behavioristic psychology. It is interesting that out of such a relationship came a man known as the father of humanistic psychology. Maslow (1954) believed that behavioral psychology should not place too much emphasis on scientific objectivity and that we should remember that science is a human creation with human motives,

[2] M. L. Maehr (1974). Culture and achievement motivation, *American Psychologist*, **29**(12), 887.
[3] A. H. Maslow (1968). *Toward a Psychology of Being*, 2d ed. New York: Van Nostrand, p. 55.

human goals, and "is created, renewed, and maintained by human beings."[4]

Throughout his life Maslow continued his plea for a humanistic science of behavior. As teachers, we would be wise to understand what he said and not lose sight of the fact that it is the behavior of *people* with which we are concerned, not just behavior.

Maslow first introduced his theory of need gratification in 1943. Basic to his theory is the assumption that in each of us there are both a positive striving to grow and forces that resist growth. Maslow said:[5]

> One set (of forces) clings to safety and defensiveness out of fear, tending to regress backward, hanging on to the past, *afraid* to grow . . . , *afraid* to take chances, *afraid* to jeopardize what he already has, *afraid* of independence, freedom and separateness. The other set of forces impels him forward toward wholeness of Self and uniqueness of Self, toward full functioning of all his capacities, toward confidence in the face of the external world at the same time that he can accept his deepest, real, unconscious Self.

A useful property of Maslow's theory of need gratification is his hierarchy of human needs. He held that some needs, especially physiological needs, are basic to others, that certain of our basic needs must be satisfied before we will be motivated to satisfy higher needs, for example, needs for achievement and recognition, or needs to know and understand (Figure 9-1).

Maslow's theory of need gratification states . . .

According to Maslow's view of motivation, physiological needs are the strongest, the most demanding of satisfaction. Consequently, the tendency is for drive reduction to be primarily toward gratification of these lowest of needs.

FIGURE 9-1 **Maslow's hierarchy of needs.**

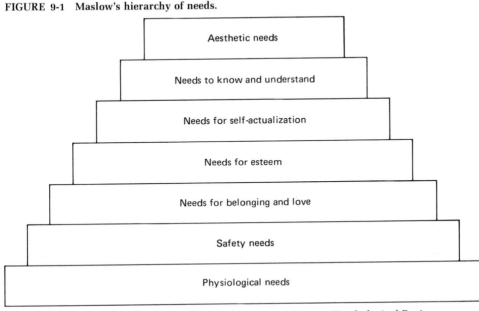

Adapted from A. H. Maslow (1943). A theory of human motivation, *Psychological Review*, **50**, 370–396. Reproduced with permission of the American Psychological Association.

---

[4] Ibid. (1954). *Motivation and Personality.* New York: Harper & Row, p. 1.
[5] Ibid. (1968). Op cit., pp. 45–46.

Once physiological needs have been satisfied, needs at the next level emerge. These are *safety* needs—drives to avoid or escape danger, be secure, and be protected. Satisfaction of safety needs is followed by motivation to be *loved* and to *belong*, to have friends and family, to become part of a group. A step beyond this is the need for *esteem*, including the desire or drive to have the respect, confidence, and admiration of others, and to gain self-confidence and self-respect. When these needs have been met, motivation is directed toward self-actualization, toward knowing and understanding, and on toward deriving satisfaction from being sensitive to the beauty of human beings, their accomplishments, and their natural environment. Maslow's self-actualized person is a highly sensitive social being who in large measure is self-motivating and self-managing.

Deficiency needs are . . .

Maslow distinguished between the first four needs in the hierarchy and the later ones. The former he termed *deficiency* needs and the latter *being* needs. Typically, gratification of deficiency needs depends on other people, whereas gratification of being needs is less dependent on other people and increasingly dependent on self and the "non-people" aspects of the environment.

Being needs are . . .

The idea of a progressive shift from relatively complete dependence on others to dependence on self and the "non-people" environment is not new with Maslow. It has always been the major goal of education. Rousseau (1762) spoke of it when he asserted that the human being is naturally good and happy. Therefore, he urged people to learn by their experiences with nature, to learn to depend on the *things* in their environment and on themselves, and to be independent of other people. The general theme of a person's striving naturally toward independence, toward becoming a self-actualized person, is seen clearly in the writing of John Dewey (1916) and, more recently, in the work of such people as Carl Rogers (1961, 1963, 1967).

Proponents of a behavioristic psychology have also been interested in causing learners to become relatively independent of their teachers, to become self-actualized persons. Their approach toward helping learners meet this goal has been considerably different, however, primarily because of differences in the basic assumptions made about the nature of motivation.

Let us look at motivation from the standpoint of a science of behavior and compare what we, as teachers, would do to motivate learners to attend to, respond to, and value learning, depending on what we believe causes them to behave. Before moving on, however, we should check our understanding of Maslow's theory of motivation, especially at the application level.

CHECKPOINT 9-1

1. Imagine you are the teacher in a grade nine course in social studies. One of your learners does not seem to be motivated to learn. He does not participate in discussions, does poorly on written assignments, and does not volunteer for group projects. He is not a discipline problem in the sense of causing a disturbance in the classroom. He simply does not attend or respond appropriately to your instruction. Using Maslow's theory of motivation as a guide, outline briefly how you will motivate your learner to attend and respond positively toward your instruction.

2. As you did item 1, were you trying to think of a specific learner whom you would like to be able to help? Yes____ No____

MOTIVATION AND
A SCIENCE OF BEHAVIOR

It has long been contended that teaching is an art, not a science. Consistent with this argument, specific methods, techniques, or strategies of instruction have been spontaneous and intuitive rather than the products of logical deductions from a science of behavior relative to teaching and learning. William James (1899), reflecting the psychology of his time, indicated in his *Talks to Teachers* that teaching is indeed an art, and that the science of psychology cannot help in the least in specific strategies of instruction.

James was probably right according to the state of the science of his times. However, it is wrong for us to believe that a practice which at one time was only an art must always remain an art. The practice of medicine, for example, was at one time little more than an art, performed spontaneously, intuitively, and often ignorantly by the local barber. Fortunately, the practice of medicine has moved beyond the level of an art. Increasingly, it is becoming a science with a well-organized, logical, and experimentally valid rationale from which are derived its specific strategies for practice.

The strategies relative to teaching and learning have been somewhat slower in their evolution. This pace has probably been the result of our comparative lack of understanding of the structure of subject matter and an absence of a scientific analysis of teaching-learning behavior. As Jerome Bruner (1960, 1966) has clearly pointed out, effective and efficient strategies of instruction depend on the structure of subject matter and the process of learning. Recently, however, as we have seen in earlier chapters, significant strides have been made, especially with a technology of education made possible by a science of behavior.

With the rules of reinforcement and procedures for doing task analyses of subject matter, we have the basis for a well-organized, logical, and experimentally valid rationale for the development of specific strategies of instruction. The concept of motivation is central to these strategies.

B. F. Skinner (1968), representing the point of view expressed by a science of behavior, talks about motivating students by means of the conditions of reinforcement that shape and maintain attending and responding behavior. He believes the question of motivation really comes down to asking what reinforces students when they study.[6]

Viewed this way, motivating the student to attend, to respond, and to value learning is a matter of arranging the conditions or reinforcement within any number of various strategies of instruction so that attending and responding will result in rewarding consequences. This calls for an application of the rules of reinforcement. However, consistent with our general theme of combining ideas rather than choosing among them, let us see how Maslow's ideas on a hierarchy of needs can be related to the concept of motivation as an arrangement of the conditions of reinforcement.

Motivation defined in terms of the rules of reinforcement is . . .

You will recall that two key ideas in Maslow's theory of motivation are that (1) there is within each of us a positive striving to grow, to have our various needs gratified; and (2) within a hierarchy of needs, certain needs must be satisfied before others can be fully gratified. This means, for example, that a desire

---

[6] B. F. Skinner (1968). *The Technology of Teaching.* New York: Appleton-Century-Crofts, p. 146.

to know and understand is not likely to occur until the needs lower in the hierarchy have been met at least in some minimal way. If we relate this idea to rules of reinforcement, we conclude that gratification of a need is a reinforcing experience. Therefore, those behaviors that result in gratification of a need will be strengthened.

Pursuing this argument brings us to an extremely useful rule for applying a science of behavior to problems of causing learners to attend and respond to learning tasks. If we use rules of reinforcement to interpret Maslow's idea that needs occur in a hierarchy, we will learn more about the conditions under which reinforcement is likely to be effective. For example, stimuli that are potentially reinforcing for attending and responding behaviors relative to knowing and understanding about arithmetic are not likely to be reinforcing for someone who feels hungry, cold, afraid, alone, unimportant, and/or doubtful that arithmetic is worthwhile. Maslow's ideas tell us that attending and responding to arithmetic are likely to be reinforcing for individuals only if they have at that time also experienced sufficient reinforcement for attending and responding behavior relative to their physical well-being, safety, belonging, esteem, and self-actualization. Stated in another way, Maslow's idea of a hierarchy of needs suggests that there is also a corresponding hierarchy of stimuli that can act as potential reinforcers for learners. This means, for example, that attending and responding to stimuli relevant to content material are not likely to be positively reinforcing until reinforcement has occurred for attending and responding behaviors that remove painful stimuli associated with hunger, loneliness, and so forth. More simply stated, learners who are hungry, cold, afraid, or lonely are not likely to find attending and responding to arithmetic problems very reinforcing.

This means two things in terms of what we will need to do as teachers to cause our learners to achieve the highest levels of affective behavior (valuing, organization, characterization) relative to their learning. We must ensure that (1) instruction is optimal for them, and (2) their lower level (deficiency) needs are met adequately. If we do not do these things, we will need to resort to punishment to cause our learners to attend and respond (the lowest levels of the affective domain). At the same time, we will very effectively keep their behavior at those minimal levels of dependency.

As you can see, Maslow provides a frame of reference for doing a task analysis relative to affective behavior. He helps us be systematic in where we look first, then next, and so on, for the source of the difficulty when our learners do not voluntarily and happily attend and respond to the instructional strategies we devise to capture their attention. He also helps us remember that our learners are more important than our strategies—that when learning does not occur, it is the strategy that must be changed or abandoned, not the learner.

The ideas of Maslow and Skinner can be synthesized by . . .

Rules of Reinforcement

The concept of motivation, from the point of view of a science of behavior, does not require assumptions about human nature, about innate tendencies, needs, or drive forces. Whether a learner attends and responds appropriately to learning tasks and values learning depends simply on whether appropriate attending and responding behaviors are reinforced. If they are, the behaviors are maintained and strengthened, and they become characteristic of the learner. If they are not reinforced, the behaviors extinguish. From this standpoint, if a learner does not attend and respond appropriately to a learning task, we do not conclude that the student is "unmotivated," but that attending and responding behaviors are not being reinforced. Our task as teachers then becomes one of examining the rules of reinforcement to see how our instructional strategy can be modified so that attending and responding will result in reinforcement.

You will recognize the following rules as those we derived from our discussion of reinforcement in Chapter 8. Notice that the first of the simple rules has been modified somewhat to accommodate Maslow's idea about the hierarchical nature of potential reinforcers.

HIGHER-ORDER RULE: *Responses that are reinforced are learned, whereas responses that are not reinforced extinguish.*

SIMPLE RULES: The simple rules of reinforcement are:

1. Since almost any stimulus can act as a reinforcer, the behavior of your learners will tell you if the reinforcers are working. If the potential reinforcers are not effective, ask yourself whether your learners have been adequately reinforced for behavior appropriate to the removal of painful stimuli associated with levels of needs lower in the hierarchy.
2. Usually, you should reinforce immediately following appropriate responses.
3. Use only enough reinforcement to get the job done. Keep your learners "hungry."
4. To begin with, reinforce each and every appropriate response. Gradually, reinforce only intermittently.
5. If necessary to cause initial responding, use reinforcers of the primary, tangible, and internal (food) type; or of the secondary, tangible, and external (stars, points, tokens) type. However, do not move so rapidly that you "lose" your learner.
6. Reinforce only appropriate responses. Withhold reinforcement from inappropriate responses.
7. Do not try to change the behavior of your learner in one big step. Follow a shaping procedure; expect gradual changes.
8. Do not try to substitute a "bag of goodies" for good teaching. Regardless of your approach, you must arrange the events of instruction so that conditions of learning are met.

APPLYING THE RULES TO
INSTRUCTIONAL STRATEGIES
THAT CAPTURE AND MAINTAIN ATTENTION

The general procedure for operant conditioning provides a useful guideline for developing specific instructional strategies that use rules of reinforcement: (1) Begin with a specific behavioral objective; (2) select a reinforcer; (3) structure the situation so that the desired behavior is likely to occur; (4) adapt your learner to the situation; and (5) begin shaping the learner's behavior by reinforcing successive approximations of the behavior stated in your objective.

One way of looking at instructional strategies that capture and maintain attending and responding behavior focuses on the kinds of reinforcers we use. Frequently, we try to motivate learners by using only a narrow range of potential reinforcers, and usually they consist of promises of future success, prestige, understanding, happiness, and so forth. Often, because they are long delayed, these potential reinforcers are weak in their motivating properties. Since they tend to be ineffective in keeping learners attending and responding, we usually find that we must resort to punishment as a means of motivation. That is, we try to motivate our learners by making nonattending and nonresponding so aversive that they will avoid or escape the punishment by doing what we demand. Most soon learn that if they at least give the impression of working at their studies, we will not hurt them for their lack of attention.

Skinner points out that to arrange good instructional contingencies, the teacher needs on-the-spot consequences.[7] Fortunately, we have a wide range of available stimuli that can serve as potential on-the-spot reinforcers. (See Figure 8-1). Haim Ginott (1965, 1969, 1971) describes how teachers and parents can reinforce and, when necessary, punish children in ways that help them become responsible, self-managing, and independent. Lipe and Jung (1971) also provide several clues about various types of reinforcers and how to use them in classrooms.

Let us look at a few examples of how we might use potentially reinforcing stimuli in instructional strategies that effectively arrange the conditions of positive reinforcement. First, we will look at some examples of *specific* strategies for capturing the attention of learners. In a later section, we will learn about a more *general* strategy for causing learners to participate actively and spontaneously in learning tasks. This strategy should have high transfer value.

EXAMPLES OF INSTRUCTIONAL STRATEGIES THAT USE CONCRETE MATERIALS   Once we have stated our objectives in specific behavioral terms, we are ready to select our reinforcers and to arrange the conditions whereby reinforcement is contingent on appropriate attending and responding behavior. An instructional strategy can be something like this:

Six rules for instructional strategies that motivate learners are . . .

1.   State the objective and share your statement with your learners.
2.   Guide (cue or prompt) initial trials so that success (reinforcement) occurs early in the experience.
3.   Initially, reinforce each appropriate response. Withhold reinforcement from inappropriate responses. Move gradually to an intermittent schedule of reinforcement.
4.   Initially, reinforce responses that are even low-level approximations of the final behavior desired. Gradually, begin to reinforce only closer approximations.
5.   Fade cues and prompts as they become unnecessary.
6.   Fade any contrived reinforcers as success in the task begins to be reinforcing, that is, as learners begin to be self-reinforcing.

A few examples will help us see how the ideas in this strategy can be applied, using concrete materials. Lipe and Jung (1971) suggest several. Among them are: (1) Give public recognition to those who perform the objectives appropriately by writing their names on the blackboard, placing tickets on their desks, or sending

---

[7] Ibid., p. 148.

notes home to parents. (2) Allow learners to watch the beginning of an interesting movie, and the rest of it only upon completion of an assignment. (3) Note the amount of time all, or certain, learners are attending and responding properly to a learning task, and reward them accordingly with free time, games, story time, and other privileges.

Food, in small quantities, is a concrete material that can be used effectively to motivate the attention and response of learners. Lessons that can be eaten have a high probability of being attended to when the food is made contingent on appropriate behaviors. Let us assume, for example, that you want your learners to write descriptive paragraphs about their observations. If this capability has not been acquired previously, it will need to be shaped gradually through a process of successive approximation. The experience can be made meaningful by using concrete materials. (Remember what Ausubel said about meaningfulness and the importance of using concrete materials with young learners, especially in discovery learning.) A small bit of food, with distinct qualities of taste, smell, feel, shape, size, and so forth, that can be eaten following, or as part of, the lesson, can function as a basis for meaningful writing experiences, and also as a stimulus that reinforces attending and responding.

As you read the following examples, try to see how the rules of reinforcement have been applied. I do not know how much help each of you will need to do this. Therefore, in example 1, I will present the situation just as it occurred. Examples 2, 3, and 4 give a bit more guidance. After completing Checkpoint 9-2, it will be helpful to reread example 1.

EXAMPLE 1   (Elementary School)

THE OBJECTIVE: *Given a concrete object, the learner is able to describe it in writing.*

The Class: Grade three; thirty-four children, grouped by past achievement in language arts into two groups; little experience in writing descriptive paragraphs.

The Lesson: The bell has just sounded the start of the school day and the children are beginning to settle into their desks. No one hurries. Some visit with one another as they hang up their coats. Several are discussing, somewhat loudly, whose turn it is to feed the hamster and clean its cage. Ronnie and Leona have an active, noisy game going at Kenny's expense: they have his cap and are trying to keep it from him.

Mr. Branson, ready to begin, moves from his desk where all the children can easily see him. In his hand is a small white box. Question marks cover the sides and top. Without saying a word, he holds it up and shakes it gently. His head tilts slightly as he strains to hear the noises coming from the box. He shakes it again and listens. Puzzlement clouds his face but does not hide the hint of a smile forming at the corners of his mouth. By the time he shakes the box a third time, he no longer needs to strain to hear. Thirty-four children are also listening. From the box comes a sound of stones or marbles falling on one another. So far, Mr. Branson has not said a word. He begins quietly.

MR. BRANSON: For composition today I thought we would start learning how to describe in writing things that we see, touch, taste, hear, and smell. I have something in this box that will help us learn to do this. (*He lifts the lid from the box and shows the children the oval-shaped peppermint candies he has brought for the lesson.*) I would like each of you to take one candy. Put it on your desk and do not touch it for now. Just look at it and see what it *looks* like to you. (*The candies are distributed.*) "Now, tell me what it *looks* like." (*Writes "looks like" on the board.*) Beth?

BETH: Mine looks round.

MR. BRANSON (*writing "round"*): Christopher?

CHRIS: It looks like a cloud.

MR. BRANSON: Good! (*writes "cloud."*) Skipper?

SKIPPER: A flying saucer.

MR. BRANSON (*writing "flying saucer"*): What does yours look like, Patty?

PATTY: A round head.

MR. BRANSON (*writing "round head"*): What *color* is it, Erica?

ERICA: White.

MR. BRANSON: Is it shiny, Erica? (*Writes "white."*) Or is it dull?

ERICA: Shiny.

MR. BRANSON: All right. (*Writes "shiny."*) What about yours, Blair?

BLAIR: Dull.

MR. BRANSON: Now, I would like you to very carefully drop your candy on your desk to see what it *sounds* like. (*Children drop candy. Then many hands are raised.*) Paul?

PAUL: Mine sounds like a rifle.

MR. BRANSON: A rifle? Good! (*Writes "sounds like—rifle."*) Rev?

REV: A pellet.

MR. BRANSON (*writing "pellet"*): Larry?

LARRY: It sounds like gravel dropped on the roof.

MR. BRANSON: Good! (*Writes "gravel dropping."*) Patrick?

PATRICK: I think it sounds like pouring rain.

MR. BRANSON: O.K. Good for you! (*Writes "pouring rain," and continues the lesson by asking the children to describe what the candies feel like and taste like. The responses are written on the board under the appropriate headings.*) Now, I want you to listen very carefully. I would like those of the Bombers who want to, to write your own composition with this heading: *My name, My candy,* and today's date. You may use any of these words, or if you have something special, use your own. Now, the Flying Saucers (*softly*), would you turn to the left as quietly as you can? (*Flying Saucers members turn desks to face the side board.*) Put your candy on your desks and leave your books closed. That's fine. Now, we need a topic sentence. What are we talking about? In a sentence, please. Dennis?

DENNIS: Candy.

MR. BRANSON: That's what we're talking about, but can you say that in a sentence?

DENNIS: I have a candy on my desk.

MR. BRANSON: Good! (*Writes "I have a candy on my desk."*) What does it look like? (*Continues the lesson with the Flying Saucers group until he has developed an outline for the "slower" group to refer to in writing their compositions.*)

The outline they developed together follows. (Time was then given to complete it, as they ate their concrete material—the candy.)

My Candy

I have a candy on my desk. It is (color) . Mine looks like (shape) . It is (dull, shiny) . When I drop it, it sounds like (sound) . It feels like (feel) . It tastes like (taste) . When I am finished writing about it, (what will happen to it) .

EXAMPLE 2   (Junior Secondary School)

One teacher in junior secondary school uses food to motivate his art students to make fancy Easter eggs with their own designs. First, he helps each person create a design. Then, after all designs have been completed, an extended art period is devoted to decorating. Each student brings a fresh egg to class. Holes are drilled in both ends of the egg and its contents are blown into a clean paper cup. A couple of mothers have been invited to help out on this day. They have brought electric skillets, and they fry bacon, scramble each student's egg, and make toast for each student who has completed the decorations on his shell.

Originally, the teacher started this procedure because of lack of motivation of his students. Now, it is something of a tradition in the school. Attending and responding in other aspects of the art class have also improved. More importantly, however, more learners in the school now choose to join art classes.

EXAMPLE 3   (Elementary School and Secondary School)

Another teacher makes food intermittently contingent on appropriate study behavior through the use of unexpected treats relating to different topics of the curriculum. When the pupils are learning about how early North American Indians dried food to prevent its spoiling, this teacher dries thin slices of meat to make jerky and parches kernels of corn. Samples of these foods are shared with her learners at appropriate times.

Important in what she does are the conditions under which the food is given. She does not use food as a tool for bargaining with the children to buy or bribe their attention to learning tasks. That is, she does not say, "Today I have a treat for you. If all of you work well until lunchtime, I will give you a sample of food." Compare this poorly contrived strategy with the more natural and effective one that the teacher used.

At a time during the study of a topic in which a particular food is a logical part of the experience, the teacher brings small samples to school. However, she does not announce that she has done so. She waits until she can "catch the learners being good," that is, attending and responding appropriately to the learning tasks. She consistently withholds reinforcement until the behavior of the class as a whole approximates what she wants it to be. At that point, she reinforces the desired behavior by saying something like, "May I please have your attention? We have been working so well that I think we can afford to take a short time for a little surprise that I have prepared for you. As you know, we have been learning about how early American Indians preserved their foods. You will remember that drying was one way they kept foods, such as meat and corn, from spoiling. It just happens that I know how to dry meat and corn and how to prepare it later for eating. Last evening I made some jerky and parched corn for you to sample. I brought it today, hoping that we would find time to enjoy it. Because we have worked so well, I think we can take time now to see how you like this type of food."

EXAMPLE 4   (Senior High School or College)

Concrete materials other than food can be effective in the instructional strategies we are discussing. Actual materials to do something with, e.g., to observe, manipulate, smell, touch, or hear, increase the probability that learners will attend and that learning will be meaningful. Doing while learning is usually more meaningful and more reinforcing than merely reading or hearing about someone else's experiences.

Attending to experiments and demonstrations is reinforcing for most learners, not just because of the novelty of such experiences, but also because learners understand clearly the instruction being presented. That is, their attending behavior is immediately reinforced by their success in the learning task. This also occurs when learners use real objects or working models, for example, in science, arithmetic, and social studies. Manipulating a model of a chemical element or compound enables learners to test their hypotheses about how the pieces fit together and to receive immediate feedback about the correctness of their respective responses. Assembling the parts of a model, such as a human heart or the bones of a skeleton, seldom requires coercion to cause learners to practice with them. The practice itself provides immediate, on-the-spot reinforcement for the learner's desired attention, response, and evaluation.

CHECKPOINT 9-2

1. Describe how each of our rules of reinforcement has been applied in the instructional strategy illustrated in example 3 above. (You may want to practice the same for examples 1, 2, and 4.)

2. Were you willing to do this activity? Yes____ No____

EXAMPLES OF INSTRUCTIONAL STRATEGIES FOR WRITTEN WORK   Much of a learner's practice occurs in writing. Written reports, essays, graphs, arithmetic problems, answers to questions, and similar exercises account for a large part of a learner's total school behavior. Much of the personal, private, and individual contact we have with our learners is through the written work they do and the comments we make on their papers. Consequently, much of what we do to motivate appropriate attending, responding, and valuing behavior is by our written communications. Therefore, the strategies we develop for handling our learners' written responses should reflect our rules of reinforcement. However, this does not always occur. Often, in grading a learner's paper, we evaluate the accuracy or completeness of the performance instead of evaluating and motivating the performance. In Chapter 13, we will learn much more about the rules of evaluation; for now, let us examine learners' written work from the point of view of motivation.

There are several ways we can apply our rules of reinforcement to strategies for shaping and maintaining appropriate attending and responding behavior through written work. First, we can ensure that reinforcement, including feedback of results, is as immediate as possible. Next, we can "catch learners being good" in written work, and we can shape those behaviors that we want to increase in quality or frequency.

Providing immediate feedback following written responses is difficult without using programmed materials and self-instructional devices. We saw in Chapter 8, however, that we can approximate this by making answers and models available to learners.

Sometimes we believe that teachers must mark all written work. This belief is unfortunate for several reasons. First, unless the learner is present during the marking session and unless the marking occurs soon after the work is written, feedback is likely to be delayed beyond the time that it will be optimally reinforcing. Second, permitting the learner always to rely on the teacher for reinforcing or corrective feedback is to be avoided if affective behavior is to occur at the higher levels of organization and characterization. Such dependence, of course, is completely contrary to our major purpose as teachers, to cause our learners to become self-motivated.

A rule of thumb relative to specific strategies for providing feedback about written work may be stated as follows: "As much as possible, encourage learners to mark their own work." This rule can and should be applied at all grade levels through graduate school. In practice, this means, for example, having children check their own written work, including tests, rather than having the teacher do it or having the students exchange papers with other persons. Thus they can monitor their own progress as they need to rather than having it evaluated only at the end of the experience. It means encouraging learners to be honest and direct about learning and to be unafraid as learners. Do not worry about your learners cheating if answers are made available. They will cheat only if instruction is bad or if they are afraid of being wrong. If a learner cheats, take this behavior as a clue that you need to improve the instruction for that person. Maybe "getting the right answers" is becoming more important than knowing, understanding, and feeling.

The foregoing is not meant to suggest that you should never mark written work. I want simply to convey that we may do more than we should. However, those papers, or parts of papers, for which we do assume major responsibility for marking, e.g., reports, exercises in creative writing, stories, expressions of opinion, or points of view, provide excellent opportunity to shape more appropriate behaviors of attending and responding. We can do this by written comments to "catch learners being good" and to provide corrective information to help them modify incorrect responses. Notice how the teacher does this in the example in Figure 9-2. Contrast teacher A's application of rules of reinforcement with teacher B's failure to apply them. Notice, also, how this example applies the conditions of learning concepts and rules we learned about in Chapter 6.

From our general rules of positive reinforcement, we can derive specific rules for marking learner's written work so that attending, responding, and valuing behavior are strengthened.

1. If you assign it, mark it, and mark it carefully.

Ten rules for marking written work are . . .

2. Return marked papers as soon as possible. Allow learners to mark their own whenever appropriate.

3. If a learner does well on some part of an assignment, ask her to show it to someone who perhaps did not do so well or who has another way of doing it.

4. Write personal and positive messages to the child: "This answer is really well written Sally!" "It is easy to follow your logic, Albert."

5. Write a positive message on the paper to the parent(s) once in awhile; do not wait until the paper is perfect.

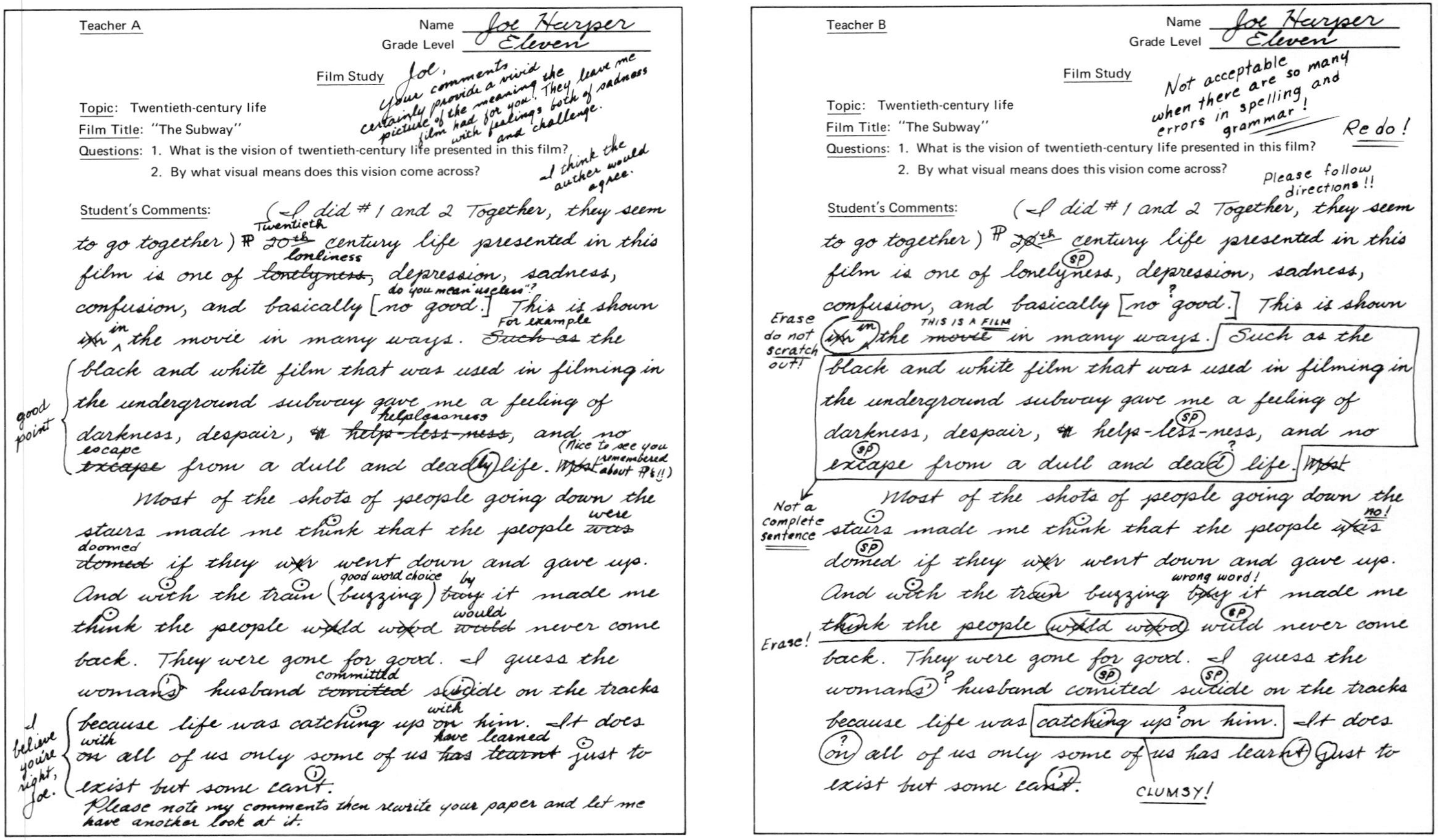

Teacher A

Name _Joe Kerger_
Grade Level _Eleven_

Film Study

Topic: Twentieth-century life
Film Title: "The Subway"
Questions: 1. What is the vision of twentieth-century life presented in this film?
2. By what visual means does this vision come across?

Student's Comments:

Teacher B

Name _Joe Kerger_
Grade Level _Eleven_

Film Study

Topic: Twentieth-century life
Film Title: "The Subway"
Questions: 1. What is the vision of twentieth-century life presented in this film?
2. By what visual means does this vision come across?

Student's Comments:

FIGURE 9-2 Applying rules of reinforcement through written comments on learners' papers.

6. Whenever possible, provide a model of the correct response instead of just pointing out that the answer is incorrect.

7. Give all the credit possible to a paper, even to the point of separate marks for various parts or aspects of the assignment: mark for correctness, spelling, neatness, and completion.

8. Write notes (personal asides) on the paper by selecting a phrase, word, or sentence, and making comments such as: "Great to read a paper that makes use of our spelling words"; "I appreciate a paper that has been double-spaced"; or "My job would be a lot easier if everyone took as much care with his work as you obviously did with this sentence!"

9. When pointing out errors, avoid smart or cutting responses.

10. Direct the learner to correct all errors and resubmit his paper.

SIMULATIONS AND GAMES: WIDELY USEFUL INSTRUCTIONAL STRATEGIES

Simulation and gaming techniques are ancient, but their use in classrooms is fairly recent. Both techniques, alone and in combination, offer potential strategies for instruction that are at once motivating and highly likely to result in meaningful learning.

Simulations are "simplified but accurate representation(s) of some aspect of the real world."[8] They may be physical, e.g., a simple static model of the solar system, an airplane, or a complex driving or pilot simulator used in driver or pilot training programs. Simulations may also be social, dealing with people, e.g., a model of some social institution or system like the family, the community, or a nation.

Simulation means . . .

A *game* is broadly defined here to mean "an activity involving interaction among individuals or groups who are attempting to achieve specific goals. The means for achieving these goals are limited by rules."[9] This definition includes the common usage of the word "games," e.g., to refer to activities such as playing basketball, cards, and checkers, and also to much of the everyday behavior of learners and teachers in classrooms. As Maidment and Bronstein (1973) point out, "a game situation occurs when individual actors or players within a system do not possess the capacity to achieve their goals alone."[10]

The term "game" means . . .

As teachers, we can draw heavily on simulation and gaming techniques to form strategies to motivate learners.

Instructional Strategies for Academic Games

Many teachers incorporate concrete objects, demonstrations, experiments, and active learner participation in instructional strategies that have gamelike qualities. Six essential properties of games are described by Coleman:[11]

---

[8] R. Maidment and R. H. Bronstein (1973). *Simulation Games: Design and Implementation.* Columbus, Ohio: Merrill, p. 1.

[9] Ibid., p. 4.

[10] Ibid., p. 5.

[11] James S. Coleman (1967). Academic games and learning, *Proceedings of the 1967 Invitational Conference on Testing Problems.* Princeton, N.J.: Educational Testing Services, p. 67.

(1) Its basic elements are players or actors, each striving to achieve his goals; (2) it is (sometimes) limited to a small, fixed set of players; (3) its rules limit the range and define the nature of legitimate actions of the players; (4) through the rules it establishes the basic order, sequence, and structure within which the actions take place; (5) it is delimited in time as well as extensivity, and an end defined by the rules; (6) its rules constitute a temporary suspension of some of the ordinary activities of life and rules of behavior by substituting for them these special time-and-space delimited ones.

Two properties of game strategies are . . .

Coleman (1967) tells us that instructional strategies with gamelike qualities establish learning contexts that have two essential properties: (1) action in an environment, and (2) reward. That is, the learner is always learning to act by acting.[12] He points out, further, that learning itself is not the goal in games, as it often is in more conventional approaches to school learning. In a game, the player learns a given skill or bit of information, not simply to have or to know it (and usually to pass a test on it), but to learn certain information and skills that will clearly help the player gain the goal or purpose of the game. Learning the rules, skills and other features of a game has the pleasing consequence of being able to participate successfully in the game. That is, learning the rules is positively reinforcing.

Game strategies that emphasize learning by experience are quite different from the more conventional classroom strategies that emphasize learning through information processing. Coleman (1973) and his colleagues have investigated these differences over the past several years, saying that "both processes have their virtues and faults, and neither is sufficient as the sole process for human learning; but the processes are partially substitutable, and one may reasonably ask, for particular things to be learned, which process will be better."[13] A comparison of the two processes is presented in abbreviated form in Table 9-1.

Coleman (1973) summarizes the characteristic properties of the two processes, pointing out that, first of all, learning through information processing can enormously reduce the time and effort necessary to learn something new. However, because this process depends heavily on a symbolic medium, usually language, efficient and effective learning within this approach requires that the symbolic media through which information is transmitted from reception to action must not be deficient or defective.

Another property of the information-processing mode of learning is related to the question of motivation. Its weakness in causing learners to attend and respond is not surprising, since, as Coleman tells us, "it must depend on artificial or extrinsic motivation. Because the action comes at the end, rather than the beginning, there is no incentive for learning until the connection between the information and the action becomes clear. . . . Thus motivation must be extrinsically supplied, as, for example, by grades in school."[14]

Game-type instructional strategies are effective because . . .

The experiential, or game, process of learning is effective because the action of the game is closely connected in time and space to the consequences of the action. Therefore, we can expect that the properties of motivation in experiential

---

[12] Ibid., p. 68.

[13] J. S. Coleman, S. A. Livingston, G. M. Fennessey, R. J. Edwards, and S. J. Kidder (1973). The Hopkins game program: Conclusions from seven years of Research, *Educational Researcher*, **2**(8), 3–7.

[14] J. S. Coleman (1967). Op. cit., p. 5.

TABLE 9-1   Two instructional strategies: Conventional and games*

INFORMATION PROCESSING (conventional)	EXPERIENTIAL LEARNING (games)
1. *Reception of information:* First there is information transmission through a symbolic medium. An example is a lecture or a book, which uses words as the symbolic medium. Information is transmitted concerning a general principle or concerning specific examples as illustrations of the general principle.	1. *Acting:* First is action in a particular instance. One carries out the action and sees the effects of that action. . . .
2. *Understanding the general principle:* This information is assimilated, and the general principle is understood. At this point one can be said to have learned the meaning of the information, to have assimilated this information as knowledge.	2. *Understanding the particular case:* Following the action and its effects, the next step is an understanding of the effects of the action. . . . At this point it could be said that the person has learned the consequences of the action, and thus has learned how to act to obtain his goals in this particular circumstance.
3. *Particularizing:* The next step is being able to infer a particular application from the general principle. This implies some cognitive abilities, general intelligence which allows one to see how a general principle applies in a particular instance, or what general principle applies to the particular instance.	3. *Generalizing:* From understanding the particular instance the next step is an understanding of the general principle under which the particular instance falls. This may require actions over a range of circumstances to gain experience beyond the particular instance and suggest the general principle. . . .
4. *Acting:* The last step is moving from the cognitive and symbol-processing sphere to the sphere of action. It involves acting, using the general principle as understood to apply to this particular instance. It constitutes, finally, the use of the information received in step 1.	4. *Acting in a new circumstance:* When the general principle is understood, the next step is its application through action for a new circumstance within the range of generalization. Here the distinction from the action of step 1 is only that the circumstance in which the action takes place is different, and that the actor anticipates the effect of the action.

* Adapted from J. S. Coleman et al. (1973). The Hopkins games program: Conclusions from seven years of research, *Educational Researcher*, **2**(8), 3–7. Reprinted by permission, Educational Research Association, Washington, D. C.

learning to be different from those in the information-processing mode of learning. Coleman suggests that motivation in experiential learning is *intrinsic*, that is, within the learning task itself. Because of this, motivation is seldom a problem for teachers, as it often is with information processing.

Coleman warns, however, that the experiential, or games, process, has some weakness. Simply "playing the game," even several times over, does not ensure that a player will infer general principles from the specific experiences of the game. Consequently, with this mode of learning, postgame discussions appear to be important.

Another property of experiential learning seems to be that it is less easily forgotten than learning through information processing. Coleman believes the reason may be that the affective associations with the concrete actions and events of games are usually positive.

A further property of academic games that can be extremely useful is the fact that they can be organized so that teams (small or large) can compete against one another. The addition of a team dimension can serve to motivate learners to practice learning tasks. An important outcome is that team members frequently tutor one another on the content (knowledge, skills) of the learning tasks required by the action of the game (DeVries and Edwards, 1973).

Let us see how these findings about academic games can be incorporated within instructional strategies that use our rules of reinforcement and cause our learners to attend to and to practice what we want them to learn. First, we will look at nonsimulation games.

NONSIMULATION GAMES

A nonsimulation game is defined as . . .

As you recall, the two essential properties of the learning context for games are (1) action in an environment toward (2) a goal. To form a game strategy we should begin by stating our objectives. Practice, leading to the attainment of the objectives, is the *action* we want learners to perform. Attainment of the objectives enables the learners to meet the *goal* of the game—to be successful at playing it. Playing successfully provides the reinforcement necessary to sustain the action of attending and responding to the parts of the learning task that need to be learned. Our rules of reinforcement will help us arrange the conditions whereby only the appropriate actions of our learners will gain reward.

EXAMPLE 1   (Senior Secondary School)
Assume that you are the teacher of a group of repeaters in grade ten. These are the young people who have failed the regular English classes in grade nine, and who are now assigned to you to learn what is commonly referred to among the students as "remedial English." This is the class you met at the beginning of the chapter.

Your objectives for the course are related to learning about English grammar. "Learning about" can reflect each of Bloom's (1956) levels of cognitive functioning.

Motivation to learn English grammar is often poor. Frequently, students attend and respond to the task in order to avoid punishment, or, as John Holt (1964) suggests, they develop strategies to avoid both learning and punishment for not learning. Frequently, only one approach to instruction is attempted. We *demand* that learners attend and respond.

Fortunately, more effective and positive approaches are available. Let us assume that you are better informed than I was when I began teaching. This means that you will try to *capture* learners' attention, to make attending and responding result in reinforcing consequences. A games approach is one way to go about it. You might begin with game action such as this:

YOU: Today, let us have some fun with words and phrases that can be used in special ways. First, as a total group, we can look at a few words and phrases. Then, as we begin to get the idea, let's form into groups of two and practice some more. Later, we can regroup as a total class and share our learning.

Here is a page of definitions and examples of words and phrases that can be used in special ways. You can refer to them as we go along. To begin, give me a naming word that can be used as a proper noun.

The students look on the page for a definition and an example of naming words that can be used as proper nouns.

PEGGY: Harry?

YOU (*writing "Harry" on the board*): Now, give a word that can be used as an "action" word, a verb in the past tense. Clifford?

The students search the page, at least some of them do.

CLIFFORD: "Laughed."

YOU (*writing "laughed"*): Give me a word or phrase that describes action words, an adverb. Madge?

MADGE: "Quietly."

YOU (*writing "quietly"*): Now, give me a word or phrase that we can use to describe a relationship between Harry and his surroundings. Give me a prepositional phrase. Dan?

DAN: Under the table."

YOU: Good! (*Writes "under the table.": You now have on the board: "Harry laughed quietly under the table."*) Give me a connecting word, one that can serve as a conjunction. Donnetta.

DONNETTA: Is "as" an example of that kind of word?

YOU: Of course! (*Writes "as."*) How about a word now that can take the place of a naming word? Give me a word that can serve as a pronoun—Debra.

DEBRA: "He."

YOU: Right! (*Writes "he."*) Now, give me another verb in the past tense—Donna.

DONNA: "Shoots." No (*pauses*)—"shot."

YOU: All right! (*Writes "shot."*) Give me a word that can be used as a common noun, plural form. Careful, now! Dave.

Everyone is now looking at the page of definitions and examples. Attention seems to be picking up.

DAVE: "Mice!"

YOU(*after pause*): Does this word qualify?

The students check the page.

PEGGY: It doesn't make much sense, but it does qualify.

YOU (*writing "mice"*): Can you end the sentence with a prepositional phrase?

Many responses are offered and, although some are a bit illogical, most are grammatically correct. One is written on the board to complete the sentence.

STUDENTS: "Through a straw."

YOU: Great! (*Writes "through a straw. The sentence now reads: "Harry laughed quietly under the table as he shot mice through a straw."*)

JUDY: Let's do another.

YOU: Why don't we do more than just another one? If you form into groups of two, I'll show you how we can do this. (*Groups are formed.*) Here are copies of several brief stories that I have written, but notice that certain words or phrases have been left out. Your job will be to put words of your own in these spaces. [See Table 9-2.]

To make the task more fun, I will give a copy of a story ("The Boy Who Cried Wolf") to only one member of each group. That person, without letting his

TABLE 9-2   Applying a games strategy

Directions:

Several words and phrases have been omitted in the following story. Where each omission occurs, insert an appropriate word or phrase of the type described for that space.

THE BOY WHO CRIED WOLF

Once upon a time, deep in the woods, there lived a _____ boy and his
                                                (adjective)
_____. Also in the woods lived an old _____ wolf. Now,
(noun—common,plural)   (adjective)
this old wolf _____ a great deal of his _____
              (verb—past tense)   (noun—common,singular)
trying to catch the _____ boy and _____ him. However,
                    (adjective)   (infinitive)
every time the wolf _____ close, the boy shouted
                     (verb—past tense)
_____ _____. His shouts were heard by the
(noun—common,singular) (noun—common,singular)
woodchoppers, who _____ nearby. They _____ came running
                    (verb—past tense)   (adverb)
with their _____ and chased the wolf _____. It _____
           (noun—common,plural)   (adverb)   (verb—past tense)
the boy greatly to see the woodchoppers running after the wolf. It was such great
_____ that one day he began shouting "Wolf! Wolf!" even
(noun—common,singular)
though the wolf was nowhere near. Of course this made the woodchoppers very
_____, so they decided to teach the _____ boy a _____
(adjective)   (adjective)   (noun—common,singular)
by ignoring his shouts of "Wolf!"

   One day soon after this, the old wolf _____ upon the boy, and finding
                                          (verb—past tense)
him playing alone, decided to have him for _____. Before the wolf
                                            (noun—common,singular)
could get near, however, the boy _____ him and began _____
                                  (verb—past tense)   (infinitive)
"Wolf! Wolf!" The woodchoppers heard his _____ but carried on
                                          (noun—common,plural)
with their _____. Soon, the boy's _____
           (noun—common,singular)   (noun—common,plural)
died away.

   The moral of the story is this: "When you 'axe' for _____,
                                                        (noun—common,singular)
make sure the 'chips' are _____."
                          (adjective)

partner see the story, will ask his partner to give him words or phrases of his own for those I have left blank. You may refer to your page of definitions and examples if you need to.

   When you finish your story, read it to your partner. Then, if you have time, do another, only this time reverse roles. Near the end of the period we can share some of our stories with the entire class.

   I see that our group has an uneven number of students. Would someone care to work with me?

A comparison of this classroom sequence with the one at the beginning of the chapter reveals some important differences in motivation. Notice how, in the latter, actions and goals are clearly related. Successful participation in the game of writing original and humorous sentences and stories requires knowing about English grammar at the application level, according to Bloom. Reinforcement is contingent on appropriate attending and responding behavior. Task-avoidance behavior is simply ignored. Shaping occurs as the difficulty of the task increases from the prompted, large-group responses at the beginning of the lesson to the less-directed, small-group responses toward the end. Shaping would continue in future lessons with increased complexity of usage and with the gradual removal of the page of prompts and cues, that is, the definitions and examples.

The most important difference, however, is the lack of punishment needed in the games strategy. Affect toward learning, toward self, and toward others is positive rather than negative. (Did you also notice in the games approach that teaching for transfer occurred—cognitive and affective, positive, vertical, and planned?)

Let us look at another example, this time one at the elementary school level, and then do a more detailed analysis of instructional strategies that combine properties of games and our rules of reinforcement.

EXAMPLE 2 (Elementary School)

Assume that you want the learners in your fourth grade class to increase their sight-vocabularies by practicing naming certain words for which they know the meaning, but which they have not yet learned to read. There are many strategies that you can construct with both the essential properties of games and the conditions of reinforcement. "Jalopy Derby," or "Drag-Strip," is one such game developed by a classroom teacher.

The format of the game is quite simple. Two to six players participate in each round, and each is to move a toy car (or some other object) through a series of spaces from start to finish. The number of moves for each player's turn is determined by the throw of dice. Number of moves corresponds to the sum of the numbers showing on the dice following a throw. The winner is the first person to move her car through all the spaces.

This basic format can be adapted for many different objectives. Here is how you can use it to cause your learners in grade four to practice sight-vocabulary:

First, get a long piece of paper. On it draw a race track with up to six lanes. Then divide the length of the track into a number of equal spaces. Label the first space "start" and the last space "finish." For each player, place the words he needs to practice, one to each space, along the lane in which his car will race. If all players need to practice the same set of words, only one set needs to be distributed along the track. Now, the first player throws the dice, and he moves his car the total number of spaces indicated by the dice, *provided* he can read all the words in those spaces. As he moves his car from space to space, he must read aloud each word his car passes. The other players act as the evaluators of his performance. (They thus participate in his practice.) When he cannot read a word, he must stop his car on that space. The turn then passes to the next player, and so on, until a player finishes and wins the game.

In the example, the object is to cause learners to practice words for sight-vocabulary. However, the same format can be used for other objectives. For instance, the spaces can contain numbers to be read, number combinations, symbols to be identified (e.g. chemical, punctuation), foreign words to be translated or pronounced, or words with letters missing to be spelled.

CHECKPOINT 9-3

1. This example of "Jalopy Derby" reflects most of the properties of academic games described by Coleman, and also our rules of positive reinforcement. Describe how our rules of reinforcement and the properties of games have been applied in this example. (What cognitive level does this task require of you?)

2. As you completed this activity, did you think about how you might go about planning your own future instructional strategies to motivate learners? Yes_____ No_____

SIMULATION GAMES

A simulation game is defined as . . .
Simulation games combine the properties of games in general with the properties of simulations. That is, they are games in which the action of the players resembles the activities of persons experiencing some real-life event. "Monopoly," for example, is a type of simulation game in which the players' action resembles the business activities of persons engaged in buying, developing, operating, and selling real estate for the purpose of profit. Since there is a clear relationship between actions and purposes (means and ends), reinforcement is likely to occur contingent on appropriate attending and responding behaviors; motivation should be positive. Transfer should also be positive and learning meaningful. (Recall the theories of transfer we learned about in Chapter 7.)

One of the games developed by the Johns Hopkins Academic Games Project (Coleman. 1967) is described as a legislative game that illustrates the properties of simulation games:[15]

> A group of 6 to 13 players constitute a legislature, and the game is a session of the legislature in which eight issues are introduced and voted upon. Each player is dealt cards each of which shows the preferences of his constituents on a certain issue.
>
> Each player has as his goal the simple task of getting reelected. But to accomplish this, he must get as many issues passed (or defeated) as he needs to satisfy the majority of his constituents. The votes for and against him in reelection after the bills are passed are determined by the number of his satisfied and dissatisfied constituents and the outcome of each issue as shows on the faces of the cards.
>
> This structure of the game induces, as one might expect, a variety of negotiations, vote exchanges, and bargains of various sorts by each player in order to gain control of the outcome on those issues important to his constituents. Thus, the principal kind of action that the player engages in is one of the kinds of actions that real legislators engage in. The player comes to see the connection between the legislator's constituency and the legislator's actions and the connection between the legislator's goals of reelection and the kind of behavior he carried out.

Five characteristics relative to simulation games can be stated in point form (Coleman, 1967). As you read the first three points, think back through the last example to see how they were applied.

_____
[15] Ibid., p. 73.

1. The players learn information relevant to the *objectives* of the game.

2. The action of the game is clearly related to the specific objectives of the game. The player always knows *why* he is learning *what* he is learning at each step.

3. The goals of the player and the constraints of his behavior are made as nearly like those of the real actor in the situation as possible.

4. Not all players infer, through the action of the game, the general principle of interdependence between legislators and constituents which makes legislatures function. Nearly everyone understands this, however, after postgame discussions. This point illustrates the belief that a game is not a self-contained learning method but one that complements verbal discussion that is often a part of the information-transmission approach.

5. This game and others encompass a wide range of skill and background. Coleman reports that the legislative game has been played by seventh graders and by graduate students in identical form. It has been played by students in a ghetto school and has provided the basis for at least two faculty members' theoretical papers on the topic of legislative decision. He points out, also, that this broad span is not merely characteristic of this game but of simulation games in general.

Several observations can be made about instructional strategies that have gamelike qualities. Academic games motivate the learner to learn the content relative to playing the game successfully, and they develop a positive affect toward goals which are clearly related to the content to be assimilated. This implies that the appropriate games for learning are those in which winning or attainment of the goal is facilitated by the knowledge and skills that the school is attempting to teach. It is likely that the most direct and powerful impact of games in school will be upon learners described as "unmotivated," for these children have never learned a goal to which school is relevant.[16]

Simulation games are likely to have positive transfer value because . . .

We are now ready to pull together what we have learned about the motivating properties of simulations, games, and our rules of reinforcement. We should be able to synthesize a higher-order instructional strategy that incorporates all these properties. Before we do so, however, let us make sure we have not forgotten Maslow's important contribution to instructional strategies based on rules of positive reinforcement.

The important point here is that even if we develop such instructional strategies, we are still likely to find some learners who do not attend and respond appropriately. Consequently, we still have the problem of deciding what to do to motivate these learners. If the activities do not capture their attention and response, should we force them to participate, hoping that if we do, they will find their participation a reinforcing experience?

Maslow is helpful here. His point of view about a hierarchy of needs suggests that we ask ourselves questions such as: "Why *isn't* it reinforcing for this learner to participate in "Jalopy Derby" or the legislative game? Can it be that he is tired, cold, hungry, afraid of being wrong, feels left out, and so on? Does it make sense to insist that he carry on with these learning activities while he has other, more immediately pressing problems? Or, is there some way I can modify this learning experience so that his particular needs can be met as he participates? How can I

---

[16] Ibid., pp. 70–71.

individualize the experience for him? That is, how can I alter the activities and the contingencies of reinforcement so that I can improve his chances of being reinforced for attending and responding behaviors that are appropriate for him at this time? How can I gradually change the nature of the learning activities for him so that, over time, he will no longer feel afraid, left out, or that he does not matter? Rather, he will find it reinforcing to *know* and to *understand*."

Games Model

In Chapter 7 we learned that general high-order rules, meaningfully learned, are more likely to transfer positively than are specific rules. Therefore, if I am to practice what I preach, before we leave the topic of motivation, we should try to synthesize a general instructional strategy of motivation that subsumes our relatively less general rules of reinforcement, simulations, and games. Furthermore, I should (1) explain how the strategy works, and (2) demonstrate it with specific examples that are likely to be meaningful and to have transfer value for you.

Games model means . . .   Briefly, what I call a *games model* is a synthesis of higher-order rules that are derived from specific rules (properties) of simulation games and simple rules of reinforcement. This model is a general plan or strategy that helps us organize the events of instruction in ways that learners will attend and respond appropriately, without the threat of punishment.

Central to the instructional strategy called the games model are the following higher-order rules:

Three rules for a games model are . . .
1. Keep actions and goals separate but related.
2. Make the actions essential to reaching the goals.
3. Make reinforcement contingent on reaching the goals.

HOW A GAMES MODEL WORKS

Keeping the actions and goals separate is our first task. We can do this by first stating our instructional objectives for the topic to which we want our learners to attend and respond. The *objectives* will constitute the basis for the *action* or practice of the game.

A games model works in this way: We are now ready to think about possible reasons why our learners might perform the actions (practice) we desire of them to meet the instructional objectives. This is the goal or purpose served by the actions. Remember, it must be clearly related to the actions in the sense that it cannot be reached unless the actions are performed appropriately. Furthermore, reaching the goal must result in pleasing experience, e.g., participating successfully in a gamelike activity, winning, or gaining recognition, awards, tokens, or food.

One of the important properties of the games model is that it is a strategy that potentially can be applied at every grade level and in nearly every topic. However, some school topics, for example, the social studies, lend themselves more readily to a games model than do other topics. This is probably because action in some topics is more clearly related to goals. Since we are social beings, we have experienced more actions and goals relative to social studies than to other topics, such as typing, mathematics, and science.

EXAMPLES OF A GAMES MODEL

Two examples will illustrate the potential range of a games model and show how it works. The first example is presented in more detail than the second, and learning about it should transfer positively to the latter.

EXAMPLE 1   (Junior Secondary School)
Topic: General Science, Grade 8, 9, and 10.
Subtopic: Factors that influence the boiling and freezing points of liquids.
Strategy:
1. State your objectives:
Cognitive
a The learner is able to define the following terms in writing: *boiling point, air pressure, solute, solvent, solution, temperature, mole.*
b The learner is able to explain how to vary the boiling and freezing point of liquids.
c The learner is able to apply simple rules for varying the boiling and freezing points of liquids.
Affective
The learner finds it satisfying to be able to apply rules of science to his daily life.
Psychomotor
Given a pressure cooker and a hand-cranked ice cream freezer, the learner can operate them successfully.
2. Set the stage for the action:
Discuss the objectives (goal) with your learners: "Today we are going to begin a unit on the factors that influence the boiling and freezing points of liquids. However, rather than learning the way we usually do, I thought we might do something different. How would you like to prepare a feast right here in the classroom, or perhaps in the home economics room? The main course could be beef stew, with homemade ice cream for dessert. By the time we finish this unit, we should have enough knowledge to manage the entire meal from the scientific preparation of it to its gastronomical conclusion!

"Of course, in order for us to do this in a completely scientific way, there are many things we must know about boiling points of liquids—how to vary and control them and how to cause melting ice to freeze a milk and cream solution to form ice cream. . . ."
3. Begin the action:
Arrange the instructional sequence so that your learners will practice those things they need to learn to scientifically prepare the meal. Note that the practice can take any number of approaches once you know what your objectives are: lectures, discussions, readings, experiments, simulations of the final performance. e.g., boiling a block of wood in a pressure cooker and freezing sugar water by adding certain amounts of salt to melting ice. (Each time I think about objectives and approaches to instruction, I am struck by the apparent paradox that freedom in teaching actually derives from structure, that is, the art derives from the science.)
4. Follow through:
Check with your learners to be sure that each person has met the objectives and is now ready to participate successfully in the final action of preparing and eating the meal. Enjoy it with them!

Four steps in doing a games model are . . .

EXAMPLE 2   (Elementary and Senior Secondary School)

Topic: Social Studies, Grades 6 to 12.

Subtopic: History of the Roman Empire.

Strategy:

1.   State your objectives: cognitive, affective, psychomotor.

2.   Set the stage for the action: Discuss the goal with your learners, e.g., "How would you like to 'live' a day in the life of a Roman citizen at the time of Julius Caesar, perhaps the day following his assasination? We could really make the day authentic if we understood well the politics, economics, social organization, issues, and so forth of that time. . . ."

3.   Begin the action: Arrange the events of instruction so that your learners gain practice in what they need to learn to live the day as a Roman citizen or slave.

4.   Follow through: Live the day—complete with as many details for which you and your learners can provide a legitimate rationale.

A WORD OF CAUTION AND A PROMISE

Before we move on to Chapter 10, in which we will consider the rules of reinforcement and punishment in classroom management, I would like to offer both a word of caution and a promise about the use of a games model.

First, the caution: A games model is only an instructional strategy. It is an approach, a technique, or a method of instruction. Consequently, if you use a games model, you must remember the higher-order rule from Chapter 6: *Regardless of the approach you select, the conditions of learning must be met.* It is not enough that your learners just "play games" and enjoy doing so, although the fun derived from games is the chief source of motivation for attending to the action. The purpose of a games model is to cause learners to want to attend, cognitively and affectively, long enough and well enough to learning tasks to learn them without being coerced.

Now, the promise: If you use a games model appropriately, you will find that discipline problems will be fewer and less severe; learners will be motivated to learn; you will become less of a "nag"; affective objectives will be met; you and your learners will be on the same team; the day is not long enough to do all you would like to do; learners will come early and stay late; your relationship with your learners will become more personal and more positive; and you will find pleasure in your work, and in your self-motivated learners.

IN PASSING

Instruction is a provisional state that has as its object to make the learner or problem solver self-sufficient.

Jerome Bruner
Toward a Theory of Instruction

ACTIVITIES

1.   Review the goals and objectives for this chapter, then write one additional instructional objective for each level of the cognitive and affective domains.

2.   As an individual or a group project, develop an instructional strategy that is based on both the rules of reinforcement and the properties of simulation games for a topic of your interest and at the grade level you plan to teach.

3.   Develop a learning hierarchy (after Bloom, Gagné, and Krathwohl) and a formative test for a unit of instruction at the grade level you plan to teach. Then show how you might apply a games model strategy to motivate the learners to participate.

4. Ask at least two learners in junior or senior secondary school to complete the story "The Boy Who Cried Wolf," from Table 9-2. (Write a story of your own and have it ready; they will want to do another.)

5. Just for fun:

At the end of Chapter 8, I shared a problem with you that we had had with our cat Lizzie. The problem, as you recall, was her habit of scratching and meowing at the bedroom door around four o'clock in the morning. I tried several "instructional" strategies before one finally worked. It was the one Donna had mentioned some weeks earlier, but before I became wise in the ways of a teacher, I tried everything from sticking reminders (plus coins) on the door for prompting and reinforcing our children to put Lizzie out, to standing quietly, sleepily, and foolishly inside the bedroom door around four o'clock to try to frighten her at the every instant she raised her voice and paw. Never once, however, did she come to the door on the nights I waited for her. Finally I ran out of alternatives except the one Donna offered in the beginning, which was just to "let her scratch." It got louder before it got better, but that was what Donna said would happen. Simple as that.

Some time ago, Lizzie ran away from home. It may have been because of the stray kitten we adopted, but I believe it was also because of some of the mistakes I made in "managing" her home environment. I think in retrospect, and how much clearer is that view than the one in prospect, punishment was too often as easy solution for motivating better behavior. Anyway, before she left, Lizzie taught me a great deal about management and mismanagement of the lives of kids and cats.

I would like to share one more episode with you in the lives of Lizzie and me. You will find it at the beginning of Chapter 10. I hope it will help us all learn about the importance of a positive approach to discipline.

REFERENCES

Atkinson, J. W. (1964). *An Introduction to Motivation.* Princeton, N.J.: Van Nostrand.

———, and G. H. Litwin (1960). Achievement motive and test anxiety conceived as motive to approach success and motive to avoid failure, *Journal of Abnormal and Social Psychology.* **60**, 52–63.

Berlyne, D. E. (1957). Conflict and information—theory variables as determinants of human perceptual curiosity, *Journal of Experimental Psychology,* **53**, 399–404.

Bloom, B. S., ed. (1956). *Taxonomy of Educational Objectives. Handbook I: Cognitive Domain.* New York: McKay.

Bruner, J. S. (1960). *The Process of Education.* New York: Vintage.

——— (1966). *Toward a Theory of Instruction.* Cambridge, Mass.: The Belknap Press of Harvard University Press.

Coleman, J. S. (1967). Academic games and learning, *Proceedings of the 1967 Invitational Conference on Testing Problems.* Princeton, New Jersey: Educational Testing Service, pp. 67–75.

———, S. A. Livingston, G. M. Fennessey, K. J. Edwards, and S. J. Kidder (1973). The Hopkins games program: conclusions from seven years of research, *Educational Researcher,* **2**(8), 3–7.

DeVries, D. L., and K. J. Edwards (1973). Learning games and student teams: their effects on classroom processes, *American Educational Research Journal,* **10**(4), 307–318.

Dewey, J. (1916). *Democracy and Education.* New York: Macmillan.

Fowler, H. (1965). *Curiosity and Exploratory Behavior.* New York: Macmillan.

Ginott, H. (1965). *Between Parent and Child.* New York: Avon Books.

——— (1969). *Between Parent and Teen-ager.* New York: Macmillan.

——— (1971). *Teacher and Child.* New York: Macmillan.

Harlow, H. F., M. K. Harlow, and D. R. Meyer (1950). Learning motivated by a manipulation drive, *Journal of Experimental Psychology,* **40**, 228–234.

James, W. (1958). *Talks to Teachers.* New York: Norton.

Lipe, D., and S. M. Jung (1971). Manipulating incentives to enhance school learning, *Review of Educational Research*, **41**(4), 249–280.

Maehr, M. L. (1974). Culture and achievement motivation, *American Psychologist*, **29**(12), 887–896.

Maidment, R., and R. H. Bronstein (1973). *Simulation Games: Design and Implementation.* Columbus, Ohio: Merrill.

Maslow, A. H. (1943). A theory of human motivation, *Psychological Review*, **50**, 370–396.

———— (1954). *Motivation and Personality.* New York: Harper & Row.

———— (1962). *Toward a Psychology of Being.* New York: Van Nostrand.

———— (1968). *Toward a Psychology of Being*, 2d ed. New York: Van Nostrand.

McClelland, D. C. (1961). *The Achieving Society.* Princeton, N.J.: Van Nostrand.

———— (1965). Toward a theory of motive acquisition, *American Psychologist*, **20**, 321–333.

Montessori, M. (1912). *The Montessori Method.* New York: Stokes.

Piaget, J. (1952). *The Origins of Intelligence in Children.* New York: International Universities Press.

Rogers, C. R. (1961). *On Becoming a Person.* Boston: Houghton Mifflin.

———— (1963). Learning to be free. In S. Faber and R. Wilson (eds.), *Conflict and Creativity: Control of the Mind.* New York: McGraw-Hill.

————, and B. Stevens (1967). *Person to Person: The Problem of Being Human.* Lafayette, Calif.: Real People Press.

Rousseau, J. J. (1762). *Emile ou de l'éducation.* Le Haye, France: Néaulme.

Skinner, B. F. (1968). *The Technology of Teaching.* New York: Appleton-Century-Crofts.

SUGGESTIONS FOR FURTHER READING

Doll, R. C., and R. S. Fleming eds. (1966). *Children Under Pressure.* Columbus, Ohio: Merrill. "The readings in this book tell how scholastic pressures on children originate; how children and parents react to these pressures; what readily identifiable social forces underlie the pressures, and what, in part, can be done to relieve the pressures."

Harlow, H. F. (1953). Mice, monkeys, men, and motives, *Psychological Review*, **60**, 23–32. In this classic paper, Harlow argues against a drive-reduction theory of learning—a theory which emphasizes the role of internal, physiological-state motivation. His point of contention is that drive-reduction theory tends to focus attention on relatively unimportant problems related to learning.

Inbar, M., and C. S. Stoll, eds. (1972). *Simulation and Gaming in Social Science.* New York: Free Press. This book provides an excellent survey, with many examples of the technique of simulation: what, how, and why.

Keislar, E. R. (1960). A descriptive approach to classroom motivation, *Journal of Teacher Education*, **11**, 310–315. Keislar takes the stand that the crucial aspects of motivation are found in the systems of reinforcements provided by a school for appropriate attending and responding behaviors.

Page, E. B. (1958). Teacher comments and student performance: A seventy-four classroom experiment in school motivation, *Journal of Educational Psychology*, **49**, 173–181. In this "naturalistic" study, Page finds that when average secondary teachers take the time and trouble to write encouraging comments on student papers, learning improves.

Segal, R. (1973). *Got No Time to Fool Around, A Motivation Program for Education.* Philadelphia: The Westminster Press. Through a series of personal and vivid accounts of boys and girls struggling against staggering odds, Segal describes the practical art of motivation applied to helping young people succeed as learners and as human beings.

Weiner, B. (1973). *Theories of Motivation, From Mechanism to Cognition.* Chicago: Markham. Weiner gives an historical review of four theories of motivation: drive theory, field theory, achievement theory, and attribution theory.

TEACHING FOR SELF-MANAGEMENT

10

Once there was a family, a black cat, Lizzie, and twelve goldfish. It was a happy home until one day the cat discovered that goldfish are good to eat. Her "misbehavior" created mixed feelings among the children since they loved their cat but they also loved the goldfish. Of course, one fish led to another, so obviously something had to be done to stop Lizzie's bad behavior.

"I'll have a talk with her," said the youngest child.

"Keep her locked in the house," suggested one of the sons.

"Buy her food with lots of fish in it and she will get tired of fish," offered another.

"Cover the fishpond with a net," volunteered the wife.

"I have it!" said the father. "We will punish her every time she tries to catch a fish. That will teach her to behave better."

Everyone agreed that this was the best way to solve the problem. And, although they did not like to hurt Lizzie, everyone knew that she needed to be "taught a lesson." Since Father was the oldest, it seemed that he should conduct the "lesson."

Father had nothing personal against Lizzie, and when no one was around to hear he explained to her that what he had to do was in no way related to how he felt toward her. He hoped that they would continue to be friends.

The next day Father sat quietly at the edge of the fishpond and waited for Lizzie to appear. He did not have to wait long, since her misbehavior had become quite regular. She settled down beside him and began to fish. Soon a fat one drifted near. Lizzie got ready for the catch, and the father got ready to catch her in the act. Just as she reached a paw toward the fish, he lifted her to the center of the pool with one smooth motion of his hands.

Lizzie was very much surprised that Father would behave this way, and it did not help much to hear him remark, as he pitched her into the pond, that this was harder on him than it was on her.

Lizzie was not in the water long. And as she ran away, she kept looking back toward him. "The lesson was a good one," thought Father. "I hope she remembers it."

However, the minds of young cats and kids forget quickly, even if not completely, and before many days Lizzie was back at her misbehavior. Obviously the lesson had not made a lasting impression. The father remarked that he was sorry, but she would have to be punished again.

This time Father had to move more carefully to get close to Lizzie as she fished. But with perseverence, he was able to catch her being "bad" and to administer the punishment. His timing was perfect, and as she hung in mid air, legs and paws thrashing wildly, he remarked firmly that he hoped this would be sufficient to teach her how a good cat should behave.

Lizzie did not pay much attention to Father's warning and, three days later, one of the kids exclaimed that Lizzie was fishing again! Father mumbled something about stubborn cats never learning as he slipped quietly toward the goldfish pond. "What am I going to do with that cat?" he thought as he crept along. This time he did not get close; Lizzie saw him coming and was gone in a flash.

Father did not see Lizzie much after that, yet the kids reported that she sneaked fish whenever he was not around, and sure enough, all the goldfish soon disappeared. Father wondered what had gone wrong with his plan. He also wondered why Lizzie no longer came to him to be petted.

CONTENTS

ONGOING SUMMARY

When our learners voluntarily attend and respond to learning tasks, we say they are motivated. Causing them to be motivated is one of the major affective concerns of teachers. In Chapter 8, we saw how the rules of a science of behavior can be applied through programmed materials and instructional devices to help make instruction optimal for each learner. In Chapter 9, we learned how to form the rules of positive reinforcement that derive from a science of behavior into strategies of instruction that capture the attention of learners, causing them to be self-motivating. Although the rules of positive reinforcement are few, the strategies that can be derived from them are limited only by our ability to be creative or inventive. We learned that combining the rules of positive reinforcement with the properties of simulations and games yields instructional strategies that have gamelike characteristics. Such strategies are highly captivating of learner attention and response.

Solving the problems of learner motivation through a synthesis of our rules of positive reinforcement and the properties of simulations and games results in the higher-order rules basic to a games model. We learned that a games model is a useful strategy for strengthening the attending, responding, and valuing behavior of learners.

ADVANCE ORGANIZER

Effective management of classroom behavior requires more than strengthening attending, responding, and valuing behavior. It also calls for weakening or suppressing inappropriate behavior. When learners attend and respond appropriately, we conclude that they are "motivated." When they do not misbehave, we conclude that they are "well disciplined." And when they behave appropriately without being bribed or coerced, we say that they are "self-motivated" and "self-disciplined," or "self-managing." Causing our learners to become self-managing is our goal as teachers.

You will recall from Chapter 2 that what we do to modify misbehavior depends on what we believe causes misbehavior. A belief in *inner causes* of misbehavior, e.g., inborn tendencies, needs, and drives, suggests action for change that is often different from the action for change that derives from a belief only in environmental causes. It is not sufficient that we use only one viewpoint or "do whatever feels right at the time" with the behavior of learners. Our action for change must be consistent, and it must derive from a humanistic view of learners that also uses the precision available in the tools from a science of behavior.

Understanding human behavior relative to teaching for self-discipline requires information about (1) the positive and negative effects of punishment, (2) alternatives to the use of punishment, and (3) ways to synthesize rules of positive reinforcement and extinction with rules of punishment and with the conditions of learning to form effective strategies for modifying behavior. Chapter 10 will help you learn about strategies that are both positive and effective in causing your learners to become self-managing individuals.

Cognitive

To become an effective teacher, the learner should be able to synthesize instructional strategies from the rules of a science of behavior and the conditions of learning that help learners become self-managing.

GOALS AND OBJECTIVES

KNOWLEDGE LEVEL

Given the following terms, the learner is able to define them in writing: *self-discipline, self-management, humanist, behaviorist, punishment, punisher, rules of punishment, positive reinforcement, negative reinforcement, reinforcer, ripple effect, Grandma's law, behavior modification, token system, a guide to behavior modification.*

COMPREHENSION LEVEL

1. The learner is able to describe the contributions of humanistic and behavioristic points of view about discipline to effective strategies for classroom management.
2. Given the rules of positive reinforcement, the rules of punishment, and the conditions of learning, the learner is able to explain how they are necessary components of effective strategies for classroom management.

APPLICATION LEVEL

Given a specific strategy for behavior modification—a token system—and a case of student misbehavior, the learner is able to state how the strategy can be used to modify the student's behavior.

ANALYSIS LEVEL

Given the details of what a teacher does to modify a student's misbehavior, the learner is able to say what the likely outcome will be.

SYNTHESIS LEVEL

The learner is able to develop a strategy that, in combining the higher-order rules of the games model and the steps included in the general guide to behavior modification, will strengthen appropriate attending and responding behavior and will weaken misbehavior.

EVALUATION LEVEL

Given the details of a case of student misbehavior and the teacher's strategy for modifying it, the learner is able to give reasons why he believes the strategy will or will not result in self-discipline.

Affective

To become an effective teacher, the learner should be able to form a personal and professional value system that emphasizes self-management of learners.

RECEIVING (ATTENDING) LEVEL

The learner recognizes that self-management is the most important goal of education.

RESPONDING LEVEL

The learner tries to understand the rationale for effective and positive strategies of classroom management.

VALUING LEVEL

The learner voluntarily examines various viewpoints on effective strategies of classroom management.

ORGANIZATIONAL LEVEL

The learner develops strategies of his own for teaching self-management.

CHARACTERIZATION LEVEL

The learner develops the habit of striving for synthesis of points of view when developing strategies for self-management.

In the opening scene of Chapter 9, you observed my effort to motivate reluctant learners to attend and respond appropriately to a boring lesson on English grammar. As you recall, my method of motivation was mainly to punish them if they did not attend appropriately.

Another observer, perhaps the school principal, might interpret my behavior differently. He might say that I was trying to maintain classroom discipline, that I was attempting to hold down or weaken behavior inappropriate to learning about English grammar. Actually, I was trying to do both even though I was not very effective at either.

In Chapter 9, we learned some things that we can do to strengthen and maintain appropriate attending and responding behavior. We called this "motivation." Strengthening appropriate behavior, however, is only part of effective classroom management. We also need to learn how to suppress or weaken undesirable behaviors of learners.

The principles and processes of motivation and discipline are as closely related as the two sides of the same coin; only on the surface are they different. You will see, as we learn more about classroom management, that in practice *self-motivation* and *self-discipline* blend imperceptibly. Effective teachers do not choose between motivation on the one hand and discipline on the other; they combine both in effective strategies for self-management.

POINTS OF VIEW ABOUT DISCIPLINE

There is little disagreement among psychologists and educators about the ultimate goal of education. Most agree that self-management (self-motivation plus self-discipline) is what we are trying to achieve with our learners. Maslow (1962), speaking for a humanistic psychology, refers to this goal when he describes self-actualized individuals. Self-management is central to Carl Roger's beliefs (1961, 1963, 1969) about becoming a person and learning to be free. B. F. Skinner (1971, 1973), speaking for a behavioral psychology, refers to the freedom of self-management as learning to depend on things rather than people.

The essential differences between so-called humanistic and behavioristic points of view about discipline or control of misbehavior are those related to *how* self-discipline is most effectively achieved. As we discuss these differences in the next two sections, you will notice a parallel with the differences, and then the blending of viewpoints that were presented in Chapter 9 about motivation. You will also notice that the ideas about the differences between *explanation* and *description* of human behavior, discussed in Chapter 2, come fully into focus because the confusion of the two terms becomes most serious and most frequent in relation to weakening the misbehavior of learners.

Self-management means . . .

A Humanistic View

Basic to a humanistic point of view is the assumption that the important prerequisite for change from dependency to relative independence is within the individual. Maslow describes the prerequisite as "an essentially inner nature which is instinctoid, intrinsic, given, 'natural', i.e., with an appreciable heredity determinant, and which tends strongly to persist. . . . This inner core shows itself as natural inclinations, propensities or inner bent."[1] You will recall that this view fits well with those of Bruner (1966, 1971), Montessori (1912), and Piaget (1952).

In this view, failure to become self-disciplined can be explained by forces from the outside world that thwart, frustrate, or suppress the natural urge to grow toward actualization, knowing, and understanding. That is, individuals behave inappropriately in their transactions with their environment because they feel afraid, unsafe, ineffective, unloved, helplessly directed by other people, and so forth. Weakening or eliminating undesirable behavior and effecting more appropriate behavior is first a matter of removing or surmounting the frightening forces that block the natural tendency to positive growth. Maslow tells us that the first step is to ensure that physiological, safety, belongingness, and esteem needs are adequately met. Once they are satisfied, the probability of self-direction is increased.

Exactly why change occurs is not entirely clear in a humanistic point of view. However, it is generally believed that improvement is facilitated by increased self-knowledge, self-awareness, and self-acceptance. Maslow points out, however, that "self-knowledge and self-improvement is very difficult for most people. It usually needs great courage and long struggle."[2] He goes on to explain that respecting and understanding the forces of fear, regression, defense, and safety make it much more possible to help oneself and others to grow toward health.

Throughout the text, we have repeatedly referred to the rule from Chapter 2 that states the relationship between our beliefs about causes of behavior and our actions to change behavior. Here again we are faced with the implications of that simple rule. If we believe (1) that misbehavior or lack of growth toward self-management is caused by inner forces that thwart or block natural tendencies for growth, and (2) that this blockage can be removed or surmounted as a consequence of self-knowledge, self-awareness, and self-acceptance, it follows that our actions for change must provide opportunity to learn about self.

A humanistic view holds that self-discipline results from . . .   Carl Rogers (1951) among others, for example, Freud (1938), Erikson (1950, 1958, 1968), Sullivan (1953), and Combs and Snygg (1959), has developed techniques for learning about self. In Roger's approach, known as *nondirective* or *client-centered* counseling, he provides a warm, personal environment in which a person can explore his problems without fear of being directed, rejected, or judged. By conveying genuine empathy and a desire to help, Rogers believes that one person can help another toward better understanding and acceptance of himself. He believes, with Maslow, that self-understanding and self-acceptance lead to the ability to solve personal problems, to behave independently, to become self-managing.

An important implication for our actions as teachers derives from a humanistic viewpoint about discipline. It is that in addition to being effective *talkers*, we must be empathic *listeners*. From this point of view, learners who have dif-

---

[1] A. H. Maslow (1968). *Toward a Psychology of Being*, 2d ed. New York: Van Nostrand, p. 190.
[2] Ibid, p. 166.

ficulty managing their own behavior, who misbehave or behave inappropriately for the situation, can be helped to change their behavior by a teacher who listens carefully to them without judging or prescribing action for them to follow. In this view, we would help our learners understand their behavior and their feelings about themselves and others. We would not accept the responsibility for deciding or telling them what they should do. This would deprive them of the very essence of what is necessary to become independent and self-actualized.

In Erikson's view, individuals are constantly, throughout life, learning in stages about themselves, developing their identity, as a consequence of the interaction between inner forces and those of the culture in which they live. Each stage presents a major task that must be overcome with the help of what was gained in the previous stage and whatever positive experiences the environment is able to provide. Erikson's descriptions of the tasks to be met provide clues about the nature of the experiences that are likely to be helpful at each stage. We will learn about the details of these stages in Chapter 11.

Briefly, a general humanistic view suggests that if we can accept learners as they are and thereby help them to better understand themselves, they will become more accepting of themselves and consequently better able to interact effectively with other parts of the environment. Because changes in outer behavior result from changes within the person, and since the person himself is really the only one who can know the inner self well enough to cause significant and lasting change to occur, it is reasonable to direct our efforts toward enhancing self-awareness. Although it is helpful to have available the skills of a trained counselor or therapist, and indeed, many schools provide these services, each of us can work toward developing warm, positive relationships with our learners so that they feel trusted, autonomous, free from guilt, industrious, and aware of who they are (the positive characteristics of Erikson's first five stages).

A Behavioristic View

Proponents of a behavioristic view of discipline and of motivation hold basic assumptions about causes of behavior that are somewhat different from those held by advocates of a humanistic approach. The greatest point of disparity concerns the locus of cause and control of behavior. Whereas humanists maintain that the mechanisms that cause and control behavior are within the individual, behaviorists argue that they reside outside the individual in the environment. B. F. Skinner states the behavioristic point of view this way: "The practice of looking inside the organism for an explanation of behavior has tended to obscure the variables which are immediately available for a scientific analysis. These variables lie outside the organism, in its immediate environment and in its environmental history."[3]

Nearly twenty years later, Skinner reiterates the same message: "We keep trying to find something wrong inside people. It's the culture that's wrong, not the people."[4]

In a behavioristic view, misbehavior is believed caused by inappropriate con-

---

[3] B. F. Skinner (1953). *Science and Human Behavior.* New York: Macmillan, p. 31.
[4] Ibid. (1971). *Beyond Freedom and Dignity.* New York: Knopf, p. 72.

In a behavioristic view, the causes of misbehavior are . . .

tingencies of reinforcement and punishment. People learn to misbehave just as they learn to behave appropriately. That is, the same rules of reinforcement and punishment shape behaviors we call dependent and undisciplined and the behaviors we describe as independent and self-managed. People do not misbehave *because* they are afraid, feel lonely, helpless, or angry. They misbehave because of the inappropriate ways in which they have been rewarded and punished by their environments. Behaviorists maintain that words such as "afraid," "lonely," "helpless," and "angry" only *describe* behavior. They do not *explain* its causes. You will recall, from Chapter 2, that using descriptive words to explain behavior results in circular reasoning. As Skinner points out, it leads us to look in the wrong places for ways to help our learners who behave badly to grow toward independence and self-management.

In a behavioristic view, the general procedure for weakening misbehavior and strengthening appropriate behavior is to manipulate certain conditions of a learner's environment so that appropriate behaviors gain reinforcement and inappropriate behaviors do not. The procedure does not require manipulation of inner states such as self-knowledge, self-awareness, or self-acceptance, although it does not deny their existence or potential usefulness as descriptions of various human conditions.

In a later section of this chapter, we will learn more about the specific details of how the main ideas of a behavioristic view can be applied in the classroom. We will also learn how some of the techniques of a humanistic view can be incorporated within a behavioristic approach, that is, how the behavioristic rules of positive reinforcement and punishment can be synthesized into humanistic strategies for self-management. Before we do so, however, we need to understand about the concept *punishment*.

CHECKPOINT 10-1

1. For the following instance of "misbehavior," describe generally how you would proceed to change Betty's behavior toward more active and spontaneous group participation if you were a (a) humanist, (b) behaviorist, (c) humanistic behaviorist.

During discussion sessions with your class of tenth grade students, Betty Smith seldom says anything. She never offers an opinion or comments on the opinions of others, but she seems to listen carefully. When asked a question, she blushes slightly and usually just shrugs her shoulders and waits quietly with her eyes fixed on the floor until the discussion passes.

2. If you had not been assigned the task of helping Betty, would you have done it anyway? Yes_____ No_____

USE AND MISUSE OF PUNISHMENT

So far in our discussion, we have said very little about punishment. It is surprising that the humanistic and behavioristic views of motivation and discipline include little mention of punishment, since its use in managing behavior is both historic and widespread. I do not know of a classroom in which punishment in some form or another does not occur. I have never known parents who reared their children without punishing them, although I have known a few who claimed they did.

Teachers *do* punish learners as they try to help them become self-motivated and self-disciplined. Frequently, however, they express their dissatisfaction with doing so. They often report that punishment does not work very well for them, but they do not know what else to do. Implied in what they say is that they are ambivalent toward the use of punishment, but also that they feel unable to help their learners toward self-management without it.

Soon you may find yourself in this position. Fortunately, considerable information is available about the effects of punishment on behavior, even though the information is not entirely conclusive. There is enough consensus, however, to do a reasonable job of sorting the myths that surround the use of punishment from the approximate facts. So, when you use punishment in your classroom, you will at least have some logical basis for doing so.

A Definition of Punishment

In its everyday use, punishment is usually thought of as an operation in which a painful stimulus follows some unwanted response, with the result that the response diminishes. Punishment in this view occurs, for example, when a learner gives an incorrect answer and feels embarrassed by the teacher's verbal comments. Punishment, in this informal usage, can take another form. When a positive reinforcer is withheld or withdrawn, punishment is said to have occurred. For example, a child, through previous experience, expects to receive a positive reinforcer—say, a smile or a word of praise—as a consequence of cleaning the chalkboards, and none comes. Another example occurs when a positive reinforcer—e.g., the choice of where to sit in the classroom—is removed as a consequence of "too much talking with neighbors."

Technically, there is more to the concept *punishment*. Potentially any stimulus can act as a *punisher*, since before a stimulus can be properly classified as such, we must observe its effect on the behavior it follows. If the behavior decreases in strength or frequency, by definition the stimulus is a punisher. The *event* is one of punishment. You will recall from Chapter 8 that this is the sort of definition required to classify stimuli as positive reinforcers. That is, both *reinforcers* and *punishers* are defined only in terms of *their effects on the behavior they follow*. Stimuli defined as positive reinforcers strengthen the behaviors they follow, whereas stimuli defined as punishers (negative reinforcers or aversive stimuli) weaken the behaviors they follow.

The event of reinforcement results in strengthening behaviors. Keeping this distinction in mind will help you understand the term *negative reinforcement*. This is an expression coined by Skinner to identify the operation in which a response results in the withdrawal of a punisher or negative reinforcer. The overall result is a strengthening of the response that terminates the punishment. An example is the event in which a learner's response of "completing his homework" results in having his name removed from the detentions list. Another is the situation in which a teacher's request of "Quiet!" is followed by a reduction of the noise in the class, or when you say "Stop that!" to someone who is irritating you, and she stops.

Punishment is defined as . . .

A punisher is defined as . . .

Reinforcement is defined as . . .

A reinforcer is defined as . . .

Negative reinforcement is defined as . . .

The concepts *punishers, reinforcers, punishment,* and *reinforcement* can easily become confused. Synthesizing them into simple rules will keep them distinctive and will help us retain them for later transfer. Notice, in the following statement of rules, that I have emphasized key parts of certain words to draw your attention to them. This is an application of what we learned in Chapter 5 about helping learners make discriminations. Note also that talking about positive reinforcers, positive reinforcement, and negative reinforcement at the same time we learn about punishers, negative reinforcers, and punishment helps to prevent the occurrence of negative transfer. That is, studying them together reduces the probability that you will get the concepts confused.

1. Positive reinforce**ment** (an event) occurs when a positive reinforc**er** (a stimulus) follows a response and the response is strengthened.
2. Negative reinforce**ment** occurs when a punish**er** (negative reinforc**er**) is withdrawn following a response and the response is strengthened.
3. Punish**ment** occurs when a punish**er** (negative reinforc**er**) follows a response and the response is weakened.
4. Punish**ment** occurs when a positive reinforc**er** is withdrawn following a response and the response is weakened.

We will learn more about the application of these rules throughout the rest of the chapter. For now, let us learn about the concept of punishment and its effects on behavior.

Why Punish?

"Why punish?" This is the fundamental question that must be answered before anything else we do relative to the use of punishment can make sense. The "standard" answer to this question is: "To cause learners to behave better." Observation in classrooms, however, suggests that there is wide interpretation of what "behave better" actually means. In many instances it appears to mean simply: "Stop that undesirable behavior!" Punishment is the penalty that must be "paid" for failure to comply with the teacher's directives. At other times, the exact function of punishment is not really clear. Often, learners are punished as a consequence of a teacher's ignorance about how learning occurs. That is, they are punished for "misbehavior" when the teacher does not know what else to do. Not infrequently, even those teachers who understand rules of human behavior allow personal feelings to interfere with professional competence in the use of punishment.

To avoid these dangers, we must constantly ask ourselves: "Why do we use punishment? In what way is punishment related to helping this specific learner modify his behavior? Is there really a lawful relationship between the use of punishment and the behavioral change desired?" We must also ask whether we are being entirely professional in our actions, that is, whether we are merely trying to cause the learner to "pay" for his misbehavior, or even whether we perhaps are trying to hurt the learner who is hurting us. I know these are serious questions and I am not always comfortable with the answers, but as professional people, we must ask. Furthermore, we must be able to answer with reason rather than with the emotion that accompanies confusion and frustration. A reasonable answer, of course, requires understanding of the effects of punishment on behavior. Let us now turn to the task of sorting the myths about punishment from the evidence supported by empirical study.

The Mythology of Punishment

The most visible myth surrounding the concept of punishment is the claim that it is of little or no value in education. Such a point of view is surprising in light of common observation and empirical evidence that clearly show punishment to be "one of the most, if not *the* most, commonly used behavioral device by parents and teachers."[5] Obviously, many people believe punishment is an effective means for controlling behavior, yet they are reluctant to admit it. The ambivalence toward the use of punishment is probably a result of the conflicting points of view of experts and laymen. Parke (1970) noted: "Possibly parents have been wiser that the 'experts' who for many years assumed that punishment was an extremely ineffective means of controlling behavior."[6]

Decisions about the effectiveness and use of punishment in education have resulted as much from social values and philosophical assumptions about the nature of the human as a learner as they have from observation and experimental evidence. Aronfreed describes the conflict in this way: "The psychology of punishment is one of the most illuminating case histories of a conflict between social values and naturalistic evidence. It seems doubtful that common observation of the interaction between parents and children would lead anyone to the general conclusion that punishment was unnatural, ineffective, or undesirable. Yet some psychologists and educators for many years have argued precisely such a general case against punishment."[7]

MacMillan, Forness, and Trumbull (1973), in their summary of the arguments that reject punishment, point out some of the typical concerns, namely, that punishment is inhumane, deplorable, unethical, nonprofessional or extremely cruel and unnecessary. In addition to such ethical concerns, Solomon (1964) added the following legends which have led to the belief that punishment is unimportant: "(a) It does not really weaken habits; (b) it is pragmatically a poor controller of behavior; and (c) it is a technique leading to neurosis or worse." [8] Let us pursue some of these claims and learn what the data do indeed support. First we will look at the effects of punishment on behavior and then examine alternatives to the use of punishment. Finally, we will synthesize some rules relative to punishment and see how those rules can become part of strategies for effective self-management.

---

[5] D. L. MacMillan, S. R. Forness, and B. M. Trumbull (1973). The role of punishment in the classroom *Exceptional Children*, **40**(2), 86.

[6] R. D. Parke (1970). The role of punishment in the socialization process. In R. A. Hoppe, G. A. Milton, and E. Simmel (eds.), *Early Experiences in the Process of Socialization*. New York: Academic, p. 81.

[7] J. Aronfreed (1968). Aversive control of socialization. In W. J. Arnold (ed.), *Nebraska Symposium on Motivation 1968*. Lincoln: University of Nebraska Press.

[8] R. L. Solomon (1964). Punishment, *American Psychologist*, **19**, 239–253.

Effects of Punishment on Behavior

The general effect of punishment on behavior is . . .

A systematic investigation of the effects of punishment must first specify the kinds of stimuli that frequently act as punishers. Next, it must describe the conditions under which punishment is used, and it must also point clearly to any undesirable side effects.

KINDS OF PUNISHERS

A continuum of potential punishers ranging from those for children who function at very immature levels to those which apply to presumably mature individuals has been proposed by MacMillan (1968). His progression extends from what are usually called *corporal* punishers to punishers that can be thought of as *awareness* of failure or incorrectness. This is the order in which he lists them: "electrical shock; spankings; withdrawal of love, affection, or approval; denial of privileges or removal from a rewarding setting; verbal reprimand, scolding, or social disapproval; the perception of being incorrect or failure to have one's expectancies confirmed; and self-disappointment."

What stimuli can act as punishers?

You will recall that the identification of stimuli as indeed being punishers depends on their effects on the behavior they follow. The stimuli classified by MacMillan as punishers may in fact function as reinforcers. For example, Meacham and Wiesen (1969) report that disruptive classroom behaviors often increase as a consequence of the greater frequency and strength of a teacher's disapproval. On the other hand, potential reinforcers, for example, words of praise, under certain conditions can function as punishers. Publicly complimenting a high school boy for a fine effort in poetry may act as a punisher on his future performance in that topic. Only the behavior of your learners can tell you how your reinforcers and punishers are working.

CONDITIONS OF PUNISHMENT

How long does a behavior last?

The question asked most frequently by teachers and parents regarding change in behavior is: "Will the change last?" Implied in this question is their concern about the permanence of the effects of punishment and reinforcement. Are the effects only temporary, or are there certain conditions under which punishment and reinforcement produce effects that are more pronounced and of longer duration? The general answer to this question is found in the consequences of the behavior: *A behavior lasts only so long as it gains reinforcement in some form or another.* As long as a behavior has positively rewarding consequences or results in the avoidance or escape from punishment, the behavior can be expected to persist. When the conditions of reinforcement and punishment change, the behavior will also change. That is, the factors that determine the lasting qualities of a behavior reside within the consequences of the behavior, not within the behavior itself. We will see evidence of this basic rule in a later section when we examine some examples of strategies of classroom management.

Three conditions that influence the effects of punishment are . . .

There are, however, certain conditions that influence the effectiveness of reinforcement and punishment. In Chapter 8, we learned about some conditions that influence the effectiveness of reinforcement; (1) timing, (2) amount or intensity, and (3) consistency. These general conditions are also related to the effectiveness of punishment and in surprisingly similar ways.

TIMING OF PUNISHMENT   One of our rules of reinforcement states that the reinforcing stimulus should occur immediately following the desired response. Similarly, maximum suppression of an undesired response is usually achieved when punishment occurs immediately following the response. Let us see what this means in terms of classroom management.

Typically, disruptive classroom behavior is *molar* rather than *molecular* in nature. Guthrie (Chapter 4) described the differences between these two types of behavior. You will recall that molar behavior consists of chains of responses, each of which serves as the stimulus for the next response. Learning molar behaviors, e.g., writing, walking, or throwing chalk, paper airplanes, or similar objects, is essentially a matter of chaining the individual or molecular parts of the larger act. Practice smoothes the performance of the total behavior. It is the disruptive or inappropriate *molar* behaviors that teachers wish to suppress when they use punishment.

The point at which punishment occurs in the response chain is an important determinant of the effects of the punishment. For the greatest suppression effects, punishment should occur early in the response sequence. The effects are considerably less when punishment occurs at the end of a total or molar act.[9] Punishment that follows immediately on a *molecular* response early in the *molar* chain has the effect of reducing the likelihood that one molecular response will act as a stimulus for the next molecular response in the sequence. Punishment breaks the chain. Aronfreed and Reber (1965), in a study of discrimination learning, reported that punishing subjects for inappropriate behavior early in a learning task resulted in faster learning than later punishing did. Early punishment also resulted in less punishment.

When should punishment occur?

MacMillan, Forness, and Trumbull (1973) report that in addition to greater suppressive effects of punishment administered early in a response sequence, the effectiveness of punishment will be greater if, instead of punishing a child after he has already completed a piece of misbehavior, you wait and punish him just as he begins to repeat the behavior. They conclude that the "evidence casts doubt on practices in which children are sent to the office for punishment 'when the principal gets around to it' or in which a teacher watches a child complete an act of misbehavior, carefully waits for him to finish, and then punishes."[10]

AMOUNT OF PUNISHMENT   One of our rules of reinforcement tells us to "use only enough reinforcement to get the job done." This admonition seems to apply also to the use of punishment. If you find it necessary to punish, you should try to judge the amount or intensity of the punishers so that they are sufficient to suppress the undesired behavior but are not excessive. Although increased intensity of punishment generally results in increased likelihood of suppression of responses for longer times, it also appears to evoke heightened levels of anxiety, especially if appropriate alternative behaviors are not clearly available to the learner.

Closely related to amount of punishment is the question of intensity. That is, if you are using punishment, should you begin with punishers that are only mildly punishing and then gradually increase their intensity? Apparently the

How much punishment should be used?

---

[9] MacMillan, Forness, and Trumbull (1973). Op. cit., p. 90.
[10] Ibid.

best answer to this question is "no," since this procedure is likely to require increasingly severe punishers administered more frequently. There is some evidence (Azrin and Holz, 1966; Mayer, Sulzer and Cody, 1968) that suggests punishment is more effective when administered initially in the full intensity required than in a sequence of gradually increasing intensities. The key idea is that if you need to use punishment, it should be intense enough to result in an initial suppressive effect, that is, you should not try to suppress misbehavior "a little at a time" through a process of successive approximation. Rather, you should try for suppression on a single trial. Once misbehavior is suppressed, you should then try to gradually reduce the intensity and frequency of punishment at the same time that you are positively reinforcing appropriate behavior.

CONSISTENCY OF PUNISHMENT   One often hears the remark that it is easier to adjust to a bad consistency than to inconsistency. The approximate truth of this old saying comes clearly into focus in regard to the use of reinforcement and punishment. As you might expect, misbehavior that intermittently gains reinforcement on the one hand, and is punished only once in a while on the other, becomes extremely resistant to the weakening effects of punishment. For learners who have experienced inconsistent reinforcement and punishment, for example, many delinquents, a relatively long time is required, even with consistent reinforcement and punishment, for significant changes to occur in their behavior. Furthermore, their behavior typically gets worse before it gets better.

Galloway, Garraway, and Chamberlain (1972) demonstrated that resistance to change is directly related to past experiences. When exposed to an experimental situation in which reinforcement and punishment were consistently and systematically applied, persons who had histories of inconsistent treatment were significantly more resistant to change than were persons who had experienced relatively less inconsistent treatment. The important finding in this and other studies is that when reinforcement and punishment are used *consistently*, behavior will eventually change, even though it may get worse before it improves.

Consistency in the use of punishment means . . .   The often-dramatic changes in behavior that can result from systematic and consistent use of reinforcement and punishment are illustrated in a classic study by Bernal, Duryee, Pruett, and Burns (1968) entitled "Behavior Modification and the Brat Syndrome."[11] In this study, a "brat" was defined as a child "who often engages in tantrums, assultiveness, threats, etc., which are highly aversive and serve to render others helpless in controlling him." The "brat" in this study was a boy, eight and a half years old, who had "frequent temper tantrums and physically attacked his mother, teachers, and peers. 'I have a right to do anything I want to do,' as he put it, was his attitude toward life." In school, he "was highly demanding of the teacher's attention and alternately bullied and tattled on the other children, depending on their physical size and strength."

His parents and teachers had "tried everything," spankings, withdrawal of privileges, verbal reprimands, social disapproval, reasoning, pleading, bargaining, and begging—all to no avail. Mostly, however, their use of reinforcement and punishment was sporadic and inconsistent, dictated by the emotional climate of the momemt rather than by reason derived from rules of a science of behavior.

---

[11] M. A. Bernal, J. S. Duryee, H. L. Pruett, and B. J. Burns (1968). Behavior modification and the brat syndrome, *Journal of Consulting Psychology*, **32**, 4, pp. 447–455.

Treatment for the boy began with changes in an important element in his environment, his mother, to help her learn to use reinforcement and punishment in a systematic and consistent way. When she began to behave toward the boy in a consistent manner, e.g., when she said she would punish him, she did, and when he behaved appropriately, she reinforced him and his behavior got better.

There were also significant affective changes in the mother-and-son relationship. Before the treatment procedure began, the mother was asked how she felt about her son. She "stated that she did not like him, and was terrified of him." After several weeks of guidance in consistent application of principles of reinforcement and punishment, she began to like him, and he in turn began to express affection for her. During week 18, the mother had the following experience after the boy had gone to bed: "He asked to talk to me. He asked if he could take piano lessons. I told him he had a bigger project first—learning to get along with others, including children—and in a few years perhaps he could take lessons. As I went out the door he said, 'I love you.' I replied the same and told him how pleased I was with him. After the door was closed I heard him say to himself, 'She's swell! I feel great!'"

UNDESIRABLE SIDE EFFECTS OF PUNISHMENT

Clearly, when used appropriately punishment can have the effect of suppressing the behavior it follows. Unfortunately, it can also have effects that are not desired: (1) *You* may become conditioned to use it more frequently; (2) your learners may avoid you; (3) punishers lose their effectiveness; and (4) the effects of punishment generalize. You will want to understand these side effects well.

Four possible undesirable side effects of punishment are . . .

CATCH THEM BEING BAD   An interesting truth in teaching and learning is simply that as you teach your learners, they also teach you (Gray, Graubard, and Rosenberg, 1974). Sometimes we are unaware of these changes in our behavior, but the fact remains that the changes occur. Furthermore, the changes are not necessarily desirable (Lipe and Jung, 1971).

Consider, for example, the situation in which you have just given a "look of disapproval" to one of your learners as a consequence of her inattention to the lesson. Suppose, further, that she then stops talking to her neighbor and "gets on" with the learning task. You have just been reinforced for using punishment to control the behaviors of your learners. Furthermore, the likelihood of your doing so on similar occasions in the future is increased. You are now one step closer to the habit of "catching them being bad" than you were before.

The potential danger is that catching and punishing misbehavior can quickly become shaped into a predominant mode for managing classroom discipline. The first limitation of such a mode is that merely suppressing misbehavior does not teach the learner appropriate behavior. This is not necessarily a problem, however, when alternative behaviors that lead to reinforcement have been learned and are available. The greatest potential risk occurs when the teacher uses punishment to control the misbehavior of learners who have not learned alternative behaviors that allow them appropriate escape or avoidance of the teacher's aversiveness (Kounin, 1970). Under these circumstances, it is possible that learners may become intensely afraid and anxious. They may indeed behave in ways that can be classified as neurotic.

The second limitation, of course, is that merely suppressing misbehavior with punishment does not help the learner gain in skills of self-management.

SH! HERE COMES THE TEACHER!   One might ask why teachers are so often responded to in this way. A likely explanation is that teachers who elicit avoidance or escape responses from their learners use punishment inappropriately. One of the consistently predictable effects of punishment is that the learner will try to escape or avoid it. When punishment occurs, the punisher is usually associated with the person administering it. Thus, the learner may become conditioned to avoid both it and the person administering it. Furthermore, the misbehavior is likely to be suppressed only in the presence of the person administering the punishment. The well-behaved class that explodes in misbehavior when the teacher leaves the room or when a substitute teacher is present is a vivid reminder of this undesirable side effect of punishment. Persons who are punished excessively and unreasonably find many ways to avoid or escape. Some of their methods are by keeping quiet or being secretive about their activities, carrying them out only when the punishing agent is not present, lying about their behavior, finding excuses, blaming others, or simply becoming inactive.

Obviously, if your learners try to avoid or escape from you, your effectiveness as a teacher will be greatly reduced. If this happens, it should be interpreted that there is something the matter with your use of reinforcement and punishment.

Not all parents and teachers who use punishment, however, are avoided. Many do not seem to be bothered by the worry that so often plagues others: "If I punish them, they won't like me." A tentative explanation for this involves two things. First, such parents and teachers have been able to form positive affective relationships with young people. It is obvious in their relationships that they care for one another. Stated more directly, these parents and teachers have learned not only to "catch learners being bad." More importantly, they also practice "catching them being good."

Punishment as natural consequences means . . .   The second factor that seems to characterize those parents and teachers who use punishment but who are not avoided by their learners is that as much as possible they allow learners to experience the natural consequences of their own behavior. Usually the punishment derives from the environment rather than being administered by someone. These persons do not assume all the responsibility for deciding how another person should behave. They help learners understand the consequences of alternative behaviors perhaps through discussion, but they do not make the decisions for action. If a learner chooses wisely for himself, the natural outcome is reinforcement, usually in the form of success. If he chooses badly, the natural outcome is usually punishing. If this is the case, the parent or teacher does not "bail the learner out." She allows him to experience the punishing consequences of his own behavior. And without anger, bitterness, moralizing, or saying "I told you so," she discusses with him in a warm, meaningful way how he might behave differently next time.

Both these characteristics of persons who have learned to use punishment without antagonizing their learners are apparent in the following exchange between a teacher and her learner in a high school biology class.

LEARNER: Why do I have to answer these questions about pollution and ecology?

TEACHER: Tomorrow we are taking a field trip to compare polluted and unpolluted areas to learn firsthand how pollution of various kinds upsets the ecology. Answering these questions will prepare you for the trip. If you are not ready for the experience, I can't see any point in your going.

LEARNER: Do you mean that if I don't do these questions, I can't go on the field trip?

TEACHER: That is correct.

LEARNER: I'm not going to do them!

TEACHER: That is your decision. However, I wish you would consider doing them. I believe you will find the experience interesting and worth your time. If there is any way I can help you with the questions, I will be happy to.

At this point the teacher moves away from the learner and leaves him to make his decision. If he decides to answer the questions and asks for help, she gives him whatever assistance she can. If he decides not to answer them, she does not plead with him or threaten punishment. She simply makes arrangements to leave him at school while the rest of the class goes on the field trip. When the class returns, she does not punish him by withholding her attention or information gained on the trip, causing him to feel bad for having missed a "great experience," or by warning him that it had better not happen again. She matter-of-factly carries on in the same way she would have had he not missed the trip.

IT ONLY HURTS FOR A LITTLE WHILE   Punishers, like reinforcers, lose their effectiveness with overuse. "A child becomes adept at 'tuning-out' the berating mother or teacher; repeated spankings become old hat, tend to be accepted as part of life, and cease to arouse much anxiety."[12] The usual consequence of declining effectiveness of overused punishers is that the teacher increases their intensity and frequency as the classroom situation goes from bad to worse.

MacMillan et al., in summarizing the evidence relative to satiation effects of reinforcers and punishers, conclude that "just as teachers need to vary positive reinforcers, so should they vary aversive consequences. Too often a teacher repeats the same phrase or call to order so incessantly that it becomes either a part of the background noise or a minor irritant to all the children in the classroom."[13]

I remember once observing in a first grade classroom in which the teacher systematically inserted a shrill "sh" sound after every fifth or sixth word while talking to the children. I'm sure she did not realize she was doing it, although I did not ask her about it. The practice had obviously become a standard part of her speech pattern while teaching. As best I could determine, the stimulus had no suppressive effect on the behavior of the children. When I was pretty sure she would not hear me, I decided to test my hypothesis. I asked one small boy if he had noticed the "sh" sound when the teacher was talking. He nodded yes.

"What does it mean?" I asked him.

"I think it means there is something wrong with her teeth," he answered.

> The fact that punishers lose effectiveness with overuse suggests . . .

ONE REPRIMAND CAN AFFECT MANY OFFENDERS—AND NONOFFENDERS   This phenomenon is known as the *ripple effect*, or *spillover*. Its name implies that the effects of punishment (and reinforcement) of one learner may generalize to other

---

[12] MacMillan, Forness, and Trumbull (1973). Op. cit., p. 91.

[13] Ibid., p. 92.

learners who witness the event. This can have both desirable and undesirable consequences (Kounin and Gump, 1958; Kounin and Ryan, 1961).

There is considerable evidence that modeling, a kind of spillover, is an effective method of learning new behaviors (Bandura, 1962). For example, if a teacher publicly punishes a learner for misbehaving, that is, if he makes an example of him, he is potentially punishing each child who observes the event. In a sense, all participate vicariously in the specific interaction between the teacher and child. Even though the suppressive effects may generalize to the class as a whole with the result that other children do not commit the observed and punished misbehavior, there are sufficient undesirable spillover effects to question the practice. McManis (1967), for example, showed that the performance of a child who was being reinforced was lowered when the child seated next to him was being reprimanded. Some researchers (O'Leary and Becker, 1968; O'Leary, Kaufman, Kass, and Drabman, 1970) have found that soft reprimands, those administered privately and quietly so that other learners in the classroom cannot hear, seem to be more effective than loud, public reprimands in the suppression of behavior.

One other possible spillover effect of punishment is of concern not only to teachers and parents but also to society in general. Teachers potentially are powerful models for the behavior of their learners. If they solve most of their management problems through the use of punishment, it is likely that our learners will solve theirs in the same way, even though we tell them they should not. Skinner's warning (1968) is worth noting: "The discipline of the birch rod may facilitate learning, but we must remember that it also breeds followers of dictators and revolutionists."[14]

Alternatives to Punishment

There are at least three things you can do that will weaken misbehavior without administering punishers. They are: (1) rewarding incompatible, alternative behavior; (2) withholding reinforcement; and (3) terminating aversive situations when behavior improves.

REWARD INCOMPATIBLE, ALTERNATIVE BEHAVIOR

The key idea in this action is that learners are unlikely to misbehave while they are participating in a rewarding experience. Your task is to provide appropriate, rewarding alternatives for your learners. This is essentially a matter of motivation, which in turn is really a matter of good instruction. That is, since learners attend and respond to rewarding events and avoid or escape those that are aversive, instructional strategies must legitimately and naturally compete successfully with distracting events for the learner's attention. If they do not, we must resort to contrived alternatives that are frequently trivial in nature and short-lived in practice, or we must make attending and responding to distracting events more punishing than attending and responding to our instruction. In

Ripple effect means . . .

Three alternatives to the use of punishment are . . .

---

[14] B. F. Skinner (1968). *The Technology of Teaching.* New York: Appleton-Century-Crofts, p. 57.

Chapters 8 and 9, we saw several examples of how instruction can be organized so that it competes successfully, e.g., Ms. Garret's use of an electromechanical device for practice with number combinations.

WITHHOLD REINFORCEMENT

We learned in Chapter 4 that an important part of our higher-order rule of reinforcement is that behaviors that are not reinforced extinguish, that is, weaken and eventually disappear. In Chapters 8 and 9, we learned how to use this idea to shape desired behaviors through differential reinforcement—reinforcing successively closer approximations of the desired behaviors and withholding reinforcement from undesired behaviors. We are ready to examine the concept *extinction* from the point of view of weakening behavior that interferes with effective school learning.

There are many kinds and degrees of misbehavior that interfere with effective school learning. It may be only mildly interfering, for example, occasional daydreaming, or it may be as severe as fighting with knives or scissors in the classroom. Misbehavior may occur infrequently or it may be relatively persistent. In addition, it may involve only one learner or every learner in the entire school, as does a student strike or walkout.

Withholding reinforcement from misbehaviors of such wide diversity and intensity as a means of causing extinction is not easy. In fact, under certain circumstances, even attempting to do so may not be desirable. MacMillan, Forness, and Trumbull point out that misbehavior that is potentially dangerous to learners, for example, "throwing other children to the ground with great force, fighting, horseplay with pencils or scissors, physical attacks and the like cannot always be handled by removal of reinforcement regardless of how sound this practice may be theoretically."[15] They continue: "If one child goes after another with a sharpened pencil, should the teacher ignore it? When a child teeters precariously on the back legs of his chair, should the teacher look the other way? Theoretically, such behavior should eventually extinguish if ignored, but common sense preempts theory. Such behaviors must be suppressed immediately."[16] Obviously, some misbehaviors cannot be ignored long enough for extinction to occur.

Typically, teachers do not control all the sources of potential reinforcement in a classroom environment. Much of the reinforcement is controlled by the learners themselves. Consequently, you may decide to ignore the misbehavior of certain learners, but your learners may not. Furthermore, it is not always abundantly clear what the source (or sources) of reinforcement are for a particular misbehavior. High school students, for example, are widely known for their ability to develop ways of misbehaving in the classroom without the teachers' becoming aware of either the identity of the specific offender or, for that matter, even the exact misbehavior. Withholding reinforcement in such instances is exceedingly difficult if not completely impossible.

In the discussion so far, I have purposely tried to cause you to question the concept of extinction. My reason for doing this is not because extinction does

---

[15] MacMillan, Forness, and Trumbull (1973). Op. cit., p. 88.
[16] Ibid., pp. 87–88.

not work, but rather, because it is not always the most appropriate technique to use to weaken misbehavior even though the literature relative to modifying behavior gives the "impression that the only techniques one needs in the classroom are positive reinforcement and extinction"[17] The point is that extinction procedures alone are not sufficient to manage the full range of potential misbehavior that can occur in your classroom. We will learn more about this fact in a later section of this chapter.

For now, let us examine some of the many situations in which extinction procedures can be used appropriately and effectively to weaken misbehavior. As a rule of thumb, situations in which extinction procedures work well are those in which the misbehavior occurs infrequently and is only mildly or moderately interfering or dangerous. Examples are behaviors such as being out-of-seat, speaking out of turn, shouting, teasing, failing to dot i's or cross t's, failing to follow directions for a game or instructional procedure, asking irrelevant questions, not listening, or playing a practical joke. If you reinforce such behaviors, the result can be a pretty miserable existence for you in the classroom. High school students, for example, can "play" some lively "games" with teachers who spend a great deal of effort and time trying to find "the culprit." Students may find it highly rewarding to play "cops and robbers" with a teacher who gets excited about trying to find who brought the dog into class. Making an issue of small things such as dotting i's and crossing t's can have the undesirable consequences of actually increasing the frequency with which the dots and crosses are missing from students' written work. The point is, you can create problems simply by trying to punish each and every act of misbehavior that occurs. The underlying principles of extinction procedures suggest that often the appropriate teacher behavior is merely to do nothing, to ignore the misbehavior, and, instead, to "catch them being good."

TERMINATE AVERSIVE SITUATIONS WHEN BEHAVIOR IMPROVES

This is the rule of negative reinforcement that I mentioned in an earlier section. It is not a form of punishment that involves administering punishers, although it can be in the sense of withholding positive reinforcers. A couple of examples will help illustrate how the rule can be used.

In a mild form, negative reinforcement is involved in many instructional situations that use a games model. That is, participation in the culminating activity, e.g., preparing and eating the feast of stew and ice cream described in Chapter 9, requires meeting the instructional objectives. Learning the material may be punishing for some learners, even within a games model. Consequently, completing the objectives results in *termination* of a punishing situation. The important point here is that the decision to terminate the punishment should be clearly the responsibility of each learner. If he chooses to learn the objective, he is then eligible to participate in the fun. If he chooses not to learn, he is not eligible to participate. The rule is as simple, straightforward, and matter-of-fact as that. Anger, administration of punishers, threats of punishment, and so forth are not a part of

---

[17] Ibid., p. 87.

the rule. The especially nice thing about a games model, however, is that termination of a punishing situation is not the only outcome for studying. It also has positive rewards of active participation, success, and winning. Sometimes this blend of games model and the rule of negative reinforcement is known as Grandma's law: "*After* you do your work, *then* you may play."

Grandma's law states . . .

Let us look at another example that uses the removal of positive reinforcement plus the rule of negative reinforcement. Suppose that you have just distributed copies of the story "The Boy Who Cried Wolf" (from Chapter 9, Table 9-2) and you notice that one team of your learners begins to fill the blank spaces with obscenities. To remove reinforcement, you would do something like this: Quietly, privately, briefly, and matter-of-factly, explain to the learners that your intent is that the activity will help them learn about English grammar and that you question the value of their specific responses; Ask them to put their copy of the story away and give them another, saying, "If you decide to take part, begin again with this new one. If you really don't want to participate, please just sit quietly and wait until the other students and I finish the activity." Then, leave them to make their decision. If just sitting is aversive for them, they will probably terminate it and begin. If they do, make sure you reinforce them. A friendly, private, and positive contact of the eyes will work wonders. If they choose not to participate, honor their decision, but privately and positively ask yourself, "What is it about this activity that fails to capture their attention? What can I do next time to capture it?" Your answers will also work wonders.

Rules of Punishment

We are now ready to synthesize the findings relative to punishment into simple rules. Later, we will combine the rules of punishment with our rules of positive reinforcement. The result of the synthesis will be some effective strategies that we can use in the task of going from motivation and discipline to self-management.

HIGHER-ORDER RULE:
   Responses that are punished are suppressed; an organism avoids or escapes from punishment.

SIMPLE RULES:
A. *Before you use punishment, ask yourself:*
   1. Why am I using punishment?
   2. Are there alternatives to the use of punishment?
   3. Is my instruction appropriate? Have all the conditions of learning been met?
B. *When you use punishment:*
   1. Almost any stimulus can act as a punisher; the behavior of your learners will tell you if your punishers are working.
   2. Punish immediately following an inappropriate response; punish at the beginning of a molar-type behavior rather than at the end.
   3. Initially, use just enough punishment to suppress the misbehavior; gradually begin to withdraw punishers.

Ten rules for the use of punishment are . . .

4. Make sure the learners have available to them appropriate, alternative behaviors.
5. Punish quietly, privately, and as a result of natural consequences.
6. Be consistent; punish every act of misbehavior; do not warn—act.
7. Be selective; punish only acts of misbehavior.
8. Be considerate; care about your learners; also "catch them being good."
9. Do not substitute punishment for motivation or good teaching.
10. Remember, your goal is self-management.

CHECKPOINT 10-2

1. Here is a classroom situation in which the teacher tries to use punishment to cause a learner to behave more appropriately. Suggest alternative actions the teacher might follow that do not rely on punishment. The learners are in sixth grade. They are doing "silent reading." Mr. Thompson is seated at his desk, also reading. Everyone except Erica is attending to the task. Her book is up in reading position, but she is not reading. Two coins are placed on edge so that they roll down the top of her desk. She is racing a penny against a nickel.

"What are you doing, Erica?" demands Mr. Thompson loudly as he moves to her desk. Everyone stops reading and watches. Erica does not answer and tries to put the coins in her desk, but Mr. Thompson is too quick for her. "What are you supposed to be doing, Erica?" asks Mr. Thompson firmly.

"Reading," answers Erica.

"And what were you doing?"

"Playing," whispers Erica.

"Throw the coins in the waste basket, please."

"I'll put them in my desk," replies Erica, moving her hand toward her desk drawer.

"You'll put them in the basket!" shouts Mr. Thompson as he grabs her hand.

"No! I can't!" Erica pleads. But Mr. Thompson has a firm grip on the situation and is determined to have his way.

2. As you responded to the item above, did you try to think of an alternative teacher action that would result in learner self-management? Yes____ No____

STRATEGIES FOR
EFFECTIVE CLASSROOM MANAGEMENT

The most effective strategies for classroom management are those that are inclusive rather than exclusive. They are plans for action that combine ideas from a humanistic psychology with rules derived from a science of behavior. In addition, the most effective strategies clearly and purposefully combine cognitive and affective objectives. They are characterized by (1) genuine and human concern for learners, (2) careful attention to the conditions of learning, (3) positive efforts to capture the attention of learners, and (4) consistent use of appropriate techniques for weakening behaviors that interfere with school learning. In concert, these characteristics of effective strategies define instructional competence that works toward learner self-management.

The Components of Effective
Strategies for Classroom Management

Let us review briefly the contribution of each of the four components that define instructional competence. Then we can pull them together into a general strategy that has wide potential for solving the many problems you will encounter in managing your classrooms. Some specific examples will then be presented to help make the general strategy meaningful.

Four major components of strategies for classroom management are . . .

A GENUINE AND HUMAN
CONCERN FOR LEARNERS

This is *always* the humanistic point from which we begin. It is the part of our strategies that reminds us that our learners are more than just the sum total of their observable responses. When we have genuine and human concern for our learners, we are aware of the importance of listening carefully to what they say, to what they do not say, and to the silent voice of their actions.

A humanistic concern directs us in the arrangement of warm, empathic, and accepting learning environments in which our learners do not avoid us or suppress sharing feelings of joy or of frustration, helplessness, and failure. In such environments, learners and teachers become unafraid of one another, honest in their communications, open in their intents, and flexible in their practices. In short, a genuine and human concern for learners puts everyone on the same team.

Without learning environments such as those described by Carl Rogers, for example, it is extremely difficult to know with certainty which of a learner's behaviors need to be changed. If your learners are afraid of you, have learned to avoid you, or are "quiet" in your presence, a tremendous source of helpful information is unavailable to you. Without the information that is held secret by your learners, your strategies for helping them change their behaviors are likely to be ineffective regardless of the logic in your application of the rules of a science of behavior.

In summary, a humanistic interpretation of behavior makes important and necessary contributions to effective strategies of classroom management. As Arthur Combs reminds us, humanism "provides a valuable tool to deal with those problems the behavioristic approach is unable to handle so effectively and efficiently."[18] More specifically, it sets the conditions of affect under which learners are unafraid to share the information about themselves that can be usefully incorporated into logical and scientific strategies for change. Second, a humanistic point of view helps keep the science a human experience. You will recall, from Chapter 9, that this is what Maslow reminds us to do.

THE CONDITIONS OF LEARNING

The contribution made by the conditions of learning to effective strategies of classroom management is largely cognitive. In this contribution is found the key to whether motivation and discipline become self-directed. If, as a part of your

---

[18] A. W. Combs (1973). Educational accountability from a humanistic perspective, *Educational Researcher*, **2**(9), 21.

strategies, you fail to ensure that the conditions of learning have been met for each learner, it is unlikely that your learners will succeed even when you cause them to stop misbehavior and to begin attending and responding appropriately. Thus, to keep them from misbehaving, you will increasingly find it necessary to continue the use of punishment on the one hand and contrived reinforcers on the other. Without success in the learning tasks, there is little opportunity for motivation to become internalized, for discipline and motivation to become self-management.

The implication of the contribution to strategies of classroom management made by the conditions of learning is that once you have captured the attention and response of your learners, you must make sure thay are able to do what you are asking of them.

MOTIVATION   Basic to a science of behavior, you will recall, is the assumption that what we practice is what we learn. Motivation represents our attempts to make the practice of certain desired responses positively and internally reinforcing. In that way, we hope to make practice of what needs to be learned a profitable and pleasurable experience for our learners. That is, we hope to strengthen and maintain appropriate attending behaviors by making it reinforcing to attend.

The contribution of motivation to effective strategies of classroom management is essentially that the rules of positive reinforcement remind us to try to *capture* the attention of our learners rather than *demand* it. It keeps us "catching them being good."

DISCIPLINE   Weakening or suppressing inappropriate behavior is the main contribution of discipline in this area. *Weakening* inappropriate behavior is usually accomplished through extinction procedures and through negative reinforcement. *Suppression* of misbehavior is usually brought about through the administration of punishers following inappropriate responses.

The importance of weakening or suppressing misbehavior is that during the time inappropriate responses are not occurring, the probability of appropriate responses being made is increased. Consequently, the opportunity to positively reinforce appropriate behavior is enhanced. As a result, desirable alternative behaviors increase in strength and frequency as misbehaviors weaken and disappear.

The implication of weakening or suppressing misbehavior as a part of our strategies of classroom management is that ignoring and punishing misbehavior can increase the opportunity for you to apply the rules of positive reinforcement.

Behavior Modification: A General Strategy for Classroom Management

At the beginning of this chapter, I mentioned that the rules of motivation and discipline are closely related. Throughout the chapter, it has been difficult to talk about one without reference to the other. In the preceding section, we saw how motivation and discipline contribute to strategies of management. At the present time, we can no longer talk specifically about motivation or discipline. Now we must talk about the more general concept *management*, that is, we must learn how motivation and discipline, as well as the conditions of learning and the affective concerns about learning environments, are meaningfully subsumed by the more inclusive concept. We must make this synthesis because effective strategies of management usually involve more than any one, two, or three of the concepts. They almost always require a combination of all of them. A general name that is frequently given to such strategies is *behavior modification.*

Behavior modification means . . .

NEEDED: A GENERAL GUIDE

Transfer occurs more effectively when we have a general guide or outline for reference when faced with the task of developing and implementing specific strategies for modifying some behavior. Without such a guide, it is comparatively easy to overlook one or more components essential to an effective strategy for change.

A danger exists, however, in having a general guide for modifying behavior. Once a guide has been developed, there is a tendency to overgeneralize it, to apply it to situations for which there is no need of it or for which it is inappropriate. Although general guides can be useful, you should not discount your own common sense when you come to arranging strategies for modifying behavior. To be effective, such strategies need not always be elaborate in design and execution. Some will be extremely simple, and some situations will not require a strategy at all. For example, a commonsense approach to modifying Lizzie's misbehavior of catching goldfish would have been far more appropriate and effective than the strategy I tried to use. Just covering the fish pond with netting would have made a great deal more sense than trying to change her behavior. In an equally simple maneuver, it may be wiser to move a learner who does not listen well closer to the front of the room than to institute a strategy for shaping better listening behavior. The learner may have a hearing problem.

You will encounter many situations in your teaching that are more effectively handled with a bit of common sense than with elaborate strategies. As a rule of thumb, you should always look first for a simple solution before you embark on a grand strategy. A grand strategy is always possible if you need it.

A GENERAL GUIDE
TO BEHAVIOR MODIFICATION

The guide is presented as a sequence of four steps:

Four general steps in strategies of behavior modification are . . .

1. *Observe, talk with, and listen to your learners regarding the problem:* Your purpose is to determine what, if any, behavior needs to be modified. It is not your purpose to find fault or to blame but to discover what the problem is and to find better ways to behave. A genuinely warm, nonjudgmental, and frankly honest environment contributes to success at this step.

2. *Decide together, as much as possible, on appropriate objectives for change:* Once you have isolated the problem, use specific behavioral terms to describe the behaviors that are to be modified. Do not be surprised if some of these behaviors pertain to the quality of your instruction. It also may need to change.

3. *Select and implement the specific procedures to be followed:* Identify the variables that cause the misbehavior. That is, observe the stimuli that immediately precede and those that immediately follow the acts of misbehavior. In this way, you will be able to isolate the stimuli that set the stage for misbehavior and the stimuli that reinforce it. Record the frequency with which the misbehavior occurs and the conditions under which it is observed. Your notes will give you a basis for defining the strength of the misbehavior and for specifying the contingencies of reinforcement and punishment that maintain it. This is the information needed for deciding how the contingencies should be changed to modify the misbehavior.

4. *"Fade out" any contrived contingencies of reinforcement and punishment as natural ones become effective:* If you have done an effective job of communicating a genuine concern for your learners, of providing the conditions of learning, and of arranging the contingencies of reinforcement and punishment, any contrived reinforcers and punishers that were used initially as part of your strategy will soon become unnecessary. The powerful and natural reinforcers of success in the learning task will be sufficient to maintain the modified behaviors in strength. If, however, the natural contingencies are not adequate to maintain the new behaviors, the change will not last. You will need to change what you are doing.

SOME EXAMPLES OF
BEHAVIOR MODIFICATION

The classroom examples that follow have been selected because they illustrate strategies for the modification of behaviors that range from the misbehavior of individual learners in classrooms to the improvement of academic achievement of many learners in several classrooms, and from behavior that is only mildly inappropriate to behavior that severely disrupts school learning. They are presented in some detail so that you will be able to see the application of the four steps that constitute the general guide. Seeing how the strategies derive from rules of human behavior should help you avoid the dangerous practice of technique adoption mentioned at the beginning of Chapter 8.

Strategies of behavior modification are widely applicable in a variety of techniques and procedures to situations other than classrooms. They range from the clinical treatment of chronic schizophrenia to helping parents live happily with their youngsters. If you are interested in learning more about the widespread application of various techniques of behavior modification, you will find some references in Suggestions for Further Reading.

A TOKEN SYSTEM FOR MODIFYING BEHAVIOR   Token systems are among the most commonly used strategies of behavior modification in the classroom. Typically, they involve tokens (chips, coins, check marks, slips of paper) that are dispensed following appropriate behaviors. The tokens are redeemable later for reinforcers such as free choice of activities, special privileges, money, free time, food, games, pencils, color crayons, tools, and model kits. Although there are many variations of token systems, most are based on the rules of positive reinforcement: (1) appropriate behaviors are described; (2) responses approximating these behaviors are reinforced positively and immediately with a token, usually paired with social reinforcement (smile, pat on back, word of praise); (3) inappropriate responses are ignored, and sometimes punished, e.g., tokens may be withdrawn, the learner may be temporarily removed from the situation, or punishers may be administered; (4) tokens are redeemed.

Most token systems begin with a schedule of continuous reinforcement and gradually move to intermittent schedules and then to the complete withdrawal of tokens and other contrived reinforcers. The following example illustrates how one token system operates. It can easily be transferred to other situations.

Ms. Murphy teaches thrity-seven children in grade six. Mostly, they enjoy one another and achievement has been about average. Lately, however, Ms. Murphy has noticed that it takes longer to get the students started on learning tasks and that study habits seem to be deteriorating. She has described, as closely as she can, the specific behaviors that appear to need modifying, and during the past week she has kept a record of the frequency with which these behaviors occur. She is now ready to discuss the situation with her learners.

When she shares her concerns with the class, there is general agreement with her specific observations. She would like to see certain changes in the following behaviors: (1) better school attendance, (2) more time spent in studying, (3) more completed assignments, and (4) more acts of sharing and kindness toward one another. Ms. Murphy explains what she means by each of these four classes of behaviors and then shows her learners the charts she has constructed that illustrate her observations of these behaviors from the previous week. She explains that these charts will serve as the baseline for evaluating their progress. They will be placed on the bulletin board where everyone can see them at all times.

Ms. Murphy now explains her strategy for changing behavior. Each morning as she checks the attendance, she will place a token (slip of colored paper, one inch square, with a "happy face" stamped on it) on the desk of each person present. The children may then write their names on the back side of their "happy faces" and at recess or noon deposit them in a container that Ms. Murphy has provided. Throughout the day, whenever Ms. Murphy "catches someone being good," that is, when the person is studying, has completed an assignment, or has acted kindly toward someone without being asked to, she will place a "happy face" on that person's desk. The more often they are caught behaving positively, the more "happy faces" they will acquire. It does not take the children long to learn this rule. At the end of each day, Ms. Murphy will ask a child to draw several "happy faces" from the container. Something nice will happen to the children whose names are on the "faces"—such as the choice of a few minutes' free activity; or the reward of food, eraser, pencil, or pad of colored paper. All the "happy faces" will then be transferred to another container. This will be done each day for a month. At the end of the month, six or seven names will be drawn from the month's accumulation of "happy faces." Ms. Murphy will take these children with her for a fun afternoon and dinner at her home. Later in the evening, she will deliver the children back to their homes and try to arrange to meet their parents. Before the year is out, she will visit all the parents of her children.

As Ms. Murphy "catches her learners being good," she tries to remember to pair social reinforcement and success in the learning task itself with the "happy faces." An important point is that initially she controls the contingencies for reinforcement; therefore, she can deliver tokens on an individual basis. If a particular child shows improvement that is significant for him she can reinforce it. She can also vary the schedule of reinforcement. As the behavior of either an individual or the group as a whole improves, she can move from a continuous to an intermittent schedule, and eventually to fading out the token system completely, replacing it with one of individual success and self-reinforcement.

A token system is defined as . . .

Noting progress on the charts of the baseline data provides additional evidence to both the children and the teacher that they are meeting their objectives.

When Ms. Murphy discontinues the use of "happy faces," she does not stop rewarding appropriate behavior. She merely changes the form in which the rewards occur. She helps the children learn to evaluate their own behavior and to become self-correcting. Occasionally she brings food into the classroom as a surprise treat for appropriate attending and responding behavior. An unexpected animal cracker or jellybean is occasionally placed on desks at appropriate times. At Christmastime and on Valentine's Day, cards with personal and positive messages appear on desks when things are going nicely. She uses lots of concrete materials that can be felt, tasted, smelled, and otherwise enjoyed. Lessons often occur in the format of games and result in success. You will recall that we learned about these ways to motivate learners in Chapter 9.

POSITIVE REINFORCEMENT AND SUCCESS IN SPELLING   This example is a combination of an original study and a later replication (Thomson and Galloway, 1970). It is of interest, first, because it illustrates a strategy for modifying behavior. Next, it involves more than one classroom. In addition, the example shows that with increased success in the learning task, contrived reinforcers can be withdrawn without lowering achievement level. The example is of further significance because it illustrates in actual practice how motivation and discipline blend to form the larger concept *self-management*.

The subjects were 192 boys and girls in six classrooms of two elementary schools. Chronological ages ranged from ten through fourteen years. During the first six weeks of the school year, teachers of the six classes taught spelling by the method of their choice, keeping records of results achieved on weekly tests for each child. This set of scores was used as a prereinforcement baseline.

Following the initial six-week period, the teachers talked with their students about trying to increase their achievement in spelling. The students agreed with the objective and the teachers then shared with them a procedure that they could use to meet the objective. They explained to the students that during the next six-week period, spelling would be taught and tested in the same manner as during the first six-week period. No new spelling words would be added to those ordinarily assigned. No extra emphasis would be given to spelling. However, with the spelling record of the previous week as a basis for comparison, inexpensive material reinforcers (pencils, rulers, erasers, candy), paired with social reinforcers (words of praise, written or verbal), would be given to each person who equaled or bettered his score of the previous week. Anyone who failed to meet this criterion of performance would not receive material reinforcement, but would be verbally encouraged to improve his performance on the next week's test. The teacher would not use the threat of the possibility of not receiving material reinforcement to try to motivate students to study spelling. The only punishment for poor performance would be withholding positive reinforcement.

The teachers did not explain to their students that during the third six-week period, material reinforcement would be delivered on an intermittent schedule rather than on a continuous one. Social reinforcement, however, would be maintained on a continuous schedule. During the fourth six-week period, material reinforcement would be withdrawn completely, although social reinforcement would be maintained on a continuous schedule.

Material reinforcement was delivered through pigeonholes, 2 inches square and 8 inches deep. Each cubicle was covered with a hinged door on which a pupil's name was printed. If a pupil achieved his individualized reinforcement criterion, he was permitted to lift the door and remove the material reinforcement. Identical apparatus in each of the six rooms was kept in view of the children throughout the second and third periods.

Results of the study demonstrate that performance in spelling can be dramatically increased, especially for initially "poor" spellers, with a strategy of behavior modification. They also show that success in the task itself, paired with social reinforcers, will maintain increased levels of performance even when material reinforcers are withdrawn; that learners, at least in regard to spelling behavior, become self-managing.

WEAKENING AND STRENGTHENING BEHAVIOR OF STUDENTS IN A SECONDARY SCHOOL CLASSROOM   The material for this example was adapted from a teacher's personal diary. It provides a candid account of a first-year teacher's struggle to devise and implement an effective strategy for modifying her own behavior and that of her twelfth grade biology students who had failed the course the previous year.

This was the only course being taken by many of the students, since they had completed all the other requirements for graduation. The students were mostly boys, some of whom were twenty years old. For several, going to school seemed to provide a handy excuse for not going to work. Here are some of the teacher's entries.

September 5. School opens tomorrow. I wonder if my section of the grade twelve biology class will be as bad as some of the teachers say it will. If I last the year I will be the first ever! If the situation is so bad, I wonder why it's never been changed. I'll have to be firm and friendly, and hope they like me.

September 6. I thought the day would never end! What a biology class! If they like me, they have a strange way of showing it! I may not last until Friday! They know every trick in the book to get the teacher and avoid the work. When I tried to go in the room, someone was holding the door closed. There was a lot of noise and laughing inside; I think mostly at me. By the time I got the principal to help me get in, everyone was sitting quietly and attentively. When he left, they all had a good laugh at me. I don't think his warnings helped any, and I tried to look firm too, but I didn't feel much like it.

They were just getting warmed-up. During roll-call, one boy answered for everyone, and at 1:45, biology books began falling on the floor, one at a time, all over the room. Everyone pretended not to notice. I did the same. As soon as the "book-thing" was over, the "coughing" began. First, one or two, then everyone. Next came the questions, polite and irrelevant. I tried to answer them but got all confused. I tried to act calm and collected, but they knew I wasn't. Already I'm beginning to hate these kids and I don't even know them. At last the end of the hour, but tomorrow comes so soon. And, to top it all off, "they" let the air out of the tires on my car. The service station man couldn't get one of them to hold air again; had to buy a new one; it didn't match the other three but still cost me $28.75, which I didn't have. He said he would trust me for it until the end of the month. I hope he knows what he is doing!

September 7. Got in the room ahead of the students today. Surprised them I think, but didn't stay ahead of them for long. Decided to say nothing about the tires, and "They" didn't mention them either. Tried to get right into a lesson but no one paid much attention until I mentioned that they should take notes. That was the wrong thing to say. All at once the room was alive with everyone moving about to beg, borrow, or steal writing materials. A great line-up formed at the pencil sharpener. Several left the room, without permission, to go to lockers for paper. I don't think all of them came back. A few apparently stopped by the washroom for a smoke. The class was gone and talking over the noise was impossible, so I wrote an assignment on the board and shouted at them to do it. I "gave" them the class period to work on it and told them to finish it for homework. I didn't know what else to do. I noticed that several began to work on the assignment but most didn't stick with it very long. One boy started several times but each time wadded his paper and threw it in the waste basket. On each trip he stopped to talk and laugh with his friends. Mostly, they just pretend to work, but they really don't do much, and they seem reluctant to take any help from me. As I approach their tables, they get busy on the assignment, but as soon as I move away, they go right back to what they were doing. Many of those who have at least a little something written on their papers quietly hide it from me with their hand as I move past. No one seriously asks me to help. Their attitude seems to be: "I *could* do it if I really wanted to, so don't bother me." I wonder if they really can? Maybe I should talk to a counselor.

September 8. Not one homework assignment was completed. Three girls and two boys turned theirs in but they were incomplete. What they did wasn't badly done—just not much of it. Gave them more seat-work today, a worksheet; and brought some extra pencils, already sharpened. One of "Them" brought a bowling ball. He wanted to know how that "struck" me. I told him to "spare" me the effort. That was the wrong thing to say! These kids know more dirty puns, actually some were really clever, though. When the puns settled down, "They" began turning the worksheets into paper airplanes. Only a few worked on the assignment.

There were new sounds in the room today. Someone "meows" like a kitten. Of course everyone pretends not to hear. I must seem pretty dumb always looking for the cat and trying to down paper airplanes. Lasted through the class but didn't teach much. It's so frustrating. Talked with a counselor after school, and he gave me a lot to think about. He said he believed that other teachers failed with that section of the biology-twelve kids every year because they played "cops and robbers" with them. They didn't do much teaching, mostly they just tried to keep the lid on the class by catching the offenders. It never works very well, the kids know too many ways to cause trouble if that's the game you are playing. I asked what he would do if he were me. He *told* me: (I thought all counselors were non-directive!)

1. Memorize their names." (He gave me last year's school pictures to practice with.)

2. "Know something about each student." (He told me about some of them and showed me the cumulative records. There was a folder for each one.)

3. "Listen to them. Teaching is as much listening as it is talking. Try to find out what they are interested in. Talk with them whenever and wherever you find them, before class, after class, lunch time, in the halls, at school-sponsored social events. Some of the boys in your class play on our football and basketball teams. Three girls and one boy in your class were in last year's all-school play. One of the boys won an acting award at the regional drama festival. You probably already know which one he is!" (He gave me a copy of Glasser's *Schools Without Failure,* and Skinner's *The Technology of Teaching.)*

4. "Students who fail usually have weak academic backgrounds, but they also have strong, personal feelings. They feel badly about not knowing and not being able to do book-things, but they don't want others to know they are 'dumb'; that hurts. As much as possible, to begin with, try to give individual help, maybe after school, but keep the tutoring *private.* One way to begin might be to organize an after-school tutoring service for elementary school children who are having trouble learning. There are two girls in your class who have already expressed interest in doing something like this. You will be surprised how helping others will result in better achievement in biology."

5. "Try to ignore misbehaviors as much as you can. For the most part, their type of misbehavior is child-like pranks done to liven-up an otherwise dull and punishing hour of biology. Learn to respond to them in a matter-of-fact way, without letting them interfere with your lesson. Don't stop everything and make a big-deal of trying to find the cat." (I wondered how he knew about the cat.)

6. "In the long run, the real key to whether you survive or not will be your teaching. Remember, many of these students have poor reading ability. Some can't read a textbook, and since even when they do attend to the lessons they usually fail, they find it less punishing simply not to attend at all. Assignments, to begin with, should be meaningful but also short and easy to accomplish, for example, filling in a few blanks with words from sentences presented in the written material. Demonstrations, using concrete materials, could substitute for much of the reading. You could ask them to write a paragraph or two, in their own words, about what they learned from the demonstrations. You should evaluate and return these paragraphs as soon as you can with lots of positive comments. Give credit for *each* bit of success they have, even if you have to give a single paper several grades, e.g., mark each item separately. For example, a paper that has ten questions, three of which are completed, could have ten grades, *A, C, B, I, I, I, I, I, I, I*, rather than just one cumulative grade of *I* or *F*. Gradually, as you and your students get better at teaching and learning, you can begin to lengthen the assignments and have the students carry more of the responsibility for managing their own learning. The material can progress in complexity to include more than just memory of information. He asked if I knew about Bloom and Krathwohl's *Taxonomy*." (I had the feeling he was also talking about Behavior Modification, but he didn't mention any of the words.)

September 9: "They" beat me to the room today. (I took a couple of extra minutes to practice with their names.) All the legs had been removed from the tables. It looked pretty funny to see everyone sitting in chairs around tables that were lying flat on the floor. "They" waited for my reaction. I ignored the situation, just pretended not to notice and began to check the roll. I didn't have to call it today. I made a point of letting them know I knew their names. "They" didn't acknowledge the fact that the tables were "odd," and neither did I. The class went pretty well. Most of the students completed the short worksheet. At least everyone turned one in.

September 10: Friday, dear Friday! Tables are back to normal. Returned the worksheet from yesterday's lesson. Merle had completed only two of the items. He looked a long time at his paper. I had marked it: (1) "A," (2) "C," (3) through (10) "Incomplete." He folded the paper carefully so that just the grade of "A" appeared. I heard him comment to his friend as he showed him his paper: "Look at that, the bitch gave me an 'A'!" I decided to let it pass.

October 14: Neela, Jill, Aileen and Fred are now tutoring children in grade three in reading and arithmetic. They go three afternoons a week to the elementary school. My own tutoring service is picking up, too, in fact, it is beginning to spread. Heard Mr. Smith, one of the English teachers, complaining in the staff room that Merle was trying to teach Betty about mitosis *during English class!* "We" lost our first football game last Saturday, John, Clint and David explained to me why "We" didn't win.

Someone put a ruler through the grill over the heat vent today. When it hit the high-speed fan that circulates the warm air, there was a great splintering sound for a while and the room was filled with fine sawdust. I kept my cool, and went right on teaching! (Combed the sawdust out of my hair after class.)

October 28: Beverly and Larry volunteered to help me set-up the demonstration for tomorrow! I think they felt badly that the mouse someone brought to class today upset things for a while. I've got to learn not to scream at mice! (We could have used "the cat" today but it hasn't been in class for some time now.)

December 12: Had an early snowstorm today. It almost wrecked the biology lesson. Sandy, what a tough kid, filled her purse with snow balls and brought them to class. Everyone knew she had them including me. (I saw her come into the building with them.) As class got started she waited for her chance to use them. I pretended not to know about the snowballs and began teaching. As I moved about the room, matter-of-factly explaining and answering questions, I paused at Sandy's side and remained there for about ten minutes. The tension mounted, but no one cracked. I assigned some written work and they got started on it. As soon as things settled down, I bent over and whispered in Sandy's ear: "If that snow melts, it could ruin your purse. Do you want to get rid of it?" She grinned and said: "Shit!" We all had a good laugh, then got back to work.

December 21: Christmas Holiday, hurrah! Going to drive home for a few days. Got an anonymous Christmas present, a new tire! Funny how it matches the other three on my car. I think I know who Santa Claus is. He is "They."

CHECKPOINT 10-3

1. Suppose that you are teaching English to ninth grade students. The topic is poetry. Suppose, further, that some of your students have expressed contempt for poetry by refusing to participate and by harassing those who try to. State how you might combine the higher-order rules for a games model (from Chapter 9) with the four steps of the general guide to behavior modification to form a strategy that is likely both to weaken and suppress misbehavior and to strengthen appropriate attending and responding behavior relative to learning about and valuing poetry.

(You will recall that the higher-order rules for a games model are: (1) keep actions and goals separate but related; (2) make the actions essential to reaching the goals; and (3) make reinforcement contingent on reaching the goals.)

2. As you did the item, did you try to synthesize the rules for a games models with the steps of the guide to behavior modification?

(Not really)   (Somewhat)   (Yes, I did)

SOME CONCERNS ABOUT BEHAVIOR MODIFICATION

In this chapter we have dealt mainly with the theory and practice of strategies for modifying behavior. We have said very little about the concerns with modifying behavior expressed by persons who are morally or ethically opposed to the manipulation of human behavior.

Not all the concern with modifying behavior comes from persons opposed to it. Behavior modifiers themselves point to the danger of parents and teachers who, in search of a quick, easy "miracle," adopt and implement techniques of modifying behavior without understanding the basic rules from which the techniques derive. There are no miracles in education; there are only hard-won and often meager gains that result from the professional competence of knowing *why* you are doing *what* you are doing. Expecting to find a miracle, ready-made in the techniques of behavior modification, reflects professional ignorance (Galloway et al., 1972). Yet, there are many instances of parents and teachers hoping in vain that a handful of "goodies" will solve their instructional problems and somehow transform their learners into self-motivated, self-disciplined, and self-managing individuals. Of course, you can arrange the contingencies of reinforcement and punishment so that your learners will avoid punishment by sitting up straight, keeping quiet, and attending to every poorly organized learning task placed before them. Unless, however, the conditions of learning are also met so that when your learners do sit up and pay attention, they succeed and feel good about succeeding, your strategy will gradually deteriorate. Then you will have no alternative other than to resort to punishment to cause them to learn. And you will begin to search for another "miracle," only this time you will be more careful; you will try to pick one that "really" works.

More specific concerns about behavior modification procedures can be found in some of the Suggestions for Further Reading.

We now turn to a consideration of the development of our learners as individuals. Our purpose will be to learn more about how we can make instruction optimal for each learner, that is, how to individualize instruction. Chapter 11 is about development and individual differences, and Chapter 12 discusses the development of a theory of instruction that we can use to derive strategies for individualizing instruction.

The child is father of the man.

Sigmund Freud

IN PASSING

ACTIVITIES

1.   Review the checkpoints for Chapters 9 and 10. Then, for each checkpoint: (1) State the level of cognitive functioning, according to the major levels of Bloom and Krathwohl's taxonomies, required to complete the activities described; and (2) write one specific instructional objective at the appropriate level that will be met when the learner is able to complete the activities.
2.   William Glasser, the author of *Schools Without Failure,* says: "For discipline to be successful, the important person—the teacher—must under no circumstances accept any excuse for a commitment not being fulfilled. If she takes an excuse, she breaks the involvement because the student then knows she really doesn't care."[19] Explain why Glasser's point of view may lead you to classify him as either a humanist, behaviorist, or behavioristic humanist.
3.   Find a teacher who will cooperate with you and together use our Guide to Behavior Modification to develop and implement a strategy for modifying the behavior of one or more of the teacher's learners.
4.   From a behavioristic point of view, does it follow logically "to hold learners responsible for behaving responsibly"? Explain your answer.
5.   Just for fun:
Recently I attended a school's staff meeting in which the teachers were discussing behavior problems of students. At the beginning of the meeting, the principal asked us to read a list of comments he had heard teachers make about the behavior of students. Then he asked us to form groups of three and to discuss several of the comments.

Just for fun, pretend that you are teachers on this principal's staff and are going to discuss the comments (listed below). One of you takes the point of view of a behaviorist, one that of a humanist, and the third person in your group combines the two views. Share your thoughts in terms of whether you agree with the teacher's comments.

Example 1 "I don't mind helping a kid who tries, but I'll be damned if I'm going to break my back helping Joe. It is useless to try to help anyone who won't try."

---

[19] W. G. Glasser (1969). *Schools Without Failure.* New York: Harper & Row, p. 23.

Example 2 "Well, I'm convinced that Mike deserves to be strapped. In my humble opinion, any kid who swears at a teacher should automatically be strapped. That will make him straighten out."

Example 3 "There is only one way to help Andy change. I've got to arrange things so he will have success. I'm not going to push him. I'm going to give him easy work, lots of praise, and lots of love."

REFERENCES

Aronfreed, J. (1968). Aversive control of socialization. In W. J. Arnold (ed.), *Nebraska Symposium on Motivation 1968*. Lincoln: University of Nebraska Press.

————, and A. Reber (1965). Internalized behavioral suppression and the timing of social punishment, *Journal of Personality and Social Psychology*, **1**, 3–16.

Azrin, N. H., and W. C. Holz (1966). Punishment. In W. K. Honig (ed.), *Operant Behavior: Areas of Research and Application*. New York: Appleton-Century-Crofts.

Bandura, A. (1962). Social learning through imitation. In M. R. Jones (ed.), *Nebraska Symposium on Motivation: 1962*, pp. 211–269. Lincoln: University of Nebraska Press.

Bernal, M. A., J. S. Duryee, H. L. Pruett, and B. J. Burns (1968). Behavior modification and the brat syndrome, *Journal of Consulting and Clinical Psychology*, **32**(4), 447–455.

Bruner, J. S. (1966). *Toward a Theory of Instruction*. Cambridge, Mass.: The Belknap Press of Harvard University Press.

———— (1971). *The Relevance of Education*. New York: Norton.

Combs, A. W. (1973). Educational accountability from a humanistic perspective, *Educational Researcher*, **2**(9), 19–21.

————, and D. Snygg (1959). *Individual Behavior: A Perceptual Approach to Behavior*. New York: Harper & Row.

Erikson, E. H. (1950). *Childhood and Society*. New York: Norton.

———— (1958). *Young Man Luther*. New York: Norton.

———— (1968). *Identity: Youth and Crisis*. New York: Norton.

Freud, S. (1938). In A. A. Brill (ed. and trans.), *The Basic Writings of Sigmund Freud*. New York: Modern Library.

Galloway, C. G., G. R. Garraway, and L. A. Chamberlain (1972). Don't expect a miracle, *The Elementary School Journal*, **73**(2), 85–90.

Glasser, W. G. (1969). *Schools Without Failure*. New York: Harper & Row.

Gray, F., P. S. Graubard, and H. Rosenberg (1974). Little brother is changing you, *Psychology Today*, **7**(10), 42–46.

Hall, E. (1972). Will success spoil B. F. Skinner?, *Psychology Today*, **6**(6), 65–72.

Kounin, J. S. (1970). *Discipline and Group Management in Classrooms*. New York: Holt.

————, and P. V. Gump (1958). The ripple effect in discipline, *Elementary School Journal*, **59**, 158–162.

————, and J. Ryan (1961). Explorations in classroom management, *Journal of Teacher Education*, **12**, 235–246.

Lipe, D., and S. M. Jung (1971). Manipulating incentives to enhance school learning, *Review of Educational Research*, **41**(4), 249–280.

MacMillan, D. L. (1968). Behavior modification: A teacher strategy to control behavior, *Report of the Proceedings of the Forty-fourth Meeting of the Convention of American Instructors of the Deaf*, 66–76.

————, S. R. Forness and B. M. Trumbull (1973). The role of punishment in the classroom, *Exceptional Children*, **40**(2), 85–96.

Maslow, A. H. (1962). *Toward a Psychology of Being*. New York: Van Nostrand.

———— (1968). *Toward a Psychology of Being*, 2d ed. New York: Van Nostrand.

Mayer, G. R., B. Sulzer, and J. Cody (1968). The use of punishment in modifying student behavior, *Journal of Special Education*, **2**, 323–328.

McManis, D. L. (1967). Marble sorting persistence in mixed verbal incentive and performance-level pairings, *American Journal of Mental Deficiency*, **71**, 811–817.

Meacham, M. L., and A. E. Wiesen (1969). *Changing Classroom Behavior: A Manual for Precision Teaching*. Scranton, Pa.: International Textbook.

Montessori, M. (1912). *The Montessori Method*. New York: Stokes.

O'Leary, K. D., and W. C. Becker (1968). The effects of the intensity of a teacher's reprimands on children's behavior, *Journal of School Psychology*, **7**, 8–11.

————, K. F. Kaufman, R. Kass, and R. Drabman (1970). The effects of loud and soft reprimands on the behavior of disruptive students, *Exceptional Children*, **37**, 145–155.

Parke, R. D. (1970). The role of punishment in the socialization process. In R. A. Hoppe, G. A. Milton, and E. Simmel (eds.), *Early Experiences in the Process of Socialization*. New York: Academic.

Piaget, J. (1952). *The Origins of Intelligence in Children*. New York: International Universities Press.

Rogers, C. R. (1951). *Client-Centered Therapy*. Boston: Houghton Mifflin.

———— (1961). *On Becoming a Person*. Boston: Houghton Mifflin.

———— (1963). Learning to be free. In S. Faber and R. Wilson (eds.), *Conflict and Creativity: Control of the Mind*. New York: McGraw-Hill.

———— (1969). *Freedom to Learn*. Columbus, Ohio: Merill.

Skinner, B. F. (1953). *Science and Human Behavior*. New York: Macmillan.

———— (1968). *The Technology of Teaching*. New York: Appleton-Century-Crofts.

———— (1971). *Beyond Freedom and Dignity*. New York: Knopf.

———— (1973). The free and happy student, *Phi Delta Kappan*, LV, **1**, 13–16.

Solomon, R. L. (1964). Punishment, *American Psychologist*, **19**, 239–253.

———— (1973). The free and happy student, *Phi Delta Kappan*, LV, **1**, 13–16.

Solomon, R. L. (1964). Punishment, *American Psychologist*, **19**, 239–253.

Sullivan, H. S. (1953). *The Interpersonal Theory of Psychiatry*. New York: Norton.

Thomson, E. W., and C. G. Galloway (1970). Positive reinforcement and success in spelling, *The Elementary School Journal*, **70**(7), 395–398.

SUGGESTIONS FOR FURTHER READING

Glasser, W. G. (1969). *Schools Without Failure*. New York: Harper & Row. This book presents a powerful and challenging synthesis of humanistic points of view about helping learners acquire self-management. Its message is all the more compelling since Dr. Glasser himself is a rare synthesis of psychiatry and common sense.

Kelman, H. C. (1965). Manipulation of human behavior: An ethical dilemma for the social scientist, *The Journal of Social Issues*, **21**(2), 31–46. Kelman points to a basic dilemma faced by practitioners and investigators of behavior change: Any manipulation of human behavior violates a fundamental value, the freedom and opportunity to choose; and education itself is a form of manipulation.

Kuypers, D. S., W. C. Becker, and D. K. O'Leary (1968). How to make a token system fail, *Exceptional Children*, **34**(11), 101–109. Catching a learner being good means more than the mechanical distribution of tokens, contingent on "good" behavior. It also means knowing why you are doing what you are doing.

Maehr, M. L. (1968). Learning theory: Some limitations of the application of reinforcement theory to education. *School and Society*, February, 108–110. Maehr warns us of the dangers of jumping on the bandwagon of behaviorism without a critical review of its claims. He reminds us that learners do not just respond, they also think about their behavior.

McKeachie, W. J. (1974). The decline and fall of the laws of learning, *Educational Researcher*, **3**(3), 7–11. The laws of reinforcement and punishment are not enough. A teacher's enthusiasms and energy, for example, are also extremely important variables in education, as is his capacity to adapt to the learner. As McKeachie points out, it is qualities such as these that make education endlessly challenging and keep it deeply humane.

O'Leary, D. K., and S. G. O'Leary, eds. (1972). *Classroom Management: The Successful Use of Behavior Modification*. New York: Pergamon. This book contains thirty-seven readings, two chapters written by the editors, and ten sets of editors' comments about managing classroom behavior. Of special interest are the twelve readings on modeling, the use of paraprofessionals, and self-management.

Smith, A. B. (1973). Humanism and behavior modification: Is there a conflict? *The Elementary School Journal,* **74**(2), 59–67. Anne Smith, a former high school teacher, says that "teachers often base their humanistic objections to behavior modification on misconceptions about these procedures." In her paper she discusses several typically "humanistic" beliefs and shows that they are largely fallacious.

Ullmann, L. P., and L. Krasner, eds. (1965). *Case Studies in Behavior Modification*. New York: Holt. Fifty case studies are reported under five section headings: Severely Disturbed Behaviors; Classic Neurotic Behaviors; Other Deviant Adult Behaviors: Sex, Tics, Stuttering; Deviant Behaviors in Children; Mental Deficiency. A 63-page introduction by the editor gives an excellent overview of the history, theory, and practices of behavior modification.

PART III

DEVELOPMENT AND INDIVIDUAL DIFFERENCES

11

CONCEPTS AND RULES OF DEVELOPMENT

The principle goal of education is to create men who are capable of doing new things, not simply of repeating what other generations have done—men who are creative, inventive, and discoverers. The second goal of education is to form minds which can be critical, can verify, and not accept everything they are offered. The great danger today is of slogans, collective opinions, ready-made trends of thought. We have to be able to resist individually, to criticize, to distinguish between what is proven and what is not. So we need pupils who are active, who learn early to find out by themselves, partly by their own spontaneous activity and partly through material we set up for them; who learn early to tell what is verifiable and what is simply the first idea to come to them.

Jean Piaget
Piaget Rediscovered

CONTENTS

ONGOING SUMMARY

In Part I we learned about the content and process of effective learning and teaching. In Part II we learned about simple and higher-order rules of reinforcement and punishment that can be synthesized into powerful strategies that lead to self-motivation and self-discipline, that is, to self-management.

Central to these strategies is the requirement that instruction be optimal for each learner.

Chiefly, we have learned about the content and process of learning and teaching and about general strategies for learning self-management as though we believed all learners are essentially the same. But all learners are not the same, and we must understand the bases for their differences if we are to ensure that our instruction is indeed optimal for each. Chapters 1 through 10 have helped us know *generally* about learners and learning; we are now ready to become more *specific,* to learn how they differ, why they are different, and what the differences mean in terms of helping them learn.

ADVANCE ORGANIZER

Ideally, optimal instruction means that the events of instruction and the strategies we use to capture and maintain attention and practice are individualized for the unique characteristics of each of our learners. Therefore, general strategies such as we have synthesized in earlier chapters must be refined and adapted to the requirements of individuals. The material in Part III will help us accomplish this task.

Chapter 11 is about development. It is a study of the concepts and rules of change, both physical and functional, over time. As teachers, we are concerned about the changes that occur in our learners, especially the functional or behavioral changes we call learning. Functional changes, however, can be adequately understood only if considered as part of the physical, biological organization that makes function possible. As D. O. Hebb (1974) reminds us, psychology is a biological science. Therefore, we will begin our study of the individual differences that result from developmental processes by learning about broad, biologically based rules and theories of development that consider human learners within the perspective of the general, higher-order rules to which *all* living organisms are subject. Then we will learn about more specific aspects of human development, intellectual, moral, social, personal, and physical.

Our search for perspective in what development is all about will lead us first into the evolutionary past of living things as we try to find meanings for such new terms as *intelligence, innate, gene action,* and *gene-environment interaction.* And as we learn about these terms, we will expand and synthesize concepts that we started learning about in the first ten chapters. The checkpoints will help us with this synthesis.

From an analysis of the biologically natural and evolutionary viewpoint, developed in large measure through the work of people such as Jean Piaget, D. O. Hebb, and Jerome Bruner, we will synthesize higher-order rules of development that have particular relevance for human development. In Chapter 12 we will see that many of these higher-order rules have specific implications for education and that they provide information needed to formulate a general theory of instruction. These contributions are of great interest to us because, with a powerful theory of instruction, we stand a good chance of at least roughly approximating our goal of making instruction truly optimal for each of our learners, the main reason for learning about human development and individual differences in the first place.

GOALS AND OBJECTIVES

Cognitive

To become an effective teacher, the learner should be able to analyze biologically based theories of developmental adaptation for their higher-order rules.

KNOWLEDGE LEVEL

Given the following terms, the learner is able to define them in writing: *biological unit; biological organization; adaptation; assimilation; accommodation; equilibration; growth; maturation; development—intellectual, moral, social, personal, and physical; gene; DNA, RNA; gene action; preprogrammed; gene-environment interaction; structure of knowledge; knowing behavior; intelligence; sensitive period; operation; sensory-motor; stage of intelligence.*

COMPREHENSION LEVEL

1. The learner is able to describe Piaget's theory of developmental adaptation.
2. Given the terms *developmental adaptation, assimilation, accommodation,* and *equilibration,* the learner is able to describe the process that interrelates them.

APPLICATION LEVEL

Given a description of the knowing behavior typical of organisms at various (1) levels of the evolutionary scale and (2) stages of development, the learner is able to describe the knowing behavior typical of both newborn and adult fish and human beings.

ANALYSIS LEVEL

Given the statement "The probability that knowing behavior can be modified through experience increases with evolutionary level," the learner can present evidence that supports it.

SYNTHESIS LEVEL

Given the following terms from Chapters 1 through 10, the learner is able to redefine them as they relate to the broadly inclusive concept of *developmental adaptation: learning, meaningful learning, rote learning, types of learning, concepts, rules, practice, retention, transfer, positive reinforcement, motivation, attention, explanation-description,* and *hierarchy of needs.*

EVALUATION LEVEL

The learner can say why he agrees or disagrees with the point of view that defining intelligence as *knowing behavior* greatly simplifies the understanding of developmental processes.

Affective

To become an effective teacher, the learner should be able to develop a broadly inclusive theoretical perspective of development from which can be derived higher-order rules with potential implications for making instruction optimal for individual learners.

RECEIVING (ATTENDING) LEVEL

The learner is willing to consider a biological approach to development that places human beings at the present endpoint of a natural and evolutionary progression of living organisms.

RESPONDING LEVEL

The learner practices the activities in the checkpoints.

VALUING LEVEL

The learner wants to learn about the bases for the individual differences he will encounter among his learners.

ORGANIZATIONAL LEVEL

The learner tries to organize a broad theoretical perspective for understanding about development.

CHARACTERIZATION LEVEL

The learner thinks about his specific instructional activities in terms of higher-order rules of development.

As you begin to teach your first group of learners, one of the things of which you will only gradually become aware is that each learner is different. At first, you can expect that they will all look pretty much alike to you except that some are girls and some are boys, some are taller or heavier than others, some have skin of a different color, some have marked physical or behavioral differences, and so forth. Only as you begin to interact with your learners will you "see" the less obvious yet potentially important differences among them that you must provide for in planning instruction that is optimal for each. That is, to meet our ultimate goal as teachers, to individualize instruction, we must know about our learners as developing, changing individuals. But where shall we start? What kinds of things are important for teachers to know about individual learners?

NEEDED: A BROAD THEORETICAL PERSPECTIVE

There are numerous dimensions to individual learners that make each one unique. We might ask, for example, why one learner is taller or heavier than another; why some learn more quickly and more thoroughly than others; why some learn effectively from complex verbal instruction, whereas others do not; why some volunteer to participate while others do so only reluctantly. In addition, we would likely ponder the two questions of great practical importance to teachers: (1) "How did each come to be the way he is?" and (2) "How might we help him change?"

These are essentially questions of development, that is, questions of *change through the process of living through time* (Stott, 1974). They are not easy questions to answer even at a knowledge (naming, defining) or comprehension (describing) level. Yet, if we are to know our learners as individuals, it is obvious that our knowing about development must be at the highest levels possible—at least at the comprehension level, with some knowing at the levels of application, analysis, and synthesis. In terms of Gagné's types of learning, this means that we need to learn concepts, simple rules, and higher-order rules of human development, since these are the types of learning that will transfer best when we come to organize our instruction so that it is individualized. You will recall from our earlier discussion of concepts and rules (Chapter 6) that a key idea relative to learning concepts or rules is that of the relationships among the parts that combine in their formation. We will realize the full importance of the idea of relationships as we learn more about the concepts and rules of development.

We will begin by trying to gain a broad perspective for understanding human development in relationship both to the processes of individual development in other living things and to *all* living things as reflected in the evolutionary history of life. The term "development" as it will be used in our discussion has a very broad meaning. We will adopt Stott's definition which stresses *continuity* and *process*, and includes "*all change* associated with time in both the structure and the functioning of the living organism."[1] By *structural* development, Stott means

Development is defined as . . .

---

[1] L. H. Stott (1974). *The Psychology of Human Development.* New York: Holt, p. 24.

Structural development means . . .

physical development that is made up of two aspects of change: *growth*, or quantitative change; and *maturation*, or change in kind or quality. A familiar example will show that both types of change are really aspects of the same fundamental process. When a child is born, some of its bone tissue is actually cartilage. With age, the total quantity of bone tissue increases; that is, growth occurs. Also, however, the quality of the bone tissue changes, it matures. Over time, a decreasing proportion of the bone tissue is cartilage; it becomes harder, more dense, and less elastic.

Changes that result from structural development are closely related to changes in *function*. "Functioning generally begins when the structure is developmentally *ready* to function."[2] You recognize that *readiness* is a concept we have encountered before. We talked about it in terms of a learner's having acquired the prerequisites for the present task, for example, the chains, associations, concepts, or rules prerequisite to a particular cognitive-type learning task.

Functional development means . . .

In a psychomotor sense, muscle tissue is ready to function, that is, to begin contractile movement, when it has acquired the growth and maturation necessary for contractile behavior to occur. As movement is experienced, however, the muscle tissue changes somewhat in its physical characteristics and in the function it is able to perform. This is the essence of development. With a bit of thought, you will see that it is also the essence of learning, broadly defined.

As we proceed through Chapter 11, you will notice that many of the concepts and rules we learned about in earlier chapters will reappear, although in slightly different contexts. For example, the concepts and rules relative to cause and effect (Chapter 2) will be extended—"spiraled up and out"—to include their physiological as well as their social characteristics. Our previous definitions and explanations of learning, practice, retention, transfer, motivation, and so on now must be accounted for in terms of the rules of physics and chemistry as well as of their function, that is, their behavioral components. We will practice the synthesis of meanings for many of these concepts in the checkpoints throughout the chapter.

To gain a meaningful and potentially useful perspective of the various concepts and rules of development and their implications for individual differences, learning, and teaching, we will need a theoretical frame of reference that is broadly inclusive yet precise enough to permit the derivation of rules that have potential implications for classroom instruction. Thus, our search for perspective will cause us to consider learners as living, evolving, biological systems, and this view will require learning first about certain general biological functions common to all living things.

For our purposes of gaining perspective about the structural and functional development of learners, a unifying, theoretical guide will be extremely useful. Such a guide will help us organize, and thus enhance, our understanding of the general concepts and rules we have learned from earlier chapters. It will also guide our attempts to assimilate new information in a logical and meaningful way so that the new information will be accommodated by the old and thus will result in continually more useful theories.

Patrick Suppes, in his presidential address to the American Educational Research Association, emphasized the crucial place of theory in education,

---

[2] Ibid., p. 25.

saying that an important contribution to our thinking is made by a powerful theory that "changes our perspective on what is important and what is superficial."[3] Without powerful statements of theory in education, we run the risk of what Suppes called "the obvious triviality of bare empiricism,"[4] or, in more direct terms, of randomly and intuitively doing what "seems to work" without having logical notions of why it "works" or fails to "work," or of how to improve it when it only "partially works."

One of the fortunate things about our search for a theoretical perspective for learning about development is that we will not need to "begin from nothing." Many persons for many years have been interested in unraveling the well-kept secrets of development. We will start with the widely general theory that Piaget and his colleagues have been developing for nearly fifty years. Then we will learn about the contributions made to more specific aspects of development by persons such as Lawrence Kohlberg on moral development, Erik Erikson on psychosocial development, Sigmund Freud on personal development, and Arnold Gesell on ages and stages of development. Finally, we will see how the educational contributions of such persons as Gagné, Skinner, Maslow, Ausubel, Bruner, and Bloom can be synthesized into a useful, yet necessarily tentative, frame of reference from which we can derive general implications for a theory of instruction as well as specific applications for individualizing instruction.

Let us turn more directly now to the task of gaining a generally meaningful and useful perspective of development, and at the same time learn how so many of the concepts and rules we learned about earlier can be synthesized into even higher-order rules of knowing about learners and learning. In so doing, we will experience firsthand what we learned in Chapter 5: that concepts and rules are never completely learned, but rather, that they continually expand and spiral up and out with each new experience. We will have more to say about this idea later.

Theory helps by . . .

Jean Piaget, Giant of Developmental Psychology

The story of the Swiss giant of development psychology, Jean Piaget (1896), tells of a fascinating lifetime search for the nature of knowledge. His is an unfinished story of revolution within philosophy, biology, and psychology, with broad and penetrating implications for education.

Piaget's genius is to be found in at least three areas; first, in the simplicity with which he has been able to state his problems so that it is indeed possible to investigate them with the tools of science. Rather than ask the traditional and essentially unanswerable philosophical question, "What *is* the nature of knowledge?" Piaget has asked the question in psychological terms: "Under what laws does knowledge *develop* and *change*?" (Inhelder, 1962.) Stated in this form, the question is open to empirical investigation and can be approached developmentally.

A second part of Piaget's genius is his breadth of vision. His view of man is

Piaget's major interest is . . .

---

[3] P. Suppes (1974). The place of theory in educational research, *Educational Researcher*, **3**(6), 4.
[4] Ibid., p. 6.

holistic, natural, and timeless. That is, he conceives of the human being as a wonderfully complex and natural biological organism in the process of becoming—of evolving and developing physically and socially, subject to all the general laws to which all living things are subject. His is the objective view of the scientist who subjects his hunches and best guesses to the scrutiny of experimental and clinical investigation. As any good scientist, he observes carefully and thoroughly (few excel Piaget as an observer of behavior), *speculates* on his observations, *devises* experimental and clinical tests of his speculations, and then *revises* or expands his theory as required.

The third part of Piaget's genius is his ability to be critical, especially of untested assumptions traditionally accepted as the givens with which philosophical thought begins. Piaget himself aptly fits the description (quoted at the beginning of this chapter) that he gives of the kind of person he believes it is the job of education to create. We will want to learn more about the logical simplicity of his theory of developmental adaptation.

Piaget's Biologically Based Theory of Developmental Adaptation

Piaget is a biologist trying to understand how living things adapt to their environments, and therefore he treats questions concerning knowledge as any other biological problem needing an answer. Even though his developmental ideas are fundamentally simple in their basic conception—"the idea of a genius, such simplicity," was the way Albert Einstein summed them up—Furth (1969) cautions that it takes time to get used to a new outlook and that there are no shortcuts.

Since Piaget's view of development is essentially biological, we should make sure that we have the prerequisites necessary to learn about it meaningfully. Therefore, before we learn more about the specific details of Piaget's theory of developmental adaptation, let us consider some of the concepts and rules basic to the biology of living things. Then we will see how Piaget fits them into his theory, and how his ideas, and those of others, can be synthesized into higher-order rules of development that have implications for a theory of instruction.

HIGHER-ORDER RULES IN NATURE

Universal
higher-order rules are
those that . . .

Within the universe as we know it, there are rules to which all things, living and nonliving, are subject. Sometimes these higher-order rules describe the basic structures of substance: "All things are composed of particles called atoms in pure form or in various combination." Other times, the rules describe certain invariant attributes of substance: "All things have weight and occupy space"; and "All things change as a function of time."

Frequently, these higher-order rules describe the general relationship or the nature of the interaction among the variables of time, space, and substance. When Sir Isaac Newton (1642–1727) stated his rules of universal gravitation, he described the general and broadly inclusive nature of the interaction between distance and substance in terms of forces of attraction. Inherent in Newton's statements is the general rule that all things, living and nonliving, tend toward balance, or a state of equilibrium. This state may be either static, such as exists between the equal and opposite forces that act when a book is at rest on a table, or dynamic, such as occurs when a reversible chemical reaction "goes" in both directions at a steady, stable rate. Later, Newton's rules were refined by Einstein to show how they must be modified to accommodate the variable of time. But this is the nature of rules, even the higher-order ones. They develop over time as a function of increasing knowledge.

HIGHER-ORDER RULES
OF LIVING ORGANISMS

Subsumed within these broad, universal higher-order rules of relationships are less inclusive rules to which all living things, including human beings, are subject. In this section we will discuss some of these rules that have particular importance for our understanding about the nature of development. Mostly these rules are contained within (1) a biological view of developmental adaptation; (2) the widely generalizable rules of gene action; (3) the interaction of heredity and experience in evolution and individual development; and (4) the evolution and development of intelligence, here defined broadly as "knowing behavior."

A Biological View
of Developmental Adaptation

Science has not been especially successful in defining what life is. However, the functions of life have been described in surprising detail. These can be roughly summarized in seven simple rules. All living things (1) move; (2) respond to conditions around them; (3) secure food; (4) use food to produce living material and/or energy; (5) excrete waste; (6) grow larger and/or change in proportions or parts; and (7) reproduce.

Seven simple biological rules of life are . . .

Let us expand a bit on some of the ideas contained in these rules. For example, we might ask about what constitutes "living things," how they are organized, and what the mechanisms are that permit them to adapt to an environment.

THE BIOLOGICAL UNIT

Piaget refers to living things as biological units: the organism, the environment, and their interaction. Furth points out that these three terms are indissociable and imply one another, that is, "one cannot conceive of an organism unless it finds itself in some meaningful exchange with the environment."[5]

Biological units are composed of . . .

ORGANIZATION AND ADAPTATION

All living things consist of parts that work together. Single-celled organisms, even those as small as bacteria and probably even viruses, contain a generalized living substance called protoplasm, nuclei containing chromosomes and genes,

---

[5] H. G. Furth (1969). *Piaget and Knowledge, Theoretical Foundations.* Englewood Cliffs, N.J.: Prentice-Hall, p. 244.

and so forth; and all the parts function as a unit. Many-celled organisms, with an even greater variety of parts, still function in an organized manner.

Biological organization means . . .
Because living things are organized in some manner or another, we call them *organisms*. Piaget (1952) believes that self-regulating mechanisms, present in all living things, have the function of conserving the organism in a steady and dynamic state of adaptation, that is, in an ongoing process of achieving balance, or equilibrium, between opposing forces in life.

KNOWING BEHAVIOR

Biological adaptation is defined as . . .
For Piaget, the basis for a biological organization is a *knowing structure* that is responsive to its environment and whose origin is not entirely outside the organism. That is, the organizational basis for responding always involves knowing structures that are (1) genetically a part of the organism, and (2) the result of experience. The process of *knowing* always results from the adaptive interaction between what is native to the organism and what is present in its environment. What is constructed in the process of knowing is a *structure of knowledge* in a true physiological sense. That is, when we interact with our environment, physiological changes occur within us, especially within the nervous system, whereby our knowledge of that interaction becomes a part of our physical self. (We will learn more about the physiological bases for knowing and knowledge in a later section on gene action.)

To know means . . .
Knowing, for Piaget, is taken in a very general sense and implies more than just conscious or reflective knowing, such as is implied when one of our students indicates that he "knows" the names of all the trees in the area. Piaget holds that an organism can respond to a stimulus only if the stimulus is, at least in some rudimentary way, meaningful or "known" to it. Biologists often use a different terminology to reflect this view of knowing; they say that an organism has some specific information about its milieu.[6] *Knowing behavior means having the capability of responding appropriately to stimuli.* Consequently, knowing behavior can be relatively simple, as, for example, when a one-celled organism "knows" how to respond to light or the presence of food, or extremely complex, as when an adult human being "knows" how to solve problems.

It follows, in Piaget's view, that adaptation, like organization, is an invariant function of all living things, since the process of interaction between a living organism and its environment implies the ongoing and dynamic process of adaptation.

ASSIMILATION AND ACCOMMODATION   Contained within Piaget's view of the dynamic process of adaptation are the bases or mechanisms for continual change over time, that is, the *development* of all organisms. These inseparable mechanisms are the two opposing activities of *assimilation* and *accommodation*, whose functioning is regulated by the internal balancing factor underlying all biological organizations. Piaget calls this regulatory factor *equilibration*. Thus, for Piaget, the process of knowing is a process of adaptation that occurs through the internally equilibrated activities of *assimilation* and *accommodation*.

Let us see what all this means in less technical terms. When an organism begins life, it has inherited potential capabilities that are the result of the evolu-

---

[6] Ibid., p. 15.

tionary learning of its species. No individual organism begins the processes of knowing its environment from zero. The fact that it is a living organism with an evolutionary history, passed on to it genetically, ensures that it will begin life with at least the basic knowledge, however rudimentary and incompletely developed, that is necessary to begin knowing, or getting along with, its environment in an adaptive, interactive way.

Assimilation can be roughly likened to the process of ingesting food into the body, where it becomes transformed chemically and eventually incorporated as a part of the structural and functional characteristics of the body (Piaget, 1970). *Accommodation,* in the metaphor of food, is defined as any structural or functional change that results within the body from the assimilation of the food; digestive processes may be stimulated toward more efficient functioning; muscle cells may become larger; or the person may become more adept at chewing, and so forth.

The activity of assimilation begins when an organism encounters a new event (stimulus) that potentially can become associated or incorporated within already-existing structures of knowledge that are in some way relevant to certain or all elements of the new event. Piaget believes that only certain environmental stimuli are *selected* for attention by any given organism, since it is obvious that not all stimuli in an environmental event can be attended to. What determines which stimuli are attended to, that is, can be assimilated, are the structures of knowledge already present within the organism. If there is none present that potentially can relate to the new environmental stimuli, the new stimuli are not meaningful. Consequently, adaptation—the process of knowing—does not occur.

On the other hand, if the relevant prerequisite structures of knowledge are present, new stimuli are assimilated; they are taken in and incorporated within the existing structures. It is important to note at this point that the *meaning* associated with new stimuli being assimilated is *constructed* by the learner and is not simply an objective and given property of the stimuli. In a very real and individual sense, each knower knows a given stimulus relative to the unique structures of knowledge he possesses at the time he encounters the stimulus. Since it is extremely unlikely that all knowers will have identical structures of knowledge (i.e., past experiences), we see in this simple idea of Piaget's the fundamental basis for individual differences in knowing behavior or, in other words, in individual capability for adaptation. An example will help us understand these ideas.

Take the situation in which one of your learners encounters for the first time the arithmetical symbol +, which means summation, or to add to. Piaget maintains that this symbol cannot be a meaningful stimulus for learners unless they already "know something," at least generally, about the process of summation; that is, unless they already have structures of knowledge relative to the concept that can accommodate or incorporate the new and related symbol. If these structures are present from previous experiences, the new information can be meaningfully learned; if not, it can only be rotely learned, since there is nothing with which the symbol can be associated. You will notice that all this sounds very much like our discussion about rote and meaningful learning in Chapters 5 and 6.

The second part of any adaptive behavior pattern is *accommodation.* This term refers to what Piaget believes happens to *existing* structures of knowledge when assimilation occurs. New information is not just brought in and added to

Assimilation means . . .

Accommodation means . . . these structures. Rather, the existing structures accommodate—they adjust or adapt to the information being assimilated. The result of accommodation is a modified structure of knowledge and thus a new level of knowing. *That is the basic action in the process of development.*

When no appropriate and relevant structure of knowledge exists within the organism into which new information can be assimilated, accommodation does not occur. The new information, if attended to at all, will result merely in the formation of new structures of knowledge unassociated with other structures except perhaps in random or contrived ways. Note that in the activities of assimilation and accommodation is found the fundamental mechanism of change, of development, both structurally and functionally as a process of the interaction of heredity and experience as a result of living through time.

EQUILIBRATION   One might ask: "What causes assimilation and accommodation to occur?" Piaget does not try to answer this question since, for him, it concerns philosophy, not science. Rather, he chooses to rephrase the question to ask: "How is the process regulated?"

To answer the latter question, Piaget looks to the higher-order rules of nature, especially those that describe the general tendency toward balance or equilibrium among all things. He postulates the presence of this tendency as a part of **Equilibration is defined as . . .** all biological units, calling this regulatory factor *equilibration*, as we noted earlier. It refers to the *stability* of knowing behavior and the tendency of the organism to maintain balance between (1) environmental information being assimilated and (2) its existing structures of knowledge.

Equilibrium is upset when an organism encounters environmental events that are new or that do not fit with present structures of knowledge. The lack of equilibrium is compensated for by a tendency toward balance that results in the spontaneous modification or restructuring of the present structures of knowledge so that the new information becomes a part of, or is accommodated by, the previous structures. With such a sequence, developmental adaptations continue to occur either until the structures achieve the limits set by the genetic characteristics of the species or until they can generalize indefinitely to the circumstances encountered.[7]

Some examples will help clarify the interaction of these invariant functions in Piaget's view of developmental adaptation. The reason examples help is itself a matter of developmental adaptation. When we encounter new information that we have difficulty learning, our existing structures of knowledge are unable to assimilate the new information. This may be either because they apparently are not relevant to the new information, or because they cannot be modified (accommodated) sufficiently to assimilate it. In either case, meaningful learning of the new information will not occur. An example helps because it has within it elements of information that either clarify the relevance of existing but apparently unrelated structures of knowledge for the new information, or it introduces other elements of information that can be assimilated by the existing structures, with the consequence that the resulting accommodation (modification) of existing structures is sufficient for them then to assimilate the new information itself.

---

[7] J. McV. Hunt (1969). The impact and limitations of the giant of developmental psychology. In D. Elkind and J. H. Flavell (eds.), *Studies in Cognitive Development, Essays in Honor of Jean Piaget.* New York: Oxford University Press, p. 9.

Now the examples. First, we will take one in the psychomotor domain, although Piaget's theory applies also, and usually simultaneously, to adaptation in the cognitive and affective domains. Suppose one of your learners encounters a boomerang for the first time. A boomerang is a flat, curved piece of wood that, when thrown just right, will return to the thrower—with luck! Considerable psychomotor know-how is required to complete a throw successfully. Now, if the requirements for the throw are not too far beyond the limits of the already-existing structures of knowledge of your learner relative to throwing things, the new information, mostly muscular and visual feedback resulting from each attempt to throw the boomerang, will be assimilated by the existing structures. Thus, the throwing experiences (practice) will lead to accommodative modifications toward greater generality and inclusiveness of the previously existing structures of knowledge relative to throwing behavior. Learning will occur.

If, on the other hand, the requirements for throwing a boomerang are too far beyond the limits of your learner's already-existing structures of knowledge relative to throwing things (e.g., knowing how to hold things for throwing; how to move the arm just right; and how to stand), the new or corrective information potentially available from each attempt to throw the boomerang will not be assimilated into existing structures nor will accommodation of these structures occur. In fact, Piaget argues that the new information will not even constitute effective stimuli for your learner, since, for the new information to be defined as meaningful stimuli, there must already exist in her structures of knowledge some structures that are appropriately relevant to throwing behavior.

Thus we see again, from a slightly different point of view, that the meaningful stimulus properties of objects or events are *constructed* by the organism in keeping with past experiences and are not solely objective and constant. Stated very simply, stimuli, for example, a boomerang, have unique meaning for each organism. Obviously, the meaning of a boomerang in terms of its potential usefulness in the development of throwing behavior is different for an ape, a human infant, a twelve-year-old boy, and a native Australian hunter.

For a second example, let us look at the cognitive aspects of an encounter with words and phrases of a different American dialect. Read the following exchange between two young boys, taken from Seymour's paper, "Black Children, Black Speech."[8]

"Cmon, man, les git goin'!" called the boy to his companion. "Dat bell ringin'. It say, 'Gitin rat now!" He dashed into the school yard.

"Aw, f'get you," replied the other. "Whe' Richuh? Whe' da' muvvuh? He be goin' to schoo'."

"He in de' now, man!" was the answer as they went through the door.

In the classroom they made for their desks and opened their books. The name of the story they tried to read was "Come." It went:

Come, Bill, come.
Come with me.
Come and see this.
See what is here.

The first boy poked the second. "Wha' da' wor'?"

"Da' wor' *is*, you dope."

---

[8] D. Z. Seymour (1971). Black children, black speech, *Commonweal*, **95**(8), 175.

"*Is*? Ain't no wor' *is*. You jivin' me? Wha' da' wor' mean?"
"Ah dunno, Jus' is."

There is little likelihood that the word "is" will be assimilated into the cognitive structure of either boy as a consequence of the reading experience. Apparently, neither boy has the needed structures of knowledge into which this word *is* can be meaningfully incorporated. The word means nothing to them; there is presently nothing that they "know about" that can be modified (accommodated) by the inclusion of the word "is"; they haven't the necessary prerequisite knowledge to make sense of the new word. Piaget would conclude that "is" has no meaningful stimulus value for the boys. The response of the last speaker reinforces the validity of Piaget's point.

We have talked about a few of Piaget's notions of developmental adaptation in the perspective of higher-order rules of nature and of living things. These rules state relationships among defined concepts such as equilibrium, organization, adaptation, and knowing behavior, and are closely related to many of the concepts and rules we learned about in earlier chapters. Checkpoint 11-1 helps you learn about the relationship with three of them.

CHECKPOINT 11-1

1. Much of the discussion in the first ten chapters has been about *learning*. In Chapter 11 it is about *development*. Describe how the two concepts are related, pointing out which of the two is the most inclusive.

2. How can Piaget's invariant processes of adaptation—assimilation, equilibration, and accommodation—be interpreted as supporting the idea that concepts are never completely learned?

3. Hunt (1969) describes a plausible relationship between Skinner's concept *reinforcement* and Piaget's concept *equilibrium*. Speculate on what it might be.

4. Do you find it difficult to consider a biological approach to human development? Yes ____ No ____

The Rules of Gene Action

In addition to the higher-order rules of the biology of living things discussed in the preceding section, there are others with which Piaget's theory of developmental adaptation must agree. Fundamental among them are the basic rules of gene action.

It is important to note that Piaget's theoretical ideas about how developmental adaptation occurs have been derived from his observations of behavior and from his knowledge of the concepts and rules of the biology of living things. As such, his ideas must be considered within the realm of psychological speculation until the biological and physical rules underlying his speculations can be shown to confirm or refute them. For these rules we will have to look to biochemistry, genetics, physiology, and psychology. Understanding about the action of genes requires a synthesis of the research data from all these areas of investigation.

When we know (1) what genes are, (2) what genes do, and (3) how genes do their work with the help of the environment, we will be able to formulate higher-order rules that provide support for many of Piaget's theoretical ideas and facilitate relatively specific and clear understanding of the bases for the individual differences among our learners. More importantly, such information will help us know better what we may do to provide instruction that is optimal for each learner.

WHAT GENES ARE

Structurally, genes are complex molecules of deoxyribonucleic acid, abbreviated DNA. Functionally, DNA is the carrier of hereditary information both in an evolutionary sense and from parent to offspring. In an evolutionary sense, DNA molecules carry the messages for the structures of knowledge relative to successful adaptation learned by each species during the eons of biological evolution that have led to its present form (Lorenz, 1965). In the sense of heredity from parent to offspring, genes are the transmitters of information necessary for a living thing to react in a specific way to a specific environment. Across all species of living things, genes show essentially the same structural and functional properties. As we will see later, this fact enables us to generalize with a good deal of confidence from the biological data available from animal studies to parallel situations involving human beings for which comparable data are difficult if not impossible to obtain.

Genes occur in great numbers in strands or chromosomes of DNA molecules within the nucleus of nearly all the cells of nearly all living organisms. A strand of DNA about one millimeter in length may contain 5,000 different genes. Callaway (1970) compares this with the total length of DNA in the forty-six chromosomes in each cell of the human body and concludes the length is about 2,000 times longer in the human being. Estimates of the average number of different genes that constitute each of these chromosomes are about 20,000. Based on the estimate of the human body's containing approximately 10^{13} cells, the strands of DNA in one body, stretched end to end, would reach across the entire solar system.

Obviously, the hereditary information carried by the genes is of great potential. Lessing (1967) estimates that human parents transmit to their offspring genetic information that would fill about 1,000 books of 500 pages each. And, with the exception of the germinal cells (sperm and egg), all this information is housed in the nucleus of each and every cell of the body. That is some library, by any standards! Whether or not this vast potential is realized, however, depends on other factors, primarily those of the environment an organism experiences. To see how environment and heredity interact, we will need to learn more about the work that genes do.

WHAT GENES DO

Very simply, genes are designed for only one function at the molecular level—the production of protein—and apparently each gene controls the production of only one type of protein molecule. This may not seem like a very important function relative to development and learning, but we must remember that protein production is fundamental to life since protein is the primary building block for cells, and protein molecules act as specific enzymes for most biochemical reactions. Since protein molecules serve as enzymes that are needed for the vast number of biochemical reactions within an organism, and since it is the

Genes are . . .

Genes produce . . .

action of genes that produces these proteins, it is easy to see how gene action is fundamentally involved in the organization, regulation, maintenance, and change (development) of an organism. However, Luria (1965) reminds us that genes could not complete their work if they were unable to receive and respond to signals relative to the ever-changing needs of the organism for particular proteins. We can see that what genes do, i.e., that they produce protein molecules (enzymes), is the starting point for development (change).

Obviously, genes do not do their work independently of the environment. Since genes and environment cooperate, that is, interact, the question of importance is how the environment affects genetic information. In brief, how do the genes and the environment interact to do their work?

HOW GENES AND THE ENVIRONMENT INTERACT TO DO THEIR WORK

By now, you are beginning to see that the potential for individual differences among our learners is nearly limitless. Fortunately for us as teachers, there are at least some approximate and predictable similarities or patterns that most learners manifest during their development. Increasingly, the reasons for the apparent regularity of these developmental patterns are being understood in terms of the interaction between the genes and the environment.

Gene-environment interaction means . . .

THE BASIC ADAPTATIONAL PROCESS: GENE-ENVIRONMENT INTERACTION   The basic adaptational process that occurs in most or all tissues is simply the increased production of material when it is in demand (Young, 1964). The demands the environment makes on the cell's metabolic resources evoke enzyme (protein) production, and, as Callaway (1970) explains, every metabolic change that uses sufficient material in the cell stimulates the production of precisely those enzymes to replace the material used. "More exactly, and this is pertinent to theories of learning and intellectual development, the material is replaced in such a way that the organism is able to meet more efficiently similar future demands."[9] Apparently the mechanisms involved in gene action for the production of protein are identical whether the gene action is in response to exercise in muscles, needed repair of skin cells, secretion by glandular cells to meet some bodily need, or brain cells involved in learning and remembering (Palay, 1964).

Structure of knowledge means . . .

GENE-ENVIRONMENT INTERACTION AND STRUCTURAL-CHEMICAL CHANGE   There is a good deal known about the structural changes in living tissue that result from gene action stimulated by environmental events. Lessing (1967) and Hyden (1966), for example, have demonstrated that practice with a previously learned skill increases the total amount of RNA (ribonucleic acid) production, whereas learning a new skill results in different kinds of RNA being produced in brain cells. This is important to know because such evidence helps establish a biological basis for (1) the role of practice, and (2) Piaget's theory of developmental adaptation. You will recall that Piaget believes assimilation and accommodation are basically two aspects of an essentially biological process that results in structural changes within the organism.

---

[9] W. R. Callaway, Jr. (1970). Modes of biological adaptation and their role in intellectual development, *Perceptual Cognitive Development Monographs*, **1**, 3.

D. O. Hebb (1966) has constructed a theoretical model to show how he pictures the structural changes that occur in the central nervous system of animals, including humans, as a consequence of experience, especially early experience. In his view, at birth the human brain is relatively unorganized and unstructured. However, as the child experiences environmental stimulation, innate but incomplete neural patterns or systems become elaborated. That is, they begin to be modified and expanded, and to work together. Hebb calls these groups of brain cells working as a unit *cell assemblies*. New experience results in greater and more complex elaboration of cell assemblies which begin to interrelate to form what Hebb calls *phase sequences*. Gradually the brain achieves widespread organization, and the child gradually becomes capable of thought that is not only rapid but also extremely complex.

Experience results in changes in. . . .

Some of the most dramatic evidence for the importance of environmental experience on structural and functional development mediated by gene action comes from the experimental work of psychologists interested in the physiology and chemistry of gene-environment interaction. The fascinating studies of Krech (1969) and Agranoff (1967) show the thrust this research has taken. Here is Krech describing his work to a group of school administrators:[10]

Some time ago we set ourselves the following problem: If the laying down (learning) of memories involves the synthesis of chemical products in the brain, then one should find that an animal which has lived replete with opportunities for learning and memorizing would end with a brain chemically and morphologically different from an animal which has lived out an intellectually impoverished life. . . . Let me tell you some of what we found.

At weaning time we divided our experimental rats into two groups, half of the rats being placed in an "intellectually enriched" environment, the other half—their brothers—in the deprived environment. While both groups receive identical food and water, their psychological environments differ greatly. The animals in the first group live together in one large cage, are provided with many rat toys (tunnels to explore, ladders to climb, levers to press), and they are assigned to graduate students who are admonished to give these rats loving care and kindness, teach them to run mazes, and in general to provide them with the best and most expensive supervised education available to any young rat at the University of California. While these rats are thus being encouraged to store up many and varied memories, their brother rats, in the deprived group, live in isolated, barren cages, devoid of stimulation by either their environmental appurtenances, fellow rats, or graduate students. After about 80 days of this differential treatment, all the animals are sacrificed, their brains dissected out and various chemical and histological analyses performed. The results are convincing. The brain from a rat from the enriched environment—and presumably, therefore, with many more stored memories—has a heavier and thicker cortex, a better blood supply, larger brain cells, more glia cells (believed to provide support and nutrition for neurons), and increased activity of two brain enzymes, acetylcholinesterase and cholinesterase, than does the brain from an animal whose life has been less memorable.

We can draw several morals from the experiments. . . . [T]he growing animal's psychological environment is of crucial importance for the development of its brain. By manipulating the environment of the young, one can truly create a "lamebrain"—with lighter cortex, shrunken brain cells, fewer glia cells, smaller blood vessels, and lower enzymatic activity levels—or one can create a more robust, a

---

[10] D. Krech (1969). Psychoneurobiochemeducation, *Phi Beta Kappan*, **L**, p. 372.

healthier, a more metabolically active brain. If it should turn out that what is true for the rat brain is also true for the human brain, and that by careful manipulation of this or that group's early environment we can develop among them bigger and better brains or smaller and meaner ones, the wondrous promises of a glorious future or the monstrous horrors of a Huxlian brave new world are fairly self-evident.

Agranoff's work (1967) synthesizes nicely with Krech's findings that experience produces structural changes in the brain cells and in their chemistry. Agranoff, working with goldfish, demonstrated that long-term memory (more than for just a few seconds or minutes) of what has been experienced (learned) is controlled by gene action, that is, by the presence of certain protein molecules that are produced by nuclear RNA. Agranoff reasoned that if long-term memory really is a function of protein production resulting from the action of genes responding to environmental stimuli, then injecting the brain of his goldfish with chemicals that prevent the formation of new proteins or nuclear RNA should prevent memory of the previous environmental experience. And indeed it did.

The structural result of learning is . . .

Agranoff trained his fish to swim to a light on one side of an aquarium to avoid an electric shock. It takes goldfish about forty minutes to learn this task, and memory of it lasts for several days. Certain chemicals were injected immediately before or just after training. The chemicals did not interfere with *learning* the task, but a day or two later, the fish showed almost no memory of the experience. Apparently production of new protein or nuclear RNA is not involved in learning a task, that is, in the short-term memory of it. Repeated trials (practice or drill), however, seem to have the effect of signaling the gene action that produces the specific protein needed for the physical structuring required in long-term memory of the event.

You might wish, at this point, to reflect on the support that the research findings of Krech and Agranoff provide for Hebb's theory of cell assemblies and Piaget's concepts of structures of knowledge and more generally for developmental adaptation. Also, you might begin to think more specifically about how environmental experience can influence gene action, which is the basis for developmental adaptation, and subsumes the concepts of *learning* and *intellectual development*—concepts of great importance to your task as a teacher. The activities of Checkpoint 11–2 will help you do this.

CHECKPOINT 11–2

1. In Chapter 4 we concluded that learning must be inferred from the changes we observe in a learner's behavior. What modifications of this statement appear justified by research data such as those of Krech, Agranoff, Lessing, and Hyden?

2. Learning is frequently defined as a relatively permanent change in a behavioral tendency that is a result of reinforced practice (Chapter 4). Redefine *learning* in terms of gene-environment interaction and structural-chemical changes. How is *retention* a part of your revised definition?

3. A major theme that we have been developing throughout the text is that "we learn what we practice." This is a psychological type of statement that has recently gained physiological support. Describe the nature and significance of this support as discussed to this point in Chapter 11.

Heredity and Experience in Evolution and Individual Development

As we learn more about how genes and the environment interact to do their work, we should return to Piaget's belief that no organism begins the process of its own developmental adaptation from zero. It always starts with the structures of knowledge, learned through its evolutionary history, that enable it to know the environment typical for its species, to respond appropriately and adaptively to it. Usually we think of this information as being innate or instinctive, although Tinbergen (Hall, 1974) and others warn us that these words are misleading since "innate" may be interpreted to mean preprogrammed information that is absolute in its structural and functional manifestations regardless of environmental influences. He suggests that the relative term "environment-resistant" is more accurate because "from the moment the egg cell is fertilized, the organism begins to interact with its environment. Therefore, to say that any characteristic of a full-grown animal is innate is an oversimplification."[11] The term environment-resistant helps us think of behavior programming as "relatively more to less 'open' programs—from less to more environment-resistant."[12]

Environment-resistant means . . .

HEREDITY PROVIDES A BASIS AND A BIAS FOR DEVELOPMENT

Today there is little argument among ethologists, such as Lorenz and Tinbergen, biologists, and psychologists over whether living organisms have environment-resistant (preprogrammed genetic) mechanisms, varying in degrees of completeness according to species, that help them respond appropriately and adaptively to their respective environments. Piaget (1952) and others, for example, Ganz (1968), Sigel (1964), Miller (1964), Koestler (1964), Melzack (1968), Lorenz (1965), and Tinbergen (Hall, 1974), have emphasized that inherited information provides the organism with a *basis* and a *bias* for later structural and functional development.

BASIS: GENERAL PLASTICITY THROUGH VAST SURPLUS OF GENETIC MATERIAL   The *basis* for development is provided in the form of the general abundance of genetic material in each organism which is typically "far greater than it is usually called upon to demonstrate. Its genetic repertoire of environmental responses is very wide, but only when a particular environment is introduced. . . does a given response occur."[13] This genetic surplus gives the organism a flexible range of potential for reacting adaptively to possible variety or changes in environmental stimuli. It gives the organism a degree of flexibility or plasticity in its developmental adaptation, and it is considerably less in lower organisms than in higher ones.

The biological basis for development is . . .

BIAS: SPECIAL SENSITIVITY THROUGH PREPROGRAMMED GENETIC MATERIAL   The *bias* in development is provided in the sense that at least some of the genetic potential of all organisms is preprogrammed, with a greater amount in organisms

---

[11] Hall, E. (1974). Ethology's warning: A conversation with Nobel Prize winner, Niko Tinbergen, *Psychology Today*, **7**(10), 70.

[12] Ibid., p. 71.

[13] E. W. Sinnot (1963). *The Problem of Organic Form*. New Haven, Conn.: Yale, pp. 189–190.

low on the evolutionary scale and a lesser amount in higher animals, including humans. Preprogramming of genetic information works in a *proactive* way. That is, preprogramming causes the new organism to orient, attend, and respond appropriately and selectively to various stimuli in its environment that have adaptive importance for it and to ignore those stimulus events that do not. In other words, an abundance of genetic material gives the organism a potential for *general plasticity*, and material that is preprogrammed gives it *special selectivity* or *sensitivity*. It is worth noting that this property of gene action describes what might be called an inborn motivation system incomplete in the human organism perhaps but nevertheless obviously present at least in inchoate form. You will recall that Bruner, Montessori, Maslow, Freud, Erikson, and others of the humanistic view of learning also believe in inborn systems of motivation.

The biological bias for development is . . .

These rules of gene action are of great importance to us as teachers. As we shall see later, they have significance for our understanding of the processes of structural and functional development. More important, they suggest relatively direct implications for educational practice since these rules form the basis for our concepts of *stages* and *sensitive periods* in the developmental adaptation of living organisms, including human learners.

The proactive-action of genes refers to . . .

EXPERIENCE AND THE PROACTIVE-REACTIVE CHARACTERISTICS OF GENES   Let us now look more closely at the proactive and reactive functions of gene action and see how experience plays a necessary part in the elaboration of preprogrammed mechanisms in both an evolutionary and an individual developmental sense.

Environment-resistant genetic mechanisms (to follow Tinbergen's usage) responsible for selectivity and sensitivity have at least two general characteristics, in addition to the fact that they are built in, which make them relevant to education. First, as Lorenz (1965) clarifies for us, preprogrammed information is manifested at the lower evolutionary levels of living organisms in terms of rigid, automatic behavior that is not influenced greatly by experience. At the higher evolutionary levels, however, behavior patterns are not nearly so "given" or set at birth. Furthermore, there is apparent in the adaptive behavior of lower organisms an *immediacy* of response dominated by physiological needs. These behavioral characteristics of lower animals are also seen to a degree in the behavior of the human infant and the young child. However, they are largely absent in the behavior of adults. Obviously, there is within the human species a *developmental* sequence away from rigidness and immediacy of response patterns.

The fact that experience is necessary, especially for organisms at the higher evolutionary levels, for elaboration of incomplete, environment-resistant mechanisms is closely related to the second general characteristic that makes these mechanisms relevant to education. The experience that must occur for the development of these preprogrammed mechanisms apparently must satisfy two criteria to be most effective. First, it must occur within *certain periods of time* during which the organism is especially sensitive to appropriate stimuli.

Second, the experience cannot be just any experience. It must be particularly relevant, or specific to the developmental task and also to the species. Krech's work and that of others suggest that the types of experience that are maximally effective for the development of incomplete, preprogrammed, adaptive mechanisms are simply, *those stimuli and responses that constitute the very behavioral responses being developed*. Usually these stimuli occur naturally in the organism's environment. For young birds learning to fly, for example, this means practice stretching and flapping the wings; for young rats learning to find their way through tunnels or passages and over, through, and under obstacles, this means exploratory practice with objects in three-dimensional space; for children learning language, "the necessary stimuli apparently involve mere exposure to the language of one's fellow-men."[14]

To summarize our discussion of the *proactive* and *reactive* characteristics of gene action, we should remember that in living organisms, including human beings, (1) gene action provides environment-resistant mechanisms that produce the structural and physiological capability to begin appropriate, adaptive interaction with the environment; and (2) structural and functional development of the rudimentary, inborn mechanisms is made possible by appropriate experiences during certain, and more or less limited, time spans.

The reactive-action of genes refers to . . .

SENSITIVE PERIODS
AND STAGES IN DEVELOPMENT

The biological characteristics of gene action–environment interaction fit very convincingly with, and add support for, another important part of Piaget's general and inclusive theory of developmental adaptation, especially the part directly concerned with the adaptive function of intellectual development: his belief in an invariant sequence of sensitive periods or stages in the development of intellectual capabilities, or intelligence.

Since much of what we do as teachers relates to the development of intellectual capabilities in our learners, we will find it helpful to understand clearly this part of Piaget's theory, and later to see how it fits with research data and the perspective of such others as Bruner, Ausubel, Maslow, Gagné, Skinner, Bloom, and Carroll. A few general words about the concepts *sensitive periods* and *stages* will serve as an advance organizer to help us more meaningfully understand how the specifics of these concepts relate to Piaget's theory, which we will learn about in the next section.

The term *sensitive period* derives from the older, more rigid, and outdated term *critical period* with which you may already be familiar. Originally the concept came from embryology, for it is well known that during early embryological stages of tissue growth, variation in stimulation of unspecific tissues, especially stimulation relative to *location* within the embryo, results in different developmental outcomes, that is, in the various specific tissues of the body. It is also well known that there are critical times during which variation in stimulation will be effective in determining the specific outcome of tissue development. The same stimulation before or after this critical period is relatively ineffective (Speman, 1938).

A sensitive period is a time during which . . .

Tinbergen (Hall, 1974) explains that it is more accurate to regard the concept of sensitive periods, in a relative sense, as the optimal period for certain experience to have its effects rather than necessarily and absolutely the only period in which it may produce its effects.

Sensitive periods imply phases or stages of development. The term "stage," in our daily conversation, generally means a stopping or resting place, or sometimes the distance (time or space) between stopping places, as on a journey. In

A developmental stage is defined as . . .

[14] E. H. Lenneberg (1967). *Biological Foundations of Language.* New York: Wiley, p. 221.

this sense, "stage" gives a stationary, inactive connotation; a period in which all forces are at rest, as in a state of static equilibrium. In development, however, "stage" generally refers to dynamic changes in kind that usually follow one another in an invariant sequence. "Change in kind" means qualitative and usually striking structural and/or functional change of the organism. Thus, a stage is a period of structural and/or functional activity that has characteristics qualitatively different from the activity before or after this period. Used in this way, the term has descriptive value and can be used as a basis for describing and measuring an individual's status with regard to some structural or functional characteristic (Stott, 1974). The familiar expression "ages and stages" is used to denote typical structural and functional characteristics of various kinds relative to age, e.g., height and weight, creeping and walking behavior, age of beginning speech, and toilet training.

Two potential misuses of the concept of stage are . . .   The concept *stage* is a useful tool. It is also a frequent source of at least two kinds of difficulty. One, it is often used inappropriately as if it had explanatory value. Stage is a descriptive term, not an explanatory one. Therefore, using it to "explain" behavior leads to circular reasoning of the type we discussed in Chapter 2; e.g., "Judy plays with only one other child." "Why does she play with only one other child?" "She is in that 'best friend' stage right now." "How do you know she is in the 'best friend' stage?" "Judy plays with only one other child." More often we hear only the pseudoexplanation, "Oh, it's just the stage he is in."

The second source of frequent difficulty derives from the first. If we believe that the sequence of stages is invariant and is somehow preprogrammed to occur naturally, it follows that if we can just "wait it out," change will occur naturally and in its own good time. For some developmental characteristics, perhaps structural ones, a "wait and see" strategy may be as good as any. As we will learn, however, for other characteristics such as the development of intellectual capabilities, waiting for things to "happen naturally" can be a mistake.

One other characteristic of the concept of stage as it is used in development needs clarifying before we look specifically at the concept relative to Piaget's theory of intellectual development. Stage, in its broad usage, is relative in terms of the time of appearance, duration, and even the individual structural and functional changes in some phenomenon that are taken as evidence to define a stage. Therefore, it is not always easy to attain agreement on what actually constitutes a stage, or if in fact stages exist at all. Is it really useful to talk about stages at all? Can the concept of stages actually hinder our seeing that developmental adaptation may be a continuous sequence of many small steps involving the same genetic and environmental mechanisms that can and do produce behavior change in the adult organism? These are the kinds of questions behavioral psychologists are asking. Are there really "uniquely developmental processes occurring in young children, to some extent qualitatively different from the processes typical of adults, and centrally important in determining the shape of adult psychology?"[15]

Consistently, for more than fifty years, Piaget has answered, with theory and experimental data, that indeed there are qualitatively different stages, at least for

---

[15] D. M. Baer and J. C. Wright (1974). Developmental psychology. In M. R. Rosenzweig and L. W. Porter (eds.), *Annual Review of Psychology.* Palo Alto, Calif.: Annual Reviews, p. 1.

intellectual development, through which all human learners must pass if they are to achieve the intellectual capabilities typical of the adult.

At this point, we have gained the broad perspective about development necessary to assimilate Piaget's concepts and rules about the development of intelligence. You will notice that, as you learn first about Piaget's ideas and then about those of others, you will experience firsthand what he is talking about. That is, your structures of knowledge will undergo continual modification as they accommodate to new information. Each new bit of information with which you are confronted will produce a lack of equilibrium between your present structures of knowledge and those necessary to assimilate the new information. Resulting from each confrontation will be a higher synthesis of the physical and functional structures of knowledge, uniquely your own, manifested by a higher level of adaptive or *knowing* behavior; that is, you will have developed to a higher level of capability for adaptation to your environment. In a word, Piaget believes that you will have become more intelligent.

CHECKPOINT 11-3

1.   Contrast the process of evolutionary learning with individual learning.

2.   What is the supporting argument for the view that the tendency to meet objectives of the type listed at the lower levels of the affective domain (Krathwohl) is preprogrammed in the human infant?

3.   Suppose it is true that motivation to attend and respond is genetically preprogrammed, at least in an incomplete form, in the human infant. What implication may this have for our use of the rules of reinforcement and punishment with a child from the time of birth?

4.   Describe how positive transfer can be considered to operate in an evolutionary sense.

5.   Speculate on a possible explanation, in terms of gene action, to account for the observation that general plasticity (flexibility) decreases with age.

6.   As you read this chapter, do you try to organize a theoretical perspective for understanding about development? Yes____   No____

The Evolution and Development of Knowing Behavior—Intelligence

The term "intelligence" has traditionally been a paradox for psychologists and educators; everyone "knows" what it is, but no one can define it adequately. Each of us knows generally what is meant when we hear that someone behaved intelligently; we know that what the person did was appropriate for the demands of the event, that he adapted well, that he knew what to do, that he figured out the event and responded correctly, or perhaps even better than we might have expected. However, if we push for a more exact definition of intelligence, even from psychologists and educators, we are not likely to get a precise statement of what intelligence is or what it means.

Questions about the nature of intelligence have been asked for centuries, and they continue to be asked today. Always, they have reflected a variety of views and have been asked for different purposes. Consider, for example, the following questions, long asked about the nature of intelligence. Note that they illustrate clearly the state of our confusion about a proper definition of the term, and that they also illuminate the breadth to which the term has been extended: "From where do general ideas of universally valid concepts derive?" "Is intelligence a fixed disposition transmitted through heredity that largely determines our capacity to behave intelligently? Do we acquire the general knowledge implied in intelligence in the same manner in which we learn any particular skill or facts? Is intelligence mainly a matter of memory?"[16]

GALTON'S VIEW OF INTELLIGENCE

Galton's view of intelligence was . . .   Sir Francis Galton (1822–1911), young cousin of Charles Darwin, was one of the first to formalize a definition of intelligence and to devise tests to measure it, although at about the same time (1872), Darwin was interested in seeing a continuity of evolution for emotions and for intelligence. Galton (1869) believed that intelligence is a result of one's sensory capabilities and that these are inherited. Therefore, he reasoned that if he could measure a person's sensory capabilities, he would have an objective measure of intelligence. Probably a major influence on Galton's belief that intelligence is inherited was his association with Darwin. Darwin's theory of evolution provided a plausible explanation for human intellect if it were defined in terms of sensory capabilities, since apparently these capabilities have survival value for the species and are obviously inherited.

Much of Galton's influence exists today in our attempts to define, nurture, and test human intelligence. His emphasis on the relationship between sensory capabilities and intellect is still seen in much of the current research on cognitive growth.

Galton was not the only person who saw the close, natural association between Darwin's theory of evolution and a theory of intelligence. Piaget also saw it. As a consequence, he has devoted the major part of his life work to building a comprehensive theory of the development of intelligence and to understanding the nature of knowledge from both an evolutionary and an individual-development point of view.

PIAGET'S VIEW OF INTELLIGENCE

Piaget defines intelligence as . . .   Piaget's view of intelligence forms a naturalistic theory in that it considers human intelligence as evolutionary and developmental processes not unlike those evolutionary and developmental processes whereby all living organisms come to "know" or adapt to their environments. His view is "natural" also in that it places the human organism in evolutionary perspective along with the rest of nature. He never removes man from this position as he tries to understand the development of his knowing behavior. In this view, Piaget finds it unnecessary to retreat to superstition or to invest supernatural entities for purposes of explanation. He avoids the age-old dichotomy of mind and body: the view that the mind is a spirit, or an essence, held in a material body. Consequently, Piaget is able to get on with the science of trying to learn how what we call *mind*, or

---

[16] H. G. Furth (1969). Op. cit., p. 3.

knowing behavior, evolves and develops as a natural and necessary part of the biological organization of living things. Searching for "the ghost in the machine" (Koestler, 1967) is a fruitless activity as far as Piaget is concerned, since, as Hebb points out, "The idea of an immaterial mind controlling the body is vitalism, no more, no less; it has no place in science . . . biological science long ago got rid of [it]."[17] Tinbergen, speaking for the view of the ethologist, sounds the same note, saying that " . . . living organisms are only special cases of the physical processes of the environment . . . they do something against it . . . and, there is just no point to vitalism. . . . living organisms are only a very, very special case of physical laws."[18]

To understand Piaget's theory of intelligence as knowing behavior, it is helpful to begin with some ideas that likely are already meaningful to you and that are also basic to his theory. In this way, positive transfer will be facilitated, since the already-familiar ideas provide the necessary structures of knowledge for assimilation of the new information. And in the process, accommodation will occur for you within these structures.

INTELLIGENCE CONSIDERED AS A BIOLOGICAL ORGAN   For Piaget, intelligence is a biological organ with structural and functional characteristics, just as the heart, brain, arms, and so forth are organs with structural and functional characteristics. Its *structural* characteristics can be thought of as the actual sensory or nerve cells and tissues of living organisms. Various structures of knowledge can be pictured in terms of the organizational patterns within sensory and other nerve cells or tissue systems. Hebb's cell assemblies and phase sequences provide an approximate physical model of structures of knowledge among various organisms that have well-defined systems of nervous tissue.

> **Intelligence can be considered an organ since . . .**

The *functional* characteristic of intelligence, considered as an organ, is the regulation of the adaptive action of a biological organism.[19] That is, the function of intelligence, or knowing behavior, is to keep the living organism interacting in dynamic equilibrium with its environment as a biological unit. Thus, as Furth tells us, "just as the organism is a living biological system, the organism's intelligence is also a living organized system."[20] And, in the same way that the total organism develops as a consequence of the interaction of heredity and experience, so also do the organism's *structures* of knowledge and its *functional* knowing behavior (its intelligence) develop as a consequence of adaptive activity. Quite literally, "Intelligence is the organ that structures itself in functioning."[21]

Consideration of intelligence as an organ for developmental and adaptive activity, manifested in the form of knowing behavior, provides a basis for continuity in the evolution and individual development of intelligence. This is an important idea that has relevance for our work as teachers: It places intelligence in perspective as a natural part of the total developing organization of a learner as a biological organism. It takes away the mystery of the "ghost in the machine" and the resulting superstition surrounding the concept. It thus enables us to look for the natural biological and psychological rules that are relevant to the development of knowing behavior. Equally important, such a view seriously questions

[17] D. O. Hebb (1974). What psychology is about, *American Psychologist,* **29**(1), 75.
[18] Hall (1974). Op. cit., p. 69.
[19] H. G. Furth (1969). Op. cit., p. 226.
[20] Ibid., p. 178.
[21] Ibid., p. 232.

the widely held assumption that the molecular and gross structure of the central nervous system, once formed, is essentially stable. It also questions the implication that intelligence, for the most part, is a fixed innate capacity.

KNOWING BEHAVIOR: WHAT INTELLIGENCE IS ABOUT   The ability to establish continuity in the evolution and individual development of knowing behavior greatly simplifies a theory of intelligence because a single set of higher-order rules can then be applied to all organisms. That is, when intelligence is considered as the knowing behavior resulting from, and giving rise to, the adaptive development of all living organisms, intelligence becomes a term that can be applied to all organisms, since even the most primitive living thing does indeed "know" its environment, that is, does respond adaptively to it. Consequently, we do not need different concepts to ref ⁃ to the adaptive, developmental behavior of different organisms. *All organisms are intelligent in this sense.* However, the characteristics of their intelligence—the *ways* in which they "know" their environment, and themselves, in the case of human beings—can be shown to be qualitatively different. Qualitative differences in knowing behavior can also be demonstrated at different periods of time (stages) in the individual development of various organisms, especially human beings.

It should be pointed out here that not all psychologists and educators agree with Piaget's view of intelligence as the development of adaptive knowing behavior. Arthur Jensen (1969), for example, expresses a belief that is quite different in several respects from Piaget's. We will discuss his theories and those of others in Chapter 12. For now, let us look more closely at Piaget's view; first in an evolutionary sense, and then, developmentally, in terms of the stages Piaget outlines for the development of intelligence in human beings.

In the broad view of intelligence presented here we see that it is appropriate to talk of lower forms of animal and even plant life as being *intelligent,* that is, as knowing their environments. Knowing behavior, relative to an environment, means that the animal or plant "acts in an adaptive, functional fashion and that environmental and social information is utilized with coordinated actions."[22]

A blade of grass is intelligent in the sense that . . .   Take, for example, a blade of grass. It "knows" its environment, chiefly with structures of knowledge preprogrammed through its evolutionary history, and responds adaptively in ways that are typical and characteristic for grass. If environmental conditions vary somewhat, e.g., having less water, more shade, or cooler temperature, this new information is assimilated by the existing structures of knowledge present within the plant. The consequence is that the structures undergo modification to accommodate the new environmental information. A new, more generally inclusive level of equilibration between the demands of the environment and the plant's structures of knowledge results from such interaction. If, however, the environmental conditions vary too drastically, e.g., if total darkness or freezing weather occurs, the present structures of knowledge will not be able to accommodate sufficiently to assimilate the new information. Developmental adaptation will not occur, that is, there will be no change in the structures of knowledge whereby the plant better knows its environment. If the changes in the environment are too drastic in any of the seven critical life processes we listed in an earlier section, the plant ceases to "know," i.e., to act intelligently toward its environment. The ultimate result is death.

---

[22] Ibid., p. 185.

Let us take another example, this time an animal, and draw some generalizations about the quality of knowing behavior (intelligence) of lower organisms. A dog can be said to "know" its environment, but obviously its ways of "knowing" it are not entirely the same as the ways in which a blade of grass or a human being knows its environment. The differences are both quantitative and qualitative, yet we can appropriately conclude that grass, dogs, and human beings are all intelligent. They "know" their environments.

Suppose environmental conditions vary somewhat for a given dog. Its present structures of knowledge accommodate to the new information and assimilate it. Perhaps the new information is a type of food never encountered before. Confronted with this change in stimulus, if the dog's present structures of knowledge relative to food are sufficiently flexible to generalize to the new food stimulus, it will be assimilated. The result is that the now-present structures of knowledge relative to food represent a higher (more generally inclusive) level of equilibration between them and the demands of the environment. Adaptive development has occurred and the dog now knows its environment "better" than it did before: very simply, the dog has become more intelligent.

If, on the other hand, the new environmental stimulus, e.g., a totally new tasting or smelling type of food, were so different that it could not be assimilated by existing structures of knowledge, adaptive development would not occur, since there would be no change in the level of knowing behavior of the dog. That is, its intelligence would remain unchanged as a consequence of the experience.

EVOLUTIONARY DIFFERENCES IN THE QUALITY AND QUANTITY OF INTELLIGENCE
You will notice that in both examples the same basic invariant mechanisms of developmental adaptation—assimilation, equilibration, and accommodation—were operating. There are some obvious and important differences, however, in the quality of knowing behavior of grass, dogs, and of course, people.

Among lower organisms, the structures of knowledge through which environments are "known" are more rigidly and more completely preprogrammed, more environment-resistant than they are among higher organisms. At the lowest levels of the plant and animal kingdom, the environment-resistant structures of knowledge are so rigidly built into the biological system that hardly any variability is left for elaboration as a function of experience. This does not mean, however, that the knowing behavior is necessarily manifested in relatively uncomplicated behavior patterns, such as simple reflexes, as it tends to be in most plants. Indeed, the behaviors may be quite complex. Take, for example, the hierarchical communication and social patterns found in colonies of ants. What environment-resistant means in this extreme form is that experience does not result in modification of knowing behavior, or that little or no learning occurs. The built-in adaptive mechanisms appear in nearly complete form at birth and change very little over time. Thus, once a particular sequence of responses is set in motion by some eliciting or releasing stimulus, the entire behavioral pattern is reeled off from beginning to end, with little hesitation or variation over trials regardless of the consequences that are obtained. This represents, in the case of lower social animals such as ants and bees, a high level of evolutionary learning (change) but little or no opportunity for individual development (learning).

Evolutionary learning means . . .

When we examine more closely the behavior of animals higher on the evolutionary scale, e.g., birds, dogs, and primates, we find a gradual change in both the quality and the quantity of intelligence, or of knowing behavior. We also

The intelligence of lower forms of life is characterized by . . .

note a gradual lengthening in the period of time required to achieve the adult form of the species. The lengthy periods of infancy and childhood among primates is itself a product of evolutionary learning that reflects this trend of gradual change in the quality and quantity of knowing behavior. The most notable changes in quality of knowing behavior are away from specific, or rigid, reflexlike reactions that are tied closely to meeting immediate physiological needs and toward more flexible, exploratory (trial-and-error) behavior that provides new information or knowledge about the environment. The function served by an extended period of infancy and childhood is simply to provide the time required to explore and to become knowledgeable about a complex environment. When great flexibility (plasticity) in adaptation is made available through a vast abundance of genetic potential, and when genetic preprogramming is relatively low and incompletely prescribed, as it apparently is in the human species, a slow period of development can be permitted without endangering the individual. The result is great variability among individuals.

DEVELOPMENTAL DIFFERENCES IN THE QUALITY AND QUANTITY OF INTELLIGENCE
Piaget maintains that a *developmental* sequence, surprisingly similar to the sequence of *evolutionary* development discussed earlier, in the quality as well as the quantity of knowing behavior can be shown to occur in children. He argues that the ways in which a child knows its environment change qualitatively as well as quantitatively as a function of its adaptive interaction with its environment over time. He maintains further that the same general, invariant processes of developmental adaptation—assimilation, equilibration, and accommodation—that are operative in the lowest of living biological organizations are also operative in the intellectual development of the child. In other words, Piaget believes that the individual development of intelligence in children is subject to the same broad rules of developmental adaptation to which all living organisms are subject.

From thousands of observations of children's adaptive behavior, he has formulated what he believes to be an invariant sequence of steps or stages in the development of intelligence in children. At the same time, Piaget says, the rate at which children progress through the stages varies as a function of many factors, such as culture, physical maturation, and opportunity for social interaction. Development takes time and experience, and the specific amount necessary for any given individual to progress through a particular stage cannot be precisely known.

Each stage is characterized by intelligence that is qualitatively different from, but includes, elements of the behavior of the stage preceding it. In this sense, the stages are hierarchical, since the structures of knowledge characteristic of each successive stage are subsumed by, and incorporated in, a higher synthesis of knowing behavior in the following stage. Piaget (Hall, 1973) explains it this way: "As soon as each stage is reached, it offers new possibilities to the child. There are no static stages as such. Each is the fulfillment of something begun in the preceding one, and the beginning of something that will lead on to the next."[23]

Piaget's two major types of human intelligence are . . .

Broadly speaking, Piaget's stages reflect two major types of structures of knowledge, manifested as adaptive, knowing behavior or intelligence in the

---

[23] Hall, E. (1973). A conversation with Jean Piaget and Barbel Inhelder, *Psychology Today*, **3** (12), 25.

developing child. The first type he calls *sensory-motor* or *practical* intelligence. It characterizes the externally oriented intellectual activity of the child from birth to around one and one-half to two years of age. The second type Piaget names *operational* intelligence to designate intellectual activity that has not only an external but also an internal function. That is, knowing behavior during the operational stage means more than merely *reacting* to external things or events. It means developing toward what can be called internalization, or *knowing about* things or events; knowing that they are distinct from the knower; and knowing that one knows. This stage typically begins with *preoperational* intelligence at around two years of age, progresses to *concrete operational* intelligence at age six or seven, and becomes *formal operational* by about eleven or twelve.

PIAGET'S STAGE OF SENSORY-MOTOR INTELLIGENCE

At birth the child's knowledge of his environment is pretty well limited to incomplete, preprogrammed mechanisms of physiological adaptation. The newborn baby's seemingly sparse knowledge about his environment must be understood, however, relative to his fantastic and flexible potential for adaptive development made possible by (1) his vast surplus of genetic material, and (2) by the long period of time from birth to adulthood, provided by his evolutionary history, in which gene-environment interaction will occur. Never again in his life will the child possess the same degree of plasticity or flexibility made possible through gene action as he does in infancy, since, as is well-known, plasticity decreases with age.

Some preprogrammed genetic mechanisms in the human infant that function proactively to give rise to behaviors, such as sucking, grasping, eye movements, crying, listening, withdrawal from aversive stimuli, and selecting certain stimuli to respond to, begin to be elaborated by environmental experience within a very few days. Others, e.g., those that control the loss of baby teeth and the development of secondary sex characteristics, remain essentially environment-resistant for several years. Then, when physiological conditions are appropriate, the preprogrammed mechanisms complete their functions and at the same time give up part of their control to certain, and usually specific, environmental stimuli.

There is evidence that certain sensitive periods crucial to later development occur during the sensory-motor stage. Two of these periods have apparent relevance for education, especially for learning language and learning to read.

Human infants are able to perceive visual patterns at birth. However, the eyes gradually lose this ability if they are not stimulated by patterned light. Before the age of three months, the human infant is able to make and remember discriminations among complex visual patterns. Furthermore, as Fantz (1965) and others have shown, infants of three months show a built-in preference for complex patterns.

Evidence such as this suggests that a sensitive period for form perception occurs during the first three months of life. You will recall, from our earlier discussion about the characteristics of sensitive periods, the implication that during this period of time, gene action is unusually sensitive to the effects of certain naturally selected environmental stimuli, in this case visual stimulation. The result of visual stimulation during this period for form perception is believed to be a facilitation of further perceptual-cognitive development, such as that necessary for learning to read.

A second sensitive period that has obvious implications for education, especially for learning to read, is believed to begin at about two years of age and extend to about four (McNeill, 1966; Chukovsky, 1966; Chomsky, 1965, 1966; Chall, 1967). During this period, incomplete, preprogrammed genetic mechanisms relative to language acquisition (called LAD—language acquisition device—by Chomsky) appear to be especially sensitive to the sounds of speech, the very environmental stimuli apparently necessary for language development to occur. This sensitivity does not mean that this is the *only* period of time during which language can be learned. Rather, it implies that the very complex patterns and rules of language are apparently less difficult to acquire during the sensitive period than at times either earlier or later.

In Piaget's terms, the elaboration of these incomplete, preprogrammed mechanisms for form perception and language acquisition as a consequence of interaction with the environment is simply another example that illustrates the dynamic quality of equilibration that occurs when existing structures of knowledge encounter and assimilate new information, and, as a result of the accommodation, adaptively develop to a higher level of knowing, or of intelligence.

The child at birth starts with a viewpoint that is completely egocentric, or self-centered; only with social experience, gained from constantly exploring his environment, will he be able to know that there are other points of view. Besides being self-centered, the infant in the sensory-motor stage is also object-oriented. In fact, it is not until near the end of this stage that the child knows objects exist independent of his own actions on them, that they are not a part of him, and that objects have permanence, that is, continue to exist even when the infant cannot see them. Piaget believes that objects are a crucial part of a child's early environment because it is from the child's sensory and motor interactions with the objects in the environment, relative to space, time, and causality, that the child begins to construct—not simply absorb—his own unique knowledge of the world. Knowing behavior, or intelligence, for Piaget, begins its construction with *physical action;* first with actions completely body-centered, then later, with actions that include external space independent from one's own body.

Sensory-motor intelligence is characterized by . . .

Whereas, early in the sensory-motor stage, the infant's behavior does not evince knowledge of cause and effect relationships, by the end of this stage he clearly shows that he knows that his actions have consequences. Piaget refers to this as logic of action; it is the beginning of thinking behavior. The child knows, for example, that shaking a rattle causes an interesting sound and that removing the wrapper from a candy exposes a sweet-tasting treat. Experimenting with things gives him practical understanding of their properties. But as Ginsburg and Opper (1969) point out, all these abilities are concrete and limited to objects immediately present. In the sensory-motor stage, the child is able to organize his reality in terms of *general* (knowing) schemes of actions, including the organization of space, time, causality, and most important, of permanent objects, among which is found the self. Yet, all this development of knowledge is on a practical plane; it concerns, in the final analysis, external actions only.[24]

---

[24] H. G. Furth (1970). *Piaget for Teachers.* Englewood Cliffs, N.J.: Prentice-Hall, p. 51.

PIAGET'S STAGES OF
OPERATIONAL INTELLIGENCE

Piaget observes that at about the second year of age, intelligence is becoming more interiorized. Knowing that has been associated almost exclusively with sensory-motor activity now is slowly elaborated into structures of knowledge and knowing behavior that Piaget calls *operations*. He refers generally to this type of knowing behavior as *operational intelligence*.

Typically, the stage of operational intelligence includes the sequence of three subtypes of knowing behavior mentioned earlier: (1) *preoperational intelligence*, (2) *concrete operational intelligence*, and (3) *formal operational intelligence*.

Three types of operational intelligence are . . .

THE STAGE OF PREOPERATIONAL INTELLIGENCE   From about two years of age until about six or seven, the child works through a lengthy transition period of development. During this period the major accomplishment is one of gradual accommodation of sensory-motor structures of knowledge that are characterized by *external actions* toward structures of knowledge that are characterized by *internal actions* or thought.

Piaget sees the knowing behavior of the child in the preoperational stage of development as primarily imitative. Through imitation, the child develops the ability to symbolize; that is, to make words or objects stand for or represent something else that need not be physically present. The child can now recall past experiences with objects. He acts like objects, pretends to be them, talks about them, recalls them, and imitates them mentally. The meaning of these actions derives from their being assimilated into schemes of knowing already available from earlier experiences of a concrete, active nature. Sometimes, however, these schemes are too primitive or inappropriate for the new information being assimilated. The results are often humorous, for example, the things children in this stage believe to be true. We saw some of these in Chapter 5: "Our father with Art in Heaven, Harold be thy name."

Characteristic of preoperational intelligence is intuitive thought; that is, reasoning is dominated by perception that usually is able to take account of only one aspect at a time of a situation or event. For example, if you first place four or five objects, say checkers, close together in a row in front of a preoperational child, she will say that there are *more* checkers in the row if you now space them farther apart in the row. She is unable to separate perception from reason: the row looks longer, although it still has the same number of checkers, just spread farther apart.

Another aspect of the knowing behavior of children in the preoperational stage is that thought activity is *irreversible*. For example, pushing the checkers back to their original positions does not help the child realize the error of her judgment since, at this stage of development, she is not able to reverse the thought process. For the child, the second action has nothing logically to do with the first.

Preoperational intelligence is characterized by . . .

Deductive reasoning (from the general to the specific) is not possible for the child with only preoperational intelligence since he does not yet know about concepts of class membership. He cannot see, for example, "All dogs have four legs; my pet is a dog; therefore, he has four legs." By the same rule, neither is inductive reasoning (specific to general) possible at this stage. Rather, the child reasons from the specific to the specific, or "transductively," as Piaget calls it "If my dog likes to swim, then your dog must also like to swim."

THE STAGE OF CONCRETE-OPERATIONAL INTELLIGENCE   So far, up until about age six or seven years, the child's knowing behavior has been essentially *prelogical*. Now, his structures of knowledge have achieved a degree of coordinated organization that makes properly logical thought possible. However, his organization of underlying structures (or more correctly, *systems*, at this point of development) is limited in its applicability to objects and events that the child considers real or concrete.

Concrete-operational intelligence is characterized by . . .

The checker-type problem no longer causes difficulty for children who have acquired concrete-operational intelligence. They perform reversible operations (logical thought processes) even when the concrete objects or events are not present.

Ordinarily it takes five or six years for equilibration to be attained within the child's systems of concrete operations. Gradually, and as a function of the interaction between experience and gene action, earlier structures of knowing become integrated into later ones. In Chapter 6 we saw another way of looking at this process: the way in which concepts increase in meaningfulness. With each new experience, accommodation of present structures of knowledge occurs until, at about eleven or twelve years of age, a qualitatively different type of knowing behavior becomes possible. Piaget calls this type of intelligence *formal operational*.

THE STAGE OF FORMAL-OPERATIONAL INTELLIGENCE   Beginning at about the eleventh year and extending onward throughout adult life is the type of intelligence characterized by formal or abstract thinking actions (operations). Attainment of this type of intelligence enables a person to reason by hypothesis, that is, to suppose that an object or event exists or occurs and then to adopt propositions about the object or event and to follow the logic, e.g., "If we suppose that all matter is made of atoms, then. . . ." In formal operational thought, the object of thought is no longer *outside* the thinking scheme as it is in earlier thought; it is now *within* the thinking scheme itself, and can even be a product of thinking. That is, the object or event of thought need not exist; it can be made up or imagined. Children who have not yet developed formal operational intelligence cannot go beyond trying to decide whether the objects or events are indeed real, or whether the original proposition about them is true.

Formal-operational intelligence is characterized by . . .

A most significant feature of formal operational intelligence is its higher degree of reversibility as compared with concrete operational intelligence. Thought in this stage of development can be interrupted, backed up, redone, twisted, and turned to include or exclude new information, even of a hypothetical nature, or temporarily and purposely set aside. Inhelder (1962) sums up the significance of formal operational intelligence by saying that the new operational abilities formed during this period are the abilities that open up unlimited possibilities for the youth to participate constructively in the development of scientific knowledge. She adds that this is so, provided his environment offers him suitable practice and a favorable intellectual atmosphere. Hunt (1961) underscores the dependence of a developing intelligence upon the interaction of heredity and environment when he reminds us that most, if not all, knowing structures and biochemical reactions underlying intelligence are modifiable through experience. He helps us understand, too, the vast potential that intelligence can realize in the human adult by pointing to the fact that the possibilities for different environmental experiences are virtually infinite. Thus, we see that knowing behavior reaches its evolutionary and individual, developmental high point in what we refer to as the intelligence typical of the adult human being.

CHECKPOINT 11-4

1. Describe how the concept *positive transfer* can be applied to Piaget's stages of intellectual development.

2. Show how the concepts *meaningful* and *rote learning* can be related to the processes of assimilation and accommodation.

3. *Readiness* is a concept we have discussed relative to Gagné's types of learning. Explain how the concept can be defined in terms of Piaget's stages of intellectual development.

4. Speculate on which of Gagné's types of learning a child would probably be capable of at each of Piaget's stages of intelligence.

5. Compare and contrast the characteristics of the intelligence of a newborn child with those of a newly hatched fish; do the same for the human adult and adult fish.

6. Do you experience a sense of wanting to learn about the bases for individual differences? Yes_____ No_____

PIAGET AND THE VIEWS OF OTHERS

Now that we have learned about Piaget's widely inclusive biological view of development and have learned some of the rules about how genes and the environment interact to do their work, let us look at the ideas of others who have contributed to our understanding of this broad topic. First, we will discuss the views of persons who have been interested in various aspects of development, such as moral, social, personal, and physical development. Then we will look briefly at the ideas about learning and teaching of some of the persons we met in earlier chapters to see how they can be combined with those of Piaget and others to provide support for those rules of development that have implications for instruction.

The Views of Other Developmentalists

We have said that development generally means change in living things over time and that change results from the ongoing interaction between living biological organisms and the varying conditions of their environments. During the lifetime of any living thing, there is a constant tendency or motivation toward balance or equilibrium within the organizational structures of the organism and with the requirements of the environment so that adaptation occurs. Generally, developmental adaptation proceeds from general to specific, simple to complex, and external-concrete to internal-abstract.

We have learned how these rules have been interpreted in Piaget's theory of intellectual development. Now let us see how they have been interpreted relative to other subtypes of human development.

KOHLBERG ON MORAL DEVELOPMENT

Moral development is defined as . . .

Moral development is closely related to the development of self-management in the sense that how persons manage their own behavior is associated with their personal values, beliefs, and standards. Consequently, if teachers have the goal of learner self-management, they also have the goal of teaching for moral development. Most teachers accept this responsibility with mixed feelings, since it is not always clear just what values should be taught and how they are learned.

Historically, moral education has proceeded from the training of virtues, e.g., temperance, pride, honesty, justice, and loyalty, during the time of Aristotle to character education in the 1920s and 1930s. At about that time, the studies of Hartshorne and May (1928) cast serious doubt on the effectiveness of educational and religious instructional programs on moral conduct. Their findings suggested that moral conduct is best thought of as relative to the characteristics of specific situations rather than to absolute character traits. That is, people behave honestly in some situations but not so honestly in others; they may say they will not cheat, but nevertheless go ahead and do so. The observation that moral behavior tends to differ among people and also within each person at different times and under different circumstances raises the question of how moral behavior develops.

Piaget's monograph *The Moral Judgment of the Child* (1932) has been the major stimulus for research in this field. More recently, Lawrence Kohlberg (1966, 1971) has extended the three-stage theory of Piaget to three levels and six stages that form an invariant sequence of moral development. In the same sense that Piaget claims all persons move through an invariant sequence of stages in intellectual development, Kohlberg claims that all persons, regardless of social or cultural background, pass through stages of moral development. This does not mean that all people necessarily reach the highest stage, but rather, that progression from stage to stage always occurs in a prescribed order. Rate and extent of movement through the progressively inclusive stages is seen to be a function of the quality of each person's social experience with the environment, not of the cultural or social *specifics* of it. Kohlberg's data suggest that most people do not progress beyond stages III or IV.

Kohlberg's theory of moral development suggests . . .

Because of the close association with Piaget's theory of intellectual development, Kohlberg's theory is mostly about the development of moral *thought* or *judgment* rather than moral *behavior* generally, although there is some evidence to suggest the two are related.

The characteristics of Kohlberg's levels and stages of moral development are summarized briefly and compared with Piaget's stages of intellectual development in Table 11–1.

To determine a learner's level of moral judgment, Kohlberg asks him to respond to a series of situation dilemmas in terms of what he believes should be done, and why he feels that it is the right thing to do. The way in which the person responds, relative to the characteristics of Kohlberg's six stages, determines his level of moral judgment.

TABLE 11-1 Kohlberg's stages of moral development

PIAGET (INTELLECTUAL DEVELOPMENT)		KOHLBERG (MORAL DEVELOPMENT)	
Age	Stage	Age	Stage
0 to 2 years	Sensorimotor (Learning tied to immediate experience; external actions on physical things and events; behavior is egocentric.)	0 to 9 years	Preconventional (Moral values derive from external physical things or events.) Stage I. Child responds to labels of right or wrong, good or bad, in deference to superior power or authority figure. Stage II. Child responds to satisfy his own and occasionally other's needs; has sense of fairness and equal sharing, but always because one good or bad deed deserves another; realizes each person has a view of right or wrong.
2 to 7 years	Preoperational (Use of language becomes important; learner no longer bound to an immediate sensory environment; intuitive, imitative learning.)		
7 to 11 years	Concrete-operational (Thought is concrete and literal; person understands functional relationships; reasons logically and reversibly.)	9 to 15 years	Conventional (Moral values derive from doing things that are conventionally good or right for the majority or are expected by others.) Stage III. Person tries to please and help others; conforms to stereotypical images; judges by intent of others. Stage IV. Person does "one's duty"; shows respect for authority and maintains the social order, or what is best for society, for its own sake.
11 years on	Formal-operational (Thought is logical, rational, and abstract; person can reason on the basis of hypothetical statements.)	16 years on	Postconventional (Moral values derive from universal principles and from internal decisions of conscience.) Stage V. Person recognizes that rules or expectations contain an arbitrary element, usually for the sake of agreement; respects right or will of others for the good of the whole society but recognizes the possibility of changing rules or contracts. Stage VI. Person is guided by his own conscience, mutual trust and respect, relative to broadly general and logically ethical principles of justice, reciprocity, equality, and human dignity.

The complexity and present lack of standardized administration and scoring procedures, however, make Kohlberg's measurements device somewhat unreliable, especially for nonspecialists like classroom teachers (Kurtiness and Grief, 1974).

Three implications of Kohlberg's theory for instruction are . . .

There are several implications for education in Kohlberg's theory of moral development. First, moral character apparently does not just happen; it develops in sequential fashion. Next, its growth seems to parallel the development of intelligence. This is important for us to be aware of, since it implies that intellectual development is prerequisite to the development of moral thought. In a practical sense, this means, for example, that teaching for moral judgment typical of stage V or VI prior to a learner's reaching the stage of formal-operational thought would likely result in failure. Also, discussing moral dilemmas before learners reach public school age makes little sense. However, there is some evidence that people prefer moral judgment one stage beyond their present level of development.

Kohlberg's theory suggests that teachers should . . .

Therefore, as teachers, we would try to organize instruction so that our learners would experience situations requiring moral judgment slightly above their present stage, but not greatly beyond it.

Another implication of Kohlberg's theory for education is that moral development is determined by interaction between people; it is not automatic. This means that learners and teachers need to participate actively in experiences designed for practice in arriving at moral judgments. The question of importance for teachers is: "What should the nature of the practice be?"

Several possibilities are open, some of which you learned about in earlier chapters. Since actual participation in a variety of social roles seems to be the type of practice Kohlberg finds helpful for moral growth, simulations and games (Chapter 9) should be highly appropriate techniques to use. You will recall that one of their positive features is their transfer value (theory of common components and generalization of principles). Also, if you choose to use simulations, remember Coleman's finding that follow-up discussions are an extremely helpful part of the total experience.

Role playing and class discussions centered on real or simulated social issues, questions, or problems are also effective techniques. The important idea is to cause your learners to become involved, to practice. This means that, as teachers, we need to be provocative and stimulating, or, as Piaget likes to think of this type of teacher action, to be challenging and confronting rather than restrictive, punitive, and moralizing.

FREUD AND ERIKSON
ON PERSONAL-SOCIAL DEVELOPMENT

The processes of learning about self and society's rules are known as *socialization,* and the developmental sequence in which the learning takes place is what

Personal-social development means . . .

we call *personal-social development.* Since none of these rules is known at birth, they must be learned as a consequence of the experiences of living through time.

To understand about personal-social development, we must know about people as personal and social beings and about the nature of the primary tasks that have to be met at various stages in our lives. In a personal and social sense, we need to understand how people change from highly dependent, helpless, and relatively simple and self-centered beings at birth to extremely complex, autonomous, and helpful adults.

Until Freud began his study of neurotic behavior, personal and social development was believed to start at about the age of entry into school, around six or seven years old. The early years were not taken seriously, since learning of any consequence would not occur until later. Children were frequently regarded as "cute playthings" or often treated cruelly as mindless beings in a period of waiting to begin learning. Freud, in his search for causes of neurotic behavior of adults, was struck with how frequently problems of adjustment in adulthood had their roots in the experiences of early childhood.

From his observations, Freud formulated the theory that each person goes through a sequence of personal-emotional stages during childhood and that the quality of each child's personal-social interactions with his environment determines in large measure the adult personality.

You will recall from our discussion in Chapter 2 that Freud postulated the existence of an inborn driving force that enables a person to respond emotionally. In his theory, this force, called the *id,* is regulated by logical and moral structures, the *ego* and *superego.* In his view, it is during the stages of childhood that the balance of these forces is, or is not, established, according to the quality of our experiences. Once the pattern of forces is established, the mold is pretty well set for our behavior on through adulthood. That is, our personal growth is over, since our personality structures are set.

Erik Erikson (1902–), one of Freud's students, expanded Freud's idea of personal-social stages in childhood to include a sequence of stages covering the entire life cycle. In his theory, Erikson tried to illustrate (1) the importance of each of his eight stages of the interaction between the person, present environmental conditions, and those in the past; and (2) the continuation of personality development throughout life.

Each of Erikson's stages is identified by the positive and negative forces surrounding a major developmental task in the form of a social conflict to be resolved at that time. Each of Erikson's stages are described briefly, along with those of Freud, in Table 11-2.

With Erikson we see great importance given to the interaction between the ego and the demand characteristics of the society in which a person lives. Development proceeds in predetermined societal stages at a rate that reflects the person's readiness to face an ever-widening social environment. In this sense, Erikson's stages are hierarchical and cumulative in nature, and readiness to meet the major developmental task of the next stage means successful resolution of the major conflicts of the preceding stages. The specific ways in which a person may resolve the demands of each stage are largely a function of the particular culture of which he is a member.

Erikson's theory stresses the creative and adaptive potential of each individual toward positive growth. Whereas Freud's theory pretty well closes the door on personal-social development by the end of childhood, Erikson is more optimistic in his belief that we are constantly in the developmental process of becoming. Furthermore, Erikson believes that favorable experiences at advanced stages can overcome the ill effects of unfortunate experiences at earlier stages.

As teachers, it is important for us to note the significance Erikson gives to *play* as a developmental, social tool. For Erikson, play, in all cultures, represents a comparatively safe technique for dealing initially with, and thus learning about, reality situations demanded by the next developmental stage. This point has rather general and direct implications for us in helping our learners success-

---

The statement "Freud discovered childhood" can be interpreted to mean . . .

In Freud's theory, personal development essentially ends in childhood, since . . .

The theories of Freud and Erikson are alike in that . . .

Erikson's eight stages of development are . . .

The theories of Freud and Erikson differ in that . . .

TABLE 11-2   The developmental stages of Freud and Erikson

AGES	FREUD'S STAGES	ERIKSON'S STAGES
0 to 1 year	*Oral Stage.* Mouth provides earliest and most satisfying sensual contact with outside world. Fixation at this stage may result in psychotic symptoms.	*Trust versus Mistrust.* Consistency, continuity, genuine regard, and sameness of experience lead to a view of the world as safe and dependable. Inadequate care or inconsistent or negative treatment leads to fear and suspicion.
2 to 3 years	*Anal Stage.* Sensual sensitivities derive from anal and urethral areas. Unfortunate experiences causing fixation at the anal stage may lead to neuroses.	*Autonomy versus Doubt.* Encouragement to try to do what he can, at own pace, and in own way leads to autonomy. If too many things done for him, if others too critical or impatient, child may doubt his own ability.
3 to 5 years	*Phallic Stage.* Sensual satisfaction derives from manipulation of and attention to the genital regions. The Oedipus complex emerges in which parent of opposite sex becomes object of sensual satisfaction. Unfortunate experiences causing fixation at this stage may lead to neuroses or inappropriate sex roles.	*Initiative versus Guilt.* If given freedom to initiate activities and careful attention to his questions, the child moves toward self-initiative. If given rigid, senseless restrictions and a sense of being a nuisance, the child will feel guilty for self-initiative.
6 to 11 years	*Latent Stage.* Sexual urges reduced; Oedipus complex resolved by identification with parent of opposite sex.	*Industry versus Inferiority.* If given recognition for the things he produces, the child develops a sense of industry. If given criticism or derision for his efforts, inferiority results.
11 to 14 years	*Pubertal Stage.* Instinctual forces move individual toward choice of love object, usually a member of opposite sex; tenderness and outgoingness.	
12 to 18 years		*Identity versus Role Confusion.* If the youth finds continuity or sameness in his personality, especially in the eyes of others, in various situations, e.g., work and leisure, then identity develops; he knows who he is. If the youth finds instability or discontinuity in his perceptions of himself in various aspects of life, role confusion results.
Young adulthood		*Intimacy versus Isolation.* Selection of a mate and the establishment of an occupational pattern lead the young adult to intimacy. Failure in either task leads to a sense of isolation from what life and society are about.

Table 11-2 (continued)

AGES	FREUD'S STAGES	ERIKSON'S STAGES
Middle age		*Generativity versus Self-Absorption.* The adult who is able to provide the growth potential for the next generation feels a sense of generativity. If the adult is unable to do so, he feels a sense of self-absorption.
Old age		*Integrity versus Despair.* If one is able to accept that his life was as it had to be, a sense of integrity results. Despair results from a view in retrospect that life was somehow a failure.

fully meet and resolve the potentially difficult social conflicts of various stages. Role playing and simulation games, for example, should prove to be highly useful instructional strategies with positive transfer value.

Other implications for instruction are suggested by the characteristics of each stage. Analysis of Table 11-2 tells us that through our instructional strategies, for example, we need consistently to convey a genuine positive regard for the learner as being capable and important; we need to provide learners opportunity and encouragement to experiment, to give things a try in their own way and in their own time; to listen attentively and patiently without being overly judgmental; to encourage and reinforce physical activity and production; and to react with open and honest consistency toward young people in the great variety of situations in which they find themselves. You will note the parallel between these implications for instruction and those that derive from other essentially humanistic views of learning, for example, those of Maslow and Rogers.

Implications for instruction from Erikson's theory are . . .

AGES AND STAGES IN PHYSICAL AND BEHAVIORAL DEVELOPMENT

One of the first persons to argue for the idea that growth and development occur in an unvarying sequence was Arnold Gesell, founder of the world-famous Gesell Institute of Child Development at Yale University during the 1930s. He believed that the growth stages in a child's life are major periods of change that occur mostly as a result of natural maturation or the unfolding of four primary types of largely predetermined characteristics: physical-motor, language, adaptive, and personal-social.

Although Gesell contended that these characteristics unfold in unvarying sequences for *all* children, he also maintained that the rate of maturation is unique for *each* person and dependent chiefly on biological preprogramming. Consequently, child development was seen to be largely a matter of internal changes initiated from within. The proper environment for such changes is one of good physical care and a generally loving atmosphere, with parents and teachers

A maturational view of development stresses . . .

adopting a helping role not entirely different from that of a well-intended midwife: "Do not guide or direct, just help things along as they begin to happen; let Nature take its course in its own good time." In this view, to systematically attempt to teach the child is believed not only undesirable but also potentially dangerous, since the child may not be maturationally "ready" for whatever you may be trying to teach. Depending on the age of the child, the result of such a mismatch may be any of the negative outcomes described by Erikson for his eight stages of the life cycle.

Developmental charts are derived from . . .   The logical implication of a strongly maturational view of growth and development is the construction of tables or charts that describe the physical and behavioral characteristics typical of the "average" child at various ages or stages. This was the main thrust of the work of Gesell and his colleagues. They systematically observed children longitudinally—from one age to the next—and recorded their physical and behavioral characteristics at each age. In this way, detailed "developmental maps" were produced that could be used as standards against which parents and teachers could compare their own children's developmental stage and rate. You will note the parallel of Gesell's approach to development with that of Piaget for intellectual development.

Here are some of the kinds of information of special interest to teachers that the Gesell type of maps shows for physical, social, and emotional development.

PHYSICAL   At four to six years of age, children are very active. Large muscles are being used mostly; boys are bigger but girls are more mature; all need to balance periods of vigorous activity with periods of rest. At ages six to ten, growth is slow and steady, with increases in height of 2 or 3 inches and 3 to 6 pounds each year; the brain has reached 90 percent of its weight, but the eyes are still immature and many children are farsighted; the children show lots of activity, e.g., running, jumping, climbing; they are learning skills of organized games and beginning to gain control of the fine muscles. At ages ten to twelve, there is a growth spurt and puberty occurs in a few girls; physical maturity differs widely at this stage; physical prowess and athletic skill especially for boys is important now; fine-muscle control is developing rapidly; there is poor posture. At ages twelve and thirteen (preadolescence), there is a brief slowdown of growth; many girls develop primary secondary sex characteristics, e.g., breasts, widening hips, a more feminine figure, menstruation. At ages thirteen to sixteen, there is another growth spurt and puberty for most persons; rapid lengthening of arms, legs, and trunk give gangly, awkward appearance and clumsy movements; there is limited physical endurance. Between sixteen and eighteen, most attain adult height; boys finally catch up to girls in physical maturity.

SOCIAL   At ages four to six years, group activity is loosely and flexibly organized. There is little sex-role influence, much make-believe play, lots of talk, and many questions asked. From six to ten years of age, friendships endure longer; the small group is important; children begin to compete. At ages ten to twelve, the small group or "gang" becomes extremely important; sex-role differences become pronounced. At ages twelve and thirteen, acceptance is sought among peers; peer codes, standards, and values become demanding of conformity. At ages thirteen to sixteen, girls are more advanced; the peer group is strong; heterosexual relationships are being formed; freedom from parents and teachers is sought; privacy becomes important; quarrels are frequent and often intense. At ages sixteen to eighteen, the peer group is dominant, the "crowd" takes over; some are becoming independent of the group, parents, and family; there is increasing concern about the opposite sex; concern with the future is growing.

EMOTIONAL At four to six years of age, there is wide and frequent emotional expression of pleasure, anger, fear, and jealousy. From ages six to ten, children become increasingly sensitive to praise, criticism, shame, and ridicule; they try to please others, especially adults. Between ages ten and twelve, character or personality traits begin to show; frustration emerges as peer and adult codes, values, and standards begin to conflict. At ages twelve and thirteen, personality traits continue to emerge and solidify; moodiness is frequent; arguments with parents are frequent and often intense. At ages thirteen to sixteen, behavior is often unpredictable, temperamental, "illogical"; youth is often highly critical and intolerant of adults; there is frequent anxiety about acceptance of opinions by peers. At age sixteen to eighteen, young people often revolt against parents, school, or "the establishment"; they are moody, anxious, and sometimes short-tempered; they are often confused and worried about what the future holds for them.

For more complete descriptions of physical and behavioral characteristics at various ages and stages, you might refer to Britton and Winans (1958), Ilg and Ames (1955), Jenkins, Schacter, and Bauer (1966), Mussen, Conger, and Kagan (1969), or Stone and Church (1972).

Developmental maps can be helpful to parents and teachers in determining whether a child exhibits physical and behavioral characteristics in advance of or behind "typical" children. For example, they have proved very useful in identifying children who are retarded. Such maps, however, have few suggestions for remedial action other than simply to "wait for something better to happen naturally, or just to accept whatever the child does since that is the nature of things and if you will only be patient, in due time he will outgrow the unfortunate stage."

Developmental maps are potentially useful for . . .

The obvious weakness of a strongly maturational view of development is that it provides little room for, or direction in, how to manage a child's learning. The experiential component of development is thus largely left to intuition or chance. You will note that at this point, the parallel with Piaget's more inclusive theory of development breaks down, since Piaget's view places tremendous importance on experience.

Two further notes of caution are in order regarding the possible misuse of Gesell-type developmental maps. The first relates to the rule from Chapter 2 on using descriptive terms as explanations. We must remember that the words we use to characterize the physical appearance and behavior of persons at various stages of development are only descriptive words and not explanations of why they appear and behave as they do at that age. That is, we must be wary of the circular reasoning that concludes, for example, that an eleven-year-old child insists on doing whatever her friends do *because* she is in the preadolescent stage of development. The explanation for her behavior is not to be found in the general description of preadolescence but, instead, in the specific operation of the rules of reinforcement and punishment that occurs between the girl and her peers, parents, school, and community.

The second note of caution about the possible misuse of developmental tables has to do with the words "should" and "expectancy." The physical and behavioral characteristics listed by age and stage on such tables represent the "average" of many observations on many individuals who may or may not be representative of a particular child you have in mind. In addition, the experiential background of your child may be very different from the "typical" experiences of the children in the comparison groups. Consequently, since experience plays such an important role in human development, you must be careful not to conclude that your child *should* be like the "typical" child of comparable age described by a developmental chart, nor to *expect* that he necessarily will be at some time or another. For example, not all young people experience the "typical" storm and stress usually expected during adolescence. The probable reason is that at least a few learn behaviors that are more helpful and appropriate for resolving potential conflicts typically faced by youth than those learned by most young people. The point is that a description of typical average behavior does not imply that it *must* or *should* occur; individual learning can make a powerful difference. Some evidence, however, suggests that if we *expect* certain behavior to occur, our prophecy will likely be fulfilled (Rosenthal and Jacobson, 1968).

Developmental charts are potentially dangerous since . . .

Piaget and the Views of Educational Researchers

In earlier chapters, we learned about the views of many persons interested in learning and teaching. To see how the main substance of some of their ideas can be combined with those of Piaget and the resulting implications for instruction, let us first look at the ideas of Ausubel, Bruner, Gagné, Bloom, Krathwohl, Harrow, Maslow, and Skinner.

PIAGET AND AUSUBEL

A major theme common to the ideas of Piaget and Ausubel relates to *meaningfulness* of experience. Subsumed within this theme are the questions of *readiness* and what Piaget refers to as the American Question: "Can the progression through the various stages of intellectual development be speeded up?" Both Piaget and Ausubel maintain that an experience cannot be assimilated meaningfully unless there already exist in cognitive structure more generally inclusive structures of knowing relevant to the new information being incorporated. Otherwise, learning that takes place will of necessity be only rote in nature. Piaget and Ausubel both support the rule that you cannot meaningfully know in *specific* until first you know *generally*.

Millie Almy (1966, 1975), specialist in young children's thinking, is also interested in the so-called American Question, as are many others. Besides questioning the issue of whether the developmental process can be speeded up or not, and at least some researchers suggest that it can (Sigel, Roeper, and Hooper, 1966), Almy asks whether it *ought* to be. She says that there seems to be "a degree of impatience with the playful, imaginative, highly personalized thought of the young child. We infer that the sooner childish thoughts are put away, the more surely and the more insightfully the person enters the intellectual kingdom set up for him by the great thinkers in the various disciplines."[25] Fur-

---

[25] M. C. Almy, E. Chittenden, and P. Miller (1966). *Young Children's Thinking.* New York: Columbia University, Teachers College, pp. 129–130.

thermore, Almy questions whether, in a long-term view, acceleration enhances the learner's ability for speculative imaginative, and creative thinking.

Another point of agreement between Piaget and Ausubel is that meaningfulness grows out of early experience with concrete objects and events. Both, however, believe that concrete objects and events become essentially unnecessary for experience to be meaningful once the learner has developed a richly meaningful cognitive structure.

These points bear on the questions of *readiness* and whether development can be speeded up. Piaget and Ausubel agree that a learner is ready for a particular environmental experience when his present cognitive organization is such that it can accommodate new information; that is, when the prerequisite knowledge or skills have been acquired and a more general structure of knowledge exists into which they can be assimilated.

Piaget and Ausubel agree on . . .

In their agreement about readiness is found Piaget and Ausubel's common response to the American Question: Speeding-up the process of development is limited by the fact that development of the structures of knowledge necessary for meaningful learning requires a vast amount of experience. Trying unduly to shortcut the time and experiences necessary to develop these structures can only result in learning that is rote (Ausubel) or unreal (Piaget).

PIAGET AND BRUNER

Both Piaget and Bruner subscribe to the view that cognitive development occurs in a sequence of stages. Bruner views the three stages in his sequence as a progression in the way that learners code information about the environment; he calls the idea of coding *symbolic representation*. Bruner believes that language plays an extremely important part in cognitive development, as do genetic factors and the cultural environment.

Both Piaget and Bruner believe that development requires activity on the child's part. Discovery learning, as you will recall, finds one of its strongest supporters in Bruner. He relies heavily on language activity, especially in the early stages, to explain cognitive development, whereas Piaget believes that physical (sensory-motor) activity is the most important basis for later intellectual development. Both believe that development occurs when the learner finds himself "off balance" and must do something to regain cognitive equilibrium. *Confrontation* is Piaget's name for the situation. Bruner refers to the process of posing puzzling questions which cause the learner to be cognitively "off balance" as *submarining*.

Both Piaget and Bruner agree that all the types of thinking represented by the various stages are available to the adult and that occasionally he will use one of the early types, especially when he encounters very difficult or unfamiliar objects or events. Bruner believes, however, that symbolic thought is possible for a child at a much younger age than does Piaget. We will see in Chapter 12 how many of their ideas can be synthesized into a theory of instruction.

Piaget and Bruner agree that . . .

PIAGET, GAGNÉ,
BLOOM, KRATHWOHL, AND HARROW

These theorists share the point of view that conceptualizes knowledge as a hierarchical organization. Piaget and Gagné share a belief in the natural ordering that emerges as successive processes of environmental experience coordinate

Piaget, Gagné, Bloom, Krathwohl, and Harrow agree that . . .

organized systems into new, more highly coordinated, and integrated systems. For Piaget, this is reflected in the successive stages of knowing behavior. For Gagné, this natural ordering of progressive inclusion is manifested in his hierarchy of types of learning, each of which requires somewhat different conditions of acquisition. For Bloom, Krathwohl, and Harrow, the natural ordering occurs in a simple to complex progression of educational objectives. All systems, it is interesting to note, show a progression from behavior that is mostly *reflexive* to behavior that is strongly *reflective*.

PIAGET AND MASLOW

Piaget and Maslow agree that . . . The main thing Piaget and Maslow share, besides the notion of a hierarchical ordering of phenomena, is the nature of the tasks that a human being must "solve" in successive order. Both Piaget and Maslow speak of a person constantly and actively in the process of "becoming," and both believe that this process begins with meeting basic physiological needs. Furthermore, they agree that progression to the higher levels of development cannot properly continue until the needs of the lower levels have been adequately met through experience.

I find it significant, first, that both Piaget and Maslow view the human's potential for development as virtually unlimited; their hierarchies remain essentially open-ended. Second, the substance of their respective systems is basically complementary. They blend affective development with cognitive development—the two, as we learned in early chapters, cannot really be separated in the first place, except in abstraction.

PIAGET AND SKINNER

Piaget and Skinner are complementary in that . . . You may find it strange to see the ideas of Piaget and Skinner fitting together—Piaget, giant of the builders of developmental theory, and Skinner, the giant of controlled laboratory experimentation who will have nothing to do with theory. For all their differences, however, a moment's reflection will suggest several important ways that their works can be seen to mesh.

Both Piaget and Skinner hold religiously to the objective methods of science; introspection plays no part in what either does; they just approach their research problems from different points of view. Each, however, is interested in behavior: Piaget in thinking, knowing behavior and Skinner in observable, "doing" behavior—he is not concerned with studying what goes on inside the head. Yet, both recognize the key importance of an organism's *actions* in the furthering of its development, including its learning.

Both are interested in development, but Piaget's interest is more comprehensive than Skinner's. Skinner's interest begins with the given assumption that every living organism naturally operates on its environment, and that these natural behaviors, called *operants*, are species-specific. He is not interested, as is Piaget, in the evolutionary or developmental origin of operants or in how they came to be a part of a species. He wants to know by what general, universal rules they are changed or modified through experience. That is, he wants to understand the rules of learning. Of course, Piaget is also concerned with the effects of experience on the developing organism, but his interest centers on the broadly generalizable effects of experience on the development of inner structures of knowledge, on the development of intelligence. He does not try to discover specific laws of learning; rather, he is interested in demonstrating the relative truth of broad and inclusive statements that constitute a theory of development. Such a theory, of course, must include laws of learning since, as you recall, development, broadly defined, means structural and functional change through the process of living through time.[26]

CHECKPOINT 11-5

1. In Chapters 8, 9, and 10, we synthesized rules of positive reinforcement and punishment relative to the topic of school learning. Given that learning is subsumed by development, how, then, might these rules be included in Piaget's theory of development?

2. Explain why, in your opinion, Piaget would support an approach to learning of either discovery, reception, both discovery and reception, or neither discovery or reception.

3. Although Piaget's broadly inclusive theory of developmental adaptation has been applied mostly to our understanding of the development of intelligence, I maintain that it also applies to our understanding of the development of psychomotor and affective capabilities. State your reasons for agreeing or disagreeing with my position.

4. In the first ten chapters, we met several educators and psychologists who approached their work from either a connectionist, a cognitive, or an eclectic point of view. Which of these approaches best describes how Piaget has gone about his work? Explain your answer.

5. Were you willing to try the activities in all the checkpoints in this chapter? Yes_____ No_____

6. As you did the reading and checkpoints for this chapter, did you think about specific instructional activities that might derive from rules of development? Yes_____ No_____

HIGHER-ORDER RULES OF DEVELOPMENT

We have seen how the ideas of Piaget and other researchers fit together; how they complement each other and help to complete the general theory of development outlined by Piaget. As this synthesis evolves, with the contributions gained from the perspective of the outstanding leaders with whose work you are familiar, plus the contributions from genetics, biochemistry, and physiology, we will begin to see the glimmerings of general rules of development that have implications for education. These will provide information for the development of a much-needed theory of instruction.

Several of these rules can now be stated, even though in necessarily incomplete and tentative form. If we check back through our discussion, several higher-order rules of development will become apparent. No doubt you are already aware of some of them. The ones that I have synthesized are summarized in the next section. In Chapter 12 we will discuss their implications for a theory of instruction from which we can derive individual and personal approaches to our task of making instruction optimal for each of our learners.

[26] L. H. Stott (1974). *The Psychology of Human Development*. New York: Holt, p. 23.

Therefore, it will suffice here simply to state the rules with little or no additional comment. This statement will serve two purposes: (1) It will summarize our discussions of a broad and biological perspective for learning what development is all about; and (2) it will provide an advance organizational structure for Chapter 12. As you are aware, both functions should facilitate positive transfer.

A Classification of Higher-Order Rules of Development

The fundamental rule of development is . . .

The most fundamental and obvious higher-order rule of development is simply: *The individual members of a given species vary, both within themselves as a function of living over time, and among themselves as a function of differences in genetic makeup and differences in experiences.* As teachers, we are concerned about understanding the rules underlying these differences. For convenience of summary and of getting ready to use them in Chapter 12, we can group them into three major categories, although in reality they are always interrelated: (1) rules of development relative to genes and gene action; (2) rules of development relative to experience; and (3) rules of development relative to the interaction of genes and experience.

RULES OF DEVELOPMENT
RELATIVE TO GENES AND GENE ACTION

What we have learned about genes and gene action relative to development can be stated in the following higher-order rules:

THE BASIC RULE OF GENE ACTION.   The major function of gene action is the production of the thousands of kinds of protein molecules that (1) serve as the primary building blocks of cells, and (2) act as specific enzymes for most biochemical reactions of life.

THE RULE OF GENERALITY.   Gene action is essentially the same across all living organisms.

THE RULE OF GENERAL PLASTICITY.   Living organisms possess genetic potential far greater than they usually demonstrate.

THE RULE OF DECREASING FLEXIBILITY.   The general plasticity of genetic potential decreases with age and lack of practice.

THE RULE OF ELABORATION.   Preprogrammed genetic mechanisms are incomplete, especially in human beings, and they must be elaborated through experience.

THE RULE OF SPECIAL SENSITIVITY, OR SENSITIVE PERIODS.   Gene action is most readily set into process during certain periods of time.

THE BASIC RULE OF FEEDBACK.   Gene action is terminated or modified by stimuli generated by feedback systems.

THE RULE OF TYPES OF GENE ACTION.   Gene action is of two general types: *proactive* or preprogrammed, and *reactive*, or modified by experience.

THE RULE OF INCREASING REACTIVITY. Early in the developmental sequence and phylogenetically, gene action is mostly *proactive*. Gradually it becomes more *reactive*.

RULES OF DEVELOPMENT
RELATIVE TO EXPERIENCE

Higher-order rules of development in which the role of experience is emphasized can be stated as follows:

THE BASIC RULE OF EXPERIENCE. Experience in development has the major function of providing the stimulation necessary to cause genes to act.

THE RULE OF HABITUATION. Experience, to be effective, must vary over time.

THE RULE OF COMPLEMENTARY ACTION. Experience is most effective when it complements the actions of preprogrammed mechanisms.

THE RULE OF THE MATCH. Experience, to be effective in stimulating gene action, must be of the appropriate kind.

THE RULE OF SPECIAL TIMING. Experience is most effective in stimulating gene action when it occurs during certain periods of time.

THE RULE OF PRACTICE. The effects of experience on gene action are more enduring with repetition.

THE RULE OF TRANSFER. Capacity for, and efficiency in, further development changes as a function of experience.

RULES OF DEVELOPMENT
RELATIVE TO THE INTERACTION
OF GENES AND EXPERIENCE

Most of our higher-order rules of development more accurately belong in this category than in either of the two previous ones. Consequently, the rules listed here will naturally overlap a bit with those we have already cited. Since interaction implies action through time, most of the rules listed in this section reflect the notion of process.

THE BASIC RULE OF INTERACTION. Development is a continuous, orderly, and lawful progression of structural and functional change that occurs within a living organism interacting with its environment over time.

THE RULE OF RECIPROCAL FEEDBACK, OR OF ACTION-REACTION. Continuing and varied interaction of individuals with their environment is necessary for development to proceed.

THE RULE OF INCREASING DELAY OF FEEDBACK. Development occurs in the order of decreasing rigidness and immediacy of response.

THE RULE OF PROGRESSIVE INTERNALIZATION. Knowing behavior develops from preprogrammed, reflective knowing toward intentional, reflective knowing.

THE RULE OF SPECIALIZATION. Development progresses from generalized, undifferentiated capabilities for responding toward specialized capabilities for responding.

THE RULE OF INCREASING SOCIALIZATION. Development progresses from individual-centered (egocentric) responding towards interindividual, social-centered responding.

THE RULE OF INCREASING COMPLEXITY. Development progresses from capabilities for basic physiological responding toward capabilities for complex cognitive and affective responding.

THE RULE OF PROGRESSIVE DIFFERENTIATION. Development progresses from a point at which individuals are most alike to a point at which they are least alike.

THE RULE OF CHANGING MOTIVATION. Development progresses from essentially preprogrammed motivation to attend and to respond toward motivation to attend and to respond that is also controlled socially and culturally.

THE RULE OF PROGRESSIVE SUBSUMPTION. The structures of knowledge that progressively develop through the interaction of genes and experience develop so that the old structures are always incorporated within the new.

THE RULE OF VARYING RATES. Development progresses at different rates within and between individuals.

Rules of development serve as a basis for . . .

It must be remembered that the above list of higher-order rules of development is tentative and certainly incomplete. Nevertheless, it can serve as a useful perspective from which we can approach our task of trying to make instruction optimal for each of our learners. Furthermore, as we mentioned before and as we will see in Chapter 12, these rules and their potential implications for education form the beginnings of a powerful theory of instruction which is important for at least two reasons. First, a theory of instruction gives us a rationale from which to plan our teaching behavior. Second, it gives us a consistent way to correct our teaching behavior when it is not working very well. Without a theory of instruction, our approaches to instruction stand little chance of rising above the level of bare empiricism about which Patrick Suppes (1974) cautioned us.

IN PASSING

This letter, [27] written by an Indian mother to the teacher of her child, is a poignant and poetic plea for the kind of individual understanding all parents hope teachers will give their children. Perhaps her letter will remind us that theories and approaches in education are only the objective tools that we devise to help us know how to behave in a consistent and humanistic way toward our learners.

Dear Teacher:

Before you take charge of the classroom that contains my child, please ask yourself why *that you are going to teach Indian children. What are your expec-*

---

[27] Author requests to remain anonymous (1973). Indian mother's plea to teacher: Treat my child with dignity, *Education* B.C., **3**(1), Reprinted by permission.

tations—what rewards do you anticipate—what ego needs will our children have to meet?

Write down and examine all the information and opinions you possess about Indians. What are the stereotypes and untested assumptions that you bring with you into the classroom? How many negative attitudes towards Indians will you put before my child?

What values, class prejudices and moral principles do you take for granted as universal? Please remember that "different from" is not the same as "worse than" or "better than," and the yardstick you use to measure your own life satisfactorily may not be appropriate for their lives. The term "culturally deprived" was invented by well-meaning middle-class whites to describe something they could not understand. Too many teachers, unfortunately, seem to see their role as rescuer. My child does not need to be rescued; he does not consider being Indian a misfortune. He has a culture, probably older than yours; he has meaningful values and a rich and varied experimental background. However strange or incomprehensible it may seem to be to you, you have no right to do or say anything that implies to him that it is less than satisfactory.

Our children's experiences have been different from those of the "typical" white middle-class child for whom most school curricula seem to have been designed (I suspect that this "typical" child does not exist except in the minds of the curriculum writers). Nonetheless, my child's experiences have been as intense and meaningful to him as any child's. Like most Indian children his age, he is competent. He can dress himself, prepare a meal for himself and clean up afterward, care for a younger child. He knows his reserve–all of which is his home—like the back of his hand.

He is not accustomed to having to ask permission to do the ordinary things that are a part of normal living. He is seldom forbidden to do anything; more usually the consequences of an action are explained to him, and he is allowed to decide for himself whether or not to act. His entire existence since he has been old enough to see and hear has been an experiential learning situation, arranged to provide him with the opportunity to develop his skills and confidence in his own capacities. Didactic teaching will be an alien experience for him.

He is not self-conscious in the way many white children are. Nobody has ever told him his efforts towards independence are cute. He is a young human being energetically doing his job, which is to get on with the process of learning to function as an adult human being. He will respect you as a person, but he will expect you to do likewise to him. He has been taught, by percept, that courtesy is an essential part of human conduct and rudeness is any action that makes another person feel stupid or foolish. Do not mistake his patient courtesy for indifference or passivity.

He doesn't speak standard English, but he is in no way "linguistically handicapped." If you will take the time and courtesy to listen and observe carefully, you will see that he and the other Indian children communicate very well, both among themselves and with other Indians. They speak "functional English" very effectively augmented by their fluency in the silent language—the subtle, unspoken communication of facial expressions, gestures, body movement and the use of personal space.

You will be well advised to remember that our children are skillful in-

terpreters of the silent language. They will know your feelings and attitudes with unerring precision, no matter how carefully you arrange your smile or modulate your voice. They will learn in your classroom, because children learn involuntarily. What *they learn will depend on you.*

Will you help my child to learn to read, or will you teach him that he has a reading problem? Will you help him develop problem-solving skills, or will you teach him that school is where you try to guess what answer the teacher wants? Will he learn that his sense of his own value and dignity is valid, or will he learn that he must forever be apologetic and "trying harder" because he isn't white? Can you help him acquire the intellectual skills he needs without at the same time imposing your values on top of those he already has?

Respect my child. He is a person. He has a right to be himself.

Yours very sincerely,
His Mother

ACTIVITIES

1. To summarize Chapter 11, write an imaginary letter to a friend. In the letter explain that you have recently become acquainted with Jean Piaget's theory of developmental adaptation and would like to share the main ideas involved in it.

2. Review each item presented in the checkpoints of Chapter 11. For each item, state the level of *cognitive* and *affective* functioning required to complete it.

3. Speculate on the implications for learning to read that may derive from the fact that a sensitive period for form perception occurs within the first three months of life.

4. As an individual, a small group, or an entire class activity, describe what an intelligence test would be like that was based on Piaget's notions of a sequence of qualitatively different stages of intellectual development. State the potential value to teachers of such a test.

5. Just for fun:

Find a teacher at the kindergarten or grade one level and another at the grade seven, eight, or nine level who will cooperate with you. Ask them to let you discuss a topic with their learners, such as making a machine to catch flies, how to improve school desks, or new ways to use paper clips, pencils, skipping rope (any familiar object). Note the responses of the learners at each grade level for indications of their stage of intellectual development according to Piaget.

REFERENCES

Agranoff, B. W. (1967). Memory and protein synthesis, *Scientific American.* **216**(6), 115–123.

Almy, M. C., E. Chittenden, and P. Miller (1966). *Young Children's Thinking.* New York: Columbia University, Teachers College.

——— (1975). *The Early Childhood Educator at Work.* New York: McGraw-Hill.

Anastasi, A. (1958). Heredity, environment and the question "How?" *Psychological Review,* **65,** 197–208.

Baer, D. M., and J. C. Wright (1974). Developmental psychology. In M. R. Rosenzweig and L. W. Porter (eds.), *Annual Review of Psychology,* Palo Alto, Calif.: Annual Reviews.

Britton, E., and J. M. Winans (1958). *Growing from Infancy to Childhood.* New York: Appleton-Century-Crofts.

Callaway, W. R., Jr. (1970). Modes of biological adaptation and their role in intellectual development, *Perceptual Cognitive Development Monographs,* **1**(1), 1–34.

Chall, J. S. (1967). *Learning to Read: The Great Debate.* New York: McGraw-Hill.

Chomsky, N. (1965). *Aspects of the Theory of Syntax.* Cambridge, Mass.: M.I.T.

——— (1966). *Cartesian Linguistics.* New York: Harper & Row.

Chukovsky, K. (1966). *From Two to Five.* Berkeley: University of California Press.

Duckworth, E. (1964). Piaget rediscovered, *Journal of Research in Science Teaching,* **2,** 172–175.

Erikson, E. (1963). *Childhood and Society.* New York: Norton.

Fantz, R. L. (1965). Visual perception from birth as shown by pattern selectivity. In Whipple, H. (ed.), New Issues in Human Development. *Annals of the New York Academy of Sciences,* **118,** 798–814.

Furth, H. G. (1969). *Piaget and Knowledge, Theoretical Foundations.* Englewood Cliffs, N.J.: Prentice-Hall.

Galton, F. (1869). *Heredity Genius,* London: Macmillan.

Ginsburg, H., and S. Opper (1969). *Piaget's Theory of Intellectual Development, An Introduction.* Englewood Cliffs, N.J.: Prentice-Hall.

Hall, E. (1973). A conversation with Jean Piaget and Barbel Inhelder, *Psychology Today,* **3,** 12, 25–32.

―――― (1974). Ethology's warning: A conversation with Nobel Prize winner Niko Tinbergen, *Psychology Today,* **7**(10), 65–95.

Hartshorne, H., and N. A. May (1928). *Studies in the Nature of Character: Studies in Deceit.* New York: Macmillan.

Hebb, D. O. (1953). Heredity and environment in mammalian behaviour, *British Journal of Animal Behaviour,* **1,** 43–47.

―――― (1966). *A Textbook of Psychology.* Philadelphia: Saunders.

―――― (1974). What psychology is about, *American Psychologist,* **29** (1), 71–79.

Hunt, J. McV. (1961). *Intelligence and Experience.* New York: Ronald.

―――― (1969). The impact and limitations of the giant of developmental psychology. In D. Elkind and J. H. Flavell (eds.), *Studies in Cognitive Development, Essays in Honor of Jean Piaget.* New York: Oxford University Press.

Hyden, H. (1966). Introductory remarks to the session on memory processes. In F. O. Schmitt and T. Melnechuk (eds.), *Neuro-Sciences Research Symposium Summaries,* vol. **1.** Cambridge, Mass.: M.I.T.

Ilg, F. and L. B. Ames (1955). *The Gesell Institute's Child Behavior.* New York: Dell.

Inhelder, B. (1962). Some aspects of Piaget's genetic approach to cognition. In W. Kessen and C. Kuhlman (eds.), *Thought in the Young Child. Monographs of the Society for Research in Child Development,* **27,** (2), Serial No. 83, 19–34.

Jenkins, G. G., H. S. Schacter, and W. W. Bauer (1966). *These Are Your Children,* 3d ed. Chicago: Scott-Foresman.

Jensen, A. R. (1969). How much can we boost I.Q. and scholastic achievement? *Harvard Educational Review,* **39**(1), 1–123.

Koestler, A. (1964). *The Act of Creation.* New York: Macmillan.

―――― (1967). *The Ghost in the Machine.* New York: Macmillan.

Kohlberg, L. (1966). Moral education in the schools: A developmental view, *School Review,* **74,** 1–30.

―――― (1971). Stages of moral development as a basis for moral education. In C. M. Beck, B. S. Crittenden, and E. V. Sullivan (eds.). *Moral Education: Interdisciplinary Approaches.* Toronto: University of Toronto Press.

Krech, D. (1969). Psychoneurobiochemeducation, *Phi Delta Kappan,* **L** (7), 370–375.

Kurtines, W., and E. B. Grief (1974). The development of moral thought: Review and evaluation of Kohlberg's approach, *Psychological Bulletin,* **81,** (5), 453–470.

Lederberg, J. (1951). *Papers in Microbial Genetics.* Madison: University of Wisconsin Press.

Lenneberg, E. H. (1967). *Biological Foundations of Language.* New York: Wiley.

Lessing, L. (1967). *DNA: At the Core of Life Itself.* New York: Macmillan.

Lorenz, K. (1965). *Evolution and Modification of Behavior* (section V). Chicago: The University of Chicago Press.

Luria, S. E. (1965). Directed genetic change: Perspectives from molecular genetics. In T. E. Sonneborn (ed.), *The Control of Human Heredity and Evolution.* New York: Macmillan.

McNeill, D. (1966). Developmental psycholinguistics. In F. Smith and G. A. Miller (eds.), *The Genesis of Language*. Cambridge, Mass.: M.I.T.

Melzack, R. (1968). Early experience: A neuropsychological approach to heredity-environment interactions. In G. Newton and S. Levine (eds.), *Early Experience and Behavior*. Springfield, Illinois: Charles C. Thomas.

Miller, G. A. (1964). Language and psychology. In E. H. Lenneberg (ed.), *New Directions in the Study of Language*. Cambridge, Mass.: M.I.T.

Mussen, P. H., J. J. Congor, and J. Kagan (1969). *Child Development and Personality*, 3d ed. New York: Harper & Row.

Nash, J. (1970). *Developmental Psychology: A Psychobiological Approach*. Englewood Cliffs, N.J.: Prentice-Hall.

Palay, S. L. (1964). The structural basis for neural action. In M. A. B. Brazier (ed.), *Brain Function, Vol. II. RNA and Brain Function: Memory and Learning*, UCLA Forum Medical Science No. 2. Los Angeles: University of California Press.

Piaget, J. (1932). *The Moral Judgment of the Child*. London: Routledge & Kegan Paul.

——— (1952). *The Origins of Intelligence*. Trans. by Margaret Cook. New York: International Universities.

——— (1960). *The Psychology of Intelligence*. Trans. by M. Piercy and D. E. Berlyne. Paterson, N.J.: Littlefield, Adams and Co. (Originally published in 1947.)

——— (1970). Piaget's theory. In P. H. Mussen (ed.), *Carmichael's Manual of Child Psychology*, Part I, 703–732. New York: Wiley.

Platt, J. R. (1968). The new biology and the shaping of the future. In R. M. Hutchins and M. Alder (eds.), *The Great Ideas Today*. Chicago: Encyclopedia Britannica.

Rosenthal, R., and L. Jacobson (1968). *Pygmalion in the Classroom*. New York: Holt.

Seymour, D. Z. (1971). Black children, black speech, *Commonweal*, **95**(8), 175–178.

Sigel, I. E. (1964). The attainment of concepts. In M. L. Hoffman and L. W. Hoffman (eds.), *Review of Child Development Research*, vol. 1, New York: Russell Sage Foundation.

———, A. Roeper, and F. H. Hooper (1966). A training procedure for acquisition of Piaget's conservation of quantity: A pilot study and its replication, *British Journal of Educational Psychology*, **36**, 301–311.

Sinnott, E. W. (1963). *The Problem of Organic Form*. New Haven, Conn. Yale.

Speman, H. (1938). *Embryonic Development and Induction*. New Haven, Conn.: Yale.

Stone, J. L., and J. Church (1972). *Childhood and Adolescence*, 3d ed. New York: Random House.

Stott, L. H. (1974). *The Psychology of Human Development*. New York: Holt.

Suppes, P. (1974). The place of theory in educational research, *Educational Researcher*, **3** (6), 3–10.

Young, J. Z. (1964). *A Model of the Brain*. Oxford: Oxford University Press.

SUGGESTIONS FOR FURTHER READING

Anastasi, A., (ed.) (1965). *Individual Differences*. New York: Wiley. This paperback of readings places the psychological study of individual differences in historical perspective with articles by such well-known researchers as Galton, Cattell, Binet, Spearman, Burt, Guilford, Pearson, E. L. Thorndike, Alice Leaky, Tryon, Hirsch, Hebb, and Anne Anastasi. Topics range from interest in measurement of individual differences to the nature of intelligence, behavior genetics, and the nature of genius.

Bruner, J. S. (1966). *Toward a Theory of Instruction*. Cambridge, Mass.: The Belknap Press of Harvard University Press. A theory of instruction must derive from a broadly based theory of development that includes a theory of knowledge. The eight essays in Bruner's book provide clues about what he believes a theory of instruction must be like. His view is developmental and broad, and it calls for synthesis of the rules of reward and punishment with the specification of content, its structure, and the sequences in which to present instructional materials.

Furth, H. (1970). *Piaget for Teachers*. Englewood Cliffs, N.J.: Prentice-Hall. Furth is an extremely clear and precise writer who understands both the technicalities of Piaget's theory and the psychology of learning and teaching. His book is especially appropriate for teachers who want to understand what use Piaget may be to them.

Ginsburg, H., and S. Opper (1969). *Piaget's Theory of Intellectual Development: An Introduction.* Englewood Cliffs, N.J.: Prentice-Hall. This volume provides a biography of Piaget that describes the evolution of his theory. The authors do an excellent job of presenting examples in a way that makes the theory both clear and comprehensible. Their detailed descriptions of children's behavior characteristic of Piaget's stages and substages are among the best available. A section of the book deals with implications for education of Piaget's theory.

Nash, J. (1970). *Developmental Psychology: A Psychobiological Approach.* Englewood Cliffs, N.J.: Prentice-Hall. Nash provides a comprehensive perspective of the biological view necessary to understand Piaget's theory of developmental adaptation. His treatment of the evolutionary and genetic influences on development is especially good.

Phillips, J. L., Jr. (1969). *The Origins of Intellect: Piaget's Theory.* San Francisco: Freeman. This is a well-organized and highly readable paperback written for teachers and students. It gives detailed descriptions of all stages and substages, and ends with implications for education: principles and examples for teaching. An interesting feature is the discussion of an intelligence test based on Piaget's theory.

Suppes, P. (1974). The place of theory in educational research, *Educational Researcher,* **3** (6), 3–10. In this brief article Suppes builds a convincing argument for the need of powerful theories in education. He points out that the alternatives to good theories are bare intuition and chaos in practice.

12

TEACHING FOR
INDIVIDUAL DIFFERENCES

Theory is in the end . . . the most practical of all things, because this widening of the range of attention beyond nearby purpose and desire eventually results in the creation of wider and farther-reaching purposes, and enables us to use a much wider and deeper range of conditions and means than were expressed in the observation of primitive practical purposes.

John Dewey
The Sources of a Science of Education

CONTENTS

ONGOING SUMMARY

Our purpose in Parts I and II was to learn about the general concepts and rules of learning and teaching. In Chapter 11 we attempted a higher-order synthesis of these concepts and rules by considering them within a general and biological theory of development. And, in doing this, we started building a widely inclusive and generally meaningful perspective for understanding what learners, learning, and teaching are all about, and for seeing how they are related developmentally. From Piaget's biologically based theory of developmental adaptation, we derived higher-order rules of development that have potential implications for education. We concluded that these rules (1) help us understand about the individual differences of our learners and (2) might be used as the basis for a much-needed theory of instruction. Thus, Piaget's major contribution to education is more appropriately viewed as an indirect than a direct one.

Chapter 12 is a continuation of Chapter 11 and is an exercise in *synthesis* and *speculation*. In it we will build toward a theory of instruction and then speculate on various approaches we might use to apply the rules of our theory to make instruction optional for each of our learners.

This is an exercise in synthesis because, currently, there is no generally recognized theory of instruction available. Consequently, we will need to construct one ourselves. Fortunately for us, many of the parts have already been identified, even though not everyone agrees on the value or appropriateness of various aspects of the different parts. However, we will not be concerned with lack of agreement, for to wait for consensus is to do nothing forever. Rather, we will put the parts together as best we can, remembering that we must always be willing to modify our product as new evidence becomes available.

Jean Piaget's biological theory of developmental adaptation will serve as the main source of information from which we will derive the basic rules for our theory of instruction. Since some investigators do not agree with Piaget, we will need to examine other views of development, especially those relative to intellectual development, to learn what modifications, if any, should be made in the rules we derived in Chapter 11. From there, we will synthesize these rules into a theory of instruction, building on the work already begun by Jerome Bruner. And last, we will examine four general approaches to instruction with the purpose of helping you decide on the type of approach with which you will feel comfortable and that will provide all the requirements of effective instruction as specified by the rules of our theory.

Our work in Chapter 12 is speculative because we will often go beyond our data. For the scientist, "staying within the data" is a fundamental rule that is observed almost religiously; for the classroom teacher, the rule is impossible. Precious little teaching would occur if we did only those things in our classrooms that are unequivocally supported by research data. Of course, we must exercise caution with our learners and try to apply the rules we have from a theory of instruction, tentative and approximate as they may be. But we also need to be bold; to dare to give a try to our hunches, best guesses, or just spontaneous intuitions. Realistically, we cannot do otherwise, since the "truths" we have relative to learning and teaching are at best part-truths, and then only temporary in nature. But, slowly and surely we are understanding better the nature of the interaction among learners, learning, and instruction, and, as you will see, a logical theory of instruction—even one that limps a bit—is of tremendous help.

Therefore, in this chapter we will remember that the theory of instruction we develop is a working assumption only. We will not worry about its absolute truth; rather, we will be concerned that its rules lead us to ask appropriate and testable questions, the tentative nature of which will, at least for now, improve our chances of making instruction optimal for each of our learners.

Cognitive

To become an effective teacher, the learner should be able to synthesize an approach to instruction that is a personally satisfying and theoretically sound one.

KNOWLEDGE LEVEL

Given the following terms, the learner is able to define them in writing: *general ability to learn, theory of instruction, approaches to instruction, feedback, corrective feedback, biofeedback, individual instruction, match, learning structure, learning sequence, readiness.*

COMPREHENSION LEVEL

1. Given Jensen's conclusion that 80 percent of human intelligence is due to heredity, the learner is able to explain why this conclusion can be only relatively true and approximately so.

2. Given the following general approaches to instruction, the learner is able to describe the major characteristics of each: *free school approach, Montessori method, open education, mastery learning.*

APPLICATION LEVEL

Given the theory of instruction developed in Chapter 12, the learner is able to apply its rules to developing his own approach to instruction.

ANALYSIS LEVEL

Given the details of a specific approach to instruction, the learner can say whether it is consistent with the theory of instruction developed in Chapter 12.

SYNTHESIS LEVEL

Given the rules of the theory of instruction developed in Chapter 12, the learner is able to construct an approach to instruction that is personally satisfying and theoretically sound.

EVALUATION LEVEL

Given four general approaches to instruction, the learner can argue in support of the approach he considers most likely to meet the requirements of effective instruction.

Affective

To become an effective teacher, the learner should be willing to speculate about the implications of higher-order rules of development for a theory of, and various approaches to, instruction.

RECEIVING (ATTENDING) LEVEL

1. The learner is aware of the fact that much of a teacher's instructional behavior is speculative.

2. Given the opportunity to reduce some of the trial and error from his instructional behavior, the learner is willing to consider ways of doing so.

RESPONDING LEVEL

The learner is willing to speculate about possible relationships between higher-order rules of development, a theory of instruction, and various approaches to instruction.

VALUING LEVEL

The learner believes it is necessary and possible to organize approaches for individualized instruction that are theoretically sound.

ORGANIZATIONAL LEVEL

The learner is developing approaches to instruction that are personally satisfying and that meet the requirements of effective instruction.

CHARACTERIZATION LEVEL

Whenever the learner reflects on how he will instruct, he always checks for the rationale behind his actions.

12

There is little point to our knowing about the genetic-environmental bases for the individual differences among our learners unless the knowledge results in instruction that provides for these differences. This is what the current movement toward *individualized instruction* is all about: making instruction optimal for each learner. (Carroll, 1963; Bloom, 1968; Block, 1971.) This movement means, of course, that many of the traditional, group-based methods of instruction must give way to methods of individual instruction. As this change occurs, the need for a theory of instruction becomes increasingly apparent, since individualizing instruction requires broad guidelines from which specific information can be derived. We need to know about (1) the kinds of experiences that *motivate* learners, (2) the organizational *structure* of information being learned, (3) most effective *sequences* for presenting materials to be learned, and (4) the *nature and schedules* of reinforcement and punishment or knowledge of results (Bruner, 1966). Bruner believes that these are the guidelines a theory of instruction must provide.

Viewed in this way, a theory of instruction is really a theory of individualized instruction. *Learning*, the object of instruction, is always a uniquely individual experience; it is only *instruction* that may sometimes be a group experience.

INDIVIDUAL DIFFERENCES
AND GENERAL ABILITY TO LEARN

Although Jean Piaget's broadly inclusive theory of developmental adaptation generally applies to all areas of development, you will recall from Chapter 11 that it has been most extensively investigated in the area of intellectual development. Intelligence, for Piaget, is both the content and the process of developmental adaptation: that is, intelligence is the structural and functional development of knowing behavior that results from the adaptive interaction of the learner with the environment over time. Intelligence, in this biological view, evolves in an invariant sequence in terms of quantity and quality as a function of time and experience. From this point of view, we found that we could derive higher-order rules of development that appear to have potential implications for instruction.

Not everyone, however, believes that intelligence can be defined as broadly as it is in Piaget's theory, or that intelligence changes appreciably as a function of time and experience. This view is frequently referred to as the *hereditarian* position. At the other extreme is the *environmentalist* position that espouses a viewpoint that questions the very usefulness of any concept of intelligence because of its lack of explanatory value. Environmentalists maintain that "intelligence" is just a descriptive term and that it often is misused in attempts to explain why some individuals learn well and others do not.

We will want to understand the bases for these apparently different standpoints because, as we learned in Chapter 2, what we believe to be true about something influences greatly what we do about it. If the views really are different in terms of their implications for instruction, of course the difference will need to be taken into account in the higher-order rules that become a part of any theory of instruction.

Let us examine the different points of view and see if we must modify our higher-order rules of development from Chapter 11 before we synthesize them with the requirements of a theory of instruction as outlined by Bruner (1966).

The View of Intelligence as General Ability to Learn

In the view of many researchers in psychology and education, intelligence is defined roughly as a general ability to learn, to reason, to grasp concepts, and to deal with abstractions (Binet, 1905; Terman, 1916); or as David Wechsler (1944) defined it, "the aggregate or global capacity of the individual to act purposefully, to think rationally and to deal effectively with his environment."[1] As you have noticed, these definitions do not differ a great deal from Piaget's definition of intelligence, especially that typical of an adult. The question that has caused division of opinion—and, at times, violent differences—is: "What accounts for the observed differences among individuals in their apparent abilities or capacities for learning?" More pointedly, the question is whether people are born with varying amounts of this general ability for learning or whether the differences are a result of variations in environmental experiences; that is, the result of differences in opportunities to learn. The question has come to be known as the "nature–nurture controversy" and it has periodically been an issue ever since people began to wonder about how they come to be the way they are. Since 1969, it is again a widely and heatedly debated topic, this time frequently labeled the Jensen Controversy, as a result of Arthur Jensen's (1969) conclusions, reported in a lengthy article, "How Much Can We Boost IQ and Scholastic Achievement?" In his article, Jensen presented data to support the view that heredity plays a substantial role in determining intelligence—about 80 percent, and that environment plays a relatively lesser role—about 20 percent. These data, taken by themselves, were not a cause of great concern. Speculation over the relative contribution to intelligence by heredity and environment has often produced similar estimates. The point of controversy in Jensen's report is his claim that there are definite differences, attributable in large measure to genetic factors, in the *average* intelligence as measured by certain tests among various populations; specifically, among *groups* of black and *groups* of white people, with the difference in the direction of higher scores associated with white populations.

The nature-nurture controversy is a debate about . . .

Jensen's data support the contention that . . .

Soon following the publication of Jensen's paper there came other reports from recognized authorities in genetics and psychology that provided support for Jensen's findings (Shockley, 1971; Herrnstein, 1971; Eysenck, 1971).

Environmentalists, those persons who attribute a relatively greater contribution to environmental experience than to heredity in determining intelligence, also responded to Jensen's assertion. Several published articles argued that Jensen's test data were biased because (1) there is unequal opportunity for Negro children to learn because of impoverished early environments, (2) the content of intelligence tests usually favors middle-class white children, (3) Negro children are not as motivated to do well on tests, and (4) Negro children are not as "test-wise" as white children. Mostly, Jensen and others have been able to present data to show that the group differences remain even after factors such as these have been taken into account. More recent data (Zajonc, 1975), however, suggest that Jensen's claim of genetically determined differences between black and white populations may be due simply to differences in average family size and average length of time between birth dates

Five possible sources of bias in Jensen's data are . . .

---

[1] D. Wechsler (1944). *The Measurement of Adult Intelligence*. Baltimore: Williams & Wilkins, p. 3.

of children within families. At this time Jensen has not yet dealt with this possibility.

If you would like to read a detailed account of the Jensen Controversy from Jensen's point of view, see the preface (67 pages) of *Genetics and Education*, by Arthur R. Jensen (1972). Also included in this book is Jensen's article that started all the controversy. To get an idea of how other authorities reacted to Jensen's article, you may want to read the Spring, 1969, issue of *Harvard Educational Review*, which contains seven invited commentaries on his article along with Jensen's rejoinder to them.[2]

Several important points about heredity, environment, intelligence, and education are brought into focus by the differences of opinions about Jensen's (1969) data. All of us who are teaching children should understand these points: (1) Differences in measures of average intelligence of populations refer to groups, not to individuals; (2) measures of intelligence are estimates of a relative, not an absolute, ability to learn; (3) intelligence is modifiable; and (4) the object of instruction is to make learning optimal for each individual, so information about how learners differ is prerequisite to individualizing instruction.

AVERAGES REFER TO GROUPS, NOT INDIVIDUALS

The relationship between group-average scores and individual scores is . . .

An average score is obtained by summing individual scores and dividing the total by the number of individual scores summed. In this process, the exact value of each individual score is lost; it becomes a part of the average. The score that is obtained helps describe the group but tells nothing that helps describe any given individual member of the group. The basic rule applies to Jensen's data and his claim that the average intelligence of Negroes is lower than that of whites. His assertion has nothing whatsoever to do with estimates of the intelligence of individual persons, either Negro or white. Great differences in measured intelligence exist within each group; considerable overlap therefore occurs among the groups; that is, in many instances the measured intelligence of individual Negroes is substantially higher than that of individual whites. The reverse is also true. This means simply that if Jensen's claim is valid, it in no way provides a basis for you to conclude that individual Negro children in your classroom are less "bright" than their white classmates, or even that they are less "bright" as a group. You must learn about each of your learners as a unique individual and not merely as a uniform representative of some stereotyped group.

MEASURES OF INTELLIGENCE ARE RELATIVE, NOT ABSOLUTE

Once again, the distinction between "relative" and "absolute" can be seen to apply to our task as teachers. By the nature of the construction of tests that

---

[2] The commentators are Jerome Kagan, J. McV. Hunt, James F. Crow, Carl Bereiter, David Elkind, Lee J. Cronbach, and William F. Brazziel. Several letters to the editor of the *Harvard Educational Review*, Spring, 1969, **39**(3), 581–631, are available (13 Appian Way, Cambridge, Mass. 02138) in a paperback reprint entitled *Correspondence: Political, Technical, and Theoretical Comments.*

purport to measure intelligence, the kinds of scores produced show how much intelligence a given person has compared with other people. (We will learn more precisely how all this works in Chapter 13; for now, this admittedly rough account will suffice.) The scores, commonly called IQ (intelligence quotient) scores, reveal nothing about the *absolute* (total, complete) amount of intelligence a person may have. IQ scores are just estimates of the magnitude of possible differences among individuals in whatever quality the test measures. In brief, the scores identify, within certain degrees of error, which individuals seem to be more or less intelligent than others, and approximately how much more or less they may be so.

This rule, as it relates to Jensen's data, is important because of possible misinterpretations that may result. In view of the relative nature of IQ scores, it would be wrong to conclude that Jensen claims the average intelligence level of Negro children is "low" or that the average intelligence level of white children is "high." An equally wrong interpretation is that Negro children do not have sufficient ability to learn or to profit from instruction. In view of what is known about the vast potential of human genetic material, its sensitivity to environmental stimuli, and the fact that gene action itself is modified by experience, potential ability to learn appears to exist in nearly every human being at a level more than sufficient to profit from instruction that has been appropriately organized. The challenge for us as teachers is to know enough about the individual characteristics of each learner to ensure that our instruction matches his or her requirements and not just those of some estimated group average.

> The fact that IQ scores are relative means . . .

INTELLIGENCE IS MODIFIABLE

Jensen's conclusion that about 80 percent of intelligence is due to heredity does not suggest that intelligence cannot be modified by experience. Quite the contrary. There is wide agreement that learning ability is enhanced by experience. The entire notion of positive transfer, either at a molecular, structural level or at a functional, behavioral level, is based on the fact that learning becomes more efficient with appropriate practice. Further, Jensen's conclusion that heredity plays a major role in determining intelligence does not preclude the notion that intelligence can be greatly modified through experience. It is just that so far it does not appear to have been so modified. Rather, his conclusion should be interpreted as indicating that current efforts at teaching children in the home and in the school do not explain as much of their ability to learn as does their genetic inheritance. This could mean, however, that with better understanding of the environmental conditions necessary for optimal learning, a relatively larger portion of intelligence could be contributed by experience than is now claimed to be the case. Jensen's estimate that 80 percent of intelligence is due to heredity, if accepted as absolute, leads to the pessimistic and completely untenable view that our efforts at instruction are generally as effective as we will ever be able to make them. At the present very limited state of our understanding of the process of learning and teaching, such a view has to be considered extremely naïve and arrogant.

> Experience could account for more of our measured intelligence if . . .

Jensen feels that our schools have not been very successful in improving children's ability to learn nor have most of the so-called special programs expressly designed to improve certain children's chances of succeeding in the regular school setting. Among the latter are the massive Head Start programs initiated during the 1960s for disadvantaged preschool children throughout the United States. A possible and at least partial explanation is our comparative ignorance of how to design instruction for individual learners. Traditionally, instruction has been group-based, and each teacher has done pretty much whatever he "felt" was best at the time to help his learners learn. As teachers, we have tended to look upon teaching as an art, mostly for lack of a powerful theory of instruction. We have had no other choice.

Jensen describes the ineffectiveness of traditional, group-based instruction in this way:[3]

> Implicit in the system as it originally developed was the expectation that not all children would succeed. These methods of schooling have remained essentially unchanged for many generations. We have accepted traditional instruction so completely that it is extremely difficult even to imagine, much less to put into practice, any radically different forms that the education of children could take. Our thinking almost always takes as granted such features as beginning formal instruction at the same age for all children (universally between ages five and six), instruction of children in groups, keeping the same groups together in lock step fashion through the first several years of schooling, and an active-passive, showing-seeing, telling-listening relationship between teacher and pupil. Satisfactory learning occurs under these conditions only when children come to school with certain prerequisite abilities and skills: an attention span long enough to encompass the teacher's utterances and demonstrations, the ability voluntarily to focus one's attention where it is called for, the ability to comprehend verbal utterances and to grasp relationships between things and their symbolic representations, the ability to inhibit large-muscle activity and engage in covert "mental" activity, to repeat instruction to oneself, to persist in a task until a self-determined standard is attained—in short, the ability to engage in what might be called self-instructional activities, without which group instruction alone remains ineffectual.

At the least, it is optimistic to believe that, with the guidelines that derive from a powerful theory of instruction, improved and individualized instructional materials, methods, and procedures will combine effectively so that experience will come to account for more of children's ability to learn than it may at the present.

KNOWLEDGE OF INDIVIDUAL DIFFERENCES: PREREQUISITE FOR INSTRUCTION

One important question that the Jensen Controversy should cause us to ask ourselves is this pointed one: "What difference will it make in our instruction if (1) heredity does indeed contribute as much as 80 percent to the intelligence of our learners, or (2) if Negro children, as a group, do not score as well as white children on measures of intelligence, possibly due to both genetic and environmental differences?" The answer to this question is to be found in the statement

---

[3] A. R. Jensen (1969). How much can we boost I.Q. and scholastic achievement? *Harvard Educational Review* **39**, Winter, pp. 1–123.

that the object of instruction is to make learning optimal for *each* individual. Estimates of the average performance of a group are of little use to us when planning the instruction for the individual members of that group. Moreover, teaching for the "average" learner is never optimally effective, since the "average" person does not exist. He is only an arithmetical abstraction.

Stated in a slightly different way, our task as teachers is not to try to cause all our learners to be identical in terms of their learning nor to cause "dull" learners to catch up with "bright" learners. Rather, it is to cause each learner to learn at a rate and in a way that is optimal for that specific individual.

Knowledge of the characteristics of individual learners must be considered prerequisite to meeting this objective. Piaget's developmental theory of intelligence as adaptive, knowing behavior provides a potentially more useful guide for gaining this knowledge than data about the relative proportion of a general ability to learn that is attributed to heredity and environment, or information that certain groups may have more or less of this ability. The idea that makes Piaget's theory such a promising guide for understanding about the characteristics of individual learners is that the invariant elements of his theory apply to *individuals,* not just to groups. Each and every individual progresses through all the various developmental stages of intelligence in exactly the same sequence. The knowing behavior typical of a given stage is characteristic of every individual at that stage of development, not just certain ones. The characteristic knowing behaviors themselves are not group averages; they describe the intelligence of any individual at that stage. Furthermore, measures of intelligence, in Piaget's view, are not just *relative* measures; they are *absolute*. That is, measures are not comparable with those of other individuals; they are comparable with an outside criterion—the various stages of intelligence. No other view of intelligence presently permits this type of individual assessment with an absolute standard.

It is not my intent to minimize the potential importance to education of data such as Jensen has provided. Even though such data may have little immediate applicability to classroom learning, they can have extensive long-range effects. If there is a strong probability that a comparatively high percentage of our ability to learn *is* contributed by genetic factors, we should do our best to identify the mechanisms whereby the genes do their work. Only then can we logically and consistently arrange learning environments that work with genetic factors to maximize the positive effects of the hereditary potential. Data such as Jensen's should stimulate this kind of research activity.

Another area of research that is likely to be influenced by data that attribute intelligence chiefly to genetic factors is that concerned with theories of development, learning, and instruction. The result should be that these theories will show a basic organizational component that is biological in nature. You will notice that this is precisely the orientation Piaget has taken in his theory of development.

We might ask how the views of a hereditarian, such as Jensen, and an environmentalist, such as Skinner, can be reconciled with the broadly inclusive and eclectic views of the interactionist, Piaget. Environmentalists usually are not much concerned with theory. Their approach, as you will remember from Chapter 4, is to conduct scientific analyses of behavior for its basic, higher-order rules and then to learn how they may use the rules for the control and

The prerequisite to individualized instruction is . . .

modification of behavior. This position avoids the debate over the relative contribution of heredity and environment to intelligence merely by refusing to be concerned about the concept in the first place. They believe it is more useful to study what the learner does under various environmental conditions with various consequences than to theorize about inner stages or properties, inherited or otherwise. For the true environmentalist, everything the organism does beyond the given operants that help define a particular living organism is the result of learning; that is, the result of the operation of the rules of reinforcement and punishment. It should not be concluded, however, that environmentalists deny that heredity has anything to do with behavior. Obviously it does, although always indirectly. For example, certain physical characteristics, such as sex, eye or hair color, overall stature, and skin color, which are widely known to be primarily the result of heredity influence an individual's behavior but always as a function of the contingencies of reinforcement and punishment that operate in

The statement "Environment and heredity interact" means . . .

the individual's environment. The inherited characteristics are not themselves important determinants of behavior. Rather, it is the reinforcement and punishment with which these characteristics become associated through the experiences of living that determine their influence on behavior. For example, consider the sex of a child. In most societies, quite different and often predictable contingencies of reinforcement and punishment operate for males and for females, and the contingencies are not entirely the same even for children of the same sex within a given family. The inherited sexual characteristics per se do not determine the individual's behavior; it is primarily the environmental rewards and punishments relative to those characteristics that determine the behavior, and that behavior, of course, is learned.

Skinner reveals the environmentalist's point of view relative to the role of heredity as a determinant, that is, as an explanation for behavior, by pointing out that "the doctrine of 'being born that way' has little to do with demonstrated facts. It is usually an appeal to ignorance. 'Heredity', as the layman uses the term, is a fictional explanation of the behavior attributed to it."[4]

Taken by itself, an environmentalist point of view must be considered incomplete. Even though it has more than adequately demonstrated its usefulness, a strictly environmentalist position is limiting in that its focus excludes interest in the learner as a biological developing organism. Such a view, for example, would not lead to the possible discovery of genetic mechanisms relevant to development or to the likelihood of organizing instruction to work with genetic factors rather than to leave such a possibility to chance in terms, say, of preprogrammed sensitive periods devoted to language and learning to read.

We saw in Chapter 11 how an environmentalist point of view is complementary to Piaget's more generally inclusive theory of developmental adaptation. In brief, and relative to Piaget's theory, a major contribution made by the environmentalist position to our understanding of the development of learners and to the eventual derivation of rules for a theory of instruction is the specification of higher-order rules of reinforcement and punishment that obtain when learners interact with their environments. Piaget's theory is noticeably deficient in these tremendously important rules. Knowing about them helps us

---

[4] B. F. Skinner (1953). *Science and Human Behavior*. New York: Macmillan, p. 6.

in a very practical way, as we learned in Chapters 9 and 10, to make decisions about sequences and strategies of instruction that capture and maintain the appropriate interacting (attending and responding) behavior of our learners.

The issue of the relative contribution to intelligence by heredity and environment has not been of particular importance in Piaget's developmental theory; both are obviously necessary. For him, the question of which is most important is much like asking which contributes more to life, the lung or the air it breathes. It is impossible to conceive a living organism without biological, genetic mechanisms, an environment, and their interaction. His question has been what he believes a more fundamental one: "What is the nature of the adaptive interaction, over time, between what is inherited and what is experienced?" Consequently, extreme points of view, such as that of environmentalists who strongly emphasize the importance of experience in the ability to learn, or that of hereditarians who place just as great an emphasis on the contribution of the genes, present little difficulty for Piaget's theory since the nature of gene-environment interaction apparently is not greatly influenced by the relative quantities of the variables involved.

If we look closely at the positions of Piaget, Jensen, and Skinner, we find that neither Jensen's nor Skinner's position contains anything that argues against a progressively developmental, adaptive interaction between a living organism and its environment. Each merely identifies a different variable as the major contributor to the interaction. Neither position precludes the possibility of knowing behavior that is qualitatively, as well as quantitatively, different at different periods of time within a given individual's life or at different levels of the evolutionary scale.

All three positions have characteristics that are remarkably similar in their implications for education: an emphasis on appropriate early experience, the insistence that experience be individualized (timing, sequence, structure), a call for diversity of experience, experience that makes a meaningful match between what the individual is currently capable of and the requirements of the new task, and the belief that development proceeds from relatively simple to complex.

Piaget's theory of intelligence subsumes hereditarian and environmentalist views in that . . .

We now understand enough about the principal elements that constitute the three major points of view about intelligence, or the general ability to learn—hereditarian, interactionist, and environmentalist—for us to see whether our higher-order rules of development from Chapter 11 need modification before being included in a potentially useful synthesis with Bruner's (1966) guide for a theory of instruction. Checkpoint 12-1 will help us with our analysis.

CHECKPOINT 12-1

1. Review the higher-order rules of development as stated in Chapter 11. For each rule, state whether you feel a strictly hereditarian or an environmentalist position points up a need for modification of the rule. Indicate the nature of any change you believe is called for.

2. Were you willing to speculate about possible modifications of the rules stated in Chapter 11? Yes____   No____

TOWARD A THEORY OF INSTRUCTION

We are indebted to Jerome Bruner (1966) for the heading of this section of Chapter 12. It is the title of the book in which he extends both the challenge to education to develop a powerful theory of instruction and suggestions about what such a theory ought to encompass. The title conveys a feeling of synthesis and speculation. Thus it establishes the frame of mind that I believe is necessary for any teacher who purposely attempts to speculate beyond tradition and the data and to organize instruction for the individual differences of learners rather than for the widespread and mythical "average" learner. It is my intent to maintain this frame of mind for the rest of this chapter.

Bruner's Contributions toward a Theory of Instruction

Bruner explains that a theory of instruction is needed in addition to theories of learning and development because the latter are descriptive rather than prescriptive. "They tell us what happened after the fact: for example, that most children of six do not yet possess the notion of reversibility. A theory of instruction, on the other hand, might attempt to set forth the best means of leading the child toward the notion of reversibility."[5] In short, a theory of instruction *prescribes* rules about effective ways of achieving knowledge and skills. In addition, it provides a way to evaluate methods or approaches to teaching or learning.

Generality is an important characteristic of all theories including a theory of instruction. Thus, a theory of instruction must set up *general* criteria and state the conditions for meeting them rather than specify conditions of instruction for specific learning outcomes.

Bruner believes that a theory of instruction has four principal features. It should specify:[6]

A theory of instruction can help us . . .

1. "The experiences which most effectively implant in the individual a predisposition toward learning—learning in general or a particular type of learning. . . .

Bruner's four principal features of a theory of instruction are . . .

2. The ways in which a body of knowledge should be structured so that it can be most readily grasped by the learner. . . .
3. The most effective sequences in which to present the materials to be learned. . . .
4. The nature and pacing of rewards and punishments in the process of learning and teaching." [Also included is the notion that a theory of instruction should specify the processes involved in changing the nature of reinforcement from *immediate* and *extrinsic* to *deferred* and *intrinsic*.]

Briefly, Bruner's four principal features of a theory of instruction are concerned with (1) motivation, (2) structure of knowledge, (3) sequence of presentation of material, and (4) knowledge or results, or positive and negative feedback. You will notice that if we operationally define motivation as attending,

---

[5] J. S. Bruner (1966). *Toward a Theory of Instruction.* Cambridge, Mass.: The Belknap Press of Harvard University Press, p. 40.
[6] Ibid., pp. 40–42.

responding, and valuing behavior maintained by appropriate contingencies of reinforcement and punishment (see Chapters 9 and 10), this feature of a theory of instruction can be incorporated within Bruner's fourth feature. Consequently, in our synthesis of the higher-order rules of development within Bruner's general features of a theory of instruction, we will combine these two and thus proceed with three rather than four major categories of specifications.

To begin the construction of our theory and to tie the three major categories of postulates together into a meaningful whole, we will state a generally inclusive basic premise relative to both learning and instruction. For each of the three major categories, we will first state the postulate, then list relevant higher-order rules of development. These will be our theorems. Next, we will speculate on the implications for instruction of these statements. Finally, in the last section of the chapter, we will examine four general approaches to individualized instruction to see how these implications may be implemented to make instruction optimal for each learner.

Beginning with a Basic Premise about Learning and Teaching

In Chapter 1 and throughout the text, we have discussed within several contexts the notion that a teacher's primary task is to cause learners to attend to appropriate learning events long enough and well enough to learn them. As you will remember, this proposition was derived from our basic assumption that we learn what we practice. Thus, the job to be done by instruction is to ensure that learners do practice appropriately; that they *attend* and *respond* effectively and come to *value* learning. Therefore, it is the basic premise of the theory being developed here that learners *will* practice effectively, provided that (1) learning materials are appropriately structured, (2) they are appropriately sequenced, and (3) corrective feedback is made appropriately contingent on attending and responding behaviors.

Briefly, and very simply, the basic premise from which the following postulates, theorems, implications, and examples for application derive can be stated this way: *Instruction must ensure that what is to be learned is practiced appropriately.*

The basic premise for our theory of instruction is . . .

The job for the postulates and theorems of our theory will be to specify the characteristics of appropriate practice relative to (1) the structure and nature of the content of the material (cognitive, affective, and psychomotor) to be practiced; (2) the sequence of practice—when, how much, and under what conditions practice should occur; and (3) effective contingencies of corrective feedback—the nature of the reinforcement and punishment that occur, and when and how they should occur. These three primary characteristics of appropriate practice are stated as the postulates of our theory of instruction.

Our theory of instruction will need to specify . . .

POSTULATE 1. EFFECTIVE
INSTRUCTION REQUIRES THAT
LEARNING EXPERIENCES BE APPROPRIATE
AND APPROPRIATELY STRUCTURED

Appropriate structure of learning experience is a matter of both the potential logic or inherent relatedness, that is, meaningfulness of the experience (or material) itself, and the substantial and organizational nature of the learner's structure of knowledge—his state of readiness (Ausubel, 1963). Learning experiences that are appropriate and appropriately structured show a match between these two requirements (Hunt, 1961).

Postulate No. 1 means . . .

Several of our higher-order rules of development from Chapter 11 are relevant to this postulate, since an important part of the definition of appropriate structure lies within the characteristic of the learner's structures of knowledge. We learned in Chapter 11 that these structures are fundamentally the result of the processes of gene-environment interaction over time.

Following are the rules of development I believe relevant to the requirement of *appropriate structure* for the effective instruction. Within each of the three major categories, I will first state the rules and then discuss their potential implications for instruction. At that point we will find it useful to recall Gagné's conditions of different types of learning (1970) and our rules of reinforcement and punishment, since, as you recall, a theory of instruction must derive from theories of development, including specific rules of learning (Bruner, 1966).

RULES   Instruction must account for the notions that:

1. The major function of gene action is the production of the thousands of kinds of protein molecules that (a) serve as the primary building blocks of cells, and (b) act as specific enzymes for most biochemical reactions of life (*the basic rule of gene action*).

2. The major function of experience in development is that it provides the stimulation necessary to cause genes to act (*the basic rule of experience*).

3. Development is a continuous, orderly, and lawful progression of structural and functional change that occurs within a living organism interacting with its environment over time (*the basic rule of interaction*).

4. Gene action is essentially the same across all living organisms (*the rule generality*).

5. Living organisms possess genetic potential far greater than they usually demonstrate (*the rule of general plasticity*).

6. Experience is most effective when it complements the actions of preprogrammed mechanisms (*the rule of complementary action*).

7. Experience, to be effective in stimulating gene action, must be of the appropriate kind (*the rule of the match*).

8. Experience, to be effective, must vary over time (*the rule of habituation*).

9. The structures of knowledge that progressively develop through the interactions of genes and experience develop so that the old structures are always incorporated within the new (*the rule of progressive subsumption*).

10. Capacity for, and efficiency in, further development change as a function of experience and time (*the rule of transfer*).

11. Development progresses from capabilities for basic physiological responding toward capabilities for complex cognitive responding (*the rule of increasing complexity*).

12. Development progresses from a point at which individuals are most alike to a point at which they are least alike (*the rule of progressive differentiation*).

IMPLICATIONS FOR INSTRUCTION   These rules of development offer several possible implications for instruction. Our job in this section will be to speculate on what they may be. In the last section of this chapter, we will attempt then to spell out how instruction may be organized to account for these implications. Right now, however, we are still talking about higher-order rules and their implications for instruction. We do not want to confuse this type of discussion with the type that deals with specific methods, materials, procedures, or techniques for applying the rules. This is the kind of distinction that, so often in education, is allowed to become clouded, with the result that frequently we intuitively adopt materials, approaches, techniques, and so forth without reference to the rules from which they should derive. We discussed this potential danger in Chapter 6, where we learned that conditions (or rules) of learning are *independent* of approaches to learning. We also learned (in Chapters 8, 9, and 10) that, whereas rules often are few, approaches are limited only by the capability for ingenuity and creativeness of each teacher.

One of the most apparent implications of all the rules listed under Postulate 1 is that instruction must ensure that learners are *active*, since structures of knowledge develop from the interaction between an individual and the environment. As a corollary to this implication is the notion, according to Piaget, that a great deal of physical activity must occur during the early years because more advanced structures of knowing derive from preprogrammed structures of knowledge that are elaborated by concrete activities (*the rule of complementary action*). Things must be acted on to be understood. "For these reasons a . . . school should encourage the child's activity, and his manipulation and exploration of objects. When the teacher tries to bypass this process by imparting knowledge in a verbal manner, the result is often superficial learning."[7]

The implication of learner activity means . . .

Activity, however, means more than just physical activity. It means mental or intellectual activity as well, especially at the stage of formal operational intelligence. Ausubel (1963) refers to the active and mental participation of learners when they are engaged in meaningful reception learning. Incorporating new information into existing cognitive structures in a meaningful, as opposed to a rote, manner requires considerable intellectual activity on the learner's part. As Piaget points out, passive observers gain little knowledge. It is the task of effective instruction to cause *both* types of activity to occur at appropriate times.

The notion that one type of action is more appropriate than another for a given stage of intellectual development brings to our attention the idea of the match (Hunt, 1961) between an individual's current structures of knowledge and the structure of the materials (experience) to be learned (*the rule of the match*). If it is true that a learner's cognitive structure reflects different developmental characteristics at different stages in terms of the types of knowing behavior he is capable of, instruction must be organized so that those parts of the structure of the material being learned will match the learner's present capabilities. This is essentially what Bruner means when he says that "any idea or problem or body of knowledge can be presented in a form simple enough so that any particular learner can understand it in recognizable form."[8]

All these ideas imply that instruction must be organized around task analyses of the bodies of knowledge and skills, including psychomotor and affective skills, that are to be learned. The hierarchies of learning outcomes proposed by Bloom (1956), Krathwohl (1964), and Harrow (1972), and of types of learning

---

[7] H. Ginsburg and S. Opper (1969). *Piaget's Theory of Intellectual Development: An Introduction.* Englewood Cliffs, N.J.: Prentice-Hall, p. 221.
[8] J. S. Bruner (1966). Op. cit., p. 440.

worked out by Gagné (1970), should prove helpful in arriving at an appropriate match between the stage of the learner's intellectual development as described by Piaget and the requirements of the learning task (*the rule of increasing complexity*). Without guides such as these to help us arrange practice that is appropriately matched to the learner's structures of knowledge, we face the danger of having our instruction become ineffective and wasteful, often because of our tendency to equate instruction with "telling." Reliance on verbalization, especially during the early years, runs the high risk of resulting in learning experiences that are rote and confused rather than meaningful, and that are aversive rather than rewarding. Under these conditions, our learners will soon find ways to escape from, and to avoid, our instruction—and probably us, as people.

It is not only in the early years that instruction which relies heavily on verbal facility can result in the ineffective and nonrewarding outcomes. At the secondary and even at the university level, the structure of the material being learned still requires an appropriate match with the structures of knowledge of the learners. Even though most of our learners by this age have developed to the stage of formal operational intelligence and thus are able to deal with concepts and rules on an abstract verbal level, their structures or knowledge do not inevitably include all those specific concepts and rules necessary to deal abstractly with a particular topic that is new for them. For our instruction to be effective in causing our learners to practice appropriately in this case, we would be wise to include experiences with concrete materials—real objects or events, models, diagrams, pictures—that can be experienced directly so as to form meaningful associations, discriminations, and concrete concepts. Defined concepts and rules relevant to the new topic can then be handled meaningfully at the abstract verbal level. Attempts to shortcut this requirement of meaningfully learned prerequisites and to "get by" on empty verbal expression is indeed risky policy. The shortcuts to learning made possible by a level of formal operational intelligence can be enjoyed only when we can be sure that our learners do indeed have richly meaningful cognitive structures that can accommodate the new material.

The implication of the match means . . .

You will notice that this discussion applies also to learning in the affective domain. Just because learners are capable of attending, responding, and valuing behavior, these structures of knowing behavior do not necessarily match the requirements of attending, responding, and valuing of some new learning task. Our instruction must include provision for ensuring that these behaviors do occur. The widespread, frequent, and essentially ineffective use of punishment in our schools, especially at the secondary levels, is sad testimony to the gross lack of attention accorded this simple idea.

The rule of complementary action implies . . .

Another implication for instruction that derives from the rules of development listed under Postulate 1 is that practice provided by instruction must be of certain kinds for the most effective elaboration of certain structures of knowledge. This, of course, is closely related to the *rule of the match*. It has particular importance, however, relative to the initial elaboration of preprogrammed structures, especially those that can be demonstrated to play a significant role in learning language and learning to read (*the rule of complementary action*). The implication for education is that instruction should be organized so that the content and the form in which practice occurs parallel the content and form of what is to be learned. In the case of language acquisition, therefore, preprogrammed mechanisms for learning language, for example the *Language Acquisition Device* postulated by Chomsky (1965), must be activated and elaborated by experiences that have the content and the form of the language that is to be learned. As you recall from Chapter 11, Lenneberg maintains that this requires "exposure to the language of one's fellow-men."[9]

There is reason to believe that learning to read is closely related to learning language. If we recall, from Chapter 11, the evidence for a sensitive period for shape and form perception that occurs within the first three months of life, and if we combine that information with the fact that a sensitive period for language acquisition begins around the second year and lasts until about four years of age (Cazden, 1968; Lenneberg, 1967; Goldman-Eisler, 1964), we are led to two conclusions. First, instruction in reading can profitably begin much earlier than the traditional ages of five or six, probably during the years between two and four. Second, the content and form of practice in beginning reading apparently should emphasize the development of associations and discriminations; that is *associations* between the sounds each letter makes and its shape and form, and *discriminations* between the different letter shapes and between their related sounds. This approach is called *code emphasis*. In this way, practice in learning to read complements and elaborates the action of preprogrammed genetic mechanisms related to language and reading.

Learning to read offers a useful example of the potential value of a theory of instruction derived from the theory and rules of development. We know about (1) gene action relative to sensitive periods, (2) preprogrammed structures of knowledge and the content and form of experience necessary to elaborate them, and (3) the prerequisite capabilities for learning to read—the structure of this task. This knowledge gives us clues about *when* reading instruction can profitably begin, and *what* the nature of the instruction should be. Having this kind of knowledge takes much of the intuition, or just plain guesswork, out of instruction for us. It also improves the probability that our learners will be successful.

You might be interested in reading more about the issues and the evidence relating to the topic of learning to read. Jeannie Chall (1967), an eminent authority on reading, has done a thorough review of the body of reading research from 1912 to 1965. Her conclusions and recommendations substantiate the speculations we made here from our theory of instruction about an effective type of instruction for learning to read.

Chall summarizes her findings this way:[10]

The [reading] results are better [with a code-emphasis], not only in terms of the mechanical aspects of literacy alone, as was once supposed, but also in terms of the ultimate goals of reading instruction-comprehension and possibly even speed of reading. The long-existing fear that an initial code-emphasis produces readers who do not read for meaning or with enjoyment is unfounded. On the contrary, the evidence indicates that better results in terms of reading for meaning are achieved with the programs that emphasize code at the start than with the programs that stress meaning at the beginning.

It should be pointed out that Chall's data do not endorse any one

[9] E. H. Lenneberg (1967). *Biological Foundations of Language.* New York: Wiley, p. 378.
[10] J. S. Chall (1967). *Learning to Read: The Great Debate.* New York: McGraw-Hill, p. 307.

code-emphasis method over another. In view of John Stephens's findings (1965) (see Chapter 2) that various methods produce essentially the same results, Chall's data are not surprising. Another point that Chall makes is that her data do not permit extrapolation beyond a method for beginning reading.

It is interesting that this type of instruction—*code emphasis*—is apparently not the most widely used by teachers. Rather, a *meaning-emphasis* type of instruction, in which word meaning is stressed first, is more popular, even though it is believed less effective. This is often the price that children have to pay for the lack of a powerful theory of instruction.

There are several other implications for instruction that derive from the rules of Postulate 1. The fact that development progresses from a point at which individuals are most alike to a point at which they are least alike (*the rule of progressive differentiation*) implies a concern for instruction that has at least two parts. First, learners in secondary school show greater variation in their structures of knowledge and knowing behavior than do infants, preschool children, and children in the elementary grades. Second, and following from the first part, since secondary school students show a greater variety or diversity in the quality and quantity of their knowing structures than younger learners do, there is a greater demand for individualized instruction at the secondary levels than in the preschool years or even in the elementary grades, although the demand is great at all levels. Because of this greater variation among older learners, however, there is also a greater variety or diversity of potential methods, techniques, materials, styles, and approaches that are possible for teachers to use at this level. The possibilities range all the way from individual tutorial by way of programmed learning to mastery learning to open education (Walberg and Thomas, 1972) to free schools (Kozol, 1972). (We will discuss these various *approaches* to instruction in the last section of this chapter.)

The rule of progressive differentiation implies . . .

It is interesting to observe that, as a rule of thumb, the further learners go in the public schools, the less individual instructional attention they receive, yet, with each year the need for individual instruction increases. Take, for example, the range in reading ability that exists in most classrooms. As a rough guide, the range increases by at least one year for each grade level. At the grade two level, then, the range in reading ability within an "average" classroom will be about two grade levels; some of the children in that group will read at only about a grade one level, whereas others in the group will read at about the grade three level. At the grade six level, the average range in reading ability will be at least six years; probably from an ability of about grade three or four to about grade nine or ten. In secondary school, the range is likely to be even greater; yet, the probability is less that instruction takes such wide variations in reading ability into account. It is this lack of instructional relevance that has prompted numerous persons, e.g., Holt (1964, 1969, 1972), Kozol (1967), Goodman (1964, 1966), Neill (1960), Illich (1971), and Kohl (1969) to criticize the public school system and to look for alternatives. Many of the alternatives, however, have not proven any more successful, probably at least partially because they also tend to be intuitive in what they do with and for learners.

A theory of instruction derived from the theory and rules of development points clearly to the educational weakness of an instructional pattern that all but neglects the fact of increasing variation among learners over time. Regardless of what grade level you are planning to teach, preschool, elementary, or secondary, you might take as a personal challenge the responsibility to organize instruction for your learners that is at least partly individualized.

Two more implications for instruction derive from the rules of Postulate 1. One derives from *the rule of transfer* and the other from *the rule of general plasticity*. The implication that derives from the fact of vast genetic potential is simply one of positive expectations for the learning capabilities of our students. Knowing about the vast genetic potential that all organisms possess beyond what they normally utilize should constantly remind us that whether that potential becomes operative for an individual depends almost entirely upon the quality of the experiences in that person's environment. In short, it should serve to remind us that if a learner is not learning, it is likely that our instruction is not appropriate for him and that it needs to be modified.

The rule of transfer is closely related to *the rule of progressive subsumption*, and together they imply that our instruction must always be prefaced with the statement to our learners: "Today you are going to learn something about . . . , later, you will learn *more* about it." The meaning in this preface is that planning for instruction must be on the basis of long-term learning, not of single, isolated lessons. Since we never learn all that can be know about a concept (Markel, 1975) each learning experience must be kept open-ended, at least in the sense that our learners are aware that what is now being learned will serve as the basis for learning more about the concept at later times. In this view, Bruner's idea of a *spiral curriculum* makes a good deal of sense. His point is that, at an early age, children can learn something of value about almost any concept and then later, as their structures of knowledge become more generally inclusive and better organized, they will be able to learn more about it, and so on. This idea has great potential usefulness to instruction and fits logically with other persons' views, e.g., Gagné, Bloom, Ausubel, Piaget, and Skinner to mention a few, even though some claim that it does not. The idea has not received the serious recognition that it merits. This is partially because it frequently is interpreted literally in the light of Bruner's bold statement that "any subject can be taught effectively in some intellectually honest form to any child at any stage of development." Thus, the idea of a spiral curriculum becomes the unfortunate target of easy criticism rather than the object of serious investigation. For example, "Thus, according to Bruner, the six-year-old minischolar can learn to think like a historian or mathematician. . . . and imagine for a moment, trying to teach a three- or four-year-old the structure of algebra or the idea that historical knowledge is relative and biased."[11] But this is not what Bruner meant.

Bruner's point is both simple and powerful. It is simple in that if we, as teachers, understand the structure of those bodies of knowledge relative to history, mathematics, political science, and so forth, we can *begin* giving meaningful instruction in them to children at an early age and *continue* to instruct meaningfully in them as the children develop rather than cause them to believe erroneously that once they have experienced some small part of a topic they have learned it, or that they are too young to understand. It is a powerful idea in that it has wide generalizability to all areas of school learning, and in that

The rules of transfer and progressive subsumption imply . . .

[11] R. C. Sprinthall and N. A. Sprinthall (1974). *Educational Psychology: A Developmental Approach.* Reading, Mass.: Addison-Wesley, pp. 255–256.

considering concept and rule learning as learning that occurs in a continuous spiral is an extremely effective way to plan long-range instruction, i.e., over several years, that *teaches* for transfer that is both *vertical* and *horizontal,* and that is *planned* rather than *incidental.* The potential danger in the idea of a spiral curriculum is that we may try to shortcut the early levels of the spiral—the concrete experiences, associations, discriminations, motor manipulations, attending and responding behaviors—or unduly speed them up, with the result that learning becomes rote rather than meaningful.

CHECKPOINT 12-2

1. Assume that you are a teacher planning educational experiences that are appropriately structured for each of your learners, for example, in the area of mathematics or the language arts. Think about the things you will need to be concerned with to ensure that the experience will be appropriately structured so that instruction will be optimal for each learner. List these concerns in point form.

2. Did you view this activity as an opportunity to practice reducing some of the trial and error from your future teaching behavior? Yes____   No____

POSTULATE 2. EFFECTIVE
INSTRUCTION REQUIRES THAT LEARNING
EXPERIENCES BE APPROPRIATELY SEQUENCED

Postulate No. 2 means . . .   The question of what constitutes an appropriate sequence of learning experience obviously involves consideration of the developmental characteristics of each learner as well as the logical sequence or progression of ideas inherent in the material to be learned. Questions such as "When should learning to read best *begin?*" and "How should reading experiences be sequenced?" can only be answered relative to the developmental characteristics of the knowing structures within the learner and the requirements at various points in a logical sequence of ideas inherent in the task of learning to read. An appropriate sequence of experience is one that continually matches the developmental level of the learner and the requirements of the task. Thus, it is obvious that there can be no one sequence for all learners.

Following are the rules of development I believe relevant to the requirement of *appropriate sequence* for effective instruction.

RULES   Instruction must account for the notions that:

1. Preprogrammed genetic mechanisms are incomplete, especially in human beings, and must be elaborated through experience (*the rule of elaboration*).
2. Knowing behavior develops from preprogrammed, reflexive knowing toward intentional, reflective knowing (*the rule of progressive internalization*).
3. Gene action is of two general types: *proactive,* or preprogrammed; and *reactive* or modified by experience (*the rule of types of gene action*).
4. Early in the developmental sequence and phylogenetically, gene action is mostly *proactive;* gradually it becomes more *reactive* (*the rule of increasing reactivity*).

5. Experience is most effective in stimulating gene action when it occurs during certain periods of time (*the rule of special timing*).
6. The general plasticity of genetic potential decreases with age and lack of practice (*the rule of decreasing flexibility*).
7. The effects of experience on gene action are more enduring with repetition (*the rule of practice*).
8. Development progresses from generalized, undifferentiated capabilities for responding toward specialized capabilities for responding (*the rule of specialization*).
9. Development progresses at different rates within and between individuals (*the rule of varying rates*).

IMPLICATIONS FOR INSTRUCTION The general implication for instruction that derives from the rules of development listed under Postulate 2 is that *first things must come first*. This idea is reflected in the notion of hierarchies of instructional objectives (Bloom, 1956; Krathwohl, 1964; Harrow, 1972), in Gagné's types of learning (1970), Maslow's basic needs (1968), and Skinner's sequences (1968) of shaping behavior through the process of reinforcing successive approximations. Several studies have attempted to validate the basic idea that higher-level skills are learned hierarchically, whereas lower-level specific and individual items of knowledge or skill are not. Richard White's study (1974) of the validation of a learning hierarchy patterned after Gagné's types of learning is one of the latest and most comprehensive. He claims that the results of his study with grade nine, ten, and eleven students given a math-science learning task support Gagné's suggestion (1968) that lower-level specific and individual items of knowledge (called *verbalized knowledge*) are not learned hierarchically though higher-level intellectual skills (concepts and rules) are. (You might find it helpful to refer to the responses for Checkpoint 5-2 for an example of a learning hierarchy after Gagné.)

The general implication that first things should come first would appear more valid at the early stages of development than at later stages, i.e., the stage of formal operations, since, with increasing verbal facility, reversibility of actions becomes possible and operations become internal as well as external. That is, learners become able to think abstractly about the order and sequence of the elements of learning events and to reorder or resequence them as they test various hypotheses about them. With this type of intellectual capability, sequencing of instruction from relatively simple to complex may be less important than when this type of capability is not present, although, as White's study (1974) showed, such sequencing is beneficial to older learners. Also, as we saw in Chapter 6, acquiring the capability to order and sequence information and events is one of the main instructional objectives of discovery learning.

The rule that first things must come first implies . . .

From the *rules of special timing and decreasing flexibility* comes an implication relevant to the importance of appropriate practice early in life: First, if instruction does not provide appropriate practice at appropriate times, the effectiveness of practice may be less than optimal; and second, since flexibility tends to decrease with age and lack of practice, it appears that appropriate practice should occur at the *earliest point in life at which it is likely to be effective*. For language acquisition and learning to read, for example, this would mean visual experience with shapes and forms and auditory experience with spoken language beginning within the first three months of life. Instruction in reading, using a code emphasis, could begin with profit by the age of two years. Delaying instruction beyond the sensitive periods for shapes, forms, and language acquisition that occur prior to about four years of age may result in increased difficulty with both language acquisition and learning to read. Readiness for language acquisition and reading apparently may actually decrease with age without appropriate experience. Callaway (1971) states it this way: "The behavioral evidence concerning early reading does not indicate a continuous growth in reading readiness. . . . Rather, it logically requires the postulation of a transitory sensitive period marked by an optimum level of readiness to learn to read."[12]

The rules of special timing and decreasing flexibility imply . . .

This means that readiness, at least for language and reading, can be thought of as being *learned* rather than simply happening as a natural part of maturational processes. The implication for instruction is that readiness can be enhanced through proper instruction, appropriately timed.

This notion regarding readiness enhancement finds support in most points of view about development, learning, and instruction. Controversy exists, however, over how much readiness can be, or should be, increased or accelerated by instruction. Environmentalists argue that readiness is mainly a matter of having learned the prerequisite knowledge and skills required in the next learning task. Readiness is always the outcome of experience and instruction. Maturationalists, on the other hand, believe that readiness evolves in its own good time, largely as a result of preprogrammed biological processes. Experience or instruction does little to increase or accelerate readiness. Of course, neither an environmentalist nor a maturationalist point of view assumes an all-or-nothing position.

Others, for example, Piaget, hold more to a middle ground in which readiness is believed to result from interaction between biological mechanisms and appropriate experience. Because both components are necessary for the interaction, Piaget maintains that increasing one, i.e., experience, will have only limited effects in increasing or accelerating readiness since the essentially unchanged level of the biological component sets the limits beyond which additional or different experiences will not be effective.

Bruner's position (1966) is somewhere between that of Piaget and the extreme environmentalists. He calls "readiness" a mischievous half-truth, explaining that "It is a half-truth largely because it turns out that one *teaches* readiness or provides opportunities for its nurture, one does not simply wait for it. Readiness, in these terms, consists of mastery of those simpler skills that permit one to reach higher skills."[13]

The rule of specialization implies . . .

The *rule of specialization* is relevant to the discussion of readiness. That development progresses from generalized to specialized capabilities has the possible implication that instruction must ensure that learners know generally about various bodies of knowledge before trying to help them know specifically about them. You will note the similarity of this implication for instruction with Ausubel's notions (1963) about the organization of instruction for meaningful reception learning that emphasizes a sequence from general to specific. The use of overviews and advance organizers is consistent with this view. Also, you will see that this implication parallels Piaget's belief, relative to the processes of

---

[12] R. W. Callaway, Jr. (1970). Modes of biological adaptation and their role in intellectual development, *PCD Monographs*, **1**(1), p. 22.

[13] J. S. Bruner (1966). Op. cit., p. 29.

assimilation and accommodation, that until you know in general you cannot know in specific.

Some of the most important implications for instruction derive from the *rules of elaboration and progressive internalization.* They concern the idea that instruction must be organized so that, over time, the responding behavior of learners develops from immediate and essentially reflexive responding guided by preprogrammed genetic mechanisms to responding that can be delayed and reflected upon. The growing evidence that many children who learn only poorly are characterized by impulsive responding and an apparent inability to attend properly to learning tasks suggests that this implication for instruction is not being dealt with adequately.

It is probably safe to say that, for many learners, very little of their instruction purposely has, as one of its major objectives, helping them develop the capability to delay responding long enough to reflect on their actions. Too often this aspect of development is left to chance or "maturation."

Children who do not learn to "think about" what they are doing before acting are found frequently in special classes. They may be labeled impulsive, inattentive, hyperactive, hyperkinetic, distractable, emotionally disturbed, and so forth. Virginia Douglas (1971) describes the behavior characteristic of children she identifies as hyperactive:[14]

> These youngsters are apparently unable to keep their own impulses under control in order to cope with situations when care, concentrated attention or organized planning are required. They tend to react with the first idea that occurs to them or to those aspects of a situation which are the most obvious or compelling. This appears to be the case whether the task requires that they work with visual, or auditory stimuli and it also seems to be true in the visual motor and kinaesthetic spheres. These deficiencies—deficiencies which I have come to think of as the inability to "stop, look and listen"—seem, too, to influence the children's social behavior. . . . On a story completion task, they are unable to react realistically to a potentially frustrating situation, and in real life, several of our older hyperactives are beginning to get into trouble with the law because of their inability to control their impulsive tendencies.

The implication for instruction is that the instruction we provide apparently does not help many of our learners develop reflective, self-controlled responding behavior. We are challenged to find ways to improve our instruction so that it does. Some of the four approaches to instruction we will discuss in the last section of this chapter will give you some clues about how you may go about this.

The rules of elaboration and progressive internalization imply . . .

The *rule of practice* allows us to speculate on at least two implications for instruction. First, instruction must provide practice, since practice is necessary for learning that results in long-term retention. A corollary of this proposition is that practice is also necessary for the retention of material previously learned, that is, for the retention of "old" material. Second, instruction must provide more practice for learning and retaining rote material than for meaningful material. Instruction that is organized so that learning is meaningful is more effective as well as more efficient than instruction whose organization results in students' learning material rotely.

---

[14] V. I. Douglas (1971). Stop, look, and listen! The problem of sustained attention and impulse control in hyperactive and normal children. Unpublished presidential address, *Canadian Psychological Association.* Montreal: McGill University, pp. 25–26.

The challenge presented by these implications is directed squarely at the traditionally established institution of group-based instruction. It is virtually impossible to organize group-based instructional materials, procedures, or techniques that will result in meaningful learning for each member of the group.

Meaning is a uniquely individual phenomenon, and its demands for individual attention bring us to the consideration of the *rule of varying rates.* This rule reminds us that developmental sequences do not always occur in smoothly uniform patterns either among all individuals or even within any given individual. Because development is the product of the interaction of biological and environmental factors, and since the specifics of these variables differ *among* individuals and also differ as a function of time *within* each individual, we can expect rather marked differences in individual rates of development. In terms of education, then, no two of your learners will ever be at exactly the same developmental point at exactly the same time, either qualitatively or quantitatively. Nor, for that matter, will any one individual ever be at exactly the same stage of development relative to all aspects of the school curriculum. That is, we cannot assume, because a learner is a certain age, that he is *at* a particular stage of development, or even that he *should* be. Whether he is or not depends on his unique biological makeup and his environmental experiences.

The rule of varying rates implies . . .   The *rule of varying rates* also means that a learner may function adequately in one area of the curriculum, for example, at a level of formal operational knowing in arithmetic, yet function only at a concrete operational level in science. The reason for such a difference in performance can likely be attributed to differences in the quality or quantity of past experiences relative to the topics of the various curriculum areas. We must remember that the stages of knowing behavior do not just evolve; they develop as a consequence of both biology and experience.

Several important implications for instruction derive from these notions about development. The most obvious one is that instruction must allow a great deal of flexibility in terms both of the *rate* at which learners may progress and of the types of instructional materials and activities that are available. Of equal importance is the idea, often overlooked by teachers, that the rate of progression and choice of materials and activities for learning must be at least partially under the control of the learner.

The logical conclusion that must be drawn from these implications for instruction is that reliance on a group-based instructional mode is a contradiction of what is well known about the varying rates of development of learners. Learners must be given both greater individual consideration in their development and greater responsibility in their own instruction. Finding ways to bring this about is a burden for our discussion in the last section of this chapter. However, we will get a few clues on "how to do it" from the rules of development relevant to Postulate 3, which deals with motivation and feedback.

CHECKPOINT 12-3

Again assume the role of a teacher planning optimal instruction for each of your learners. This time, however, think through the kinds of things with which you will need to be concerned to ensure that the experiences will be appropriately *sequenced* for each learner. List these concerns in point form.

POSTULATE 3. EFFECTIVE
INSTRUCTION REQUIRES THAT
LEARNING EXPERIENCES INCLUDE
APPROPRIATE CONTINGENCIES
OF CORRECTIVE FEEDBACK

In Chapters 5 and 6, we learned that a general condition necessary for all of Gagné's types of learning is knowledge of results, or feedback. In Chapters 8, 9, and 10, we saw that positive reinforcement and punishment are frequently observed forms in which feedback occurs.

Bruner reminds us that "learning depends upon knowledge of results at a time when and at a place where the knowledge can be used for correction. Instruction increases the appropriate timing and placing of corrective knowledge."[15] He also points out that both (1) the *conditions* under which knowledge of results is useful in learning and (2) the *form* in which corrective information is received are important for us to consider if we are to make our instruction effective. This means we must specify these conditions and forms. You will notice that we have already done so to some extent through our discussions, in Chapters 8, 9, and 10, of the rules of reinforcement and punishment relative to the task of helping learners become self-managing.

**Postulate No. 3
means . . .**

The following rules of development from Chapter 11, I believe, are relevant to the requirement of appropriate contingencies of corrective feedback for effective instruction.

RULES   Instruction must account for the notions that:

1.   Gene action is terminated or modified by stimuli generated or transported by feedback systems (*the basic rule of feedback*).
2.   Continuing and varied interaction of individuals with their environment is necessary for development to proceed (*the rule of reciprocal feedback, or of action-reaction*).
3.   Development progresses from genetically preprogrammed motivation to attend and to respond toward motivation to attend and respond that is controlled also socially and culturally (*the rule of changing motivation*).
4.   Development occurs in the order of decreasing rigidness and immediacy of response (*the rule of increasing delay of feedback*).

IMPLICATIONS FOR INSTRUCTION   We learned in Chapter 5 that attending-responding behavior and knowledge of results, including feedback of possible reinforcing and punishing consequences, are included among the general conditions for all the types of learning described by Gagné (1970). If these conditions, among others, are not met by an individual learner, then learning of associations, discriminations, concepts, and rules will not occur for him. In short, unless the learner attends and responds to a learning task, and gets feedback about the effectiveness of his responses, learning will not occur for him—his performance on the task will not change; he will not improve. *Attention* guides our responses and *feedback* gives us the information that enables us to modify our next response to make it more effective.

The implications for instruction of these two ideas are that instruction must

---

[15] J. S. Bruner (1966). Op. cit., p. 500.

be organized so that it (1) causes each learner to attend and respond appropriately, and (2) provides feedback in the appropriate *form* and at the appropriate *time* for it to be useful in modifying later responses. We will discuss each of these general implications in terms of specific rules of development listed above.

The rule of changing motivation implies . .

The rule of changing motivation suggests that individuals are born with incomplete, built-in mechanisms for attending and responding to certain environmental stimuli. Continued development and elaboration of these mechanisms depend on appropriate practice. The challenge to instruction is to provide that practice rather than to assume that appropriate attending and responding behavior exists naturally within each learner—or that it "should," regardless of age or past experiences. Apparently, the preprogrammed attending and responding behaviors of many learners have been so modified by the experiences even before kindergarten or grade one that appropriate school learning is greatly impaired. Virginia Douglas (1971) described the behavior of some of these children, labeled *hyperactive*. Dennis Stott (1974) talks about kindergarten-age children who already have learned how *not to learn*. He also describes his training program aimed at improving their attending and responding behavior:[16]

> By the time a child reaches school age, he has developed his own style of coping with problems, and this becomes the learning style that he uses in school tasks. Some children, either by temperament or by training, develop excellent styles. They forge ahead, register high intelligence quotients, and do well academically. Other children, from handicap of temperament or cultural disadvantage, use a style that results in failure. Failure in turn generates a variety of ways of avoiding a situation. Avoidance may take the form of seeking distractions or retreating into dullness. . . . We make similar observations (that some children do not know how to learn) about children who come to us with a diagnosis of perceptual handicap. In their initial responses they certainly failed to discriminate between letters of the alphabet, but we noticed that they did not give themselves time to make the discrimination. Until they changed their hit or miss habits, we had no way of discovering, by test or otherwise, what their perceptual ability might be.

Stott continues, describing the challenge to instruction imposed by the fact that many young learners have not developed the appropriate attending and responding behavior for success in school-type tasks:[17]

> The reluctance to teach children the elements of reading and number in kindergarten stems from the feeling that by postponing academic learning we are granting the young child a little more time of stress-free happiness. But academic studies are not inevitably unpleasant and fraught with stress. What matters with a young child, irrespective of the content of the curriculum, is that he enjoys learning. Obviously, if he is exposed to material that discourages and bewilders him, and hence provides none of the rewards of success, it will be impossible to fulfill these conditions. If he is given suitably graded experiences to help him form his associations and concepts, he is reinforced by feelings of competence.

What Stott is describing here is the fact that appropriate attending and

---

[16] D. H. Stott (1974). A preventive program for the primary grades, *Elementary School Journal,* **74**(5), pp. 300–304.
[17] Ibid., p. 307.

responding behavior (motivation to learn) is maintained by its consequences, which are made known to the learner as knowledge of results, or as feedback. The implication for instruction is that for attending and responding behavior to be maintained appropriately, the feedback provided by instruction *must be positive*. As we learned from Chapters 4, 8, 9, and 10, this means that the *learner must be successful*. Of course, as we learned also, the consequences do not need to be positive on each and every occasion to maintain appropriate attending and responding behavior. In fact, such behavior will probably be maintained in great strength on an intermittent schedule of positive consequences. The point, however, is that continual negative feedback will *not* maintain appropriate attending and responding behavior, even with the use of punishment to which we often resort.

The basic rule of feedback in development is currently gaining much attention by way of research in biofeedback. Primarily, this research is demonstrating the vital role of feedback in learning, especially in learning to control many of our bodily functions that have traditionally been believed to be beyond our conscious control, e.g., rate of heart beat, brain waves, blood pressure, and control of sphincter muscles. Results of some studies (Brown, 1974) show that persons can learn to control the firing of a single nerve in the brain through biofeedback. The main idea underlying biofeedback is that, given knowledge of results of our responses, we can learn to control any of our bodily activities, including those that have usually been regarded as unconscious or automatic. The key to such control is in gaining corrective feedback. This is the way George Harris (1974) describes the working concept of biofeedback: "Body processes generate specific electrical waves. These can be measured by electronic sensors and reported by an indicator—often like the pointer on a speedometer. By watching the indicator, we can follow what goes on inside of us."[18] When we make a response, we can see or feel immediately the effects of our response on the part of our body to which we are "hooked up" electronically. With biofeedback (knowledge of results), we are able to modify our next response and thus gradually learn to respond in ways that produce lower blood pressure, firing of a particular nerve, and so forth.

The area of biofeedback is indeed an exciting one in several respects besides the fact that it shows, in another way, the crucial importance of feedback for learning and that applications may one day be commonplace in your classroom. For one thing, data from biofeedback research lend support to Piaget's theory of developmental adaptation in which intelligence is broadly defined as knowing behavior. As you will recall, his theory is that knowing behavior has evolved in a evolutionary sense from a primitive sensory type of knowing to the conscious reflecting type of knowing characteristic of the adult human. You will remember that his theory also holds that newer, more complex types of knowing behaviors evolve out of, and incorporate, older, more primitive ones. Thus, one would expect that even though human beings are characterized by a conscious or reflective-type intelligence, they would also retain a more primitive and less adaptively important sensory type of knowing behavior that is for the most part cut off from awareness. Many investigators have for years been interested in human behavior that appears to be a function of levels of awareness below

Biofeedback is a technique that . . .

---

[18] T. G. Harris (1974). Barbara Brown's body, *Psychology Today*, **8**(3), p. 45.

consciousness. Chief among these were Sigmund Freud and his followers, who postulated the existence of an unconscious area of the mind and studied its role in human behavior. Biofeedback research offers the exciting possibility of bridging the gap between Freud and Piaget and of bringing *both* levels of knowing behavior under conscious control.

The *rules of increasing delay and the changing conditions of feedback* suggest possible implications for instruction that fit Bruner's belief that as learning progresses, there is a point at which it is better to shift from extrinsic to intrinsic rewards and also a point at which immediate reward should be replaced by deferred reward.[19] The implications are that appropriate practice must be arranged with appropriate contingencies of reinforcement so that (1) the nature of what constitutes positive reinforcement for an individual changes from the type classified (Chapter 8) as *primary, tangible,* and *internal* or *external* to the *secondary, intangible,* and *internal* type; and (2) delayed rewards will have greater reinforcing potential than immediate rewards. For the teacher, these implications require knowing about the properties of reinforcement and punishment so that they can be used appropriately. Also, instruction must be arranged so that learners discover that striving toward a more distant and perhaps more educationally useful goal carries the probability of greater reward than striving toward a lesser and more immediate goal.

Finally, these implications suggest that instruction must be arranged so that reinforcing experiences coincide with and enhance the individual's developing capability to interpret the world from another person's point of view. Sometimes this process is referred to as becoming *other-* or *group-centered* rather than remaining *self-centered.* However, the important thing for us to remember, regardless of what the process is called, is that appropriate practice is necessary to cause it to happen. In short, this practice must provide feedback to the learner that other-centered behavior, or caring about others, is potentially more reinforcing than self-centered behavior—caring only about one's self. Somehow it must become more rewarding for the individual at least sometimes to behave in ways that will enhance the welfare, the freedom, and the dignity of others rather than always of himself. This growth toward maturity is what the following books are really about: *Beyond Freedom and Dignity* (Skinner, 1971); *Toward a Psychology of Being* (Maslow, 1968); *On Becoming a Person* (Rogers, 1961); *Toward a Theory of Instruction* (Bruner, 1966); *Childhood and Society* (Erikson, 1950); and *Moral Education in the Schools* (Kohlberg, 1966), to name only a few.

CHECKPOINT 12-4

1. Speculate on the kinds of things you will need to be concerned about in organizing learning environments that will cause each of your learners to (a) attend to and practice at learning tasks long enough and well enough to succeed in them; and (b) become responsible for his own learning behavior as well as for helping others learn. List your concerns in point form.

2. Do you believe it is necessary and possible to organize approaches to instruction that are theoretically sound? Yes____   No____

[19] J. S. Bruner (1966). Op. cit., pp. 41–42.

TOWARD THE APPLICATION
OF A THEORY OF INSTRUCTION

We are now ready to consider possible approaches that we may use to organize our instruction to take into account as many of the preceding implications as possible. To make this task a bit easier, I have summarized our postulates and theorems (rules) and their implications for instruction in Table 12-1. As is obvious from even a quick examination of the table, our theory is only a rough

TABLE 12-1   Toward a theory of instruction

BASIC PREMISE

We learn what we practice. Therefore, instruction must ensure that what is to be learned is practiced appropriately.

Postulate 1

Effective instruction requires that learning materials (experiences) be appropriate and appropriately structured.

   Theorems.   The theorems of Postulate 1 include the rules of (1) gene action, (2) experience, (3) interaction, (4) generality, (5) general plasticity, (6) complementary action, (7) the match, (8) habituation, (9) progressive subsumption, (10) transfer, (11) increasing complexity, and (12) progressive differentiation.

   Implications for instruction.   Instruction must ensure that (1) learners are active; (2) actions include physical, manipulative activity with concrete objects, especially early in life; (3) the learner's structures of knowledge match the requirements of the learning task; (4) the content and form of practice parallels the content and form of what is to be learned; (5) variations among learners in terms of their structures of knowledge are provided for; (6) what is learned today enhances learning that will occur later.

Postulate 2

Effective instruction requires that learning experience be appropriately sequenced.

   Theorems.   The theorems of Postulate 2 include the rules of (1) elaboration, (2) progressive internalization, (3) types of gene action, (4) increasing reactivity, (5) special timing, (6) decreasing flexibility, (7) practice, (8) specialization, and (9) varying rates.

   Implications. Instruction must ensure that: (1) first things come first; (2) practice occurs, and that it occurs at appropriate times; (3) appropriate practice occurs at the earliest point in life at which it is effective; (4) practice is individualized and flexible; (5) biological readiness is elaborated through appropriate practice; (6) learners are helped to know *in general* before *in specific;* (7) responding behavior of learners progresses from immediate and reflexive to delayed and reflective; (8) learners have a part in managing the sequence and the nature of their practice.

Postulate 3

Effective instruction requires that learning experiences include appropriate contingencies of corrective feedback.

   Theorems.   The theorems of Postulate 3 include the rules of: (1) feedback, (2) action-reaction, (3) changing motivation, (4) increasing delay of feedback, and (5) changing conditions of feedback.

   Implications.   Instruction must ensure that: (1) through appropriate contingencies of reinforcement and punishment, learners attend and respond appropriately; (2) feedback is provided in the appropriate form and at the appropriate time so that it can be used to modify later responses; (3) positive reinforcement for an individual becomes *secondary, intangible,* and *internal;* (4) delayed rewards have greater reinforcing potential than immediate rewards; (5) reinforcing experiences coincide with and enhance the individual's developing capability to interpret the world from another person's point of view.

approximation of all that must occur between teachers and learners, yet it will give us at least more to go on than the "bare empiricism" of which Patrick Suppes (1974) spoke. Also, and equally important, it will give us a guide that we can use to evaluate our instructional efforts and gradually improve them. We will learn more about this aspect of a theory of instruction in Chapter 13.

The relationship between a theory of instruction and approaches to instruction is . . .

One of the really nice things about instruction is that there is no "one-and-only" or absolutely "best" approach. There are many "best" approaches, each of which is "best" relative to (1) how well it provides for the requirements of effective instruction, such as those identified by our theory of instruction; and (2) how personally satisfying it is to you and to your learners. While it is comforting to realize that great flexibility exists in approaches to instruction, you may also be disconcerted to realize both that you must develop your own personalized approach to instruction and that, regardless of your approach, you must accept the responsibility for ensuring that all the requirements of effective instruction are met. It is at this point that the full value of a theory of instruction can be realized.

Four popular approaches to instruction are . . .

Here we will examine four of the better-known general approaches to instruction that have gained the attention of education both historically and currently because of their focus on the individual learner, that is, on *individualized instruction*. We will be interested in analyzing these approaches for their probability of meeting the requirements of effective instruction as specified in our theory. The specific approaches we will look at can be grouped under the two general approaches we learned about in Chapter 6, *discovery* and *reception* learning. Within these major categories, we will consider (1) the free school approach, (2) the Montessori method, (3) open education, and (4) mastery learning. From our discussion of these general approaches with their various materials and procedures, you should get some ideas that will be helpful in the development of approaches that in a large measure will be uniquely your own. You will find additional references for these approaches in the Suggestions for Further Reading.

Discovery Approaches

Discovery learning requires . . .

There are no universally accepted criteria that define precisely what is meant by a discovery approach. Generally, it implies emphasis on the *processes* of learning, sometimes almost completely excluding concern about the specific content of learning. The social and emotional development of learners is frequently stated as a primary objective of discovery approaches. Another frequent characteristic is emphasis on activities that are learner-initiated and guided rather than planned and controlled by the teacher. In discovery approaches, the teacher's role tends to be that of a consultant-discussant, poser of questions, and supplier of resources rather than that of planner, organizer, and manager of lessons. It will be well to remember, however, that discovery learning is essentially an analysis- and synthesis-level activity. Therefore, whenever you elect to use a discovery approach, you must ensure that your learners have indeed met the cognitive prerequisites of the knowledge, comprehension, and application levels.

Of course, there is no hard-and-fast dichotomy between discovery and reception approaches, and the two following examples illustrate the range of differences that exist even within a single approach. The free school approach reflects an extreme type of discovery learning, whereas Marie Montessori's method clearly shows elements of both the discovery and reception approaches. We will devote a bit more space to our discussion of free schools than to the other approaches since we will need to consider the meaning of the term *freedom* relative to schooling and to education. Each person who teaches must arrive at his own operational definition of the concept *freedom* because it is central to all approaches to instruction, including the ones you will eventually synthesize for yourself.

THE FREE SCHOOL APPROACH

The term *free school,* as it is used today, designates a school that is established by persons who for various reasons are dissatisfied with public schools and want to provide alternatives to compulsory education. Often the source of dissatisfaction centers on what Richmond (1973) has termed the Absolute Paradox: schooling *or* education—the idea that traditional schooling prevents education.

The term free school means . . .

Richmond asks: "What's wrong with compulsory schooling anyway?" He then answers his question with the following eleven statements:[20]

1. School conditions everyone to the acceptance of schooling as necessary.
2. It is an impersonal process.
3. It lacks opportunities for worthwhile activity.
4. It distorts values.
5. It makes nonsense of the concept of equality of opportunity.
6. It discourages independent learning.
7. It provides an inferior learning environment.
8. It is geared to the covert objectives of a technocratic society.
9. It creates an artificial demand for more schooling.
10. It splits society into factions.
11. It stands in the way of liberal education so long as it remains compulsory.

In large measure, the free school movement has been an attempt to remedy many of these frequently expressed charges against formal schooling.

One of the earliest persons to speak out against formal learning was Jean Jacques Rousseau. In his book *Émile* (1762), he argued that education should be natural, child-centered, spontaneous, and pleasant; it should free the child to learn spontaneously and naturally. John Dewey (1938), one of the most influential of all American philosophers, argued for a *progressive* education. The reform that he called for was to make educational experience relevant to each learner in terms of the *continuity* the experience provides with past and later learning and the *interaction* the experience causes between the learner and his environment. For Dewey, progressive education meant a process of living in the present, not a preparation for living at some time in the future.

The traditional schooling that Dewey spoke out against is the kind that teaches

---

[20] W. K. Richmond (1973). *The Free School.* London: Methuen, pp. 25–84.

only for cognitive objectives and leaves affect to chance, or worse. He contended that enduring and positive attitudes toward learning should be the primary goals of education.

The most famous of the progressive free schools, Summerhill, was founded in England by A.S. Neill (1883–1973), and it has been operating for more than forty years. The basic assumption upon which it was established was Neill's belief in the natural realness and wisdom of each learner; that if just "left to himself without adult suggestion of any kind, he will develop as far as he is capable of developing."[21]

FREEDOM IN SCHOOLING AND EDUCATION   Obviously, freedom is a key concept relative to free schools, but it is not always defined in the same way by various proponents of alternative schools. Neill explained that freedom does not mean license. "In the disciplined home, the children have *no* rights. In the spoiled home, they have *all* the rights. The proper home is one in which children and adults have *equal* rights. And the same applies to school."[22] Application of Neill's notion of equal rights takes several forms. Each of the fifty or so students in the school has an equal vote on all decisions relative to the management and the operation of the school. Town-hall meetings are held for the purpose of making those decisions, and all teachers, all students, and Neill attend. All have equal rights to take part in the discussions and to vote on the propositions. The guiding rules for these discussions and the decisions that are made are, first, that no one has license to infringe on the individual rights of another. Second, all persons are responsible for their own behavior and must accept its consequences.

Freedom in Neill's type of free school also means deciding for oneself what one will do; what will be studied, in what way, how much, and when. Class attendance is not compulsory, nor are assignments such as reports, papers, or homework. Classroom and school behavior is not rigidly prescribed; it is jointly decided upon by students and teachers. Through a democratic process of decision making, rules for conduct are formulated, e.g., to smoke or not to smoke in class, the type of dress, hair style, or makeup that is acceptable. According to Neill, there have been a few instances in which individuals have not attended class for several years.

The concept of freedom is viewed in various ways, however. Whereas Neill and others, as we shall soon see, interpret individual freedom as the right to move and speak freely, openly, and honestly without fear of suppression, unjust punishment, or of being oppressed for holding a particular view or for demanding one's personal rights, Dewey's view of freedom is significantly different. I believe this difference is important for beginning teachers to understand clearly, since the concept of freedom will undoubtedly continue to be an issue in all types of schools. What you understand and believe about this concept will play an enormous part in what you actually do with, for, or to your learners every minute of every day you teach. But back to Dewey and his view about freedom.

Dewey (1938) labeled the type of freedom that I have described earlier as

---

[21] A. S. Neill (1960). *Summerhill.* New York: Hart, p. 4.
[22] Ibid., p. 107.

"freedom of activity," and he remarks that the commonest mistake made about freedom is [23]

> to identify it with freedom of movement, or with the external or physical side of activity. Now this external and physical side of activity cannot be separated from the internal side of activity; from freedom of thought, desire and purpose. . . . but the fact still remains that an increased measure of freedom of outer movement is a *means*, not an end. The educational problem is not solved when this aspect of freedom is obtained. Everything then depends, so far as education is concerned, upon what is done with this added liberty. What end does it serve? What consequences flow from it?

The danger Dewey warned us about is the belief that simply liberating our learners from their desks and obligations for learning makes them free. He points out that merely removing external controls is no guarantee for the production of intelligent self-management. If you try to free your learners from all external controls, they will find themselves in another and, Dewey believed, a more dangerous form of external control; that of impulses and desires that are ordered not by intelligence but by accidental circumstances. He maintained that a person whose conduct is controlled in this way has only the illusion of freedom, and that actually he is directed by forces over which he has no command.[24]

The *end* that Dewey saw being facilitated by the *means* of an external freedom of activity is the formation of intelligent purposes. This process involves helping our learners gain the capabilities required to postpone immediate action upon impulse, desire, or whim.[25]

> Since freedom resides in the operation of intelligent observation and judgment by which a purpose is developed, guidance given by a teacher to the exercise of the pupil's intelligence is an aid to freedom, not a restriction upon it. Sometimes teachers seem afraid even to make suggestions to the members of a group as to what they should do. I have heard cases in which children are surrounded with objects and materials and left entirely to themselves, the teacher being loath to suggest even what might be done with materials lest freedom be infringed upon. Why, then, even supply materials, since they are a source of some suggestion or other? But what is more important is that the suggestion upon which pupils act must in any case come from somewhere. It is impossible to understand why a suggestion from one who has a larger experience and a wider horizon should not be at least as valid as a suggestion arising from some more or less accidental source.

Dewey cautioned, however, that it is possible to abuse your power as a teacher and to force your learners into activities that express only your purpose rather than that of your learners. But this does not mean that you should take the other extreme and withdraw your guidance entirely. Rather, the purpose of education should be a cooperative enterprise, not a dictation.

The difference between A. S. Neill's relatively narrow definition of freedom and Dewey's definition may account for the reports of many graduates of Summerhill who say that, although their school experiences helped them learn about freedom in the physical sense that we have talked about it here—self-confidence,

---

[23] J. Dewey (1938). *Education and Experience.* New York: Macmillan, pp. 61–62.
[24] Ibid., p. 65.
[25] Ibid., p. 71.

respect for the rights and responsibilities of others, maturity—these experiences were uninspiring and lacked academic opportunity and dedicated teachers (Bernstein, 1968). Some of the fifty graduates interviewed by Bernstein felt that their experiences at Summerhill had led them to find more difficulty in life than they might have otherwise experienced. Most of the graduates of Summerhill did not send their own children to Neill.

As a teacher, you will have to decide for yourself just what freedom relative to schooling and education means. Will it be more than the physical freedom Dewey referred to, or will it mean, for you, that your children should be free to do their "own thing," that you should not try to "teach," but rather that you should serve as a protector of their individual rights by providing a nonthreatening, a nonjudgmental, and an unconditionally accepting environment in which learners will discover and promote their own natural tendencies to develop?

Relative to the concept *free school* is the issue of whether "teaching" should even be a legitimate function of the persons designated as teachers, or the "facilitators," "catalysts," or "assistants," as they are sometimes called in free schools. This issue has typically created heated differences of opinion regarding teaching what Kozol (1972) calls the "hard skills," especially reading. Kozol, a white teacher working with black children and their parents in a Boston ghetto, is forthright in his views about the question of *teaching* in a free school. He says that, although some children learn to read pretty much on their own, "for an awful lot of children, for as many as one-quarter of the children in a Free School situation, it is both possible and necessary to go about the teaching of reading in a highly conscious, purposeful and sequential manner."[26] He says that "it is just not true that the best teacher is the grown-up who most successfully pretends that he knows nothing."[27] Kozol is clear in his continuing belief that all education should be child-centered, open-structured, individualized, and unoppressive. He expresses concern, however, with[28]

> the ways in which some of the people who first come into the context of the Free Schools often seek to *force* their new found orthodoxies in between the teeth and down the throats of black and Spanish-speaking children and their mothers and their fathers. Many of the young people who come into Free Schools straight from college are incredibly dogmatic and, ironically, "manipulative" in their determination to *coerce* the parents of poor children to accept their notions about noncoercive education.

Kozol, like Dewey before him, recognizes a broader definition of freedom than that which allows teachers to adopt a "do-nothing" or an "I don't want to lay my influences on them" interpretation of their teaching role. He points out that you *can* teach reading and that if your children cannot read, it is necessary that you help them learn. Sometimes, however, it is difficult to detect those children who cannot read. As Kozol tells us, for many learners, reading has been associated with so many painful and intimidating memories that they completely avoid all written material. And "if (a learner) is ingenious and sophisticated, as many of the fourteen-year-old street kids in the South End are, he may be able to disguise

---

[26] J. Kozol (1972). *Free Schools*. Boston: Houghton Mifflin, pp. 30–31.
[27] Ibid., p. 31.
[28] Ibid.

his fear of words to a degree that will successfully deceive the young white teachers. 'He's beautiful,' as the young utopian volunteers will characteristically remark. 'He just likes cinema and weaving more than books. When he's ready for books . . . when he senses his organic need . . . he'll let us know.'"[29]

What Kozol finds upsetting about this point of view is that many teachers and volunteers in free schools believe that if an individual is not learning, he merely has not yet reached the appropriate point of organic readiness and that the proper teacher action is simply to take no action, or in Dewey's terms, to offer no suggestions. Kozol points to the fallacy in this belief by noting that:[30]

> children can get messed up very badly by that foolish and insistent obviation of the simple truth that they are in real trouble. It is too much like looking into the windows of a mental hospital and making maniacal observations on the beautiful silence of the catatonic patients. Children who are psychologically shell-shocked in regard to reading are not "beautiful" and are not in the midst of some exquisite process of "organic" growth. They are often in real trouble; they are, in the most simple and honest terms, kids who just can't do a damn thing in the kinds of cities that we live in. There must be a million unusual, non-manipulative but highly conscious ways of going about the task of freeing children from these kinds of misery. There is only one thing that is unpardonable. This is to sit and smile in some sort of cloud of mystical, wide-eyed, non-directive and inscrutable meditation—and do nothing.

Kozol's idea of a free school emphasizes . . .

If you decide to use any of the ideas from a free school approach, you will find it helpful to read books that present greater detail than we have been able to offer here. Several books, other than those already mentioned by Kozol and Neill, are listed in Suggestions for Further Reading. As you read these books and try to arrive at an approach to instruction that will be personally satisfying to you, you should also refer back to our theory of instruction and ask yourself how well the approach you are considering will provide for the requirements for effective instruction implied by our theory. If you do not find a completely satisfactory answer in the free school approach, perhaps the Montessori method will give you a few more ideas to think about.

THE MONTESSORI METHOD

The Montessori method is an approach to instruction that has the basic aim of freeing the learner's potential for self-instruction or self-development in a prepared environment. The philosophy behind this aim is the belief stated by Maria Montessori (1870–1952) that *no one can be free unless he is independent*. It follows, then, that the thrust of the approach to instruction developed by Montessori is toward causing learners to become self-managing: self-motivated, self-disciplined, and self-taught.

The method of instruction developed by this Italian physician-educator, who began work with children in a Roman slum, is often thought of as a system of prepared materials and prescribed exercises to be used by the preschool-aged child (three to six) in designated ways for certain purposes. Actually, her method of instruction is just the visible and applied part of a comprehensive theory about

---

[29] Ibid., p. 34.
[30] Ibid., pp. 34–35.

child development and education. In fact, as we shall see, her beliefs about child development show a surprising parallel with the views of Piaget. The ways in which her ideas about freedom, relative to schooling and education, are applied through her method of instruction show the inclusive definition of freedom described by Dewey.

So here we have three persons, two men and a woman, in three different parts of the world, living at about the same time, whose ideas of theory and application about the development and education of children are similar in surprising detail. I think both Piaget and Dewey would be pleased with the agreement of their ideas with those of Montessori and with her ability to extend her ideas in the practical application of them. It should also be pleasing to all three to see the tremendous growth that has only recently occurred in the demand for Montessori education. In 1958 there was only one Montessori school in the United States. In 1970 there were about 700 (Orem, 1971). Today, the number is probably more than double the 1970 figure.

In Montessori's total approach, "the child is seen as not only capable of but motivated toward auto-formation (self-development) and auto-education (self-teaching). Each child . . . should be provided the freedom to work on self-chosen tasks in an attractive environment especially designed and equipped to meet his needs."[31] The task of the teacher is to provide and maintain an appropriate and responsive learning environment that can be acted upon directly by learners. In short, the teacher prepares the instructional environment and protects the learning process.

In this approach to instruction, the teacher is an observer or a follower of learners (very much in agreement with Piaget's beliefs), who assists indirectly when needed, not by doing it for the learner, but by following up the child's responses and helping him see how he can do it for himself. In this sense, once the environment has been prepared for learning, the teacher moves into the background and *follows* the learning rather than *pushing* or leading it along. Much of what the teacher does and says occurs spontaneously during each teacher-pupil interaction. However, a large share of the teacher's responses is prescribed either generally or specifically by the Montessori method.

To get a better idea of the Montessori approach, we can look at the basic points or elements of the method, listed in summary form below, then take a couple of examples to see how they are applied. (Orem, 1971).

TWELVE CARDINAL POINTS OF THE MONTESSORI METHOD

1. *Training in observation for perceptual, then conceptual proficiency*
The Montessori-trained child becomes an increasingly accurate and rapid perceiver and classifier in tasks ranging from concrete sensory discrimination to abstract intellectual decisions.

2. *Programmed preparation, practice, precision, and perfection*
The child's work with Montessori "didactic apparatus" involves sequentially ever-more complex sensory, motor, and intellectual exercises for sense training,

---

[31] R. C. Orem (1971). *Montessori Today*. New York: Putnam, p. 17.

muscular coordination, and mental development. In the Montessori environment, the child has adequate preparation and practice to develop proficiency in individual and social skills.

3. *Self-processes and individuality*

The intrinsically motivated, "normalized"[32] child strives for mastery of self and environment, achieving auto-construction, self-development, and self-discipline through auto-education. These children work at their own pace on self-selected Montessori materials and exercises.

4. *Movement, activity, and work*

Montessori "active education" involves the child in sensory training for perceptual efficiency, movement in muscular education, and the application of knowledge gained through intellectual work. Concentration, tactile manipulation, and exercises of practical life are also important in "learning to do by doing." By completing cycles of interest, activity, and work, the child learns "habits of work and order."

5. *Freedom and spontaneity*

The child growing under laws of natural development achieves ever-greater independence, expressing spontaneous individuality through immersion in interesting, self-chosen tasks in an "expansive education."

6. *Prepared environment*

The Montessori milieu, with stimuli measured by gradients of material containing control of error, provides an "adaptive environment" to meet the child's inner needs for full functioning of his learning capacities.

7. *Sensitive periods*

During his development, the child experiences a series of crucial transitory periods of special sensitivity to particular learnings. The child's "great work" from birth to age six ("formative period") is to absorb and organize environmental stimuli under the guidance of his unique laws of learning, to "make" his self ("auto-construction").

8. *Rhythm—balance—order.*

In nature and in the universe, order and continuity make the life process possible. People, creatures of "rhythm," require self-control and social cohesiveness—liberty within limits—for optimum development of their physical, emotional, mental, and spiritual "energies."

9. *Discovery and development*

Objective study of normal, natural development from birth onward and skilled observation of free children at work in an experimental "learning laboratory" will culminate in a "science of child care" and scientific pedagogy, both of which will contribute to the emergence of superior human beings—a "new mankind" able to master the new environment.

The key words in the Montessori method are . . .

10. *The child as adult-to-be*

The adult must be centrally concerned with all hygienic prerequisites for realizing the child's potential, indirectly serving the child's inner drive for self-actualization and demonstrating faith in the "adult-to-be" while respecting his rights.

---

[32] Montessori uses the term "normalized" to refer to the self-confident, competent learner, physically and psychically healthy. The term is in contrast with "deviated," designating the child who has been denied the full development of his potential for creative functioning.

11. *New teacher as exemplar*

The Montessori teacher (directress), prepared in "spirit and skills," is a careful observer; he or she reflects the best values, guards the learning process, communicates effectively with the child, and programs his educative development creatively.

12. *To know, love, and serve*

The "new person" balances meditation with action and concern for the collective interest with his individual perfectionment. His threefold mission is to know, love, and serve.

As you probably noticed when reading these twelve points, the Montessori method subsumes many ideas we have learned about before. It applies Bruner's notions of a spiral curriculum (point 2) and discovery learning (point 9); Piaget's ideas about activity and concrete experience (point 4), stages of sequential development (point 1), sensitive periods (point 7), rhythm, balance, and order (point 8); the notions of Piaget, Dewey, Maslow, Rogers, and Bruner about self-processes, freedom, spontaneity, and individuality (points 3, 5, and 10); Skinner's views on the definition of teaching and what constitutes individualized instruction (points 2, 6, and 11); the basic ideas of Gagné, Carroll, and Bloom that underlie sequential, hierarchically organized progressions of learning tasks leading to mastery of self and the material (points 2, 3, 4, and 6); and Dewey's beliefs in learning by doing, the progressive organization of subject matter, and in freedom as coming with self-competence (points 4, 5, and 11).

A comparison of Montessori and traditional approaches to instruction is shown in Table 12-2. It was prepared by Eugene Haggerty of the Gateway Montessori School in San Francisco (Orem, 1971).

It is hard to understand how an instructional approach based on a philosophy that subsumes so many of the key ideas of the world's outstanding theorists of development, learning, and education could have gone relatively unnoticed, particularly in the United States and Canada, for a period of nearly fifty years. Yet, from the time her first book, *The Montessori Method*, was published in 1912 until the 1960s there were only a few places in the world where the Montessori method and materials were being used.

THE METHOD AND MATERIALS IN ACTION: SOME EXAMPLES Let us look at two examples of the method and materials in action. We can start with a statement of the "ground rules" for operating the method and for using the individualized and self-corrective materials. This description was written by Jo Wood Savoye, directress of the New World Montessori School in Hackensack, New Jersey.[33]

The role of the learner in the Montessori approach is . . .

Any child is free to work with any material displayed in the environment so long as he uses it respectfully. He may not harm the material, himself, or others. He may not use it in a way that disturbs the activities of others.

A child may work on either a rug or table—whichever is suitable to the work he has chosen. Children do not work at or on display shelves, as their presence there would obstruct the other children's access to materials.

The child restores the environment during and after an exercise. He is responsible for mopping his own spills (after demonstrations by teacher). He puts his own

---

[33] R. C. Orem (1971). Op. cit., p. 58.

TABLE 12-2   A comparison of the Montessori approach and traditional approaches to instruction*

MONTESSORI	TRADITIONAL
Self-humanization as root motivation	Pervasive emphasis on grades, scores, social conformity
Nongraded (two- or three-year-age span)	Children grouped chronologically, one age per class
Students work at tables, on floor; freedom of movement	Class seated at desks much of time for lessons
Children pursue their own self-paced curriculum, individually or in small groups, in various parts of learning environment	Class, as a group, studies one subject at a time
Children in direct contact with environment; i.e., they have natural, sensory and cultural experiences	Children taught by "truth middlemen" (teachers, society's conforming values)
Long blocks of time permit invaluable concentration	Class schedules limit child's involvement
Relatively few interruptions	Relatively frequent interruptions: bells, adult interventions
Critical cognitive skills developed before age six	Postponement of cognitive development until first grade
Multisensorial, more flexible writing and reading opportunities	Basal readers
Children learn from peers, self-correcting materials; "teacher's" role as guide	Teacher, society "corrects" pupils' "errors"

* R. C. Orem (1971). *Montessori Today*. New York: Putnam. Reprinted with permission.

rug away after rolling it neatly. If he has been working at a table, he pushes his chair under his place at the table.

No child touches the work of another child or interferes with another's activity. This provides security for the child involved in an exercise to continue it to completion. His right to initiate, complete, or repeat an exercise is protected by this ground rule. If he must leave his exercise temporarily, he is confident that his work will be as he left it and he can resume the activity.

Children are not coerced into joining a group activity. It is the child's right to keep working at individual exercises during group activities. It is also his right to stand as an observer of group activity without becoming an active participant. A child is not allowed to interfere or disrupt an activity in which he has chosen not to participate.

A child is not forced or even encouraged to share with another child an exercise which he has chosen to work with by himself. Generosity develops from within as a child matures and gains self-security. If materials are adequate and ground rules are effective, sharing will come naturally, in cases where sharing is appropriate or necessary.

A child is free to "do nothing" if he desires, as long as he does not disturb the activities of others. He may be learning by observing others working, or he may be thinking, or simply relaxing.

The second example comes from a description of a Montessori school in the Virgin Islands.[34]

"The visitor . . . is usually struck first by the atmosphere of concentration. The room is pleasant and orderly. The furniture is childsize, with individual tables and chairs and low shelves neatly arranged with many types of equipment. Color catches the eye. There is the sound of quiet conversation as small groups work together or a child leaves his table to obtain or return a piece of apparatus.

The teacher moves unobtrusively. She stops to work with one child on rods representing number values. She explains another device to a group. She imposes lessons on no one. She guides and assists each child according to his needs. She checks his comprehension, and she introduces him at the right moment to the next step in his work.

Toward midmorning, refreshments are served by the children. Cookies and glasses of juice are courteously passed and received. Assigned youngsters wash and put away the dishes. An outdoor recess of about fifteen minutes usually follows, and energy is released in activities with swings, trees, sandbox, and climbing equipment. The child then returns to the classroom for music, artwork, or story reading, or to some activity of his own if he prefers.

A few more words should be said about the self-instructional and corrective nature of the Montessori materials and the attitude in which they are used, since the idea of corrective feedback, including knowledge of results, often in the form of reinforcing or punishing sequences, is one of the three major postulates of our theory of instruction. Note in the following excerpts the frequency with which Montessori's ideas parallel the ideas and concepts we learned about in earlier chapters.

"The Montessori 'didactic materials,' or learning games, are so designed and constructed that the child can use them without the aid of a teacher or other outside help. These materials provide cues which enable the child to tell when he has made a mistake and to correct it."[35]

Montessori believed that readiness or preparation for a learning task, such as ordering, comparing, or discriminating among sets of objects such as blocks, shapes, or forms that are sequentially patterned along one or more dimension (size, color, sound, weight, length), "includes mastery of every subtask fundamental to its execution. An ideal sequence of presentation of tasks is one which is so graded and matched to the child's current level of functioning as to ensure him a reasonable chance of success."[36] Montessori believed, also, that the "ready" or prepared mind is one capable of manipulating increasingly subtle and complex (from concrete to abstract) relationships. "Every task that the child performs has, in effect, roots in the past and seeds for the future, having been thoroughly prepared for and serving, in turn, as preparation for yet another more involved activity."[37]

Most supporters of Montessori agree that the single most important aspect of the didactic materials is the fact that they provide self-corrective feedback. "A child who does a task incorrectly will find spaces unfilled or pieces left over. While the child is working on the problem, the teacher is not hovering or crit-

[34] Ibid., p. 59.
[35] Ibid., p. 60.
[36] M. Montessori (1912). *The Montessori Method.* New York: Stokes, p. 60.
[37] Ibid.

icizing and will help only if asked. If the child cannot finish the project, he can return it to its place and find something else. Inevitably, he will return when ready and tackle the problem again."[38]

The issue of reinforcement and punishment is handled naturally in Montessori's approach. She believed that natural motivation for the child is an innate characteristic. That is, the tendency to attend and to respond appropriately to the environment is preprogrammed and will be elaborated and developed fully as a consequence of interaction with environmental stimuli which offer a "reasonable chance of *success.*" Reinforcement, for Montessori, cannot be bought by what she called "those degrading things," i.e., contrived rewards for accomplishment. In her view, the only real rewards are the joy of discovery and the satisfaction of success. In short, the child's motivation for learning derives from the pleasure he or she finds in it.

Ideally, punishment in terms of administering aversive stimuli (Chapter 10) has no place in the Montessori approach. Punishment as the cessation or withdrawal of rewarding consequences, however, does occur. That is, if a child does not manage the materials or his own freedom to learn in an appropriate manner, they are withdrawn from him until he feels he is ready to try again. He may just sit, walk around, stand, or lie down if he chooses to. The only restriction is that whatever he does, it may not interfere with the activity of others.

One other comment about the Montessori method is in order before we consider the open-education approach to instruction. Although the Montessori approach has had its greatest application to the education of children three to four years of age, and mainly in specially created Montessori schools, its basic philosophy applies to all levels of education. Increasingly, Montessori classes are being established in public schools and are being offered to older learners, through secondary school in some instances. Many schools (or classes in a public school) start with Montessori's approach with preschool-age children and then expand the program as the children grow older.

Finding Montessori materials for older learners is a bit of a problem. If you are interested in using a Montessori approach in your teaching of older learners, you would be wise to focus on the main ideas of the method rather than on the specific details of the materials designed for preschoolers. If you understand the theory behind Montessori, you should be able to arrange for your own materials either by selecting them from the many currently available auto-instructional materials—prepared programs, instructional devices—or by constructing your own. Chapter 8 gave a few clues about doing this. Such is the power of a theory of development which includes a theory of learning and instruction: it provides the basic substance out of which specific techniques, procedures, sequences, and materials can be logically derived, tested, and modified. Understanding the theory is the key. The other things can then be invented by each person who tries to apply the basic ideas.

Reception Approaches

The two approaches we will consider under this heading are *open education* and *master learning.* As will become apparent from the discussion, the open educa-

The Montessori approach includes these concepts learned about in earlier chapters:

---

[38] Ibid., p. 61.

tion approach does not fit neatly into the model of meaningful reception learning that we learned about in Chapter 6. It more nearly represents a compromise, as does the Montessori method, between discovery and reception approaches. However, it is my opinion that open education has more in common with mastery learning than with a free school approach to instruction.

THE OPEN EDUCATION APPROACH

The basic assumptions underlying open education are . . .

The concept *open education*, developed initially in England, is another approach toward the major goal of breaking down a lockstep or group-based method of instruction. Like the free school and Montessori approaches, it is an attempt to individualize instruction. The approaches, however, differ in how each tries to achieve the goal. The open education approach is more like the Montessori approach than like the approach of most free schools. It is based pretty much on the same assumptions and cardinal points about learners and learning as the Montessori method. That is, it assumes that learners want to learn, are capable of learning, and are free only when they have acquired the knowledge and skills that enable them to learn without direct supervision of teachers. Thus, an open education approach is characterized by a structured learning environment in which there are definite instructional goals and objectives and organized learning experiences, planned and prepared ahead of time by teachers. This sounds like a pretty traditional educational approach until we add the dimension of crucial differences: The learners do not all do the same things at the same time and in the same way, and the learners, not the teachers, are the essential actors. In this approach, teachers organize and arrange appropriate learning situations (events and materials) that offer various options of what might be learned as well as the approach that might be used.

Let us look at a list of themes that characterize typical open classrooms.

Eight themes of open education are . . .

EIGHT THEMES OF OPEN EDUCATION   This list was prepared by Walberg and Thomas (1972) as a result of an exhaustive review of the literature on open education, and visits and interviews with teachers in more than forty open classrooms in the United States and Britain.[39]

1. *Provisioning* for learning
Manipulative materials are supplied in great diversity and range with little replication, i.e., not class sets. Children move about the room without asking permission. Talking among children is encouraged. The teacher does group children by ability according to tests or norms. Children generally group and regroup themselves through their own choices.
2. *Humaneness*, respect, openness, and warmth
Children use "books" written by their classmates as part of their reading and reference materials. The environment includes materials developed or supplied by the children. Teacher takes care of dealing with conflicts and disruptive behavior without involving the group. Children's activities, products, and ideas are reflected abundantly about the classroom.
3. *Diagnosis* of learning events
Teacher uses test results to group children for reading and/or math. Children expect

---

[39] H. J. Walberg and S. C. Thomas (1972). Open education: A classroom validation in Great Britain and the United States, *American Educational Research Journal*, **9**(2), 200–201.

the teacher to correct all their work. Teacher gives children tests to find out what they know. To obtain diagnostic information, the teacher closely observes the specific work or concern of a child and asks immediate, experience-based questions.

4. *Instruction,* guidance, and extension of learning

Teacher bases her instruction on each individual child and his interaction with materials and equipment. The work children do is divided into subject matter areas. The teacher's lessons and assignments are given to the class as a whole. Teacher bases her instruction on curriculum guides or text books for the grade level she teaches. Before suggesting any extension or redirection of activity, teacher gives diagnostic attention to the particular child and his particular activity.

5. *Evaluation* of diagnostic information

Teacher keeps notes and writes individual histories of each child's intellectual, emotional, physical development. Teacher has children for a period of just one year. Teacher uses tests to evaluate children and rate them in comparison to their peers. Teacher keeps a collection of each child's work for use in evaluating his development. Teacher views evaluation as information to guide her instruction and provisioning for the classroom.

6. *Seeking* opportunities for professional growth

Teacher uses the assistance of someone in a supportive, advisory capacity. Teacher has helpful colleagues with whom she discusses teaching.

7. *Self-perception* of teacher

Teacher tries to keep all children within her sight so that she can make sure thay are doing what they are supposed to do.

8. *Assumptions* about children and learning process

The emotional climate is warm and accepting. The class operates within clear guidelines made explicit. Academic achievement is the teacher's top priority for the children. Children are deeply involved in what they are doing.

Obviously, individualizing instruction through an open education approach radically alters the traditional role of the teacher. Teaching as group lecturing is largely replaced by individual tutoring; that is, of (1) posing questions (*confrontation* in Piaget's terms, and *submarining* in Bruner's) and following up on learner's responses; (2) providing information as it is needed; and (3) constant, ongoing evaluation as an aid to learning rather than for the assignment of marks (Hassett and Weisberg, 1972).

The role of the teacher in open education is . . .

The open education approach can be an engaging and demanding experience for you as a teacher. All your students, rather than working simultaneously on a particular lesson, may be working at many different tasks for varying lengths of time. The instructional requirements placed on you by your students for time, materials, guidance, evaluation, can be absolutely overwhelming if you try to do it all yourself. You will recall we talked about this in Chapter 8 on auto-instruction. Montessori recognized the fact that it was impossible for a teacher, if unaided by self-instructional materials, to cope with more than just a few learners at once. She also saw the value of teaching learners to become self-managing, self-teaching, independent learners. You would be wise to consider the use of these types of learning materials if you decide to use an open education approach in your instruction. Also, you might weigh the value of having assistance in your teaching: paid aides, older students, parents, grandparents, and other teachers on your staff.

One major problem in open education is . . .

Several sources of information are available on open education. You may find them useful if you would like to know more about this approach. References are listed in the Suggestions for Further Reading.

THE MASTERY LEARNING APPROACH

By now you have probably been asking yourself the question that most of us who are interested in schools and education ask continually: "Is it possible for me to provide the kind of guidance and organization of instruction that will meet the requirements implied in our theory of instruction without causing my learners to feel that learning must be traditionally impersonal, irrelevant, and painful, and that I am manipulating them?" We have examined three approaches to instruction that may provide some clues that will help you find your personal answer to this question. We are now ready to have a look at a fourth approach, *mastery learning*. Of course, this approach is not new for us at this point. We have examined its basic assumptions and method of application in earlier chapters (Chapters 1 and 4 especially). It remains to remind ourselves briefly of these assumptions and methods and then to place them in perspective relative to alternative ways of using this approach.

As you can see, and as was apparent in the Montessori method, the role of the teacher with thirty or more learners can become extremely complex, since, rather than prepare one standard lesson for all learners, the teacher must plan learning experiences largely on an individual basis. Moreover, the teacher must evaluate and monitor the progress of individuals rather than just that of "the group" since, as in the open education approach, progress is paced by the individual and not by the prescribed text, the calendar, or the desire of the teacher.

The mastery approach requires that . . .   Briefly, the basic assumption from which a mastery learning approach derives is that most learners can master what we want to teach them *if* instruction is optimal for each individual and if enough time is allowed. You will recall that in a mastery approach, instruction is defined as optimal when (1) objectives are clear and precise; (2) learners are motivated to attend and practice the material; (3) they are able to proceed at their own rate; (4) learning tasks are organized, where possible, in a progressively inclusive manner (following some hierarchial guide such as Gagné's conditions of learning); (5) learners gain appropriate, corrective feedback as they learn the material; (6) reinforcement (mostly in the form of success) is contingent on appropriate performance; and (7) sufficient review and practice are provided for retention.

The crucial outcome of individualized instructional approaches such as a mastery approach is simply that they seek a uniformly high level of achievement for most learners and, as Kifer's (1975) data suggest, continued school achievement *leads to* positive personality characteristics, e.g., positive judgment about one's self and one's abilities.

Clearly, organizing instruction for a mastery approach involves many of the ideas inherent in the Montessori method and in open learning. About the only ideas common with a free school approach, however, are, first, the main idea that learners are capable, and second, that they should be allowed to learn at their own rates. Both Montessori and open learning approaches share the following ideas with a mastery approach:

1. Specific instructional objectives. (In a mastery approach, they are arrived at either by the teacher or cooperatively with learners, stated precisely, and behaviorally, and shared with learners. They are teacher-formulated in a Montessori approach and are implied largely by the activities. In open education, instructional objectives are teacher-formulated and implied through the arrangement of activities and materials, or they are arrived at cooperatively with learners.)

2. Prepared, organized, and guided activities. (The degree of teacher guidance is probably more apparent in a mastery approach.)

3. Encouragement of learners to attend to and practice certain activities. (Encouragement is made explicit in a mastery approach and implied by the contents and arrangement in the Montessori and open education approaches.)

4. Sequential and hierarchical organization of learning tasks.

5. Individual rates of progress controlled by the learners.

6. Continuously available corrective feedback. (Probably they are more so in Montessori and mastery approaches than in open education.)

7. Reinforcement largely from success in the learning tasks.

8. Emphasis on self-reliance, self-instruction, and freedom within a prepared environment.

9. Individual and ongoing evaluation for the purpose of helping each learner meet the instructional objectives.

I believe the reason we see so many of the same major ideas inherent in the Montessori, open education, and mastery learning approaches, but not so many in the free school approach, is that these three approaches derive from beliefs about development, learning, and instruction that are theoretically and practically very similar. The free school approach, on the other hand, has been derived largely from reaction against the all-too-obvious ills of traditional public schooling rather than from a powerful theoretical statement that gives clues about how instruction should be organized to best enhance the process. Consequently, instruction within the free approach is, as often as not, the result of bare empiricism—of trial and error—and without the guide of theory, there is little chance for the corrective feedback so necessary for improvement. As Kozol has so often pointed out, free schools fail because they do not teach. Corrective feedback is a necessary condition of all types of learning, including our own learning about how to improve our instruction. Without a theoretical guide, such corrective, evaluative feedback is difficult, if not impossible, to gain. Thus, we can never adequately answer the two questions fundamental to teaching: "Is my approach to instruction effective?" and "How can I improve it?"

A possible reason free schools typically last only a short time is . . .

Soon you will face the responsibility for planning and organizing instruction that is optimal for each of your learners. As you go about the task of synthesizing approaches that are personally satisfying to you and your learners, you should also refer back to the rules of our theory of instruction to see whether your approaches meet the requirements for effective instruction implied by the theory. In this way, you will be able to do a logical assessment of the two key questions just mentioned.

These are the two questions for the last major topic we will learn about in this text: evaluating learning and teaching. The material in Chapter 13 will help you answer them. As a result, it will add to the information needed to develop your own unique approach to making instruction optimal for each of your learners.

Once upon a time, the animals decided they must do something heroic to meet the problems of "a new world." So they organized a school.

IN PASSING

They adopted an activity curriculum consisting of running, climbing, swimming, and flying. To make it easier to administer the curriculum, *all* the animals took *all* the subjects.

The duck was excellent in swimming, in fact better than his instructor; but he made only passing grades in flying and was very poor in running. Since he was slow in running, he had to stay after school and also drop swimming in order to practice running. This was kept up until his web feet were badly worn and he was only average in swimming. But "average" was acceptable in school, so nobody worried about that except the duck.

The rabbit started at the top of the class in running, but had a nervous breakdown because of so much makeup work in swimming.

The squirrel was excellent in climbing until he developed frustration in the flying class, where his teacher made him start from the ground up instead of from the treetop down. He also developed "charlie horses" from overexertion and then got "C" in climbing and "D" in running.

The eagle was a problem child and was disciplined severely. In the climbing class, he beat all the others to the top of the tree, but he insisted on using his own way to get there.

At the end of the year, an abnormal eel that could swim exceedingly well, and also run, climb, and fly a little, had the highest average and was valedictorian.

The prairie dogs stayed out of school and fought the tax levy because the administration would not add digging and burrowing to the curriculum. They apprenticed their children to a badger and later joined the groundhogs and gophers to start a successful private school.

Does this fable have a moral?[40]

ACTIVITIES

1. To summarize the main points of Chapter 12, outline an approach to instruction that feels comfortable for you. Show how your approach can be expected to provide for all the requirements of effective instruction indicated by our theory of instruction. (Would you do this activity even if it were not assigned? Yes_____ No_____)

2. Assume that you are a teacher. About half the learners in your classroom are black; the others are white. What does this information suggest to you about the type of approach to instruction that you should use? Explain your answer relative to (a) the rules of our theory of instruction; and (b) the two major conclusions from Jensen's study (1969).

3. *Evaluate* the following statement: A theory of instruction applies to *all* learners in *all* learning situations.

4. As an individual, small group, or entire class activity, select (or develop) an approach to instruction. Then describe the steps that will be involved in applying it to teaching some cognitive, affective, or psychomotor behavior, e.g., reading a compass, keeping the room tidy, playing the piano.

5. Find a teacher who will work with you and observe the instructional approach she uses. Try to determine from her teaching behavior the assumptions she makes about the requirements for effective instruction as indicated by our theory. Discuss your observations with the teacher.

6. Just for fun:
Choose one of your own college courses and analyze it in terms of how well the approach being used meets the requirements for effective instruction.

REFERENCES

Ausubel, D. P. (1963). *The Psychology of Meaningful Verbal Learning.* New York: Grune & Stratton.

Bernstein, E. (1968). What does a Summerhill old school tie look like? *Psychology Today,* **2**(5), 37–70.

Binet, A., and H. Simon (1905). Application des methodes nouvelles au diagnostic du niveau intellectuel chez enfants normaux et anormaux d'hospice et d'école primaire, *L'Année Psychologigue,* **11**, 245–266.

---

[40] Reavis, G. H. (1953). The animal school: A fable for school people. *The Educational Forum,* **17**(2), p. 141.

Block, J. H., ed. (1971). *Mastery Learning: Theory and Practice.* New York: Holt.

Bloom, B. S., ed. (1956). *Taxonomy of Educational Objectives. Handbook 1: Cognitive Domain.* New York: McKay.

—— (1968). Learning for mastery, *Evaluation Comment,* **1**(2). Los Angeles: University of California, Center for the Study of Evaluation of Instructional Programs.

Brown, B. (1974). *New Mind, New Body.* New York: Harper & Row.

Bruner, J. S. (1966). *Toward a Theory of Instruction.* Cambridge, Mass.: The Belknap Press of Harvard University Press.

Callaway, R. W., Jr. (1970). Modes of biological adaptation and their role in intellectual development, *PCD Monographs,* **1**(1), 1–34.

Carroll, J. A. (1963). A model of school learning, *Teachers College Record,* **64,** 723–733.

Cazden, C. B. (1968). Some implications of research on language development for preschool education. In R. D. Hess and R. M. Bear (eds.), *Early Education.* Chicago: Aldine.

Chall, J. S. (1967). *Learning to Read: The Great Debate.* New York: McGraw-Hill.

Chomsky, N. (1965). *Aspects of a Theory of Syntax.* Cambridge, Mass.: M.I.T.

Dewey, J. (1929). *The Sources of a Science of Education.* New York: Liveright.

—— (1938). *Education and Experience.* New York: Macmillan.

Douglas, V. I. (1971). Stop, look, and listen!: The problem of sustained attention and impulse control in hyperactive and normal children, unpublished presidential address, *Canadian Psychological Association,* Montreal: McGill University.

Eysenck, H. J. (1971). *The I.Q. Argument.* New York: The Liberty Press.

Gagné, R. M. (1968). Learning hierarchies, *Educational Psychologist,* **6,** 1–9.

—— (1970). *The Conditions of Learning,* 2d ed. New York: Holt.

Ginsburg, H., and S. Opper (1969). *Piaget's Theory of Intellectual Development: An Introduction.* Englewood Cliffs, N.J.: Prentice-Hall.

Goldman-Eisler, F. (1964). Discussion and further comments. In E. H. Lenneberg (ed.), *New Directions in the Study of Language.* Cambridge, Mass.: M.I.T.

Goodman, P. (1964). *Compulsory Miseducation.* New York: Horizon Press.

—— (1966). *Compulsory Miseducation and the Community of Scholars.* New York: Vintage.

Harris, T. G. (1974). Barbara Brown's body, *Psychology Today,* **8**(3), 45–46.

Harrow, A. J. (1972). *A Taxonomy of the Psychomotor Domain.* New York: McKay.

Herrnstein, R. (1971). I.Q., *The Atlantic,* **228**(3), 43–64.

Holt, J. (1964). *How Children Fail.* New York: Pitman.

—— (1969). *The Underachieving School.* New York: Pitman.

—— (1972). *Freedom and Beyond.* New York: Dutton.

Hunt, J. McV. (1961). *Intelligence and Experience.* New York: Ronald.

Illich, I. (1971). *Deschooling Society.* New York: Harper & Row.

Jensen, A. R. (1969). How much can we boost IQ and scholastic achievement? *Harvard Educational Review,* 39, Winter, 1–123.

—— (1972). *Genetics and Education.* London: Methuen.

Kifer, E. (1975). Relationships between academic achievement and personality characteristics: A quasi-longitudinal study, *American Educational Research Journal,* **12**(2), 191–210.

Kohl, H. (1969). *The Open Classroom.* New York: Vintage.

Kozol, J. (1972). *Free Schools.* Boston: Houghton Mifflin.

Krathwohl, D. R., B. S. Bloom, and B. B. Masia (1964). *Taxonomy of Educational Objectives. Handbook II: Affective Domain.* New York: McKay.

Lenneberg, E. H. (1967). *Biological Foundations of Language.* New York: Wiley.

Markle, S. M. (1975). They teach concepts, don't they?, *Educational Researcher,* **4**(6), 3–9.

Maslow, A. H. (1968). *Toward a Psychology of Being,* 2d ed. Princeton, N.J.: Van Nostrand.

Montessori, M. (1912). *The Montessori Method.* New York: Stokes.

Neill, A. S. (1960). *Summerhill*. New York: Hart.

Orem, R. C. (1971). *Montessori Today*. New York: Putnam.

Reavis, G. H. (1953). The animal school: A fable for school people, *The Educational Forum*, **17**(2), 141.

Richmond, W. K. (1973). *The Free School*. London: Methuen.

Rogers, C. R. (1961). *On Becoming a Person*. Boston: Houghton Mifflin.

Rousseau, J. J. (1762). Émile ou de l'éducation. Le Haye, France: Neaulme.

Shockley, W. (1971). Negro IQ deficit: Failure of a "malicious coincidence" model warrants new research proposals, *Review of Educational Research*, **41**(3), 227–248.

Skinner, B. F. (1953). *Science and Human Behavior*. New York: Macmillan.

——— (1968). *The Technology of Teaching*. New York: Appleton-Century-Crofts.

——— (1971). *Beyond Freedom and Dignity*. New York: Knopf.

Sprinthall, R. C., and N. A. Sprinthall (1974). *Educational Psychology: A Developmental Approach*. Reading, Mass.: Addison-Wesley.

Stephens, J. M. (1965). *The Psychology of Classroom Learning*. New York: Holt.

Stott, D. H. (1974). A preventive program for the primary grades, *Elementary School Journal*, **74**(5), 299–308.

Suppes, P. (1974). The place of theory in educational research, *Educational Researcher*, **3**, (6), 3–10.

Terman, L. M. (1916). *The Measurement of Intelligence*. Boston: Houghton Mifflin.

Walberg, H. J., and S. C. Thomas (1972). Open education: A classroom validation in Great Britain and the United States, *American Educational Research Journal*, **9**(2), 197–208.

Ward, E. F. (1971). *The Montessori Method and the American School*. New York: Arno Press and The New York Times.

Wechsler, D. (1944). *The Measurement of Adult Intelligence*. Baltimore: Williams & Wilkins.

White, R. T. (1974). The validation of a learning hierarchy, *American Educational Research Journal*, **11**(2), 121–136.

Zajonc, R. B. (1975)). Dumber by the dozen, *Psychology Today*, **8**(8), 37–43.

SUGGESTIONS FOR FURTHER READING

The following references are grouped according to their relevance for discovery or reception approaches to instruction.

DISCOVERY APPROACHES

Ashton-Warner, S. (1963). *Teacher*. New York: Simon & Schuster. This book describes what is known as the language-experience approach to learning to read. It is a method developed by Ashton-Warner that begins with words that are meaningful to the learner. Thus each child produces his own initial reading material.

Bhaerman, S., and J. Denker (1972). *No Particular Place to Go: The Making of a Free High School*. New York: Simon & Schuster. This is the story of two teachers in public high school who helped a group of students in the Washington, D. C., area create an alternative to schools they found boring and oppressive. The alternative school was built on the foundation of communal living.

Dennison, G. (1969). *The Lives of Children*. New York: Vintage. The main theme of Dennison's book is that education *is* living, not just preparation for later living, and that public schools *do not* practice this truth.

Hassett, J. D., and A. Weisberg (1972). *Open Education: Alternatives within Our Tradition*. Englewood Cliffs, N. J.: Prentice-Hall.

Kohl, H. (1967). *36 Children*. New York: New American Library. Kohl's approach to instruction is to "plant" the learner's environment with as many interesting things as possible and then wait for his spontaneous responses. Instruction begins at that point and goes wherever each learner wants to take it. *36 Children* describes the "places" his sixth grade children in a Harlem elementary school "took" their interests.

———— (1969). *The Open Classroom*. New York: Vintage. In this book Kohl draws on his teaching experiences with a free-school approach to offer several suggestions not just about free schools but also about education in general.

Kozol, J. (1972). *Free Schools*. Boston: Houghton Mifflin. Kozol's biases, poignantly and honestly stated, about what free schools should and should not be make this book a must for anyone thinking about trying to begin a free school, joining one, or just trying to understand the movement. He lists 21 pages of contacts, leads, and addresses for free schools.

Montessori, M. (1912). *The Montessori Method*. New York: Stokes. This is the basic text for the Montessori approach. It exposes the reader to the method and the materials. It is great!

———— (1948). *From Childhood to Adolescence*. New York: Schocken. In this book Montessori comes to grips with the educational concerns of older learners—adolescents and even university students. The parallels between her views about development and those of Piaget are apparent in this volume.

Orem, R. C., ed. (1971). *Montessori Today*. New York: Putnam. Orem gives a recent, cross-section view of the Montessori movement in America. Nearly 700 Montessori schools were examined in detail for information about their specific methods, beliefs, and materials. Dozens of these are included. The appendix gives a guide about how to start a Montessori school and where you might go to get Montessori teacher training.

RECEPTION APPROACHES

Block, J. B., ed. (1971). *Mastery Learning: Theory and Practice*. New York: Holt. This is probably the most concise yet comprehensive statement available about mastery learning. It includes theory and descriptions of programs that have used a mastery learning approach.

Bloom, B. S., J. T. Hastings, and G. F. Madaus, eds. (1971). *Handbook on Formative and Summative Evaluation of Student Learning*. New York: McGraw-Hill. This encyclopedia-type book of 932 pages gives broad coverage of a mastery learning approach to instruction, with a major focus on evaluation of learning and teaching relative to this approach. An important feature of the volume is its guide to evaluation within specific context areas and of affective objectives.

Daniels, S. (1971). *How 2 Gerbils, 20 Goldfish, 200 Games, 2000 Books, and I Taught Them How to Read*. Philadelphia: Westminster. Daniels's approach is totally eclectic. He uses whatever works, and finds—finally—that a combination of firmness, positiveness, and plenty of captivating things to do is a really effective approach.

Engelmann, S., and E. C. Bruner (1969). *Distar Reading: An Instructional System*. Chicago: Science Research Associates. The Distar programs are highly structured sequences of reception learning, originally developed for preschool and primary grade children who have had difficulty learning reading, language, and arithmetic from other materials. The sequences are structured from task analyses, are teacher-directed, mastery-oriented, and apply rules of reinforcement and punishment.

Nyquist, E. B., and G. R. Hawes, eds. (1972). *Open Education: A Sourcebook for Parents and Teachers*. New York: Bantam. If you want an overall perspective of what *open education* means to various people, this book is a good source.

Perrone, V. (1972). *Open Education: Promise and Problems*. Bloomington, Ind.: Phi Delta Kappa. This book is a firsthand account of the open education movement in North Dakota, center of interest in open education in the United States.

Plowden, Lady B., et al. (1967). *Children and Their Primary Schools: A Report of The Central Advisory Council for Education* (The Plowden Report). London: Her Majesty's Stationary Office. This is the most comprehensive account of open education available.

The study, done in England, advocates the open education approach be widely adopted as a model for elementary education.

Walberg, H. J., and S. C. Thomas (1972). Open education: A classroom validation in Great Britain and the United States, *American Educational Research Journal,* **9**(2), 197–208. Walberg and Thomas compared open education and traditional classrooms and developed a list of eight themes that they believe characterize the open education approach.

PART IV

EVALUATION OF LEARNING AND TEACHING

EVALUATING LEARNING AND TEACHING

13

Evaluating student work calls upon the teacher to make critical judgments and the best a teacher can do is present his evaluation as his own and not as an unquestioned objective truth about the student's work. Obviously there are some cases, for example in the correcting of math or spelling exercises, where qualitative judgment isn't as relevant as in writing or in other creative activities. However, it is one thing to say a word is spelled incorrectly or an addition is wrong, and another to understand why a particular child made a particular mistake the moment it was made. The latter requires considerable perception and judgment and can more effectively help a student to learn than a mere cross or a zero.

Herbert Kohl
The Open Classroom

CONTENTS

ONGOING SUMMARY

With Chapter 12 we completed our discussion of two of the three major questions that face all teachers: "What do I want learners to learn?" and "How can I help learners learn?" Our discussion began with a broad purpose of education to change the behavior of learners. Bearing in mind this primary purpose of education and the proposition that learners learn what they attend to and practice, we commenced the essentially cognitive task of learning about what we have called the *content* and *process* of learning and teaching (Part I).

But, as we have seen, there is more to learning and teaching than describing and analyzing the content to be learned and specifying the conditions necessary for learning to occur. Education also has an important *affective* component. We must know about helping learners to attend and respond profitably to learning tasks, to be committed to the importance of learning, and to become self-managing individuals (Part II).

With the information about learning and teaching provided by Parts I and II, we were ready to analyze Piaget's broadly inclusive and biologically based theory of developmental adaptation. From our analysis of his ideas and those of researchers in genetics, biochemistry, and physiology, and with what we had learned earlier, we were able to synthesize higher-order rules of development, many of which have rather clear implications for education. These rules gave us the broad perspective necessary to expand on Bruner's notions about the requirements of a much-needed theory of instruction. Such a theory, incomplete and approximate as it is, gives us a general basis from which we can develop any number of approaches to instruction, each of which can be designed for the individual needs of specific individuals, and all of which can be examined to ensure they are theoretically sound (Part III).

Now we are ready to consider the third major question faced by all teachers: "How can I check on the effectiveness of *their* learning and *my* teaching?"

ADVANCE ORGANIZER

In Chapter 13 we will learn what evaluation in education is all about, rather than attempt to learn all about evaluation. This frame of reference, as you will recognize, is consistent with the way we have approached most of the other major topics that we have studied, for example, development, learning, motivation, and discipline.

Especially, we will see the value in keeping approaches, methods, and techniques of evaluation consistent with the concepts and rules of evaluation, just as we saw that our approaches to instruction must provide for the rules of our theory of instruction.

You will notice that our study of evaluation brings us back fullcycle to where we began, with specific instructional objectives, for indeed that is where evaluation and instruction begin. However, you will see that we are now beyond where we first started. Our cycle has been a spiral, not just a flat circle; that is, we have *learned* in the process.

In Chapter 13 we will challenge some of the traditional assumptions made about the intellectual ability of our learners and speculate about the differences that can result in instruction and learning *if* we adopt alternative and more optimistic assumptions that learners can learn effectively *if* we can learn to be effective teachers. As we learn how we can do so, we will notice that teaching and testing blend together as two aspects of the same process.

GOALS AND OBJECTIVES

Cognitive

To become an effective teacher, the learner should be able to evaluate learner capabilities, classroom learning, and his own instruction.

KNOWLEDGE LEVEL

Given the following terms or phrases, the learner is able to define them in writing: *evaluation, measurement, testing, prediction, selection, feedback/correction, validity-content, curricular, predictive, concurrent, construct-, reliability, objectives-achievement chart, rules of evaluation, methods of evaluation, classroom questions, teacher-made test, standardized test, the normal curve, norm-referenced evaluation, criterion-referenced evaluation.*

COMPREHENSION LEVEL

1. Given the statement, "*Methods* of evaluation must agree with *rules* of evaluation," the learner is able to explain it.
2. The learner can explain why test items can rarely be 100 percent valid and reliable.

APPLICATION LEVEL

Given an individualized approach to instruction, the learner is able to outline in writing an appropriate method of evaluating the learning and instruction.

ANALYSIS LEVEL

Given a description of a classroom teacher's *construction* and use of a teacher-made test, the learner is able to say whether it is likely to give valid and reliable information about learner achievement.

SYNTHESIS LEVEL

Given the major concepts and rules of Piaget's theory of intellectual development and the requirements of a criterion-referenced test, the learner is able to specify the basic components of a criterion-referenced test of intellectual development.

EVALUATION LEVEL

Given the opportunity to judge the effectiveness of his own instruction, the learner will be able to provide an argument to support the view that if his learners are meeting the objectives, he is an effective teacher.

Affective

To become an effective teacher, the learner should be able to display confidence in his ability to evaluate the effectiveness of his teaching, to judge the worth of his approaches to teaching, and to be willing to change when new information demonstrates the need to do so.

RECEIVING (ATTENDING) LEVEL

The learner is aware of the abuses in instruction and evaluation that are usually associated with group-based approaches to instruction.

RESPONDING LEVEL

The learner readily questions traditional assumptions about an individual's ability to profit from instruction.

VALUING LEVEL

The learner voluntarily discusses methods and rationale for evaluating learning and instruction.

ORGANIZATIONAL LEVEL

The learner conceptualizes instruction and evaluation as parts of the same process.

CHARACTERIZATION LEVEL

As a standard procedure, whenever the learner devises approaches to instruction and evaluation, he checks to ensure that they agree with the concepts and rules of instruction and evaluation.

"Today, I have a surprise for you," begins Mr. Owens, as his grade twelve students get ready for another lesson in their study of the major causes of poverty in the world today.

"He's got our tests," whispers Ted.

"Well, hurrah for him, he's only had them a little over a month!" Ann responds sarcastically. "I can hardly remember what the test was all about, except that it was another of his little 'surprises'."

I am seated nearby as an observer to evaluate the instruction of Mr. Owens, who is in his first year of teaching. As Ann's eyes meet mine, I can tell that she knows I heard her. I look away because I understand how she must feel, but I do not know what message to send back to her; I cop out for now, but I would like to talk with her later.

Mr. Owens continues, "I'm pleased with how well some of you did on the exam. Your answers, especially to the essay items, show that a few of you understand the major concepts and rules related to the political, economic, and social conditions in the modern world. And, as I have repeatedly pointed out, a good grasp of these concepts and rules is necessary to understand the major causes of poverty in the world today.

Many of your answers, however, are pretty weak, and I'm really disappointed in a few of them. There were a couple of papers that I couldn't read completely because the handwriting was so messy. In general, though, they are about what I would have predicted. As Brian returns your papers, I will put the distribution of grades on the board. You will notice that they are very nearly a normal curve."

Brian hands back the papers, being careful to place them face down on each desk.

Mr. Owens explains that of the thirty-nine papers, four received an "A," six received a "B," twenty-one were awarded a "C," five received a "D," and three were failures. He asks the pupils to look over their papers.

"Are there any questions?" queries Mr. Owens.

"How come I only got a 'C'," demands Ann.

"You missed nearly half the multiple-choice questions, and I don't think you covered the essay topic, Ann," replies Mr. Owens. "You certainly wrote enough for a 'B' or an 'A,' but your thoughts rambled and you didn't actually come to grips with the issues. It was hard for me to know if you really understood what you were talking about. Are there any other questions?"

"Well, what *were* the main issues that you marked us on and that you wanted us to 'grip'?" Ann asks disgustedly.

"But, that was the main purpose of the test, Ann, to find out who could isolate the issues and then discuss them intelligently," replies Mr. Owens, with a touch of impatience in his voice.

"Oh, neat to know that, *now!*" sighs Ann as she drops her paper on her desk. I think she knows her case is closed.

"Some of us didn't have enough time to finish, Mr. Owens," begins Shirley.

"It wasn't a long test, Shirley, there were only ten multiple-choice items."

"I know," replies Shirley, "but your questions had so many catches in them and some of the words were so hard for me that I had to read them over and over before I knew what you were getting at. And I still can't see what question 6 has to do with the topic."

"Yes, they were a bit tricky, weren't they?" responds Mr. Owens with a faint smile. "But they really do separate those who have studied from those who haven't. You are right about item 6—it requires only logical thought. I included it because that is what this course requires to be successful in it. Now, are there any more questions?" asks Mr. Owens, again. Janet starts to raise her hand, but decides not to when she notices Mr. Owens's look of impatience. "Well then, put away your papers and let us go on with the major causes of poverty in the world today. And I want to warn you right now, there will be a comprehensive exam at the end of this topic, also. Now, as we were saying. . . ."

At lunchtime, I notice Ann and a small group of her classmates sitting on the lawn. They are talking about the exam. Ted, one of the four persons who received an "A," is looking over Ann's paper. There are several red checkmarks, question marks, and X's on it. There are two comments on her response to the essay question; one says, "Watch your use of the word 'economy'," and the other, "I don't think this is really an important issue." The only other evidence of evaluation on Ann's paper is a letter grade of "C" written beside her name.

The papers of Ann's classmates carry similar markings. On Ted's paper is Mr. Owens's only comment: "Nice job."

Larry is laughing about the comment on his paper. Beside the letter grade of "D" is the phrase: "Consider this mostly a gift!" Larry says, "I never had a clue about what Mr. Owens would ask on this test, so I just wrote a bunch of stuff and tried to make it sound good."

There are many questions I would like to ask these kids: "Did you really understand the topic? Do you know what you were supposed to learn from the topic? Do you know why you got an 'A,' 'C,' or 'D'? Do you know what is right and what is wrong with what you did? Do you know what to do to improve your performance? Do the letter grades, checks, X's, question marks, and comments help you learn from your errors?" When I asked these questions, the only answer I got was "No." When I asked Nancy why she felt she got only a "C," she shrugged her shoulders and replied, "I get so frightened and confused on tests, and I guess I've always been just a 'C' student."

Ann interrupted, saying, "Maybe we've got just a 'C' teacher."

The look Ann gave me as she stated her simple conclusion was a challenge that each of us as teachers must answer. We must not only evaluate and try to improve the performance of our learners directly, but also we must strive indirectly for their improvement by evaluating and trying to improve the cognitive and affective aspects of our instruction. Otherwise, we will be hopelessly condemned to the mediocrity of which Ann spoke so pointedly.

Chapter 13 will help us develop a positive approach to instruction and evaluation, and we will return several times to the opening scene with Mr. Owens as we learn better ways to evaluate learning. The checkpoints will be used to do this.

EVALUATION IN EDUCATION

Evaluation means . . . "Evaluation" is a word frequently confused with the related terms "measurement" and "testing." Generally, *evaluation* is a broadly inclusive term that refers to the ongoing process of gathering information, making judgments about the information, and then arriving at decisions. *Measurement* usually means the process of developing or obtaining, and then using, some testing device or rating scale to collect information. *Testing* has a more restricted meaning. It defines the specific conditions and steps involved in administering and scoring tests of various kinds for various purposes. These are only general definitions, but they will be sufficient to get us started in our discussion of the purposes and procedures of evaluation in education. As we go along, we will modify them as the need arises.

Traditionally, the purpose of evaluation in education has been conceived in a narrow sense of grading and classifying learners, such as we observed in the scene with Mr. Owens and his students. This conception of evaluation is based on a similarly narrow yet widely held view that at any level of education, only a few selected learners are actually capable of learning all that the school offers. Bloom, Hastings, and Madaus describe this parochial view of education as a pyramid in which learning tasks become presumably more difficult from year one to the last year of formal schooling, and in which fewer and fewer learners are believed to have the native endowments or acquired skills and attitudes to complete them successfully.[1] The major purposes of evaluation in this conception of education are *prediction* and *selection*: the prediction of an individual's probability of success at the next educational level, and the selection of the most appropriate alternative.

The classification of learners is usually accomplished on the basis of examination results and teacher judgments that are converted into a grading system, typically one patterned after a normal distribution (Chapter 4). In this system of classification, only a few learners receive relatively high marks, about the same small percentage get poor and failing marks, and most receive average marks. In such a grading or selection system, the marks received by an individual tend to be highly consistent from one grade or level to the next. As Nancy, in Mr. Owens's class said, "I've always been just a 'C' student."

Bloom, Hastings, and Madaus have expressed concern about the consequences for learning and for the welfare of the individual learners in an educational system in which the major purposes of evaluation are prediction and selection. "The result of this method of categorizing individuals is to convince some that they are able, good and desirable from the viewpoint of the system and others that they are deficient, bad, and undesirable. It is not likely that this continual labeling has beneficial consequences for the individual's educational development, and it is likely that it has an unfavorable influence on many a student's self-concept."[2]

If we define the purpose of education as providing instruction that is individually optimal for each learner rather than as providing merely a fixed curriculum consisting of a graded set of learning tasks which is optimal for only a select few of our learners, we find that evaluation has another major purpose in education besides prediction and selection. In earlier chapters, we noted the necessity for corrective feedback for change in behavior, which is what education is all about. Evaluation can and must provide this feedback for use in the improvement of learning and teaching.

Taken by themselves, the uses typically made of evaluation processes—prediction and selection—are insufficient in that they are not directed primarily

Measurement means . . .

Testing means . . .

Three major purposes of evaluation are . . .

---

[1] B. J. Bloom, J. T. Hastings, and G. F. Madaus, eds. (1971). *Handbook of Formative and Summation Evaluation of Student Learning.* New York: McGraw-Hill, p. 7.
[2] Ibid.

toward improvement of learning and teaching. With the current and more realistic redefinition of the purpose of education meaning to produce maximum desirable *change* in each learner rather than to *select* at each level those few who "can" from those who "cannot," there is a tremendous need for evaluative information in the form of corrective feedback.

Let us look more closely at each of these three primary forms of evaluative information in education and see what proper use we may make of each. Once we understand these three purposes, we will be ready to learn about various methods of measurement and evaluation both in traditional, group-based approaches to education and in the alternative individual approaches we discussed in Chapter 12. Eventually, you will need to synthesize for yourself the useful methods that are appropriate for your approaches to instruction.

Prediction and Selection in Education

Much of our job as teachers calls for predictions about the kinds and magnitude of changes in learner behavior that are likely to result from various educational experiences. Decisions based on our predictions must be made, often many times each day, about the selection of (1) learners for certain experiences, and (2) materials and techniques for instruction that will match each learner's state of readiness. Prediction, viewed in this sense, is essentially a matter first of determining the prerequisite capabilities necessary for success in the new learning task, and second, of making an assessment of the learner to determine whether he has acquired them. The decision that we make from this information is usually to place, or to begin, selected learners at appropriate spots with appropriate experiences in a learning sequence according to their acquisition of the prerequisite capabilities.

The purpose of prediction is . . .

Most often, our predictions serve as bases for decisions in the ongoing, day-by-day business of moving learners ahead in sequences of various topics of the curriculum (cognitive, affective, and psychomotor) appropriate to their level of development. For example, Mr. Owens has to decide which of his learners are ready to begin the study of the major causes of poverty in the world today. That is, he must predict which learners will profit from this next learning task in the sequence of social studies. Based on his predictions, we would expect that he may begin selected students at various points in the sequence with various materials and approaches. However, as you will recall from our brief peek into his classroom, it is unlikely that he will do this. Rather, Mr. Owens seems to have made the decision to keep the entire class together and proceed to the next topic, using group-based instruction even though it is obvious from the tests written by

The purpose of selection is . . .

his learners that many are not ready to go on. The outcome of his decision will probably be that only a few of his learners will do well in the following topics of the sequence. I imagine that this is also his expectation.

Although Mr. Owens's approach to evaluation provides some potential feedback information about his learners' performance and the effectiveness of his instruction, it is not being used for the improvement of either. Rather, it simply confirms what he expected, since it is Mr. Owens's opinion that his is just an average group of learners. Based on the related assumption that success in learning is a function of essentially fixed learner capabilities, Mr. Owens sees no useful purpose of evaluation procedures other than to confirm the prediction of success and failure for given learners, and to provide information for the selection of certain learners for certain course marks.

Fortunately, most teachers make better use of the predictive and selective information available from evaluation procedures than does Mr. Owens. Evaluation for them is a planned part of instruction rather than something thought about at the end of an instructional sequence and then tacked on as an afterthought or for grade purposes before continuing on to the next topic. Information that results from planned evaluation procedures helps most teachers ensure that each learner will be placed at an appropriate place within each learning sequence and that each will experience instruction from which he can profit.

Although, as we mentioned before, most of the placement decisions that result from our predictions about learner success relate to day-by-day classroom instruction, many are of a slightly different nature. For example, at the secondary school levels, often we must help decide which of several possible programs of study will probably be best for a particular learner to pursue. Selection of occupational or postsecondary educational experiences involves decisions about learners' futures commonly encountered by counselors in most high schools. At the elementary school level, predictions, then decisions, must be made about placement of selected learners in remedial, enriched, or advanced programs of special instruction to meet various needs of individual learners deemed too atypical for the regular classroom teacher to teach effectively.

With such a variety of decisions to be made about which learners should do what things, immediately or in terms of longer-range plans, a variety of predictive information is needed. Since as teachers we must help make most of these decisions, we will want to know more about the kinds of predictive information available.

SOURCES OF PREDICTIVE INFORMATION

The kind of evaluative information needed depends on the kind of decisions of selection and placement we have to make. Sometimes the decision requires information about a learner's *general* ability or achievement level. For example, we may want to select certain secondary school learners for particular types of educational programs for the next year, e.g., occupational, commercial, or academic. Or we may need to select certain learners for placement in essentially the same educational program, say at the fifth grade level, but with groups using different approaches, e.g., discovery or reception.

At other times, information is needed about *specific* learner aptitudes, capabilities, or achievement level in a particular topic. For example, we may need to decide whether Sammy Brown, Alice Jones, and George Jay are ready to begin the next level of work in arithmetic, music, or reading. We may need to select certain learners to participate in various athletic events, such as running, jumping, and throwing, when our classroom challenges Mr. Johnson's to a track and field contest.

The information needed to make the many decisions of selection and placement typically comes from sources of evaluation that range from a teacher's informal or casual day-to-day observation of learners to formal and individual tests given and interpreted by an expert in measurement and testing. Included in this range of potential sources of predictive information are the general and subjective opinions that all teachers form about each of their learners without being able to say precisely what the opinion is based on. Specifically planned observations and interviews, structured as well as unstructured, are also common sources of predictive information, as are daily assignments and teacher-made tests, since one of the best predictors of a learner's future performance is simply present performance in similar or related behaviors.

Toward the more formal end of the range of potential sources of predictive information are commercially available *standardized* tests. These tests, administered either individually or in groups, are designed to provide evaluative information of several kinds that can be useful in predicting the future performance of learners. They can be classified according to what they attempt to measure and the kind of information they provide. We will list a few of the more commonly used types here, and in a later section, learn about their special characteristics.

TYPE OF STANDARDIZED TEST	ATTEMPTS TO MEASURE
1. Intelligence	General learning ability
2. Aptitude	Special capabilities, e.g., verbal and numerical facility, abstract and logical reasoning, mechanical reasoning, musical ability, physical dexterity
3. Achievement	General achievement in various curriculum areas, e.g., reading, spelling, mathematics, science, social studies
4. Diagnostic	Specific achievement of specific prerequisite knowledge and skills in various curriculum areas, e.g., reading comprehension or vocabulary; computation and number facts for addition, subtraction, multiplication, and division
5. Interest	Preference for various types of activities, or likes and dislikes for them

There are many things to be considered in getting accurate predictive information from observing and testing learners for the purpose of selection and placement. They have to do with the basic concepts and rules of evaluation, but we are not quite ready for that discussion. First, we need to learn about the third major form that evaluative information takes in education; that of *correction* or *corrective feedback*.

Correction in Education

Once evaluative information has helped us decide on the selection and placement of learners relative to particular learning experiences, we must concern ourselves with the effects of the instruction on each learner. Does each learner profit from the instruction with which he has been matched? Does each receive corrective feedback that enables him to modify his next trials? Does the teacher get feedback from the learner's efforts that helps him know how to improve instruction?

You will recall from Chapters 11 and 12 that one of our rules of development, the basic rule of feedback, implies that corrective feedback is necessary for development, including learning. Knowing the results of our responses helps us modify and improve our next ones. Since our job as teachers is essentially to produce change in the behavior of our learners and in ourselves, the importance of corrective feedback is apparent.

The importance of correction in learning is . . .

We need to become a bit more specific about corrective feedback in instruction and its effective use to improve learning and teaching.

THE NATURE AND USE OF
CORRECTIVE FEEDBACK IN INSTRUCTION

To be specific about the use of corrective feedback, we must be specific about what is to be learned. As you will remember, this is the first of the three major questions teachers have to answer. In Chapters 3 and 4, we learned that instructional objectives, stated precisely and in terms of learner behavior, help us answer this question and are useful in at least three ways relative to evaluation: (1) before instruction (pretesting), (2) during instruction (formative evaluation), and (3) after instruction (summative evaluation). We are now ready to learn more about the relationship between specific instructional objectives and the evaluation and improvement of learning and teaching, especially in terms of how objectives are a necessary part of a teaching-learning cycle: response→feedback→correction→response. . . .

The principal benefit for evaluation from a statement of specific instructional objectives, formulated prior to instruction and shared with learners, is that everyone knows ahead of time both what is to be learned and what the criteria are for evaluation. If our objectives are stated clearly in terms of learner behavior, we know even before instruction occurs what evaluation tasks our measuring instruments must include. Since the criteria for evaluation are simply the objectives described, these measuring instruments are referred to as *criterion-referenced* tests. Pretesting our learners on these or parallel tasks helps us to select and place our learners in appropriate experiences according to what each needs to learn, rather than to expose *all* learners to the same experiences, whether they are likely to profit from them or not.

A teaching-learning cycle is defined . . .

Once learners are appropriately placed in an instructional sequence, objectives and evaluation interact in a formative way to help them form or attain the knowledge, skills, attitudes, and so forth to be learned. Formative evaluation, as you recall from Chapter 4, provides information about the effectiveness of the teaching and learning process as it proceeds, not just when the process is over. In this way, evaluative information can be used in a corrective way at the time when it will be effective.

James Block (1971) describes this feedback/correction aspect of formative evaluation procedures as making the same kind of systematic instructional adjustments as would a tutor. When the learner makes an error, instruction is immediately changed somewhat; new cues are presented, more practice is provided, or the nature and quantity of reinforcements are altered.

Block goes on to explain the relationship of instructional objectives to a teaching-learning cycle based on a feedback/correction system. He points out that the factor that makes the procedure effective is the ongoing, criterion-referenced measurements that are taken directly from the instructional objectives. You will recall from our discussion of mastery learning in Chapters 4 and 12 that formative-type, diagnostic tests are given throughout instruction to check on each learner's progress toward the objectives. On the basis of this feedback information, corrective action may be taken by the teacher whenever it is needed, e.g., reteaching the entire class, individual tutoring by the teacher or other learners, or using programmed materials with some auto-instructional device.

Formative evaluation means . . .

You will notice that the idea of an ongoing instructional cycle is not new for us at this point. We recognize it as the central process in Skinner's (1968) definition of teaching (Chapter 8). We also saw the cycle applied as an integral part of various approaches to instruction, e.g., in the Montessori method and in mastery learning (Chapter 12).

The cyclic nature of both teaching and learning needs to be emphasized so that it points boldly to the insufficiency of a conceptualization of teaching and learning as a linear, one-way only, or noncyclic process. School learning needs to be seen as a back-and-forth process of learners responding, checking their results, and using that feedback for making further responses that successively approximate the objectives of the effort.

Our teaching must also be viewed as a feedback/corrective cycle both with individuals and groups of learners for a given objective and from one group to another. Otherwise, it stands little chance of improvement. The big questions in doing this, however, are, first, knowing how to provide individual corrective feedback to each learner in an entire class, and, second, at what time the feedback will be most helpful. Chapter 8 gave us some ideas about how to solve these problems through the use of programmed materials and auto-instructional devices. However, we should remember that the key use of corrective feedback is to modify *instruction* because learning is not likely to improve until there is an improvement in teaching. When learners, such as Nancy in Mr. Owens's class, remark that they have "always been just a 'C' student" it is a pretty good bet that, as Ann put it, they have "always had just 'C' teachers"; that is, teachers who have viewed instruction as a one-way trip through the material rather than a cycle that regularly offers the possibility of improvement.

CHECKPOINT 13-1

1.   State what you believe Mr. Owens's purpose was for testing his learners.

2.   If Mr. Owens had used the results from his test as a formative part of the teaching-learning cycle, how would he have proceeded?

3.   Were you previously aware of the abuses in group-based instruction and evaluation described in the exchange between Mr. Owens and his students? No____ Somewhat____ Completely____

BASIC CONCEPTS AND RULES OF EVALUATION

Now that we know about the major purposes or uses of evaluation in education, it will be helpful for us to understand some basic concepts and rules that we must account for in whatever methods of evaluation we decide to use. Just as the rules of a theory of instruction must be built into each of the various approaches to instruction, so also must approaches to evaluation agree with concepts and rules of evaluation. Unless the agreement is as good as we can make it, evaluation procedures, just like instructional procedures, become meaninglessly random and intuitive, and so does learning.

In measuring and evaluating teaching and learning for whatever purpose, the first rule is that our procedures and tools must be as *valid* (appropriate), and *reliable* (consistent) as we can make them. Knowing about each of the defined concepts in this rule will help us do a better job of approximating the ideal. Referring back to the insight made by Debra (one of Mr. Johnson's learners in Chapter 6) during an arithmetic lesson about the concept and rules of estimation will help us get started. Debra, as you will recall, formulated the extremely important rule that "all measurements are really just estimates of reality." Her rule, as you recognize, is a specific example of the higher-order rule we learned about in Chapter 2: *Truth is only relative and approximate.* As we learn about the concepts and rules of measurement and evaluation, we will want to keep Debra's rule clearly in mind. We will constantly want to be aware of the relative and approximate nature of the information we gather with our measuring tools and to remember that the measurements we make of our learners' abilities, achievement, interests, motivations, and so forth are only *estimates,* and not the reality of these qualities and quantities. We must know that our estimates *always* contain error of a variety of potential kinds, usually associated with the lack of validity and reliability of our tools and procedures. An obvious rule that derives from this observation is that *our estimates are only as accurate as our measurements.* Therefore the worth of our evaluation judgments and decisions is limited by the accuracy of the information we gather from our estimates.

> The statement "A measurement is only an estimate" means . . .

With this bit of advance caution, let us now discuss the major defined concepts and rules of measurement and evaluation. We will examine the concepts *validity* and *reliability.* Then, in later sections, we will see how these concepts and their related rules can be approximated in various methods of evaluation, both in traditional group-based approaches to instruction and in some of the more individualized approaches we learned about in Chapter 12.

Validity

To be useful in forming judgments from which educational decisions can be made, evaluative information must be *valid;* that is, it must be *appropriate* information. It must serve the purpose intended (TenBrink, 1974). A brief look at a few of the judgments and decisions faced by teachers will help illustrate this important requirement.

Suppose you need to select one assistant for the science laboratory from five student applicants. *Valid* information for making this decision is any information that helps you select the best person for the job. It may include knowledge about the applicants' previous work experience; their familiarity with laboratory equipment, supplies, and procedures; their attitudes and interests regarding science; their general ability to learn; achievement in science courses; and opinions of other teachers. Information from all these sources together likely has a greater

> Validity is defined generally as . . .

validity for our purpose of selecting the best person for the job than does information from any one source.

Information that is likely to have low or no validity for our purpose of selecting an effective lab assistant would include information that is unrelated to the requirements of the task. It could include things such as knowledge about the applicant's sex, skin color, height or weight, attitudes and interests in sports, place of residence, and length of hair.

Discriminating between valid and invalid evaluative information is relatively easy when the judgments and decisions to be made call for rather specific information of a known type. For example, tests of running speed, jumping, and throwing are pretty good ways to get highly valid information for deciding who should compete in which events in an upcoming track and field competition. Test scores in reading, typing, science, or auto mechanics, however, are obviously not likely to be highly valid predictors of ability to run the 100-meter dash or to throw the javelin.

Many of our judgments and decisions are not so easy to make as selecting the fastest runner or even the best lab assistant. Yet, we need information for these decisions that is as valid as possible. Suppose, for example, that you are a counselor in a secondary school and you need to help some of your grade twelve clients decide on occupational or further educational experiences after graduation, or perhaps to help one of your clients decide whether to drop out of school. For judgments and decisions such as these, it is not easy to get really valid information, since they are extremely complex decisions and we really do not know exactly what kind of information is likely to be helpful in making them. From observation and research, however, we have developed some techniques for increasing the validity of the information we use for making educational judgments and decisions. We will learn about some of these techniques in later sections.

Thus, right to begin with, we can see that the concept of validity is a specific term that has meaning only relative to the purpose (decision) for which we need evaluative information. Consequently, whenever we speak of the validity of certain tools, e.g., tests, check lists, and questionnaires, or procedures, such as testing, observations, and analysis, for gaining evaluative information, we must ask: "Valid for what purpose—selection, placement treatment, or correction?"

Once we know the purpose, we have already taken the first major step toward getting valid information. However, as we just saw, knowing the purpose is often more complicated than it may appear. For example, if our purpose is to decide whether Johnny Frog is ready to begin the next unit in arithmetic, it is fairly easy to construct or select evaluative tools and techniques that are likely to give highly valid information to help us make the decision. The reason is that we can be pretty sure of the criteria necessary for Johnny to meet to be successful at the next level. We know the specific kind of information we need to make the decision.

If, however, we must judge whether Johnny can profit from instruction in a regular classroom or whether he should be placed in a special group for special instruction, it becomes difficult to be confident about which tools and techniques will give us valid information for this decision. The problem we face, like that of the high school counselor, is that we do not know for sure what constitutes all the criteria for success in school-type tasks. Therefore, although we know what decision we need to make, we do not know exactly what kind of evaluative information is most valid for the purpose.

We do know several things, however, that can help us make such judgments and decisions of placement. For one thing, we know that the level of past achievement in school-type tasks as reflected by course marks is a fairly good predictor of future achievement in similar school-type tasks. Scores on tests of general ability, usually in the form of IQ scores, also help predict future probability of success. Also, teachers' observations, subjective as they may be, are usually a source of fairly valid predictive information. But, for most of the educational decisions you will face, less than completely valid information can be obtained, and usually the validity obtainable is related to the type of judgment being made. Consequently, it is useful to think of validity of several types.

TenBrink reminds us that "most evaluative judgments used in educational decision making fall into two types: Those where present ability is being judged (estimates) and those where future performance is being judged (predictions)."[3] The evaluative information we need to make these types of judgments and decisions calls for somewhat different, yet overlapping, types of validity. Judging present ability, e.g., achievement level in a course or proficiency in some skill like typing, driving a car, or public speaking, requires information that has what Robert Ebel (1965) designates as *direct* validity, and which Thorndike and Hagan (1955) describe as depending primarily on rational analysis and professional judgment. Predicting future performance calls for evaluative information that has *derived* validity[4] and that depends, for the most part, on empirical and statistical evidence.[5]

Two major types of validity are . . .

DIRECT VALIDITY

Typically, we check on the validity (appropriateness) of the evaluative information, e.g., readiness of learners for the next task and needed modifications of our instruction, by analyzing the evaluative information we get from daily assignments, tests, major projects, and informal observations. Our purpose is to see how well our instructional objectives in all domains are apparently being met by each learner. Two questions we usually try to answer from this direct approach are, first, "Is our evaluative information really a *true measure* of the objectives of instruction?" and second, "Is it an *adequate sample* of the objectives of instruction?" These are questions of *curricular* and *content* validity, respectively.

Curricular validity is determined by judging the degree to which the evaluative information obtained from observations, tests, daily assignments, and so forth is a true measure of our instructional objectives.

Curricular validity means . . .

Content validity is estimated by checking to see whether the evaluative information represents an adequate sample of all the objectives relative to the decisions being made. Both these types of validity can be checked with an objectives-achievement chart such as that outlined in Figure 13-1. This type of

Content validity means . . .

---

[3] T. D. TenBrink (1974). *Evaluation: A Practical Guide for Teachers.* New York: McGraw-Hill, p. 40.

[4] R. L. Ebel (1965). *Measuring Educational Achievement.* Englewood Cliffs, N. J.: Prentice-Hall, p. 381.

[5] R. L. Thorndike and E. Hagen (1955). *Measurement and Evaluation in Psychology and Education.* New York: Wiley, pp. 109–110.

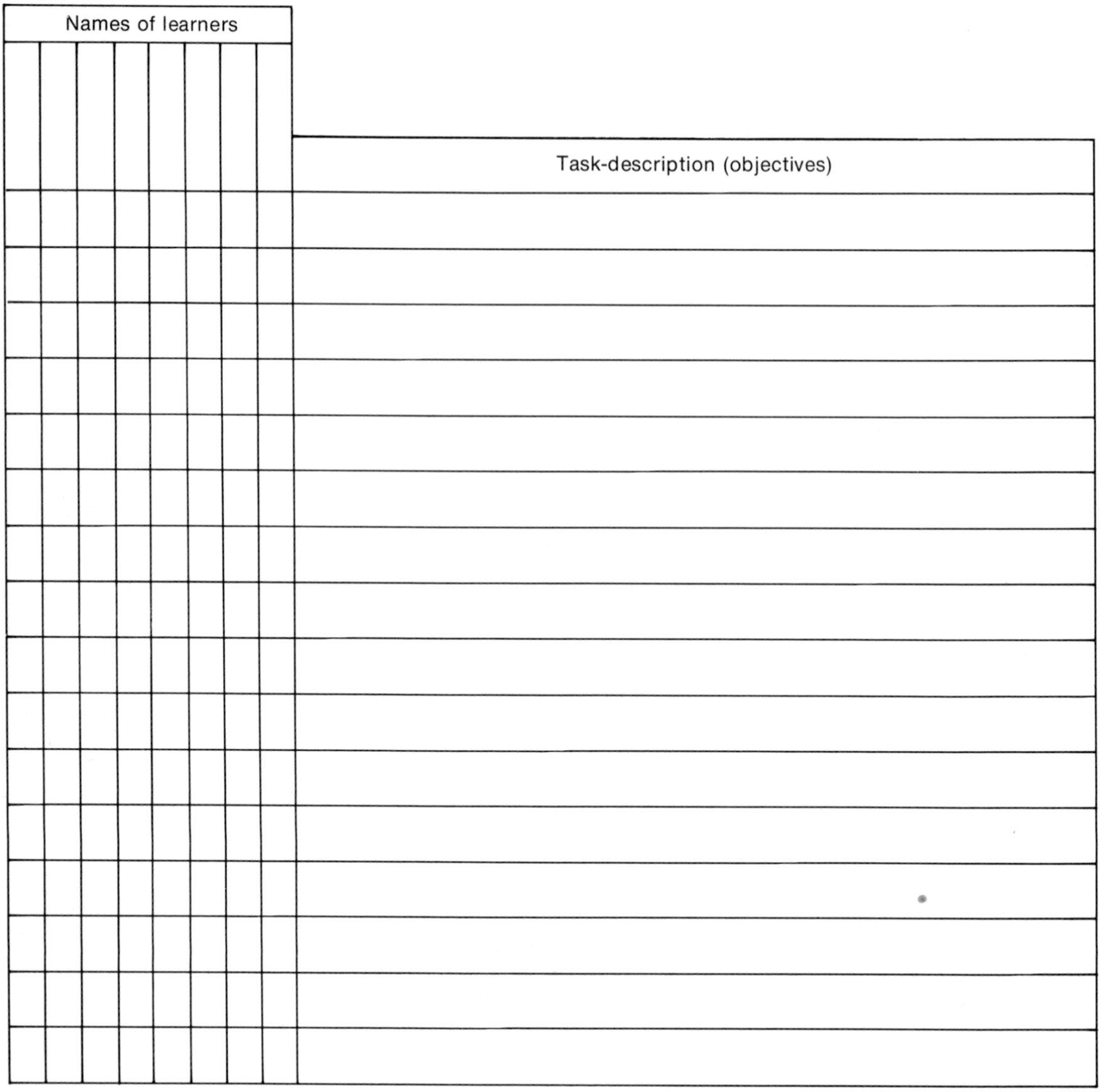

Names of learners									Task-description (objectives)

FIGURE 13-1   An outline of an objectives-achievement chart.

chart gives us, in addition, a way of keeping track of which learners have achieved which objectives.

To check on the curricular and content validity of evaluative information, compare your evaluative information or plans to get it with your chart of objectives to judge whether (1) the information is a true measure of the objectives, and (2) it is an adequate sample of those objectives.

An example will help illustrate these two types of validity and show how we can check on them. Suppose you have several instructional objectives for your learners of a psychomotor type at what Harrow (1972) terms the Skilled Movement level. The general goal described by these objectives is that the learner is able to play volleyball, and it includes instructional objectives that describe the specific skills needed for serving and returning the ball, setting it up at the net, and so forth. Suppose, further, that after a period of instruction, you want to know if your learners have achieved all the specific objectives. You tell your learners that you are going to test each of their skills at volleyball by watching them perform in a game situation that will last ten minutes. At the end of the test game, whatever evaluative information you have gathered is likely to be high in *curricular* validity but low in *content* validity. The evaluative information probably represents a reasonably true measure of the objectives (skills) assessed, but it probably does not constitute an adequate sample for each learner of the objectives (skills) of concern.

In such a brief observation period, it is not likely that each of some twenty learners had ample opportunity to display his level of achievement for each of the several specific skills that describe the general task of playing volleyball. A more valid method of estimating achievement should be found. That is, a method is needed to gain a more representative or adequate sample of each learner's achievement of each skill. This can be done by using the objectives-achievement chart as a checklist.

To use an objectives-achievement chart as a checklist for obtaining evaluative information whose content validity is relatively high for estimating achievement, we would simply arrange several real or simulated situations in which each learner had reasonable opportunity to perform the requirements of each objective. In the case of the volleyball skill, we would have each learner demonstrate his level of achievement for each of the specific skills listed on the chart as objectives. This could be done either in several actual game situations or in a simulated situation in which only "serves" or "setups at the net" would be performed. As each learner attempted a particular skill, the teacher would check the appropriate box beside the learner's name with a mark designating "complete" or "incomplete."

An objectives-achievement chart is . . .

A similar procedure can be used for learning tasks in cognitive and affective domains. For example, if you wish to check on the curricular and content validity of a paper-and-pencil test you have prepared for a unit in social studies, you will compare your test items with your objectives-achievement charts. In this way, you will be able to judge whether (1) your test items are a reasonably true measure of the content of the objectives, and (2) the items are a representative sample of all the objectives, and do not contain too many items from one or more parts of the unit and too few from others.

Affective objectives can also be arranged on an objectives-achievement chart and the chart used to check the curricular and content validity of information gathered as an estimate of our learners' achievement of them. Gathering the information, however, often involves more than assessing the results of paper-and-pencil tests and assignments, or observing learner performance in real or simulated situations. We will learn about some of these methods of obtaining evaluative information in a later section.

DERIVED VALIDITY   The validity (appropriateness) of the information we obtain for making instructional judgments and decisions about our learners is not always possible to estimate by comparing the information directly with our in-structural objectives listed on an objectives-achievement chart. Sometimes these judgments and decisions are about future performance. In these cases we want to know how valid whatever information we have is for helping us make accurate predictions about the likely performance of our learners on some criterion measure at a later date.

Predictive validity is defined as . . .

PREDICTIVE VALIDITY   Sometimes we want to estimate the validity of our evaluative information for making judgments and decisions about the probability of our learners success on future tasks, e.g., success at the next grade level or in a special educational program, as a future classroom teacher, or satisfaction with a particular occupational choice. Obviously, there is no simple, direct way of checking on the predictive validity of information we have presently available for learner performance that has not yet occurred. We must carry out some experiments over time to see how appropriate (valid) certain evaluative information is for predicting learner performance in the future. Fortunately, we do not have to begin from zero for many of the predictions we need to make. Educators, psychologists, and test makers for years have been conducting experiments and gathering data for a great number of the kinds of predictions frequently made by teachers, counselors, and employers. For example, it is well known that information about past performance on school-type tasks, i.e., course marks or grades, is a relatively good predictor of future performance on school-type tasks. So are general ability (IQ) test scores and scores on standardized achievement tests. Standardized tests of special aptitudes and interests provide evaluative information that has some predictive validity for success and satisfaction in various occupations. For the most part, however, information from standardized tests is only *generally* valid. Since such information relates generally to great numbers of learners only somewhat similar to your groups of learners, and even less to specific individuals in your groups, it will need to be supplemented with evaluative information from your own observations and experiments with your own learners.

An expectancy table shows . . .

One useful way to handle the evaluative information you want to use for prediction and then decision making, usually on selection and placement, is to construct *expectancy tables*. These tables help interpret evaluative information for learners and they also help us check on the predictive validity of the information. An example of how evaluative information might be presented in an expectancy table is shown in Table 13-1. The table was prepared by a counselor in a secondary school for use with grade eleven students who were trying to decide whether to take a physics course in grade twelve.

To interpret students' grade-point average in the prerequisite math courses taken in grades 9, 10, and 11 in terms of their probability of obtaining a particular grade-point in the physics course, the counselor refers students to the appropriate rows and columns corresponding to their grade-point average in the prerequisite math courses. The entries at these points show the probability, based on the performance of previous students over several years in this school in these courses, of attaining a particular grade-point in physics. For example, if a particular student's grade-point average for the three prerequisite math courses is 2.8, then the probability of her attaining a grade in the physics course of "D" is at least 91 percent; of "C" at least 87 percent; of "B" at least 54 percent; and of "A," at least 26 percent.

The predictive validity of expectancy tables such as the one in Table 13-1

TABLE 13-1   An expectancy table for achievement in grade twelve physics

GRADE-POINT AVERAGE IN PREREQUISITE MATH COURSES (GRADES 9, 10, 11).	PROBABILITY OF EARNING A GRADE-POINT OF AT LEAST:			
	1.00 ("D" Average)	2.00 ("C" Average)	3.00 ("B" Average)	4.00 ("A" Average)
3.5–4.0	100%	95%	80%	58%
3.0–3.4	100	90	68	35
2.5–2.9	91	87	54	26
2.0–2.4	86	80	37	19
1.5–1.9	72	54	6	3
1.0–1.4	23	18	4	1
0.5–0.9	10	5	1	0

changes somewhat as conditions relative to success on the criterion measure vary. The actual content of the courses may change from year to year; different teachers, with different teaching capabilities or views on grading, may teach the courses; motivations to do well in these types of courses may change with shifts in political or economical values in society, as they did, for example, after the launching of Sputnik. Changes such as these influence the relationship between the evaluative information and the criterion being predicted. Consequently, expectancy tables must be constantly revised to update their information and maintain and improve their predictive validity.

With just a bit of thought, we see that expectancy tables, especially those based on the evaluative information of learners in the local area, can have relatively high predictive validity and thus be clearly useful to teachers and students for making decisions of selection and placement. The evaluative information these tables contain may range from scores on standardized tests of readiness, general intelligence, and special aptitudes to scores on standardized preference or interest inventories, and to scores on teacher-made tests and informal classroom observations of learner performance in various cognitive, affective, and psychomotor areas. Judgments and decisions for which such information may show predictive validity can include deciding whether a learner is likely to profit from instruction in reading, calculus, or advanced swimming; be successful and enjoy a particular occupational choice; or succeed in his first university year.

CONCURRENT VALIDITY   Many times we have evaluative information available from more than one source that helps us form judgments and decisions. If the information from each source, e.g., teacher observation, course marks, daily assignments, or test scores, leads to the same judgments and to the same decisions, we can say that these measures have *concurrent* validity. When this is the case, the various forms of evaluative information show a high degree of relationship with one another, that is, they are highly correlated in terms of what they measure. It is often useful to know that two or more forms of evaluative information are concurrently valid because one form of information may then be substituted for the other. Moreover, if one form is easier to obtain than another or costs less in

**Concurrent validity is
defined as . . .**

money, time, or skill required, its use can result in substantial savings without appreciable differences in validity. An example of this is seen in the evaluative information obtained from group and individual intelligence tests, since both tests measure the same general abilities. Consequently, most schools that use intelligence tests administer standardized *group* rather than *individual* tests as a general practice because the group tests are less expensive, less time-consuming, require less skill to give and interpret, and provide at least a rough approximation of the evaluative information gained from individual tests. However, when a more precise breakdown of abilities is desired, individual tests are given.

CONSTRUCT VALIDITY   Our concern with the validity of all the various types of evaluative information we obtain about our learners always centers on whether the information is really a representative, true measure of what we attempt to evaluate. More simply, we want to know whether we are indeed measuring what we think we are. Checking with objectives-achievement charts for the *content* and *curricular* validity of the evaluative information we obtain is a fairly direct way of trying to answer the question. Indirectly, we check on the appropriateness of our information for certain judgments and decisions by observing the future performance of learners and constructing expectancy tables to illustrate the *predictive* validity of the information. Also indirectly, we check on the appropriateness of our information by comparing it with other types. If they all appear to estimate essentially the same things, we conclude that they are *concurrently* valid and that one type of information may be substituted for another.

When more than a single criterion is being measured, such as the performance required to meet an instructional objective, establishing the *content, curricular, predictive,* or *concurrent* validity of evaluative information, however, does not help answer the fundamental question: "Are we actually measuring what we think we are?" When the criterion to be estimated is some concept or construct that is obviously complex, general, and theoretical in nature, e.g., a personality trait or characteristic, general ability, or intelligence, we must try to validate our information by an empirical process. That is, we must try to determine *what* we are measuring through experimentation. This process of experimentation begins with an operational definition of the theoretical construct—of what we think the construct involves. Next, we try to develop ways to measure the behaviors specified in our definition. Finally, we check to see how well the measures agree with our definition. Often we have to redefine the construct somewhat and start the process all over again. In this sense, construct validity is really never fully achieved.

One of the main problems in obtaining valid measures of theoretical constructs is that not everyone agrees on how they should be defined. For example, what exactly should be meant by constructs such as *intelligence, anxiety,* or *creativity?* Robert Ebel believes that one obstacle to defining constructs in operational terms is "a persistent belief that what a word (or a construct) like 'anxiety' or 'intelligence' or 'creativity' means can somehow be discovered by research or by analysis of data."[6] Ebel points out, however, that, since language is always invented, what a term means must always be determined by agreement or consensus among users of the term, both past and present. He continues, saying that

---

[6] R. L. Ebel (1965). Op. cit., p. 384.

"research can discover what people *do* mean by the term 'anxiety.' It cannot reveal what anxiety *ought* to mean. Tests cannot reveal what intelligence *really* is; they can only illustrate what certain test constructors believe that the term 'intelligence' ought to mean."[7]

You will remember from Chapters 11 and 12 that many people have defined the construct *intelligence* differently. Galton (1869) defined intelligence in terms of sensory capabilities; Piaget, in terms of the knowing behavior characteristic of different forms of living things and of different stages of development; Binet (1905) and Terman (1916), in terms of general ability to learn, to reason, to grasp concepts, to deal with abstractions; and Wechsler (1944), as "the aggregate or global capacity of the individual to act purposefully, to think rationally, and to decal effectively with his environment."[8] Imagine the difficulty test makers have had trying to construct instruments that account for all the differences in the definition of the term *intelligence*. No wonder tests constructed by various persons produce evaluative information with slightly, and sometimes vastly, different meanings, and consequently different uses. We will see how the definition of intelligence is related to how a test for it is constructed when, in a later section, we compare tests of intelligence as defined by the behavioral characteristics of Piaget's developmental stages and as defined more traditionally as the general ability to learn.

As teachers, we do not often construct tests to measure abstract constructs of personality or intelligence. However, practically every school-aged child in North America has at some time or another had his intelligence estimated by such tests, and it will be our job to interpret the results. Thus we must be concerned about the validity of such theoretical constructs as *intelligence, creativity, anxiety, drive, need,* and *special aptitudes,* since many of the judgments and decisions we make about the lives of our learners are based on the evaluative information derived from instruments that purport to measure these constructs. It seems only logical that we should constantly question: "What, exactly, do they measure?" "What do the test manuals say the tests measure?" and "What do we want to measure?" One place to look for some of these answers is in Buros's *Seventh Mental Measurements Yearbook* (1972), which presents critiques, prepared by experts in the field of measurement and evaluation, for most commercially available standardized tests.

Construct validity is defined as . . .

Reliability

The second most important concept of measurement and evaluation, next to the *validity* of information, is its *reliability*. To have confidence in information for the judgments and decisions we need to make about selection, placement, and correction, we must know, first, that it is appropriate (valid) information for our purposes, and, second, that it is relatively free from error of measurement (reliable). Cronbach (1969) points out that reliability information tells how much confidence we can place in a measurement. And, as Debbie, in Mr. Johnson's class (Chapter 6), put it: "Measuring is just estimating. Rulers and scales aren't

---

[7] Ibid.

[8] D. Wechsler (1944). *The Measurement of Adult Intelligence.* Baltimore: Williams & Wilkins.

all exactly the same, and people can make mistakes when they use them. Even with a ruler, you can't measure—*exactly*. You just estimate—better than you can without a ruler."

Reliability means . . .

Reliability, according to Cronbach, always refers to the *consistency* of evaluative information obtained throughout a series of measurements. He says that since evaluative information varies from one trial to another, we should not trust any one measure absolutely. The information is only a rough indication of the level of the person's ability or typical behavior. Any evaluative information we obtain about our learners will always contain some error of measurement, or, in other words, will always be somewhat unreliable. Our task as teachers is to try to increase the reliability of our observations about our learners, since inconsistency of our data reduces their validity and can lead only to inaccurate judgments and decisions. Or, more directly, our tests cannot be valid unless they are also reliable.

Three possible sources of unreliability of evaluative information are . . .

To minimize the error in our evaluative information, we need to understand its possible sources. Most evaluative information has three main sources of possible unreliability: (1) within the *tools* for gathering information, (2) within the *process* of acquiring evaluative information, and (3) within the *learner*. Let us look more closely at each of these potential sources.

POSSIBLE ERROR WITHIN THE TOOLS

Ebel (1965) writes that the appropriateness and definiteness of the task from which evaluative information is obtained affect the reliability of the information. When directions are ambiguous, poorly worded, or hard to read, or when the intent is unclear, it is difficult to interpret the meaning of learners' responses to them. The problem is that we do not know how much of a learner's error is due to inability to perform the task and how much is due to uncertainty about what is being asked. Ambiguity is always a serious concern in terms of the reliability of evaluative information. It is especially serious when the total observations, e.g., number of test questions, items on a questionnaire, problems on an assignment, or times spent watching learners are few. As a rule of thumb, longer tests, questionnaires, assignments, observation periods, and so forth provide more reliable information than do relatively short ones; they are more likely to provide a truly representative sample of the information desired, and ambiguity within a single element of the longer instrument represents a smaller proportion of the total information than it does in a shorter one.

Examples of error within the tools are . . .

Years ago, Percival Symonds (1931) issued a warning, loudly and clearly, about the unreliability of inadequate samples of learner behavior. His words are just as valid today as they were then:[9]

> A single observation is unreliable, a single rating is unreliable, a single test is unreliable, a single measurement is unreliable, a single answer to a question is unreliable. Reliability is achieved by keeping up observations, ratings, tests, questions, measures. . . . If you ask one teacher for her judgment of a boy's trustworthiness, you obtain what she has been able to observe in those few narrow classroom situations that appeared when her attention was particularly directed to some act involving honesty. An adequate rating (representative sample), on the other hand, requires the judgment of several raters in several situations at several different times. Reliable evidence is multipled evidence.

---

[9] P. M. Symonds (1931). *Diagnosing Personality and Conduct*. New York: Appleton-Century, p. 5.

If the elements within the information-gathering tool are too easy or too difficult for the learners, reliability is reduced because, in both cases, the details of the learner's true ability or achievement level is masked. If the elements are too easy and a learner gets all of them correct, we do not know how well he could have performed if at least some of the elements had been more difficult. If the elements are too hard and a learner is unable to perform any of them correctly, we know only what he *cannot* do; we have no information about what he *can* do.

POSSIBLE ERROR WITHIN THE PROCESS

There are two main sources of potential measurement error within the information-gathering process: the conditions under which the information is *obtained*, and those under which it is *scored*. Both types of error reduce the reliability and thus the validity of evaluative information.

Any condition in an information-gathering situation that influences a learner's performance, other than those conditions being estimated, potentially can reduce the reliability of the information obtained. For example, conditions of unclear or complicated directions, distractions such as noise, cramped quarters, poor ventilation, and excessive heat or cold, and improper or deficient equipment like poorly duplicated copies of tests can significantly alter the information obtained. In addition, not providing sufficient time for each learner to complete the tasks, unless rate of performance is one of the qualities being estimated, also contributes to unreliability.

Possible errors within the process are . . .

Scoring and recording evaluative information, whether by the teacher or by learners when they score and record their own work, can result in error that reduces reliability. This is especially the case when responding, scoring, and recording procedures are complicated as, for example, when separate answer sheets are used and then scored with perforated overlays that require several steps in the process, or when the criterion is not specified clearly, as often occurs in essay-type exam items or in poorly defined affective objectives.

Clearly, there are many conditions relative to the use of tools for gathering evaluative information that operate to reduce reliability. There are perhaps more, however, that are related to the learners themselves; these, of course, interact with the sources of error within both the tools and the process.

POSSIBLE ERROR WITHIN THE LEARNER

The performances of our learners change over time. Consequently, so do the scores we obtain from our observations of them. These variations are due to several factors, such as physical growth, learning, changes in motivation, development, health, and chance (changes for which we cannot account). Some of these changes occur somewhat gradually, for example, those associated with growth and development, including learning, whereas other changes, such as those related to interest, motivation, and health, tend to fluctuate more frequently, sometimes daily.

As a teacher, it is important to be aware of the characteristics of learners that are potential sources of error. Robert Thorndike (1949) made a list of most of these and then classified them according to whether the characteristics were *lasting* or *temporary*, and *general* or *specific*. His four categories are shown in Table 13-2 along with a few examples.

Four types of possible error within the learner are . . .

TABLE 13-2 **Possible sources of error within the learner***

I Lasting and general characteristics of the individual
   1. General skills (e.g., reading)
   2. General ability to comprehend instructions, test wiseness, techniques of taking tests
   3. Ability to solve problems of the general type presented in this test
   4. Attitudes, emotional reactions, or habits generally operating in situations like the test situation (e.g., self-confidence)
II Lasting and specific characteristics of the individual
   1. Knowledge and skills required by particular problems in the test
   2. Attitudes, emotional reactions, or habits related to particular test stimuli (e.g., fear of high places brought to mind by an inquiry about such fears on a personality test)
III Temporary and general characteristics of the individual (systematically affecting performance on various tests at a particular time)
   1. Health, fatigue, and emotional strain
   2. Motivation, rapport with examiner
   3. Effects of heat, light, ventilation, etc.
   4. Level of practice on skills required by tests of this type
   5. Present attitudes, emotional reactions, or strength of habits (insofar as these are departures from the person's average or lasting characteristics—e.g., political attitudes during an election campaign)
IV Temporary and specific characteristics of the individual
   1. Changes in fatigue or motivation developed by this particular test, (e.g., discouragement resulting from failure on a particular item)
   2. Fluctuations in attention, coordination, or standards of judgment
   3. Fluctuations in memory for particular facts
   4. Level of practice on skills or knowledge required by this particular test (e.g., effects of special coaching)
   5. Temporary emotional states, strength of habits, etc., related to particular test stimuli (e.g., a question calls to mind a recent bad dream)
   6. Luck in the selection of answers by "guessing"

* R. L. Thorndike (1949). *Personnel Selection*. New York: Wiley. Reprinted with permission.

You might want to keep Thorndike's list handy to check the evaluative information you obtain whenever you wonder about its reliability. Each entry points you to possible sources of error either for your group of learners as a whole or for any given individual. Each potential source of error you identify should cause you to lower your confidence in the reliability of your evaluative information. It should also give you a clue about how to remedy the situation in future testing.

CHECKPOINT 13-2

1. In the exchange between Mr. Owens and some of his learners, evidence can be found that leads one to question the reliability and the validity of the evaluative information he obtained. Analyze the exchange for the potential measurement error of each of the three types discussed earlier (within the *tool*, *process*, and *learner*), and list them briefly in point form.

2. Did you voluntarily discuss this item with anyone? Yes_____   No_____

METHODS OF EVALUATION IN TRADITIONAL GROUP-BASED APPROACHES TO EDUCATION

Methods of evaluation are the means that we use to try to find out what our learners' abilities, interests, and preferences are, what they have learned, and where they may be having difficulties in their physical and functional development. Our methods include the tools and procedures that help us find out about our learners. Since our approach to school learning has traditionally and nearly exclusively been group-based rather than individualized, it is only natural that the methods of evaluating learners' abilities and achievement have also been largely group-referenced. I mean by this term that learners' abilities, achievement, interests, and so forth have been measured and evaluated in a *comparative* or relative sense rather than in an absolute or criterion sense.

Especially with regard to general and specific abilities, interests, personality characteristics, and physical growth, the object of measurement and evaluation has been first to determine the "normal" or average performance of individuals grouped on the basis of some common characteristic, such as age, sex, or year in school. Then, with a *norm* (or standard) performance or characteristic established, the object has been to measure each individual's performance (achievement, abilities, interests) and compare it with the norm. Various mathematical and statistical techniques have been worked out to describe how much an individual's performance or score varies or deviates from the group average (norm, standard). These techniques usually result in the placement of each learner's score on a continuum or a distribution from "poor" to "good" relative to the average of the group being used for comparison. Such a distribution of scores tells us that an individual's performance is a certain amount higher or lower than the group average or the score of some other individual.

In this approach, an individual's performance is valued in relation to how others of his group or a comparable one performed on the same or similar tasks. A "good" performance is one that is "more than" the group average; a "poor" performance is one that is below the group norm. Typically, grades or marks are assigned on this basis of relative "goodness" and "poorness" of performance, and it is usually the average performance of the group, e.g., the class, that is taken as evidence by the teacher that instruction for the group is effective, or that it needs to be modified.

The performance of individuals, either "very good" or "very poor," has little to do with bringing about modification of instruction, since these cases are relatively few compared with the rest of the group. The wide deviance in their performance is usually interpreted by teachers as due to individual pecularities rather than to inadequacies in instruction. Thus, teaching is geared to the group norm, "average" learning becomes the goal, and methods of group-based measurement and evaluation tend to keep it that way.

In the last sections of this chapter, we will learn about rules and methods of measurement and evaluation that are based more on individual performance (ability and achievement) relative to stated criteria than on the performance of other members of a group. But, since many of the methods of gathering evaluative information are common to both group-based approaches to instruction and the more individualized approaches we learned about in Chapter 12, we will discuss these methods in the present section. For convenience, we will group the methods into "informal" and "formal."

Method of evaluation means . . .

Norm-referenced methods of evaluation are those that . . .

By *informal* we will mean those ways of finding out about our learners' abilities, interests, and achievement that traditionally have been more or less unstructured, spontaneous, or casual. Teacher's observations, planned as well as incidental, and teacher's classroom questions are the two methods we will discuss.

When we talk of *formal* methods of measurement and evaluation, we will mean testing in the sense that time is set aside specifically for the purpose of asking learners to respond to questions that were prepared ahead of time. The tests may be either teacher-made or standardized, they may be paper-pencil or oral, or they may require a physical performance. They may measure general or specific abilities, interests, achievement, or learner characteristics such as height, weight, hearing, vision, and personality traits.

Informal Methods of Measurement and Evaluation

Obviously the oldest methods of measurement and evaluation in education are those of observation and questioning. Their importance as ongoing and spontaneous methods of evaluating and enhancing learning has been well established since the time of Socrates (470?–399 B.C.). Typically, teacher observations, with or without the use of guides such as checklists, rating scales, open-ended sentences, and daily diaries, have been used to measure and evaluate the affective and psychomotor behavior of learners. Classroom questions, on the other hand, have been used nearly exclusively to measure and evaluate cognitive behavior of learners, that is, their achievement in school subjects. Both methods can be used to obtain evaluative information to improve learning and instruction.

Three methods of informal evaluation are . . .

Until the past few years, these two methods of measuring and evaluating learner behavior have been used spontaneously and intuitively by most teachers. In fact, spontaneous and intuitive observations and questioning are even today seen by many as the central process that makes teaching an art. With the development of taxonomies of educational objectives for the cognitive, affective, and psychomotor domains (Chapter 3), however, and the specification of the rules of reinforcement and punishment that derive from a science of behavior (Chapters 8, 9, 10), a great deal of the intuition can be removed from our observations and classroom questions as methods of measurement and evaluation. Let us see how this can be done in terms of the affective behavior of learners, first using teacher observation techniques, for example, open-ended sentences, checklists, and rating scales. Then we will see how the taxonomy for the cognitive domain can serve as a guide to help us improve the quality of our classroom questions and also reduce our intuitive use of them.

EVALUATING AFFECTIVE BEHAVIOR

The place to start, in measuring and evaluating the affective behavior of our learners and our instruction, is with our affective objectives. Earlier in this chapter and in Chapter 3, we discussed the importance of instructional objectives prior to, during, and after instruction. At this point we need to understand the specific relevance of those early arguments for the measurement and evaluation of affective behaviors of learners. The essence of these arguments, I believe, is simply that if we feel the affective development of our learners is an important part of our instructional task, we must specify our affective objectives in precise terms, we must teach for them, and we must also evaluate our efforts to do so.

In earlier chapters we learned to write specific instructional objectives (task description) for the affective domain and to analyze them (task analysis) for purposes of instruction. Throughout the text, we have worked our way through several examples of teaching for affective objectives, and, as Bloom points out, we must develop some methods of evaluating these objectives. To do so, we should return to our purposes for gathering evaluative information—prediction, selection, and correction—since affective objectives can be evaluated for any of these purposes, with the overall goal of improving learning and instruction. Perhaps an important point, however, is that evaluation of affective objectives as a part of school learning largely should be directed toward obtaining feedback information that can be used to modify instruction as it occurs both in individual and group approaches. This suggests a need for formative and summative evaluation methods, that is, for an emphasis on helping learners develop affective behavior rather than on grading it.

There are several methods of evaluating affective development to obtain information that can be used in a formative way, once we have described our affective objectives precisely and specifically. You will recall from Chapter 3 that Krathwohl's *Taxonomy* (1964) for the affective domain provides a useful guide for describing affective objectives in hierarchical order: (1) receiving or attending, (2) responding, (3) valuing, (4) organization, and (5) characterization. (It may be helpful to review Table 3-7 in Chapter 3, since the following discussion of methods of evaluating affective objectives is based on Krathwohl's system of classification.)

Once our affective objectives have been stated, we can evaluate the effectiveness of our instruction toward them by methods such as (1) informal daily observation of learner behavior, often guided by an objectives-achievement chart; (2) interviews, structured or unstructured, individual and private or groupwide discussions; and (3) paper-and-pencil questionnaires with multiple-choice items, open-ended questions, stories, or situations.

Three methods of evaluating affective objectives are . . .

To get an idea of how you might use some of these methods, let us work our way through an example, and, to take advantage of the effects of positive transfer, let us use an example that we already know something about. In Checkpoint 3-7, we wrote affective objectives for a unit in social studies, the Amazon Basin. Suppose we take those affective objectives and see what methods we might use to evaluate whether our learners are meeting them. (See Responses for Checkpoint 3-7 in the Appendix.)

The first thing we might do with this set of affective objectives would be to enter them on an objectives-achievement chart such as the one outlined in Figure 13-1. In Figure 13-2, this general outline is used to list the specific affective objectives written for our unit on the Amazon Basin.

Since one of our basic assumptions about school learning is that learners learn what they practice (Chapter 1), we would analyze the objectives to get clues about the nature of the practice that should be included in the instruction. Note how each objective suggests activities as well as materials that will be needed. Note also that each objective gives us a description of some affective behavior whose acquisition we can estimate for each learner by using one or more of the methods of evaluation listed earlier. For example, we can use the ob-

etc.	Ann Brown	Bob Bowles	Tracy Aims	John Adams	Task-description
					Names of learners
					1.0 Receiving (Attending)
					1.1 Awareness. The learner is aware that people in different parts of the world have values that are different from his or hers.
					1.2 Willingness to receive. The learner is able to accept the fact that skin color has nothing to do with the worth of an individual.
					1.3 Controlled or selected attention. When given the opportunity to choose his or her own reading material, the learner chooses stories related to the people of the Amazon Basin.
					2.0 Responding
					2.1 Acquiescence in responding. Even though he or she may believe that food from the Amazon Basin will taste strange to him, the learner is willing to taste some.
					2.2 Willingness to respond. Given the information that the class is going to perform a dramatic sketch of a day in the life of a native family of the Amazon Basin, the learner will volunteer to participate.
					2.3 Satisfaction in response. The learner enjoys playing games typical of those played by children of the Amazon Basin.
					3.0 Valuing
					3.1 Acceptance of a value. The learner believes it is important to communicate with peoples of other lands.
					3.2 Preference for a value. The learner assumes responsibility for writing a letter to a pen-pal in the Amazon Basin.
					3.3 Commitment. When given the choice to discontinue writing to his or her pen-pal over summer holidays, the learner will choose to continue to write.
					4.0 Organization
					4.1 Conceptualization of a value. Through a study of the people of the Amazon Basin, the learner will be able to gain support for the value statement: "all people are important."
					4.2 Organization of a value system. The learner is able to form judgments about how respect for human dignity can be related to the way in which his or her country responds to the needs of the people of the Amazon Basin.
					5.0 Characterization by a value or value complex
					5.1 Generalized set. When given the opportunity to choose a classmate to work with, the learner chooses a partner on the basis of the requirements of the task, behavioral characteristics of the person, and so forth, rather than on the basis of race, color or religion.
					5.2 Characterization. The learner's actions toward people who differ from him or her in various ways (color, beliefs, values) are consistent with verbal statements about them.

FIGURE 13-2   Affective objectives for a unit on the Amazon Basin.

jectives-achievement chart as a basis for informal, ongoing, daily observations of our learners as we carry out the activities suggested by the objectives: choosing reading material, tasting food from the Amazon Basin, planning and doing a dramatic sketch, playing games typical of those played in the Amazon Basin, writing to a pen pal, discussing the qualities that make people important, and so forth. We can use the chart in a more formal way as the basis for individual and private interviews with certain selected learners who do not seem to be meeting the objectives very well, or as the basis for a general, classwide discussion to check on how we are progressing as a group. Information obtained from these observations and interviews will tell us a great deal. It gives us feedback about the effectiveness of our instruction and how it can be corrected for the entire class or for given individuals.

The objectives-achievement chart can be used as the basis for paper-and-pencil methods of evaluation. For example, we could construct a questionnaire with multiple-choice items derived from some of our objectives. (You will note, however, that paper-and-pencil responses are usually not adequate for evaluation at the characterization level. The learner must perform, that is, *live* his beliefs to qualify as having met objectives at this level. Teacher observations or self-reports are probably better methods of evaluating objectives at this level.)

1. When you have free time during which you choose to read, what type of stories do you select?
_____ Mystery stories
_____ Stories of discovery or adventure
_____ Stories of people from other lands
_____ Science-fiction stories

2. If our class decides to perform a dramatic sketch of a day in the life of a native family of the Amazon Basin, would you like to take part?
_____ Yes!
_____ Maybe I would
_____ I don't think so.
_____ No!

3. How much did you like the Brazilian games we played during our study of the people of the Amazon Basin?
_____ A lot
_____ Some
_____ Not much
_____ Not at all

Our questionnaire could also include open-ended questions, such as the following:

1. Studying about the people of the Amazon Basin has caused me to believe more strongly that all people _____

2. I believe our country should _____

3. When I choose someone to work with, I choose on the basis of _____

5. The part of our unit on the people of the Amazon Basin that I liked best was _____

6. I didn't like it much when we _____

Let us now turn our attention to an informal method of obtaining evaluative information in the cognitive domain. It is probably used more extensively, and often more poorly, than any other methods of evaluating learner achievement. It is the method of classroom questioning.

CHECKPOINT 13-3

Assume that you are Mr. Owens and that you have written the following affective objectives for your learners for the next unit, a study of the major causes of poverty in the world today. For each objective, describe a method to evaluate whether your learners have met it.

1. *Valuing Level.* The learner will volunteer to participate in a classroom debate on the major causes of poverty in the world today.

2. *Organizational Level.* Given a choice of topics on which to write a term paper for social studies, the learner will elect to write on the causes of poverty in the world today.

3. *Characterization Level.* The learner spends part of his free time assisting organizations dedicated to fighting poverty in the world.

4. Did you work with another person on these items? Yes_____ No_____

USING CLASSROOM QUESTIONS

It is a common observation that teachers everywhere consider asking questions a necessary part of the teaching-learning-evaluation process. It is also commonly recognized that teachers too often rely on classroom questions that require students to do little more than recall isolated bits of knowledge. For many children, education is thus defined as the requirement merely to gather information for the sole purpose of recalling it. It is obvious, however, that education must be more than memory of factual information. Therefore, the many questions we ask our learners in the course of daily instruction must be carefully selected and formulated. They must accurately reflect what we are trying to help our learners learn, and they must provide useful formative-type information about how well learning is occurring. Therefore, the classroom questions we ask our learners must derive from our instructional objectives. As we will soon see, the problem of knowing what questions to ask our learners is largely resolved when specific instructional objectives have been written in answer to the question: "What do I want them to learn?"

Norris Sanders (1966) has shown how Bloom's *Taxonomy of Educational Objectives: Cognitive Domain* might be used as a guide for constructing classroom questions that require children to function at various intellectual levels beyond simple recall. Using the major categories of the *Taxonomy*, Sanders has developed what he calls a "Taxonomy of Questions" (Table 13-3).

Once a teacher has mastered the characteristics of each major category in Bloom's *Taxonomy* (knowledge, comprehension, application, analysis, synthesis, and evaluation) and for a particular unit of study has formulated specific instructional objectives at the various levels, it becomes relatively easy for her to formulate questions that reflect the intellectual performances desired. The objec-

TABLE 13-3   Memory of information is at the base of all types of thinking†

						EVALUA-TION
					SYNTHE-SIS	Synthe-sis
				ANAL-YSIS	Anal-ysis	Anal-ysis
			APPLICA-TION	Appli-cation	Appli-cation	Appli-cation
		INTERPRE-TATION	Interpre-tation	Inter-preta-tion	Interpre-tation	Interpre-tation
	TRANSLA-TION	Transla-tion	Transla-tion	Trans-lation	Transla-tion	Transla-tion
MEMORY	Memory	Memory	Memory	Memory	Memory	Memory

† N. M. Sanders (1966). *Classroom Questions: What Kinds?* New York: Harper & Row, p. 10. Reprinted with permission.

tives themselves, if well stated, suggest what the essence of the questions should be. Questions of this sort are not only those statements that are followed by question marks but also any intellectual exercises that call for a response. They would include problems, projects, and exercises as well as questions as such, and they would represent a variety of levels of intellectual functioning complying with the major categories of the *Taxonomy*.

Classroom questions derive from . . .

Sometimes, however, it is difficult to gain agreement even among experts as to the appropriate classification of a given objective or question. Even though the descriptions of the categories in Bloom's *Taxonomy* appear to be discrete and separate entities, in reality they are only approximations of discrete categories. However, as Sanders (1966) points out, this is really not a serious problem for the teacher. He says that since the categories blend gradually from one to the next, it is exceedingly difficult to be precise about the level of a particular question, but that the important point for teachers to remember is that failure to precisely classify a question does not detract from its quality.

Sanders describes three other factors that enter into classifying a question. First, he tells us that the nature of the question itself, and second, the nature of the knowledge each learner brings to the classroom, must be considered in terms of classification in the *Taxonomy*.

Let us look at these two points more closely, since the way in which learners answer our questions largely determines the decisions we then make about what to do next. Suppose you have just completed a math exercise with one group of learners in your classroom and have asked them to solve a problem that requires the application of a rule just learned. Although, for apparent purposes, the problem you have assigned is an application-level question, it may turn out to be a memory-type one for some of the learners. It is possible that a student may have overheard you ask the same question during a lesson you taught earlier with another group in the same classroom. Consequently, that learner's response may not reflect an intellectual performance that can be classified as application. It may be only memory, yet, since he has answered it correctly, you may unknowingly conclude that he has mastered the application of the rule and is now ready to go on to analysis- or synthesis-level tasks involving that rule.

A third factor that Sanders says enters into the classification of questions concerns the instruction that precedes the asking of a question. For example, you may ask learners a question which in your opinion requires an analysis-level performance. It may turn out to be a memory-level requirement if the answer was given in the text or in other reading material. Although a teacher can never be absolutely certain about the learners' prior knowledge on a particular topic, for the most part she can anticipate the mental processes that they will find necessary to use to arrive at an answer. As Sanders points out, there are exceptions, and it is wrong to assume that a single question inevitably leads to a single category of thinking or that all students are necessarily using the same mental processes to arrive at an answer. Notice how this thinking relates to our earlier discussion of the reliability of observations and how reliability can be improved by getting a larger sample, that is, by not relying on a single question.

Classification of classroom questions requires that . . .

One further point should be made about classroom questions that can be derived from the *Taxonomy of Educational Objectives: Cognitive Domain*. This is the fallacy in believing that a question which requires the use of information (Chapter 3), or intellectual functioning beyond memory, is necessarily more difficult than a question which requires a memory-level performance. This need not be so. For example, remembering point by point all the details of the story "The Three Pigs" may be as difficult as, if not more difficult than, answering a higher-level question such as one on what the story is about (comprehension).

Although, in our discussion, we have objected to the use of questions that require only a memory-level performance, it is important to restate that there is nothing "wrong" with the accumulation of knowledge and asking questions to evaluate and help form it. The points I want to make are that too often accumulation of knowledge becomes the primary focus of what education is about, and that a more reasonable balance is needed between the questions we ask to help learners *acquire* information and those we ask to help them *use* information. As Table 13-3 illustrates, acquiring and remembering information is a necessary prerequisite for *every* kind of thinking. Thus it is important that we ask our learners questions that let us know whether they are acquiring it.

ASKING SIMPLE AND COMPLEX QUESTIONS   Within each category of the *Taxonomy*, it is possible to formulate both simple and complex questions. For example, a memory-type question may require only the recall of one small bit of information, such as: "Who was the main character in the story we just read?" On the other hand, a memory-type question may require the learner to recall an entire series of sequence, as in the memorization of the poem "The Cremation of Sam Magee." Sanders (1966) suggests that all teachers from the primary grades through graduate school should be able to use every category of questions. He points out that the differences in the questions used at various grade levels and with relatively slow or rapid learners should be in *complexity* (simple to complex) of thinking, rather than in *kind* (various levels) of thinking.

What Sanders is suggesting here is that it is a mistake to believe that slow learners are capable of performing only memory-type tasks. Many teachers believe learning to *remember* certain "essential" information is about all that can be expected of children who do not perform well. Furthermore, this assumption has often become part of a closed and wasteful cycle in which inappropriate expectations are set for learners—and met.

Who should be asked what type of questions?

It may be educationally sound to focus a good deal of attention, especially in the primary grades, on the accumulation of information. However, it must also be just as educationally unsound to completely neglect the teaching for, and evaluation of, the higher cognitive processes with young children. As in most other educational issues, however, there certainly are differences of opinion with regard to the intellectual abilities of young children. For example, as you recall from Chapters 12 and 13, Jean Piaget and his followers maintain that higher cognitive processes (synthesis-evaluation levels) are not possible for children of early school age. On the other hand, Jerome Bruner and others believe that you can teach anything to anyone *given that certain prerequisites have been acquired*, especially those related to language acquisition. Somewhere in the middle are classroom teachers, such as yourself, who must translate the often-contradictory opinions of authorities into specific classroom practices. A guiding rule of thumb might well be to set your expectations for a learner's performance as if he were indeed capable, and then to modify those expectations downward if your experience indicates the need to do so. For example, it may be wise to expect that learners will be able to synthesize and evaluate information, given your ability to structure the learning situation so that each child has at least a reasonable chance of being able to perform at that level. This means that in your teaching and evaluating, you will need to ascertain that the child has acquired the prerequisite skills and information necessary for a synthesis-type performance. You will need to test to make sure that he can (1) *remember* the necessary information, (2) *translate* it into his own terms, (3) *interpret* it in light of his own past experience, (4) *apply* that information to the specific task at hand, and (5) make an *analysis* of the requirements of the problem and thus *construct* a solution unique to himself.

A learner should be able to answer higher-level questions if . . .

Let us check on your mastery of the ideas involved in writing classroom questions that require the type of cognitive performance reflected by each major level of Bloom's *Taxonomy*. Checkpoint 13-4 will help us do this.

CHECKPOINT 13-4

Write one question that derives from the objectives I wrote for each of Bloom's six major categories for the story "The Three Bears." (See Responses for Checkpoint 3-6 in the Appendix.)

Formal Methods of Measurement and Evaluation

When we talk of formal methods of measurement and evaluation, we usually have in mind something to do with tests in one way or another. What most people mean by the word "test" is really some task, often with more than one part, that is set by one person and administered to others for the purpose of estimating their capabilities for performing the task. How well they perform is taken as evidence of the degree to which they possess whatever qualities are believed to be required to complete the task. This evidence is then used as the basis for forming judgments and making decisions about various aspects of the test-taker's life.

This has been the central idea in testing for thousands of years and it still is today. The ancient Egyptians, for example, devised a simple test (task) to estimate whether a person had sufficient mental ability to manage his own affairs of daily living or whether he should be declared incompetent and thus relieved of his responsibilities—and, no doubt, his assets. The person, brought to the attention of the authorities probably as a consequence of informal observation or questioning, was given the task of solving a problem of logic or of "common sense." The standard procedure was this: The person suspected of incompetence was brought into a bare but comfortable room and seated on a bench in front of a huge water jar placed on a low table. A short hollow reed extended from the bottom of the jar to a much smaller empty vessel. The end of the reed was stopped with a small wooden plug. The subject was given a small shallow dipper and the following directions by the examiner: "Soon, I will pull the plug from the hollow reed and water will begin rushing into the small empty vessel. You are not to allow the water in it to overflow and you are not to spill any on the floor. You may not ask me any questions. When I pull the plug, begin." The examiner would then pull the plug and leave the room, taking the plug with him. At this point, with the empty vessel filling quickly, some subjects would begin dipping water back into the huge reservoir jar, carefully at first and then not so carefully as the level of water in the small vessel gained on them. Eventually and consistently, this approach to the task ended in a subject's failure—and in the *judgment* of incompetence. The *decision* to relieve him of his responsibilities for himself usually followed.

Some subjects did not try to dip faster than the water could drain into the small vessel. They just put a finger into the end of the hollow reed and shut off the flow. On the basis of their performance, these persons were judged as competent and the decision was made that they should manage their own lives.

As you are well aware, not all tests are as simple as this Egyptian competency test in terms of construction, administration, scoring, and interpretation, i.e., only one test item, one direction, a single score of either pass or fail, and only one judgment. Yet, even though we would question the validity and reliability of this ancient test, most of the concepts relative to present-day testing procedures are reflected in it. We can see that this is so by examining a few of the kinds of tests and testing procedures teachers frequently use with their learners. We can look first at procedures for developing, administering, scoring, and interpreting teacher-made tests that are intended primarily for measurement and evaluation relative to group-based approaches to instruction. Then we can learn more about these procedures as seen in commercially available standardized tests.

TEACHER-MADE TESTS

Earlier in this chapter we described the cyclic nature of teaching and in Chapter 6 we talked of learning, especially concept learning, as a never-ending upward spiral. One of the elements which permits both these processes to occur is, of course, that of ongoing *feedback/correction*. Teacher-made tests are one of the most widely used methods of providing this kind of information. When used effectively, they serve as valuable learning experiences in the sense that they derive from the objectives, occur frequently throughout the period of instruction as well as at the end, and form the bases for needed modification of teacher and learner behavior. In short, teacher-made tests can be a useful method of formative and summative evaluation.

Teacher-made tests are generally used to . . .

Unfortunately, many teachers overlook the important potential for formative evaluation of their tests and use them almost exclusively as a means of arriving at grades for their learners, as did Mr. Owens, whom we met at the opening of this chapter. Understanding about the characteristics of teacher-made tests that make them effective instruments for learning, including the evaluation of learning, will help us avoid their restricted use only for purposes of grading.

CHARACTERISTICS OF TEACHER-MADE TESTS   The most important characteristics of teacher-made tests, as with all measurement tools, are their validity and reliability. Since most teacher-made tests are criterion-referenced (measuring achievement of specific content), content and curricular validity are not often serious problems, especially if test items are derived from objectives-achievement charts such as the ones we discussed earlier, and if the test includes both *objective* (true-false, matching, multiple-choice, completion) and *subjective* (essay) items. The main problem with using only essay items is that, since learner responses to them are time-consuming, it is difficult to ensure that a representative sample of the objectives are being evaluated; thus, content and curricular validity are likely to be low. This weakness can be compensated for, however, by writing objective-type items to estimate achievement of some of the objectives, especially those at the levels of knowledge, comprehension, application, and analysis. Using essay-type items for objectives at the levels of synthesis and evaluation will probably help improve the validity estimates of your learners' achievement of objectives that require them to *contrast, compare, develop, devise, construct,* and *evaluate.*

The important characteristics of teacher-made tests are . . .

Although content and curricular validity of teacher-made tests can be checked fairly easily, reliability is often more difficult to determine. This is an important point since, as we said earlier, the reliability of any measuring tool affects its validity. This is so simply because the greater the error of measurement (lack of consistency) associated with the use of any measuring instrument, the less confidence we can have in the information it gives, even when we can be reasonably sure that it is an appropriate or useful estimate of whatever we are trying to measure.

We can do several things that will help ensure an acceptable level of reliability in the construction and use of our teacher-made tests. They derive mostly from the points of our earlier, more general discussion about three major sources of potential unreliability of evaluative information: the tools, the process, and the learner. Since we already know *generally* about these potential sources of error, it remains now for us to know only how they relate *specifically* to potential error in the case of teacher-made tests. Merely stating this information in the form of rules, with an example or two when appropriate, should suffice. Note here that, just now, we have again experienced what is meant by the expression "teaching and learning for transfer," and that, in terms of meaningful learning, we will have gone from "knowing generally" to "knowing specifically" according to Piaget and Ausubel (Chapters, 6, 7, 11).

1. Making the *tool* more reliable:

    a. Include more than a single test item for each objective evaluated; use as many as you feel you need to get a representative sample of each learner's achievement of each objective.

    b. Include a combination of objective and essay-type items to ensure that objectives at all levels are evaluated.

    c. Try for a range of difficulty in your test items; include items that are easy enough for all learners to answer correctly and some items that you believe only your most capable learners will be able to answer; however, avoid "tricky" items, e.g., catchwords, double negatives, difficult vocabulary, and material that was not taught.

    d. State the test items clearly, simply, and as briefly as possible.

    e. Make sure test copies are of legible quality.

There are many important subparts to each of these rules that we lack space to discuss here. However, there are several excellent books that can help in the step-by-step preparation and use of teacher-made tests. Four of them are listed in Suggestions for Further Reading.

2. Making the *process* more reliable:

    a. State the directions clearly, simply, and as briefly as possible; include sample problems whenever you believe your instruction may not be understood exactly, e.g., when the procedure is new for your learners or is complex.

    b. Eliminate all distracting elements from the testing situation, e.g., extraneous noise, unnecessary interruptions, uncomfortable environment (stuffiness, excessive heat or cold, cramped space), and insufficient or inadequate testing materials.

    c. Plan sufficient time for all learners to complete the test; also make clear what those learners who finish early are to do until the end of the testing period.

    d. Prepare an answer key for both objective and subjective items before giving the test to your learners.

    e. Take the test yourself.

    f. Score the test and return the results as soon as possible; objective items can often be scored immediately by each learner; essay items will usually require your attention. (Refer to Chapter 9 and our rules for marking learners' papers.)

    g. Avoid bias in scoring, especially of essay-type items. Try to keep the identity of each paper unknown to you as you score it; on essay items, score only one item on *all* papers before going on to the next item; do not score papers when you are likely to be subject to excessive distractions, e.g., fatigue, emotion, or illness.

3. Making the *learner* more reliable.
You will be able to increase the reliability of learners' responses to your test items if you keep the following rules in mind and make provision for the individual differences of which they remind us:

    a. Some of your learners may not have the general abilities or attitudes required to report accurately what they are able to do. They may lack the necessary reading or writing skills, specific vocabulary, or facility with numbers; they may not be able to understand your directions; they may have poor know-how for test taking, lack self-confidence in test situations, or feel that tests are a waste of time.

b. At the time of testing, some of your learners may be ill, excessively tired, upset about something, or overly involved in other things in their lives, e.g., school play, getting a driver's license, a part-time job, or preparations for a holiday.

c. During the testing situation, some of your learners may become discouraged by a particular item or by their own slowness in responding, and therefore may stop trying to do their best; they may experience a temporary lapse of memory for a particular fact; some may hurry, become careless, and begin to guess just to finish early or to keep from being the last one to finish; others may believe they do not have a chance in the first place and consequently do not try at all; they just take their chances at guessing.

Three general areas of error within learners are . . .

As a rule of thumb, one of the best ways to check on the reliability and validity of the items on your teacher-made tests is simply to enable each learner to discuss with you any item that he fails to respond to correctly. If you do not make this provision, you will almost certainly make judgments and decisions about the performance of your learners and about the adequacy of your instruction that are frequently based on invalid and unreliable test information. There is just no way of perfecting your test-item writing so that your items will be 100 percent valid and reliable for all your learners all the time. Encouraging your learners to tell you about the items they miss will go a long way toward correcting your errors of measurement—and your resulting errors of judgment and decision.

A rule of thumb to check on reliability and validity of teacher-made tests is . . .

STANDARDIZED TESTS

There are some principal differences between tests that are teacher-made and those that are standardized. First, we saw that there are several types of standardized tests commonly used by classroom teachers—achievement, general ability or intelligence, special aptitudes, diagnostic, and interest. Teacher-made tests are usually for the purpose of evaluating achievement of certain *specific* objectives. Standardized achievement tests are often used to evaluate *general* achievement within various curriculum areas; for example, a general level of reading comprehension may be tested, rather than the learner's comprehension of a particular passage within a particular story, as might be tested by a comprehension-level item on a teacher-made test. Another difference is that teacher-made tests are usually criterion-referenced and standardized tests often are norm-referenced, although this is not entirely the case. Recently, publishers of standardized tests have begun making available to classroom teachers vast lists of instructional objectives with accompanying test items for various topics of the school curriculum. A teacher can select the objective of interest to him and the test publisher will prepare a test specifically for him.

In terms of the more commonly used standardized tests, however, test items are intended to discriminate between learners who score high and those who score low on the content of the test. In the development of a standardized test, the items are given to large groups (usually thousands) of learners who are believed to be representative of the learners who will eventually use the test.

These are called norms or *comparison groups.* Teacher-made tests are not ordinarily tried out on anyone other than the learners for whom the test is constructed. The purpose of giving a standardized test to widely representative groups of learners is to provide you, when you give that test to your learners, with a basis on which to compare their scores with those of similar learners. Being able to do this gives you a bit more information about how learners are doing and how they may be expected to compete with other learners in some common future experience, for example, a beginning college mathematics course, a public speaking contest, or perhaps a program of auto mechanics.

A standardized test is one that . . .

In this sense, the scores on most standardized tests have meaning only *relative* to the scores of others with which they are being compared. They do not have *absolute* meaning in terms of telling us how much of some specific criterion, e.g., an instructional objective, the score represents. On the other hand, teacher-made tests whose items derive from specific objectives do offer this possibility, although unfortunately they are not always used in this way.

Standardized tests also differ from teacher-made tests in that they have prescribed (standard) procedures, such as time allowed, sequence, and help permitted, for administration and scoring. Also, they usually have guides for interpreting the test results. The purpose for standard procedures is to assure that the tests are given to all learners in a uniform manner. If they are not, the results cannot be meaningfully interpreted nor can comparisons be made among learners within a group or between groups. As in a controlled experiment, all variables need to be held constant except the variable you want to examine, which may be the general learning ability, special aptitude, achievement level, interest, or other behavior of your learners.

CHARACTERISTICS OF STANDARDIZED TESTS   Aside from the differences noted here in teacher-made and standardized tests, both have very similar characteristics. Standardized tests must be valid for the purposes for which we intend to use them, and they must provide reliable estimates of those qualities. Note that the rules we stated for making teacher-made tests more reliable apply also to standardized tests, since they were derived from the more general requirements for satisfactory levels of reliability in *all* methods or approaches for evaluation.

The test manual that accompanies a standardized test usually describes its appropriate uses and its limitations, and reports the levels of reliability obtained with the test on various norm groups. If we remember to use a test only in the intended way, and if we adhere to the directions for administration, scoring, and interpretation, we will have done about all we can to ensure its validity and reliability. What we have to be maximally clear about is that the standardized test we decide to use does indeed estimate what we want to measure. Many times these tests do not. To go ahead and use them anyway is always a mistake.

Three ways to check on validity and reliability of standardized tests are . . .

If you are unsure about whether to use a particular standardized test, for whatever purpose, you would be wise to obtain other opinions of the technical qualities of the test you have in mind. One good source of such information is the *Seventh Mental Measurements Yearbook* (Buros, 1972). Another way is to contact persons knowledgeable about the selection and use of standardized tests, for example, persons in the educational psychology departments of faculties of education in colleges or universities in your area, or persons responsible for a school district's testing program.

Even though most manuals for standardized tests do at least a fair job of describing the technical qualities of the tests and of giving suggestions for their appropriate use, there are general assumptions made in the construction of some types (e.g. intelligence) that are not usually mentioned. In schools, we do a lot about children's knowing behavior or intelligence, including trying to measure and change it. Moreover, as we learned from the higher-order rules in Chapter 2, what you *assume* to be true about some phenomenon is closely related to what you then *do* about it. Therefore, it seems only prudent that we understand the assumptions made in the construction of standardized tests designed to estimate intelligence and the possible implications these assumptions can have for our instruction.

A BASIC ASSUMPTION IN INTELLIGENCE TESTING   You will recall that, in the example of an early Egyptian test at the beginning of this section, the users of the test made a basic assumption about an abstract characteristic of the persons tested, a *construct* called *mental ability*. They also assumed that the task they devised was a valid, reliable test for the presence or absence of an amount of this quality deemed necessary to manage one's affairs and to live responsibly in the community. Implicit in the test was the belief that all people had *some* of this quality but not necessarily in equal amounts. The belief, of course, agreed reasonably well with experience, since the belief derived from informal, ongoing observations of the effectiveness with which various persons were able to organize the events of their lives; that is, the belief derived from experience.

This ancient assumption about a distribution of varying mental ability is still with us today, although the tests for it have been greatly refined. Some of the tasks are still essentially the same but many new ones have been added, so that scores can now be obtained for persons that estimate not only whether they have a specified amount of the quality compared with other people, but also how much more or less they have.

A basic assumption in intelligence testing is . . .

It is important that as teachers, we understand this basic assumption in intelligence testing even though we do not ordinarily construct our own tests of this type. Often, however, we do administer intelligence tests to our learners, or at least use the results of such tests, and, as the higher-order rule in Chapter 2 reminds us, our beliefs—whether valid or not—influence our actions. For an excellent review of the social and political history of mental testing, see Lee Cronbach's (1975) paper: "Five decades of public controversy over mental testing."

THE NORMAL CURVE   Another higher-order rule from Chapter 2 is pertinent to our discussion here: "In our constant press for economy of effort, discoveries or developments in one area are often generalized to other areas that appear to be related to it." This has been the case in the development and refinement of the belief that mental ability is differentially distributed among individuals. In an attempt to specify the nature of the quantitative distribution, an abstract model was borrowed from mathematics. This is the defined concept *normal curve* that we first learned about in Chapter 4. Since this concept has been so overgeneralized and misused in education, especially in connection with evaluation of both ability to learn and achievement, we must understand its limitations or we are also likely to use it inappropriately.

A normal distribution (curve) is an abstract, mathematical concept with the characteristics shown in Figure 13-3.

A normal distribution does not exist in reality; only relative approximations

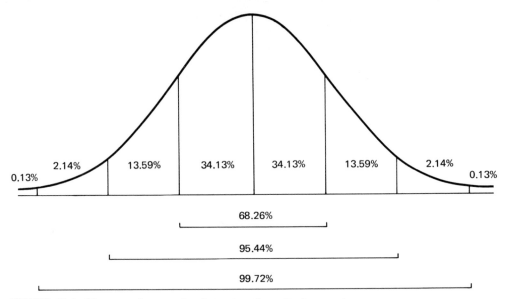

FIGURE 13-3   **The normal curve: An abstract mathematical concept.**

do, and then only for random or chance events for which large numbers (thousands) of observations are available. What a normal curve shows is the mathematical probability with which certain values of some randomly occurring event will be different from the average of all the cases possible. In brief, it can be seen that in a normal or chance distribution, the characteristic in question is estimated to be distributed uniformly from the very high ranges to the very low ranges, with most of the cases occurring in the middle. Also, it can be seen that progressively fewer cases occur as the differences become greater from the average case at the midpoint of the curve. That is, most of the cases observed are neither extremely greater nor far less than the average. An example will help.

A normal curve is defined as . . .   Suppose in the fall you gather *all* the leaves from *all* the oak trees growing in North America. In addition to having the raw material for a dandy bonfire, you will also have the basis for a normal distribution. Now, if you measure the width of each of these hundreds of millions of oak leaves and record the measurements on a bar graph, you can expect to have a graph that looks like that in Figure 13-4. If you now smooth out the tops of each of your bars, you will find that your curve is an excellent approximation of the abstract mathematical distribution shown in Figure 13-3. You would get a very similar curve with other randomly occurring characteristics, including such human characteristics as height, weight, and length of index finger, *if* you had sufficiently large numbers of cases to measure, e.g., all the people in the world.

Let us suppose, however, that you really do not have the time or the facilities to gather and measure *all* the oak leaves in North America or all the people in the world. Rather, suppose you are able to measure only a sample (a small number) of all those possible. As a rule, you will discover that the smaller and more select your sample becomes, the less likely your curve will resemble the normal distribution.

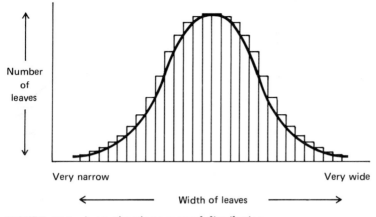

FIGURE 13-4   Approximating a normal distribution.

The concept *normal distribution* has played a key role in the history of testing for intelligence, or general mental ability. Since one of the main purposes of such testing is to identify or select those persons who apparently have more or less of this quality, it is helpful to have tests that can be used to gather information about a given individual and then to compare his scores with those of large numbers (usually thousands) of others with characteristics similar to his (e.g., age, sex). In this way, we can say whether an individual has more or less of this ability than the average of those persons included in a particular norm group.

If, however, in the construction of the test, we select items in such a way that the scores of the persons in the norm groups approximate a normal distribution, we then have a mathematical way of saying *how much* more or less any individual's test score deviates from the average. And by *inference* we conclude how much more or less an individual's intelligence is than average.

We just touched on an extremely important point about test construction that is often overlooked in our use of tests of general mental ability and achievement: The shape of the distribution we get with a test depends on the way the test is constructed, not on the way the quality being measured is distributed among the individuals of the population. This means, for example, that the scores on general mental ability tests of individuals in norm groups approximate a normal curve because the test items were designed to get this type of curve, not because general mental ability is necessarily distributed in nature according to the proportions reflected by the normal curve. General intelligence may or may not be normally distributed, but standardized tests of mental ability do not offer proof one way or the other.

Let us look at an example of how test construction determines the shape of the distribution of scores rather than necessarily reflecting the true distribution of the quality being tested. Item difficulty is the main idea involved: *You can change the shape of the distribution of test scores merely by changing the difficulty of the test items.* Figure 13-5 shows the distribution curves of scores on tests whose items were (1) easy, (2) neither easy nor difficult, (3) difficult for the individuals in the group tested.

You can change the shape of the distribution in any way you choose. In tests

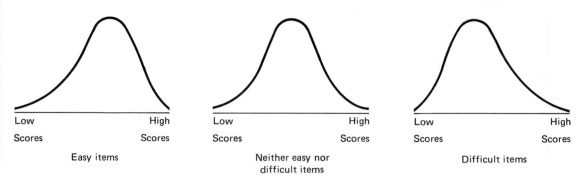

FIGURE 13-5   The shape of a distribution of test scores is determined by the difficulty of the items.

of general mental ability, the items can be made so easy that nearly everyone can complete them; they can be constructed so that only certain proportions of the group will get them correct; or, they can be made so difficult that practically no one can do any of the items.

This is an important idea for us chiefly because it gets lost so easily. As a consequence, we begin to believe erroneously that the way our learners score on our tests is a function, either directly or indirectly, of certain characteristics, especially general ability to learn. We also assume that these characteristics are normally distributed among our learners merely because standardized tests for these characteristics are constructed to give scores that approximate the normal curve.

Some serious widespread and frequent abuses in instruction and evaluation of learners derive from the belief that general ability to learn truly is normally distributed within the total population. These abuses are even more serious when the belief is generalized to indicate that learning ability is normally distributed within classroom-sized groups of learners. The two main abuses that derive from this belief are (1) being satisfied, or even expecting, that many learners will be able to learn only part of what is taught, and (2) grading on the curve.

TEACHING FOR PARTIAL LEARNING   Returning once again to the higher-order rule, stated in Chapter 2, that relates our beliefs about the causes of behavior and our actions to change behavior, we can see how the essential idea of this rule works to the disadvantage of our learners when we assume that many of them are unable to learn all of what we teach them *because* they have only limited general learning ability. The disadvantage is often compounded by the additional assumption that intelligence is mostly a matter of inherited or genetic characteristics.

These beliefs are translated into educational abuse usually through a group-based approach to instruction. It occurs something like this:

"If I have a group of thirty-five or so learners, of whom I believe only a few have enough learning ability to profit fully from my instruction, most have only enough to learn partially, and a few do not have enough intelligence to learn much of anything I teach, my organization for instruction is likely to be directed toward my estimate of the average ability of the group. I teach for, expect, and usually, get mediocre achievement of my learners. And the sad part of all this is that I am satisfied with my performance and that of my learners. When I get a

The shape of a distribution is determined by . . .

normal-looking distribution of scores that range from poor to excellent on the evaluation instruments I use to check on my instruction and my learners' achievement, I see that most learned only part of what I tried to teach them. This is what I expected, since I assumed that most have only an average amount of learning ability. Furthermore, I see no reason why I should modify my instruction for the next cycle since the reason so many learn only partially is their relative inability to profit from instruction. If my instruction is fair, meaning the same for each learner, each will learn the most he can from it, using whatever ability he has available to learn with. And when it comes to grading the achievement of my learners, it seems reasonable to expect that relatively few should receive excellent marks. These marks reflect the fact that they have been able to learn considerably more than the majority who receive average marks, and substantially more than those few who should receive poor to failing marks. 'Grading on the curve' seems to be a logical method of reporting the wide range of learner achievement that can be counted on to result from group-based instruction in which I 'teach *for* the curve.'"

Grading on the curve means . . .

In this view, the quality of instruction appears to be only marginally related to the level of achievement of the learners; whether learners learn depends upon their ability to learn and has little to do with the teacher's ability to instruct.

Fortunately, there are alternatives to this point of view, and the related abuses of instruction and evaluation need not occur. Two steps that can be taken to lessen the abuses are, first, to reexamine our basic assumptions that general ability to learn is mostly inherited and normally distributed, and second, to move from group-based approaches to instruction toward alternative, individualized approaches that provide for the rules included in our theory of instruction (Chapter 12).

Let us turn now to a brief discussion of these two steps. You will notice as we proceed that the concepts and rules we learned earlier about mastery learning (Chapters 4 and 12), Piaget's developmental theory of knowing behavior (Chapter 11), and our theory of instruction (Chapter 12) will now transfer in a *cognitive, positive, horizontal,* and *planned* way to helping us learn about methods of evaluation in approaches to education that attempt to individualize instruction.

CHECKPOINT 13-5

Assume once again that you are Mr. Owens. You have completed the next unit of study and have given your learners an exam of it. This is approximately the way the scores were distributed among your thirty-nine students:

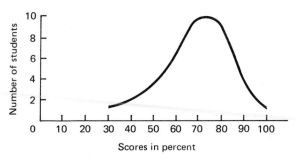

1. Describe your feelings about the way your class performed on the test.

2. If you had been individualizing the instruction in your class, would you be pleased with the test results? Explain.

3. Do you question traditional views that assume only a few learners can learn well? Yes_____ No_____

4. Do you view instruction and evaluation as two parts of the same process of learning? Yes_____ No_____

METHODS OF EVALUATION IN INDIVIDUALIZED APPROACHES TO EDUCATION

One of the main differences between group-based and individualized instruction is our focus of attention. In group-based approaches we tend to direct our instruction to the average of the group, knowing full well that it is beyond the ability of some of the learners, about right for many, and boring for others. On the other hand, instruction that is individualized attends to the abilities and the achievement level of each learner.

The focus of evaluation is also quite different in these two general approaches to education, although the methods of evaluation are often the same ones: informal observations (checklists, questionnaires, classroom questions) and formal tests of abilities and achievement, both formative and summative. In group-based approaches, an individual's abilities and achievement are evaluated and judged as they relate to the abilities and achievement of other learners in the group. We have spoken of this before as *norm-based* evaluation.

Toward the Development of Criterion-based Tests

Criterion-based evaluation means . . .

Evaluation in individualized approaches focuses on estimating each individual's abilities and achievement relative to some *absolute* criterion rather than relative to the abilities and achievement of others in the group. Absolute criteria may include sets of instructional objectives or they may be the stages, levels, or steps described in some developmental sequence, for example, of physical growth, Maslow's need gratification, or Piaget's intellectual development. In this view, evaluative information is used to form judgments about each individual's performance relative only to the criteria of concern and not just to the performance of others in the group on those tasks. This focus of evaluation is what we described earlier as *criterion-based*.

We should now follow up this distinction between evaluation in group-based and in individualized approaches to instruction to see what differences they make in terms of the major purpose of evaluation: to improve learning and instruction. We can do this, as suggested in the previous section, first by reexamining our basic assumptions that general ability to learn is mostly inherited and normally distributed, and next by thinking through the implications for instruction that derive from the different basic assumptions that *ability to learn* may not be mostly inherited, but that *opportunity to learn* may be a variable that is normally distributed.

As you notice, since these questions are theoretical, they are open to investigation, and indeed a great amount has already been conducted—by Piaget, Jensen, and Skinner, to mention only a few persons with whom we are familiar. It will not be our purpose here to argue the absolute truth of either point of view, but rather, to search for the potential usefulness for improving learning and teaching offered by the alternative assumptions.

Criterion-based Tests of Intelligence

In the Activities of Chapter 11, I invited you to speculate on what an intelligence test would be like if it was based on Piaget's stages of intellectual development. I also asked you to consider the potential value of such a test for teachers. Now that we have learned a bit more about measurement and evaluation, let us return to these questions.

One of the first things to be accomplished in the construction of a norm-based intelligence test is the determination of what the items should be. In norm-based tests, this is usually done by first deciding what general areas of competency are to be included in the construct *intelligence*, for example, verbal facility, abstract and logical reasoning, and spatial relationships. Next, test items are written and tried out on samples of persons drawn from the population with which the test is eventually to be used. On the basis of how these persons respond, the items are modified, deleted, and new ones added until they meet a statistical criterion of discrimination among persons of different age groups. Typically, the shape of the distribution of scores approximates the normal curve by the time the test makers are satisfied with their test. Once its validity and reliability have been established and the procedure for administration, scoring, and interpretation standardized, the test is ready to be used to select those persons who have more or less of the qualities measured and to specify statistically how much more or less of the qualities they have than does some hypothetical, but comparable, average person.

This type of evaluative information is useful for purposes of prediction. Knowing how an individual scores on a norm-based test of intelligence allows us to estimate his future performance from our expectancy tables, since we know how others who have scored in a similar way have performed in specific courses, study programs, and other learning situations. Thus, our knowledge, gained from evaluative information, helps us make judgments and decisions about our learners' probable success in various future learning environments.

Prediction, however, is about the only purpose of evaluation that can be legitimately served by traditional norm-based tests of intelligence. They have little, if anything, to offer in terms of improving classroom instruction and learning or of enhancing the very qualities they claim to measure.

At the present time, there is no widely recognized test of intelligence commercially available that is based on a theory of intellectual development such as that of Piaget, although some work in this direction has been done (Pinard and Laurendeau, 1964; Educational Testing Service, 1965). However, a criterion-based test of intelligence derived from Piaget's theory of intellectual develop-

A criterion-based test
of intelligence is
characterized by . . .

ment would be quite different from norm-based tests. For one thing, the test items would be generated from Piaget's theory, and they would be designed to help the test user determine the stage of intellectual development of any given individual. This could be accomplished by using items that require a particular quality of thinking to solve tasks usually solved by individuals at the various stages of intellectual development (see Chapter 11 for examples of typical behaviors).

The procedure for administering such a test would need to be considerably more flexible than in traditional intelligence tests since the follow-up of incorrect answers can often reveal useful information about why the individual answered as she did. Scoring a criterion-based test of intelligence would be in terms of the match between an individual's responses to the items and the requirements of a particular stage. Her score would not be numerical, but rather, it would consist of a descriptive statement of the quality of her thinking at the time of testing. Its meaning would be interpreted in terms of the quality of thought typical of learners at Piaget's various stages of intellectual development. You will recall from Chapter 11 that this is essentially the way Kohlberg (1966) went about the development, administration, and scoring of his test of moral development.

Table 13-4 shows some of the main differences between traditional norm-based tests of intelligence and those based on the criteria described by Piaget's theory of intellectual development.

The potential usefulness of such evaluative information, beyond prediction, selection, and placement, is immediately apparent: It can be helpful in the instructional cycle. For example, knowing the quality of intellectual thought of which a particular learner is currently capable and not capable can guide us in organizing her instruction at a level which she is likely to be able to handle. Such information also can help us avoid instruction that requires intellectual abilities that are beyond a learner's present stage of development. In a word, evaluative information that might be obtained from such a criterion-based test of intelligence could be helpful in ensuring that an appropriate match occurs between each learner's present level of intellectual development and the specific requirements of the learning tasks.

THE ASSUMPTION OF
EQUAL OPPORTUNITY TO LEARN

In Chapter 11 we learned that, according to Piaget and others, experience is necessary for the development of intelligence. Consequently, with a criterion-based test of intelligence, the assumptions are made that an essential part of what we are measuring is the result of experience and that experience, or opportunity to learn, has not necessarily been the same for each person tested. Difference in experiences is one of the main explanations for differences in test performances since without opportunity for learning (experience), genetically preprogrammed characteristics will not be elaborated; that is, development will not occur. As you recall from our earlier discussions, however, opinions differ about the degree to which intellectual development can be enhanced, or "speeded up" by experience. Yet, part of the explanation for failing to perform intellectually at a particu-

TABLE 13-4   Comparison of traditional and Piaget-based intelligence tests‡

CHARACTERISTIC OF TEST	TYPE OF TEST	
	Traditional (norm-based)	*Piaget (criterion-based)*
Standardization	"Level" determined statistically. Items selected that discriminate between specified chronological age groups.	"Level" derived from theory. Intellectual development studied; problems devised to reveal various levels of mental process. Statistical analysis, to determine average age of each acquisition, is done later.
Administration	Highly structured. With few exceptions, same questions asked of all subjects who respond to a given item. Exceptions are questions designed to clarify pass-fail distinction. Only right answers are important	Less structured. Each question determined by subject's answer to preceding ones. Questions designed to reveal quality of subject's thinking. Wrong answers are important.
Scoring	Determined by numbers of items passed with a limited range of difficulty. Failing an item at one level can be compensated for by passing one at a different level.	Determined by quality of responses to a standard set of items. "Level" is quality of response rather than difficulty of items passed. Items not passed or failed, but evaluated for stage inclusion.

‡ J. L. Phillips, Jr. (1969) *The Origins of Intellect: Piaget's Theory.* San Francisco: Freeman, p. 125. Adapted and reprinted with permission.

lar stage of development is that the learner has not yet acquired (learned) the structures of knowledge prerequisite for success at that level.

Quite in contrast with this viewpoint is the assumption, made in norm-based tests of intelligence, that what are measured are differences only in inherited qualities of the individuals, since it is *assumed* that all persons tested have had equal opportunity to learn; that is, that they have had equal experiences with the content of the items and with the process of testing. The assumption is also made that motivation to do well on the test is equally distributed among all individuals who take the test. Of course, both these assumptions are only approximately true, even though a great deal of effort may have gone into making the test "fair" for everyone.

It may be useful for us as teachers to take a slightly different point of view: that opportunity to learn has *not* been equal among our learners and that what is measured by norm-based tests of intelligence is chiefly the results of differences

The assumption of equal opportunity to learn means . . .

in appropriate past experience among learners, rather than differences in inherited ability. This view is not apt to lead to abuse of instruction and learners, but offers the optimistic probability of resulting in more nearly ideal and individualized instruction. Let us look at the implications of this alternate assumption.

Teaching, Testing, and Grading in Individualized Approaches to Instruction

Suppose, for a moment, that I am again the teacher for the class of thirty-five learners we used to illustrate the abuses often associated with group-based instruction and evaluation procedures that result in "grading on the curve." This time, however, let us assume that I believe all my learners have sufficient ability to learn what is taught. Naturally, my instruction will reflect this belief. I will feel responsible for instruction that is adequate for each learner, for, if even one does not learn well, instruction for him must not have been adequate. Perhaps the objective was inappropriate for him at this time; maybe I incorrectly assumed he had acquired the prerequisite knowledge, skills, or attitudes necessary to profit from the instruction planned for him; perhaps my directions were unclear; or perhaps there were a hundred or so other reasons. The point is that my instruction has not been effective for *him* and it must be changed until it is; that is, it must be individualized.

I know that each learner's history of experience shows a varying degree of opportunity to learn. Consequently, each learner is different in his overall acquired ability to learn and in his knowledge and skills relative to specific learning tasks. To pretend my learners are not different is to submit most of them to the instructional abuse of the standard lesson taught to the mythical average learner who certainly does not exist, and to partial learning or complete failure. But I will not do this so easily if I believe they *all* can learn *if* only I can find ways to make instruction optimal and can provide the time necessary for each learner. And, as I search for ways to improve instruction, the learners and I will use whatever methods of evaluation we find effective in giving us the ongoing information we need to tell *who* is likely to profit from *which* learning experiences and how the instruction must be organized for *each* student. As we do these things together, almost imperceptibly teaching and testing will blend to form a single process; my learners will become self-confident, capable individuals, and I will become more than just a "C" teacher. I will become an effective teacher.

But effective *teaching* is not all that will be required of you in the classroom. The job will likely also demand that you *grade* the learning performances of your learners. For several reasons, this is often a confusing and distasteful part of the role of a teacher.

Some of the confusion about the practice of grading is legitimate and *should* cause teachers concern. Some, however, is not, and we should not let it influence our actions. First, let us examine the bases for legitimate concern.

Typically, grades are awarded on the basis of the evaluative information we gather about our learners' achievement in the various topics of the cirriculum. Usually the grades represent our estimate of how well each learner achieved compared with others in the group. There are two legitimate concerns that derive from this practice. First, we should remember that our estimates can never be more accurate than the evaluative information from which they derive, and that information is always just an approximation. Throughout this chapter we have learned of the many things that can reduce its validity and reliability, sometimes drastically so. Consequently, the grades we give our learners based on such information should be viewed with suspect.

Two legitimate concerns about grading derive from . . .

Second, we legitimately need to question the meaning of grades awarded on a comparative basis of achievement. What does a grade of "A," "B," or "F" mean other than approximately how well a particular learner did compared with others in the group? Unless we also know a great deal about the other learners, the course, and the teacher, the grade tells us very little about the learner's cognitive achievement. It also tells us little, if anything, about the student's individual affective achievements; how they feel about the specific material, about the topic in general, about learning, and about themselves.

It is from this second legitimate concern about grading that most of the illegitimate concerns derive. The widespread acceptance of comparative or normative evaluation and the wholesale adoption of the normal curve in education have led us to believe that comparative grading *should* occur; that it is the *natural* outcome of effective educational practices. Furthermore, it has caused us not only to feel guilty about even questioning the practice, but also, and more important to be embarrassed when our learners achieve better than a normal distribution would predict. In short, comparative grading practices establish an expectation of mediocrity both for the learner and for the teacher since, in the very beginning of an educational experience, everyone knows that only a few are expected to be highly successful. Usually, it is also understood that some will fail.

Fortunately, there is a movement afoot in education at all levels that is beginning to gain ground against comparative instruction as well as against comparative grading (Thorndike, 1975). It is associated with the movement toward individualized instruction, and the resulting transformation of grading into a more informative, individualized system of reporting the achievement of each learner relative to the stated objectives of learning. The system is taking many forms, ranging from general reports of "complete-incomplete" to comprehensive, detailed, and written statements about each learner's performance on each objective taught for. In a view of individualized instruction, comparative grading makes little sense other than as a report of the rate at which a learner is achieving. So far, few teachers have felt it appropriate to assign a letter grade just for relative rate of learning.

But the current movement toward reporting, based on criterion-referenced evaluation, is not widespread (Pratt, 1975). And as T. H. Huxley said, "it is the customary fate of new truths to begin as heresies and to end as superstitions." Consequently, you may find yourself in the unfortunate position of being required to apply a grading system based on comparative evaluation procedures to an individualized approach to instruction. The confusion that is likely to result is both obvious and illegitimate. You will wrongly be caused to worry about rewarding your learners with the high marks that most will earn from optimal instruction because helping *everyone* learn well may be inconsistent with many people's expectations. Yet, you cannot simply ignore the problem; you will need to do something when this concern arises.

Confusion about the purpose of schooling causes us unjustified concern about . . .

Although I do not know the answer that you should reach, I do know what I do. I believe with Thelen (1960) that "the confusion over marks is a symptom of the larger confusion over the mission of the school."[10] Therefore, I try to concentrate on helping each learner to learn and not to be embarrassed if he and I are able to do the job well. I am also learning to be bold about reporting learners' success and my grade sheets weigh heavily in "A's" and "B's." And at the same time, I am working toward the clarification of the primary mission of the school that will allow each of my learners the full expectation of success.

I wish you well in your work as a teacher, a friend, and a person.

IN PASSING

I shall pass through this world but once. Any good thing therefore that I can do, or any kindness that I can show to any human being, let me do it now. Let me not defer it or neglect it, for I shall not pass this way again.

Saint Paul

ACTIVITIES

1. To summarize the main ideas in Chapter 13, make a list of all the higher-order and simple rules of evaluation stated or implied in the content. (One way to organize your list would be to review the headings of the Table of Contents.)
2. Using the outline of an approach to instruction that you did for item 1 of the Activities for Chapter 12, describe the methods you would use to evaluate learning and instruction in that approach.
3. Find a teacher who will share with you a copy of one of her teacher-made tests. Discuss with her how she checks on its validity and reliability.
4. As an individual, a small group, or an entire class activity, examine the items included in some well-known group test of intelligence for their independence from "opportunity to learn." Discuss what you believe to be the test maker's definition of the construct *intelligence*.
5. Just for fun:

Following is a checklist that someone used to evaluate the teaching behavior of Socrates. Although it is intended as a satire on the worth of such evaluation tools, it may be fun to discuss the validity and reliability of the items.

Teacher Evaluation†

TEACHER: SOCRATES

A. PERSONAL QUALIFICATIONS

	Rating (high to low) 1 2 3 4 5	Comments
1. Personal appearance	☐ ☐ ☐ ☐ ☑	Dresses in an old sheet draped about his body.
2. Self confidence	☐ ☐ ☐ ☐ ☑	Not sure of himself; always asking questions.
3. Use of English	☐ ☐ ☐ ☑ ☐	Speaks with a heavy Greek accent.
4. Adaptability	☐ ☐ ☐ ☐ ☑	Prone to suicide by poison when under duress.

[10] H. A. Thelen (1960). The triumph of achievement over inquiry in education. In R. C. Sprinthall and N. A. Sprinthall (eds.), *Educational Psychology: Selected Readings*. New York: Van Nostrand Reinhold, 1969, p. 323.

Teacher Evaluation†

TEACHER: SOCRATES

	Rating (high to low)	Comments
	1 2 3 4 5	

B. CLASS MANAGEMENT

1. Organization	☐ ☐ ☐ ☐ ☑	Does not keep a seating chart.
2. Room appearance	☐ ☐ ☐ ☑ ☐	Does not have eye-catching bulletin boards.
3. Utilization of supplies	☐ ☐ ☐ ☐ ☑	Does not use supplies.

C. TEACHER-PUPIL RELATIONSHIPS

1. Tact and consideration	☐ ☐ ☐ ☐ ☑	Places student in embarrassing situation by asking questions.
	1 2 3 4 5	
2. Attitude of class	☐ ☑ ☐ ☐ ☐	Class is friendly.

D. TECHNIQUES OF TEACHING

1. Daily preparation	☐ ☐ ☐ ☐ ☑	Does not keep daily lesson plans.
2. Attention to course of study	☐ ☐ ☑ ☐ ☐	Quite flexible; allows students to wander to different topics.
3. Knowledge of subject matter	☐ ☐ ☐ ☐ ☑	Does not know material; has to question pupils to gain knowledge.

E. PROFESSIONAL ATTITUDE

1. Professional ethics	☐ ☐ ☐ ☐ ☑	Does not belong to professional associations or PTA.
2. In-service training	☐ ☐ ☐ ☐ ☑	Complete failure here—has not even bothered to attend college.
3. Parent relationships	☐ ☐ ☐ ☐ ☑	Needs to improve in this area—parents are trying to get rid of him.

Recommendation: Does not have a place in Education. Should not be rehired.

† J. Gauss (1962). Teacher evaluation. *Phi Delta Kappan*, January, back cover. Reprinted by permission.

Binet, A., and H. Simon (1905). Application des methodes nouvelles au diagnostic du niveau intellectual chez des enfants normaux et anormaux d'hospice et d'école primaire, *L'Année Psychologique*, **11**, 245–266.

Block, J. H. (1971). Criterion-referenced measurements: Potential, *School Review*, **79**(2), 289–298.

Bloom, B. S., M. D. Engelhart, E. J. Furst, W. H. Hill, and D. R. Krathwohl (1956). *Taxonomy of Educational Objectives. Handbook I: Cognitive Domain*. New York: McKay.

———, J. T. Hastings, and G. F. Madaus, eds. (1971). *Handbook of Formative and Summative Evaluation of Student Learning*. New York: McGraw-Hill.

Buros, O. K., ed. (1972). *Seventh Mental Measurements Yearbook*, Highland Park, N.J.: Gryphon Press.

REFERENCES

Cronbach, L. J. (1969). *Essentials of Psychological Testing*, 3d ed. New York: Harper & Row.

Cronbach, L. J. (1975). Five decades of public controversy over mental testing, *American Psychologist*, **30**(1), 1–14.

Ebel, R. L. (1965). *Measuring Educational Achievement*, Englewood Cliffs, N.J.: Prentice-Hall.

Educational Testing Service (1965). *Let's Look at First Graders: A Guide to Understanding and Fostering Intellectual Development in Young Children*. New York City: Board of Education.

Galton, F. (1869). *Hereditary Genius*. London: Macmillan.

Harrow, A. J. (1972). *A Taxonomy of the Psychomotor Domain*. New York: McKay.

Kohl, H. (1969). *The Open Classroom*. New York: Vintage Books.

Kohlberg, L. (1966). Moral education in the schools: A developmental view, *The School Review*, **74**, 1–30.

Krathwohl, D. R., B. S. Bloom, and B. B. Masia (1964). *Taxonomy of Educational Objectives. Handbook II: Affective Domain*. New York: McKay.

Osgood, C., G. Suci, and P. Tannenbaum (1967). *The Measurement of Meaning*. Urbana: The University of Illinois Press.

Pinard, A. and M. Laurendeau (1964). A scale of mental development based on the theory of Piaget: Description of a project, trans. by A. B. Givens, *Journal of Research in Science Teaching*, **2**, 253–260.

Pratt, D. (1975). A competency-based program for training teachers of history, *Teacher Education*, **8**(Spring), 81–91.

Sanders, N. M. (1966). *Classroom Questions: What Kinds?* New York: Harper & Row.

Skinner, B. F. (1968). *The Technology of Teaching*. New York: Appleton-Century-Crofts.

Symonds, P. M. (1931). *Diagnosing Personality and Conduct*. New York: Appleton-Century.

TenBrink, T. D. (1974). *Evaluation: A Practical Guide for Teachers*. New York: McGraw-Hill.

Terman, L. M. (1916). *The Measurement of Intelligence*. Boston: Houghton Mifflin.

Thelen, H. A. (1960). The triumph of achievement over inquiry in education. In R. C. Sprinthall, and N. A. Sprinthall, eds. (1969). *Educational Psychology: Selected Readings*. New York: Van Nostrand Reinhold.

Thorndike, R. L. (1949). *Personnel Selection*. New York: Wiley.

———, and E. Hagen (1955). *Measurement and Evaluation in Psychology and Education*. New York: Wiley.

Thorndike, R. L. (1975). Mr. Binet's test 70 years later, *Educational Researcher*, **4**(5), 3–7.

Wechsler, D. (1944). *The Measurement of Adult Intelligence*. Baltimore: Williams & Wilkins.

SUGGESTIONS FOR FURTHER READING

The first reference is a comprehensive handbook that deals with formative and summative evaluation in each major subject field and level in education. One chapter is on evaluation techniques for affective objectives.

Bloom, B. S., J. T. Hastings, and G. F. Madaus, eds. (1971). *Handbook of Formative and Summative Evaluation of Student Learning*. New York: McGraw-Hill.

The next three references provide excellent guidance in planning, constructing, and using teacher-made tests.

Ebel, R. L. (1965). *Measuring Educational Achievement*. Englewood Cliffs, N.J.: Prentice-Hall. The chapters on how to write test items are especially helpful.

Stanley, J. C. (1964). *Measurement in Today's Schools*, 4th ed. Englewood Cliffs, N.J.: Prentice-Hall. It has an excellent chapter on the historical development of measurement.

TenBrink, T. D. (1974). *Evaluation: A Practical Guide for Teachers.* New York: McGraw-Hill. This book offers an easily understood model of the evaluation process from beginning to end of each teaching-learning cycle.

The next reference describes the major defined concepts and rules relative to testing and measurement. It is a handy guide for understanding about the types of scores used in standardized tests, and it has a good glossary.

Lyman, H. B. (1963). *Test Scores and What They Mean.* Englewood Cliffs, N.J.: Prentice-Hall.

Few texts are available that help the classroom teacher with the daily job of informal diagnosis of learning difficulties in cognitive, affective, and psychomotor areas. The following one is excellent in this respect. In addition, it has a very pointed and informative chapter entitled "The Educational Irrelevance of Intelligence," with a section that explains what intelligence tests can and cannot do.

Smith, R. M., ed. (1969). *Teacher Diagnosis of Educational Difficulties.* Columbus, Ohio: Merrill.

The last reference is a useful guide to making and asking questions. It should help us ensure that the questions we ask our learners require more than mere memory of information.

Sanders, N. M. (1966). *Classroom Questions: What Kinds?* New York: Harper & Row.

APPENDIX

RESPONSES FOR THE CHECKPOINTS

CHAPTER TWO   2-1

All the comments reflect circular reasoning that confuses description with explanation. Note that the key words in each comment are summary-type, descriptive terms improperly used as explanations: "doesn't like it" describes Sam's behavior toward arithmetic; "low IQ" describes how Karen scores on an intelligence test; "short attention span" describes Joe's behavior relative to certain school-type tasks.

                                                                       2-2

1. Each comment has an element common to all the others: the assumption that the cause of misbehavior is within the learner. This point of view relies on the same assumption that has been made about the causes of human misbehavior since the Dark Ages. Fortunately, more useful ways of looking at causes of human behavior are presently available. Essentially, behavior is considered to be subject to the operation of laws or rules of learning. Stated briefly, we *learn* to behave as we do. And we can learn to behave differently. This optimistic view of human behavior will be discussed in detail in later chapters.

CHAPTER THREE   3-1

1. Long-range goal

2. Specific instructional objective

3. Long-range goal

4. Specific instructional objective

Objectives 1 and 3 are stated from the teacher's point of view. They tell what the *teacher* plans to do. Objectives 2 and 4 are stated from the learner's point of view. They describe what the *learner* will be able to do after meeting the objectives.

1. Aloud, no assistance, within ten seconds.

2. A basketball, 90 percent accuracy, shooting with one hand, from a distance of 20 feet.

3. Given the direction to name five major export products of South America, other than coffee and meat, the learner is able to do so from memory.

4. Given two short stories, one by H. G. Wells and the other by D. H. Lawrence, the learner is able to contrast them by describing in no more than 500 words, how each author uses dialogue, foreshadowing, and mood.

1. Knowledge
2. Comprehension (translation)
3. Comprehension (interpretation)
4. Application
5. Analysis
6. Synthesis
7. Synthesis
8. Evaluation

Part I. Acquiring information

1. *Knowledge:* Without referring back to the story, the learner is able to state why Goldilocks was in the woods.

Part II. Using information

2. *Comprehension* (translation): Given the sentence: "They lived in a little house in the wood," the learner is able to convey the same meaning by using words other than "They," "lived," "little house," and "wood." Or *Comprehension* (interpretation): Given the direction to "be Father Bear," the learner is able to dramatize the actions and sounds Father Bear made when he found that someone had tasted his porridge.

3. *Application:* Given the situation that there were also three hairbrushes in the Bears' home (Papa's, Mama's, and Baby's) and that Goldilocks used them, the learner is able to suggest what Goldilocks would have done and said about each one.

4. *Analysis:* Given a definition of the word "consistent," the learner is able to find evidence in the story that supports the idea that Goldilocks acted "consistently" whenever she encountered one of the Bears' belongings.

5. *Synthesis:* Given the situation that Goldilocks could not get the door open when she ran downstairs, the learner is able to create a new ending for the story which takes this into account.

6. *Evaluation:* When asked if he believes that Goldilocks should or should not have gone into the Bear's home, the learner is able to state his opinion and provide reasons in support of it.

1.0 Receiving (attending)

1.1 *Awareness.* The learner is aware that people in different parts of the world have values that are different from his.

1.2 *Willingness to Receive.* The learner is able to accept the fact that skin color has nothing to do with the worth of an individual.

1.3 *Controlled or Selected Attention.* When give the opportunity to choose his own reading material, the learner chooses stories related to the people of The Amazon Basin.

2.0 Responding

2.1 *Acquiescence in Responding.* Even though he may believe that food from the Amazon Basin will taste strange to him, the learner is willing to taste some.

2.2 *Willingness to Respond.* Given the information that the class is going to perform a dramatic sketch of a day in the life of a native family of the Amazon Basin, the learner will volunteer to participate.

2.3 *Satisfaction in Response.* The learner enjoys playing games typical of those played by children of the Amazon Basin.

3.0 Valuing

3.1 *Acceptance of a Value.* The learner believes it is important to communicate with peoples of other lands.

3.2 *Preference for a Value.* The learner assumes responsibility for writing a letter to a pen pal in the Amazon Basin.

3.3 *Commitment.* When given the chance to discontinue writing to his pen pal over summer holidays, the learner will choose to continue to write.

4.0 Organization

4.1 *Conceptualization of a Value.* Through a study of the people of the Amazon Basin, the learner will be able to gain support for the value statement: "All people are important."

4.2 *Organization of a Value System.* The learner is able to form judgments about how respect for human dignity can be related to the way in which his country responds to the needs of the people of the Amazon Basin.

5.0 Characterization by a Value or Value Complex

5.1 *Generalized Set.* When given the opportunity to choose a classmate to work with, the learner chooses a partner on the basis of the requirements of the task, behavioral characteristics of the person, and so forth, rather than on the basis of race, color, or religion.

5.2 *Characterization.* The learner's action toward people who differ from him in various ways (color, beliefs, values) are consistent with his verbal statements about them.

1. **a** Given any necessary equipment, the learner is able to demonstrate a minimum increase, from pretest to post-test, of: (*a*) five push-ups, (*b*) four chin-ups, (*c*) thirty sit-ups, (*d*) 10 feet in the softball throw, (*e*) 1 foot in the running broad jump, (*f*) 2 inches in the high jump, (*g*) running speed so that, for the 50-yard dash, his time is reduced by one second, (*h*) 5 pounds in grip strength, (*i*) cardiovascular endurance by decreasing the resting heart rate, (*j*) reaching 2 inches closer to the floor when doing forward hip bends without bending the knees.
b Given a 10-inch playground ball, the learner is able to pat-bounce it with one hand five times without missing.

CHAPTER FOUR

1. Note that in this item it is not sufficient simply to state the rule of classical conditioning. *Interpretation* requires that you say what the rule *means*. This is what I believe the rule means, or is *about*: The rule of classical conditioning is a lawful statement that specifies the conditions under which learning, especially affective learning (as defined in Chapter 3), will occur.

2. First, ensure that the occasion for speaking to the class is pleasant, e.g., perhaps the presentation of a brief announcement that is likely to be positively received by the class members. Second, make sure that each person speaking can successfully complete his message; help him practice ahead of time, if necessary, so that he knows what he will say and knows how to say it. Third, listen attentively to what he has to say. When all these stimuli occur together, the learner will not try to avoid speaking in front of the class.

4-2

Applying Guthrie's rule of learning requires several steps:

1. a. Make sure the children understand the desired procedure, step by step, so that they can repeat it.
b. Practice the sequence, trying not to have any errors occur.
c. If errors do occur somewhere in the chain, go back to the room, have everyone sit down, and begin again.
d. Upon successful completion of the entire chain, reward the children, e.g., with smiles, words of praise, or perhaps a game of their choice. (NOTE: Reward is not strictly a part of Guthrie's theory. It is something others have added—and it works!)
e. After a few trials, the chain will become firmly established.

4-3

1. a. *"Don't leave well enough alone"* means that if I want appropriate behavior to continue, I must see that it is positively reinforced.
b. *"Catch kids being good,"* means that if I want learners' behavior to "improve," I must attend to the "good" things they do and make sure those behaviors are rewarded—even if they are not as "good" as I hope they eventually will be. If I am consistent in catching the "good" behavior, it *will* improve.

2. a. *"Don't leave well-enough alone."* If Johnny Brown, for the first time today, is doing what I believe he should be doing ("well enough"), I should not let his behavior go unrewarded. I should do something positive about it, such as giving him a word of encouragement, a pat on the shoulder, a smile, or a hug.
b. *"Catch kids being good."* Suppose Johnny Brown is in the habit of putting away his work materials in a manner that makes them difficult for the next person to use. What I should do to help change his "messy" behavior is not to catch him being "messy." Rather, I should "catch" him when he has done a "relatively good" job of putting them away and make sure that this behavior gets rewarded.

4-4

Our task, from a cognitive interpretation of learning, is to help our learners discover what the wind is "about," to understand about "windness," not just to learn to state the physical characteristics of the wind or to illustrate how it behaves. To do this, ideally our learners need to experience the wind, that is, they need to watch it, to feel, smell, and hear it, to interact with it, to guess about and to test it. Understanding about the wind means experiencing the wind, discovering how it makes them feel when they are in it, or when they listen to it from the warmth and safety of their beds, or when it whispers gently or howls angrily.

The descriptions of the wind will not be complete nor will they reflect real understanding until each learner has discovered for himself what is meant by "windness." The teacher sets the occasions so that experiences with the wind occur and she helps each learner become involved, but learning itself is personal and individual, and it is as much a process as it is a product. When the learner has experienced and thus discovered the wind, he will be able to describe it.

1. NOTE: The following task analysis is by no means complete, but it is probably detailed enough to help you get an idea of what is involved in doing one. We will work with others in Chapters 5 and 6.

   A. Higher-order rule required: *The area of a rectangle (square) is found by multiplying its length times its width.* Others are possible; for example, the area of a rectangle (square) can be found by marking off the surface into square units (square inches), and then summing them.

   B. Rules (principles):
   (**1**) Yardsticks measure distances.
   (**2**) An inch is a unit of distance.
   (**3**) A rectangle has a distance called length and a distance called width.
   (**4**) Area is expressed in terms of square units.
   (**5**) Multiplication is a quick way to sum number values.

   C. Defined concepts: The learner must be able to demonstrate his understanding of the following concepts, perhaps by defining them, e.g., by answering such questions as "What is meant by measure?" or "What is a yardstick?"

(**1**) Yardstick	(**5**) Distance	(**9**) Area
(**2**) Measure	(**6**) Length	(**10**) Multiplication (and the subconcepts in-
(**3**) Inch (length)	(**7**) Width	volved in it, e.g., addition, number
(**4**) Inch (square)	(**8**) Rectangle (square)	values, etc.)

   D. Concrete concepts: The learner must be able to demonstrate that he can identify the following concepts, perhaps by naming them or by pointing to the concept when he hears its name, e.g., "What is this?" (yardstick); "Show me the area of your desk-top"; "Show me a distance on the yardstick."

(**1**) Desk-top	(**4**) Area	(**7**) Inch (length)
(**2**) Yardstick (and its subdivisions)	(**5**) Length	(**8**) Inch (square)
(**3**) Distance	(**6**) Width	

   E. Discriminations: The learner must be able to demonstrate that he can tell the difference between the following stimulus objects, perhaps by pointing without needing to name the objects:
   (**1**) Desk-tops and other square or rectangular surfaces
   (**2**) Yardsticks and ordinary sticks or rulers
   (**3**) Inches and yards, or inches and feet
   (**4**) Areas and lengths

   F. Chains (motor and verbal): The learner must be able to demonstrate that he can link together the necessary, individual responses (motor, verbal) needed to:

   (*Motor*) Manipulate the yardstick, paper, pencil, etc., to make the necessary measurements and do the calculations required.
   (*Verbal*) (Memorized sequences of words are probably not of primary concern for this type of task)

1. If *each* learner is allowed the time *he* needs to learn to some level, and if he *spends* the *required time* attending to the learning task, then he *will* learn it.

2. The model is concerned with ensuring that *each* child learns successfully. If a child is experiencing success in his learning, he finds it easier to attend, to respond, to value, to organize his values, and to behave consistently in accordance with his values than if he is experiencing failure. In brief: "You do not find many positively-affective kids who are failing in school-type tasks."

3. Degree of learning $= f \left(\dfrac{\text{(1) time allowed \quad (2) perseverance}}{\substack{\text{(3) aptitude \quad (4) quality of instruction} \\ \text{(5) ability to understand instruction}}} \right)$

4. **a.** Is sufficient time for learning being allowed Sally?
    b. Does she attend to the learning task?
    c. How much time does Sally need to learn this task? (For example, does she have the prerequisites for this task or will she need time to learn them also?)
    d. Is the quality of instruction optimal for Sally?
    e. Is Sally able to profit (learn) from the instruction offered?

5. Children attend to (persevere at) those tasks from which they gain reinforcement, especially success.

6. Level 1, knowledge level; level 2, interpretation; level 3, analysis; level 4, application; level 5, application.

CHAPTER FIVE   5-1

1. (a) All three; (b) all three; (c) task description; (d) task description; (e) task analysis; (f) mastery learning; (g) all three.

2. <u>b</u> Motor chains
    <u>c</u> Verbal chains
    <u>a</u> Discriminations
    <u>g</u> Concrete concepts
    <u>e</u> Defined concepts
    <u>f</u> Simple rules
    <u>d</u> Higher-order rules

                                                                                      5-2

A sample task analysis for the instructional objective: Given written examples of proper fractions, the learner is able to reduce each of them to lowest terms.

HIGHER-ORDER RULES   To reduce a proper fraction to its lowest terms, divide both the numerator and the denominator by the largest possible number that will divide both of them evenly.

RULES
1. "To estimate, I . . ."
2. "If an estimate is too large, try a smaller number . . ."
3. "If an estimate is too small, try a larger number . . ."
4. "To divide, I . . ."
5. "To multiply, I . . ."
6. "To subtract, I . . ."
7. "When I get an answer, I check to see if it can be reduced further . . ."
8. "When the numerator and the denominator can no longer be divided evenly by the same number, I stop; I'm finished."

DEFINED CONCEPTS   (The learner must be able to demonstrate an understanding of the following concepts, e.g., define the concept, explain its meaning, give an example of the concept, or illustrate how it "works.")

1. A fraction can be defined as . . .
2. Proper fractions are those fractions that . . .
3. To reduce to lowest terms means . . .

4. To estimate means . . .
5. To divide means . . .
6. To divide evenly means . . .
7. To multiply means . . .
8. To subtract means . . .
9. The term numerator is defined as . . .
10. The term denominator is defined as . . .
11. The meaning of each of the symbols $\div$, $\times$, $=$, and $\dfrac{x}{y}$ is . . .
12. The meaning of each of these arithmetic sentences is . . .
    a. $1 \times 2 =$ ____   **b.** $2 \div 2 =$ ____   **c.** $4 \div$ ____ $= 2$
13. Numberness, e.g., "tenness," "twelveness," and so forth
14. Numeralness, e.g., the figure 7 represents the name for seven objects, things, ideas, and so on
15. Even, uneven
16. None, less, more
17. Above, below

CONCRETE OBJECTS   (The learner must be able to demonstrate that he can identify the following concepts, e.g., by pointing, naming, or by manipulating actual objects.)

1. Fractions and objects or numerals that are not fractions
2. Proper fractions and fractions that are not proper fractions
3. Numerator
4. Denominator
5. Symbols, e.g., $\div$, $\times$, $=$, and $\dfrac{x}{y}$

DISCRIMINATIONS   (The learner must be able to demonstrate that he can tell the difference between the following stimulus objects, e.g., he can point to the group of objects that has more objects in it than the others.)

1. Fractions and whole numbers
2. Proper and improper fractions
3. More and less
4. Above and below
5. Even and uneven
6. Equal and unequal
7. Symbols such as $\div$, $\times$, $=$, and $\dfrac{x}{y}$
8. The value of numbers, e.g., 10 as different from 12
9. The verbal or written direction "to estimate" as being different from the direction "to calculate."

CHAINS   (The learner must demonstrate that he can link together, and reproduce from memory, the necessary individual responses for verbal and motor sequences such as the following:)

VERBAL CHAINS
1. "To reduce a proper fraction to its lowest terms, divide both the numerator and the denominator by the largest possible number that will divide both of them evenly."
2. "To estimate, I . . ."
3. "To divide, I . . ."
4. "To multiply, I . . ."
5. "To subtract, I . . ."
6. "A fraction is . . ."
7. "The numerator is the part of a fraction that . . ."
8. "The denominator is the part of a fraction that . . ."
9. "The symbols $\div$, $\times$, $=$, and $\dfrac{x}{y}$ tell me to . . ."

10. "$1 \times 2 =$ _____, $2 \times 2 =$ _____, $3 \times 2 =$ _____, ... $12 \times 12 =$ _____"

11. "$2 \div 2 =$ _____, $4 \div 2 =$ _____, $6 \div 2 =$ _____, ... $144 \div 12 =$ _____"

12. "$2 \div$ _____ $= 1$, $4 \div$ _____ $= 2$, $6 \div$ _____ $= 3$, ... $144 \div$ _____ $= 12$"

13. "$1 + 1 =$ _____, $1 + 2 =$ _____, $1 + 3 =$ _____, ... $10 + 10 =$ _____"

14. "$1 - 1 =$ _____, $2 - 1 =$ _____, $3 - 1 =$ _____, ... $10 - 10 =$ _____"

MOTOR CHAINS

1. To manipulate writing materials so that written symbols and numerals are clearly and accurately formed and spaced.
2. To arrange the component parts of the task on paper in an appropriate form so that confusion in recording information does not occur.
3. To copy or transcribe information accurately and clearly from some source to a worksheet.

5-4

This is a synthesis-level performance. To complete the task, we will need to use what we have learned about the conditions of learning chains. My solution would be to cause Mike to practice forming his numerals and symbols in the context of an appropriate pattern for writing number sentences that include fractions. If I want Mike *also* to learn certain numerals and symbols, I would have him practice them in an appropriate size, form, and pattern. The rule is that if I want transfer to occur, I must teach for it in as many ways as I can. That is, I should make practice sessions as similar to the application situations as possible. Consequently, instead of having Mike practice writing isolated lines of the same properly formed numerals and symbols, I would have him practice writing properly formed number sentences that include whole numbers, fractions, and symbols, all in appropriate relationship with each other.

In the beginning practices, I would guide his efforts so that he is likely to do a good job and thus be reinforced early. This not only increases the likelihood that more responses will be made; it also sets the learner's expectation that he can succeed. In addition, I would make sure that neat and legible number work that was appropriately organized and presented would "count" in *all* aspects of written assignments.

A few examples of what I would have Mike do may help me communicate what I mean. I would ask Mike to practice a sequence something like this:

A. "Trace over these figures. Use your felt pen and the plastic overlay."

1. $\dfrac{4}{6} = \dfrac{2}{3}$ 　　 2. $\dfrac{9}{12} = \dfrac{3}{4}$ 　　 3. $\dfrac{7}{4} = 1\dfrac{3}{4}$ ...

B. "Look closely at these numbers. In the space below each example, copy the example as carefully as you can. When you finish each one, push the overlay forward so that you can check your work before going on to the next example."

1. $\dfrac{10}{12} = \dfrac{5}{6}$ 　　 2. $\dfrac{34}{60} = \dfrac{17}{30}$ 　　 3. $\dfrac{3}{16} = \dfrac{12}{64}$ ...

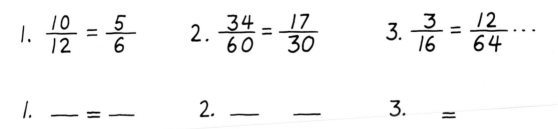

1. ___ = ___ 　　 2. ___ ___ 　　 3. ___ = ___

C. "Copy the following examples on a sheet of lined paper. Try to make your copies look exactly like the examples."

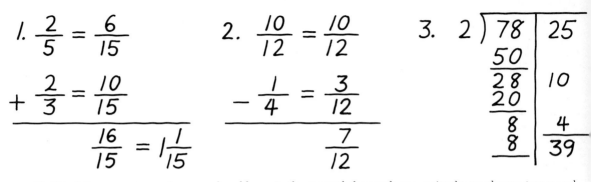

1. $\dfrac{2}{5} = \dfrac{6}{15}$

$+ \dfrac{2}{3} = \dfrac{10}{15}$

$\dfrac{16}{15} = 1\dfrac{1}{15}$

2. $\dfrac{10}{12} = \dfrac{10}{12}$

$- \dfrac{1}{4} = \dfrac{3}{12}$

$\dfrac{7}{12}$

3. $2\overline{)78}\ \big|\ 25$

$\quad\ 50$

$\quad\ 28\ \big|\ 10$

$\quad\ 20$

$\quad\ \ 8\ \big|\ \ 4$

$\quad\ \ 8\ \big|\ 39$

D. "Read these number sentences and problems. In the spaces below each one, write the number sentences and problems. Use numerals and symbols rather than words. Compare your work with an answer sheet."

   1. Four-sixths equals two-thirds.

   2. Two-fifths plus two-thirds equals one and one-fifteenth.

   3. Fourteen-thirds equals four and two-thirds.

   4. . . . .

5-5

To discriminate "to" and "too," I think I note that one of the words has two letters in it and the other has three. I know that one of the two words means to "add," which has three letters, too. Consequently, when I want to use the word that means "in *addition* to," I remember that "too" has three letters that matches the three letters of "add," whereas "to" has only two and doesn't match. It's somewhat complicated, but it works.

5-6

When I have acquired the meaning associated with potentially meaningful stimulus events, I do not need to rely on the distinctiveness of cues relevant to the stimuli in order to make discriminations among them. Reason forms the basis for telling them apart. The meaning that I associate with the two stimulus events in the example is as follows:

   1. **a.** Rule 1 means that some number of objects is being "broken" into parts that are smaller than one whole. The question is how many "pieces," each smaller than one whole, will result if each piece is "broken" into pieces the size of the fraction? If the problem is, for example, $3 \div \frac{1}{3} = $?, this means that each whole is being divided into three equal-sized pieces. How many pieces will result from such a division? Simple: There are three whole objects, each of which contains three pieces. Therefore, $3 \times \frac{3}{1} = 9$ pieces.

      b. Rule 2 means that there is some number of "pieces" of objects, each of which is less than one whole. The question is, how many whole objects will result if all the pieces are combined? For example, if the problem is $3 \times \frac{1}{3} = $? , this means that there are three "pieces" of objects, each one-third of a whole in size. The question is, how many whole objects are all three "pieces" equivalent to? Again, the process is simple: There are three pieces, each of which is one-third of a whole. So, $3 \times \frac{1}{3} = \frac{3}{3}$, or one whole object. Meaning makes discrimination easy—and accurate—and consistent!

CHAPTER SIX

6-1

1. *Exemplars*

   a. Real triangles of various sizes, colors, shapes, and materials, placed in various positions and locations.

Nonexemplars

   a. Real squares, rectangles, angles, cones, balls, boxes, pyramids, circles, trapezoids, and so forth, of various sizes, colors, and materials.

   b. Line drawings of triangles of various sizes and shapes.

   c. Real objects and/or pictures, e.g., buildings, shadows, or pyramids that contain triangles and nontriangles.

   b. Line drawings or all the real objects in (*a*).

2. *Relevant attributes*
   a. Three sides
   b. Three angles
   c. Two dimensions
   d. Closed figure
   e. Straight lines

Irrelevant attributes
   a. Color   **e.** Shape
   b. Type of material   **f.** Location
   c. Size   **g.** Weight
   d. Position

3. This is probably done best by directly comparing and contrasting the attribute, e.g., three sides of various exemplars of a triangle with exemplars of another stimulus object (say, a box) that is very different from a triangle. Verbal cues can be used to direct a learner's attention to important differences and similarities, such as "Notice that . . ."; "Look here . . ."; or "Triangles have . . ., whereas pyramids have . . . ." Holding, touching, and manipulating various exemplars and nonexemplars help the learners learn which attributes belong to the concept and which do not.

                                                                           6-2

Smooth (visual-tactile)

1. Present *smooth* first as a visual concept, later as a tactile concept. Demonstrate the concept with a piece of cloth, which is first identified ("This is a cloth"), and then is smoothed out, perhaps over a chair or table. Introduce the concept statement. "This cloth is *smooth*. Say it." Wrinkle the cloth. "This cloth is *not* smooth. Is this cloth smooth? . . . No, this cloth is (clap) *not* smooth." The concept is expanded by presenting pictures of water and sand, which are identified as being either smooth or not smooth.

2. Demonstrate the tactile version of smooth by presenting, behind the child's back, textures which can be felt but not seen. This convention avoids a great deal of confusion because it prevents the child from formulating the concept according to some visual cues. To acquaint the child with the concept, present something smooth, perhaps a piece of paper. "This is paper. This paper is smooth. Say it." Next, present something that is not smooth, perhaps a piece of sandpaper. "This is sandpaper. This sandpaper is not smooth. Say it." After the child has been exposed to different smooth and not-smooth things and has mastered the *yes-no* questions, ask the child to produce the concept statement. "What can I say about this piece of wood?"[1]

    Between is the last preposition that should be introduced. It is different from the others because its statement form contains the word "and." The concept can be nicely illustrated with a chalkboard diagram of a house, a man, and a car. After the objects are identified, point to the man, and ask, "Where is the man?" and answer, "The man is *between* the house (point) and the car (point)." The basic statement is repeated, and questions are asked about house, man, and car. "Is the house between anything? . . . No, it is not between. Is the car between? . . . No. Is the man between? . . . Yes, see where he is? He is between this house and this car." Replace the house with a car and repeat the series of questions and statements. During subsequent exercises, place the house in the middle and flank it with perhaps two men, perhaps two other houses, etc. The teaching of the concept *between*, since it involves a more complicated procedure than that of the other positional words, is best presented as a chalkboard task. The relationship between the three elements on the board and the structure of the statement can be made clear.[2]

---

[1] C. Bereiter and S. Engelmann (1966). *Teaching Disadvantaged Children in the Preschool.* Englewood Cliffs, N.J.: Prentice-Hall, p. 147.

1. When a person has learned a rule, he should be able to:
   a. State or explain the main idea of the rule.
   b. Illustrate or demonstrate the meaning of the rule.

2. The conditions of learning rules are:
   General
   a. The learner must attend to the learning task, actively participate, and optimally, he should "learn by doing" rather than solely by seeing or hearing.
   b. Objectives must be clearly understood, that is, learners need to know that they will be required to describe or state, and illustrate or demonstrate, a rule.
   c. The learner must have meaningfully learned and be able to recall the prerequisite concepts that chain to form the rule, and the relevant verbal chains and discriminations prerequisite to the concepts.
   d. The learner needs to know whether his responses are correct; usually feedback should occur at each step and not just at the end. Prompts, cues, questions, and telling the learner that he is right or wrong can all be used for this purpose. Being right usually serves as a powerful reinforcement for responding.

   Specific
   a. Situations need to be arranged that provide cues, often verbal statements plus concrete materials, that lead the learner to put the appropriate concepts together in proper order to form the rule.
   b. Contiguity appears to be a necessary condition of learning rules. Presentation of concrete materials and verbal cues that guide the learner's attention and direct him to respond in certain ways should occur in proper sequence so that the appropriate parts of the rule are meaningfully associated. For example, the familiar word "guess" and the less familiar word "estimate" should occur in close contiguity.
   c. Repetition (practice) is probably not an important factor in learning rules. If all other conditions of learning rules are met, learning the main idea of a rule seems to occur without specific practice. Repetition, however, is important for *generalization* of a rule. Even though rules, once meaningfully learned, are highly resistant to forgetting, practice can serve the purpose of overcoming the effects of interference—of possible confusion with other rules learned, especially those similar in meaning or appearance. Confusion of the rule for multiplication of fractions with the rule for comparison of ratios and with the rule for division of fractions is a good example of how rules can be confused. Practice helps to reduce the confusion; discrimination becomes easier.

CHAPTER SEVEN   7-1

1. *Cognitive, positive, horizontal, and planned:* Perhaps some of the most obvious instances of this type of transfer occur within the language arts. For example, learning about words, to read, and to spell transfers positively and horizontally to reading, writing, listening, and speaking in all other parts of school experiences, including arithmetic, science, and social studies. Other instances of this type of transfer are plentiful in geography and history. Knowing about the geography of an area helps to understand about its history. Examples of this type of transfer can also be planned in less obvious associations, e.g., observations in nature to serve as raw material for design in art work.

2. *Affective, positive, vertical, and incidental:* An instance of this type of transfer may occur accidentally, for example, a learner may answer some question correctly, yet completely by trial and error. If his response gains satisfying consequences, his willingness to respond later in similar situations is strengthened. It is the wise teacher who ensures that pleasing things happen to learners when they "spontaneously" attend or respond appropriately; they "catch them being good!"

3. *Psychomotor, negative, vertical, and planned:* An example of this type of transfer occurs when teachers encourage learners not to use their lips and fingers during silent reading. Another is when teachers help learners learn to verbally express themselves clearly and accurately without the use of hand and arm movements. Teaching for this type of transfer can also involve trying to prevent skills of body contact learned in football from transferring to playing basketball.

1. Gestalt, wholeness, or cognitive-field theory of transfer.
2. The major arguments:
    a. The important unit for transfer is the *whole* learning situation.
    b. Transfer from one situation to another occurs only when the learner recognizes them as being similar in total configuration, including cognitive content, affective context, and psychomotor activity.
    c. Similarity is recognized in terms of relationships among the facts, processes, affect, physical activity, and principles that combine to form the total experiences. Thus, the more meaningful the initial relationships are for the learner, the greater the probability of transfer to other similar situations.

1. The word "prerequisite" means an act or thing that is required ahead of time as a necessary condition. For example, holding a pencil is prerequisite for writing. Being able to read is a prerequisite for solving story-problems. Addition and subtraction are prerequisites for multiplication and division.
2. My word-pictures of these terms look like this:

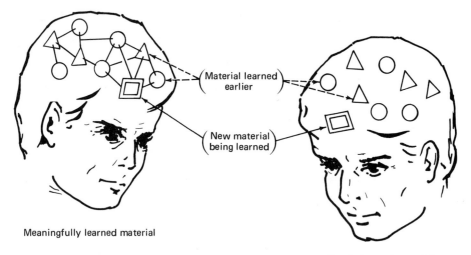

Meaningfully learned material

Rotely learned material

3. I picture a rich and meaningfully organized cognitive structure something like this:

A learner whose *cognitive structure* is *rich* and *meaningfully organized* knows a great many things that are interrelated and are sequenced from generally inclusive rules to highly specific chains. (See page 493.)

CHAPTER EIGHT

1. **A.** *Task description:* "Through consistent and careful listening to the comments of others, the learner demonstrates his beliefs that each person has a right to express a point of view." (Characterization Level.)

A rich and meaningfully organized cognitive structure

B. *Task analysis:* We could ask: "What must the learner be able to do to complete the objective as described?" Several types or levels of affective behavior are apparently involved.
The learner must:

(1) *Receiving (Attending)*
   a. Be aware that another person is speaking or wants to speak.
   b. Be willing to accept points of view other than his own.
   c. Be able to sustain his attention to another's comments long enough and well enough to hear what the other person is saying.

(2) *Responding*
   a. Comply with rules about listening, e.g., "Wait until the other person finishes his comments before beginning your own."
   b. Assume responsibility for following the rules about listening to others.
   c. Enjoy listening to the comments of others.

(3) *Valuing*
   a. Accept the importance of ensuring that each person in a democratic society be guaranteed the right to be heard.
   b. Assume responsibility for helping classmates and the teacher listen consistently and carefully to the comments of others.
   c. Speak out, when necessary, in support or defense of another's right to be heard.

(4) *Organization*
   a. Try to learn the reasons or basic assumptions that underlie a person's right to express a point of view.
   b. Develop ways or techniques for himself that will help him listen consistently and carefully to the comments of another even when he is strongly opposed to the point of view being expressed.

(5) *Characterization*
   a. Illustrate through his actions that he has confidence in his ability to tolerate differences in points of view expressed by others.
   b. In a variety of contexts, listen consistently and carefully to the comments of others.

C. *Conditions of learning:* The *general* conditions of learning cognitive-type behaviors are probably also important conditions of learning affective and psychomotor-type behaviors. For example, learning to "wait until the other person finishes his comments before beginning your own" probably requires general conditions such as: (1) knowing the *objective*; (2) understanding *prerequisites* such as the words used by the other person; having previously learned the clues, verbal and nonverbal, that indicate when another has finished speaking; being able to discriminate between the sounds made by the speaker and those from other sources, e.g., others' whispering while the speaker is talking; (3) *attending* to the other person—*receiving* his message; (4) *getting feedback* that his responses of attending, listening, and waiting are adequate; and (5) being *reinforced* for attending, listening and waiting.

One difficulty you will encounter, when trying to generalize the conditions of learning cognitive-type behaviors to learning those of the affective and psychomotor types, is that one of the general conditions of learning cognitive behaviors is an essentially affective behavior—"attending to the task." The question is: What are the conditions of learning to attend to the task? Probably they are the same general conditions of learning other behaviors: (1) a clear objective; (2) prerequisites being met, e.g., being able to see, hear, or feel; (3) knowledge of results, e.g., seeing, hearing and feeling when he makes attending responses; and (4) reinforcement for making attending responses.

The *specific* conditions of learning affective and psychomotor-type responses are likely the conditions of learning cognitive-type behaviors: (1) contiguity of response, feedback, and reinforcement; and (2) practice in a variety of forms and contexts.

D. *Events of instruction:* It follows that if the conditions of learning affective types of behaviors are similar to the conditions of learning cognitive-type behaviors, then the events of instruction will also be similar. That is, organizing instruction for learning affective or psychomotor-type behaviors will involve: (1) gaining and controlling attention, (2) clarifying the objectives, (3) ensuring that prerequisite capabilities have been met, (4) presenting the stimuli inherent to the learning task, (5) providing guidance for appropriate responding, (6) providing feedback about adequacy and appropriateness of responses (this can also be a source of reinforcement), and (7) providing practice.

E. *Differential Reinforcement:* Only those responses that are approximations of the performance described in the objective are reinforced. All others are ignored. For example, when your learner asks (organizational level) for an explanation of why it is important to ensure that each person has an opportunity to be heard, his response of asking must be reinforced. On the other hand, any responses he makes that indicate an indifference to finding reasons why each person has a right to express a point of view must not be reinforced; e.g., during a discussion of the topic of freedom of speech, he asks questions about the arithmetic assignment. See Figure 8-1 for suggestions about possible reinforcing stimuli.

F. *Shaping:* In the present example, this can mean, at the attending or receiving level, that, to begin with, any and all responses, even those remotely approximating the desired response of listening to another as he speaks, will be reinforced. Responses such as glancing toward, looking at, or stopping talking, even of short duration, will be reinforced. Gradually, however, the attending responses will need to become more specific and more sustained before being reinforced. Finally, only those responses described in the objective—listening carefully and consistently in a variety of contexts—will gain reinforcement.

G. *Maintenance:* Once the listening behaviors have been established, they need to be reinforced only occasionally in order to be maintained in strength.

8-2

1. Programmed materials that teach must include:
   a. A logical, sequential, and step-by-step progression of the ma'erials
   b. Opportunity for the learner to respond frequently and accurately; prompts and cues built into the program
   c. Feedback about the correctness of responses
   d. Differential reinforcement—immediate reinforcement of *correct* responses and disregard of *incorrect* ones
   e. Ways for the learner to know how to modify incorrect responses
   f. Gradual shaping so that increasingly closer approximations of the terminal behavior must be made before being reinforced

2. The steps required in constructing programmed materials that teach are:
   a. Writing a description of the terminal (instructional) objective in specific behavioral terms, e.g., after Bloom
   b. Completing an analysis of the terminal objective, e.g., after Gagné
   c. Determining the *general* and *specific* conditions of learning for each behavior in the task analysis
   d. Determining an appropriate sequence of the material to be learned
   e. Composing sequential steps of experiences for each behavior that

(**1**) Present a small amount of information

(**2**) Require the learner to respond

(**3**) Ensure that the learner is successful

f. Providing feedback, that is, reinforcement, about the correctness of the learner's response

g. Showing the learner how to modify his incorrect responses, e.g., providing additional information or directing him to redo parts of the program

h. Gradually removing prompts or cues

i. Gradually requiring a higher level of performance before reinforcement until the learner is able to complete the responses required by the terminal behavior on his own

8-3

1. **a.** A *bicycle* is a vehicle that has only two wheels. People ride a *bicycle* by using their feet to press pedals that make the wheels go around. Copy the word here:

b. The word has two parts. The first part, *bi*, comes from the Latin word *bis*, which means "two" or "twice." *Cycle* comes from the Greek word *kyklos* which means "circle."

b □ c y c □ e

c. When both parts of the word are put together, they mean a vehicle that has two wheels.

□ □ c y c □ □

e. Notice that the letter in the center of the word is a *y*. It has a *c* on both sides of it.

□ □ □ y □ □ □

f. Boys and girls enjoy riding a _____.

This task requires a synthesis-level performance. Transfer is *cognitive, positive, vertical,* and *planned.*

8-4

Neither Materials A nor Materials B are programmed materials. The difficulty with both sets of materials is that they *present* material, that is, they *tell* the learner what to do. Neither *teaches* in the sense of providing opportunity both to respond and to have responses verified with feedback. There are no contingencies of reinforcement built into the materials. In the absence of immediate feedback with its property of differential reinforcement, the learner is held responsible for teaching himself as best he can. Materials A are like a lesson plan or guide to writing programmed materials. They *present* the substance of what to do, but they do not teach the learner to do it. Materials B are in a format typical of worksheets for practice of skills learned earlier, and for purposes of testing a learner's achievement. Without feedback, however, they do not qualify as materials that *teach*.

CHAPTER NINE   9-1

In Maslow's point of view, a learner is *always* motivated. Therefore, our task is to offer guidance and direction so that the drive forces result in gratification of needs. In the case of your grade nine learner who apparently is unmotivated to know and understand about social studies, this probably means that currently he is striving to gratify needs at lower levels. Until these lower needs are gratified, the need to know and understand about social studies is not likely to emerge. Consequently, you would first try to determine whether his physiological needs were being met adequately. Next, you would try to determine whether he feels safe in the presence of yourself, his peers, and the topic being studied. You would try to answer the questions of whether he feels that he belongs, that others care about him, whether he feels self-worth, and so forth. Wherever you find his needs ungratified, that is where you begin to offer your assistance. You would not force or threaten your learner; rather, try to understand and respect him.

1. Food is the reinforcing stimulus chosen by the teacher.

   Reinforcement comes immediately after appropriate attending and responding behaviors.

   The learners receive only a small amount of food. Therefore, they are not likely to become satiated.

   Since the teacher controls the contingencies for reinforcement, she can easily manage the schedule of reinforcement, first making it continuous then intermittent as necessary.

   Food is paired with success in the learning task. Gradually, it can be withdrawn as success increases in its potential reinforcing value.

   Since the teacher is "catching them being good," she is reinforcing only appropriate attending and responding behavior. She ignores inappropriate behavior.

   Because the teacher controls the contingencies of reinforcement, she can carry out a shaping procedure over a period of time so that a desired level of attending and responding behavior can be gradually approximated.

   A "bag of goodies" is not being substituted for good teaching. The "goodies" become a part of effective instruction, and success will result in self-motivation.

RULES OF POSITIVE REINFORCEMENT

   Reinforcement for attending and responding occurs as feedback about correctness of reading responses, moving ahead, and winning.

   Reinforcement is immediate, following appropriate reading responses.

   Reinforcement is in relatively small amounts. The player does not easily become satiated.

   It may be necessary to use a primary reinforcer, e.g., food, contingent on winning, to cause players initially to attend and respond to the game; then the teacher moves as quickly as possible to reinforcers that more naturally occur as part of the fun of playing the game, *success*.

   Only appropriate reading responses are reinforced. Words incorrectly read are not reinforced.

   Shaping procedures can be applied through the game in the sense that over time increasingly complex or difficult words can be placed in the spaces as each learner adds to his sight vocabulary. Furthermore, the shaping sequence can be individualized for each learner.

   Positive reinforcement is a natural part of the events of instruction, not a "bag of goodies" substituted for effective instruction. Players practice the actions necessary because those actions are reinforced through success in moving toward the goal of the game.

PROPERTIES OF ACADEMIC GAMES

   Each player is striving to achieve the goal of winning the game.

   Only a small group of players participates in each game.

   The rules for playing are clear.

   There is a basic order, sequence, and structure for the action of the game.

   There is a definite goal or purpose to be achieved through the action of the game. That is, learning to read the words enables the learner to play the game successfully and to have a chance to win. Consequently, to enjoy participating in the action of the game, he must attend to and practice the words long enough and well enough to learn them.

   The rules of the game substitute temporarily for the usual rules of classroom life.

(The cognitive level of this task is *analysis*.)

CHAPTER TEN

1. **a.** As a teacher with a strictly humanistic point of view, you would: (1) establish a warm and friendly relationship with Betty; (2) convey to her that you understand the uncomfortable feelings she might have during

class discussions; (3) let her know that you care about her and are available if she would like to talk privately; (4) listen carefully to her words and feelings and reflect them to her without judging or directing; (5) allow Betty to proceed at her own rate as she tries to work out her own solution to her problems.

b. As a teacher with a strictly behavioristic point of view, you would: (1) determine the contingencies of reinforcement and punishment that are maintaining Betty's present behaviors; (2) discuss privately with her the difficulties she seems to have becoming actively involved in class discussions; (3) decide together on specific changes to be made in her behavior; (4) change the contingencies so that "participating" responses are likely to result in rewarding consequences, rather than punishing ones, for Betty. This will require a shaping procedure so that she can *learn* the kinds of responses that are likely to gain positive reinforcement.

c. As a teacher with both a humanistic and a behavioristic point of view, you would (1) begin with items 1–3 from a humanistic point of view; (2) listen carefully to Betty's words and feelings, then decide together which, if any, of her behaviors should be changed; (3) determine the contingencies of reinforcement and punishment that are maintaining the undesirable behaviors; (4) change the contingencies so that undesirable behaviors are not reinforced; (5) institute a shaping procedure so that she can learn the responses that will gain positive reinforcement.

10-2

The important rule here is: "Don't make a mountain out of a mole hill." The commonsense action that is both humanistically and behavioristically sound is simply to ask Erica, quietly and privately, if she realized that racing her coins may be disturbing to others. Asking her to put them away and begin reading is probably all that is required. A key to the effectiveness of this action, however, is what *you* do after you have "caught the learner being bad," even if you have caught her in a way that shows consideration for her as a human being. As soon as she begins to behave more appropriately, you should "catch her being good." That is, you should reinforce her appropriate behavior as soon as it occurs following the termination of misbehavior. This is easy to accomplish, even at a distance, because learners always steal a brief glance at the teacher soon after their "misbehavior" has ended and they are behaving appropriately. *Defensive checking* is a name frequently used to refer to this process. In that brief instant when you eyes meet, you can deliver a reinforcing message that says: "Good student!" The message you get in return will say: "Good teacher!"

10-3

1. a. Discuss the situation with your students. Listen carefully to what they say and "feel" about poetry. Maintain an atmosphere of genuinely honest and nonjudgmental inquiry.

b. Decide together on appropriate instructional objectives for the unit on poetry. State the objectives in specific behavioral terms.

c. Decide together on some reason why your students would want to be able to do the things described in the objectives. The reason should be some experience that the students will find rewarding and that also will require them to learn the information and skills described in the objectives.

d. Select and implement the specific procedures to be followed. Reinforce any behaviors that are consistent with meeting the objectives. Withhold reinforcement for those that are not. Use punishment, if necessary, to suppress misbehavior long enough for appropriate alternative behaviors to occur and be reinforced.

e. Follow through with the performance of the pleasing activity for which the students were learning the objectives.

f. As your students get better at poetry, fade-out any contrived reinforcement and punishment. Their success with the newly learned information and skills relative to poetry will be sufficient motivation to ensure appropriate attending and responding behavior.

Following is a brief account of how one teacher applied the synthesis of rules above to help his reluctant junior high school students learn about poetry:

In class discussion the teacher encouraged his students to express freely how they felt about poetry. They reported a dislike for it that may have derived from lack of understanding, a narrow interpretation of poetry as "glorified nursery rhymes," and unpleasant past experiences of being forced to memorize and recite words and phrases that were often meaningless. From their discussion, the students learned that poetry could take any number of different imaginative forms of language to express thoughts and feelings other than ordinary speech, or the sing-song rhythm of simple rhymes.

The students agreed to let the teacher think about their comments for a couple of days to see what he could come-up with. When he returned to the topic some time later, this is how he began: "How would you like to present a pop-concert to the rest of the school? I mean with all the popular music, sound and lighting effects that go with it. What I would like you to think about doing is choose some music you especially like, something that says something to you, and work-out some way of conveying to others how the music makes you feel. This could be actions, words, sound effects, special lights and shadows, or any combination of these. You could work alone or in teams. I hope that you might write something of your own to read using your choice of music as back-up to set the mood for your words. We could arrange for a practice room, and later we could present our work during lunch hour for anyone who wanted to hear us."

The students were reluctant at first but the more they discussed the possibilities the more positive they became. Three boys said they wanted no part of it. The teacher accepted their decision and gave them a choice of alternatives: to write reactions to certain pieces of poetry; or to choose a particular style of poetry and report on it.

The presentations were mostly team efforts and most wrote their own material. One of the boys who originally decided not to participate, eventually did. It took five lunch hours to complete the presentations, but not because the presentations required that much time. Most were less than three minutes. Since the room would hold only about two hundred students, it took five lunch hours to meet the demands of the student body to hear the presentations.

CHAPTER ELEVEN 11-1

1. *Development* is the more inclusive. *Learning* is but one aspect of the overall change that results from living through time; other changes are physical growth and maturation.

2. Each time we are confronted with a new experience relating to a particular concept and that experience is assimilated by an existing structure of knowledge, that structure "grows"; it becomes more generally inclusive relative to the class to which the specific information belongs. Since the possibilities for environmental experiences about a given concept are virtually infinite and each experience increases the generality of the concept, it follows that concepts are extremely unlikely ever to be learned completely.

3. When a learner is confronted with a new situation, an initial lack of equilibrium occurs between the requirements for assimilation of the new information and the presently existing structures of knowledge. Reinforcement consists in successfully achieving equilibrium as a consequence of the accommodative action of the existing structures. Notice how similar Hunt's account of reinforcement is to the notion, presented in Chapters 8, 9, and 10, that the most basic and lasting source of reinforcement is simply *success* at the task at hand.

11-2

1. Their data suggest that learning has more than a *functional* component; it also has a physical or structural basis in terms of increased numbers and kinds of *molecules of DNA, RNA, protein, nerve (glial) cells, and nervous tissue* in the central nervous system.

2. Learning is a relatively permanent change in behavioral tendency and physical-chemical structure of the central nervous system that is the result of practice sufficient to produce the protein molecules necessary for long-term retention.

3. The studies of Lessing (1967) and Hyden (1966) show that practice of an already-learned skill increases the total amount of RNA in applicable cells (thereby facilitating long-term memory), but that practice learning a new skill results in the production of *different kinds* of RNA in affected brain cells. The significance of this is simply that "these findings establish the fact that certain ordinarily dormant sections of DNA, i.e., genes, are stimulated into activity in the process of [practice] learning new skills."[1] Notice how these findings support Piaget's notions about assimilation and accommodation.

Agranoff's (1967) findings are also important here since they demonstrate the direct relationship between practice and the protein production necessary for learning that results in long-term retention of the material learned.

11-3

1. Evolutionary learning is frequently and often erroneously considered as instinct. The error is in believing that somehow the instinctive behavior of organisms is innately a part of the organism; that it was never learned. All behavior of all organisms has been learned, either through the nearly infinite number of experiences of evolutionary ancestors or through the thousands of experiences each individual encounters in his own lifetime as he takes up living at the point his ancestors left off, beginning with the accumulated learning that they were able to pass on to him in the form of a genetic code.

2. You will recall from Chapter 3 that the objectives at the lower end of the affective domain refer to *attending* and *responding* behavior. The argument rests on evidence that the human infant is born with an incipient motivational system ("bias"), that is, a tendency to *attend* and to *respond* to certain selected environmental stimuli. The stimuli selected for attention and response are those that appear to be necessary for proper and complete elaboration of incomplete, preprogrammed mechanisms that have survival value for the infant.

3. I believe the implication is that we need to be concerned that indiscriminate use of punishment may suppress a natural motivational tendency and that, later, the child may be motivated to attend and respond only through external contrived reinforcers, or more punishment.

4. Throughout evolutionary history, each time a change occurred in the genetic material of an organism and adaptation was made easier or more complete, the basis for positive transfer was enhanced, since that organism's progeny had an increased probability of successful adaptation. An evolutionary sequence is itself evidence of positive transfer of learning.

5. My speculation is this: We know that gene action modifies our experience, but we also know that gene action is modified by experience. Furthermore, most genes, except perhaps those that act proactively, commence and continue their action only when stimulated by specific environmental experience. Furthermore, there is convincing evidence that sensitive periods obtain, especially early in life, during which certain genes are more easily set into action than at a later time. There is some evidence (Luria, 1965) that with age, many genes lose all or part of their reactive potential, especially as a function of lack of stimulation. Taken together, these points suggest at least a partial explanation for decreasing plasticity with age: Over time, fewer and fewer genes are potentially and maximally available for gene-environment interaction.

11-4

1. The knowing behavior that develops at each stage facilitates and becomes a part of the development of the knowing behavior characteristic of the following stage. In fact, Piaget believes that development of the knowing behavior characteristic of a later stage will not occur until development characteristic of the earlier stage has occurred. Positive transfer between stages is a logical necessity.

2. Accommodation implies meaningfulness. The fact that an existing structure of knowledge assimilates new infor-

---

[1] W. R. Calloway, Jr. (1970). Modes of biological adaptation and their role in intellectual development, *Perceptual Cognitive Development Monographs*, **1**(1), 16.

mation and makes an accommodative adjustment to it *means* that the new information is incorporated meaningfully. It becomes a part of the existing structure and also modifies it.

When new information can find no existing, relevant structure of knowledge into which it can be assimilated, it forms an isolated structure of its own. It *means* nothing larger than itself; existing structures are unchanged by its inclusion among them; the new information has been rotely learned. And, as this way of looking at rote learning shows, transfer value of such material is clearly limited.

3. You will have noticed how Piaget's theory helps us put some of our "old" concepts into new perspective and thus increase their meaningfulness. (He would say this shows the processes of assimilation and accommodation at work.) *Readiness* and *positive transfer* come into a wider perspective relative to Gagné's types of learning and Piaget's stages of intelligence. Their meanings blend so that they make sense only when considered together: Readiness, in terms of Piaget's stages, means having developed the structures of knowledge that will transfer positively to make development in the next stage possible.

4. Speculation is always a bit dangerous, but we would make very little progress without it. The thing that is potentially hazardous about speculating on the correspondence between Gagné's types of learning and Piaget's stages of intelligence is that we may forget we are just making an educated guess, not a statement of proven fact.

My *guess* at their possible correspondence is roughly this:

PIAGET'S STAGES OF INTELLIGENCE	GAGNÉ'S TYPES OF LEARNING
Sensory-motor (0–2 years)	Motor and verbal chains; discriminations
Preoperational (2 years–6 or 7 years)	Motor and verbal chains; discriminations; concrete concepts
Concrete-operational (6 or 7 years–11 or 12 years)	Motor and verbal chains; discriminations; concrete concepts; defined concepts; simple rules
Formal-operational (11 or 12 years–adult)	Motor and verbal chains; discriminations; concrete concepts; defined concepts; simple rules; higher-order rules

5. You will remember from Chapters 5 and 6 that similarities and differences are more easily discriminated if the items to be compared and contrasted are presented in close proximity. This is one of the useful features of tables for presenting information that is to be compared and contrasted. Therefore, my response to this item is presented in the following table.

Characteristics of Knowing Behavior (Intelligence)

	FISH	HUMAN
NEWLY BORN	Rigid; reflexive; acts immediately; mostly preprogrammed; little variability left for individual learning; narrow, specifically directed toward meeting physiological needs; specific responses controlled by specific stimuli; little variation among individuals; nonreversible; behavior, especially the motor patterns, not very modifiable by experience.	Rigid; reflexive; acts immediately; mostly preprogrammed; great variability left for individual learning; narrow, specifically directed toward meeting physiological needs; specific responses controlled by specific stimuli; some variation among individuals; nonreversible; behavior greatly modifiable by experience, including both its quality and quantity.
ADULT	Rigid; reflexive; acts immediately; mostly preprogrammed; little variability left for individual learning; narrow, specifically directed toward meeting physiological needs; specific responses controlled by specific stimuli; little variation among individuals; nonreversible; not very modifiable by experience, especially as to motor patterns.	Flexible; reflective; responses can be delayed; little preprogramming; broad, great variability for individual learning; directed toward meeting Maslow's higher-level needs; responses controlled by a variety of stimuli; great variation among individuals; reversible; greatly modifiable by experience, both quantity and quality.

1. Even though there is convincing evidence that human infants have preprogrammed motivating mechanisms, there is also strong evidence that preprogrammed genetic mechanisms in human beings are nearly always incomplete and rely heavily on experience for their elaboration. Thus, from a very early point in life (perhaps even before birth), experience is a fundamental variable in developmental adaptation. Consequently, the reinforcing and punishing properties of experience, i.e., the rules of reinforcement and punishment, are key variables in *any* theory of development. Once the infant initially gets started, the way he then develops is largely a matter of the reinforcing and punishing consequences of his experiences.

2. I believe Piaget's thinking on approaches to learning are much like Ausubel's (Chapter 6): Discovery learning has its greatest importance early in life—during the time that exploration of objects and people and their interactions can be meaningful only through direct, concrete association with them. Later, as symbolic and abstract thought becomes possible, there is less need for discovery learning; meaningful reception learning becomes an effective approach, and an efficient one.

3. The reasons for my position are these: Intelligence, considered broadly as *knowing behavior,* permits the extension of the same sets of higher-order rules of developmental adaptation that apparently apply to intellectual development to the development of *other* subtypes of knowing, in this case, the development of psychomotor and affective knowing. Piaget's theory, viewed in this way, provides a logical guide for our search for the characteristics of the developmental sequence of structures of psychomotor and affective knowledge as reflected in psychomotor and affective knowing behavior. To the present time, unfortunately, this potentially powerful and inclusive aspect of his theory has received little or no attention.

4. In terms of how we defined *cognitive* and *connectionist* in Chapter 4, Piaget clearly takes a cognitive approach; he is interested in what happens *inside* the organism. The tremendous power of his theory, however, derives from the fact of his unusual ability to analyze and synthesize (the stuff of discovery); that is, to *combine* ideas from a variety of sources, e.g., biology, physics, chemistry, philosophy, ethology, psychology, and epistemology.

CHAPTER TWELVE

Neither Jensen's conclusions nor the views presented by environmentalists alter the higher-order rules of development we derived in Chapter 11. Since Piaget's theory of development subsumes both Jensen's and Skinner's views, no modifications of his general rules of development are required. The data of Jensen and Skinner help clarify certain parts of Piaget's theory by contributing specific information about certain of the rules of development, but they do not add new or different rules.

1. **a.** The stage of general intellectual development of each learner.

  b. Each learner's current structures of knowledge relative to the topic to be learned about next, in this case, in mathematics or language arts. That is, has each learner acquired the prerequisites necessary to complete the next topic to be learned?

  c. Long-range planning for learning outcomes (goals) in the major topic and in those related to it, and short-range planning for outcomes (objectives) in specific aspects of the major topic—task description and task analysis.

  d. Specification of the learning subtasks of the topic relative to the dimensions: simple to complex, concrete to abstract, and general to specific.

  e. Presentation of the materials in an instructional form (concrete materials, pictures, models, verbal descriptions) that matches the characteristics of the developmental level of each learner.

1. The stage of general intellectual development of each learner.

2. Each learner's current structures of knowledge relative to the topic to be learned about next (prerequisites).

3. Long-range goals and short-range instructional objectives (task description and task analysis).

4. Arrangement of learning subtasks in a hierarchical sequence from simple to complex, concrete to abstract, and general to specific.

5. Presentation of the materials in an instructional sequence, the rate and content of which can be controlled by each learner.

1. **a.** All the concerns listed in Checkpoints 12-2 and 12-3.
   b. Providing a wide variety of instructional materials, in terms of specific content, general interest level and concreteness or abstractness, many of which are auto-instructional and provide immediate corrective feedback.
   c. Devising ways to monitor and follow up each individual's responses, especially those that are in error, with appropriate corrective experiences.
   d. Arranging schedules of reinforcement so that personal success in learning and sharing in the success of others becomes more reinforcing for learners than contrived reinforcers.

CHAPTER THIRTEEN

1. The most obvious purpose was *selection:* To select those who had learned well from those who had not, and to assign grades accordingly. Although not so obvious, another purpose was probably *correction:* If everyone had failed the test, or if everyone had gotten all items correct, Mr. Owens no doubt would have used that information as an indication that his instruction needed modifying. However, since the distribution of marks was as he expected—"nearly a normal curve"—there was no apparent need for instructional change.

2. He would have followed up with each learner to determine what the problems were for each and then retaught each person until all were able to meet all the objectives. He would not merely record the scores, file the exams, and continue on to the next unit.

1. Tricky or catchy items; difficult vocabulary; small number of items; item 6 is irrelevant.

2. Insufficient time for some; unclear criteria for scoring the essay item; vague, confusing directions.

3. Fear of tests and perhaps the teacher; guessing; poor writing and reading skills.

   All these sources of error would reduce the validity of the test, since to be a valid measure, a test must also give reliable or consistent results.

13-3

1. If our class planned a debate on the major causes of poverty in the world today, would you like to participate?
   ____ **a.** Yes!   ____ **c.** I don't think so.
   ____ **b.** Maybe I would. ____ **d.** No!

2. The topic I have chosen to write my term paper on is. . . .

3. The ways in which I spend my free time are. . . .

13-4

1. Why was Goldilocks in the woods?

2. Using other words for the words in the story "they," "lived," "little," "house," and "wood," show that you can say this sentence in another way and still have it mean the same thing: They lived in a little house in the wood.

3. Show the rest of the class what Father Bear acted like and sounded like when he found that someone had been eating his porridge.

4. What do you suppose Goldilocks would have done and said if she had noticed three hairbrushes in the Bears' home?

5. The word "consistent" can mean to act in the same way at different times; for example, to say "Hello" to Mrs. Jones whenever you see her—at home, at school, at the store. Do you think Goldilocks acted consistently in what she did and said in the Bears' home? Tell us why you do or do not think so.

6. Suppose that when Goldilocks ran downstairs, she could not get the door open. Make up a new ending for the story that tells what Goldilocks might have done and said in that case.

7. Do you believe that Goldilocks should have gone into the Bears' home? Why? Why not?

13-5

1. Since, as Mr. Owens, I assume that many of my learners will not be able to learn everything I teach, I would probably be happy with the results of this exam. It is skewed in favor of higher scores, with only six or seven persons scoring less than 50 percent correct. The results of this test are apparently better than those of the previous test, described at the beginning of the chapter.

2. No, I would not, since my assumption is now that each learner can learn only *if* I can make instruction optimal. Obviously, from the results, I have been less than successful. Very few of my learners actually learned most of what I tried to teach them. I will have to find out what is missing in my instruction for most of my learners and then teach again.